PREMIER LEAGUE

THE PLAYERS

A complete guide to every player 1992-93

Compiled by

Barry J. Hugman
and Alan Platt

Published by Tony Williams Publications

© Hugman Enterprises Limited 1992

ISBN 1-869833-15-5

Typesetting and Film Origination: Character Graphics, Taunton.
Design: Bob Bickerton.
Illustrations: Empics, Nottingham.
Printed by: Ian Allan Printing, Addlestone.

Distributed by Little Red Witch Book Distribution,
24a Queen Square, North Curry, Taunton, Somerset TA3 6LE
Tel: 0823 490080 Fax: 0823 490281

CONTENTS

ACKNOWLEDGEMENTS

As the managing editor, I would like to thank the many various experts, without whose help this book would not have been possible to produce within the allotted time available.

Firstly, co-author Alan Platt, who helped me to produce all of the player profiles, once again came to the rescue. He is a freelance transport planner whose recent assignments have all been overseas and who invariably gets back just in time to help me with whatever football book I am working on at that moment. Some holiday! Unlike many schoolboys he did not take an interest in soccer until the age of 14, but once involved he was hooked. From 1960 onwards he has kept detailed records on all Football League clubs. From 1985 to 1986 he contributed to the Chesterfield (where he lives when in England) match programme. He first met me in 1981, following the publication of my original Football League Players' Records, which we are currently in the process of bringing out again and impressed by the depth of research and attention to detail, volunteered his assistance to all future additions. His "assistance" has always been gratefully accepted and none more so than this year when thrown in at the deep end, we co-wrote 708 player biographies inside 12 weeks.

Another to help has been Michael Featherstone. Michael has been involved with me since Football League Players' Records back in 1975 and is a keen sporting statistician who works in the accounts department of a large public company. He started out many years ago by collecting both cricket and soccer information, which he obtained from the Colindale National Newspaper Library. Several years later he joined Ray Spiller's Association of Football Statisticians. After we had first met, he began intensive research into post-war League footballers. He has contributed to several books, apart from Football League Players' Records, including The British Boxing Yearbook, The Olympic Games: Complete Track & Field Results, 1896-1988, The Cricket Who's Who and many others. He was responsible for researching all of the associated schoolboy and trainee signing dates and international appearances within these covers.

He in turn was helped by A. Evans (Welsh FA), D Morris (Scottish FA), D Bowen (Northern Ireland FA), D Painter (Welsh Schools), Jim McDonnell (Northern Ireland Schools), Marshall Gillespie, Malcolm Stammers and Dave Barber.

In acquiring club information, I am most grateful to David Miles and Gary Lewin (Arsenal), Debbie Lowe (Aston Villa), John Howarth (Blackburn Rovers), Ron Hockings (Chelsea), George Dalton (Coventry City), Terry Byfield (Crystal Palace), Les Helm (Everton), Mike Noye and Peter Trevillyn (Ipswich Town), Alan Sutton (Leeds United), Sheila Watts and Steve Heighway (Liverpool), Terry Farrell (Manchester City), Marie and Cliff Butler (Manchester United), Roger Dermont and Tommy Johnson (Middlesbrough), Kevan Platt and Mike Davage (Norwich City), John Perkins (Nottingham Forest), Gordon Lawton and Lisa Brogan (Oldham Athletic), Sheila Marson (Q.P.R.), Jane and Andrew Pack (Sheffield United), Alan Smith (Sheffield Wednesday), John Hughes (Southampton), John Fennelly (Tottenham Hotspur) and Reg Davis (Wimbledon).

On the production front, I must thank Neal Simpson and Paul Marriott of Empics Photo Agency, 26 Musters Road, West Bridgford, Nottingham (0602 455885) for the quality and amount of pics supplied that helped to make the book such an attractive product; Bob Bickerton, who made a great job on designing and laying out the picture spreads for The Premier League Players and both Mark and Graham of Character Graphics, who with their knowledge of soccer, coupled with their excellent typesetting, almost made the book a pleasure to work on.

Both the publisher, Tony Williams and myself, are indebted to Suzannah Dwyer, who produced the captain's pages quite brilliantly, Steve Whitney, who supplied non-League details and to all the anonymous club scouts, who helped enormously with the skill factor information for each of the 708 players involved in the book, a mammoth task.

Finally, I take my hat off to the publisher, Tony Williams, whose great enthusiasm and support has made the publication of this book and others possible.

Barry J. Hugman

THE ART OF CAPTAINCY by Ron Atkinson

"Captaincy is an art", states Ron Atkinson. It could be argued that in recent times the need for a captain on the field has become less necessary than in the past, but Atkinson does not agree. "In an ideal world we would all take responsibility for ourselves and that would be beautiful. The reality, however, is that someone is always needed to harness together great talents in a team game".

Normally he feels that people have an aptitude for leadership which is the basis of good captaincy. He reasons that there is no specific "type" of person, rather that the right person tends to emerge and become the obvious choice.

"There are not as many natural leaders about as I would like to see", he said. "There seem to be fewer personalities than in the past, but that might be the consequence of too much brainwashing within the system.

I do think that there are two types of captain. The first leads by example. He is a fairly quiet individual but he has a commanding presence. Then you have the rip-roarer – he leads by example too, but he's vocal and plays every move of the game himself, or seems to!

But both types are brave men. Even on days when they are not playing well as individuals, they don't disappear. They are still prepared to do what's necessary-encourage, support, keep battling.

It's easy to be captain when the team is performing well and it takes a lot of character to continue to fight when a game seems to be slipping away and heads have dropped, but there are many who thrive on that kind of challenge.

There are great players who have not turned out to be great captains and sometimes the reverse is true. At the turn of the '80s when Nottingham Forest was one of the best teams in England, or Europe, their captain, John McGovern, was an unsung hero. He was, arguably, the least talented player in the side, but his strength lay in moulding those gifted stars into a force that was exceptional. A good captain must lead by example first. The level of his commitment must never be questioned; in a crisis there can only be one boss. He must, on occasions, act as a buffer between the team and the manager – so he does require the talents of a diplomat and a negotiator. Perhaps the ability to make decisions on the pitch is less critical now than it was in the past – the game is more tactical today. I do think that a captain can function more effectively from midfield or central defence. He does need to be able to view the game from as many angles as possible.

Most great captains have had presence. Think of Bobby Moore and Franz Beckenbaur. Dave Mackay was a thinking captain – Danny Blanchflower was an intellectual. One of the most inspirational captains I have ever seen was Billy Bremner – amazing courage and determination. Today? Well, Bryan Robson is a legend. Ray Wilkins is another fine captain – always encouraging. And Graeme Souness, of course there was never any doubt that he was captain where ever he played. He had the nerve to accept responsibility and the courage to tackle the difficult. I suppose the best kind of captain is the one who has the ability to take a game by the scruff of its neck and turn a lost cause into a victory".

So who was the best captain that Ron Atkinson ever played with? "Me, of course".

In highlighting the Premier League club captains as a special feature of the book, we felt it would be a good idea to ask one of the most experienced managers in the game, Ron Atkinson, to express his views in the art of captaincy. Ron's thoughts were penned by Suzannah Dwyer, who provided the splendid captain's profiles.

INTRODUCTION

With the advent of the new FA Premier League for 1992-93, it was quickly agreed by Tony Williams, the publisher and myself, that in order to celebrate what has often been called the world's strongest League, we should produce and annual title, portraying every professional player signed up for the coming season. To make it both attractive and easy to follow, it was decided to split the book into two sections; club and player profiles and to include over 400 action packed photographs.

The club section at the beginning of the book shows the current staff as at 1 July 1992, by playing position, club debut and 1991-92 appearances and goals. Players who have left since the beginning of last season are also shown, along with the current trainees. Where a players name is written in *italic* in the line-up for the team photo, it denotes that he is no longer with the club. Included in this section is an original feature on the present club captain giving them recognition for the responsibility they have accepted.

Good captains can make a great deal of difference to a team's performance and indeed to the atmosphere and spirit within a club. We are featuring the men who are taking responsibility at the Premier League clubs and we have also asked club officials to let us know which other players, currently on their books, have captained the side. As a bit of fun, we are showing a "captains' table" at each club where the current skipper has "invited" former captains to join him. Just imagine the stories that could be told if these men could really get together.

The decision to produce career records of all the players in alphabetical order and not within the club section was made because over the coming 12 months many of them will change clubs and it will therefore be easier to identify them in this fashion. The club section will also act as a cross reference and an * in the statistical box denotes players' current clubs at the time of going to press. When Alan Platt and myself started to write the player profiles, the initial aim was provide a factual account of each individual career in an objective and neutral manner. When we stood back and reviewed our early efforts, the results seemed uniformly bland and uninteresting. Hardly any two players careers are alike, yet our descriptions made it seem as though they were all too similar.

It was therefore decided to take a different approach. In order to provide more "colourful" and distinguishing features for each players, we included what was considered to be both the highlights and low points of their careers to date. Instead of being wholly objective it was decided to become more subjective and thus, arguably, betray our biases for and against certain players. It was not the intention to be controversial, but this may be the inevitable result of expressing "opinions". If any player, or manager, or supporter etc, is offended by the viewpoints in question, one can only apologise and state that we believe our opinions to be fair comment based on the information available to us at the time. Career details have been researched thoroughly and diligently given the time available, but it is possible that with over 700 players included in the book many of them being first year pros and recent signings from the trainee ranks, certain information may have escaped our attention. The aim for next year's book onwards, is to have an individual club expert covering "their" players in greater detail, regarding the past season and future aspirations.

The Position/Skill Factor element of the player biographies were supplied by a senior club scout, who has a knowledge and love for the game that is possibly unrivalled, being ably supported by many other former leading players working in the same capacity. They kindly provided background information and a description of the playing style of each player in question. It was decided at an early stage only to portray a player's qualities and attributes and not his weaknesses, as one could arguably do a hatchet job on many individuals that could well be construed as negative and ultra-critical.

Regarding the statistical box, the first club stated is that of the player in question's first Football League side and does not cover any previous playing information, which can be found in amongst the text. Also, because of a lack of information, we have not filled in appearances and goals for non-League, Scottish and European clubs, but will endeavour to produce the requisite information for all future editions. Appearances and goals are broken down by Football League, League Cup, FA Cup and others, which includes European competitions, Play-Off games, the Charity Shield and the Zenith Cup etc. The transfer fee shown is the one that would have been reported in the press at the time and in some cases where player exchanges have taken place, adjustments have been made to take that into account.

The authors are long standing supporters of the sport and it is not unusual for the opinions of fans and the media to be at variance with those of football managers. The history of soccer is littered with examples of players who were great crowd pleasers, but were overlooked and spurned by their managers. Football, as the national game, generates great interest because of different opinions – managers usually know far more about players' abilities and characters that the average fan who can only form a judgement from what he sees on the field of play, or on television. But managers are also sometimes guilty of irrational bias and over the years players who appear to be a worthless investment with one club have gone on to become "worldbeaters" with a change of scenery. Like everything else, football is all about opinions and we hope that what is expressed in this book will make it more interesting to read and provoke argument and discussion, without causing offence.

Barry J. Hugman

PREMIER LEAGUE CLUB SECTION

ARSENAL
1886

THE GUNNERS

Team Manager George Graham
Club Address Arsenal Stadium, Avenell Road, Highbury, London N5 1BU
Record Attendance 73,295 v Sunderland Div. 1, 9 March 1935
Turned Professional 1891
Previous Names Dial Square, Royal Arsenal, Woolwich Arsenal
Club Honours Football League: Div. 1 Champions 1930-31, 1932-33, 1933-34, 1934-35, 1937-38, 1947-48, 1952-53, 1970-71, 1988-89, 1990-91. FA Cup: Winners 1930, 1936, 1950, 1971, 1979. League Cup: Winners 1987. European Fairs Cup: Winners 1969-70
League History 1893-1904 Div. 2; 1904-13 Div 1; 1913-19 Div. 2; 1919 Div. 1

Most League Points in a Season (2 for a win) 66 in Div. 1 1930-31. (3 for a win) 83 in Div. 1 1990-91
Most League Goals in a Season 127 in Div. 1 1930-31
Record League Victory 12-0 v Loughborough T. in Div. 2, 12 March 1900
Record League Defeat 0-8 v Loughborough T. in Div. 2, 12 December 1896
Consecutive League Wins 10 in 1987
Consecutive League Defeats 7 in 1977
Record League Appearances David O'Leary, 517 between 1975-92
Record League Goalscorer—Career Cliff Bastin, 150 between 1930-47
Record League Goalscorer—Season Ted Drake, 42 in Div. 1 1934-35

1991-92 Record

Football League First Division (4th): Played 42, Won 19, Drawn 15, Lost 8, Goals For 81, Goals Against 46, Points 72
FA Cup Third Round: Wrexham (A)1-2

League Cup Second Round: Leicester C. (A)1-1 (H)2-0; Third Round: Coventry C. (A)0-1
European Cup First Round: Austria Vienna (H)6-1 (A)0-1; Second Round: Benfica (A)1-1 (H)1-3

1991-92: Back Row L-R: Gary Lewin (Physio), Pat Rice (Youth Team Coach), Paul Davis, Andy Linighan, David O'Leary, Tony Adams, Steve Bould, Alan Smith, Paul Merson, Colin Pates, Stewart Houston (First Team Coach), George Armstrong (Reserve Team Coach).
Front Row: *Craig McKernon*, Perry Groves, David Seaman, Kevin Campbell, David Rocastle, Anders Limpar, George Graham (Manager), David Hillier, *Siggi Jonsson, Michael Thomas,* Alan Miller, Lee Dixon, Nigel Winterburn.

Playing staff for 1992-93 (As at 1 July 1992)   ARSENAL

PLAYERS	CLUB DEBUT (Football League)	1991-92 APPEARANCES				1991-92 GOALS			
		Lge	FL Cup	FA Cup	Others	Lge	FL Cup	FA Cup	Others
GOALKEEPERS									
Miller, Alan	–								
Seaman, David	Wimbledon (A) 25 August 1990	42	3	1	5				
Will, James	–								
DEFENDERS									
Adams, Tony	Sunderland (H) 5 November 1983	35	3	1	5	2			
Bould, Steve	Wimbledon (A) 27 August 1988	24+1			0+1	1			
Dixon, Lee	Luton T. (H) 13 February 1988	38	3	1	5	4			
Gaunt, Craig	–								
Linighan, Andy	Chelsea (H) 15 September 1990	15+2	1+1		2				1
Lyderson, Pal	Norwich C. (A) 8 April 1992	5+2							
Marshall, Scott	–								
Morrow, Steve	Norwich C. (A) 8 April 1992	0+2							
O'Leary, David	Burnley (A) 16 August 1975	11+14	0+1	1	2				
Pates, Colin	Sheffield Wed. (A) 17 February 1990	9+2	2		2				1
Webster, Ken	–								
Winterburn, Nigel	Southampton (H) 21 November 1987	41	2	1	5	1			
MIDFIELDERS									
Clements, Steve	–								
Davis, Paul	Tottenham H. (A) 7 April 1980	12	2		4				
Flatts, Mark	–								
Hillier, David	Leeds U. (A) 29 September 1990	27		0+1	1	1			
Lee, Justin	–								
Parlour, Ray	Liverpool (A) 21 January 1992	2+4				1			
Rocastle, David	Newcastle U. (H) 28 September 1985	36+3	3	1	5	4			
Selley, Ian	–								
FORWARDS									
Bacon, John	–								
Campbell, Kevin	Everton (A) 7 May 1988	22+9	2	1	5	13			1
Carter, Jimmy	Nottingham F. (A) 8 December 1991	5+1		1					
Cole, Andrew	Sheffield U. (H) 29 December 1990				0+1				
Dickov, Paul	–								
Groves, Perry	Luton T. (A) 13 September 1986	5+8	1+2	0+1	0+3	1			
Heaney, Neil	Sheffield U. (A) 18 April 1992	0+1							
Limpar, Anders	Wimbledon (A) 25 August 1990	23+6	1		3	4			1
Merson, Paul	Manchester C. (H) 22 November 1986	41+1	3	1	5	12	1		
Read, Paul	–								
Shaw, Paul	–								
Smith, Alan	Liverpool (H) 15 August 1987	33+6	2	1	5	12		1	4
Wright, Ian	Southampton (A) 28 September 1991	30	3			24	2		
PLAYERS MAKING APPEARANCES IN 1991-92 (No longer with the club)									
PLAYERS	CURRENT CLUBS								
Thomas, Michael	Liverpool (December 1991)	6+4	2		1+2	1			

TRAINEES

Jason C. Brissett, Stuart J. Campbell, Adrian J. Clarke, Anthony Connolly, Graeme B. Hall, Paul R. T. Harford, Ryan M. Kirby, Mark McCardle, Christopher McDonald, Gavin G. McGowan, Roy J. O'Brien, Matthew Rawlins, Matthew Rose, Nicholas C. I. Rust, Joel T. Swain, Soner Zumrutel

The Arsenal Captain

Tony Adams

When Tony Adams runs out onto the pitch at Highbury there is no mistaking the fact that this is his stage and his club. His height accentuates his commanding presence; he is the player who leads by example and although he is perhaps less vocal than some, there is never any doubt that he is captain. His ability to organise with the minimum of fuss is a valuable asset on the pitch. The captain is invariably an extension of the manager during a game and Tony Adams and George Graham have obviously developed a fine working relationship.

Adams is a good player in his own right. His ability alone has earned him the respect of his colleagues and the Arsenal supporters. The club means everything to him and he indicates that in the manner in which he conducts himself on the field. When games are not going well he never hides and when he makes an error, no-one is more anguished than Adams himself, but he is swift to recover and make amends.

George Graham could be forgiven for taking a leaf out of Dave Bassett's book by hanging up the Christmas decorations early in the marble halls, because Arsenal did not get off to a very promising start last season and then there was a bit of a slump (by Arsenal's standards) in mid-season. Nevertheless, there were many teams in the upper ranks of the League table who felt that Arsenal was the best and most complete footballing side that they had played. The signing of the explosive and exciting Ian Wright, added a new dimension to Arsenal's already formidable attack. He settled quickly, having got off to a dream start and George Graham was faced with the nightmare that most manager's long for – so much quality from which to select.

Tony Adams reasons that the old adage of "boring Arsenal" is now defunct. He believes that, currently, he captains the most exciting team in the land and that as the season progressed the "Gunners'" games provided fantastic entertainment. With four forwards who all netted more than ten goals each last season, there's every reason to be optimistic about next year, he feels. Adams insists that his team has performed with style despite a long injury list and "a dressing room which looked like a home for the walking wounded"! Even he admits that had the season started in February, Arsenal would have been leading the field.

Adams pays tribute to the Arsenal supporters for their loyalty. He has nothing but admiration for the core of 20-25,000 fans who stuck with the team through thick and thin, significantly after the defeat at Wrexham. He appreciates that it cannot be easy to follow a football team all over the country in the middle of a recession.

In his programme notes before the game against Sheffield Wednesday on 15 February, Tony Adams hinted that "we've got a few things to pull out of the bag". He could never have imagined a 7-1 victory. Could he?

Captain's Table

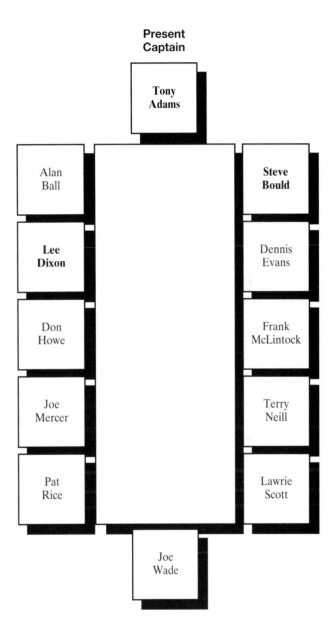

Present Captain

Tony Adams

Alan Ball | Steve Bould
Lee Dixon | Dennis Evans
Don Howe | Frank McLintock
Joe Mercer | Terry Neill
Pat Rice | Lawrie Scott

Joe Wade

Tony Adams heads an impressive table with his guests, including many famous post-war club captains both past and present. Those still on the club books are denoted in **bold** print.

ASTON VILLA
1874

THE VILLANS

Team Manager Ron Atkinson
Club Address Villa Park, Trinity Road, Birmingham B6 6HE
Record Attendance 76,588 v Derby Co., FA Cup 6th Round, 2 March 1946
Turned Professional 1885
Previous Names None
Club Honours Football League: Div. 1 Champions 1893-94, 1895-96, 1896-97, 1898-99, 1899-1900, 1909-10, 1980-81; Div. 2 Champions 1937-38, 1959-60; Div. 3 Champions 1971-72. FA Cup: Winners 1887, 1895, 1897, 1905, 1913, 1920, 1957. Football League Cup: Winners 1961, 1975, 1977. European Cup: Winners 1982-83. European Super Cup: Winners 1982-83
League History 1888-1936 Div. 1; 1936-38 Div. 2; 1938-59 Div. 1; 1959-60 Div. 2; 1960-67 Div. 1; 1967-70 Div. 2; 1970-72 Div. 3; 1972-75 Div. 2; 1975-87 Div. 1; 1987-88 Div. 2; 1988- Div. 1

Most League Points in a Season (2 for a win) 70 in Div. 3, 1971-72. (3 for a win). 78 in Div. 2, 1987-88
Most League Goals in a Season 128 in Div. 1, 1930-31
Record League Victory 12-2 v Accrington Stanley in Div. 1, 12 March 1882
Record League Defeat 0-7 v Blackburn Rov. in Div. 1, 19 October 1889, v West Bromwich A. in Div. 1, 19 October 1935 and v Manchester U. in Div. 1, 24 October 1964
Consecutive League Wins 9 in 1897
Consecutive League Defeats 11 in 1910 and 1963
Record League Appearances Charlie Aitken, 561 between 1961-76
Record League Goalscorer—Career Harry Hampton, 213 between 1904-20 and Billy Walker, 213 between 1919-34
Record League Goalscorer—Season "Pongo" Waring, 49 in Div. 1, 1930-31

1991-92 Record

Football League First Division (7th): Played 42, Won 17, Drawn 9, Lost 16, Goals For 48, Goals Against 44, Points 60
FA Cup Third Round: Tottenham H. (H)0-0 (R)1-0; Fourth Round: Derby Co. (A)4-3; Fifth Round: Swindon T. (A)2-1; Sixth Round: Liverpool (A)0-1
League Cup Second Round: Grimsby T. (A)0-0 (H)1-1
Zenith Cup Second Round: Coventry C. (A)2-0; Third Round: Nottingham F. (H)0-2.

1991-92: Back Row L-R: Bryan Small, *Derek Mountfield,* Ugo Ehiogu, *Kent Nielson,* Les Sealey, Nigel Spink, *Ivo Stas, Paul Mortimer, Chris Price,* Kevin Richardson. **Middle Row:** Jim Barron (First Team Coach), *Ian Ormondroyd,* Neil Cox, *Ian Olney,* Dalian Atkinson, Cyrille Regis, *Kevin Gage,* Mark Blake, Steve Staunton, *Andy Gray* (Assistant Manager). **Front Row:** Jim Walker (Physio), Dwight Yorke, Shaun Teale, *Stuart Gray,* Ron Atkinson (Manager), *Gary Penrice, Gordon Cowans,* Tony Daley, Roger Spry (Fitness Consultant).

Playing staff for 1992-93 (As at 1 July 1992)   ASTON VILLA

PLAYERS	CLUB DEBUT (Football League)	1991-92 APPEARANCES				1991-92 GOALS			
		Lge	FL Cup	FA Cup	Others	Lge	FL Cup	FA Cup	Others
GOALKEEPERS									
Bosnich, Mark	Luton T. (A) 24 April 1992	1							
Livingstone, Glen	–								
Oakes, Michael	–								
Sealey, Les	Everton (A) 19 October 1991	18		4	2				
Spink, Nigel	Nottingham F. (A) 26 December 1979	23	2	1					
DEFENDERS									
Barrett, Earl	Manchester C. (A) 29 February 1992	13							
Boden, Chris	–								
Crisp, Richard	–								
Ehiogu, Ugo	Arsenal (H) 24 August 1991	4+4		0+1	1				
Kubicki, Dariusz	Southampton (A) 31 August 1991	23	2	4+1	1				
McGrath, Paul	Nottingham F. (A) 19 August 1989	41	2	5		1			
Small, Bryan	Everton (A) 19 October 1991	8		2+1	2				
Staunton, Steve	Sheffield Wed. (A) 17 August 1991	37	2	4		4			
Teale, Shaun	Sheffield Wed. (A) 17 August 1991	42	2	5	2		1		
MIDFIELDERS									
Berry, Trevor	–								
Blake, Mark	Luton T. (A) 14 October 1989	14	1	2	2	2			
Breitkreutz, Matthias	Sheffield Wed. (H) 18 January 1992	7+1							
Cox, Neil	Notts Co. (A) 10 March 1992	4+3			1				
Froggatt, Stephen	West Ham U. (A) 26 December 1991	6+3		2+1				1	
Parker, Garry	Oldham Ath. (A) 30 November 1991	25		5		1		1	
Richardson, Kevin	Sheffield Wed. (A) 17 August 1991	42	2	5	2	6			
Williams, Lee	–								
FORWARDS									
Atkinson, Dalian	Sheffield Wed. (A) 17 August 1991	11+3	1	1	1	1			
Beinlich, Stefan	Nottingham F. (A) 18 April 1992	0+2			0+1				
Carruthers, Martin	Wimbledon (A) 8 February 1992	2+1		0+1	0+1				
Daley, Tony	Southampton (A) 20 April 1985	29+5		5	2	7			
Davis, Neil	–								
Farrell, David	–								
Fenton, Graham	–								
Parrott, Mark	–								
Regis, Cyrille	Sheffield Wed. (A) 17 August 1991	39	2	5		11			
Yorke, Dwight	Crystal Palace (A) 24 March 1990	27+5	2	5	1	11		5	1

PLAYERS MAKING APPEARANCES IN 1991-92 (No longer with the club)

PLAYERS	CURRENT CLUBS	Lge	FL Cup	FA Cup	Others	Lge	FL Cup	FA Cup	Others
Gowans, Gordon	Blackburn Rov. (November 1991)	10+2	2		0+1				
McLoughlin, Alan	Southampton (Loan – September 1991)				1				
Mortimer, Paul	Crystal Palace (October 1991)	10+2	2			1			
Mountfield, Derek	Wolverhampton W. (November 1991)	2							
Nielson, Kent	Brondby (February 1992)	3+3			1				
Olney, Ian	Oldham Ath. (May 1992)	14+6	0+1		2	2			1
Ormondroyd, Ian	Derby Co. (September 1991)	0+1							
Penrice, Gary	Q.P.R. (October 1991)	5+3			1				
Price, Chris	Blackburn Rov. (February 1992)	2+1			1				

TRAINEES

Lee A. Aston, Paul Browne, Steven M. Cowe, Darren Evans, Nicki D. J. Finney, Garry M. Harrison, Otis Hutson, Ian J. King, Scott McLaughlin, Christopher J. Pearce, Dennis A. Pearce, Riccardo Scimeca, Graeme E. Williams, John M. Wiltshire

The Aston Villa Captain

Kevin Richardson

Kevin Richardson had played on many notable stages in England prior to his Spanish sojourn. Goodison Park, Vicarage Road (in its heyday, and Highbury – the continental call was followed by the ultimate summons – Villa Park and English football was revisited. "It did take a little while to readjust", Richardson remembers. "It seemed even quicker and stronger than I had thought. On the continent things are not physical at all and you do get used to that. But it was not too long before I was back into the English game.

I remember the week that I was asked to be captain – Gordon Cowans had been dropped and the manager said 'Richo – you're captain – come and have a word tomorrow'. I was stunned. I couldn't believe it. I'd not been there that long and there were so many other great players to choose from. Anyway, I accepted the responsibility proudly. The game that Saturday was against Notts Forest at home. We won 3-1 and I scored; it couldn't have been a better start.

I suppose you could say that as captain, you're the middle man. There's a lot to do off the pitch as well as on it – sorting out tickets and the like. In a heated situation I have to calm things down. I am a reasonably experienced player so it's not a problem. On the pitch I deal with everyone in the same way – there's no special treatment for senior professionals. I do remember one away game against Sheffield United – it was freezing and the pitch was rock-hard. The ball had bounced over Cyrille Regis' head and I said a few strong words. When he turned round to look at me he seemed to expand and he's a big fellow to start with! But all that's over in that split second – Cyrille's a great professional. But he is big"!

There are many who have praised Ken Richardson's captaincy of Aston Villa this season. He has unified a side which has changed frequently – injuries and new players have meant that the team sheet has never been predictable, but he has never lost his will to win and he admits that he is still a very bad loser. (Though his son, Jake, can give him a run for his money and not bat an eyelid).

Richardson is the kind of player that supporters take to their hearts because he never gives up whatever is happening on the pitch. He believes that Villa, who finished seventh in the League, could have been at least in fourth place had they not thrown so many games away. But he feels that next season the blend of players that manager, Ron Atkinson, has brought together will begin to bear fruit. "He has the nerve to keep changing things until he's got what he's looking for", he says of Atkinson. "He's a great manager. He does not go on about tactics before a game. There are no long pre-match lectures with great detailed things to remember. Once, before a critical game against Leeds, all he said was 'Go out and treat it like a five-a-side game'. So we did and we played really well. He believes in players' ability and that makes people relax and try things – it's a great feeling for players to know that".

Captain's Table

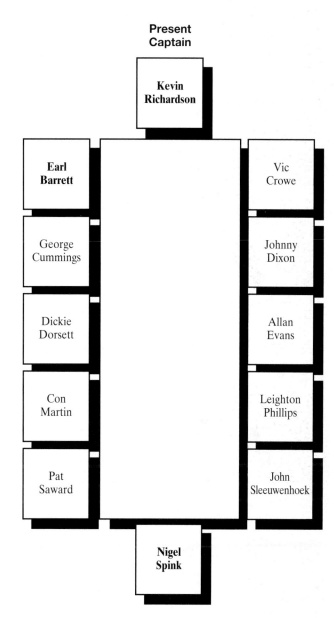

Kevin Richardson heads an impressive table with his guests, including many famous post-war club captains both past and present. Those still on the club books are denoted in **bold** print.

BLACKBURN ROVERS
1875

ARTE ET LABORE

THE BLUE & WHITES

Team Manager Kenny Dalglish
Club Address Ewood Park, Blackburn BB2 4JF
Record Attendance 61,783 v Bolton W., FA Cup 6th Round, 2 March 1929
Turned Professional 1880
Previous Names Blackburn Grammar School OB
Club Honours Football League: Div. 1 Champions 1911-12, 1913-14; Div. 2 Champions 1938-39; Div. 3 Champions 1974-75. FA Cup: Winners 1884, 1885, 1886, 1890, 1891, 1928
League History 1888-1936 Div. 1; 1936-39 Div. 2; 1946-47 Div. 1; 1947-57 Div. 2; 1957-66 Div. 1; 1966-71 Div. 2; 1971-75 Div. 3; 1975-79 Div. 2; 1979-80 Div. 3; 1980-92 Div. 2; 1992- Div. 1

Most League Points in a Season (2 for a win) 60 in Div. 3, 1974-75. (3 for a win) 77 in Div. 2, 1988-89
Most League Goals in a Season 114 in Div. 2, 1954-55
Record League Victory 9-0 v Middlesbrough in Div. 2, 6 November 1954
Record League Defeat 0-8 v Arsenal in Div. 1, 25 February 1933
Consecutive League Wins 8 in 1980
Consecutive League Defeats 7 in 1966
Record League Appearances Derek Fazackerley, 596 between 1970-86
Record League Goalscorer—Career Simon Garner, 167 between 1978-92
Record League Goalscorer—Season Ted Harper, 43 in Div. 1, 1925-26

1991-92 Record

Football League Second Division (6th): Played 46, Won 21, Drawn 11, Lost 14, Goals For 70, Goals Against 53, Points 74

FA Cup Third Round: Kettering T. (H) 4-1; Fourth Round: Notts Co. (A)1-2
League Cup First Round: Hull C. (H)1-1 (A)0-1
Zenith Cup First Round: Port Vale (A)0-1

1991-92: Back Row L-R: Robert Dewhurst, Mark Atkins, Darren Collier, Bobby Mimms, *Terry Gennoe,* Tony Dobson, Keith Hill, Steve Livingstone, Kevin Moran, Peter Thorne. **Middle Row:** *Don Mackay* (Manager), Mike Pettigrew (Physio), Nicky Reid, Stuart Munro, *Howard Gayle,* Jason Wilcox, Chris Sulley, Craig Skinner, *Alan Irvine,* David May, *Peter Baah, Scott Sellars,* Tony Parkes (Assistant Manager), Jim Furnell (Youth Team Manager). **Front Row:** Asa Hartford (Reserve Team Manager), Lee Richardson, *Mike Duxbury,* Darren Donnelly, *Lenny Johnrose, John Butterworth,* Simon Garner, Richard Brown, *Matthew Holt,* Paul Shepstone, Steve Agnew, Sammy Chung (Chief Scout).

Playing staff for 1992-93 (As at 1 July 1992)   BLACKBURN ROVERS

PLAYERS	CLUB DEBUT (Football League)	1991-92 APPEARANCES				1991-92 GOALS			
		Lge	FL Cup	FA Cup	Others	Lge	FL Cup	FA Cup	Others
GOALKEEPERS									
Collier, Darren	Ipswich T. (A) 13 May 1989								
Dickins, Matt	Wolverhampton W. (H) 14 April 1992	1							
Mimms, Bobby	Charlton Ath. (A) 1 January 1991	45	2	2	4				
DEFENDERS									
Brown, Richard	Port Vale (H) 14 September 1991	24+2		2	1				
Dewhurst, Robert	Hull C. (H) 28 August 1990								
Dobson, Tony	Ipswich T. (H) 19 January 1991	4+1	2		1				
Hendry, Colin	Charlton Ath. (A) 9 November 1991	26+4		0+1	3	4			
Hill, Keith	Middlesbrough (H) 26 September 1987	31+1		2	1				
May, David	Swindon T. (A) 1 April 1989	12	1		4				
Moran, Kevin	Stoke C. (H) 27 January 1989	37+4	2	2	3	2			1
Munro, Stuart	Ipswich T. (H) 31 August 1991	1							
O'Shaughnessy, Brendan	–								
Pickup, Jonathan	–								
Price, Chris	Leeds U. (H) 23 August 1986	11+2			2	3			
Sulley, Chris	Stoke C. (H) 14 March 1987	7	2						
Wright, Alan	Grimsby T. (H) 26 October 1991	32+1		2	3	1			
MIDFIELDERS									
Agnew, Steve	Portsmouth (H) 17 August 1991	2	2						
Atkins, Mark	Chelsea (A) 27 August 1988	40+4	2	2	3	6			
Cowans, Gordon	Middlesbrough (H) 30 November 1991	26		2	3	1		1	
Makel, Lee	–								
Reid, Nicky	Hull C. (A) 15 August 1987	8+13	2	1+1	0+1	1			
Richardson, Lee	Bristol C. (A) 25 August 1990	18+6	0+1		2+2	1			
Sellars, Scott	Leeds U. (H) 23 August 1986	28+2		2	3	7			1
Shepstone, Paul	Bristol C. (A) 25 August 1990	1	1						
Sherwood, Tim	Middlesbrough (A) 22 February 1992	7+4							
Skinner, Craig	Bristol C. (H) 15 December 1990	7+2		1	1				
FORWARDS									
Donnelly, Darren	Charlton Ath. (H) 13 April 1991								
Garner, Simon	Newcastle U. (A) 9 September 1978	14+11	2	0+2	1	5			
Lindsay, Scott	–								
Livingstone, Steve	Ipswich T. (H) 19 January 1991	6+4	1			1			
McGarry, Ian	–								
Newell, Mike	Barnsley (H) 16 November 1991	18+2		2	3	6		3	2
Shearer, Duncan	Barnsley (A) 28 March 1992	5+1			0+1	1			
Speedie, David	Portsmouth (H) 17 August 1991	34+2	2	2	3	23		1	2
Tallon, Gary	–								
Thorne, Peter	–								
Wegerle, Roy	Bristol Rov. (A) 7 March 1992	9+3				2			
Wilcox, Jason	Swindon T. (H) 16 April 1990	33+5			1	4			

PLAYERS MAKING APPEARANCES IN 1991-92 (No longer with the club)

PLAYERS	CURRENT CLUBS	Lge	FL Cup	FA Cup	Others	Lge	FL Cup	FA Cup	Others
Baah, Peter	F/T (May 1992)	1							
Beardsmore, Russell	Manchester U. (Loan – December 1991)	1+1							
Duxbury, Michael	Bradford C. (March 1992)	5							
Gayle, Howard	F/T (April 1992)	1+3	0+2		1				
Irvine, Alan	F/T (May 1992)	4+2	1		0+1				
Johnrose, Len	Hartlepool U. (February 1992)	7			1			1	

TRAINEES

Paul B. Ainscough, Christopher J. Bardsley, Ian J. Berry, James S. Berry, Andrew J. Gifford, Wayne J. Gill, Steven J. Grunshaw, Daniel J. Goodall, Darren Grasby, Lee. A. Hitchen, Joshua H. Metcalf, Lee A. Moss, Alec D. Ridgway, Andrew M. Scott, Damian Sweeney, Scott L. Thornton

The Blackburn Rovers Captain

Kevin Moran

Kevin Moran's footballing career began after he was spotted playing for the University College Dublin team, Pegasus. Since then his winged heels have taken him to Manchester United, Sporting Gijon and then re-routed him to Blackburn Rovers two seasons ago.

He is a quiet man, a responsible person whose "never say die" attitude to play is an inspiration to the patchwork quilt of talents gathered together at Ewood Park for 1991-92. Moran was a crucial component in Jack Charlton's glorious Eire side and he played in all five matches in Italia 90.

Kevin Moran is described as a very likeable man, gentle of nature, who has had a career plagued by injuries and a certain Cup-Final. He is popular with management and colleagues and is easily the most experienced player in the side. He has spent most of his working like as a defender, or on the left side of midfield.

At the beginning of the year few at Ewood Park could have dreamed that the club was about to undergo a mind-blowing metamorphosis. After a shaky start to the season, manager Dave Mackay was removed and Tony Parkes took the reins. Matches were won and life was a little more relaxed than in October and after much Press speculation, Kenny Dalglish signed as Blackburn Rovers' new manager. Gates which had previously registered at 6/7,000, now swelled to 12/14,000 and eventually to bursting point when 19,000 fans squeezed in. By now, thanks to millionaire Chairman, Jack Walker, Blackburn Rovers had a bank balance that was the envy of every club in the League. Surrounded by a recession, Rovers had hit the jackpot. Just before Christmas the club rose from the lower half of the Division Two to the top and stayed there, apparently immovable. The bookies stopped taking bets on Blackburn Rovers and promotion seemed inevitable. But in football you have to put all your eggs in one basket and there's always risk. A player was injured, another was suspended and the winning rhythm was disturbed. And just as suddenly, Ewood Park was struggling and people who had not said anything of the sort, were saying I told you so.

There was a memorable game in the Semi-Final of the Play-Offs against Derby. Rovers had gone two down and all seemed irrecoverable, but just before half-time, in went their first goal and they won 4-2.

Plymouth Argyle will remember Blackburn Rovers with some pain. In Dalglish's first home game as manager, they won 5-2 and Moran scored. At the tailend of the year, when Argyle were battling to stay up and Rovers were pitching for a place in the Play-Offs, David Speedie got a hat-trick.

The Play-Off final was an emotional game, especially for those who were there when the club had gone down in 1966. It was hard work and none toiled more effectively than captain, Kevin Moran. He seemed to be everywhere that day. And there are many who felt that he should have been awarded the accolade of "Man of the Match".

Captain's Table

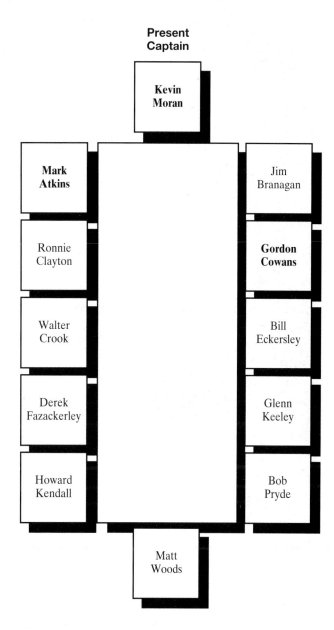

Kevin Moran heads an impressive table with his guests, including many famous post-war club captains both past and present. Those still on the club books are denoted in **bold** print.

CHELSEA
1905

THE BLUES

Team Manager Ian Porterfield
Club Address Stamford Bridge, Fulham Road, London SW6 1HS
Record Attendance 82,905 v Arsenal, Div. 1, 12 October 1935
Turned Professional 1905
Previous Names None
Club Honours Football League: Div. 1 Champions 1954-55. Div. 2 Champions 1983-84, 1988-89. FA Cup: Winners 1970. Football League Cup: Winners 1965. European Cup Winners Cup: Winners 1970-71
League History 1905-07 Div. 2; 1907-10 Div. 1; 1910-12 Div. 2; 1912-24 Div. 1; 1924-30 Div. 2; 1930-62 Div. 1; 1962-63 Div. 2; 1963-75 Div. 1; 1975-77 Div. 2; 1977-79 Div. 1; 1979-84 Div. 2; 1984-88 Div. 1; 1988-89 Div. 2; 1989- Div. 1
Most League Points in a Season (2 for a win) 57 in Div. 2, 1906-07. (3 for a win) 99 in Div. 2, 1988-89
Most League Goals in a Season 98 in Div. 1, 1960-61
Record League Victory 7-0 v Lincoln C. in Div. 2, 29 October 1910, v Walsall in Div. 2, 4 February 1989 and 9-2 v Glossop in Div. 2, 1 September 1906
Record League Defeat 1-8 v Wolverhampton W. in Div. 1, 26 September 1953 and 0-7 v Nottingham F. in Div. 1, 20 April 1991
Consecutive League Wins 8 in 1927 and 1989
Consecutive League Defeats 7 in 1952
Record League Appearances Ron Harris, 655 between 1962-80
Record League Goalscorer—Career Bobby Tambling, 164 between 1958-70
Record League Goalscorer—Season Jimmy Greaves, 41 in Div. 1, 1960-61

1991-92 Record

Football League First Division (14th): Played 42, Won 13, Drawn 14, Lost 15, Goals For 50, Goals Against 60, Played 63
FA Cup Third Round: Hull C. (A)2-0; Fourth Round: Everton (H)1-0; Fifth Round: Sheffield U. (H)1-0; Sixth Round: Sunderland (H)1-1 (R)1-2

League Cup Second Round: Tranmere Rov. (H)1-1 (A)1-3
Zenith Cup Second Round: Swindon T. (H)1-0; Third Round: Ipswich T. (H)2-0; Fourth Round: Crystal Palace (A)1-0; Semi-Final: Southampton (A)0-2 (H)1-3

1991-92: Back Row L-R: Andy Myers, Gareth Hall, Damien Matthew, *Jason Cundy,* Kevin Hitchcock, Alan Dickens, Steve Clarke, Joe Allon, Graeme le Saux. **Middle Row:** Eddie Niedzwiecki (Reserve Team Coach), Bob Ward (Physio), David Lee, Kerry Dixon, Paul Elliott, Dave Beasant, Ken Monkou, Ian Pearce, Erland Johnsen, Dave Collyer (Youth Team Coach), *Stan Ternent* (First Team Coach). **Front Row:** Graham Stuart, Dennis Wise, Vinny Jones, Gwyn Williams (Assistant Manager), Ian Porterfield (Manager), Andy Townsend, *Tom Boyd, Kevin Wilson.*

PLAYERS	CLUB DEBUT (Football League)	1991-92 APPEARANCES				1991-92 GOALS			
		Lge	FL Cup	FA Cup	Others	Lge	FL Cup	FA Cup	Others
GOALKEEPERS									
Beasant, Dave	Crystal Palace (H) 14 January 1989	21	1	1					
Chatfield, Ian	–								
Hitchcock, Kevin	Southampton (H) 26 March 1988	21	1	4	5				
DEFENDERS									
Clarke, Steve	Norwich C. (A) 24 January 1987	31	2	1	3	1			
Elliott, Paul	Wimbledon (H) 17 August 1991	35	2	5	5	3			
Hall, Gareth	Wimbledon (A) 5 May 1987	9+1		4	1				
Johnsen, Erland	Q.P.R. (A) 9 December 1989	6+1							
Lee, David	Leicester C. (H) 1 October 1988	1							
Monkou, Ken	Stoke C. (H) 1 May 1989	31	2		3				
Myers, Andy	Luton T. (H) 6 April 1991	9+2	0+1	2	1	1			
Pearce, Ian	Aston Villa (A) 11 May 1991	0+2			0+1				
Sinclair, Frank	Luton T. (H) 6 April 1991	8		1					
MIDFIELDERS									
Barnard, Darren	West Ham U. (H) 4 April 1992	1+3							
Burley, Craig	Nottingham F. (A) 20 April 1991	6+2			2				
Dickens, Alan	Wimbledon (A) 19 August 1989	6+4			1				
Jones, Vinny	Luton T. (H) 31 August 1991	35	1	4	5	3		1	2
Le Saux, Graeme	Portsmouth (A) 13 May 1989	39+1	2	3	4+1	3			
Matthew, Damian	Crystal Palace (H) 16 April 1990	2+5	1						
Newton, Eddie	Everton (A) 2 May 1992	0+1				1			
Townsend, Andy	Derby Co. (H) 25 August 1990	35	2	5	3	6	1		
FORWARDS									
Allon, Joe	Wimbledon (H) 17 August 1991	2+9	0+2		2+1	2			1
Cascarino, Tony	Crystal Palace (H) 8 February 1992	11		2		2			
Dixon, Kerry	Derby Co. (H) 27 August 1983	32+3	2	4+1	3	5			1
Rowe, Zeke	–								
Stuart, Graham	Crystal Palace (H) 16 August 1990	20+7		3+1	2+1			1	
Wise, Dennis	Derby Co. (H) 25 August 1990	37+1	2	4	4	11	1	2	1

PLAYERS MAKING APPEARANCES IN 1991-92 (No longer with the club)

PLAYERS	CURRENT CLUBS	Lge	FL Cup	FA Cup	Others	Lge	FL Cup	FA Cup	Others
Allen, Clive	West Ham U. (March 1992)	15+1		4+1		7		2	
Boyd, Tommy	Glasgow Celtic (February 1992)	22+1	2	2	5				
Cundy, Jason	Tottenham H. (March 1992)	12		5	2	1			
Gilkes, Michael	Reading (Loan – January 1992)	0+1			0+1				
Wilson, Kevin	Notts Co. (March 1992)	15+7	2	1+2	2+1	3			

TRAINEES

Stan R. Bowder, Nicholas V. Colgan, Terry W. Christie, Jeremy M. Davies, Ryan N. J. Goddard, John P. Hughes, Mustafa K. Izzet, Steven M. Martin, Jason D. McLennan, Christian W. Metcalfe, Craig T. Norman, Landilane Salako, Barry Scott, Neil J. Shipperley, Terence J. Skiverton, Paul S. Yates

The Chelsea Captain

Andy Townsend

Andy Townsend has been described a one of the most aesthetically pleasing midfielders in Europe. Creative, cerebral, elegant and with the kind of touch that made Liam Brady a name to lift the senses, Andy Townsend has captained Chelsea through a difficult year both on and off the pitch. While others have battled with the seige of Stamford Bridge, the players and popular manager, Ian Porterfield, faced the task of maintaining an equilibrium on the playing field so that supporters continued to attend, despite uncertainties regarding the club' future. Added to that external problem, Chelsea's pitch was appalling and injuries and illnesses, the perennial scourge of a convoluted and punishing League schedule all took their toll on clubs last season and Chelsea was no exception. When Townsend arrived at Stamford Bridge from Norwich for a mighty £1.2 million, he was heralded as the "complete midfielder" – he can defend and win the ball, he has the vision to turn defence into attack in one move, his passing is accurate, he rarely loses possession, he is a superb support player and he scores goals. To select such a player as captain can sometimes be self-destructive, but Townsend is a brave and strong-minded leader – his playing example is enough to inspire the mercurial talents of the intelligent and exciting Graham le Saux, as well as it serves to temper the more volatile, but so passionately committed, Vinny Jones and Dennis Wise. At the back though, Townsend is nobly supported by the experienced Paul Elliott, who has taken over the captain's armband when the Northern Ireland International has been unavailable through injury or illness.

There were some memorable games last season, but there are two which have stayed in Andy Townsend's personal bank. On 1 February, Chelsea beat Liverpool at Anfield for the first time in 56 years. For Townsend it was not just the victory but the manner in which his team played that pleased him most. "We played so well as a unit and we didn't just scrape home either. We thoroughly deserved to win. And to win a penalty at Anfield is an event in itself"!

There was a special atmosphere for the Fifth Round Cup tie against Sheffield United later on in the same month. It was Stamford Bridge's biggest crowd of the season. "The place was packed out", Townsend recalls. "And there was real buzz among the supporters and among the players. All the anticipation associated with a FA Cup-run was in the air – you could feel the expectations of absolutely everyone – it was electric. And we won with that magnificent goal from Stuart".

The clever Graham Stuart showed great enterprise during the game, but it was obvious that he was positively encouraged by the ubiquitous Townsend.

And back to the future? The pitch has been treated to a facelift, the ground is no longer under threat and the team has remained almost stable as the transfer market steadies. Chelsea and Townsend know that all will be well this season.

Captain's Table

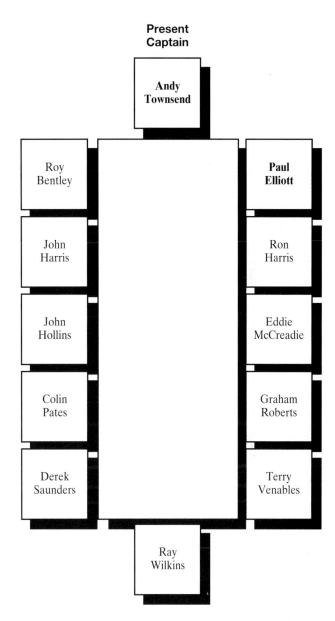

Present Captain

Andy Townsend

Roy Bentley	**Paul Elliott**
John Harris	Ron Harris
John Hollins	Eddie McCreadie
Colin Pates	Graham Roberts
Derek Saunders	Terry Venables

Ray Wilkins

Andy Townsend heads an impressive table with his guests, including many famous post-war club captains both past and present. Those still on the club books are denoted in **bold** print.

COVENTRY CITY
1883

THE SKY BLUES

Team Manager Bobby Gould
Club Address Highfield Road Stadium, King Richard Street, Coventry CV2 4FW
Record Attendance 51,455 v Wolverhampton W., Div. 2, 29 April 1967
Turned Professional 1893
Previous Names Singers
Club Honours Football League: Div. 2 Champions 1966-67; Div. 3 Champions 1963-64; Div. 3(S) Champions 1935-36. FA Cup: Winners 1987
League History 1919-25 Div. 2; 1925-26 Div. 3(N); 1926-36 Div. 3(S); 1936-52 Div. 2; 1952-58 Div. 3(S); 1958-59 Div. 4; 1959-64 Div. 3; 1964-67 Div. 2; 1967- Div. 1
Most League Points in a Season (2 for a win)
60 in Div. 4, 1958-59 and in Div. 3, 1963-64. (3 for a win) 63 in Div. 1, 1986-87
Most League Goals in a Season 108 in Div. 3(S), 1931-32
Record League Victory 9-0 v Bristol C. in Div. 3(S), 28 April 1934
Record League Defeat 2-10 v Norwich C. in Div. 3(S), 15 March 1930
Consecutive League Wins 6 in 1964
Consecutive League Defeats 9 in 1919
Record League Appearances George Curtis, 486 between 1956-70
Record League Goalscorer—Career Clarrie Bourton, 171 between 1931-37
Record League Goalscorer—Season Clarrie Bourton, 49 in Div. 3(S), 1931-32

1991-92 Record

Football League First Division (19th) Played 42, Won 11, Drawn 11, Lost 20, Goals For 35, Goals Against 44, Points 44
FA Cup Third Round: Cambridge U. (H)1-1 (R)0-1

League Cup Second Round: Rochdale (H)4-0 (A)0-1; Third Round: Arsenal (H)1-0; Fourth Round: Tottenham H. (H)1-2
Zenith Cup Second Round: Aston Villa (H)0-2

1991-92: Back Row L-R: Micky Gynn, Stewart Robson, *Trevor Peake,* Robert Rosario, Andy Pearce, Peter Billing, Peter Ndlovu, Craig Middleton. **Middle Row:** George Dalton (Physio), Brian Borrows, Lee Hurst, Steve Ogrizovic, Paul Edwards, Lloyd McGrath, Brian Eastick (Reserve Team Coach), *Mick Mills* (Assistant Manager). **Front Row:** Kenny Sansom, Ray Woods, Kevin Drinkell, *Terry Butcher* (Player/Manager), David Smith, Dean Emerson, Kevin Gallacher.

PLAYERS	CLUB DEBUT (Football League)	1991-92 APPEARANCES				1991-92 GOALS			
		Lge	FL Cup	FA Cup	Others	Lge	FL Cup	FA Cup	Others
GOALKEEPERS									
Davies, Martin	–								
Ogrizovic, Steve	Aston Villa (A) 25 August 1984	38	3	2	1				
DEFENDERS									
Atherton, Peter	Q.P.R. (A) 24 August 1991	35							
Billing, Peter	Charlton Ath. (A) 28 October 1989	17+5	4	2		1			
Booty, Martyn	Chelsea (H) 2 November 1991	2+1	1	2					
Borrows, Brian	Manchester C. (H) 17 August 1985	34+1	3	2	1			1	
Busst, David	–								
Carr, Gerard	–								
Chadwick, Luke									
Edwards, Paul	Sheffield Wed. (H) 17 March 1990	4+1	2		1				
Greenman, Chris	Crystal Palace (H) 19 October 1991	4			1				
Hurst, Lee	Wimbledon (A) 2 February 1991	8+2	2+1	1					
Pearce, Andy	Leeds U. (A) 9 March 1991	36	4	2	1	2			
Sansom, Kenny	Manchester C. (H) 23 March 1991	21		2					
Smith, Ricky	–								
MIDFIELDERS									
Crews, Barry	–								
Flynn, Sean	Sheffield U. (A) 26 December 1991	21+1				2			
Gynn, Micky	Watford (A) 27 August 1983	21+2	1	1		3			
McGrath, Lloyd	Southampton (A) 28 April 1984	38+2	4	2	1	1	1		
Middleton, Craig	Tottenham H. (A) 14 April 1990	1	1						
Robson, Stewart	Leeds U. (A) 9 March 1991	37	2	1	1	3			
Sheridan, Anthony	–								
Wilson, Carl	–								
FORWARDS									
Drinkell, Kevin	Manchester U. (H) 21 October 1989	2+2							
Fleming, Terry	Wimbledon (A) 2 February 1991								
Furlong, Paul	Manchester C. (H) 17 August 1991	27+10	4	1+1	1	4	1		
Gallacher, Kevin	Chelsea (H) 3 February 1990	33	4	1	1	8	2		
Ndlovu, Peter	Q.P.R. (A) 24 August 1991	9+14	2		0+1	2			
Rosario, Robert	Norwich C. (A) 6 April 1990	26+3	2+1	2	1	4	2		
Smith, David	Manchester U. (A) 6 February 1988	23+1	1	1		4			
Stephenson, Michael	–								
Woods, Billy	–								
Woods, Ray	Crystal Palace (H) 2 March 1991	9	1						

PLAYERS MAKING APPEARANCES IN 1991-92 (No longer with the club)

PLAYERS	CURRENT CLUBS	Lge	FL Cup	FA Cup	Others	Lge	FL Cup	FA Cup	Others
Baker, Clive	F/T (May 1992)		1						
Butcher, Terry	Retired (January 1992)				1				
Emerson, Dean	Hartlepool U. (May 1992)	10+11	2+1		0+1				
Heald, Paul	Leyton Orient (Loan – March 1992)	2							
Sealey, Les	Aston Villa (Loan – March 1992)	2							

TRAINEES

Jamie Barnwell, Timothy A. Blake, David Carmichael, Jamie A. Cleland, David J. Coleman, Graham Hepburn, Richard J. Jones, Thomas L. Keetings, Craig J. Melrose, Paul W. O'Brien, Gavin F. O'Toole, Lee Rogers, Stephen D. Williams, Scott C. Young

The Coventry City Captain

Stewart Robson

Last season, Stewart Robson was voted "Player of the Year" by the Coventry fans. This must rank as some achievement since it was Robson's first year as captain, though he is not happy that his team finished so low in the table, only just avoiding relegation.

Robson is a brave, intelligent man, a student of football, a player who has without doubt endured more than his fair share of serious injury. He has strong views about all areas of football and has the ability to express his thoughts cogently. However, on the pitch he prefers to lead by example; he understands that during a game no amount of ranting and raving is ever effective, but a captain whose own game is full of running and heart can do far more to energise a flagging side.

Stewart Robson has always epitomised the ultimate in professionalism – even during the close season he was still training regularly. He is looking forward to the new season, though the departure of Don Howe was a disappointment. Last year Coventry only won two games out of the last 25, despite being fifth in the table at one time, so Robson is anxious to erase that memory from his supporters' minds with an enthusiastic start in August. He believes that the side battled hard throughout the year but suffered badly from a spell of goal starvation.

As a captain he is emphatic about the need to encourage players, support them when they are low in self-esteem and rally a unified response to difficult times in the year. Too much negative thinking and reporting leads to loss of self-belief and the self-fulfiling prophecy is set in motion – tell a player too many times that he has played badly and in no time at all he believes that he can never play well again.

Nevertheless, Robson was delighted with the team's performance against Manchester United at Highfield Road. "They were top of the table at the time and we outplayed them", he recalls. "It was a marvellous result".

On a personal note, he enjoyed the victory over West Ham away from home. "The West Ham supporters gave me a great reception". Interestingly, Robson reserves his admiration for captains of sports outside football where he feels that their role allows them more freedom to exercise individual philosophies and strengths. He particularly admires Will Carling, the England Rugby Union captain and Mike Brierley, who captained England's cricket side with such individual flair. He thinks that Germany's Mattheus and Bryan Robson are both inspirational captains, both players whose presence on the pitch is almost as significant as their game.

Not so long ago, when Robson was a young Arsenal player for whom much was hoped, he found himself pencilled in by Bobby Robson as a replacement for Bryan Robson, when the England captain was doubtful for an international. The call did not come and several appalling pelvic operations and clubs later finds Robson still determined, still optimistic. When he becomes a manager he will be worth watching!

Captain's Table

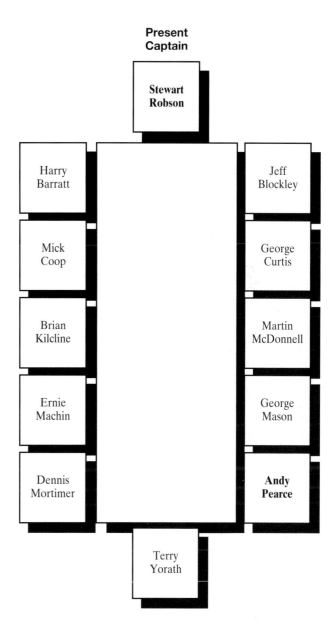

Stewart Robson heads an impressive table with his guests, including many famous post-war club captains both past and present. Those still on the club books are denoted in **bold** print.

CRYSTAL PALACE
1905

THE EAGLES

Team Manager Steve Coppell
Club Address Selhurst Park, London
SE25 6PU
Record Attendance 51,482 v Burnley, Div. 2,
11 May 1979
Turned Professional 1905
Previous Names None
Club Honours Football League: Div. 2
Champions 1978-79; Div. 3(S) Champions
1920-21
League History 1920-21 Div. 3(S); 1921-25
Div. 2; 1925-58 Div. 3(S); 1958-61 Div. 4;
1961-64 Div. 3; 1964-69 Div. 2; 1969-73 Div. 1;
1973-74 Div. 2; 1974-77 Div. 3; 1977-79 Div. 2;
1979-81 Div. 1; 1981-89 Div. 2; 1989- Div. 1
Most League Points in a Season (2 for a win)
64 in Div. 4, 1960-61. (3 for a win) 81 in Div. 2,
1988-89
Most League Goals in a Season 110 in Div. 4,
1960-61
Record League Victory 9-0 v Barrow in Div.
4, 10 October 1959
Record League Defeat 0-9 v Liverpool in
Div. 1, 12 September 1989
Consecutive League Wins 8 in 1921
Consecutive League Defeats 8 in 1925
Record League Appearances Jim Cannon,
571 between 1973-88
Record League Goalscorer—Career Peter
Simpson, 154 between 1930-36
Record League Goalscorer—Season Peter
Simpson, 46 in Div. 3(S), 1930-31

1991-92 Record

Football League First Division (10th): Played 42, Won 14, Drawn 15, Lost 13, Goals For 53, Goals Against 61, Points 57
FA Cup Third Round: Leicester C. (A)0-1
League Cup Second Round: Hartlepool U. (A)1-1 (H)6-1; Third Round: Birmingham C. (A)1-1 (H)1-1 (R)2-1; Fourth Round: Swindon T. (A)1-0; Fifth Round: Nottingham F. (H)1-1 (R)2-4
Zenith Cup Second Round: Southend U. (H)4-2; Third Round: Q.P.R. (A)3-2; Fourth Round: Chelsea (H)0-1

1991-92: Back Row L-R: Ricky Newman, *Jeff Hopkins, Garry Thompson, Martin Chester, Tony Witter,* Chris Coleman, *Alan Pardew,* Gareth Southgate, Dean Gordon. **Middle Row:** Alan Smith (Assistant Manager), Wally Downes (Coach), Spike Hill (Kit Manager), *Paul Bodin,* Paul Brazier, *Rudi Hedman,* Stan Collymore, Jimmy Glass, Nigel Martyn, Andy Woodman, *Perry Suckling,* Andy Thorn, John Salako, Torje Eike (Physio), David West (Physio), Dave Garland (Youth Team Coach). **Front Row:** Jamie Moralee, Eddie McGoldrick, John Humphrey, Simon Rodger, Mark Bright, Geoff Thomas, Steve Coppell (Manager), *Andy Gray, Ian Wright,* Eric Young, Simon Osborn, Richard Shaw, David Whyte.

CRYSTAL PALACE

PLAYERS	CLUB DEBUT (Football League)	1991-92 APPEARANCES				1991-92 GOALS			
		Lge	FL Cup	FA Cup	Others	Lge	FL Cup	FA Cup	Others
GOALKEEPERS									
Glass, Jimmy	–								
Martyn, Nigel	Tottenham H. (H) 18 November 1989	38	8	1	3				
Woodman, Andy	–								
DEFENDERS									
Budden, John	–								
Coleman, Chris	Chelsea (H) 26 October 1991	14+4	2+2		2	4			
Edwards, Russell	–								
Gordon, Dean	Tottenham H. (H) 22 December 1991	2+2	0+1		0+1				
Humphrey, John	Luton T. (A) 25 August 1990	36+1	4+2	1	0+1				
Patterson, Darren	–								
Shaw, Richard	Reading (A) 19 September 1987	9+1							
Sinnott, Lee	Manchester C. (A) 24 August 1991	35+1	5	1	1				
Southgate, Gareth	Liverpool (A) 23 April 1991	26+4	6		3				
Thorn, Andy	Manchester U. (A) 9 December 1989	33	7	1	3		2		
Young, Eric	Luton T. (A) 25 August 1990	30	7	1	3	1			1
MIDFIELDERS									
Bowry, Bobby	–								
Hawthorne, Mark	–								
Holman, Mark	–								
McGoldrick, Eddie	Chelsea (A) 14 January 1989	36	8	1	3	3			1
Mortimer, Paul	Coventry C. (A) 19 October 1991	17+4		1	3	2			
Newman, Ricky	–								
O'Connor, Martyn	–								
Osborn, Simon	Tottenham H. (H) 17 April 1991	13+1	4		1+2	2			
Rodger, Simon	Sheffield Wed. (A) 5 October 1991	20+2	6	0+1	0+1				
Thomas, Geoff	Huddersfield T. (A) 15 August 1987	30	5	1	2	6	1		2
FORWARDS									
Barnes, Andy	Q.P.R. (A) 2 May 1992	0+1							
Bright, Mark	Ipswich T. (H) 15 November 1986	42	8	1	3	16	4		1
Collymore, Stan	Q.P.R. (H) 16 February 1991	4+8	1+2			1	1		
Moralee, Jamie	Coventry C. (H) 1 February 1992	2+4							
Salako, John	Barnsley (H) 24 January 1987	10	1			2			
Thompson, Niall	–								
Watts, Grant	–								
Whyte, David	Wimbledon (A) 26 December 1991	7+4	1+2		0+1	1	1		
PLAYERS MAKING APPEARANCES IN 1991-92 (No longer with the club)									
PLAYERS	CURRENT CLUBS								
Bodin, Paul	Swindon T. (January 1992)	3+1	1						
Gabbiadini, Marco	Derby Co. (January 1992)	15	6	1	3	5	1		1
Gray, Andy	Tottenham H. (March 1992)	25	7	1	3	2	4		1
Hedman, Rudi	F/T (May 1992)	0+3							
Pardew, Alan	Charlton Ath. (November 1991)	3+5	1						
Suckling, Perry (N/C)	Watford (June 1992)	3							
Sullivan, Neil	Wimbledon (Loan – May 1992)	1							
Wright, Ian	Arsenal (September 1991)	8				5			

TRAINEES

Paul Charlton, Timothy J. Clark, Steven G. Cornish, Sean F. Daly, Edward Dixon, Kevin Hall, Glenn Little, Andrew McPherson, George E. Ndah, Marcus Rourke, Chris Roberts, Eric Smith, Paul Sparrow, Paul D. Stokoe, Jamie R. Vincent, David Williams

The Crystal Palace Captain

Geoff Thomas

People at the Palace speak very highly of Geoff Thomas. He's known as a tough, competitive and inspirational captain whose all-round game has certainly improved since he received International recognition. Geoff Thomas is one of the game's most professional players so happy to have been plucked from the lower slopes of the league and still slightly amazed to be where he is.

Perhaps it is significant that he is not a player endowed with a natural talent, but he has used the strengths he has to operate crucially for Crystal Palace – so much so that when he has been absent throught injury, the club has missed the driving force he brings to the side.

He claims that this has been a hard season for Crystal Palace even though they finished tenth in the League. They were dogged by media attention early on and the cup-runs were disappointing after so much success in previous years. The dreadful injury to John Salako at the start of the season was a terrible blow for everyone at the club. "John was so young and he was just beginning to emerge as a fine player. He'd had a great time in Australia with the national squad and no-one could have envisaged that he would have been out for a whole season. But he's back training now and looking fit and hungry".

Thomas was sad to lose Ian Wright "to a bigger stage". "Ian has to be one of the best players to watch – he has flair, skill, pace and he can always do something out of the ordinary. It did take us a while to get used to a different style of play and Mark Bright has done ever so well. Ian Wright was a great servant to Crystal Palace".

As the team was altered for one reason or another, Steve Coppell was able to play youngsters who might not normally have expected to play first team football. Geoff Thomas appreciated that this has not always been too pleasing for spectators and maintains that the new faces are improving all the time and that this season should be much easier for them. "For all the disappointments we've had this season there have been as many pluses hidden in those young players whom we might not have seen.

The highlight of the season has to be winning the 'double' over Liverpool. To be honest the victory at Anfield was a bit special. We performed well and we could have scored more; it was a very professional display and was most definitely a turning point.

As for beating Arsenal – well. We have to reach the standard set by Arsenal who play a similar game to ours, but it is more refined. We are compact as a team and that is one of our major strengths.

This season we plan to get off to a really good start and hope that things snowball. The squad is really hyped-up and ready to go. You can't just be content to compete in the Premier League – you have to go for trophies and League positions. And that place in Europe"!

Captain's Table

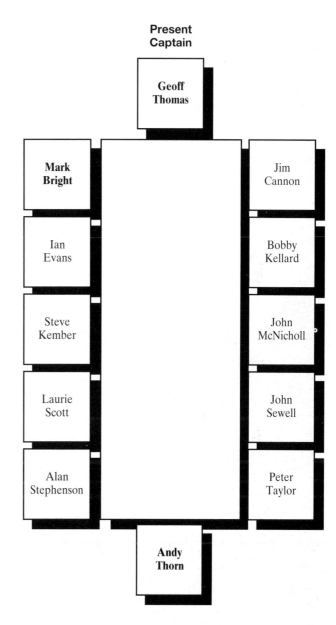

Geoff Thomas heads an impressive table with his guests, including many famous post-war club captains both past and present. Those still on the club books are denoted in **bold** print.

EVERTON
1878

THE TOFFEEMEN

Team Manager Howard Kendall
Club Address Goodison Park, Liverpool L4 4EL
Record Attendance 78,299 v Liverpool, Div. 1, 18 September 1948
Turned Professional 1885
Previous Names St Domingo
Club Honours Football League: Div. 1 Champions 1890-91, 1914-15, 1927-28, 1931-32, 1938-39, 1962-63, 1969-70, 1984-85, 1986-87; Div. 2 Champions 1930-31. FA Cup: Winners 1906, 1933, 1966, 1984. European Cup Winners Cup: Winners 1984-85
League History 1888-1930 Div. 1; 1930-31 Div. 2; 1931-51 Div. 1; 1951-54 Div. 2; 1954- Div. 1
Most League Points in a Season (2 for a win) 66 in Div. 1, 1969-70. (3 for a win) 90 in Div. 1, 1984-85

Most League Goals in a Season 121 in Div. 2, 1930-31
Record League Victory 9-1 v Manchester C. in Div. 1, 3 September 1906 and v Plymouth Arg. in Div. 2, 27 December 1930
Record League Defeat 4-10 v Tottenham H. in Div. 1, 1984-85
Consecutive League Wins 12 in 1894
Consecutive League Defeats 6 in 1930, 1958 and 1972
Record League Appearances Ted Sagar, 465 between 1929-53
Record League Goalscorer—Career "Dixie" Dean, 349 between 1925-37
Record League Goalscorer—Season "Dixie" Dean, 60 in Div. 1, 1927-28 (Football League record)

1991-92 Record

Football League First Division (12th): Played 42, Won 13, Drawn 14, Lost 15, Goals For 52, Goals Against 51, Points 53
FA Cup Third Round: Southend U. (H)1-0; Fourth Round (A) Chelsea 0-1

League Cup Second Round: Watford (H)1-0 (A)2-1; Third Round: Wolverhampton W (A) 4-1; Fourth Round: Leeds U. (H) 1-4
Zenith Cup Second Round: Oldham Ath. (H) 3-2; Third Round: Leicester C. (A)1-2

1991-92: Back Row L-R: Andy Hinchcliffe, *Eddie Youds,* Neville Southall, Martin Keown, Gerry Peyton, Dave Watson, Alan Harper.
Middle Row: Les Helm (Physio), Jimmy Gabriel (Reserve Team Coach), *Raymond Atteveld,* Robert Warzycha, *Neil McDonald, Mike Newell,* John Ebbrell, Peter Beagrie, Pat Nevin, Colin Harvey (First Team Coach) **Front Row:** *Kevin Sheedy,* Ian Snodin, Mark Ward, Howard Kendall (Manager), *Kevin Ratcliffe,* Tony Cottee, Peter Beardsley.

PLAYERS	CLUB DEBUT (Football League)	1991-92 APPEARANCES				1991-92 GOALS			
		Lge	FL Cup	FA Cup	Others	Lge	FL Cup	FA Cup	Others
GOALKEEPERS									
Kearton, Jason	–								
Peyton, Gerry	–								
Southall, Neville	Ipswich T. (H) 17 October 1981	42	4	2	2				
DEFENDERS									
Ablett, Gary	Nottingham F. (H) 19 January 1992	17		1		1			
Doolan, John	–								
Hinchcliffe, Andy	Leeds U. (H) 25 August 1990	15+3	3		2				
Jackson, Matthew	Aston Villa (H) 19 October 1991	30		2	1	1			
Jenkins, Iain	Q.P.R. (A) 11 May 1991	1+2							
Keown, Martin	Sheffield Wed. (A) 30 August 1989	39	4	2	1				
Moore, Neil	–								
Unsworth, David	Tottenham H. (A) 25 April 1992	1+1				1			
Watson, Dave	Nottingham F. (H) 23 August 1986	35	4	2	2	3			1
MIDFIELDERS									
Ebbrell, John	Wimbledon (H) 4 February 1989	39	4	2	1	1			
Harper, Alan	Nottingham F. (A) 17 August 1991	29+4	1+1	1	2				
Kenny, William	–								
Priest, Christopher	–								
Snodin, Ian	Sheffield Wed. (H) 17 January 1986								
Ward, Mark	Nottingham F. (A) 17 August 1991	37	2	2	1	4			
FORWARDS									
Barlow, Stuart	Wimbledon (H) 10 April 1991	3+4							
Beagrie, Peter	Aston Villa (A) 5 November 1989	20+7	1+1	2	0+1	3	2		
Beardsley, Peter	Nottingham F. (A) 17 August 1991	42	4	2	2	15	3	1	1
Cottee, Tony	Newcastle U. (H) 27 August 1988	17+7	3+1	1+1	2	8	1		1
Johnston, Mo	Notts Co. (H) 23 November 1991	21	1	1	1	7			
Nevin, Pat	Newcastle U. (A) 27 August 1988	7+10	3	1+1	1	2			
Quinlan, Phil	–								
Warzycha, Robert	Nottingham F. (H) 23 March 1991	26+11	1+1	1+1	1	3			
Wood, Kenneth	–								

PLAYERS MAKING APPEARANCES IN 1991-92 (No longer with the club)

PLAYERS	CURRENT CLUBS	Lge	FL Cup	FA Cup	Others	Lge	FL Cup	FA Cup	Others
Atteveld, Raymond	Bristol C. (March 1992)	8+5	3+1		0+2		1		
McDonald, Neil	Oldham Ath. (October 1991)	7+10	3	1+1	1	2			
Newell, Mike	Blackburn Rov. (November 1991)	8+5	2+1		1	1	1		1
Ratcliffe, Kevin	F/T (May 1992)	8+1	2						
Sheedy, Kevin	Newcastle U. (February 1992)	16	2		1	1			
Youds, Eddie	Ipswich T. (November 1991)		0+1		1				

TRAINEES

David Astley, John J. Carridge, Richard Emery, Anthony J. Grant, Peter I. Holcroft, Terence P. Jones, Alan D. McMahon, Mark A. Powell, Christopher Price, Steven T. Reeves, Glenn L. Renforth, Sean M. Roberts, Carl J. Ruffer, Alex P. Smith, Dean A. Smith, Paul Tait, Lee J. Williams

The Everton Captain

Dave Watson

hen Kevin Ratcliffe left Everton on a free transfer it could have been an impossible task to fill the void of his fine and enduring captaincy. But Howard Kendall had no doubts at all that the best man for the job was Dave Watson. He was, in fact, the automatic choice.

Kendall believes that Watson is a super captain. "He leads by example as do all the top-class captains". Known for his strong personality and vigorous defending, Watson also has tremendous character – a quality needed to take over a post which had been held so well by his predecessor. To follow in the footsteps of someone successful is never easy but Watson has made the transition effortlessly and with style.

His manager maintains that he gives 110 per cent in every game, unfailingly. "If you had 11 Dave Watsons in your side you'd not go far wrong", Kendall adds. "When he was out of the team through injury we had some poor results – he was greatly missed. His performances are so consistent and this inevitably rubs off onto the other players. One of the most important things a captain can do is to inspire his colleagues to be better than they think they are – and he does that every week". Kendall has much respect for Watson and he has not been surprised by the way in which he had led the Everton side. "Watson has always been a favourite with supporters so it was natural that that support followed him in his role as captain" – it's something that Watson both appreciates and values. Howard Kendall observes that some players win the affection of the crowd immediately and Watson was such a player. He knows that the Goodison faithfuls have waited far too long for something to put in the trophy cabinet and his determination to do just that will not have diminished during the close season. His partnership with Martin Keown has matured into one of the most potent central defences in the League.

For Everton, the season fell into two distinct sections. Until Christmas everything looked comfortable and the mood at Goodison Park was one of restrained optimism. However, things began to fall away after the New Year. Injuries disrupt any team's rhythm and the second-half of the season found the side struggling now and then. Both Howard Kendall and Dave Watson are determined that next season will be more balanced and though many teams would have been more than content with Everton's final eighth position in the League table, nothing but the best is ever good enough for Dave Watson.

Because Watson is such a consistent player, Howard Kendall found it impossible to select a particular game when his captain was outstanding. "He is always outstanding", he said. "He never has a bad game".

Captain's Table

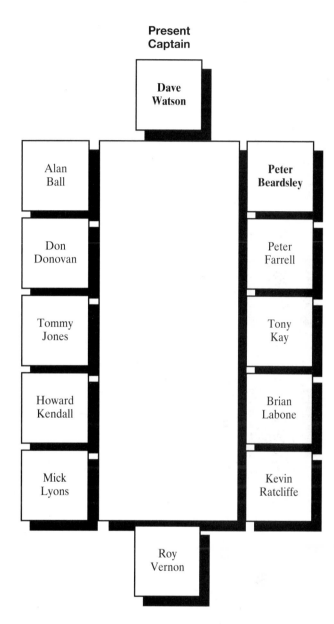

Dave Watson heads an impressive table with his guests, including many famous post-war club captains both past and present. Those still on the club books are denoted in **bold** print.

IPSWICH TOWN
1878

·IPSWICH·
TOWN·F·C

THE BLUES or TOWN

Team Manager John Lyall
Club Address Portman Road, Ipswich IP1 2DA
Record Attendance 38,010 v Leeds U., FA Cup 6th Round, 8 March 1975
Turned Professional 1936
Previous Names None
Club Honours Football League: Div. 1 Champions 1961-62; Div. 2 Champions 1960-61, 1967-68, 1991-92; Div. 3(S) Champions 1953-54, 1956-57. FA Cup: Winners 1978. UEFA Cup: Winners 1980-81
League History 1938-54 Div. 3(S); 1954-55 Div. 2; 1955-57 Div. 3(S); 1957-61 Div. 2; 1961-64 Div. 1; 1964-68 Div. 2; 1968-86 Div. 1; 1986-92 Div. 2; 1992- Div. 1
Most League Points in a Season (2 for a win)

64 in Div. 3(S), 1953-54 and in 1955-56. (3 for a win) 84 in Div. 2, 1991-92
Most League Goals in a Season 106 in Div. 3(S), 1955-56
Record League Victory 7-0 v Portsmouth in Div. 2, 7 November 1964, v Southampton in Div. 1, 2 February 1974 and v West Bromwich A. in Div. 1, 6 November 1976
Record League Defeat 1-10 v Fulham in Div. 1, 26 December 1963
Consecutive League Wins 8 in 1953
Consecutive League Defeats 10 in 1954
Record League Appearances Mick Mills, 591 between 1966-82
Record League Goalscorer—Career Ray Crawford, 204 between 1958-69
Record League Goalscorer—Season Ted Phillips, 41 in Div. 3(S), 1956-57

1991-92 Record

Football League Second Division (1st): Played 46, Won 24, Drawn 12, Lost 10, Goals For 70, Goals Against 50, Points 84
FA Cup Third Round: Hartlepool U. (H)1-1 (R)2-0; Fourth Round: Bournemouth (H)3-0; Fifth Round: Liverpool (H)0-0 (R)2-3

League Cup Second Round: Derby Co. (A)0-0 (H)0-2
Zenith Cup First Round: Bristol Rov. (A)3-1; Second Round: Luton T. (H)1-1; Third Round: Chelsea (A)2-2

1991-92: Back Row L-R: Glenn Pennyfather, *Steve Greaves,* David Lowe, *Tony Humes,* Neil Thompson, Gavin Johnson, David Gregory, *Neil Gregory, David Hill.* **Middle Row:** Simon Milton, Steve Palmer, Jason Dozzell, Phil Whelan, Craig Forrest, *Phil Parkes, Brian Gayle,* Gary Thompson, Lee Honeywood, *Simon Betts.* **Front Row:** *Romeo Zondervan,* Mike Stockwell, Paul Goddard, David Linighan, Frank Yallop, Chris Kiwomya, Steve Whitton.

Playing staff for 1992-93 (As at 1 July 1992)   IPSWICH TOWN

PLAYERS	CLUB DEBUT (Football League)	1991-92 APPEARANCES				1991-92 GOALS			
		Lge	FL Cup	FA Cup	Others	Lge	FL Cup	FA Cup	Others
GOALKEEPERS									
Forrest, Craig	Stoke C. (A) 27 August 1988	46	2	5	3				
Winters, Jason	–								
DEFENDERS									
Honeywood, Lee	–								
Linighan, David	Stoke C. (A) 27 August 1988	36	2	5	2	3			
Thompson, Neil	Barnsley (H) 19 August 1989	45	2	5	3	6			
Wark, John (N/C)	Leicester C. (H) 29 March 1975	36+1	1	5	3	3			
Whelan, Phil	Southend U. (A) 4 April 1992	8			1	2			
Yallop, Frank	Everton (A) 17 March 1984	9+8	2	0+1	2				
Youds, Eddie	Derby Co. (A) 16 November 1991	1							
MIDFIELDERS									
Dozzell, Jason	Coventry C. (H) 4 February 1984	45	1	5	3	11		4	1
Durrant, Lee	–								
Gregory, David	Chelsea (A) 26 December 1988	0+1	0+1		1				
Johnson, Gavin	Barnsley (H) 21 February 1989	33+9	1	5	1	5		1	
Milton, Simon	Swindon T. (A) 28 December 1987	31+3	1	5	3	7		1	
Palmer, Steve	Oxford U. (A) 23 September 1989	16+7		5	1+1				
Pennyfather, Glenn	Portsmouth (A) 28 October 1989	2+1		0+1					
Stockwell, Mike	Coventry C. (A) 26 December 1985	46	2	5	2	2			
Tanner, Adam	–								
FORWARDS									
Goddard, Paul	Millwall (H) 2 February 1991	19+5	1	0+1	1	4			
Kiwomya, Chris	Bradford C. (H) 24 September 1988	43	2	5	1	16		1	2
Lowe, David	Aston Villa (H) 15 August 1987	7+7	1		2+1	1			3
Thompson, Gary	–								
Whitton, Steve	West Bromwich A. (H) 12 January 1991	43	2	5	2	9		1	

PLAYERS MAKING APPEARANCES IN 1991-92 (No longer with the club)

PLAYERS	CURRENT CLUBS	Lge	FL Cup	FA Cup	Others	Lge	FL Cup	FA Cup	Others
Edmonds, Darren	F/T (May 1992)	0+2			0+1				
Gayle, Brian	Sheffield U. (September 1991)	5							
Humes, Tony	Wrexham (March 1992)	5							
Moncur, John	Tottenham H. (Loan – October 1991)	5+1							
Zondervan, Romeo	NEC Breda (June 1992)	25+3	2	0+1	2				

TRAINEES

Graham Connell, Leo S. Cotterell, Gavin P. Dolby, Jeremy J. Eason, Graham P. Mansfield, Philip J. Morgan, Peter R. Mortley, Lee R. Norfolk, David W. Pirie, Darren L. W. Powley, Richard Ryland, James B. Scowrcroft, Theodoros Theodorou, Anthony J. Vaughan, Kenneth Weston, Matthew Weston

The Ipswich Town Captain

David Linighan

t the start of last season nobody at Portman Road could have dreamed up such an end to the year – automatic promotion into the Premier League.

This was David Linighan's second term as captain and he still can't quite believe what has happened. He will join his three brothers in the Premier League next year – who do parents watch in that situation? David Linighan is over six feet tall, a height which seems to be a pre-requisite these days for the position of centre-half, where he has always played. From central defence, Linighan feels that he is well-placed to monitor the game, be aware of everyone else and attend to his own playing role comfortably. He enjoys his captain's role and was particularly flattered when new manager John Lyall selected him. He is reluctant to sing his own praises and maintains that responsibility on the pitch is a collective thing, something he shares with other experienced members of the side.

The team has enormous respect for Lyall as does the whole football industry. To be managed by a man who quietly commands so much admiration has an enriching effect on players and Linighan is the first to recognise this. "His knowledge of football is so vast that you could sit and talk to him about the subject all day and he wouldn't repeat himself once", he says. "He's really given our players self-belief and a will to win".

Ipswich's directors asked John Lyall what he would like to achieve most at Portman Road and this was before he had been appointed as manager. The reply was not the standard wish to win something. John Lyall is made of the stuff of dreams. "I want us to play football that will capture the imagination of people in Suffolk". He started as he meant to go on.

Linighan feels that the previous year when Ipswich finished 17th in the Second Division was a good learning experience for everyone at the club. "This season we have been lucky with injuries, had a few good runs and we ended up four points clear and still learning"!

He remembers the home game against Blackburn, just before Christmas as a significant victory. "They were top, buying players like mad and playing well too. It was a cracking game and we completely overpowered them to win 2-1. I think that was the catalyst that we needed to set us on our way. That's when the self-belief really became rock solid".

He recalls the Barnsley game, won 2-0, primarily because he was injured and missed eight games. No joke at that point in the season. But then came Oxford and Linighan sat on the bench. "That 1-1 draw sealed it. We were up but not champions. Even though I did not play I was still so proud".

But the dreams continue into next season. "Our aim now is to go on producing good football, passing quick and early". Consistency will be the challenge. And capturing the imaginations of the whole of the Premier League.

Captain's Table

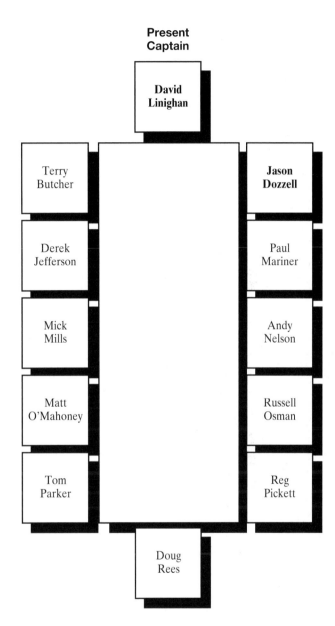

David Linighan heads an impressive table with his guests, including many famous post-war club captains both past and present. Those still on the club books are denoted in **bold** print.

LEEDS UNITED
1904

THE WHITES

Team Manager Howard Wilkinson
Club Address Elland Road, Leeds LS11 0ES
Record Attendance 57,892 v Sunderland, FA Cup 5th Round replay, 15 March 1967
Turned Professional 1920
Previous Names Leeds City
Club Honours Football League: Div. 1 Champions 1968-69, 1973-74, 1991-92. Div. 2 Champions 1923-24, 1963-64, 1989-90. FA Cup: Winners 1972. Football League Cup: Winners 1968. European Fairs Cup: Winners 1967-68, 1970-71
League History 1920-24 Div. 2: 1924-27 Div. 1; 1927-28 Div. 2; 1928-31 Div. 1; 1931-32 Div. 2; 1932-47 Div. 1; 1947-56 Div. 2; 1956-60 Div. 1; 1960-64 Div. 2; 1964-82 Div. 1; 1982-90 Div. 2; 1990- Div. 1

Most League Points in a Season (2 for a win) 67 in Div 1, 1968-69. (3 for a win) 85 in Div. 2, 1989-90
Most League Goals in a Season 98 in Div. 2, 1927-28
Record League Victory 8-0 v Leicester C. in Div. 1, 7 April 1934
Record League Defeat 1-8 v Stoke C. in Div. 1, 27 August 1934
Consecutive League Wins 9 in 1931
Consecutive League Defeats 6 in 1947
Record League Appearances Jack Charlton, 628 between 1953-73
Record League Goalscorer—Career Peter Lorimer, 168 between 1962-86
Record League Goalscorer—Season John Charles, 42 in Div. 2, 1953-54

1991-92 Record

Football League First Division (1st): Played 42, Won 22, Drawn 16, Lost 4, Goals For 74, Goals Against 37, Points 82
FA Cup Third Round: Manchester U. (H)0-1
League Cup Second Round: Scunthorpe U. (A)0-0

(H)3-0; Third Round: Tranmere Rov. (H) 3-1; Fourth Round: Everton (A)4-1; Fifth Round: Manchester U. (H)1-3
Zenith Cup First Round: Nottingham F. (H)1-3

1991-92: Back Row L-R: Bobby Davison, Chris Whyte, Gary McAllister, John Lukic, Mervyn Day, Peter Haddock, Lee Chapman, Rod Wallace. **Middle Row:** Alan Sutton (Physio), Ray Wallace, Steve Hodge, Chris Fairclough, *John McClelland, Mike Whitlow,* Mel Sterland, Mick Hennigan (Coach). **Front Row:** David Batty, Gary Speed, Imre Varadi, Howard Wilkinson (Manager), Gordon Strachan, Tony Dorigo, *Chris Kamara.*

Playing staff for 1992-93 (As at 1 July 1992)　　　　　　　**LEEDS UNITED**

PLAYERS	CLUB DEBUT (Football League)	1991-92 APPEARANCES				1991-92 GOALS			
		Lge	FL Cup	FA Cup	Others	Lge	FL Cup	FA Cup	Others
GOALKEEPERS									
Cousin, Scott	–								
Day, Mervyn	Fulham (A) 17 August 1985								
Lukic, John	Brighton & H. A. (A) 13 October 1979	42	5	1	1				
DEFENDERS									
Dorigo, Tony	Nottingham F. (H) 20 August 1991	38	5	1	1	3			
Fairclough, Chris	Portsmouth (H) 25 March 1989	30+1	3+1	1	1	2			
Haddock, Peter	Blackburn Rov. (A) 23 August 1986								
Kerr, Dylan	Brighton & H.A. (H) 15 April 1989								
Newsome, Jon	Wimbledon (A) 2 November 1991	7+3			1	2			
Sterland, Mel	Newcastle U. (A) 19 August 1989	29+2	5	1	1	6	1		
Wallace, Ray	–								
Wetherall, David	Arsenal (H) 3 September 1991	0+1							
Whyte, Chris	Everton (A) 25 August 1990	41	5	1	1	1			
MIDFIELDERS									
Batty, David	Swindon T. (H) 21 November 1987	40	4		1	2			
Hepworth, Richard	–								
Hodge, Steve	Sheffield Wed. (H) 24 August 1991	12+11	3+2	1		7			
McAllister, Gary	Everton (A) 25 August 1990	41+1	4	1		5			
Nicholls, Ryan	–								
Speed, Gary	Oldham Ath. (H) 6 May 1989	41	4	1	1	7	3		
Strachan, Gordon	Portsmouth (H) 25 March 1989	35+1	4			4			
Tinkler, Mark	–								
FORWARDS									
Cantona, Eric	Oldham Ath. (A) 8 February 1992	6+9				3			
Chapman, Lee	Blackburn Rov. (A) 13 January 1990	38	5	1		16	4		
Davison, Bobby	Swindon T. (H) 21 November 1987	0+2		0+1					
Henderson, Damian	–								
Kelly, Garry	Nottingham F. (A) 22 December 1991	0+2	0+1						
O'Connell, Patrick	–								
Shutt, Carl	Bournemouth (H) 1 April 1989	6+8	2+1		1	1	1		
Varadi, Imre	Hull C. (H) 10 February 1990	2+1							
Wallace, Rod	Nottingham F. (H) 20 August 1991	34	3	1	0+1	11	2		1

PLAYERS MAKING APPEARANCES IN 1991-92 (No longer with the club)

PLAYERS	CURRENT CLUBS	Lge	FL Cup	FA Cup	Others	Lge	FL Cup	FA Cup	Others
Agana, Tony	Notts Co. (Loan – February 1992)	1+1							
Grayson, Simon	Leicester C. (March 1992)				0+1				
Kamara, Chris	Luton T. (November 1991)	0+2	0+1		1				
McClelland, John	F/T (May 1992)	16+2	2+1						
Snodin, Glyn	Rotherham U. (February 1992)				1				
Whitlow, Mike	Leicester C. (March 1992)	3+7		0+1		1			
Williams, Andy	Notts Co. (February 1992)		1+1	1					

TRAINEES

Richard Atkinson, Robert A. Bowman, Alexander Byrne, David M. Connor, Andrew J. Couzens, Kevin Daly, Mark S. Ford, Stephen Hill, Michael S. Hoyle, Martin Littlewood, Gary M. Lynam, Gary J. O'Hara, Simon Oliver, Matthew P. Smithard, Steven Tobin, Noel Whelan

The Leeds United Captain

Gordon Strachan

here is a familiar quote from the plundered bard which suggests that "There is a tide in the affairs of men, which, when taken at the flood, leads on to fortune". There is also a familiar quote from the wise men of football which implies that there is a time in a footballer's working life – the age of 30 which acts as a watershed; the player either stagnates or moves forwards in a new direction. Gordon Strachan is proof that passing through that venerable age and stage is a matter of talent, courage and application. Howard Wilkinson is a man of deep wisdom, a man who believes in the pursuit of knowledge for its own sake. Yet for all his astuteness, his serious and truly professional approach to his work, Wilkinson has always been a bit of a romantic. His surprise signing of Gordon Strachan from Manchester United in 1989, in the proverbial 11th hour before the transfer deadline, led some Yorkshire stalwarts to wonder at the sanity of their manager.

Youth was not on Strachan's side, but Wilkinson was to admit later, "It was the best stroke of business that I've done as a manager. I bless the day I signed him". For Strachan, this was possibly that moment of peak flooding – he was inspired for Leeds that season and not long afterwards he earned a recall to Scotland's national team at the age of 32. He displayed an appetite for the game usually seen in players just setting out on their careers. And as Leeds United stirred and became a force to be noticed, it was Strachan who was the Machiavellian in midfield. If his influence was far-reaching, his captaincy was extraordinary. He played football which was simply inspirational and led one well-known journalist to record that Gordon Strachan was one of the few professional footballers of recent times whom the football press, without exception, would pay to watch.

150,000 fans applauded the team on its triumphant journey around the town after the First Division League Championship was theirs. The average gate at Elland Road this season has been 29,500 – the highest for 15 years and the fans began to return soon after Strachan was signed. When this season began, Wilkinson expressed the realistic hope that his team should finish in the top four – certainly he felt that they should improve on their previous position even though they had only just returned to the First Division. They did not play on the opening game of the season, but by the end of October they were at the top. Manchester United dogged the Leeds' slipstream for match after match, yet, amazingly, the Yorkshire side did not drop out of the first two all year. But nothing was ever taken for granted and the final sprint for the title was one of the most exciting and unpredictable for years.

Gordon Strachan cost Leeds United £300,000 – a very small fortune for the man who was to lead Leeds on to the League Championship

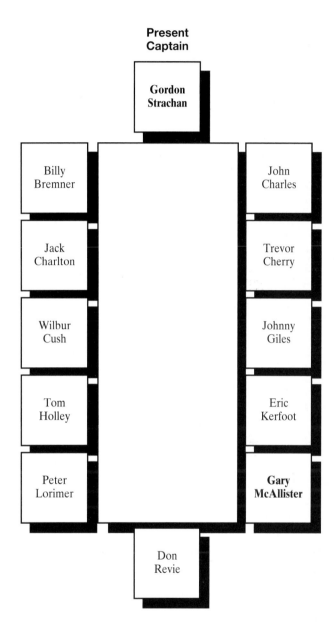

Captain's Table

Present Captain

Gordon Strachan

Billy Bremner

John Charles

Jack Charlton

Trevor Cherry

Wilbur Cush

Johnny Giles

Tom Holley

Eric Kerfoot

Peter Lorimer

Gary McAllister

Don Revie

Gordon Strachan heads an impressive table with his guests, including many famous post-war club captains both past and present. Those still on the club books are denoted in **bold** print.

LIVERPOOL
1892

THE REDS or POOL

Team Manager Graeme Souness
Club Address Anfield Road, Liverpool 4 0TH
Record Attendance 61,905 v Wolverhampton W., FA Cup 4th Round, 2 February 1952
Turned Professional 1892
Previous Names None
Club Honours Football League: Div. 1 Champions 1900-01, 1905-06, 1921-22, 1922-23, 1946-47, 1963-64, 1965-66, 1972-73, 1975-76, 1976-77, 1978-79, 1979-80, 1981-82, 1982-83, 1983-84, 1985-86, 1987-88, 1989-90; Div. 2 Champions 1893-94, 1895-96, 1904-05, 1961-62. FA Cup: Winners 1965, 1974, 1986, 1989, 1992. Football League Cup: Winners 1981, 1982, 1983, 1984. League Super Cup: Winners 1985-86. European Cup: Winners 1976-77, 1977-78, 1980-81, 1983-84. UEFA Cup: Winners 1972-73, 1975-76. European Super Cup: Winners 1977
League History 1893-94 Div. 2; 1894-95 Div.

1; 1895-96 Div. 2; 1896-1904 Div. 1; 1904-05 Div. 2; 1905-54 Div. 1; 1954-62 Div. 2; 1962- Div. 1
Most League Points in a Season (2 for a win) 68 in Div. 1, 1978-79. (3 for a win) 90 in Div. 1, 1987-88
Most League Goals in a Season 106 in Div. 2, 1895-96
Record League Victory 10-1 v Rotherham U. in Div. 2, 18 February 1896
Record League Defeat 1-9 v Birmingham C. in Div. 2, 11 December 1954
Consecutive League Wins 11 in 1982
Consecutive League Defeats 9 in 1899
Record League Appearances Ian Callaghan, 640 between 1960-78
Record League Goalscorer—Career Roger Hunt, 245 between 1959-69
Record League Goalscorer—Season Roger Hunt, 41 in Div. 2, 1961-62

1991-92 Record

Football League First Division (6th): Played 42, Won 16, Drawn 16, Lost 10, Goals For 47, Goals Against 40, Points 64
FA Cup Third Round Crewe Alex. (A)4-0; Fourth Round: Bristol Rov. (A)1-1 (R)2-1; Fifth Round: Ipswich T. (A)0-0 (R)3-2; Sixth Round: Aston Villa (H) 1-0; Semi-Final: Portsmouth 1-1 (R)0-0; Final: Sunderland 2-0

League Cup Second Round: Stoke C. (H)2-2 (R)3-2; Third Round: Port Vale (H)2-2 (R)4-1; Fourth Round: Peterborough U (A)0-1
UEFA Cup First Round: Kuusysi Lahti (H)6-1 (A)0-1; Second Round: Auxerre (A)0-2 (H)3-0; Third Round: Swarovski Tirol (A)2-0 (H)4-0; Fourth Round: Genoa (A)0-2 (H)1-2

1991-92: Back Row L-R: *Steve Staunton, Glenn Hysen,* Nick Tanner, Mike Hooper, *Gary Gillespie,* Bruce Grobbelaar, Mark Wright, *Gary Ablett,* Jan Molby. **Middle Row:** Roy Evans (First Team Assistant Coach), Mike Marsh, Steve McManaman, Barry Venison, Ian Rush, *Jimmy Carter,* Ronny Rosenthal, *David Speedie,* Ron Moran (Chief Coach), Phil Boersma (Physio and Coach). **Front Row:** Dean Saunders, Ray Houghton, John Barnes, Steve Nicol, Graeme Souness (Manager), Ronnie Whelan, *Steve McMahon, Peter Beardsley,* David Burrows.

Playing staff for 1992-93 (As at 1 July 1992)   LIVERPOOL

PLAYERS	CLUB DEBUT (Football League)	1991-92 APPEARANCES				1991-92 GOALS			
		Lge	FL Cup	FA Cup	Others	Lge	FL Cup	FA Cup	Others
GOALKEEPERS									
Grobbelaar, Bruce	Wolverhampton W. (A) 29 August 1981	37	4	9	5				
Hooper, Mike	Newcastle U. (A) 23 August 1986	5	1		3				
James, David	–								
DEFENDERS									
Brydon, Lee	–								
Burrows, David	Coventry C. (H) 22 October 1988	30	5	6	7	1			
Jones, Rob	Manchester U. (A) 6 October 1991	28		9	2+1				
Matteo, Dominic									
Nicol, Steve	Birmingham C. (A) 31 August 1982	34	3	8	7	1			
Scott, John	–								
Tanner, Nicky	Manchester C. (A) 2 December 1989	32	5	2	5+1	1			
Venison, Barry	Manchester C. (H) 25 August 1986	9+4		1+2	0+2	1			1
White, Tom	–								
Wright, Mark	Oldham Ath. (H) 17 August 1991	21	1	9	4				
MIDFIELDERS									
Charnock, Philip	–								
Gelling, Stuart	–								
Harkness, Steve	Q.P.R. (H) 27 August 1991	7+4	2+1	1	3+1				
Houghton, Ray	Luton T. (A) 24 October 1987	36	3	8	4	8	1	1	2
Hutchison, Don	Notts Co. (H) 31 March 1992	0+3							
Kenny, Marc	–								
Kozma, Istvan	Norwich C. (A) 22 February 1992	3+2		0+2					
McAree, Rodney	–								
Marsh, Mike	Charlton Ath. (H) 1 March 1988	19+15	3+1	4+2	7+1				1
Molby, Jan	Norwich C. (A) 25 August 1984	25+1	3	5+1	5	3		1	1
Paterson, Scott									
Redknapp, Jamie	Southampton (A) 7 December 1991	5+1		2	1+1	1			
Thomas, Michael	Tottenham H. (A) 18 December 1991	16+1		5		3		2	
Whelan, Ronnie	Stoke C. (H) 3 April 1981	9+1		3				1	
FORWARDS									
Barnes, John	Arsenal (A) 15 August 1987	12		4	1	1		3	
Cousins, Tony	–								
Fowler, Robert	–								
Jones, Lee	–								
McManaman, Steve	Sheffield U. (H) 15 December 1990	26+4	5	8	8	5	3	3	
Rosenthal, Ronny	Southampton (H) 31 March 1990	7+13	0+3	1+2	1	3			
Rush, Ian	Ipswich T. (A) 13 December 1980	16+2	3	4+1	5	4	3	1	1
Saunders, Dean	Oldham Ath. (H) 17 August 1991	36	5	8	5	10	2	2	9
Walters, Mark	Oldham Ath. (H) 17 August 1991	18+7	4	2+1	4+1	3	2		1
PLAYERS MAKING APPEARANCES IN 1991-92 (No longer with the club)									
PLAYERS	CURRENT CLUBS								
Ablett, Gary	Everton (January 1992)	13+1	2+1		6				
Hysen, Glenn	Gais (March 1992)	3+2	2			1			
McMahon, Steve	Manchester C. (December 1991)	15	4		5	1			

TRAINEES

Wayne A. Dennis, Daniel C. Embleton, Sean P. F. Fallon, Michael J. Fox, Ian Frodsham, Robert J. Holcroft, Stuart J. Jones, Christian Li, Anthony Matthews, Stephen Morris, Ashley J. Neal, Terry Nestor, Paul G. O'Donnell, Paul Snape, Mark E. Stalker

The Liverpool Captain

Mark Wright

There are people who knew Mark Wright when he was much younger who simply cannot believe that the quiet, reserved person they thought he was could ever have achieved the status of England centre-back and captain of Liverpool Football Club.

Wright was a gentle fellow, a trusting person. Those qualities remain with him, but he has grown in many ways which old friends could never have believed possible.

Malcolm Elias used to teach Mark Wright and Martin Keown – an astonishing coincidence, or perhaps a testament to the importance of the genuine mentor in the lives of gifted individuals. Elias no longer teaches, but he is still involved in youth work and he cites Mark Wright often; he sees him as an example for all youngsters to try to emulate.

Now the quiet lad from Oxford has shown that he can be forceful, that he knows what he wants in his professional life. On the pitch he has learned to become the complete competitor and he will stand up for himself and anyone else in his team and hang the cost! There is no questioning his bravery. He is still trusting, but that aspect of his nature is now allied to mature leadership. In the dressing-room he is a dominant character. He will defend all his colleagues. When Graeme Souness made Wright the captain of Liverpool it was perhaps because he could see elements of himself in Wright's character. He sets high standards for himself and is not happy if he lets those standards slip. As a leader he is a magnificent motivator. And to lead Liverpool, especially last season, he needed to draw on reserves of strength that perhaps he did not know were there. Other professionals respect him for his honesty and his directness. He never sits on the fence – he always has the courage to seize the day and trust that everyone else will bring the same commitment to the job in hand. Wright's father comes from Liverpool and now it is Mark Wright's task to win the absolute affection of the Liverpool fans – injury has courted him cruelly last season and he will be determined to prove his all round worth to the people who watch him every week. But he thrives on that kind of challenge.

The Cup Final is always a very special occasion for any player but for Wright, who has weathered a storm or two in recent years, it was a particularly exquisite moment. When he lifted the Cup above his head, words almost failed him!

Elias has watched all the significant moments in Wright's football career but he admits that he has never been so worried as he was during the 1992 FA Cup Final. "I just didn't want him to make a mistake. But I don't know why I was concerned. He just oozed with confidence. I should have known that he would come through. He always does".

Captain's Table

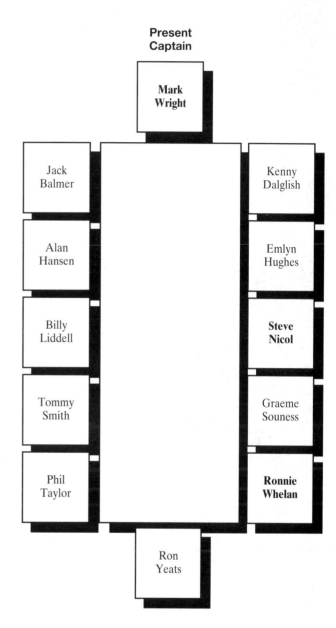

Mark Wright heads an impressive table with his guests, including many famous post-war club captains both past and present. Those still on the club books are denoted in **bold** print.

MANCHESTER CITY
1887

THE BLUES or CITY

Team Manager Peter Reid
Club Address Maine Road, Moss Side, Manchester M14 7WN
Record Attendance 84,569 v Stoke C., FA Cup 6th Round, 3 March 1934
Turned Professional 1887
Previous Names Ardwick
Club Honours Football League: Div. 1 Champions 1936-37, 1967-68; Div. 2 Champions 1898-99, 1902-03, 1909-10, 1927-28, 1946-47, 1965-66. FA Cup: Winners 1904, 1934, 1956, 1969. Football League Cup: Winners 1970, 1976. European Cup Winners Cup: Winners 1969-70.
League History 1892-99 Div. 2; 1899-1902 Div. 1; 1902-03 Div. 2; 1903-09 Div. 1; 1909-10 Div. 2; 1910-26 Div. 1; 1926-28 Div. 2; 1928-38 Div. 1; 1938-47 Div. 2; 1947-50 Div. 1; 1950-51 Div. 2; 1951-63 Div. 1; 1963-66 Div. 2, 1966-83

Div. 1; 1983-85 Div. 2; 1985-87 Div. 1; 1987-89 Div 2; 1989- Div. 1
Most League Points in a Season (2 for a win) 62 in Div. 2, 1946-47. (3 for a win) 82 in Div. 2, 1988-89
Most League Goals in a Season 108 in Div. 2, 1926-27
Record League Victory 11-3 v Lincoln C., in Div. 2, 23 March 1895
Record League Defeat 1-9 v Everton in Div. 1, 3 September 1906
Consecutive League Wins 9 in 1912
Consecutive League Defeats 6 in 1910 and 1960
Record League Appearances Alan Oakes, 564 between 1959-76
Record League Goalscorer—Career Eric Brook, 159 between 1927-39
Record League Goalscorer—Season Tommy Johnson, 38 in Div. 1, 1928-29

1991-92 Record

Football League First Division (5th): Played 42, Won 20, Drawn 10, Lost 12, Goals For 61, Goals Against 48, Points 70
FA Cup Third Round: Middlesbrough (A)1-2

League Cup Second Round: Chester C. (H)3-1 (A)3-0; Third Round: Q.P.R. (H)0-0 (R)3-1; Fourth Round: Middlesbrough (A) 1-2
Zenith Cup Second Round: Sheffield Wed. (A)2-3

1991-92: Back Row L-R: Neil Pointon, David White, Paul Lake, Niall Quinn, *Colin Hendry,* Mark Brennan. **Middle Row:** *Roy Bailey* (Medical Trainer), Tony Book (First Team Coach), *Clive Allen,* Andy Hill, Tony Coton, Martyn Margetson, Gary Megson, *Wayne Clarke,* Sam Ellis (Assistant Manager). **Front Row:** *Adrian Heath,* Ian Brightwell, Steve Redmond, Peter Reid (Player/Manager), Keith Curle, *Jason Beckford,* Michael Sheron.

Playing staff for 1992-93 (As at 1 July 1992) MANCHESTER CITY

PLAYERS	CLUB DEBUT (Football League)	1991-92 APPEARANCES				1991-92 GOALS			
		Lge	FL Cup	FA Cup	Others	Lge	FL Cup	FA Cup	Others
GOALKEEPERS									
Coton, Tony	Tottenham H. (A) 25 August 1990	37	5	1					
Dibble, Andy	Hull C. (A) 27 August 1988	2							
Margetson, Martyn	Manchester U. (A) 4 May 1991	3			1				
DEFENDERS									
Curle, Keith	Coventry C. (A) 17 August 1991	40	4	1	1	5			
Edgehill, Richard	–								
Foster, John	–								
Hill, Andy	Luton T. (H) 5 March 1991	36	5			4			
Limber, Nicky									
Pointon, Neil	Tottenham H. (A) 25 August 1991	39	5	1	1	1			
Redmond, Steve	Q.P.R. (H) 8 February 1986	31	5	1	1	1			
Sliney, Gary	–								
Vonk, Michel	Nottingham F. (A) 21 March 1992	8+1							
MIDFIELDERS									
Brennan, Mark	Aston Villa (H) 5 September 1990	13	2		1	3	1		
Brightwell, David	Wimbledon (A) 22 February 1992	3+1							
Brightwell, Ian	Wimbledon (H) 23 August 1986	36+4	5	1	1	1			
Flitcroft, Gary	–								
Kerr, David	–								
Lake, Paul	Wimbledon (A) 24 January 1987								
Lomas, Steve	–								
McMahon, Steve	Norwich C. (H) 26 December 1991	18		1					
Megson, Gary	Oldham Ath. (A) 14 Janaury 1989	18+4	3	0+1					
Quigley, Mike	Aston Villa (A) 7 December 1991	0+5			1				
Reid, Peter	Everton (A) 17 December 1989	29+2	1	1				1	
Simpson, Fitzroy	Q.P.R. (A) 7 March 1992	9+2				1			
Thomas, Scott	–								
Wallace, Michael	–								
FORWARDS									
Harkin, Sean	–								
Hughes, Michael	Nottingham F. (H) 6 April 1991	24	5	1	1	1			
Mike, Adrian	Notts Co. (H) 25 April 1992	2				1			
Quinn, Niall	Chelsea (H) 21 March 1990	35	4	1		12	2		
Sheron, Mike	Everton (H) 17 September 1991	20+9	2+1	0+1	1	6	1		
White, David	Luton T. (A) 27 September 1986	39	3	1		19	3		

PLAYERS MAKING APPEARANCES IN 1991-92 (No longer with the club)

PLAYERS	CURRENT CLUBS	Lge	FL Cup	FA Cup	Others	Lge	FL Cup	FA Cup	Others
Allen, Clive	Chelsea (December 1991)	0+3	1+1			2	1		
Clarke, Wayne	Walsall (June 1992)	0+5				1			
Heath, Adrian	Stoke C. (March 1992)	20+8	5	1	1	1	1		
Hendry, Colin	Blackburn Rov. (November 1991)	0+6	0+1		1	1			2
Hoekman, Danny	Southampton (January 1992)	0+1	0+2						
Mauge, Ronnie	Bury (Loan – September 1991)				0+1				

TRAINEES

Christopher Beech, James Bentley, Matthew K. Foster, Joseph Harkin, Rae Ingram, Joseph L. Lydiate, Stephen A. McDowell, Darren R. McHugh, Joseph McLean, Nevin Riches, David Roe, John J. Sharpe, Greg Thompson, David E. Turner, David A. Walker

The Manchester City Captain

Keith Curle

When Manchester City finished in sixth place in the League last season, captain Keith Curle was not surprised. He was made captain in his first year, having signed from Wimbledon for an exalted fee. This was Peter Reid's second season as Player/Manager and Curle knew from the start that everything would fall into place for his team.

For this Bristol-born player, suddenly everything seemed to happen at once – a dream move to a club rich in tradition and expectation, a call to join the England squad and the coveted captain's armband – lesser mortals might have bowed under so much. But Keith Curle draws strength from demanding situations. Curle is an elegant and swift centre-back, a relaxed player whose enjoyment of the game is obvious. In the excellent match against Sheffield Wednesday at Hillsborough, Manchester City met an "Owls'" side on the day when everyone played well at the same time. In the City defence, Curle and Coton were inspired and that day spectators were treated to English football at its best. Despite the onslaught from Wednesday's attack, Curle was still able to enjoy himself, teasing David Hirst in his own area. Hirst grinned, Coton roared and the crowd loved it! Pete Reid looked up to heaven.

Keith Curle admits that he always enjoys the challenge of playing against more talented opponents. "I thrive on the fact that for the full 90 minutes I have to concentrate totally when facing someone like Gary Lineker". Hirst he knew well, having joined him on the tour of Australia with the national side last summer.

From his days as a winger at Bristol City, Keith Curle has always been recognised as a sprint king and as an extremely vocal player. He brings both those assets to his captain's role and has enjoyed his first year at the helm of Maine Road. He maintain's, with a laugh, that City has 11 captains but he's the boss on the pitch! Fortunately, he is the kind of person who relishes responsibility and his all-round play seems to have grown along with his commitment to captaincy.

When Manchester City beat Leeds 4-0, there were many who thought that Curle's side were doing their rivals at Old Trafford a favour – but nothing could have been further from the truth. Keith Curle was particularly proud of his team's performance that day – it was a result for their supporters to cherish. Of course the Manchester "derbies" rank high in Keith Curle's memory bank for last season, especially the 1-1 draw at Old Trafford. To take and score the equalising penalty was a very poignant moment for Curle. "To do that in front of 40,000 people and know that you are the captain of your side, well . . " and the pride in his voice says it all.

He and his wife have been quite overwhelmed by the warmth of the Maine Road Club and its supporters and he is certain that those factors have contributed greatly to the ease with which he has been able to slip into the side as captain and player.

Captain's Table

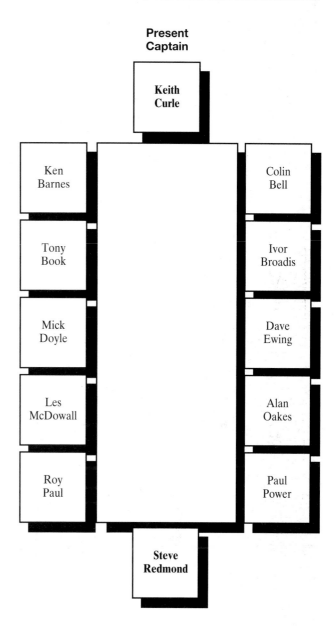

Present Captain

Keith Curle

Ken Barnes

Tony Book

Mick Doyle

Les McDowall

Roy Paul

Colin Bell

Ivor Broadis

Dave Ewing

Alan Oakes

Paul Power

Steve Redmond

Keith Curle heads an impressive table with his guests, including many famous post-war club captains both past and present. Those still on the club books are denoted in **bold** print.

MANCHESTER UNITED
1878

THE RED DEVILS

Team Manager Alex Ferguson
Club Address Old Trafford, Manchester M16 0RA
Record Attendance 76,962 Wolverhampton W. v Grimsby T., FA Cup Semi-Final, 25 March 1939
Turned Professional 1885
Previous Names Newton Heath
Club Honours Football League: Div. 1 Champions 1907-08, 1910-11, 1951-52, 1955-56, 1956-57, 1964-65, 1966-67; Div. 2 Champions 1935-36, 1974-75. FA Cup: Winners 1909, 1948, 1963, 1977, 1983, 1985, 1990. Football League Cup: Winners 1992. European Cup: Winners 1967-68. European Cup Winners Cup: Winners 1990-91
League History 1892-94 Div. 1; 1894-1906 Div. 2; 1906-22 Div. 1; 1922-25 Div. 2; 1925-31 Div. 1; 1931-36 Div. 2; 1936-37 Div. 1; 1937-38 Div. 2; 1938-74 Div. 1; 1974-75 Div. 2; 1975- Div. 1

Most League Points in a Season (2 for a win) 64 in Div. 1, 1956-57. (3 for a win) 81 in Div. 1, 1987-88
Most League Goals in a Season 103 in Div. 1, 1956-57 and in 1958-59
Record League Victory 10-1 v Wolverhampton W. in Div. 2, 15 October 1892
Record League Defeat 0-7 v Blackburn Rov. in Div. 1, 10 April 1926, v Aston Villa in Div. 1, 27 December 1930 and v Wolverhampton W. in Div. 2, 26 December 1931
Consecutive League Wins 14 in 1904-05
Consecutive League Defeats 14 in 1930
Record League Appearances Bobby Charlton, 606 between 1956-73
Record League Goalscorer—Career Bobby Charlton, 198 between 1956-73
Record League Goalscorer—Season Dennis Viollet, 32 in Div. 1, 1959-60

1991-92 Record

Football League First Division (2nd): Played 42, Won 21, Drawn 15, Lost 6, Goals For 63, Goals Against 33, Points 78
FA Cup Third Round: Leeds U. (A)1-0; Fourth Round: Southampton (A)0-0 (R)2-0
League Cup Second Round: Cambridge U. (H)3-0 (A)1-1; Third Round: Portsmouth (H)3-1; Fourth Round: Oldham Ath. (H) 2-0; Fifth Round: Leeds U. (A)3-1; Semi-Final: Middlesbrough (A)0-0 (H)2-1; Final: Nottingham F. 1-0
European Cup Winners Cup First Round: PAE Athinaekos (A)0-0 (H)2-0; Second Round: Atletico Madrid (A)0-3 (H)1-1

1991-92: Back Row L-R: Lee Martin, Steve Bruce, Lee Sharpe, Gary Walsh, Peter Schmeichel, *Jim Leighton,* Mike Phelan, Neil Webb. **Middle Row:** Paul Ince, Clayton Blackmore, Mark Robins, Brain Kidd (Youth Development Officer), Jim McGregor (Physio), Norman Davies (Kit Manager), Denis Irwin, Russell Beardsmore, Darren Ferguson. **Front Row:** Andrei Kantchelskis, Gary Pallister, Brain McClair, Bryan Robson, Alex Ferguson (Manager), Mal Donaghy, Mark Hughes, Danny Wallace.

Playing staff for 1992-93 (As at 1 July 1992)   MANCHESTER UNITED

PLAYERS	CLUB DEBUT (Football League)	1991-92 APPEARANCES				1991-92 GOALS			
		Lge	FL Cup	FA Cup	Others	Lge	FL Cup	FA Cup	Others
GOALKEEPERS									
Pilkington, Kevin	–								
Schmeichel, Peter	Notts Co. (H) 17 August 1991	40	6	3	3				
Walsh, Gary	Aston Villa (A) 13 December 1986	2	1		1				
Wilkinson, Ian	–		1						
DEFENDERS									
Blackmore, Clayton	Nottingham F. (A) 16 May 1984	19+14	4+1	1	1	3	1		
Brazil, Derek	Everton (H) 10 May 1989								
Bruce, Steve	Portsmouth (A) 19 December 1987	37	7	1	4	6	1		
Carey, Brian	–								
Donaghy, Mal	Everton (A) 30 October 1988	16+4	3+1	2					
Irwin, Dennis	Coventry C. (H) 25 August 1990	37+1	7	3	2	4			
Martin, Lee	Wimbledon (H) 9 May 1988	0+1	1		1+2				
Pallister, Gary	Norwich C. (H) 30 August 1989	37+3	8	3	3+1	1			
Parker, Paul	Notts Co. (H) 17 August 1991	24+2	6	3	2				
Whitworth, Neil	Southampton (A) 13 March 1991								
MIDFIELDERS									
Beardsmore, Russell	West Ham U. (H) 24 September 1988				1				
Davies, Simon	–								
Doherty, Adrian	–								
Ferguson, Darren	Sheffield U. (A) 26 February 1991	2+2							
Ince, Paul	Millwall (H) 16 September 1989	31+2	6+1	3	3	3			
Lawton, Craig	–								
Phelan, Mike	Arsenal (H) 19 August 1989	14+4	2+1		4				
Robson, Bryan	Manchester C. (A) 10 October 1981	26+1	5+1	2	3	4	1		
Sharpe, Lee	West Ham U. (H) 24 September 1988	8+6	1+3	0+1		1	1		
Toal, Kieran	–								
Webb, Neil	Arsenal (H) 19 August 1989	29+2	6	3	3	3			
FORWARDS									
Burke, Raphael	–								
Giggs, Ryan	Everton (H) 2 March 1991	32+6	6+2	2+1	1	4	3		
Hughes, Mark	Southampton (H) 21 January 1984	38+1	6	2+1	4	11		1	2
Kantchelkis, Andrei	Crystal Palace (A) 11 May 1991	28+6	4	2	1	5	2	1	
McClair, Brian	Southampton (A) 15 August 1987	41+1	8	3	4	18	4	1	1
McKee, Colin	–								
Maiorana, Giuliano	Millwall (H) 14 January 1989								
Robins, Mark	Wimbledon (A) 22 October 1988	1+1	0+3		2+1		2		
Switzer, George	–								
Wallace, Danny	Manchester C. (A) 23 September 1989				1+1				

Bryan Robson

t has been said that Bryan Robson is at his most significant when he is not playing because only then can his full worth be measured, by his absence.

Neil Webb has clear memories of meeting Bryan Robson for the first time in the national squad. "He was a very quiet person, very down to earth", Webb remembers "and he was totally aware of how unnerving it was for those of us coming up from the lower divisions to the national scene".

Most current managers would love to be able to pencil Bryan Robson's name onto their team sheets, in any capacity, such is his reputation. Neil Webb sums up his national and League team skipper's qualities quite simply. "He leads by example, he never wants to lose, he's unbelievably determined and perhaps, most important of all, when you are in a pickle – which does happen – he can rally the troops in the last ten minutes, even if you're losing".

Webb firmly believes that the ability to captain well is instinctive and cannot be learned. "I've tried captaincy", he says ruefully. "The added responsibility makes players and supporters expect something extra from you for every game. It can affect your game and certainly, when I took over from Steve Bruce for two months, it did mine", he adds, honestly.

"Bryan Robson is such a consistent player", he maintains. "He doesn't shy away from difficult situations. A captain needs to talk all the time", says Webb "and the more gritty players seem able to do this quite easily. Because a mid-field player works up and down the park, he can see the game in total perspective. Bryan does that constantly and at the same time he can praise people or pick them up – whatever is necessary".

Obviously teams get to know one another throughout the seasons so the manager's pre-match pep talk can sometimes seem a touch redundant. Out on the pitch it's a different matter. Neil Webb thinks that a good captain is needed most when things are going wrong because he will take responsibility as a leader.

Over the years Webb has had cause to be grateful to Bryan Robson on several occasions. "If I'm having a bad game, he'll come and have a quiet encouraging word. No-one else would be aware. He's like that. But you need to respect a man before you can accept that kind of advice".

Bryan Robson captained Manchester United and England in exactly the same swashbuckling and committed manner. There is no fear of confrontation, no fear of anything. "If the ball's there and there's a bit of grass around it, it's his. I must admit that I wince sometimes", Webb laughs.

He believes that Robson was most missed in mid-March to early April when United should have won several games, but marked time instead. He thinks that Bryan Robson is incomparable.

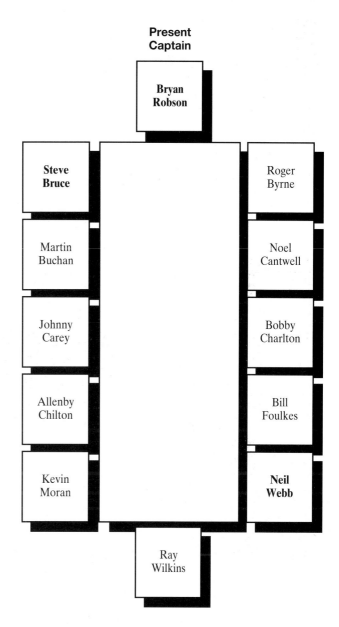

Bryan Robson heads an impressive table with his guests, including many famous post-war club captains both past and present. Those still on the club books are denoted in **bold** print.

MIDDLESBROUGH
1876
THE BORO

Team Manager Lennie Lawrence
Club Address Ayresome Park, Middlesbrough, Cleveland TS1 4PB
Record Attendance 53,596 v Newcastle U., Div. 1, 27 December 1949
Turned Professional 1889
Previous Names None
Club Honours Football League: Div. 2 Champions 1926-27, 1928-29, 1973-74
League History 1899-1902 Div. 2; 1902-24 Div. 1; 1924-27 Div. 2; 1927-28 Div. 1; 1928-29 Div. 2; 1929-54 Div. 1; 1954-66 Div. 2; 1966-67 Div. 3; 1967-74 Div. 2; 1974-82 Div. 1; 1982-86 Div. 2; 1986-87 Div. 3; 1987-88 Div. 2; 1988-89 Div. 1; 1989-92 Div. 2; 1992- Div. 1
Most League Points in a Season (2 for a win)

65 in Div. 2, 1973-74 (3 for a win) 94 in Div. 3, 1986-87
Most League Goals in a Season 122 in Div. 2, 1926-27
Record League Victory 9-0-v Brighton & H.A. in Div. 2, 23 August 1958
Record League Defeat 9-0 v Blackburn Rov. in Div. 2, 6 November 1954
Consecutive League Wins 9 in 1974
Consecutive League Defeats 8 in 1954
Record League Appearances Tim Williamson, 563 between 1902-23
Record League Goalscorer—Career George Camsell, 326 between 1925-39
Record League Goalscorer—Season George Camsell, 59 in Div. 2, 1926-27 (Div. 2 record)

1991-92 Record

Football League Second Division (2nd): Played 46, Won 23, Drawn 11, Lost 12, Goals For 58, Goals Against 41, Points 80
FA Cup Third Round: Manchester C. (H)2-1; Fourth Round: Sheffield Wed. (A)2-1; Fifth Round: Portsmouth (A)1-1 (R)2-4
League Cup Second Round: Bournemouth (H)1-1

(A)2-1; Third Round: Barnsley (H)1-0; Fourth Round: Manchester C. (H)2-1; Fifth Round: Peterborough U. (A)0-0 (R)1-0; Semi-Final: Manchester U. (H)0-0 (A)1-2
Zenith Cup Second Round: Derby Co. (H) 4-2; Third Round: Tranmere Rov. (A)0-1

1991-92: Back Row L-R: Jimmy Phillips, Nicky Mohan, Paul Wilkinson, Alan Kernaghan, Willie Falconer, Robbie Mustoe, *Gary Hamilton.* **Middle Row:** Tommy Johnson (Physio), *Ian Arnold,* Curtis Fleming, Steve Pears, Ian Ironside, Stuart Ripley, *Owen McGee,* Ray Train (Reserve Team Coach). **Seated:** Gary Parkinson, Mark Proctor, Lennie Lawrence (Manager), *Tony Mowbray,* John Pickering (Assistant Manager), Bernie Slaven, John Hendrie.

PLAYERS	CLUB DEBUT (Football League)	1991-92 APPEARANCES				1991-92 GOALS			
		Lge	FL Cup	FA Cup	Others	Lge	FL Cup	FA Cup	Others
GOALKEEPERS									
Collett, Andrew	–								
Ironside, Ian	Wolverhampton W. (A) 2 May 1992	1							
Pears, Steve	Cardiff C. (H) 5 November 1983	45	8	4	2				
DEFENDERS									
Falconer, Willie	Millwall (H) 17 August 1991	25	1+1			5			
Fleming, Curtis	Ipswich T. (A) 24 August 1991	23+5	2+1		1+1				
Gilchrist, Philip	–								
Kernaghan, Alan	Notts Co. (H) 27 February 1985	38	8	3	2	2		2	
Mohan, Nicky	Southampton (A) 14 January 1989	27	5	4	1	2			
Parkinson, Gary	Port Vale (H) 23 August 1986	23+4	6	4	1		1		
Phillips, Jimmy	Blackburn Rov. (H) 17 March 1990	43	8	4	2	2			1
Todd, Andy	–								
MIDFIELDERS									
Kavanagh, Graham	–								
Lake, Robert	–								
Moore, Alan	–								
Mustoe, Robbie	West Ham U. (H) 25 August 1990	28+2	7+1	4	2	2	1		
Peake, Andy	Blackburn Rov. (A) 30 November 1991	20+3		4					
Pollock, Jamie	Wolverhampton W. (H) 27 April 1991	21+5	6+1	4	2	1			
Proctor, Mark	Birmingham C. (A) 22 August 1978	27+9	4+2	0+2	2	2			
FORWARDS									
Hendrie, John	West Ham U. (H) 25 August 1990	38	7	3+1		3	1	1	
Payton, Andy	Bristol C. (H) 23 November 1991	8+11		1+3		3			
Peverell, Nick	–								
Ripley, Stuart	Oldham Ath. (H) 5 February 1985	36+3	7	4	1	3	1		
Slaven, Bernie	Leeds U. (A) 12 October 1985	28+10	6+1	1+1	2	17	1		1
Wilkinson, Paul	Millwall (H) 17 August 1991	46	8	4	2	15	3	4	2
Young, Michael	Southend U. (H) 2 November 1991	0+1			0+1				
PLAYERS MAKING APPEARANCES IN 1991-92 (No longer with the club)									
PLAYERS	**CURRENT CLUBS**								
Arnold, Ian	F/T (May 1992)	0+1			0+1				
Gittens, Jon	Southampton (Loan – February 1992)	9+3							
Hewitt, John	Glasgow Celtic (Loan – September 1991)	0+2							
Marwood, Brian	Sheffield U. (Loan – October 1991)	3	1			1			
Mowbray, Tony	Glasgow Celtic (November 1991)	17	3			1			
Shannon, Rob	Dundee (Loan September 1991)	0+1	1						

TRAINEES

Michael J. Barron, Paul J. Dwyer, Neil D. Illman, Ian Johnson, Anthony S. Lee, Stephen McGargle, Kevin A. Maddick, Paul Norton, Michael Oliver, Ben J. Roberts, Philip L. Stamp, Mark S. Taylor

The Middlesbrough Captain

Alan Kernaghan

Lennie Lawrence has a crusade to follow – he wants to build something that will last and Alan Kernaghan must feel that fate was quite determined that he should be part of that crusade. At the end of last season he had spent three months on loan to Charlton, then managed by Lawrence, who tried to sign Kernaghan from Middlesbrough. However, the north east club was not too keen. "Anyway, I came back to Ayresome Park, played in the Play-Offs and now, when I look back, maybe things did seem a bit strange", Kernaghan recalls with a laugh. "I'd gone in to collect something and someone said 'the new manager's on the pitch'. And it was Lennie! I said 'What're you doing here?' But after that, things couldn't have turned out better for me or the club".

Now 25 and six feet two inches tall, Kernaghan has matured into a powerful centre-half. "It's a good position from which to captain the side. I can see most things that are happening, read the pattern of the game easily. I'm very vocal on the pitch, always have been so captaincy is not a problem – it does not affect my game. I like responsibility anyway. You do need to have someone who can communicate well, who has a good knowledge of the game, able to think quickly. I do my best", he laughs again.

"I have a great respect for our manager. He's never played professional football and he brings such a fresh outlook to the game – he's not, how can I put it? . . ., entrenched in old traditions. He's given us a completely fresh start".

Alan Kernaghan recalls the first game of last season vividly. "It was against Millwall at home – the gaffer's first game and we did well. Won 2-0 and that was so important – we stayed at the top of the League for about eight weeks after that. At the beginning of the season we did believe that we could go up but then, from November to the end of January, we played terribly away from home. At Ayresome Park we were winning well then we'd lose away – we were like two different teams.

I remember the Rumbelow's Cup Semi-Final against Manchester United. It was 0-0 at home on the first leg and then we lost 2-1 in extra-time at Old Trafford. That was a real turning point. Instead of feeling dejected it gave us a boost. They were at the top of the First Division and we had given them a good game. We knew we had nothing to fear and from then on our away form picked up.

On the morning of the day we were due to play Wolves at Molyneux, the stand had been burnt down. Obviously, this put the game in jeopardy and there we were sitting in our hotel, just waiting – it was strange. Eventually, the game was played. I'd missed the previous six games through injury and I watched the first-half from the bench but couldn't bear anymore. I went out and bought a sandwich and a paper and by the time I returned in the second-half, we'd had a player sent off! But then we scored – twice. And that clinched promotion for us".

Captain's Table

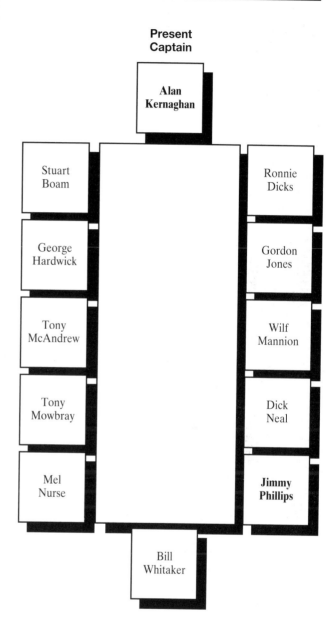

Present
Captain

Alan Kernaghan

Stuart Boam

George Hardwick

Tony McAndrew

Tony Mowbray

Mel Nurse

Bill Whitaker

Ronnie Dicks

Gordon Jones

Wilf Mannion

Dick Neal

Jimmy Phillips

Alan Kernaghan heads an impressive table with his guests, including many famous post-war club captains both past and present. Those still on the club books are denoted in **bold** print.

NORWICH CITY
1905

THE CANARIES

Team Manager Mike Walker
Club Address Carrow Road, Norwich NR1 1JE
Record Attendance 43,984 v Leicester C., FA Cup 6th Round, 30 March 1963
Turned Professional 1905
Previous Names None
Club Honours Football League: Div. 2 Champions 1971-72, 1985-86; Div. 3(S) Champions 1933-34. Football League Cup: Winners 1962, 1985
League History 1920-34 Div. 3(S); 1934-39 Div. 2;1939-58 Div. 3(S); 1958-60 Div. 3; 1960-72 Div. 2; 1972-74 Div. 1; 1974-75 Div. 2; 1975-81 Div. 1; 1981-82 Div. 2; 1982-85 Div. 1; 1985-86 Div. 2; 1986- Div. 1
Most League Points in a Season (2 for a win)

64 in Div. 3(S), 1950-51. (3 for a win) 84 in Div. 2, 1985-86
Most League Goals in a Season 99 in Div. 3(S), 1952-53
Record League Victory 10-2 v Coventry C. in Div. 3(S), 15 March 1930
Record League Defeat 0-7 v Walsall in Div. 3(S), 13 September 1930 and v Sheffield Wed. in Div. 2, 19 November 1931
Consecutive League Wins 9 in 1985-86
Consecutive League Defeats 7 in 1935 and 1957
Record League Appearances Ron Ashman, 592 between 1947-64
Record League Goalscorer—Career Johnny Gavin, 122 between 1948-58
Record League Goalscorer—Season Ralph Hunt, 31 in Div. 3(S), 1955-56

1991-92 Record

Football League First Division (18th): Played 42, Won 11, Drawn 12, Lost 19, Goals For 47, Goals Against 63, Points 45
FA Cup Third Round: Barnsley (H)1-0; Fourth Round: Millwall (H) 2-1; Fifth Round: Notts Co. (H)3-0; Sixth Round: Southampton (A)0-0 (R)2-1; Semi-Final: Sunderland 0-1

League Cup Second Round: Charlton Ath. (A)2-0 (H)3-0; Third Round: Brentford (H)4-1; Fourth Round: West Ham U. (H)2-1; Fifth Round: Tottenham H. (A)1-2
Zenith Cup Second Round: Q.P.R. (H)1-2

1991-92: Back Row L-R: Robert Fleck, David Phillips, Daryl Sutch, John Polston, Dale Gordon, Ian Culverhouse, Mark Bowen. **Middle Row:** Mike Walker (Reserve Team Manager), Chris Sutton, Tim Sheppard (Physio), Tim Wooding, Darren Beckford, Colin Woodthorpe, Mark Walton, *Tim Sherwood*, Bryan Gunn, Rob Newman, Ian Butterworth, Ruel Fox, Keith Webb (Youth Team Manager), Ian Crook, *David Williams* (Assistant Manager). **Front Row:** Jason Minett, Jeremy Goss, *Henrik Mortensen*, Lee Power, *Dave Stringer* (Manager), *Steve Ball*, Paul Blades, David Smith, Robert Ullathorne.

Playing staff for 1992-93 (As at 1 July 1992)   NORWICH CITY

PLAYERS	CLUB DEBUT (Football League)	1991-92 APPEARANCES				1991-92 GOALS			
		Lge	FL Cup	FA Cup	Others	Lge	FL Cup	FA Cup	Others
GOALKEEPERS									
Gunn, Bryan	Tottenham H. (H) 8 November 1986	25	5	1	1				
Walton, Mark	Aston Villa (A) 28 April 1990	17		5					
DEFENDERS									
Blades, Paul	Sunderland (H) 25 August 1990	26	5	1	1				
Bowen, Mark	Southampton (H) 19 August 1987	35+1	5	4	1	3		1	
Butterworth, Ian	Aston Villa (A) 20 September 1986	31	3	4	1	1			
Culverhouse, Ian	Carlisle U. (A) 12 October 1985	21		4					
Johnson, Andrew	Sheffield Wed. (A) 20 April 1992	2							
Minett, Jason	Leeds U. (A) 1 September 1990								
Newman, Rob	Sheffield U. (H) 17 August 1991	41	5	6	1	7	1	1	
Pennock, Adrian	Southampton (A) 27 February 1990								
Polston, John	Sunderland (H) 25 August 1990	16+3	0+1	5+1		1			
Ullathorne, Robert	Nottingham F. (A) 24 April 1991	20	4	2		3			
Wooding, Tim	–								
Woodthorpe, Colin	Sheffield U. (A) 11 May 1991	12+3	0+2	4	0+1	1			
MIDFIELDERS									
Collins, Sean	–								
Crook, Ian	Chelsea (A) 23 August 1986	20+1	2+1	1+2		1			
Goss, Jeremy	Coventry C. (A) 12 May 1984	29+4	4	6	1	1			
Phillips, David	Sheffield Wed. (A) 19 August 1989	34	4	4	1	1		1	
Smith, David	Derby Co. (A) 21 April 1990	1							
Sutch, Daryl	Manchester U. (A) 26 December 1990	5+4		0+1					
FORWARDS									
Beckford, Darren	Sheffield U. (H) 17 August 1991	25+5	3+2	2+1	1	7	3		1
Fleck, Robert	Wimbledon (A) 18 December 1987	35+1	5	6		11	6	2	
Fox, Ruel	Oxford U. (H) 29 November 1986	27+10	4+1	5	1	2	1		
Power, Lee	Aston Villa (A) 28 April 1990	2+2				1			
Sutton, Chris	Q.P.R. (H) 4 May 1991	16+5	2	6		2		3	

PLAYERS MAKING APPEARANCES IN 1991-92 (No longer with the club)

PLAYERS	CURRENT CLUBS	Lge	FL Cup	FA Cup	Others	Lge	FL Cup	FA Cup	Others
Ball, Steve	F/T (May 1992)	0+2	0+2						
Gordon, Dale	Glasgow R. (November 1991)	15	3		1	4	1		
Mortensen, Henrik	Retired (February 1992)				1				
Sherwood, Tim	Blackburn Rov. (February 1992)	7	1						

TRAINEES

Adeola P. Akinbiyi, Deryn P. J. Brace, Shaun P. Carey, Jamie Cureton, Darren M. Eadie, Scott R. Ewins, Alistair P. Gibb, Justin D. Harrington, Stacey J. Kreft, Neil J. Liffen, Andrew J. Marshall, Richard C. Mellon, Marcus J. Oldbury, Glyn S. Roberts, Barry O. Ruse, Scott Snowling, Gary W. Weston, Jonathan Wright

The Norwich City Captains

Mark Bowen

Mark Bowen/Ian Culverhouse

In recent years, Norwich City have played some of the most entertaining and attractive football in the First Division. Free-flowing, short-passing patterns with quicksilver movement, outstanding technique and speed of thought, were the natural order of things at Carrow Road since Dave Stringer arrived there five years ago. This year Norwich reached the Quarter-Finals of the FA Cup for the third time in four seasons. Yet it has not been the easiest of years for Stringer and as a consequence he decided to resign from his post, feeling that the time had come for a new face to take the helm and steer the "Canaries" back to a more stable League position.

By mid-February, Norwich had slipped down the League list and the fans were getting restless to say the least. And in general, Norwich supporters are a patient lot, but perhaps the kudos earned by previous season's high praise, raised expectations somewhat and down in East Anglia, the worm began to turn, just a little. Dave Stringer was so upset by events that he spoke on national radio, defending himself and his players. Fortunately, on the afternoon of the broadcast, Norwich beat Notts County otherwise Stringer's appeal could have been his swansong.

When he had taken on the role of manager, Norwich were down at the bottom of Division One and relegation seemed inevitable. Scarely had 18 months passed when Norwich reached the FA Cup Semi-Final, and achieved their highest League position in the club's 87 year history.

Norwich could perhaps be described as a homespun club by some of its more worldly Premier League colleagues. There are no great reservoirs of finance available to the Norwich management, yet the club traditionally has been a breeding ground for young players, a nursery where talent was fostered and encouraged. Sadly, this meant that the bright young stars did not stay for long – the likes of Drinkell, Townsend, Linighan and Bruce are soon snapped up by the more wealthy clubs.

To captain a team such as Norwich demands a very particular type of player. To work with a team of shifting talent is not easy. The job has required spirit and strength of character, someone capable of unifying a collection of youngsters hungry for success and moulding them into a team with older, more experienced players. This season Mark Bowen and Ian Culverhouse have worn the captain's armband for Norwich and both have given gutsy commitment to the job in hand despite the difficulties that seemed to plague the club all season.

In that game against Notts County, way back in February, Norwich certainly showed the greater conviction of the two sides. The purist's might not have been happy with the direct route football that Norwich adopted to win this match, but as David Phillips the "Canaries'" Welsh international said: "It's not the Norwich way that is loved and admired, but we have our backs up against the wall". Desperate times call for desperate measures.

Captain's Table

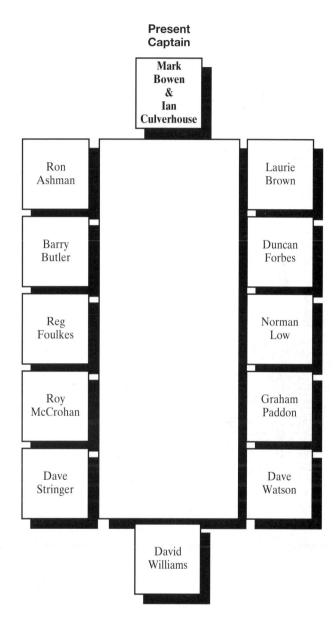

Present Captain

Mark Bowen & Ian Culverhouse

Ron Ashman

Barry Butler

Reg Foulkes

Roy McCrohan

Dave Stringer

Laurie Brown

Duncan Forbes

Norman Low

Graham Paddon

Dave Watson

David Williams

Mark Bowen and Ian Culverhouse head an impressive table with their guests, including many famous post-war club captains both past and present. Those still on the club books are denoted in **bold** print.

NOTTINGHAM FOREST
1865
FOREST
THE REDS

Team Manager Brian Clough
Club Address City Ground, Nottingham NG2 5FJ
Record Attendance 49,945 v Manchester U., Div. 1, 28 October 1967
Turned Professional 1889
Previous Names None
Club Honours Football League: Div. 1 Champions 1977-78; Div. 2 Champions 1906-07, 1921-22; Div. 3(S) Champions 1950-51. FA Cup: Winners 1898, 1959. Football League Cup: Winners 1978, 1979,1989, 1990. European Cup: Winners 1978-79, 1979-80. European Super Cup: Winners 1979-80.
League History 1892-1906 Div. 1; 1906-1907 Div. 2; 1907-1911 Div. 1; 1911-22 Div. 2; 1922-25 Div. 1; 1925-49 Div. 2; 1949-51 Div. 3(S); 1951-57 Div. 2; 1957-72 Div. 1; 1972-77 Div. 2; 1977- Div. 1

Most League Points in a Season (2 for a win) 70 in Div. 3(S), 1950-51. (3 for a win) 74 in Div. 1, 1983-84
Most League Goals in a Season 110 in Div. 3(S), 1950-51
Record League Victory 12-0 v Leicester C. in Div. 1, 12 April 1909
Record League Defeat 1-9 v Blackburn Rov. in Div. 2, 10 April 1937
Consecutive League Wins 7 in 1892-93, 1906, 1921 and 1979
Consecutive League Defeats 14 in 1913
Record League Appearances Bob McKinlay, 614 between 1951-70
Record League Goalscorer—Career Grenville Morris, 199 between 1898-1913
Record League Goalscorer—Season Wally Ardron, 36 in Div. 3(S), 1950-51

1991-92 Record

Football League First Division (8th): Played 42, Won 16, Drawn 11, Lost 15, Goals For 60, Goals Against 58, Points 59
FA Cup Third Round: Wolverhampton W. (H)1-0; Fourth Round: Hereford U. (H)2-0; Fifth Round: Bristol C. (H)4-1; Sixth Round: Portsmouth (A)0-1
League Cup Second Round: Bolton W. (H)4-0 (A)5-2; Third Round: Bristol Rov. (H)2-0; Fourth Round: Southampton (H)0-0 (R)1-0; Fifth Round: Crystal Palace (A)1-1 (R)4-2; Semi-Final: Tottenham H. (H)1-0 (A)2-1; Final: Manchester U. 0-1
Zenith Cup Second Round: Leeds U. (A)3-1; Third Round: Aston Villa (A)2-0; Fourth Round: Tranmere Rov. (A)2-0; Semi-Final: Leicester C. (A)1-1 (H)2-0; Final Southampton 3-2

1991-92: Back Row L-R: *Garry Parker,* Roy Keane, Tommy Gaynor, *Brian Rice,* Terry Wilson, *Des Walker,* Scot Gemmill, *Nigel Jemson.* **Middle Row:** Ron Fenton (Assistant Manager), Liam O'Kane (Coach), Brian Laws, Carl Tiler, *Steve Sutton,* Steve Chettle, Mark Crossley, Teddy Sheringham, *Alan Mahood,* Graham Lyas (Physio), Archie Gemmill (Coach). **Front Row:** Nigel Clough, Lee Glover, Gary Charles, Brian Clough (Manager), Stuart Pearce, Ian Woan, Gary Crosby.

NOTTINGHAM FOREST

PLAYERS	CLUB DEBUT (Football League)	1991-92 APPEARANCES				1991-92 GOALS			
		Lge	FL Cup	FA Cup	Others	Lge	FL Cup	FA Cup	Others
GOALKEEPERS									
Crossley, Mark	Liverpool (H) 26 October 1988	36	9	4	5				
Davies, Chris	–								
Marriott, Andrew	Manchester U. (H) 18 March 1992	6	1		1				
Smith, Mark	–								
DEFENDERS									
Boardman, Craig	–		0+1						
Byrne, Raymond	–								
Charles, Gary	Arsenal (H) 6 November 1988	30	7	2+1	3+1	1			
Chettle, Steve	Chelsea (A) 5 September 1987	17+5	3+1	0+1	3+1	1			
Forrest, Cuan	–								
Hope, Chris	–								
Laws, Brian	West Ham U. (A) 12 November 1988	10+5	3+2	2	2+1				
Pearce, Stuart	Luton T. (A) 17 August 1985	30	9	4	5	5	1	2	1
Tiler, Carl	Everton (H) 17 August 1991	24+2	5+1	1	1	2			
Williams, Brett	Birmingham C. (A) 26 December 1985	9	1						
Wright, Dale	–								
MIDFIELDERS									
Black, Kingsley	Sheffield Wed. (A) 7 September 1991	25	8	3	4+1	4	2		1
Bowyer, Gary	–								
Gemmill, Scot	Wimbledon (A) 30 March 1991	39	8+1	4	6	8	2		3
Glasser, Neil	–								
Howe, Steve	–								
Keane, Roy	Liverpool (A) 28 August 1990	39	8	4	5	8	4		2
Kilford, Ian	–								
McKinnon, Ray	–								
Orlygsson, Toddy	Southampton (H) 17 December 1989	5							
Stone, Steven	West Ham U. (A) 2 May 1992	0+1							
Warner, Vance	–								
Wilson, Terry	Southampton (H) 2 September 1987	1							
Woan, Ian	Norwich C. (A) 2 January 1991	20+1	3+1	1	2	5			1
FORWARDS									
Clough, Nigel	Ipswich T. (H) 26 December 1984	35+1	7	3	4+1	5	1	2	
Crosby, Gary	Charlton Ath. (H) 16 January 1988	31+2	8	3+1	6	3			2
Gaynor, Tommy	West Ham U. (A) 21 November 1987	3+1	2		0+1		3		
Glover, Lee	Charlton Ath. (A) 15 August 1987	12+4	2+2	2+1	2+1		2		
Kaminsky, Jason	Luton T. (A) 14 April 1992	0+1							
McGregor, Paul	–								
Sheringham, Teddy	Everton (H) 17 August 1991	39	10	4	6	13	5	2	2

PLAYERS MAKING APPEARANCES IN 1991-92 (No longer with the club)

PLAYERS	CURRENT CLUBS	Lge	FL Cup	FA Cup	Others	Lge	FL Cup	FA Cup	Others
Jemson, Nigel	Sheffield Wed. (September 1991)	6				1			
Parker, Garry	Aston Villa (November 1991)	5+1	3		1	1			
Walker, Des	Sampdoria (May 1992)	32+1	9	4	6				
Wassell, Darren	Derby Co. (June 1992)	10+4	4+1	3	4+2				1

TRAINEES

Craig Armstrong, Nathan Drury, John Finnigan, Stephen Guinan, Paul Haywood, Daniel Hinshelwood, Luke Hughes, Lee Marshall, Carl Rookyard, Richard Smith, Mark Statham, Lee Stratford, Justin Walker

The Nottingham Forest Captain

Stuart Pearce

One week after their glorious victory over Tottenham Hotspur in the Rumblelows League Cup Semi-Final, Nottingham Forest were London bound again, this time to face Southampton in the Zenith Data Systems Cup Final. Minutes into the game, Forest's captain, Stuart Pearce twisted his left knee.

Treatment administered, he carried on playing, but it was obvious that he was moving with difficulty. As the trainer ran around the pitch to be near Pearce, the Forest crowd held its collective breath. All eyes were on their captain, but he waved the trainer away and there was an audible sigh of relief.

Stuart Pearce is a player whose pride for his team and his club would never allow him to continue playing if he was unable to give his best. The job has to be done well and an injury means "get off, get fit and get back", in that order. Though a player of consummate bravery, he is not foolhardy. His colleagues describe him as one of the most honest professionals in the game and though to leave the pitch during a Cup Final must have broken his heart, it was the right thing to do. And Stuart Pearce will always do the right thing.

He leads by magnificent example, always aware of the playing strengths of his team-mates, always aware of his responsibilities to the paying public. When he limped off the Wembley turf, at 3.15 p.m., having handed the captain's armband to Des Walker, Nottingham Forest supporters gave him a standing ovation. All the way back to the players' tunnel, his slow, painful journey was accompanied by a deafening and moving chorus of "We love you Psycho – we do". Just for a moment the game seemed inconsequential – something which Pearce would not have wanted, though he recognises and appreciates deeply the feelings the fans have for him. The vocal tribute was perhaps one of the most eloquent expressions of affection and regret ever heard at the old stadium.

The match won, despite some heart-stopping moments, the team prepared to go up to receive the Cup. It was no surprise to watch Stuart Pearce quietly insist that Des Walker, the captain on the day, should lead the team up those famous steps and be the one to lift the glittering prize. Pearce was the last player to climb the steps and the last to hold the Cup above his head. Once again his name rolled round the arena.

During the following week investigations proved that the injury was much more serious than originally suspected. Chances of him playing in the Rumblelow's Cup Final were beginning to look remote. Stuart Pearce could still lighten the dense disappointment he must have felt with a spot of dry humour. "I was sick when I came off the field at Wembley", he admitted, "but my knee was in worse danger sitting on the bench between the boss and Alan Hill. The knee wasn't too bad until 'Hilly' grabbed it when Southampton scored one of their goals and for a minute I thought I would be better off back on the pitch"!

Captain's Table

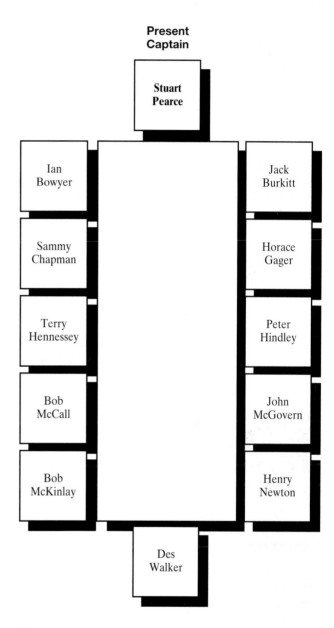

Present Captain

Stuart Pearce

Ian Bowyer	Jack Burkitt
Sammy Chapman	Horace Gager
Terry Hennessey	Peter Hindley
Bob McCall	John McGovern
Bob McKinlay	Henry Newton

Des Walker

Stuart Pearce heads an impressive table with his guests, including many famous post-war club captains both past and present. Those still on the club books are denoted in **bold** print.

OLDHAM ATHLETIC
1894

THE LATICS

Team Manager Joe Royle
Club Address Boundary Park, Oldham OL1 2PA
Record Attendance 47,671 v Sheffield Wed., FA Cup 4th Round, 25 January 1930
Turned Professional 1899
Previous Names Pine Villa
Club Honours Football League: Div. 2 Champions 1990-91; Div. 3(N) Champions 1952-53; Div. 3 Champions 1973-74
League History 1907-10 Div. 2; 1910-23 Div. 1; 1923-35 Div. 2; 1935-53 Div. 3(N); 1953-54 Div. 2; 1954-58 Div. 3; 1958-63 Div. 4; 1963-69 Div. 3; 1969-71 Div. 4; 1971-74 Div. 3; 1974-91 Div. 2; 1991- Div. 1
Most League Points in a Season (2 for a win) 62 in Div. 3, 1973-74. (3 for a win) 88 in Div. 2,

1990-91
Most League Goals in a Season 95 in Div. 4, 1962-63
Record League Victory 11-0 v Southport in Div. 4, 26 December 1962
Record League Defeat 4-13 v Tranmere Rov. in Div. 3(N), 26 December 1935
Consecutive League Wins 10 in 1974
Consecutive League Defeats 8 in 1932-33 and 1934-35
Record League Appearances Ian Wood, 525 between 1966-80
Record League Goalscorer—Career Roger Palmer, 141 between 1980-92
Record League Goalscorer—Season Tom Davis, 33 in Div. 3(N), 1936-37

1991-92 Record

Football League First Division (17th): Played 42, Won 14, Drawn 9, Lost 19, Goals For 63, Goals Against 67, Points 51
FA Cup Third Round: Leyton Orient (H)1-1 (R)2-4

League Cup Second Round: Torquay U. (H)7-1 (A)2-0; Third Round: Derby Co. (H)2-1; Fourth Round: Manchester U. (A)0-2
Zenith Cup Second Round: Everton (A)2-3

1991-92: Back Row L-R: *Neil Redfearn, David Currie, Paul Warhurst,* Willie Donachie, *Paul Kane.* **Middle Row:** Ronnie Evans (Kit Manager), Bill Urmson (Coach), Gunnar Halle, John Keeley, Paul Moulden, Jon Hallworth, Richard Jobson, *Frankie Bunn,* Ian Liversedge (Physio). **Front Row:** Roger Palmer, Andy Barlow, Ian Marshall, *Earl Barrett,* Joe Royle (Manager), Rick Holden, Nicky Henry, Andy Ritchie, Neil Adams.

Playing staff for 1992-93 (As at 1 July 1992) OLDHAM ATHLETIC

PLAYERS	CLUB DEBUT (Football League)	1991-92 APPEARANCES				1991-92 GOALS			
		Lge	FL Cup	FA Cup	Others	Lge	FL Cup	FA Cup	Others
GOALKEEPERS									
Gerrard, Paul	–								
Hallworth, Jon	Leicester C. (H) 30 September 1989	41	4	2					
Keeley, John	Manchester C. (H) 2 May 1992	1			1				
DEFENDERS									
Barlow, Andy	Birmingham C. (H) 25 August 1984	28	3		1	2			
Donachie, Willie	Birmingham C. (H) 25 August 1984								
Fleming, Craig	Norwich C. (H) 24 August 1991	28+4	2+1	2	1	1			
Hall, David	–								
Halle, Gunnar	Port Vale (H) 16 February 1991	10	1						
Harriott, Marvin	–								
Holden, Andy	Manchester C. (H) 14 January 1989								
Jobson, Richard	Portsmouth (H) 1 September 1990	36	3	2	1	2	1		
McDonald, Neil	Southampton (H) 5 October 1991	14+3	2			1			
Marshall, Ian	Swindon T. (H) 12 March 1988	41	3	2	0+1	10			
Miller, Robert	–								
MIDFIELDERS									
Bernard, Paul	Middlesbrough (H) 7 May 1991	16+5	1+1	2	0+1	5			
Everingham, Nicholas	–								
Henry, Nicky	Hull C. (H) 19 September 1987	42	3	2	1	6	1		
Makin, Chris	–								
Milligan, Mike	Sheffield U. (A) 12 April 1986	36	4		1	3	1		1
Wilson, Greg	–								
FORWARDS									
Adams, Neil	Manchester C. (H) 14 January 1989	21+5	0+1	2		4		1	
Holden, Rick	Blackburn Rov. (A) 19 August 1989	38+4	3+1	2	1	5	1		1
Moulden, Paul	Sheffield U. (H) 28 March 1990	0+2				1			
Olney, Ian	–								
Palmer, Roger	Leyton Orient (H) 22 November 1980	14+7	1+1	2		3	1	1	
Ritchie, Andy	West Bromwich A. (A) 15 August 1987	7+7	1		1	3	4		
Sharp, Graeme	Liverpool (A) 17 August 1991	42	4	2	1	12	2	1	
Tolson, Neil	–								

PLAYERS MAKING APPEARANCES IN 1991-92 (No longer with the club)

PLAYERS	CURRENT CLUBS	Lge	FL Cup	FA Cup	Others	Lge	FL Cup	FA Cup	Others
Barrett, Earl	Aston Villa (February 1992)	29	4	2	1	2			
Currie, David	Barnsley (September 1991)	1+3				1			
Kane, Paul	Aberdeen (November 1991)	1+3	2		1				
Kilcline, Brian	Newcastle U. (February 1992)	8	2						
Snodin, Glynn	Leeds U. (Loan – August 1991)	8	1			1			

TRAINEES

Christian Adams, Matthew Berry, Liam T. Boden, Matthew J. Booth, John R. Eyre, Paul D. Feltham, John A. Frost, Richard E. Graham, Ian J. Gray, Robert C. Hilton, Anthony P. Hoolikin, Stephen C. Knapman, Steven Lane, Richard J. Lockley, Martin C. Pemberton, Stephen J. Price, Paul S. Rickers, Carl Serrant, Matthew I. Speak, Andrew N. Woods

The Oldham Athletic Captain

Mike Milligan

Oldham Athletic are living proof that creativity grows out of limitations. With little to spend on famous names, Joe Royle gathered together a team of courage and character and in 1991 they reached Division One for the first time in 83 years. Not only did they win promotion, they also won the Second Division Championship – and for once, justice prevailed.

Current captain, Mike Milligan, familiar with the vicissitudes of those exciting years, was more than happy to return to his old club after an unsatisfactory spell at Everton. For Milligan it was a relief to come back to a manager and coach whom he trusted completely. Not much had changed, including the salaries, he joked, though inevitably the squad had altered slightly. He admits that there is a little more pressure, but with Joe Royle as manager, problems are always diffused by humour.

First Division status has brought new fans to Boundary Park and certainly Oldham Athletic has not been outclassed by more famous clubs this season. Milligan believes that previous Cup-runs against mighty opposition has taken away the mystique surrounding some sides. He does feel that his team is more motivated to do well against good sides, often playing badly against teams from lower leagues. "I would like us to be more consistent", he says. "We manage it against top opposition – if only we could achieve that against the minnows", he laughs. Milligan has always played in midfield and feels that his position means that he can talk from the front or the back of play. He believes that midfielders are traditionally self-motivated players, who because they have to cover everything on the pitch, are naturally disposed to the captain's role.

He likes the responsibility, accepts that it is "part and parcel of the job", but admits that his players think he goes over the top sometimes! He jokes about everything, including himself. "The players say I moan, but I do encourage – they forget that", he says. "I'm especially conscious of our new players who perhaps need support now and then". And he claims that the hardest part of captaincy is trying to guess which side the coin is going to land at the start of the game! "It's always good to choose – that does affect the game", he insists with another laugh.

He was not pleased to lose the last home game of the season to Manchester City and he thinks that the team still needs more strength in depth. But there are some good memories, especially the away performance at Highbury where though beaten, Oldham played particularly well as a team and that always pleases Mike Milligan. Then there was the exciting tussle with Liverpool at the season's start when the "Latics" could so easily have won. But he enjoyed the victory over Manchester City at Maine Road best, when Graham Sharp put three wonderful goals past Tony Coton. Once, Milligan was on City's books – such victories remain sweetly within the soul.

Captain's Table

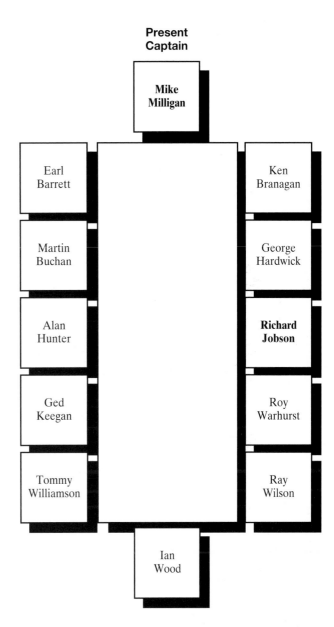

Present Captain

Mike Milligan

Earl Barrett	Ken Branagan
Martin Buchan	George Hardwick
Alan Hunter	**Richard Jobson**
Ged Keegan	Roy Warhurst
Tommy Williamson	Ray Wilson

Ian Wood

Mike Milligan heads an impressive table with his guests, including many famous post-war club captains both past and present. Those still on the club books are denoted in **bold** print.

QUEENS PARK RANGERS
1885

THE R's or RANGERS

Team Manager Gerry Francis
Club Address Rangers Stadium, Shepherds Bush, London W12 7PA
Record Attendance 34,353 v Leeds U., Div. 1, 27 April 1974
Turned Professional 1898
Previous Names St Jude's Institute
Club Honours Football League: Div. 2 Champions 1982-83; Div. 3(S) Champions 1947-48; Div. 3 Champions 1966-67. Football League Cup: Winners 1967
League History 1920-48 Div. 3(S); 1948-52 Div. 2; 1952-58 Div. 3(S); 1958-67 Div. 3; 1967-68 Div. 2; 1968-69 Div. 1; 1969-73 Div. 2; 1973-79 Div. 1; 1979-83 Div. 2; 1983- Div. 1
Most League Points in a Season (2 for a win) 67 in Div 3, 1966-67. (3 for a win) 85 in Div. 2, 1982-83
Most League Goals in a Season 111 in Div. 3, 1961-62
Record League Victory 9-2 v Tranmere Rov. in Div. 3, 3 December 1960
Record League Defeat 1-8 v Mansfield T. in Div. 3, 15 March 1965 and v Manchester U. in Div. 1, 19 March 1969
Consecutive League Wins 8 in 1931
Consecutive League Defeats 9 in 1969
Record League Appearances Tony Ingham, 514 between 1950-63
Record League Goalscorer —Career George Goddard, 172 between 1926-34
Record League Goalscorer—Season George Goddard, 37 in Div. 3(S), 1929-30

1991-92 Record

Football League First Division (11th): Played 42, Won 12, Drawn 18, Lost 12, Goals For 48, Goals Against 47, Points 54
FA Cup Third Round: Southampton (A)0-2

League Cup Second Round: Hull C. (A)3-0 (H)5-1; Third Round: Manchester C. (A)0-0 (R)1-3
Zenith Cup Second Round: Norwich C. (A)2-1; Third Round: Crystal Palace (H)2-3

1991-92: Back Row L-R: Dennis Bailey, Les Ferdinand *Roy Wegerle,* Michael Meaker, *Mark Falco,* Jan Stejskal, Alan McDonald, Peter Caldwell, Darren Peacock, *Paul Vowles,* Karl Ready, *Dominic Iorfa.* **Middle Row:** Des Bulpin (Youth Team Manager), Ron Berry (Kit Manager), Frank Sibley (First Team Coach), *Paul Bromage,* David McEnroe, Maurice Doyle, Bradley Allen, Tony Roberts, Andy Tillson, Brian Law, Alan McCarthy, Andy Impey, Roger Cross (Reserve Team Manager), Brian Morris (Physio), Les Boyle (Youth Team Trainer). **Front Row:** Ray Wilkins, David Bardsley, Rufus Brevett, Andy Sinton, Clive Wilson, Gerry Francis (Manager), *Paul Parker,* Simon Barker, Danny Maddix, Justin Channing, Roberto Herrera.

Playing staff for 1992-93 (As at 1 July 1992)   QUEENS PARK RANGERS

PLAYERS	CLUB DEBUT (Football League)	1991-92 APPEARANCES				1991-92 GOALS			
		Lge	FL Cup	FA Cup	Others	Lge	FL Cup	FA Cup	Others
GOALKEEPERS									
Caldwell, Peter	–								
Roberts, Tony	Coventry C. (H) 18 December 1987	1			1				
Stejskal, Jan	Leeds U. (A) 20 October 1990	41	4	1	1				
DEFENDERS									
Bardsley, David	Derby Co. (H) 16 September 1989	41	4	1	2		1		1
Brevett, Rufus	Tottenham H. (A) 23 March 1991	6+1	1						
Channing, Justin	Luton T. (A) 1 November 1986				1				
Finlay, Darren	–								
Gallen, Stephen	–								
Herrera, Roberto	Liverpool (A) 28 April 1990		0+1						
Law, Brian	Sheffield Wed. (H) 23 April 1988								
McCarthy, Alan	Arsenal (H) 24 November 1990	3							
McDonald, Alan	Wolverhampton W. (A) 24 September 1983	27+1	1	1	1				
Maddix, Danny	Sheffield Wed. (A) 28 November 1987	19	4		1				
Peacock, Darren	Derby Co. (A) 23 December 1990	39	4	1	2	1			
Ready, Karl	Wimbledon (H) 1 February 1992	1	0+1						
Tillson, Andy	Derby Co. (A) 23 December 1990	9+1	2		1				
Wilson, Clive	Nottingham F. (A) 25 August 1990	40	4	1	2	3			
Witter, Tony	–								
MIDFIELDERS									
Barker, Simon	Manchester U. (A) 27 August 1988	31+3	4	1	2	6	2		
Doyle, Maurice	–								
Holloway, Ian	Arsenal (A) 17 August 1991	34+6	3	1	1+1				
Impey, Andy	Coventry C. (A) 11 January 1992	13	0+1		0+2				1
McEnroe, David	–								
Meaker, Michael	Manchester C. (A) 1 December 1990	0+1							
Sinton, Andy	Sheffield Wed. (A) 25 March 1989	38	3	1	2	3			1
Waddock, Gary	Swansea C. (A) 15 September 1979								
Wilkins, Ray	Crystal Palace (A) 2 December 1989	26+1	1	1	1	1			1
FORWARDS									
Allen, Bradley	Wimbledon (A) 14 January 1989	10+1				5			
Bailey, Dennis	Arsenal (A) 17 August 1991	19+5	3	1	1	9	2		
Ferdinand, Les	Coventry C. (A) 20 April 1987	21+2	1+1		1	10			
Freedman, Douglas	–								
Penrice, Gary	Aston Villa (H) 2 November 1991	13+6	1	0+1	1	3	1		
Thompson, Garry	Norwich C. (H) 21 August 1991	10+5	3		1	1	3		

PLAYERS MAKING APPEARANCES IN 1991-92 (No longer with the club)

PLAYERS	CURRENT CLUBS	Lge	FL Cup	FA Cup	Others	Lge	FL Cup	FA Cup	Others
Iorfa, Dominic	Galatsaray (December 1991)	0+1							
Walsh, Paul	Tottenham H. (Loan – September 1991)	2							
Wegerle, Roy	Blackburn Rov. (March 1992)	18+3	1	1		5			

TRAINEES

Marvin L. Bryan, Trevor M. Challis, John R. Cross, Joseph L. Davey, Daniele S. E. Dichio, Steven D. Dickinson, Kevin A. Gallen, Lee Goodwin, Paul A. Goodwin, Mark R. Graham, Stephen Jackson, Robert D. Magill, Martyn L. D. Millard, John S. Peacock, Benjamin K. Pratt, Gary R. Wilkinson

The Queens Park Rangers Captain

Ray Wilkins

The only detrimental remark that anyone at Queen's Park Rangers could find to say about their captain was that "he frowned too much on television"! The frown disguises a man who loves to tease, though never maliciously and a man who despite so many achievements has "no airs and graces whatsoever". For many years he played alongside Bryan Robson so he learned early the value and importance of good captaincy. At Q.P.R. he is immensely popular both on and off the pitch. Younger players are inevitably influenced by their senior professionals and when that senior is as experienced and civilised as Ray Wilkins then the benefit to the club is priceless. Wilkins is an intelligent man with a vast knowledge of the game. One official at Q.P.R. said, "You will never hear a bad word said against Ray. He is a complete gentleman both on and off the pitch. It is not often that a player and his wife recognise what goes on in the administrative side of a football club – they both have an appreciation of what makes a club tick".

Ray Wilkins was never known for his pace so as the years roll on, the affect on his game is barely perceptible; time has simply added a maturity and authority to his captaincy. Always the general, marshalling forces from a deep midfield position, he really does seemed to have enjoyed last season in particular as his young and exciting side strode proudly through to defeat teams who seemed destined for honours until they reached South Africa Road.

Manchester United were dismissed less than lightly and on an arctic evening in March this year, so were Leeds. That night, Wilkins was so totally in command, he was awe-inspiring. He completely eclipsed both Gordon Strachan and David Batty and once the heart of Leeds had been cut out, there was nothing left. At the time the Yorkshire side was one of the leading contenders for the League Championship so victory was especially sweet. On an equally chilly Saturday on 28 December, Rangers faced Sheffield Wednesday at home. Rangers' team performance was excellent, but the match is remembered for Ray Wilkins' outrageously calm chip over the head of Chris Woods. When Wednesday equalised in the last minute of the game even "Owls'" fans said it was a miscarriage of justice.

The opening game of any season is always critical but against Arsenal, Wilkins proved that like all the best captains his absence was a crucial factor of the game. Ray Wilkins played for 60 of the 90 minutes and he came off the field when Queen's Park Rangers were 1-0 up and dominant. Rangers loss was Arsenal's gain and they eventually drew 1-1.

Ray Wilkins' enthusiasm for the game has never waned. In the close season last year he underwent a minor knee operation and was wretched with frustration while he waited for the word that he could begin training again. Age has definitely not wearied him – if anything he has improved like a good champagne. Vintage Wilkins is a most valuable asset and at Queen's Park Rangers he has earned the great respect which they afford him.

Captain's Table

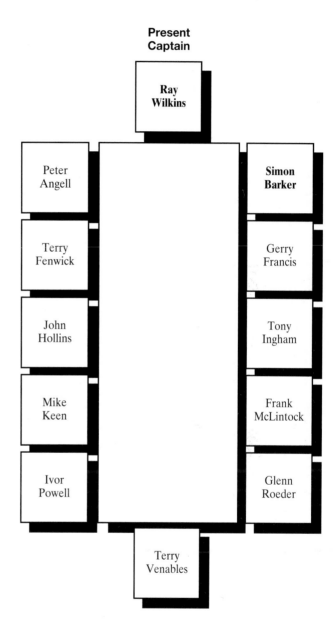

Present Captain

Ray Wilkins

Peter Angell		**Simon Barker**
Terry Fenwick		Gerry Francis
John Hollins		Tony Ingham
Mike Keen		Frank McLintock
Ivor Powell		Glenn Roeder

Terry Venables

Ray Wilkins heads an impressive table with his guests, including many famous post-war club captains both past and present. Those still on the club books are denoted in **bold** print.

SHEFFIELD UNITED
1889
THE BLADES

Team Manager Dave Bassett
Club Address Bramall Lane Ground, Sheffield S2 4SU
Record Attendance 68,287 v Leeds U., FA Cup 5th Round, 15 February 1936
Turned Professional 1889
Previous Names None
Club Honours Football League: Div. 1 Champions 1897-98; Div. 2 Champions 1952-53; Div. 4 Champions 1981-82. FA Cup: Winners 1899, 1902, 1915, 1925
League History 1892-93 Div. 2., 1893-1934 Div. 1; 1934-39 Div. 2; 1946-49 Div. 1; 1949-53 Div. 2; 1953-56 Div. 1; 1956-61 Div. 2; 1961-68 Div. 1; 1968-71 Div. 2; 1971-76 Div. 1; 1976-79 Div. 2; 1979-81 Div. 3; 1981-82 Div. 4; 1982-84 Div. 3; 1984-88 Div. 2; 1988-89 Div. 3; 1989-90 Div. 2; 1990- Div. 1

Most League Points in a Season (2 for a win) 60 in Div. 2, 1952-53. (3 for a win) 96 in Div. 4, 1981-82
Most League Goals in A Season 102 in Div. 1, 1925-26
Record League Victory 10-0 v Port Vale in Div. 2, 10 December 1892 and v Burnley in Div. 1, 19 January 1929
Record League Defeat 3-10 v Middlesbrough in Div. 1, 18 November 1937
Consecutive League Wins 8 in 1893, 1903, 1958 and 1960
Consecutive League Defeats 7 in 1975
Record League Appearances Joe Shaw, 629 between 1948-66
Record League Goalscorer—Career Harry Johnson, 205 between 1919-30
Record League Goalscorer—Season Jimmy Dunne, 41 in Div. 1, 1930-31

1991-92 Record

Football League First Division (9th): Played 42, Won 16, Drawn 9, Lost 17, Goals For 65, Goals Against 63, Points 57
FA Cup Third Round: Luton T. (H)4-0; Fourth Round: Charlton Ath. (A)0-0 (H)3-1; Fifth Round: Chelsea (A) 0-1
League Cup Second Round: Wigan Ath. (A)2-2 (H)1-0; Third Round: West Ham U. (H)0-2
Zenith Cup Second Round: Notts Co. (H)3-3

1991-92: Back Row L-R: Ian Bryson, Michael Lake, *Vinny Jones,* Brian Deane, Phil Kite, *Bob Booker,* Paul Beesley, Jamie Hoyland, Glyn Hodges. **Middle Row:** Derek French (Physio), Chris Wilder, Carl Bradshaw, John Pemberton, Simon Tracey, Colin Hill, *Tony Agana,* John Gannon, Geoff Taylor (Assistant Manager). **Front Row:** Brian Marwood, Dane Whitehouse, Richard Lucas, Dave Bassett (Manager), Clive Mendonca, Mitch Ward, Tom Cowan.

Playing staff for 1992-93 (As at 1 July 1992)   SHEFFIELD UNITED

PLAYERS	CLUB DEBUT (Football League)	1991-92 APPEARANCES				1991-92 GOALS			
		Lge	FL Cup	FA Cup	Others	Lge	FL Cup	FA Cup	Others
GOALKEEPERS									
Kite, Phil	Derby Co. (A) 29 August 1990	4	3	1	1				
Rees, Mel	Liverpool (H) 11 March 1992	8							
Tracey, Simon	Huddersfield T. (H) 11 March 1989	29		3					
DEFENDERS									
Barnes, David	West Bromwich A. (A) 19 August 1989	15		3					
Beesley, Paul	Derby Co. (A) 29 August 1990	38+2	2	4	1	2			
Cowan, Tom	Norwich C. (A) 17 August 1991	20	2	1	1				
Fickling, Ashley	–			1					
Gage, Kevin	Tottenham H. (A) 23 November 1991	22		2+2		1			
Gayle, Brian	Notts Co. (H) 17 September 1991	33	3	3	1	4		1	1
Hill, Colin	West Bromwich A. (A) 19 August 1989	11+4	1	2+2		1			
Kent, Shane	–								
Lucas, Richard	Aston Villa (A) 1 December 1990	0+1							
Pemberton, John	Liverpool (H) 25 August 1990	19+1	1		1				
Walton, David	–								
Wilder, Chris	Shrewsbury T. (A) 24 January 1987	4	1						
MIDFIELDERS									
Cherrill, Matthew	–								
Gannon, John	Blackpool (H) 25 February 1988	32	3	4	1	1			
Hartfield, Charles	Crystal Palace (A) 31 August 1991	6+1	1						
Hoyland, Jamie	Liverpool (H) 25 August 1990	23+3	2+1	1	1	4	1		
Lake, Michael	Newcastle U. (A) 25 November 1989	8+10	1+2	4	0+1	4		1	
Littlejohn, Adrian	Southampton (H) 24 August 1991	5+2			1				
Marwood, Brian	Leeds U. (H) 23 September 1990	1+4		0+1		1			
Rogers, Paul	Luton T. (A) 22 February 1992	13							
Whitehouse, Dane	Blackpool (A) 15 October 1988	25+9	3	3+1	1	7		1	2
FORWARDS									
Bradshaw, Carl	Plymouth Arg. (A) 16 September 1989	15+3	2	2	1	1		1	
Brocklehurst, David	–								
Bryson, Ian	Reading (A) 27 August 1988	29+5	3	3+1	1	9			
Cork, Alan	Sheffield Wed. (A) 11 March 1991	7+1				2			
Deane, Brian	Reading (A) 27 August 1988	30	1	4		12	2	2	
Duffield, Peter	Leicester C. (H) 17 October 1987	0+2							
Hodges, Glyn	Manchester C. (A) 19 January 1991	22+4		3+1		2		1	
Mendonca, Clive	Brighton & H.A. (A) 2 May 1987	4+6	0+2		0+1	1			
Peel, Nathan	Tottenham H. (A) 23 November 1991	0+1							
Reed, John	Wimbledon (A) 2 May 1992	0+1							
Ward, Mitch	Manchester C. (H) 8 September 1990	4+2	0+1	1		2			
PLAYERS MAKING APPEARANCES IN 1991-92 (No longer with the club)									
PLAYERS	CURRENT CLUBS								
Agana, Tony	Notts Co. (November 1991)	13	3			4			
Booker, Bob	Brentford (November 1991)	8+4							
Davison, Bobby	Leeds U. (Loan – March 1992)	6+5				4			
Day, Mervyn	Leeds U. (Loan – May 1992)	1							
Jones, Vinny	Chelsea (August 1991)	4							
Wood, Paul	Bournemouth (October 1991)	3+1							

TRAINEES

Graham J. Anthony, Tony Battersby, Timothy Butterfield, Steven Cope, Ian Dickerson, Matthew Foreman, Lee M. Innes, Steven Kennedy, Simon C. Letts, Craig P. McGovern, Craig Myhill, Gregory Pearson, Christopher A. Stammers, Jason K. Tee, Martin Thomson, Danny Wainwright, Lee Wainwright, Barry L. Zivkovic

The Sheffield United Captain

Brian Gayle

Christmas will be a little early this year at Bramall Lane. Sheffield United have decided to start the season where they usually begin it, after Christmas.

On New Year's Day they lost at Anfield and then proceeded to have a run of 17 games with just one defeat, finishing ninth in the League table. It was a fine effort for a team which was seriously out of fortune by Christmas Eve.

For captain Brian Gayle and the "Blades" this was their best season since returning to senior flight football. So Dave Bassett decided to bring the side in for pre-season training a fortnight before everyone else go back to work. He even jests that the club's Christmas party will be held in August this year to try and hoodwink his team into thinking that they are already on their way up to the higher plains of the Premier League.

Without a doubt, Sheffield as a city has as powerful a pair of footballing sides as Manchester, or London, or Liverpool. And the Steelmen are more prepared this year for the toughness and importance of their opening encounters. There is less apprehension now and players have more self-belief.

Perhaps Sheffield United might be forgiven for feeling slightly peeved that the team on the other side of town gains accolades for its more refined style. United earn more industrious metaphors – where The "Owls" "flow" and play "a lyrical passing game", the "Blades" "battle" and play "scrapping, combative football". To win a comprehensive "double" over rivals, Sheffield Wednesday, was particularly sweet. (Not forgetting Forest and Tottenham!)

The first victory at Bramall Lane was critical because it moved the team away from the bottom of the First Division and put a stop to talk of relegation. Brian Deane was back after a two month absence with the debilitating illness, glandular fever and Brian Gayle's authoritative marshalling of United's defence ensured that Wednesday were unable to penetrate the "Blades'" ten yard box. After the game even Wednesday's manager, Trevor Francis, admitted that the opposition played with far more passion. It is not insignificant to note that there are more home-grown players in Sheffield United's side, a critical factor in any "derby" game.

The new season holds no fears for Gayle or anyone else in his vastly improved side. Mike Lake and John Gannon have both developed into commanding defenders and with Gayle at the helm, the "Blades'" back four looks rock solid. The team feels well-equipped to challenge for honours because all the players want to improve together and that can only be good. United believe that they can match anything that Wednesday achieved last season – nothing is impossible according to Dave Bassett. Finances at Bramall Lane are a touch less healthy than at the other Yorkshire clubs, but lack of brass has never stopped Yorkshiremen from following dreams.

Captain's Table

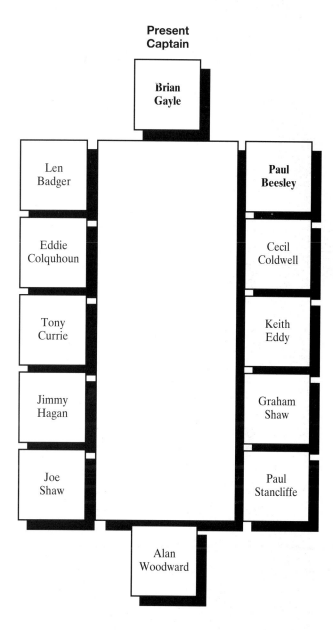

Present Captain

Brian Gayle

Len Badger

Eddie Colquhoun

Tony Currie

Jimmy Hagan

Joe Shaw

Paul Beesley

Cecil Coldwell

Keith Eddy

Graham Shaw

Paul Stancliffe

Alan Woodward

Brian Gayle heads an impressive table with his guests, including many famous post-war club captains both past and present. Those still on the club books are denoted in **bold** print.

SHEFFIELD WEDNESDAY
1867

THE OWLS

Team Manager: Trevor Francis
Club Address Hillsborough, Sheffield S6 1SW
Record Attendance 72,841 v Manchester C., FA Cup 5th Round, 17 February 1934
Turned Professional 1887
Previous Names The Wednesday
Club Honours Football League: Div. 1 Champions 1902-03, 1903-04, 1928-29, 1929-30; Div. 2 Champions 1899-1900, 1925-26, 1951-52, 1955-56, 1958-59. FA Cup: Winners 1896, 1907, 1935. Football League Cup: Winners 1991
League History 1892-99 Div. 1; 1899-1900 Div. 2; 1900-20 Div. 1; 1920-26 Div. 2; 1926-37 Div. 1; 1937-50 Div. 2; 1950-51 Div. 1; 1951-52 Div. 2; 1952-55 Div. 1; 1955-56 Div. 2; 1956-58 Div.1; 1958-59 Div. 2; 1959-70 Div. 1; 1970-75 Div. 2; 1975-80 Div. 3; 1980-84 Div. 2; 1984-90 Div. 1; 1990-91 Div. 2; 1991- Div. 1

Most League Points in a Season (2 for a win) 62 in Div. 2, 1958-59. (3 for a win) 88 in Div. 2, 1983-84
Most League Goals in a Season 106 in Div. 2, 1958-59
Record League Victory 9-1 v Birmingham C. in Div. 1, 13 December 1930
Record League Defeat 0-10 v Aston Villa in Div. 1, 5 October 1912
Consecutive League Wins 9 in 1903-04 and 1904-05
Consecutive League Defeats 7 in 1893
Record League Appearances Andy Wilson, 502 between 1900-20
Record League Goalscorer—Career Andy Wilson, 200 between 1900-20
Record League Goalscorer—Season Derek Dooley, 46 in Div. 2, 1951-52

1991-92 Record

Football League First Division (3rd): Played 42, Won 21, Drawn 12, Lost 9, Goals For 62, Goals Against 49, Points 75
FA Cup Third Round: Preston N.E. (A)2-0; Fourth Round: Middlesbrough (H)1-2

League Cup Second Round: Leyton Orient (A)0-0 (H)4-1; Third Round: Southampton (H)1-1 (R)0-1
Zenith Cup Second Round: Manchester C. (H)3-2; Third Round: Notts Co. (A)0-1

1991-92: Back Row L-R: Richie Barker (Assistant Manager), Phil King, *Steve McCall*, Peter Shirtliff, Viv Anderson, Kevin Pressman, Carlton Palmer, *Chris Turner*, Paul Warhurst, Nigel Worthington, *Darren Wood*, Gordon Watson, Alan Smith (Physio). **Front Row:** Roland Nilsson, Paul Williams, John Harkes, David Hirst, Trevor Francis (Player/Manager), Nigel Pearson, Danny Wilson, *Steve Mackenzie*, John Sheridan.

Playing staff for 1992-93 (As at 1 July 1992)   SHEFFIELD WEDNESDAY

PLAYERS	CLUB DEBUT (Football League)	1991-92 APPEARANCES				1991-92 GOALS			
		Lge	FL Cup	FA Cup	Others	Lge	FL Cup	FA Cup	Others
GOALKEEPERS									
Beresford, Marlon	–								
Key, Lance	–								
Pressman, Kevin	Southampton (A) 5 September 1987	1							
Robinson, Paul	–								
Woods, Chris	Aston Villa (H) 17 August 1991	41	4	2	2				
DEFENDERS									
Anderson, Viv	Hull C. (H) 12 January 1990	15+7	4	1+1	2	3	1		
Flint, Jonathan	–								
King, Phil	Nottingham F. (A) 4 November 1989	38+1	4	2	2	1			
Linighan, Brian	–								
Linighan, John	–								
Nilsson, Roland	Luton T. (H) 9 December 1989	39	3	2	1	1			
Palmer, Carlton	Wimbledon (A) 25 February 1989	42	3	2	2	5			
Pearson, Nigel	Nottingham F. (A) 17 October 1987	31	2	1	1	2			
Shirtliff, Peter	Peterborough U. (A) 19 August 1978	12							
Stewart, Simon	–								
Warhurst, Paul	Aston Villa (H) 17 August 1991	31+2	2	1	1				
Watts, Julian	–								
MIDFIELDERS									
Bart-Williams, Chris	Arsenal (H) 23 November 1991	12+3		1	0+1			1	
Frank, Ian	–								
Harkes, John	Oldham Ath. (H) 3 November 1990	14+15	3	2	2	3			
Hyde, Graham	Manchester C. (A) 14 September 1991	9+4	1	1+1	1				1
Jones, Ryan	–								
Sheridan, John	Nottingham F. (A) 4 November 1989	24	2	1		6		1	
Simpson, Ronald	–								
Williams, Mike	–								
Wilson, Danny	Ipswich T. (A) 25 August 1990	35+1	4	0+1	1+1	3			
Worthington, Nigel	Brighton & H.A. (H) 25 February 1984	34	3	2	1	5			
Wright, Jeremy	–								
FORWARDS									
Chambers, Leroy	–								
Curzon, Richard	–								
Francis, Trevor (N/C)	Millwall (H) 3 February 1990	0+20	0+1	0+1		1	2		
Hirst, David	Charlton Ath. (A) 23 August 1986	33	3	1	2	18	1	1	1
Jemson, Nigel	Norwich C. (A) 18 September 1991	11+9	1+2	1	1+1	4			1
Johnson, David	Aston Villa (A) 18 January 1992	5+1							
Rowntree, Michael	–								
Waddle, Chris	–								
Watson, Gordon	Notts Co. (A) 2 March 1991	4	1	1	0+1				
Williams, Paul	Ipswich T. (A) 25 August 1990	31+9	3	1	2	9	1		
PLAYERS MAKING APPEARANCES IN 1991-92 (No longer with the club)									
PLAYERS	CURRENT CLUBS								
Mackenzie, Steve	Shrewsbury T. (March 1992)	0+3							
Wood, Darren	F/T (May 1992)		1+1		1				

TRAINEES

Carl A Baird, Lee Briscoe, Matthew J. Burkill, Marc L. Burrows, Simon Carter, Simon J. Dean, David P. Faulkner, Mark A. Guest, Darren P. Holmes, Daniel M. Jacks, Scott Parker, Neil Rodgers

The Sheffield Wednesday Captain

Nigel Pearson

Nigel Pearson is a highly-respected professional. He would probably behave in exactly the same manner on the pitch even if he was not Sheffield Wednesday's captain. When he took over the armband from Mel Sterland several years ago, he did not find it easy to replace a much-liked and local player. That season the team just escaped relegation, but sadly were demoted the following year. For Pearson, it was all part of a learning process.

"During the bad times you have, as captain, to absorb much of the criticism that people feel in general. And even though you might not feel too optimistic at the time, you must project a positive attitude", he maintains. "Your pride, both personal and professional, has been dented by something like relegation. It's deflating. You feel you have failed everyone, including yourself.

But the test of character is to put right something you put wrong. At that time no-one left the club. Several players who could easily have transferred back to the First Division, chose to stay and that following season was fantastic. We were geared for success – it was based on a very strong foundation and though we went back into the First Division from third place, we were the best team".

The Rumbelow's Cup-Final against Manchester United in 1991 was a triumph for Nigel Pearson. He earned fine praise from the discerning media the next day and he was unanimously voted "Man of the Match". He was described as "a towering figure who handled the threat of McClair and Hughes almost single-handedly". And it was Pearson's decisive challenge on Pallister that led to John Sheridan's fiercely driven shot – the matchwinner.

"Of course, it's easy to enjoy things when you're doing well, but I do think we play football as it should be played. We do have a lovely collection of individuals at the club and that makes all the difference. The game is still rich with characters – just as many as there were years ago.

I enjoyed the game against Manchester City. I think every one did. It was one of those games that sent you home feeling that everything is worthwhile. The Tottenham draw at home was another fine game. A 0-0 draw, but a measure of the type of football that we can play in this country.

The Crystal Palace result was not the one we wanted. Afterwards in the dressing-room, you'd think we had been relegated! We had not been out of the first six all season – the first time under pressure and we failed! But you have to keep things in perspective – take stock and then change things.

We did not lose two games on the trot all year and after those two heavy defeats against Leeds and Arsenal, we came back to win the following week. We are really looking forward to playing in the European competitions. Many of our squad are already experienced internationals. I can't wait for the home legs – what a carnival that's going to be at Hillsborough"!

Captain's Table

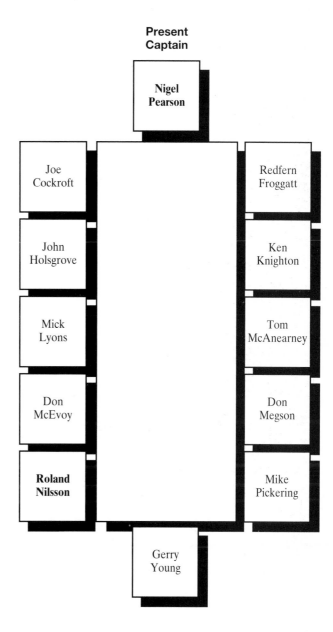

Nigel Pearson heads an impressive table with his guests, including many famous post-war club captains both past and present. Those still on the club books are denoted in **bold** print.

SOUTHAMPTON
1885

THE SAINTS

Team Manager Ian Branfoot
Club Address The Dell, Milton Road, Southampton SO9 4XX
Record Attendance 31,044 v Manchester U., Div. 1, 8 October 1969
Turned Professional 1894
Previous Names Southampton St Marys
Club Honours Football League: Div 3(S) Champions 1921-22; Div. 3 Champions 1959-60. FA Cup: Winners 1976
League History 1920-22 Div. 3(S); 1922-53 Div. 2; 1953-58 Div. 3(S); 1958-60 Div. 3; 1960-66 Div 2; 1966-74 Div. 1; 1974-78 Div. 2; 1978- Div. 1
Most League Points in a Season (2 for a win) 61 in Div. 3(S), 1921-22 and in Div. 3, 1959-60. (3 for a win). 77 in Div. 1, 1983-84

Most League Goals in a Season 112 in Div. 3(S), 1957-58
Record League Victory 9-3 v Wolverhampton W. in Div. 2, 8 September 1965 and 8-2 v Coventry C. in Div. 1, 28 April 1984
Record League Defeat 0-8 v Tottenham H. in Div. 2, 28 March 1936 and v Everton in Div. 1, 20 November 1971
Consecutive League Wins 6 in 1964 and 1992
Consecutive League Defeats 5 in 1927, 1957, 1967-68 and 1988-89
Record League Appearances Terry Paine, 713 between 1956-74
Record League Goalscorer–Career Mike Channon, 182 between 1966-82
Record League Goalscorer–Season Derek Reeves, 39 in Div. 3, 1959-60

1991-92 Record

Football League First Division (16th): Played 42, Won 14, Drawn 10, Lost 18, Goals For 39, Goals Against 55, Points 52
FA Cup Third Round: Q.P.R. (H)2-0; Fourth Round: Manchester U. (H)0-0 (R)2-2; Fifth Round: Bolton W (A)2-2 (R)3-2; Sixth Round: Norwich C. (H)0-0 (R)1-2

League Cup Second Round: Scarborough (A)3-1 (H)2-2; Third Round: Sheffield Wed. (A)1-1 (R)1-0; Fourth Round: Nottingham F. (A)0-0 (R)0-1
Zenith Cup Second Round: Bristol C. (A)2-1; Third Round: Plymouth Arg (A)1-0; Fourth Round: West Ham U. (H)2-1; Semi-Final: Chelsea (H)2-0 (A)3-1; Final: Nottingham F. 2-3

1991-92: Back Row L-R: Jason Dodd, *Andy Cook,* Alexei Cherednik, Jon Gittens, *Sergei Gotsmanov.* **Third Row:** Stephen Roast, Nicky Banger, Francis Benali, Neil Maddison, Tom Widdrington, Matthew Bound, David Hughes, Jeff Kenna, Paul Tisdale. **Second Row:** *Alan McLoughlin,* Matthew le Tissier, *Steve Davis,* Ian Andrews, Paul Moody, Tim Flowers, *Neil Ruddock,* Richard Hall, *Paul Rideout,* Lee Powell. **Front Row:** Lew Chatterley (First Team Coach), Micky Adams, *Russell Osman,* Glenn Cockerill, Ian Branfoot (Manager), Kevin Moore, Barry Horne, Alan Shearer, Don Taylor (Physio).

Playing staff for 1992-93 (As at 1 July 1992) SOUTHAMPTON

PLAYERS	CLUB DEBUT (Football League)	1991-92 APPEARANCES				1991-92 GOALS			
		Lge	FL Cup	FA Cup	Others	Lge	FL Cup	FA Cup	Others
GOALKEEPERS									
Andrews, Ian	Derby Co. (H) 10 March 1990	1							
Flowers, Tim	Manchester U. (A) 13 September 1986	41	6	7	6				
DEFENDERS									
Adams, Micky	Arsenal (H) 25 March 1989	34	6	4	5	3			
Benali, Francis	Derby Co. (H) 1 October 1988	19+3		6	3				
Bound, Matthew	Oldham Ath. (H) 25 April 1992	0+1							
Cherednik, Alexei	Liverpool (A) 31 March 1990								
Dodd, Jason	Q.P.R. (A) 14 October 1989	26+2	6	4	3				
Ferguson, Gary	–								
Gittens, Jon	Birmingham C. (A) 19 April 1986	9+2	4		1				
Hall, Richard	Wimbledon (H) 11 May 1991	21+5	4+1	5	3	2		2	
Kenna, Jeff	Derby Co. (A) 4 May 1991	14		3+1	3				
Moore, Kevin	Manchester U. (H) 15 August 1987	15+1	2	2	1				1
Wood, Steve	Norwich C. (H) 19 October 1991	15		1	4			1	
MIDFIELDERS									
Cockerill, Glenn	Luton T. (A) 19 October 1985	36+1	6	5+1	3	4	2		
Gray, Stuart	Arsenal (H) 28 September 1991	10+2	5	4	1			1	
Horne, Barry	Arsenal (H) 25 March 1989	34	5+1	7	5	1	1	2	
Hughes, David	–								
Hurlock, Terry	Manchester U. (H) 14 September 1991	27+2	4	5	6				1
McKilligan, Neil	–								
Maddison, Neil	Tottenham H. (A) 25 October 1988	4+2		0+1					
Powell, Lee	Luton T. (H) 21 March 1992	1+3							
Roast, Stephen	–								
Thomas, Martin	–								
Tisdale, Paul	–								
Widdrington, Tom	Everton (A) 1 April 1992	2+1							
FORWARDS									
Banger, Nicky	Norwich C. (A) 8 December 1990	0+4	0+1		1				
Dowie, Iain	Luton T. (A) 4 September 1991	25+5	1+3	4	4	9			
Lee, Dave	Leeds U. (H) 28 August 1991	11+8		0+1	1+1				
Le Tissier, Matthew	Norwich C. (A) 30 August 1986	31+1	6	7	6	6	1	1	7
MacDonald, Callum	–								
Moody, Paul	Tottenham H. (H) 17 August 1991	2+2		0+1					
Shearer, Alan	Chelsea (A) 26 March 1988	41	6	7	6	13	3	2	3
Wilson, Barry	–								

PLAYERS MAKING APPEARANCES IN 1991-92 (No longer with the club)

PLAYERS	CURRENT CLUBS	Lge	FL Cup	FA Cup	Others	Lge	FL Cup	FA Cup	Others
Gilkes, Michael	Reading (Loan – March 1992)	4+2							
McLoughlin, Alan	Portsmouth (March 1992)	0+2	0+1						
Osman, Russell	Bristol C. (October 1991)	1+3							
Rideout, Paul	Notts Co. (September 1991)	4							
Ruddock, Neil	Tottenham H. (June 1992)	30	5	6	4			1	

TRAINEES

Keith Accison, Peter Allen, Neal Bartlett, Anthony G. Cleeve, Kevin T. Doherty, Paul Harper, Neil Hopper, Aron A. McNally, Russell Meara, Kevin Murphy, Matthew R. Robinson, Richard M. Rowe, Benjamin D. Shiers, James Winstanley

The Southampton Captain

Glenn Cockerill

Glenn Cockerill does not lead so much as command his team who have this season only masqueraded under the nickname of "Saints"! The rugged midfield duo of Cockerill and Terry Hurlock, with Neil Ruddock shoring up the rear, puts one in mind of one of those old films where gods and warriors roamed the earth in search of an adventure or two. It would seem that a few of them stopped off at the Dell, watched the "Saints" train and decided to stay for the season.

After the sacking of Chris Nicholl, the first time a manager at Southampton had been dismissed in 36 years, Ian Branfoot breezed in pledging that the club would soon rediscover the days of glory still remembered from the early 1980s. Branfoot desires success and he is not afraid to admit it. He worked at the Dell as youth team coach and recalls Keegan, Channon and Ball vividly. Last season saw the emergence of Alan Shearer as a bright new star, but he was destined to flicker only momentarily at the Dell and this year will see him playing for Kenny Dalglish's Blackburn Rovers. Though the Southampton manager will be sad to see Shearer go, he accepts the inevitability of such moves. But he remains proud of the tradition at Southampton for bringing on youngsters like Shearer and the Wallace brothers, who departed to Leeds a season ago.

This has been Glenn Cockerill's 16th season as a professional footballer. Since signing from Sheffield United in 1985 he has played more than 300 times in Southampton's midfield. He can be justly proud of the way that he has helped his team to avoid relegation. He is the kind of captain who can take hold of a departing game and turn things around before the opposition knows what has hit them – literally or metaphorically.

He firmly believed that his side would win the ZDS Final against Nottingham Forest and he was almost proved right. The game was a testament to the dual nature of English football – the refined versus the robust – and the margin between the two was so narrow that day. Both teams played with such courage and commitment in their own very particular styles and pity it was that there had to be a loser. Cockerill's contribution was total, the competitive edge sometimes veering towards the suicidal. There were one or two who thought that he was lucky to remain on the pitch. But his absence would have been as heartbreaking for Southampton as the loss of Pearce was to Forest.

Cockerill hoped that Shearer would stay, along with the gifted Matthew le Tissier, but he is philosophical about the reality of those hopes. "We're building for the future", he says. "Whether some players stay with us remains to be seen. I hope they do because you need quality players around.

But if they leave, I'm sure they'll be adequately replaced. One or two players don't make a team and we'll be successful in the future, with or without them".

Captain's Table

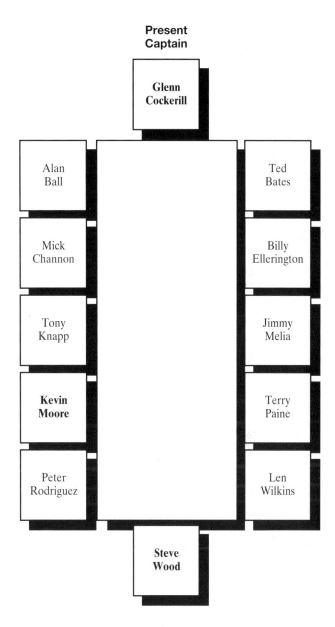

Glenn Cockerill heads an impressive table with his guests, including many famous post-war club captains both past and present. Those still on the club books are denoted in **bold** print.

TOTTENHAM HOTSPUR
1882
THE SPURS

Team Manager Terry Venables
Club Address White Hart Lane Ground, 748 High Road, Tottenham, London N17 0AP
Record Attendance 75,038 v Sunderland, FA Cup 6th Round, 5 March, 1938
Turned Professional 1895
Previous Names Hotspur
Club Honours Football League: Div. 1 Champions 1950-51, 1960-61; Div 2 Champions 1919-20, 1949-50. FA Cup: Winners 1901, 1921, 1961, 1962, 1967, 1981, 1982, 1991. Football League Cup: Winners 1971, 1973. European Cup Winners Cup: Winners 1962-63. EUFA Cup: Winners 1971-72, 1983-84
League History 1908-09 Div. 2; 1909-15 Div. 1; 1919-20 Div. 2; 1920-28 Div. 1; 1928-33 Div. 2; 1933-35 Div. 1; 1935-50 Div. 2; 1950-77 Div. 1; 1977-78 Div. 2; 1978-Div. 1

Most League Points in a Season (2 for a win) 70 in Div. 2, 1919-20. (3 for a win) 77 in Div. 1, 1984-85
Most League Goals in a Season 115 in Div. 1, 1960-61
Record League Victory 9-0 v Bristol Rov. in Div. 2, 22 October 1977
Record League Defeat 0-7 v Liverpool in Div. 1, 2 September 1978
Consecutive League Wins 13 in 1960
Consecutive League Defeats 5 in 1912, 1955 and 1975
Record League Appearances Steve Perryman, 655 between 1969-86
Record League Goalscorer–Career Jimmy Greaves, 220 between 1961-70
Record League Goalscorer–Season Jimmy Greaves, 37 in Div. 1, 1962-63

1991-92 Record

Football League First Division (15th): Played 42, Won 15, Drawn 7, Lost 20, Goals For 58, Goals Against 63, Points 52
FA Cup Third Round: Aston Villa (A)0-0 (R)0-1
League Cup Second Round: Swansea C. (A)0-1 (H)5-1; Third Round: Grimsby T. (A)3-0; Fourth Round: Coventry C. (A)2-1; Fifth Round: Norwich C. (H)2-1; Semi Final: Nottingham F. (A)1-1 (H)1-2
European Cup Winners Cup Prelim Round: SV Stockerau (A)1-0 (H)1-0; First Round: Hajduk Split (A)0-1 (H)2-0; Second Round: FC Porto (H)3-1 (A)0-0; Third Round: Feyenoord (A)0-1 (H)0-0

1991-92: Back Row L-R: *John Moncur, Andy Polston,* Gudni Bergsson, Erik Thorstvedt, *Mitchell Thomas,* Ian Walker, David Tuttle, Steve Sedgley, Justin Edinburgh. **Middle Row:** Doug Livermore (Assistant Manager), *Philip Gray, Brian Statham,* Pat van den Hauwe, Vinny Samways, David Howells, Paul Moran, Nayim, John Hendry, Ray Clemence (Reserve Team Manager). **Front Row:** *Paul Walsh, Mark Robson,* Paul Stewart, Terry Fenwick, *Peter Shreeves* (Manager), Gary Mabbutt, *Gary Lineker, Paul Gascoigne,* Paul Allen.

Playing staff for 1992-93 (As at 1 July 1992)   TOTTENHAM HOTSPUR

PLAYERS	CLUB DEBUT (Football League)	1991-92 APPEARANCES				1991-92 GOALS			
		Lge	FL Cup	FA Cup	Others	Lge	FL Cup	FA Cup	Others
GOALKEEPERS									
Dearden, Kevin	–								
Heath, Michael	–								
Thorstvedt, Erik	Nottingham F. (H) 15 January 1989	24	6	2	7				
Walker, Ian	Norwich C. (A) 10 April 1991	18	1		2				
DEFENDERS									
Austin, Dean	–								
Bergsson, Gudni	Luton T. (H) 26 December 1988	17+11	3+2	0+1	5+1	1			
Culverhouse, David	–								
Cundy, Jason	Coventry C. (H) 28 March 1992	10							
Edinburgh, Justin	Wimbledon (H) 10 November 1990	22+1	1+2		3				
Fenwick, Terry	Watford (H) 1 January 1988	22+1	4	2	5				
Hendon, Ian	Aston Villa (A) 16 March 1991	0+2	1		0+1				
Mabbutt, Gary	Luton T. (H) 28 August 1982	40	6	2	9	2			1
McDonald, David	–								
Mahorn, Paul	–								
Marlowe, Andrew	–								
Nethercott, Stuart	–								
Ruddock, Neil	Charlton Ath. (H) 18 April 1987								
Sedgley, Steve	Luton T. (H) 19 August 1989	21+13	6+1	2	5+3				
Tuttle, David	Chelsea (A) 1 December 1990	2	1		1				1
Van den Hauwe, Pat	Aston Villa (A) 9 September 1989	35	6	2	7		1		
Young Neil	–								
MIDFIELDERS									
Allen, Paul	Watford (H) 17 August 1985	38+1	7	2	7+1	3	2		
Caskey, Darren	–								
Gray, Andy	Leeds U. (H) 7 March 1992	14				1			
Howells, David	Sheffield Wed. (A) 22 February 1986	27+4	5	1	7	1			
Minton, Jeffrey	Everton (H) 25 April 1992	2				1			
Nayim, Mohamed	Norwich C. (H) 21 February 1989	22+9	4+2	0+1	7	1			
Potts, Anthony	–								
Samways, Vinny	Nottingham F. (A) 2 May 1987	26+1	6+1	2	7+1	1	1		
Stewart, Paul	Manchester U. (H) 1 October 1988	38	7	2	9	5	1		
Turner, Andrew	–								
Watson, Kevin	–								
FORWARDS									
Anderton, Darren	–								
Barmby, Nicky	–								
Beadle, Peter	–								
Durie, Gordon	Southampton (A) 17 August 1991	31	6	1	8	6	2		3
Hendry, John	Norwich C. (A) 10 April 1991	1+4	0+1			1			
Hodges, Lee	–								
Houghton, Scott	Manchester U. (H) 28 September 1991	0+10	0+2		0+2	2			
McMahon, Gerard	–								
Morah, Ollie	–								
Moran, Paul	Everton (A) 11 May 1987				0+1				
PLAYERS MAKING APPEARANCES IN 1991-92 (No longer with the club)									
PLAYERS	CURRENT CLUBS								
Lineker, Gary	Grampus (May 1992)	35	5	2	9	28	5		2
Moncur, John	Swindon T. (March 1992)		0+1						
Walsh, Paul	Portsmouth (May 1992)	17+12	2+1	2	1+3	3	1		

TRAINEES

Ijah M. Anderson, Spencer C. Binks, Sulzeer J. Campbell, James R. Clapham, Christopher N. Day, Daniel F. Foot, Darren M. Grogan, Junior L. Haynes, Daniel R. L. Hill, William G. Hudson, Gareth R. Knott, Christopher S. Landon, Neil E. LeBihan, David E. J. McDougald, Andrew J. Quy, Andrew Reynolds, Christopher C. Reynolds, Stephen Robinson, Robert A. Simpson, Leon Townley

The Tottenham Hotspur Captain

Gary Mabbutt

Gary Mabbutt has spent ten years at Tottenham and for five of those years he has captained the side. The season of 1990-91 began as the worst of times because of the club's much-publicised financial situation, but it certainly ended as the best of times when the team won the FA Cup.

The team had begun the season with flair, flying high on the coat-tails of the England team's success in the World Cup and the significant part in that triumph played by two Tottenham players, Gary Lineker and Paul Gascoigne. However, the club's finances began to draw more media attention than the team's efforts on the pitch and it became necessary for the players to begin to rally together in the face of great pressure and somehow they began to believe that a Cup Final place was a strong possibility.

It has been said that Gary Mabbutt is the one captain that all managers would like to be able to field in their respective sides. Quiet, calm and resolute, Mabbutt is also a powerful player and when he is on the pitch there is never the remotest indication that he is a diabetic. His condition is not one which he tries to disguise and his open and frank attitude to something which could have halted his playing career has been an inspiration to many with less critical problems.

Gary Mabbutt is proud but modest and insists that Tottenham's FA Cup success was a result of teamwork, rather than his leadership qualities. "It had been a difficult season and the team showed great character. All the players worked for one another so it wasn't at all tough for me. We did have a lot of press interest so by the end of the week it really was a relief to go out and play football. To play two stunning games as we did in the Semi-Final and the Cup Final was more than memorable. It was strange after the Semi, staged at Wembley, to just leave – go home with no presentations. But the actual Final? Well, I think we experienced every possible emotion you could feel in football in the first ten minutes of the game. Paul was badly injured, Forest scored from the resulting free-kick, Gary Lineker had a goal disallowed, then a penalty saved . . . what more could have happened? Then in the second-half everything came together. To win? There were all the emotions you could think of – a personal dream for me after the disappointment of Coventry in 1987. The only reason that I didn't run up the steps was because I was so exhausted!

We began this season well and up until Christmas everything was looking rosy – then, within three or four weeks it all dropped away and our League form suffered. But it was great to be back playing European opposition again. In the last ten years we have been third in the League twice so this season it would be good to make a sustained chase for the Championship. We have lost two world-class players but there are some excellent youngsters coming through, one or two on the verge of becoming great players – everything will gel together next season, I'm sure".

Captain's Table

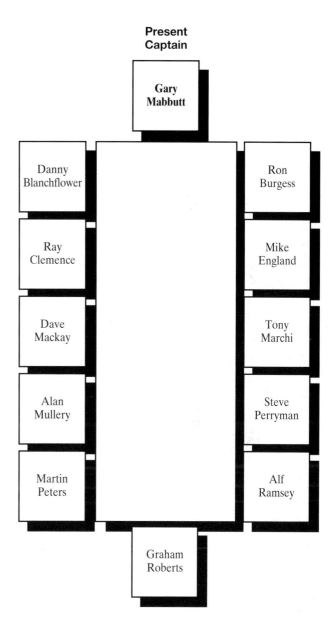

Present Captain

Gary Mabbutt

Danny Blanchflower

Ray Clemence

Dave Mackay

Alan Mullery

Martin Peters

Ron Burgess

Mike England

Tony Marchi

Steve Perryman

Alf Ramsey

Graham Roberts

Garry Mabbutt heads an impressive table with his guests, including many famous post-war club captains both past and present. Those still on the club books are denoted in **bold** print.

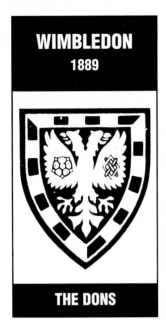

WIMBLEDON
1889

THE DONS

Team Manager Joe Kinnear
Club Address Selhurst Park, London
SE25 6PU
Record Attendance 18,000 v HMS Victory,
FA Amateur Cup 3rd Round, 1934-35
Turned Professional 1964
Previous Names Wimbledon Old Centrals
Club Honours Football League: Div. 4
Champions 1982-83. FA Cup: Winners 1988
League History 1977-79 Div. 4; 1979-80 Div 3;
1980-81 Div. 4; 1981-82 Div. 3; 1982-83 Div. 4;
1983-84 Div. 3; 1984-86 Div. 2; 1986- Div. 1
Most League Points in a Season (2 for a win)
61 in Div. 4, 1978-79. (3 for a win) 98 in Div. 4,
1982-83

Most League Goals in a Season 97 in Div. 3,
1983-84
Record League Victory 6-0 v Newport Co. in
Div. 3, 3 September 1983
Record League Defeat 1-6 v Carlisle U. in
Div. 2, 23 March 1985 and v Gillingham in
Div. 2, 13 February 1982
Consecutive League Wins 7 in 1983
Consecutive League Defeats 4 in 1982
Record League Appearances Alan Cork, 352
between 1978-92
Record League Goalscorer–Career Alan
Cork, 145 between 1978-92
Record League Goalscorer–Season Alan
Cork, 29 in Div. 3, 1983-84

1991-92 Record

Football League First Division (13th): Played 42, Won
13, Drawn 14, Lost 15, Goals For 53, Goals Against 53,
Points 53
FA Cup Third Round: Bristol C. (A)1-1 (R)0-1

League Cup: Second Round: Peterborough U. (H)1-2
(A)2-2
Zenith Cup Second Round: Brighton & H.A. (A)2-3

1991-92: Back Row L-R: Joe Dillon (Kit Man), Neal Ardley, Steve Cotterill, Scott Fitzgerald, Paul Miller, Chris Perry, Neil Sullivan, Stewart Castledine, Dean Blackwell, Aiden Newhouse, Brian McAllister, Warren Barton, Ron Suart (Chief Scout). **Middle Row:** Syd Neal (Kit Manager), Roger Joseph, John Scales, Robbie Earle, Lawrie Sanchez, Steve Anthrobus, Hans Segers, John Fashanu, *Alan Cork,* Carlton Fairweather, *Jamie McCarthy,* Terry Phelan, Steve Allen (Physio). **Front Row:** *Don Howe* (Coach), Andy Clarke, Gerald Dobbs, Paul McGee, Terry Gibson, *Ray Harford* (Manager), Gary Elkins, Vaughan Ryan, Justin Skinner, Michael Bennett, Joe Kinnear (Reserve Team Manager).

Playing staff for 1992-93 (As at 1 July 1992)   WIMBLEDON

PLAYERS	CLUB DEBUT (Football League)	1991-92 APPEARANCES				1991-92 GOALS			
		Lge	FL Cup	FA Cup	Others	Lge	FL Cup	FA Cup	Others
GOALKEEPERS									
Segers, Hans	Everton (H) 1 October 1988	41	2	2	1				
Sullivan, Neil	Aston Villa (A) 20 April 1991	1							
DEFENDERS									
Barton, Warren	Arsenal (H) 25 August 1990	42	2	2	1	1			
Blackwell, Dean	Manchester C. (H) 16 September 1989	1+3	1			1			
Elkins, Gary	Chelsea (H) 17 November 1990	15+3	1		1	1			
Fitzgerald, Scott	Tottenham H. (H) 28 April 1990	34+2	2	2	1	1			
Jennings, Paul	–								
Joseph, Roger	Arsenal (H) 27 August 1988	25+1	2						
McAllister, Brian	Arsenal (H) 13 January 1990	9+1							
Perry, Chris	–								
Phelan, Terry	Watford (A) 15 August 1987	37	2	2	1	1			
Scales, John	Watford (A) 15 August 1987	41	2	2	1				1
Skinner, Justin	–								
MIDFIELDERS									
Anthrobus, Steve	Aston Villa (A) 24 February 1990	10		2					
Ardley, Neal	Aston Villa (A) 20 April 1991	7+1							
Bennett, Michael	Arsenal (H) 13 January 1990	5	1+1		0+1	1			
Castledine, Stewart	Norwich C. (A) 25 April 1992	0+2							
Dobbs, Gerald	Nottingham F. (H) 2 April 1992	2+2							
Earle, Robbie	Chelsea (A) 17 August 1991	40	2	2	1	14			1
Fear, Peter	–								
Kruszynski, Detzi	West Ham U. (A) 2 January 1989	1							
McGee, Paul	Arsenal (A) 17 May 1989	15+1	1	2	1	2	1		
Ryan, Vaughan	Tottenham H. (H) 22 April 1988	16+5	1		1	2			
Sanchez, Lawrie	Birmingham C. (H) 22 December 1984	16		2		3			
Talboys, Steven	–								
FORWARDS									
Allen, Leighton	–								
Clarke, Andy	Norwich C. (H) 2 March 1991	13+21	1+1	0+1		3	1		
Cotterill, Steve	Tottenham H. (H) 15 April 1989								
Fairweather, Carlton	Brighton & H.A. (A) 29 December 1984	6							
Fashanu, John	Portsmouth (A) 29 March 1986	38	2	2	1	18	1	1	
Gibson, Terry	Derby Co. (A) 29 August 1987	7			1				
Miller, Paul	Watford (A) 15 August 1987	22				2			
Newhouse, Aiden	Charlton Ath. (A) 17 April 1990	5+7		2		1			
Payne, Grant	–								

PLAYERS MAKING APPEARANCES IN 1991-92 (No longer with the club)

PLAYERS	CURRENT CLUBS	Lge	FL Cup	FA Cup	Others	Lge	FL Cup	FA Cup	Others
Cork, Alan	Sheffield U. (March 1992)	12+7	0+2		0+1	2			
Hayes, Martin	Glasgow Celtic (Loan – February 1992)	1+1							

TRAINEES

Daniel P. Brooker, Marc B. Cable, Jason Cunningham, Franco di Rubbo, Neil Fairbairn, Gavin A. Fell, Barry J. Laker, Peter C. Lingley, David Mosley, Kieron Swift, Mark L. Thomas

The Wimbledon Captain

John Fashanu

Not too many players have been able to lead a forward line successfully and captain the team at the same time. One exception is John Fashanu of Wimbledon – an original and innovative man in all areas of his life, he takes captaincy in his stride.

He accepts that to captain from the position of centre-forward is unusual, but he feels that his game has altered slightly in the last few years – he often drops back to take free-kicks now and he will slip into defence when necessary. "As I tire a bit towards the end of the game I tend to slide back into midfield anyway", he says.

He thinks that captains are important people on the pitch and that much is expected of them. Fashanu feels that a captain needs to be someone who has the ability to concentrate on his own job and yet be able to create a calming atmosphere in the changing room, inspire the team on the pitch and at the same time command the respect of the majority of the players. He does believe that captains are born not made, that they need a certain arrogance and self-belief. "When the pressure's on you need to know that your players will obey without question – a captain must have authority in a crisis. And this he must earn along with respect. A captain must know how to help his colleagues both on and off the pitch, on a personal level as well as on a professional level. And if he can't help himself, then he must be able to direct players to someone who can. That's very important.

I try to use my captaincy in a positive way. I have more space because I have more time to think now. Everyone expects more from a captain than from other players so there is less margin for error but I must admit, I still enjoy the one on one confrontation that exists between forwards and defenders! Some areas of the job are not easy – when you're having a real drumming and you may for a moment feel like giving up, but you can't. Then it's into the training room to sort it out – not always easy. But you are not paid to be liked, you are paid to do a job".

Wimbledon played Sheffield United on the last day of the season and the game stays in Fashanu's memory for several reasons. "Yes. I missed my first penalty ever. We were winning 3-0 and if I'd given it to Robbie Earle he'd have had a hat-trick. But I thought it was our best team performance of the season".

Over the last 14 years of his footballing career, Fashanu has known many captains and the best of them all was Bryan Robson, under whom he played at International level. And he pays Robson a most simple and eloquent tribute: "If he's there, everything is all right".

Captain's Table

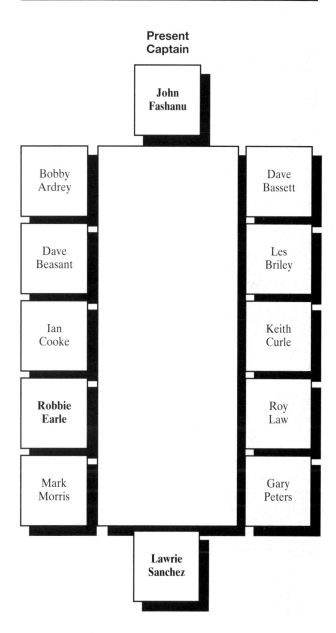

John Fashanu heads an impressive table with his guests, including many famous post-war club captains both past and present. Those still on the club books are denoted in **bold** print.

Gary Pallister (Manchester United) – The PFA "Player of the Year" for 1992.

July, 1992

Transfers into the Premier League: Phil BABB £500,000 (Bradford City – Coventry City), Steve BLATHERWICK (Notts County – Nottingham Forest), Anthony COLE (Newcastle United – Middlesbrough), Jon GOULD (W.B.A. – Coventry City), John JENSEN £1,100,000 (Brondby – Arsenal), Alan KELLY £150,000 (Preston North End – Sheffield United), Stuart MASSEY (Sutton United – Crystal Palace), Geraint WILLIAMS £650,000 (Derby County – Ipswich Town), John WILLIAMS £250,000 (Swansea City – Coventry City), Tommy WRIGHT £650,000 Leicester City – Middlesbrough).

Transfers within the Premier League: Kerry DIXON £575,000 (Chelsea – Southampton), Jon GITTINS (Southampton – Middlesbrough), Barry HORNE Tribunal (Southampton – Everton), Ray HOUGHTON £900,000 (Liverpool – Aston Villa), Stuart RIPLEY £1,300,000 (Middlesbrough – Blackburn Rovers), David ROCASTLE £2,000,000 (Arsenal – Leeds United), Scott SELLARS £800,000 (Blackburn Rovers – Leeds United), Alan SHEARER £3,600,000 (Southampton – Blackburn Rovers), David SPEEDIE £400,000 (Blackburn Rovers – Southampton), Paul STEWART £2,300,000 (Tottenham Hotspur – Liverpool).

Trainee Signings: Craig ARMSTRONG (Nottingham Forest), Russell MEARA (Southampton), Craig MEL-ROSE (Coventry City), Colin MURDOCK (Manchester United).

Transferred outside the Premier League: Andy COLE (Arsenal – Bristol City), Kevin DRINKELL (Coventry City – Falkirk), Paul FURLONG (Coventry City – Watford), Michael HUGHES (Manchester City – Strasbourg), David LOWE (Ipswich Town – Leicester City), Duncan SHEARER (Blackburn Rovers – Aberdeen), Paul SHEPSTONE (Blackburn Rovers – Freed), Barry VENISON (Liverpool – Newcastle United).

ABLETT Gary Ian

Born: Liverpool, 19 November 1965

Height: 6'0" Weight: 11.4

International Honours: E "U21"-1, E"B"

Position/Skill Factor: Natural left footed player, adept at "one-twos" and a great passer of the ball. Joins up in the attack at every opportunity as a provider, rather than scorer. Principally a central defender, he is versatile enough to play anywhere along the back four.

Career History: Liverpool born and bred, he signed associated schoolboy forms for the "Reds" in October 1981 and apprentice forms in June 1982. He actually made his FL debut for Derby County, while on loan, at home to Bournemouth on 30 January 1985 and also had further FL experience on loan to Hull City before playing his first League match for Liverpool in December 1986, deputising for Alan Hansen. He established a regular place in the Liverpool team from February 1988, alternating between left-back and central defence until the 1989 close season. However, his progress was retarded by the signings of David Burrows (left-back) and Glenn Hysen (central defence) and although playing quite frequently in 1989-90 and 1990-91, it was as cover for the four defensive positions and not as first choice. A member of the Liverpool side that lifted the FA Cup in 1989 when beating Everton 3-2, he also won two League Championship medals with the club in 1987-88 and 1989-90. Had a golden opportunity to re-establish himself in the heart of the Liverpool defence in 1991-92, following the departure of Gary Gillespie and injuries to Glen Hysen and new signing

Mark Wright. Although he formed a partnership with the previously untried Nicky Tanner, he was lacking in confidence and it was he and not Tanner, who made way when Wright returned. His transfer from Anfield was perhaps inevitable, although it was a surprise when he moved to city rivals, Everton. Settled down well at Goodison Park, however, playing both at left-back and in central defence.

Clubs	Signing Date	Transfer Fee	APPEARANCES				GOALS			
			Lge	FL Cup	FA Cup	Others	Lge	FL Cup	FA Cup	Others
Liverpool	11.83	–	103+6	10+1	16+2	9	1			
Derby County	1.85	Loan	3+3			2				
Hull City	9.86	Loan	5							
Everton*	1.92	£750,000	17		1		1			

ADAMS Anthony (Tony)
Alexander

Born: Romford, 10 October 1966

Height: 6'1" Weight: 12.1

International Honours: E Yth, E "U21"-5, E"B", E-19

Position/Skill Factor: Key, commanding central defender, who is exceptional in the air inside both six yard boxes. Also specialises in striking good long balls behind an opponent's defence.

Career History: Came through Arsenal's junior ranks, signing associated schoolboy forms in November 1980, before becoming an apprentice in April 1983. After making his FL debut at Highbury against Sunderland on 5 November 1983, two months prior to turning professional, he eventually graduated as the club's youngest ever captain. Recognised at full international level, he made his England debut against Spain in Madrid on 18 February 1987 and, two months later, was at Wembley, playing in Arsenal's 2-1 League Cup Final win over Liverpool. And at the end of that season he was honoured by the PFA as their "Young Player of the Year". He was a regular choice for his country for two years, participating in England's ill-fated appearance in the European Championships in West Germany, June 1988, until losing his place to Des Walker. Scaled the heights in 1988-89, when he led the "Gunners" to the League Championship, following a famous last match of the season victory over Liverpool at Anfield. But two years later he was disgraced, when he was absent from the team for three months, following a well publicised jail conviction for a drink driving offence. However, he was soon back in charge, leading Arsenal to yet another League Championship title, the tenth in the club's history and, perhaps surprisingly, winning two more England caps, both against the Republic of Ireland, after being overlooked for two years by the England management. Played in all but seven League games during 1991-92, an up and down season for Arsenal and his international career looked to be over, when he was not selected for any of England's mid-term games, or the European Championships.

Clubs	Signing Date	Transfer Fee	APPEARANCES				GOALS			
			Lge	FL Cup	FA Cup	Others	Lge	FL Cup	FA Cup	Others
Arsenal*	1.84	–	248+1	33+1	18	9	20	2	1	1

Tony Adams

ADAMS Michael (Micky) Richard

Born: Sheffield,
8 November 1961

Height: 5'6"

Weight: 10.4

International Honours:
E Yth

Position/Skill Factor: Versatile player who can operate at left-back or in defensive left-sided midfield positions. Can go past defenders to create chances and crosses well. A willing worker, he is always prepared to help team-mates in trouble.

Career History: Signed as a Gillingham apprentice in August 1978 and made his FL debut at Swindon Town on 19 April 1980 when coming on as a substitute. After four seasons with the Kent side, he moved into the First Division with Coventry City and became an instant hit with the fans when he scored on his home debut. Yorkshire-born, he spent little more than three years at Highfield Road before returning to his home county with Leeds United. Proved to be a shrewd acquisition when helping the club to the 1987 FA Cup Semi-Final, but following the arrival of Glyn Snodin, he found it difficult to hold down a first team place. Moved south to Southampton, settling into the left-back berth, until forced to miss a huge chunk of the 1989-90 season due to injury. Came back as strong as ever, sharing the position with young Francis Benali. A consistent first choice at left-back in 1991-92, apart from a spell out of the team from February to April 1992.

Clubs	Signing Date	Transfer Fee	APPEARANCES				GOALS			
			Lge	FL Cup	FA Cup	Others	Lge	FL Cup	FA Cup	Others
Gillingham	11.79	–	85+7	5	6		5			
Coventry City	7.83	£75,000	85+5	9	7	2	9	1		
Leeds United	1.87	£110,000	72+1	4	6	6	2		1	
Southampton*	3.89	£250,000	86+1	12	6	6	3			

ADAMS Neil James

Born: Stoke,
23 November 1965

Height: 5'8"

Weight: 10.1

International Honours:
E "U21"-1

Position/Skill Factor: Right-winger with plenty of pace and enthusiasm. Runs at defenders and often drives balls in from crossing positions.

Career History: Stoke City plucked him out of local junior football and he made his FL debut away at Charlton Athletic in the number three shirt on 21 September 1985 and held his place for the remainder of the season. Everton moved in smartly for him, but after three years at Goodison and only limited appearances, he signed for Oldham Athletic in the summer of 1989, after impressing manager Joe Royle during a spell on loan in 1988-89. However, he was unable to command a regular place, often selected as substitute, but proved a valuable member of the squad that won the Second Division title in 1990-91. In and out of the team during Oldham's first campaign in Division One for 68 years, sharing the number seven shirt with Roger Palmer, his appearances were restricted by frequent tactical team changes.

Clubs	Signing Date	Transfer Fee	APPEARANCES				GOALS			
			Lge	FL Cup	FA Cup	Others	Lge	FL Cup	FA Cup	Others
Stoke City	6.85	–	31+1	3	1	3	4			
Everton	6.86	£150,000	17+3	4+1		5+1		1		
Oldham Athletic	1.89	Loan	9							
Oldham Athletic*	6.89	£100,000	60+24	7+1	8+2	1+1	14	1	2	

AGNEW Steven (Steve) Mark

Born: Shipley, 9 November 1965

Height: 5'9" Weight: 10.6

Position/Skill Factor: Midfield player with great passing ability and superb vision. Can play both short or long and hits some tremendous diagonal passes. Always dangerous at free-kicks.

Career History: Began his career with Barnsley as an apprentice in July 1982, before turning professional early in 1983-84. Played just one match that season when coming on as a substitute for his FL debut at Oakwell against Charlton Athletic on 14 April 1984. After appearing in the next two seasons, a broken leg suffered during 1985-86 threatened to end his FL career. However, he made a remarkable comeback in 1986-87, not in his original forward role, but as a forceful midfielder with a powerful shot. For the next four seasons he was an essential part of the Barnsley engine room and achieved the professional's ambition of being ever present in 1989-90. During his time at Oakwell, the team often challenged for promotion, but twice fell just short of reaching the Play-Offs in 1988-89 and 1990-91. In the summer of 1991 he was signed by Don Mackay for the ambitious and ultra-wealthy Blackburn Rovers. Tragically, after only four games with his new club, he suffered a serious ankle injury which ruled him out for the remainder of 1991-92. With the chance of playing in the top flight for the first time in his career, he will be looking to be fully match fit in time for the start of the new season.

Clubs	Signing Date	Transfer Fee	APPEARANCES				GOALS			
			Lge	FL Cup	FA Cup	Others	Lge	FL Cup	FA Cup	Others
Barnsley	11.83	–	186+8	13	20	6+1	30	3	4	
Blackburn Rovers*	6.91	£700,000	2	2						

ALLEN Bradley James

Born: Romford,
13 September 1971

Height: 5'7"

Weight: 10.0

International Honours:
E Yth, E "U21"-4

Position/Skill Factor: Up and coming striker who is very skilful. Turns quickly and looks to get his shots in, he will almost certainly be another goalscorer in the family mould.

Career History: Another member of the Allen footballing family who have succeeded at the top level, starting with his uncle, Les. Was an associated schoolboy (March 1987) at Loftus Road before turning pro and making his FL debut for Queens Park Rangers at Wimbledon on 14 January 1989, the only first team match he played that season. After three seasons of only occasional appearances he finally earned an extended run in QPR's first team in the closing weeks of 1991-92, scoring five goals in ten games. He was rewarded with a call up to the England Under 21 squad for the annual end of season tournament in Toulon, France. Clearly has a bright future in the Premier League.

Clubs	Signing Date	Transfer Fee	APPEARANCES				GOALS			
			Lge	FL Cup	FA Cup	Others	Lge	FL Cup	FA Cup	Others
Q.P.R.*	9.88	–	14+8	0+1	0+1	1	7			

ALLEN Leighton

Born: Brighton, 22 November 1973

Height: 6'0" Weight: 12.11

Position: Forward.

Career History: Signed on the dotted line for Wimbledon during the summer of 1992, having first come to the club as a trainee in July 1990. No first team experience.

Clubs	Signing Date	Transfer Fee	APPEARANCES				GOALS			
			Lge	FL Cup	FA Cup	Others	Lge	FL Cup	FA Cup	Others
Wimbledon*	6.92	–								

ALLEN Paul Kevin

Born: Aveley, 28 August 1962

Height: 5'7" Weight: 9.12

International Honours: E Yth, E "U21"-3, E"B"

Position/Skill Factor: Very under-rated wide midfield player with a tremendous workrate. Can produce crosses at one end of the park and in the next minute be seen making tackles in a defensive role.

Career History: From a famous footballing family, uncles Les and Dennis, cousins Martin, Bradley and Clive, have all played League soccer. Learnt his trade at the West Ham United "Academy" where he came up through the junior ranks, first as an associated schoolboy (March 1977) and later as an apprentice (July 1978). Made FL debut at home to Burnley as the youngest player ever to turn out for the "Hammers" on 29 September 1979. He went on to play 31 matches that term as well as making history as the youngest player to appear in an FA Cup Final, when helping West Ham to a 1-0 win over Arsenal, at 17 years and nine months of age. His appearances were restricted the following season as the "Hammers" concentrated on promotion back to the First Division, but from then on he matured in the first team under the guidance of players like Billy Bonds and Trevor Brooking. He was sold in the 1985 close season to Tottenham Hotspur and among his new team mates was his cousin, Clive. Has held down a first team place since that day, despite several challenges. Played in his second FA Cup Final, albeit a losing one, when turning out for "Spurs" against Coventry City in 1987 and was ever present in 1991 when Tottenham beat Nottingham Forest 2-1 in extra-time to win the trophy for the eighth time. As consistent as ever in what was a generally disappointing season for his club, missing only three League games in 1991-92. Although a very solid performer, his career has not realised the heights predicted at the time he first burst on the scene.

Clubs	Signing Date	Transfer Fee	APPEARANCES				GOALS			
			Lge	FL Cup	FA Cup	Others	Lge	FL Cup	FA Cup	Others
West Ham United	8.79	–	149+3	20+4	15+3	2+1	6	2	3	
Tottenham Hotspur*	6.85	£400,000	238+16	38+3	17+1	12+2	20	4	1	

ALLON Joseph (Joe) Ball

Born: Gateshead, 12 November 1966

Height: 5'11" Weight: 12.2

International Honours: E Yth

Position/Skill Factor: An old fashioned goalscorer, who by sheer hard work gets into good scoring positions. Once in front of goal, he is a clinical finisher.

Career History: A Newcastle United discovery, signing as an associated schoolboy in July 1981, he was reckoned by many to be a top prospect, while playing in the club's youth side alongside Paul Gascoigne. Later made his FL debut for United at home to Stoke City on 1 December 1984. Lost his way after only a handful of matches and found himself playing Third and Fourth Division football. His 28 FL goals for Hartlepool United were instrumental in the club being promoted to the Third Division for the first time since 1969. Broke United's transfer record when signing for Chelsea in August 1991, but the fee, decided by the FL Tribunal, was much below Harlepool's valuation. After numerous appearances as substitute and scoring on his Chelsea debut with a late equaliser at home to Wimbledon, manager Ian Porterfield apparently decided he wasn't up to standard and ignored him for selection after November. Thereafter, his only League action was on loan to Second Division Port Vale, struggling unsuccessfully against relegation, but to no great effect.

Clubs	Signing Date	Transfer Fee	APPEARANCES				GOALS			
			Lge	FL Cup	FA Cup	Others	Lge	FL Cup	FA Cup	Others
Newcastle United	11.84	–	9	1			2			
Swansea City	7.87	–	27+7	2	2	2	12			1
Hartlepool United	10.88	–	112	5	6+1	7	51	2	5	2
Chelsea*	8.91	£250,000	2+9	0+2		2+1	2			1
Port Vale	2.92	Loan	2+4							

ANDERSON Vivien (Viv) Alexander

Born: Nottingham, 29 August 1956

Height: 6'0" Weight: 11.1

International Honours: E "U21"-1, FL Rep, E"B", E-30

Position/Skill Factor: Very experienced right-back, cum central defender, who is good in the air and always dangerous at set plays. Not as quick as he once was, but uses his guile to defend and can still use those long legs of his to great effect.

Career History: The first black player to represent England, he joined Nottingham Forest as an associated schoolboy (August 1972), before becoming an apprentice (November 1972) a few month later. Went on to make his FL debut at Sheffield Wednesday on 21 September 1974 and was a regular at right-back when Brian Clough arrived in January 1975. In 1976-77 he was a key player as Forest were promoted to the First Division as runners-up and the next season the club won a League Championship and League Cup double. After many sound displays with Forest it came as no great surprise when he was finally recognised at full international level and made his England debut at Wembley against Czechoslovakia on 29 November 1978. This was followed by European Cup and Super Cup winners medals. After nearly 12 years at the club it came as some surprise when he was allowed to move on to Arsenal where he picked up yet another League Cup medal when the "Gunners" defeated Liverpool in 1987. Still as reliable as ever, he was transferred to Manchester United in the 1987 close season and played in 30 League matches as the club finished in second place behind Liverpool. More recently, with mount-

102

ing competition from the likes of Clayton Blackmore and Lee Martin and following the signing of Dennis Irwin, he was allowed to move to Second Division Sheffield Wednesday on a free transfer. Immediately settled into the defence in the absence of the injured Roland Nilsson as the club gained promotion to the First Division in third place. Since Nilsson's return, he has provided cover for the central defensive positions and in 1991-92 assisted the "Owls" to their highest League position for 30 years.

Clubs	Signing Date	Transfer Fee	APPEARANCES				GOALS			
			Lge	FL Cup	FA Cup	Others	Lge	FL Cup	FA Cup	Others
Portsmouth	2.90	–	53+9	3+2	7	2	7	1	5	
Tottenham Hotspur*	5.92	£1,750,000								

ANDREWS Ian Edmund

Born: Nottingham, 1 December 1964

Height: 6'2" **Weight:** 12.2

International Honours: E Yth, E "U21"-1

Position/Skill factor: Goalkeeper who always cuts an imposing figure. Very agile, he always comes for crosses. Recognised for his strong left foot volley kicking, which can reach the opposition's box.

Career History: Was an associated schoolboy with Nottingham Forest (March 1980), before being released to start an apprenticeship at Mansfield Town. However, Leicester City who were looking for a long-term replacement for Mark Wallington, were sufficiently impressed for him to complete his apprenticeship at Filbert Street and snapped him up in June 1981. Was loaned out to Swindon Town to gain experience and made his FL debut there against Bristol City on 24 January 1984. Once he had taken over the 'keeper's jersey permanently from Wallington during 1984-85, he missed only three games in just under three seasons. But in 1986-87, although ever present, the club was relegated into the Second Division and he began to lose confidence. On losing his place to Paul Cooper, he was sold to Celtic where he became understudy to Pat Bonner, but after spending just over a year at Parkhead, Southampton signed him as cover for Tim Flowers. Made only one appearance in 1991-92 and since leaving Leicester his career has stalled badly with only 12 League appearances spread over four seasons.

Clubs	Signing Date	Transfer Fee	APPEARANCES				GOALS			
			Lge	FL Cup	FA Cup	Others	Lge	FL Cup	FA Cup	Others
Leicester City	12.82	–	126	6	7					
Swindon Town	1.84	Loan	1							
Glasgow Celtic	7.88	£300,000	5	2		1				
Leeds United	12.88	Loan	1							
Southampton*	12.89	£200,000	5			1				

ANDERTON Darren Robert

Born: Southampton, 3 March 1972

Height: 6'0"

Weight: 11.7

International Honours: E Yth

Position/Skill Factor: Excellent left-winger with lovely skill and control. Has the ability to go past defenders to cross good early balls into the danger zone. Scores goals as well.

Career History: Potentially brilliant left winger who hit the headlines during Portsmouth's long FA Cup run last season. Came to Fratton Park, first as an associated schoolboy in September 1986, before moving through the ranks as a trainee in February 1988 to professional status at the beginning of 1990. After showing early promise, he made his FL debut at home to Wolverhampton Wan-. derers on 3 November 1990 and towards the end of 1990-91 was challenging strongly for a first team place. During 1991-92 he established himself firmly in the "Pompey" team from the start of the season and showed such good form that he was the subject of transfer speculation even before the club started its FA Cup run, during which he came into the national spotlight. Scored both goals in "Pompey's" Fourth Round victory over Leyton Orient and another brace in the astonishing 4-2 Fifth Round victory over Middlesbrough at Ayresome Park – a ground where 20 previous visitors had managed to score only 11 goals between them. In the Semi-Final, he scored a breakaway goal in the 20th minute of extra time against Liverpool – a goal which seemed certain to take Portsmouth to Wembley for the first time since 1939 until the "Reds'" last last equaliser. The dream was ended in the replay, but only after a penalty "shoot out" at the end of extra time. With so much attention, it was inevitable that Portsmouth would lose their prize asset, who signed for Tottenham Hotspur soon after the end of the season and can now look forward to a glittering career.

Clubs	Signing Date	Transfer Fee	APPEARANCES				GOALS			
			Lge	FL Cup	FA Cup	Others	Lge	FL Cup	FA Cup	Others
Nottingham Forest	8.74	–	323+5	39	23+1	33	15	5	1	
Arsenal	7.84	£250,000	120	18	12		9	3	3	
Manchester United	5.87	£250,000	50+4	6+1	7	2	3	1	1	
Sheffield Wednesday*	1.91	–	36+8	4	4+1	2	5	1	2	

ANTHROBUS Stephen (Steve) Anthony

Born: Lewisham, 10 November 1968

Height: 6'2" **Weight:** 12.13

Position/Skill Factor: Winger who is very strong physically and difficult to knock off the ball. Useful in the air, with a good left foot, he is extremely dangerous at the far post.

Career History: Came up through Millwall's junior ranks and made his FL debut for the club away to Plymouth Argyle wearing the number 11 shirt on 20 October 1987. After playing a further couple of games, he was replaced by Jimmy Carter, but the following season when the latter switched flanks, he got back into the side again. Created such a good impression that he was snapped up by

Wimbledon, initially replacing Michael Bennett, but has made only limited League appearances for the "Dons". As also seems to be the case with Michael Bennett, there is no role for orthodox wingers in Wimbledon's direct and robust playing style.

Clubs	Signing Date	Transfer Fee	APPEARANCES				GOALS			
			Lge	FL Cup	FA Cup	Others	Lge	FL Cup	FA Cup	Others
Millwall	8.86	–	19+2	3		1	4			
Wimbledon*	2.90	£150,000	23		2					

ARDLEY Neal Christopher

Born: Epsom, 1 September 1972

Height: 5'11" Weight: 11.9

Position/Skill Factor: A strong tackling midfielder who is not easily beaten. He is also a good passer of the ball and gets forward eagerly when the opportunity presents itself.

Career History: Joined Wimbledon while still at school when signing associated schoolboy forms in January 1988, before graduating to trainee status in July 1989. His FL debut, his one and only match in 1990-91, came in a 2-1 victory for the "Dons" at Aston Villa on 20 April 1991. Given further first team opportunities in 1991-92, both in midfield and at full-back, but has yet to establish a regular place.

Clubs	Signing Date	Transfer Fee	APPEARANCES				GOALS			
			Lge	FL Cup	FA Cup	Others	Lge	FL Cup	FA Cup	Others
Wimbledon*	7.91	–	8+1							

ATHERTON Peter

Born: Orrell, 6 April 1970

Height: 5'11" Weight: 12.3

International Honours: E Sch, E"U21"-1

Position/Skill Factor: Consistent centre-back who can defend tenaciously and will improve with experience in the higher grade.

Career History: He first came through Wigan Athletic's junior ranks as an associated schoolboy (October 1984), before signing as a trainee in July 1986. Prior to turning professional, he made his FL debut at Blackpool on 24 October 1987 in a 0-0 draw and played a further 14 League games during 1987-88. Since claiming a regular place the following season, apart from one appearance as a substitute, he has not missed a match and was twice voted Wigan's "Player of the Year". Obviously impressed Coventry City manager Terry Butcher, in two FA Cup ties between Wigan and the "Sky Blues" in January 1991 and moved to highfield Road in the first week of the 1991-92 season. Quickly established a place in the heart of the City defence and earned an England Under 21 cap in October 1991. A mainstay in one of the tightest of defences, a bright future in the Premier League and maybe at international level seems assured.

Clubs	Signing Date	Transfer Fee	APPEARANCES				GOALS			
			Lge	FL Cup	FA Cup	Others	Lge	FL Cup	FA Cup	Others
Wigan Athletic	2.88	–	145+4	8	7	12+1	1			
Coventry City*	8.91	£300,000	35							

ATKINS Mark Nigel

Born: Doncaster, 14 August 1968

Height: 6'1"

Weight: 12.0

International Honours: E Sch

Position/Skill Factor: A tireless midfield worker who seems to cover acres of ground in an effort to plug any gaps. Very competitive, he is also useful in the air.

Career History: Came through the Scunthorpe United junior sides to make his FL debut as a substitute at Wrexham on 27 April 1985, whilst still a schoolboy, three and a half months short of his 17th birthday and yet to sign professional forms. Had to wait until October 1986 for his next taste of action, but became a regular selection in a variety of positions, including both full-back slots, central defence and midfield. In 1987-88 he continued his role as a utility player until December, but lost his place and played little further part in the campaign. It was therefore a surprise when Second Division Blackburn Rovers signed him in the summer of 1988, presumably as an investment for the future. It was an even bigger surprise and a great feather in the cap of Rovers' manager, Don Mackay, that he started the 1988-89 at right-back and held his place throughout the campaign, not missing a single game and scoring six goals from open play into the bargain – a tremendous achievement for a young player in his first season with a new club. It was almost a promotion season as Blackburn reached the Play-Off Final only to be denied by a goal in the 27th minute of extra-time which sent Crystal Palace up at Rovers' expense. It was the same story the following term, with Rovers failing in the Play-Offs, as he enjoyed another excellent season with 41 FL appearances and seven goals. 1990-91 by contrast, was almost disastrous as Rovers just staved off relegation and he lost his place for a while. In 1991-91 he was switched from right-back to midfield early in the season to cover for injuries to other players. He remained in this role for most of the season at the end of which, Rovers achieved their ambition of Premier League football the hard way, through the Play-Offs, after appearing to be runaway Second Division Champions in February.

Clubs	Signing Date	Transfer Fee	APPEARANCES				GOALS			
			Lge	FL Cup	FA Cup	Others	Lge	FL Cup	FA Cup	Others
Scunthorpe United	7.86	–	45+5	3+1	5	6+1	2			
Blackburn Rovers*	6.88	£45,000	162+11	11	7	13	22	3		1

ATKINSON Dalian Robert

Born: Shrewsbury,
21 March 1968

Height: 5'11"

Weight: 11.7

International Honours:
E "B"

Position/Skill Factor: Physically strong, striker, who is not easy to dispossess, especially when in full flow. Extremely quick, he often commits defenders by running straight at them. Also, dangerous in the air.

Career History: Began with Ipswich Town, signing as an associated schoolboy in December 1982, before becoming an apprentice in July 1984. Made his FL debut as a substitute for Town away to Newcastle United on 15 March 1986 and impressed. After only occasional appearances for Ipswich, he finally established a first team place in February 1988, scoring eight goals in only 13 full appearances to the end of the season, including a magnificent hat-trick of "solo" goals against promotion bound Middlesbrough and the maturing Gary Pallister. Transferred to Sheffield Wednesday, he immediately became a favourite with the Hillsborough faithful. Only stayed for 12 months, before being sold to the Spanish side, Real Sociedad, with the "Owls" pocketing well over £1 million profit on the transaction. After one year in Spain, where he scored 12 League goals in 29 games in partnership with John Aldridge for the San Sebastian team, he was re-signed in the 1991 close season by his former manager at Hillsborough, Ron Atkinson, who by then had taken over at Aston Villa. Scored on his debut for Villa, by a remarkable coincidence at Hillsborough, in an opening day 3-2 victory over Wednesday. Sadly, it was to prove his only first team goal of the season, as a constant succession of niggling injuries prevented him from winning a regular place in the team. However, he played in the titanic Fifth Round FA Cup struggle with Liverpool at Anfield and looked the player most likely to make the breakthough (on either side), but it was the "Reds" who prevailed with a single goal. After such a dismal first season at Villa Park, through no fault of his own, his first season in the new Premier League can only be an improvement.

Clubs	Signing Date	Transfer Fee	APPEARANCES				GOALS			
			Lge	FL Cup	FA Cup	Others	Lge	FL Cup	FA Cup	Others
Ipswich Town	6.85	–	49+11	5+1		2+1	18	3		
Sheffield Wednesday	7.87	£450,000	38	3	2	2	10	3	1	1
Real Sociedad (Spain)	8.90	£1,700,000								
Aston Villa*	7.91	£1,600,000	11+3	1	1	1	1			

AUSTIN Dean Barry

Born: Hemel Hempstead, 26 April 1970

Height: 6'0" Weight: 12.4

Position/Skill Factor: Strong right-back who is very quick into the tackle. Also has the ability to pass the ball and join in.

Career History: Signed by Southend United from Vauxhall League club, St Albans City, after previous experience with Hendon in the same league, he slotted straight into the club's Third Division promotion winning side, making his FL debut as a right-back at Burnley on 10 April, 1990 and holding his place till the end of the season. Made 44 FL appearances in 1990-91 as the "Shrimpers" achieved promotion to Division Two for the first time in their history, finishing second in the Third Division, after heading the table for most of the season. Played 45 FL games in Southend's debut season in Division Two, during which they reached second place in January, only to "tail-off" disappointingly to finish in mid-table. For much of the season, he was the subject of transfer speculation and soon afterwards, was signed by Tottenham Hotspur. The fee of £375,000, plus an additional £150,000 for club appearances and an international cap, fixed by the Transfer Tribunal, seemed a reasonable one in the circumstances, but the Southend chairman, in a fit of pique, stated that no more Southend players would be sold to "Spurs" in future.

Clubs	Signing Date	Transfer Fee	APPEARANCES				GOALS			
			Lge	FL Cup	FA Cup	Others	Lge	FL Cup	FA Cup	Others
Southend United	3.90	£12,000	96	4	2	7	2			
Tottenham Hotspur*	5.92	£375,000								

BACON John Patrick Gerrard

Born: Dublin, 23 March 1973

Height: 5'11" Weight: 12.5

International Honours: IR "U21"-1

Position/Skill Factor: Talented striker with lovely skills who is also good in the air.

Career History: He first went to Highbury as a trainee in September 1989 and had progressed to the professional ranks during the 1990 close season. Spent the tail end of 1991-92 on loan to Shamrock Rovers in the League of Ireland and has yet to play League football.

Clubs	Signing Date	Transfer Fee	APPEARANCES				GOALS			
			Lge	FL Cup	FA Cup	Others	Lge	FL Cup	FA Cup	Others
Arsenal*	7.90	–								
Shamrock Rovers	1.92	Loan								

BAILEY Dennis Lincoln

Born: Lambeth,
13 November 1965

Height: 5'10"

Weight: 11.6

Position/Skill Factor: Striker, or winger, who is quick off the mark with lovely skills to match. Is extremely dangerous, either with his back to goal, or when he runs at the opposing defence.

Career History: Joined Fulham as a non-contract player from Barking in 1986, before moving on to Farnborough Town of the then Vauxhall Opel League, without making a FL appearance. However, Crystal Palace signed him and he made his FL debut at Hull City on 19 December 1987. After a few sporadic appearances at Selhurst Park, he got an opportunity to show what he could do when going on loan to Bristol Rovers, then managed by Gerry Francis. During the 1989 close season he was transferred to Birmingham City and after topping their goalscoring charts in his first season with 18 League goals, he dried up the following season and was allowed to return to Bristol Rovers on loan. It was assumed that Gerry Francis would sign him permanently for the "Pirates". In fact, Francis did sign him, but for his new club, Queens Park Rangers, a remarkable change in his fortunes. Although presumably signed as cover for the forward positions at Loftus Road, he started the season in the first team and was a fairly regular selection through the first half of 1991-92. On New Years Day he achieved a personal "high water mark" in his career with a hat-trick at Old Trafford against the League leaders and Championship favourites, Manchester United. Rangers' 4-1 victory inflicted United's first home defeat and was one of the "turn-ups" of the season. Perhaps the attendant publicity affected him as one month later he lost his place to Les Ferdinand and played no part in the remainder of the campaign.

Clubs	Signing Date	Transfer Fee	APPEARANCES				GOALS			
			Lge	FL Cup	FA Cup	Others	Lge	FL Cup	FA Cup	Others
Crystal Palace	12.87	£10,000	0+5				1			
Bristol Rovers	2.89	Loan	17			1+1	9			1
Birmingham City	8.89	£80,000	65+10	6	6	3+3	23	2		
Bristol Rovers	3.91	Loan	6				1			
Q.P.R.*	6.91	£175,000	19+5	3	1	1	9	2		

BANGER Nicholas (Nicky) Lee

Born: Southampton, 25 February 1971

Height: 5'8" Weight: 10.6

Position/Skill Factor: Winger who can play up front, he twists and turns well on the edge of the box. Always causing defenders problems with quick darting runs.

Career History: Locally born and bred, he was an associated schoolboy (September 1985) and then a trainee (July 1987) before turning pro for Southampton and making his FL debut at Norwich City on 8 December 1990. Although yet to score in a League match, the first time he played for "Saints" was in the second round of the League Cup on 9 October 1990 and he marked that occasion with a hat-trick in the 3-0 home defeat of Rochdale. Made a few substitute appearances in 1991-92, but with Alan Shearer and Iain Dowie holding down the strikers' role, has yet to make a first team breakthrough.

Clubs	Signing Date	Transfer Fee	APPEARANCES				GOALS			
			Lge	FL Cup	FA Cup	Others	Lge	FL Cup	FA Cup	Others
Southampton*	4.89	–	0+10	1+1		1		3		

BARDSLEY David John

Born: Manchester,
11 September 1964

Height: 5'10"

Weight: 10.0

International Honours:
E Yth

Position/Skill Factor: Attacking right-back, with a wonderful right-foot, who is brilliant at striking long balls behind the opposing full-backs. Very effective when he gets forward and is a intelligent crosser of the ball.

Career History: Began his career at Blackpool where he was an associated schoolboy (May 1981) and an apprentice (July 1981). He made his FL debut at Bury on 18 May 1982, signing professional forms four months later. Immediately becoming a regular, it wasn't long before other clubs were casting envious eyes in his direction and he eventually moved to Watford. In his first season at Vicarage Road, he helped the club to their first ever Wembley appearance where they were beaten 2-0 by Everton in the 1984 FA Cup Final. Three years later, Oxford United, looking for a replacement for David Langan, were surprised to find him available and signed him for a club record fee. His time there proved disappointing as the club were relegated to the Second Division, although they had earlier reached the Semi-Finals of the League Cup. After beginning the 1989-90 season in United's colours, he joined Queens Park

Rangers for a substantial fee, plus striker Mark Stein and after making his debut in a right sided midfield role, he reverted to his favoured defensive position later in the season. A consistent defender, he has only missed three League games in three seasons at Loftus Road. Very few forwards will get the better of him in the new Premier League.

Clubs	Signing Date	Transfer Fee	APPEARANCES				GOALS			
			Lge	FL Cup	FA Cup	Others	Lge	FL Cup	FA Cup	Others
Blackpool	9.82	–	45	2	2			1		
Watford	11.83	£150,000	97+3	6	13+1	1	7	1	1	
Oxford United	9.87	£265,000	74	12	5	3	7			
Q.P.R*	9.89	£500,000	110	8	10	3	1	1		1

BARKER Simon

Born: Farnworth,
4 November 1964

Height: 5'9"

Weight: 11.0

International Honours:
E "U21"-4

Position/Skill Factor: An attacking midfield player with a good football brain. Directs passes, short and long, very early and is quite capable of opening up the tightest of defences.

Career History: Spent six years as a pro with Blackburn Rovers, having been at the club as an associated schoolboy (July 1980) and an apprentice (July 1981). Made his FL debut away to Swansea City on 29 October 1983 and immediately established himself as a regular in the side. He went from strength to strength and was soon regarded as one of the best midfield players in the Second Division. It came as no surprise when he finally left Rovers, when they failed to win promotion to Division One in 1988, following their defeat by Chelsea in the end of season Play-Offs. Although unable to establish himself at Queens Park Rangers in his first season, after the arrival of Ray Wilkins he settled down to play some good football and was a major influence in Q.P.R.'s bid to stave off relegation in 1990-91. A consistent performer in 1991-92, partnering Ian Holloway and Ray Wilkins in midfield, he did not miss a game until February 1992, when he lost his place ostensibly to Andrew Impey, although in fact Ian Holloway was switched from the right-wing to fill the midfield slot. Afterwards he was mainly used as substitute.

Clubs	Signing Date	Transfer Fee	APPEARANCES				GOALS			
			Lge	FL Cup	FA Cup	Others	Lge	FL Cup	FA Cup	Others
Blackburn Rovers	11.82	–	180+2	11	12	8	35	4		2
Q.P.R.*	7.88	£400,000	107+15	13+2	13+1	7	11	3	2	

BARLOW Andrew (Andy) John

Born: Oldham,
24 November 1965

Height: 5'9"

Weight: 11.1

Position/Skill Factor: Left-back with two good feet and a lovely striker of the ball. Alway prepared to support the attack, he will go all the way at times. Often spells danger with his long throws.

Career History: A one club man, he signed as an associated schoolboy for Oldham Athletic in November 1982, while at Hulme Grammar School and made his FL debut, one month after turning pro, at home to Birmingham City on 25 August 1984. In his first five seasons, he struggled to hold down a regular first team place, alternating between midfield and the full-back slots. Since 1989-90, however, he has been automatic first choice at left-back and although Oldham failed to gain promotion that season they achieved miracles in the two cup competitions, reaching the Semi-Final of the FA Cup, before going out after a replay to Manchester United and then losing 1-0 in the League Cup Final to Nottingham Forest. It paved the way to the "Lactics" joining the elite and in 1990-91 he was ever present, winning a Second Division Championship medal as the club finally realised its ambition of First Division football. Absent through injury at the start of 1991-92, he returned to the team in October, holding his place till the end of the season, exept for short intermission in the New Year when the team was re-organised, following a 6-3 home thrashing by Manchester United.

Clubs	Signing Date	Transfer Fee	APPEARANCES				GOALS			
			Lge	FL Cup	FA Cup	Others	Lge	FL Cup	FA Cup	Others
Oldham Athletic*	7.84	–	234+13	20	17	6	5			

BARLOW Stuart

Born: Liverpool, 16 July 1968

Height: 5'10" Weight: 11.0

Position/Skill Factor: A hard working young striker who is still making his way in the game. Has good pace and runs well off the ball.

Career History: Signed from Sherwood Park of the Liverpool Sunday League in the Summer of 1990, he made the gigantic leap from junior club soccer to the First

Division inside 12 months when making his FL debut for Everton at home to Wimbledon on 10 April 1991. Joined Rotherham on loan in 1991-92, but his one League appearance as substitute for the "Millers" was cancelled out when Aldershot resigned from the Football League. Returned to Goodison Park and enjoyed a short run in the first team at the end of the season in place of Mo Johnston.

Clubs	Signing Date	Transfer Fee	APPEARANCES				GOALS			
			Lge	FL Cup	FA Cup	Others	Lge	FL Cup	FA Cup	Others
Everton*	6.90	–	3+6							
Rotherham United	1.92	Loan				0+1				

BARMBY Nicholas (Nicky) Jonathan

Born: Hull, 11 February 1974

Height: 5'6" Weight: 11.3

International Honours: E Sch, E Yth

Position/Skill Factor: Very skilful striker who holds the ball up well and is adept at bringing his supporting players into the game.

Career History: Joined Tottenham Hotspur as an associated schoolboy in March 1990, before accepting trainee status on leaving school in August 1990. Turned professional early in 1991, having spent some time at the Lilleshall Centre of Excellence. Made no first team appearances during 1991-92.

Clubs	Signing Date	Transfer Fee	APPEARANCES				GOALS			
			Lge	FL Cup	FA Cup	Others	Lge	FL Cup	FA Cup	Others
Tottenham Hotspur*	2.91	–								

BARNARD Darren Sean

Born: Rintel, Germany, 30 November 1971

Height: 5'10" Weight: 11.0

International Honours: E Sch

Position/Skill Factor: Predominately a winger, he has an excellent left foot and is a lovely crosser of the ball. Also has the ability and skill to go past defenders in order to create goalscoring chances.

Career History: Son of an armed forces serviceman, hence his foreign birthplace. Signed by Chelsea from Wokingham Town of the Vauxhall (now Diadora) League in the 1990 close season. His talent was recognised early by the FA, who selected him for the England Schoolboys under 18 side in 1989-90. After waiting patiently for a first team chance, he made his FL debut at Stamford Bridge, when he came on as a substitute against West Ham United on 4 April 1992. Selected for the next three games, he played his first full game at Aston Villa on 20 April.

Clubs	Signing Date	Transfer Fee	APPEARANCES				GOALS			
			Lge	FL Cup	FA Cup	Others	Lge	FL Cup	FA Cup	Others
Chelsea*	7.90	£50,000	1+3							

BARNES Andrew (Andy) John

Born: Croydon, 31 March 1967

Height: 5'10" Weight: 11.0

Position/Skill Factor: Goalscoring forward, who although new to professional football, is adaptable and displays great enthusiasm.

Career History: A remarkable "rags to riches" story. In September 1990, at the age of 23, he was playing football at a very minor level for Chipstead, a Croydon area club, of the Dan Air League. One year later he found himself signing for a First Division club for a large fee. He first came to prominence after Sutton United of the Vauxhall Conference League signed him from Chipstead in November 1990. Although Sutton were subsequently relegated to the Diadora League at the end of the season, he had been a great success with 22 goals in 40 appearances. After scoring eight goals in seven games for Sutton at the start of 1991-92, Crystal Palace pounced, paying £70,000 with more to follow if he made the grade. Tragically, he suffered a serious knee injury in his first game for Palace reserve team, thus delaying his introduction to the First Division. However, he regained fitness by the end of the season and made his FL debut as a substitute in the last match away to Queens Park Rangers on 2 May 1992. Palace manager Steve Coppell has a knack of picking up future international players from non-league football, witness Andy Gray and Ian Wright, so Barnes' progress is worth watching in 1992-93.

Clubs	Signing Date	Transfer Fee	APPEARANCES				GOALS			
			Lge	FL Cup	FA Cup	Others	Lge	FL Cup	FA Cup	Others
Crystal Palace*	9.91	£70,000	0+1							

BARNES David

Born: Paddington, 16 November 1961

Height: 5'10"

Weight: 11.4

International Honours: E Yth

Position/Skill Factor: A very experienced left-back who knows just when to tackle, he is a more than capable defender. Has a good left foot and makes excellent use of the ball, with either short or long passes. A player with plenty of nice touches.

Career History: Served as an apprentice with Coventry City (August 1978), before turning pro and making his FL debut at Bolton Wanderers on 15 April 1980. Only played the odd match at Highfield Road and signed for Ipswich Town on a free, but again infrequent appearances were the order of the day. On moving to Wolverhampton Wanderers, he managed to hold down a regular place, but the team were struggling and during his three years at Molineux, they dropped from the Second to the Fourth Division. Following that, he had a spell with Aldershot, but after two years at the foot of Division Four, Dave Bassett surprisingly took him to Sheffield United where he shared the left-back spot with Wilf Rostron. In his first season, the club were promoted from the Second Division as runners-up and he certainly didn't look out of place when playing 28 First Division matches in 1990-91. Displaced by the signing of Tom Cowan in the first half of 1991-92, he won his place back in January 1992 and held it till the end of the season, assisting the "Blades' " remarkable rise from the foot of the table to a final placing of ninth.

Clubs	Signing Date	Transfer Fee	APPEARANCES				GOALS			
			Lge	FL Cup	FA Cup	Others	Lge	FL Cup	FA Cup	Others
Coventry City	5.79	–	9		4					
Ipswich Town	5.82	–	16+1							
Wolverhampton W.	10.84	£35,000	86+2	7	6	6	4			
Aldershot	8.87	£25,000	68+1	2	2+2	4	1			
Sheffield United*	7.87	£50,000	67	4	11	4	1			

BARNES John

Born: Jamaica, West Indies, 7 November 1963

Height: 5'11" Weight: 11.10

International Honours: E"U21"-2, FL Rep, E-67

Position/Skill Factor: Can play in any position up front, but most frequently appears on the left flank. He has wonderful natural skill, with the ball seemingly tied to his foot at times. Very quick from a standing start, where his pace and strength takes him past defenders as if they didn't exist.

Career History: Came out of local junior football with Sudbury Court to turn professional at Watford and made an immediate impact. he made his FL debut for the "Hornets" at home on 5 September 1981 against Oldham Athletic and has rarely looked back. Was soon collecting international honours, making his full England debut against Northern Ireland in Belfast in 1983 when coming on as a substitute in a 0-0 draw, but the lasting international memory of him will surely include the marvellous solo goal he scored in England's 2-0 victory over Brazil in Rio de Janeiro, June 1984, proving that he could live with the best. Was an instant success at Anfield, scoring 15 times in 38 FL matches in his first season, 1987-88, helping the club to the League Championship in the process. Another League Championship medal came his way at the end of the 1989-90 season, with the club looking for the "Double" until losing 4-3 to Crystal Palace in the semi-final of the FA Cup. He was voted "Footballer of the Year" by the FWA in both 1988 and 1990 and the

PFA's "Player of the Year" in 1988. His consistently brilliant performances for Liverpool since 1987, mark him out as the outstanding forward of his generation. Sadly it seems that at international level he will forever remain an enigma, the majority of his performances being merely

competent rather than inspired. Often alleged to have a desire to play in the warmer climes of Italian Football, he was persuaded to sign a one year contract to remain with Liverpool for 1991-92. It proved a highly expensive decision for the club, as due to a succession of injuries, starting from the second game of the season, he played only 12 League games and in those he was clearly below par and not 100 per cent fit. In fairness to Barnes, his contributions in the FA Cup rescued Liverpool's season from total disaster. On his first comeback in January 1992, he scored a hat-trick at Crewe Alexandra in the Third Round. On his second comeback, he supplied the perfectly weighted through ball to set up Michael Thomas for the only goal of the Fifth Round clash with Aston Villa.

John Barnes

On his third comeback in the first Semi-Final game against Portsmouth, his free kick against the post in the closing minutes of extra time created the opportunity for Ronnie Whelan to save the day for the "Reds". Sadly, another thigh injury sustained in the last game of the season, cost him a place in Liverpool's Cup Final team and ultimately excluded him from the England squad for the 1992 European Championship in Sweden.

Clubs	Signing Date	Transfer Fee	APPEARANCES				GOALS			
			Lge	FL Cup	FA Cup	Others	Lge	FL Cup	FA Cup	Others
Watford	7.81	–	232+1	21	31	7	65	7	11	
Liverpool*	6.87	£900,000	152	10	32	5	62	2	14	2

BARRETT Earl Delisser

Born: Rochdale, 28 April 1967

Height: 5'10" Weight: 11.2

International Honours: E "U21"-4, FL Rep, E"B", E-1

Position/Skill Factor: An extremely athletic central defender, who can also play at full-back. Has tremendous pace and can change up a gear. Gets forward well, he is a difficult defender to get the better of.

Career History: Began as an apprentice with Manchester City, signing in April 1984, but made his FL debut whilst on loan with Chester City at Mansfield Town on 4 March 1986, before his City debut at home against Luton Town on 3 May 1986. Did not make progress at Maine Road and was transferred to Oldham Athletic. Made a good start at Boundary Park until sidelined through injury for a spell during his first season, but was soon back on regular

duty at left-back. In 1989-90 he exchanged his number three shirt for that of centre-back and was ever present as the club were losing League Cup Finalists and progressed to the Semi-Final of the FA Cup. The following season again saw him at the heart of "Lactics' " defence and for the second successive term he played in every match and hardly put a foot wrong as the club won the Second Division title. Rewarded for his fine displays at club level, he was selected for the international tour of Australasia in the summer of 1991 and made his England debut against New Zealand. In his first season in the First Division, he struggled a little in the heart of the leakiest defence at that level, but held his place, whilst his defensive partners were chopped and changed. it was a great disappointment to "Lactics' " fans when he was transferred to Aston Villa in February 1992, but it was for a fee that a small club such as Oldham could hardly refuse. At Villa Park he slotted in at right-back, but is probably regarded as the long term replacement for Paul McGrath in the middle of the defence.

Clubs	Signing Date	Transfer Fee	APPEARANCES				GOALS			
			Lge	FL Cup	FA Cup	Others	Lge	FL Cup	FA Cup	Others
Manchester City	4.85	–	2+1	1						
Chester City	3.86	Loan	12							
Oldham Athletic	11.87	£35,000	181+2	20	14	4	7	1	1	
Aston Villa*	2.92	£1,700,000	13							

BARTON Warren Dean

Born: Stoke Newington, 19 March 1969

Height: 6'0" Weight: 11.0

Position/Skill Factor: Excellent attacking full-back who is very much suited to the sweeper system, but can play equally well in midfield. Will attack at every opportunity and is a lovely crosser of the ball.

Career History: Signed for Maidstone United from Vauxhall League side, Leytonstone & Ilford, prior to the club embarking on their first Football League campaign. He made his FL League debut at Peterborough United on 19 August 1989 and after a difficult introduction to League football, Warren, who had started his career as a Leyton Orient trainee (August 1986), won a permanent place at right-back and helped the "Stones" to reach a Play-Off position. Wimbledon had been suitably impressed with his displays and he was signed for a £300,000 fee, of which £30,000 went to Leytonstone & Ilford. His first game for the "Dons" saw him substituted against Arsenal at Highbury, but that was only a temporary setback as he firmly established himself in midfield, missing only one League match in 1990-91. Enjoyed another excellent season in 1991-92, playing in every single competitive game for Wimbledon, but in a more defensive role than in his initial season in the First Division.

Clubs	Signing Date	Transfer Fee	APPEARANCES				GOALS			
			Lge	FL Cup	FA Cup	Others	Lge	FL Cup	FA Cup	Others
Maidstone United	7.87	£10,000	41+1	0+2	3	7		1		
Wimbledon*	6.90	£300,000	79	4	5	2	4			

BART-WILLIAMS Christopher (Chris) Gerald

Born: Sierra Leone, 16 June 1974

Height: 5'10" Weight: 11.0

International Honours: E Yth

Position/Skill Factor: Midfield player with plenty of stamina, he keeps his passing simple and is not afraid to get his foot in. Progressing all the time.

Career History: Began with Leyton-Orient as an associated schoolboy in October 1988 and progressed to trainee status in July 1990. A teenage footballing prodigy, he made his FL debut at the age of 16 years and 4 months, as Orient's youngest ever debutant as a substitute at Grimsby Town on 23 October 1990 and later scored for the "O's" after only ten minutes of his full FL debut at home to Tranmere Rovers on 2 February. Thereafter he was established in midfield for the remainder of the season, still at the tender age of 16, as First Division scouts became alerted to his talent. An automatic first choice for Orient in 1991-92, he was signed up by Sheffield Wednesday manager Trevor Francis in November 1991, a few weeks after the two teams had met twice in a League Cup tie. Francis announced cautiously that he was "one for the future" and that he didn't intend pitching him into First Division action immediately. One week later, Bart-Williams was playing with the composure of a veteran on his Wednesday debut against League Champions, Arsenal! He held his place until January before being rested and making occasional appearances thereafter. It is always dangerous to make extravagant predictions on behalf of young players, but provided he maintains his present progress and does not allow flattery to go to his head, he is surely an international player of the future.

Clubs	Signing Date	Transfer Fee	APPEARANCES				GOALS			
			Lge	FL Cup	FA Cup	Others	Lge	FL Cup	FA Cup	Others
Leyton Orient	7.91	–	34+2	4		2	2			
Sheffield Wednesday*	11.91	£275,000	12+3		1	0+1			1	

BATTY David

Born: Leeds, 12 December 1968

Height: 5'5" Weight: 10.0

International Honours: E "U21"-7, E"B", E-10

Position/Skill Factor: Great midfield competitor and a very strong tackler and ball winner in the Norman Hunter mould, who is also a constructive passer of the ball. Causes many opposing defences problems, especially in their penalty area, with his long throws.

Career History: Has been at Leeds since signing as an associated schoolboy in November 1983. Becoming an apprentice footballer in August 1985, he went on to make his FL debut against Swindon Town at Elland Road on 21 November 1987. Despite turning out regularly for the club and playing well over 100 FL games, he had only scored

two League goals in five seasons coincidentally both against Manchester City. Was a driving force, collecting a Second Division Championship medal while playing 39 times, in Leeds' surge back to the First Division in 1989-90. Towards the end of his first season of First Division football, his fine displays brought him a place in the England squad and he made his debut against the USSR at Wembley on 21 May 1991, coming on as a substitute.

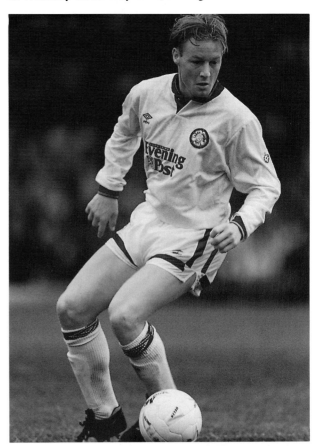

Despite his paucity of goals, he is hugely popular with the Elland Road faithful for his non-stop energy and aggression and his work-rate and ball winning tenacity, was a major factor in Leeds United's first League Championship triumph since 1974. After playing in England's first two internationals of 1991-92, he was "rested", while England manager Graham Taylor examined the credentials of Geoff Thomas and Carlton Palmer. His place seemed in doubt, but he was included in the squad of 20 for the European Championship Finals in Sweden and made two appearances, one of them, surprisingly in the the right-back position as England gave way to the host country, Sweden.

Clubs	Signing Date	Transfer Fee	APPEARANCES				GOALS			
			Lge	FL Cup	FA Cup	Others	Lge	FL Cup	FA Cup	Others
Leeds United*	7.87	–	163+9	15	9	12	3			

BEADLE Peter Clifford

Born: Lambeth, 13 May 1972

Height: 6'0" Weight: 11.12

Position/Skill Factor: Big striker who leads the line well and is useful in the air.

Career History: Made his FL debut for Gillingham as a 16-year-old junior at home to Cardiff City on 11 March 1989, when he came on as substitute. Initially, he joined the club as an associated schoolboy in December 1986, later signing on as a trainee in July 1988. Made ten more appearances at the start and end of the 1989-90 season, before turning professional. Played both in midfield and up front during 1990-91, demonstrating his goal scoring potential with seven FL goals in 12 full appearances, plus ten as substitute. Started 1991-92 as a forward, but found goals hard to come by and finished the season in midfield. Increasingly the subject of transfer speculation, he was signed by Tottenham Hotspur at the end of the season.

Clubs	Signing Date	Transfer Fee	APPEARANCES				GOALS			
			Lge	FL Cup	FA Cup	Others	Lge	FL Cup	FA Cup	Others
Gillingham	5.90	–	42+25	2+4	1+1	1	14	4		
Tottenham Hotspur*	5.92	£300,000								

BEAGRIE Peter Sydney

Born: Middlesbrough, 29 November 1965

Height: 5'8" Weight: 9.10

International Honours: E "U21"-2, E"B"

Position/Skill Factor: Clever left sided wingman who deceives opponents with a various array of trickery. Often feinting to cross and then going on with the ball, checking from one foot to the other, he has great balance.

Career History: Was an associated schoolboy with Hartlepool United, signing forms in January 1980, before going to Ayresome Park. Made his FL debut for Middlesbrough at Oldham Athletic on 2 October 1984. Signed for Sheffield United prior to the start of the 1986-87 season, establishing himself as joint leading goalscorer with nine to his credit that term and won his first and only international honours at under 21 level. Transferred to Stoke City following the "Blades' " relegation to the Third Division. His displays for the "Potters" attracted the attention of several First Division clubs, before Everton moved in for him in an effort to revive their declining fortunes. Not performing consistently at the highest level with the "Toffees" during his first two years at Goodison, he was in and out of the side. Indeed, for the first two months of 1991-92, was ignored for selection behind Pat Nevin, Mark Ward and Robert Warzycha for the wing slots. When loaned to Sunderland in September, a permanent transfer out of Goodison seemed imminent. However, he was recalled by manager Howard Kendall and reinstated in the first team. A brilliant performance in his comeback game against Wolverhampton Wanderers in the League Cup in October, when scoring two goals and creating another, resulted in his remaining in the first team squad for the remainder of the season, although frequently relegated to substitute.

Clubs	Signing Date	Transfer Fee	APPEARANCES				GOALS			
			Lge	FL Cup	FA Cup	Others	Lge	FL Cup	FA Cup	Others
Middlesbrough	9.83	–	24+8	1		1+1	2			
Sheffield Wednesday	8.86	£35,000	81+3	5	5	4	11			
Stoke City	6.88	£210,000	54	4	3		7		1	
Everton*	11.89	£750,000	48+15	1+1	5+2	5+1	5	2		1
Sunderland	9.91	Loan	5			1				

BEARDSLEY Peter Andrew

Born: Newcastle, 18 January 1961

Height: 5'8" Weight: 11.7

International Honours: E "B", E-49

Position/Skill Factor: Quick thinking, skilful striker, who is a veritable box of tricks. Very good on the ball, he always looks dangerous when he runs at defenders, or when coming from deep positions.

Career History: Carlisle United picked him up as an 18-year-old, when he was playing for a Wallsend Boys Club in his native Tyneside. Made his FL debut at home to Blackburn Rovers on 21 August 1979 and spent three years at Brunton Park before trying his luck in North America with Vancouver Whitecaps. Beardsley's success in the States, alerted Manchester United and they brought him back to Britain, but within six months he was back in Vancouver, without playing a single game for the first team. A year later, Arthur Cox, then manager of Newcastle United, signed him as a striking partner for Kevin Keegan and in his first season, 1983-84, the club were promoted to the First Division in third place when he scored 20 League goals to complement Keegan's 27. Following Keegan's retirement, he was leading scorer in the next two First Division campaigns and although the

Peter Beardsley

goals dried up in 1986-87 it came as a great shock to the Geordie faithful when he was allowed to leave for Liverpool. While at Newcastle, he had won 18 full England caps after making his debut against Egypt in Cairo on 29 January 1986, when coming on as a substitute. A late and surprise inclusion for England's World Cup squad for the Finals in Mexico in 1986, his partnership with Gary Lineker revived a flagging campaign and helped establish the latter as one of the world's great strikers with six goals in the tournament. He was subsequently a regular international performer until 1990, but a lack of goals (only eight in 49 games for England) ended his England career somewhat prematurely. Along with John Barnes he inspired another golden era for the "Reds", winning a League Championship medal in his first season at Anfield, which was followed by an FA Cup Winners medal in 1989 and another League title triumph in 1989-90. As much a creator, as scorer, he was never prolific for Liverpool until 1990-91, when he netted 11 goals in his first 11 games, including a hat-trick against deadly rivals, Manchester United. Surprisingly, it was the beginning of the end of his Anfield career. Losing his place through injury, he was then ignored by manager Kenny Daglish, when fit again. Although restored to first team duty after Daglish's amazing departure, he seemed to have lost his zest and failed to recapture his early season form as Liverpool faded out of the championship race. It was still a major shock when new manager Graham Souness discarded him during the summer of 1991 to make way for Dean Saunders and he moved to local rivals, Everton. It was also a questionable decision, as Beardsley was undoubtedly the star of a generally disappointing and lack lustre campaign by the "Toffees", top scoring with 15 League goals, plus four in cup competitions. His form prompted some to suggest a recall to the England team, but no doubt his age counted against him. He remains one of the few forwards with real star quality.

Clubs	Signing Date	Transfer Fee	APPEARANCES				GOALS			
			Lge	FL Cup	FA Cup	Others	Lge	FL Cup	FA Cup	Others
Carlisle United	8.79	–	93+11	6+1	15		22		7	
Vancouver (NASL)	4.81	£275,000								
Manchester United	9.82	£300,000		1						
Vancouver (NASL)	3.83									
Newcastle United	9.83	£150,000	146+1	10	6	1	61			
Liverpool	7.87	£1,900,000	120+11	13+1	22+3	5	46	1	11	1
Everton*	8.91	£1,000,000	42	4	2	2	15	3	1	1

BEARDSMORE Russell Peter

Born: Wigan, 28 September 1968

Height: 5'6" Weight: 9.0

International Honours: E "U21"-5

Position/Skill Factor: Midfield player who sees passes early and is a lovely passer of the ball, both short and long. Produces excellent crosses when he can get wide.

Career History: Joined Manchester United first as an associated schoolboy (April 1984) and then as an apprentice (June 1985), before being given his FL debut two years after turning professional, at home to West Ham United on 24 September 1988, coming on as a substitute. Can play both as a full-back and as a right sided midfielder. Enjoyed an outstanding match against Liverpool on 1 January 1989, creating one goal and scoring another

as United fought back from one down with three in the last 25 minutes to win 3-1 with an under full strength team. Appeared to be the natural successor to Gordon Strachan when the latter moved on to Leeds United, but following the big money signings of Paul Ince and Mike Phelan during the 1989 close season, he has found himself on the sidelines, more frequently selected as a substitute than as first choice. In 1991-92, he was not even considered for first team duty during United's ultimately unsuccessful Championship bid and a short loan period with Blackburn Rovers failed to revive his flagging fortunes. Needs a new start to reactivate what seemed to be a promising career only three years ago.

Clubs	Signing Date	Transfer Fee	APPEARANCES				GOALS			
			Lge	FL Cup	FA Cup	Others	Lge	FL Cup	FA Cup	Others
Manchester United*	9.86	–	30+26	3+1	4+4	2+3	4			
Blackburn Rovers	12.91	Loan	1+1							

BEASANT David (Dave) John

Born: Willesden, 20 March 1959

Height: 6'3" Weight: 13.0

International Honours: E "B", E-2

Position/Skill Factor: Big, strong, brave goalkeeper, who never stops talking to his defenders. One of the first goalies to run the ball out of his own penalty area in an effort to increase his distance. Also, sets up attacks with good throws.

Career History: Discovered by Wimbledon while playing for non-League Edgware Town, he made his FL debut at home to Blackpool on 12 January 1979. Became a regular for the "Dons", not missing a League match from the beginning of 1981-82, until he left for Newcastle United, a total of 304 consecutive FL matches. During that time he won both Division Four and Division Two Championship medals as the club moved up to Division One. His last game for the club was the sensational 1988 FA Cup Final against Liverpool, which saw him save John Aldridge's penalty. The first spot kick saved in Cup Final history at Wembley as Wimbledon held on to take the trophy back to south London. It was not a great surprise when he was sold at the end of that season to Newcastle United, but it was perhaps not a good move for either the player or his new club. The "Magpies" struggled at the foot of the First Division during his short stay and he had little opportunity to further his reputation or become accepted by their fans. No doubt unsettled by his move from his native London, he was "rescued" by Chelsea after only six months on Tyneside for a slightly reduced fee and assisted them to the Second Division Championship. In the summer of 1990, his consistent displays were finally recognised at international level when coming on as a substitute for England against Italy on 7 July 1990, but after appearing in the first 10 games for Chelsea in 1990-91, his incredible run of 394 consecutive FL games came to a halt when he was ruled out with an injured hand. In 1991-92 he was no longer automatic first choice 'keeper for the "Blues", swapping first team duties with Kevin Hitchcock throughout the season and it will be interesting to see who starts 1992-93 as the number one 'keeper.

Clubs	Signing Date	Transfer Fee	APPEARANCES				GOALS			
			Lge	FL Cup	FA Cup	Others	Lge	FL Cup	FA Cup	Others
Wimbledon	8.79	£1,000	340	21	27	3				
Newcastle United	6.88	£800,000	20	2	2	1				
Chelsea*	1.89	£725,000	116	11	5	8				

a minor role in the "Canaries'" FA Cup run. Recalled to the first team in March, he scored a hat-trick against Crystal Palace, but was surprisingly overlooked for the Semi-Final against Sunderland when Norwich scarcely managed a "shot in anger" against the Second Division team in a disappointing team performance. He has two younger brothers; Jason, who also started with Manchester City, but is now with Birmingham City, and Andy who has only played outside the Football League with a number of East Midlands clubs, most recently Leicester United.

Clubs	Signing Date	Transfer Fee	APPEARANCES				GOALS			
			Lge	FL Cup	FA Cup	Others	Lge	FL Cup	FA Cup	Others
Manchester City	8.84	–	7+4	0+1						
Bury	10.85	Loan	12				5			
Port Vale	3.87	£15,000	169+9	12	14	9+1	71	3	4	3
Norwich City*	7.91	£925,000	25+5	3+2	2+1	1	7	3		1

BECKFORD Darren Richard

Born: Manchester,
12 May 1967

Height: 6'1"

Weight: 11.1

International Honours:
E Sch, E Yth

Position/Skill Factor: Free scoring striker, who will be suited to the Premier Division. Has good skills for a big lad and is very good in the air.

Career History: Started his career with Manchester City as an associated schoolboy (November 1981) and graduated as an apprentice (April 1984), before making his FL debut at Middlesbrough on 20 October 1984. After nearly seven years at Maine Road and limited opportunities, he was transferred to Port Vale. Earlier, he had given a glimpse of what he was capable of when on loan at Third Division Bury. Became an automatic choice for Vale and topped the club's goalscoring lists every season from 1987-88. His 20 League goals were also an important factor when the club climbed out of Division Three in 1988-89 and included a cracking hat-trick in a 4-1 win at Notts County. Transferred to First Division Norwich City for a massive club record fee in the summer of 1991, considered excessive by some. He struggled to justify the fee and was in and out of the side all season, scoring only seven FL goals, plus four more in cup competitions and played only

BEESLEY Paul

Born: Liverpool,
21 July 1965

Height: 6'1"

Weight: 11.5

Position/Skill Factor: Footballing central defender who passes the ball, rather than clearing his lines. Intercepts through balls well and is always looking to get his own attack moving.

Career History: Was playing for Marine, in the Northern Premier League, before signing pro with near neighbours, Wigan Athletic. Made his FL debut at Reading on 3 October 1984, but only appeared once more that term. Gradually established himself at the heart of the Wigan defence, before being transferred to Leyton Orient, who paid a club record fee to get their man. Although he only played 32 League matches in his first season 1989-90, the Orient players voted him their "Player of the Year". Moved to Sheffield United during the 1990 close season and proved a shrewd investment as he established a regular place in their defence. Struggled at the start of 1991-92 as the "Blades" made their customary disastrous start, but then formed a highly effective defensive partnership with Brian Gayle, newly signed from Ipswich, which stabilised the back four and assisted United to a remarkable recovery, culminating in a final placing of tenth in the First Division. Absent for only two matches of the FL programme, he has missed only three League matches since signing for the "Blades".

Clubs	Signing Date	Transfer Fee	APPEARANCES				GOALS			
			Lge	FL Cup	FA Cup	Others	Lge	FL Cup	FA Cup	Others
Wigan Athletic	9.84	–	153+2	13	6	11	3			
Leyton Orient	10.89	£175,000	32		1	2	1			1
Sheffield United*	7.90	£300,000	75+2	6	4	3	3			

BEINLICH Stefan

Born: Berlin, Germany, 13 January 1972

Height: 5'11" Weight: 11.2

Position/Skill Factor: A quality striker with very good first touch, his skilful twists and turns, create goalscoring chances for both himself and others.

Career History: Signed along with Matthias Breitkreutz from an obscure regional club in East Berlin by the name of Bergmann Borsig in October 1991 for a combined fee of £200,000. He made less impact than his German colleague, with only two first team appearances as a substitute at the end of the season, the first being his FL debut at Nottingham Forest on 18 April 1992. Should have more opportunities this season as none of Villa's present forwards seem able to score consistently.

Clubs	Signing Date	Transfer Fee	APPEARANCES				GOALS			
			Lge	FL Cup	FA Cup	Others	Lge	FL Cup	FA Cup	Others
Aston Villa*	10.91	£100,000	0+2			0+1				

BENALI Francis Vincent

Born: Southampton, 30 December 1968

Height: 5'9" Weight: 11.0

International Honours: E Sch

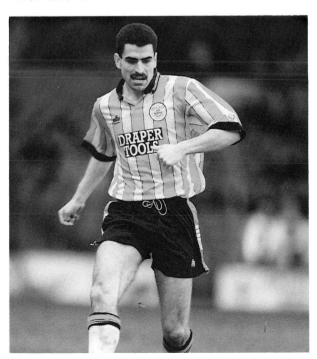

Position/Skill Factor: Very determined left-back, who is aggressive in the tackle. With a lovely left foot, he strikes the ball well and is an excellent crosser.

Career History: Locally born and bred, he signed associated schoolboy forms for Southampton in January 1983 and graduated as an apprentice in July 1985, before turning pro and making his FL debut as a substitute at home to Derby County on 1 October 1988. After a further couple of appearances as a substitute, he got a chance to impress, following a long term injury to Micky Adams. Originally a left-winger, he was given an extended run at left-back in 1989-90, along with Jason Dodd, another youngster playing at right-back during an injury crisis at the Dell. Subsequently, played second fiddle to Micky Adams until January 1992 when recalled to the "Saints' " team on the left flank in partnership with Adams, instead of his deputy. Held his place until the end of the season, at left-back in Adams' absence, and further forward when the latter was available.

Clubs	Signing Date	Transfer Fee	APPEARANCES				GOALS			
			Lge	FL Cup	FA Cup	Others	Lge	FL Cup	FA Cup	Others
Southampton*	12.86	–	54+14	7+4	11	3				

BENNETT Michael Richmond

Born: Lambeth, 27 July 1969

Height: 5'11" Weight: 11.3

International Honours: E Yth

Position/Skill Factor: Right-winger with a great physique. Has plenty of pace and is a good early crosser of the ball with either foot.

Career History: Signed as an apprentice for Charlton Athletic in July 1985, he actually made his FL debut at home to West Ham United on 7 March 1987 before he had turned pro. Had played only 11 full League games prior to 1988-89, but on coming into the side early that season on the right-wing, he created a tremendous impression on all who saw him. Unfortunately, he suffered a serious knee injury during at match at Queens Park Rangers, which put him out for the rest of the season and created severe doubts as to whether he could recover his magical form. Come back he did, though, the following November and impressed Bobby Gould, the then Wimbledon manager, sufficiently to buy him. His opportunities at Plough Lane and latterly Selhurst Park, have been few and far between, however, despite a dream start, scoring the winning goal at Arsenal on his Wimbledon debut in January 1990. He made only five appearances in 1991-92 and a promising career appears, hopefully, only temporarily at a halt. It is also doubtful whether genuine wingers have a great deal of scope within Wimbledon's direct down-the-middle style of play and a change of club might be necessary to reactivate a once promising career.

Clubs	Signing Date	Transfer Fee	APPEARANCES				GOALS			
			Lge	FL Cup	FA Cup	Others	Lge	FL Cup	FA Cup	Others
Charlton Athletic	4.87	–	24+11	4	1	6+1	1			
Wimbledon*	1.90	£250,000	12+6	1+1	0+1	1+1	2			

BERESFORD Marlon

Born: Lincoln, 2 September 1969

Height: 6'1" **Weight:** 12.6

Position/Skill Factor: Very sound young goalkeeper with good technical ability, who often, as the last line of defence, displays great bravery. Also a good long kicker.

Career History: Signed for Sheffield Wednesday firstly as an associated schoolboy (June 1985) and then as a trainee (July 1986), before going pro. Has yet to play for the Wednesday, having been loaned to a succession of clubs in order to further his experience. Made his FL debut for Bury at Preston North End on 26 August 1989 and conceded two goals in a 3-2 defeat. However, he kept seven clean sheets in 13 games while at Northampton Town in 1990-91 and later that season appeared three times for Crewe Alexandra. Started the 1991-92 season as fourth choice keeper at Hillsborough behind Chris Woods, Kevin Pressman and Chris Turner and was farmed out on loan to Northampton Town for a second time from August to November. The "Cobblers" would have been happy to sign him permanently, but "Owls'" manager Trevor Francis obviously felt he still had a future with Wednesday and recalled him.

Clubs	Signing Date	Transfer Fee	APPEARANCES				GOALS			
			Lge	FL Cup	FA Cup	Others	Lge	FL Cup	FA Cup	Others
Sheffield Wednesday*	9.87	–								
Bury	8.87	Loan	1							
Northampton Town	9.90	Loan	13			2				
Crewe Alexandra	3.91	Loan	3							
Northampton Town	8.91	Loan	15							

BERGSSON Gudni

Born: Iceland, 21 July 1965

Height: 5'10"

Weight: 10.7

International Honours: Iceland Int

Position/Skill Factor: Predominately a right-back, he can play fittingly as well in a centre-back role, where his main strength is in defending. His great pace makes him difficult to beat and he loves to get forward.

Career History: First played in his native country for Valur, before having a spell on trial with Aston Villa in October 1985, but returned home having failed to impress. Came back to Britain in November 1988, this time at the invitation of Tottenham Hotspur and after a brief trial period he made his FL debut at home to Luton Town on 26 December 1988. Unable to secure a regular place at "Spurs", he became a vital member of the first team squad. Played more FL games in 1991-92 than in his previous three seasons, in a variety of different shirt numbers, but operating nearly always at right-back. However, he was unable to hold a place after the turn of the year and with Justin Edinburgh and Pat van den Hauwe firmly established in the full-back positions at White Hart Lane, he may need a change of club to find regular first team football.

Clubs	Signing Date	Transfer Fee	APPEARANCES				GOALS			
			Lge	FL Cup	FA Cup	Others	Lge	FL Cup	FA Cup	Others
Tottenham Hotspur*	12.88	£100,000	51+15	4+2	2+1	5+1	3			

BERNARD Paul Robert James

Born: Edinburgh, 30 December 1972

Height: 5'9"

Weight: 11.0

International Honours: S"U21" - 3

Position/Skill Factor: Very positive midfielder, he trains all day long and has a marvellous attitude to the game. With two great feet, and good passing ability and physical toughness, he is a manager's dream.

Career History: An associated schoolboy (January 1987) and a trainee (November 1989), before turning pro in the summer of 1991 with Oldham Athletic, he made his FL debut in the penultimate match of the season, a 2-0 win, at home to Middlesbrough on 7 May 1991, whilst still a trainee. He retained his place for the final match of the season at home to Sheffield Wednesday, remarkably scoring the equaliser after Oldham had been losing 2-0 and when Neal Redfearn converted a penalty in injury time, the club were promoted as Second Division Champions. It was amazing that manager Joe Royle should "blood" an untried youngster at such a critical stage of the season. Played in Oldham's first match in Division One for 68 years against Liverpool at Anfield, but did not win a regular place until the New Year when again, remarkably, he scored four goals in consecutive League games and a fifth goal after seven matches. This indicated his attacking inclinations; few of his goals were spectacular, but he had a talent for putting away loose balls in the penalty area. Meanwhile, he was called up into the Scottish Under 21 squad, making one full appearance and two as substitute during the season. Clearly a player with a promising future.

Clubs	Signing Date	Transfer Fee	APPEARANCES				GOALS			
			Lge	FL Cup	FA Cup	Others	Lge	FL Cup	FA Cup	Others
Oldham Athletic*	7.91	–	18+5	1+1	2	0+1	6			

BERRY Trevor John

Born: Haslemere, 1 August 1974

Height: 5'7" Weight: 10.8

International Honours: E Yth

Position: Midfielder.

Career History: A recent Aston Villa professional signing, in return for a small fee, he had initially joined Bournemouth as an associated schoolboy in February 1989 and at the time of the move, he had been on the club's books as a trainee since September 1990. A promising player, he has yet to make his FL debut.

Clubs	Signing Date	Transfer Fee	APPEARANCES				GOALS			
			Lge	FL Cup	FA Cup	Others	Lge	FL Cup	FA Cup	Others
Aston Villa*	4.92	£50,000								

BILLING Peter Graham

Born: Liverpool,
24 October 1964

Height: 6'2"

Weight: 12.7

Position/Skill Factor: Strong defending central defender who loves a battle. Good in the air and strong on the ground, he is a good long kicker and relishes free-kicks.

Career History: Played for South Liverpool in the Northern Premier League before signing for Everton and prior to going into non-League football had been an associated schoolboy (January 1979) with Bolton Wanderers. Made his FL debut at Goodison Park against West Ham United on 5 May 1986, his only appearance for the "Toffees" before joining Crewe Alexandra where he spent two and a half season and was a cornerstone in their successful promotion drive to the Third Division in 1988-89. During the 1989 close season, he was transferred to Coventry City and although not holding down a regular place, he proved a more than capable deputy for Brian Kilcline when required. Remained a useful squad player

in 1991-92, rather than automatic first choice, despite the departure of Kilcline (to Oldham) and Trevor Peake (to Luton) at the beginning of the season. Instead, their places were taken by new arrivals Andy Pearce and Peter Atherton, with Billing first choice as cover.

Clubs	Signing Date	Transfer Fee	APPEARANCES				GOALS			
			Lge	FL Cup	FA Cup	Others	Lge	FL Cup	FA Cup	Others
Everton	1.86	–	1			4				
Crewe Alexandra	12.86	£12,000	83+5	1+1	5	9	1			
Coventry City*	6.89	£120,000	48+7	9+1	7	2	1			

BLACK Kingsley

Born: Luton, 22 June 1968

Height: 5'8" Weight: 10.11

International Honours: E Sch, NI "U21"-1, NI-22

Position/Skill Factor: Ball playing left-winger with lovely skills. A good crosser, he has the ability to create chances, both on and off the ball.

Career History: Local lad who first as an associated schoolboy for Luton Town in March 1986 and shortly afterwards turned professional. Made his FL debut at Queens Park Rangers on 26 September 1987, but was then kept out of the side by Ian Allinson, who had just joined the "Hatters" from Arsenal. However, remarkably, he did win a place in the side that faced Arsenal in the 1988 Cup Final, only his seventh first team game. His lively runs on the left-wing, helped to keep the favourites at bay until midway through the second-half and after Luton fell behind he helped his team to stage a remarkable late comeback to defeat the "Gunners" 3-2. Within three days of that great victory, he made his full international debut when coming on as a substitute for Northern Ireland versus France at Belfast on 27 April 1988. Earned a permanent place in 1988-89 and was again a member of the side as they reached a second successive League Cup Final. This time they lost to Nottingham Forest, but more importantly, his eight League goals that term helped Luton avoid relegation by just two points. Town's escape the following season was even more dramatic, with the club needing to win their final three League matches to avoid the drop. Kingsley netted one of the two that beat Arsenal and then after a win against Crystal Palace, his two goals secured a 3-2 victory at Derby on the final day of the season. 1990-91 was just as tense and the club once again stayed in the First Division by winning their last game against Derby, while Sunderland were losing. With Luton unable to survive financially on attendances of 10,000, his eventual sale was inevitable and he joined Nottingham Forest early in 1991-92. Despite scoring some spectacular goals for Forest, in particular one against local rivals Notts County, his first team place was not guaranteed and he alternated with Ian Woan for the left-wing slot and Gary Crosby for the right-wing place. However, he was selected for his third League Cup (now Rumbelows Cup) Final in five years - a remarkable record - but for the second time he was on the losing side as a tired Forest team playing their 20th game in 72 days were unable to reply to Manchester United's early goal.

Clubs	Signing Date	Transfer Fee	APPEARANCES				GOALS			
			Lge	FL Cup	FA Cup	Others	Lge	FL Cup	FA Cup	Others
Luton Town	7.86	–	123+4	14+2	6+2	4+2	25	1	2	1
Nottingham Forest*	9.91	£1,500,000	25	8	3	4+1	4	2		1

BLACKMORE Clayton Graham

Born: Neath, 23 September 1964

Height: 5'9" Weight: 11.3

International Honours: W Sch, W Yth, W "U21"-3, W-31

Position/Skill Factor: Full-back who can play in midfield, he is a great striker of the ball with either foot and is quite capable of scoring from free kicks and 30 yard shots. A great competitor, he enjoys the physical side of the game.

Career History: First signed for Manchester United as an associated schoolboy (November 1978), then as an apprentice (June 1981), before joining the professional ranks and making his FL debut at left-back at Nottingham Forest on 16 May 1984. And after only two appearances for United, he made his full international debut for Wales against Norway, when coming on as a substitute for Jeff Hopkins on 5 June 1985 in Bergen. Since then he has been a regular first choice for his country. In most of his early games for United, he played in midfield, usually on the flanks, but in a defensive capacity rather than as a traditional winger. Since 1988 he has been deployed more frequently as a full-back. His versatility has perhaps

handicapped his career, as he has been used as cover for both defensive and midfield places, but rarely able to claim one position as his own. Not until 1990-91 was he selected consistently throughout the season. Prior to then, he was frequently chosen as substitute. Despite his defensive role in the team, he is not afraid to go forward and has frequently scored vital goals for United as the record shows. In 1989-90, he popped up to net the winner in a Fourth Round FA Cup tie at Hereford United and on reaching Wembley, he came on as a sub during the drawn match with Crystal Palace. He didn't play in the replay, but still picked up a FA Cup winners medal when United won 1-0. Also, after scoring the first goal for the club on their return to Europe, in the European Cup Winners Cup, he played in every round right through to the Final, when Barcelona were defeated 2-1. On a less euphoric

note, however, he was a member of the United side that lost 1-0 in the League Cup Final against Sheffield Wednesday. In 1991-92 he reverted to his role of squad man, alternating between occasional outings at full-back and midfield and frequent appearances as substitute. Thus he played less of a part in United's unsuccessful Championship bid than he would have wished and perhaps surprisingly was excluded from the team which defeated Nottingham Forest 1-0 in the 1992 League Cup Final.

Clubs	Signing Date	Transfer Fee	APPEARANCES				GOALS			
			Lge	FL Cup	FA Cup	Others	Lge	FL Cup	FA Cup	Others
Manchester United*	9.82	–	138+34	22+2	15+5	14	19	3	1	4

BLACKWELL Dean Robert

Born: Camden, 15 December 1969

Height: 6'1" Weight: 12.10

International Honours: E "U21"-6

Position/Skill Factor: Central defender who is good in the air, attacks the ball and has plenty of pace.

Career History: Was a Wimbledon associated schoolboy (May 1985) and then a trainee (July 1986), prior to turning pro with the club and making his FL debut, when coming on as a substitute, at home to Manchester City on 16 September 1989. Made two more substitute appearances that season and had a spell on loan with Second Division Plymouth Argyle. Started 1990-91 on the bench, but following a reshuffle, he was given the number five shirt at the end of September and made the position his own, missing just one match throughout the rest of the season. He was also selected for the England Under 21 squad, making five full appearances, plus one, as a substitute. Well established in the heart of the "Dons' " defence, he was most unfortunate to suffer a hernia type injury before 1991-92 was properly underway and on coming back into the side for a few first team games in October, he sustained a leg injury which then put him out for the rest of the season.

Clubs	Signing Date	Transfer Fee	APPEARANCES				GOALS			
			Lge	FL Cup	FA Cup	Others	Lge	FL Cup	FA Cup	Others
Wimbledon*	7.88	–	32+10	2	3	1	1			
Plymouth Argyle	3.90	Loan	5+2							

BLADES Paul Andrew

Born: Peterborough, 5 January 1965

Height: 6'0"

Weight: 11.0

International Honours: E Yth

Position/Skill Factor: Central defender with good pace. Is a lovely striker of the ball, who intercepts passes well and is very constructive when in possession.

Career History: Made his FL debut for Derby County at Leeds United on 18 September 1982, while still an apprentice, having been signed in July 1981. Played just ten matches in the next two seasons as Derby slipped into the Third Division, but came to the fore as the "Rams" re-emerged from the doldrums. Promotion from the Third Division in third place, in 1985-86, was followed the next season by the club regaining its First Division status. Paul took over the right-back slot from the injured Mel Sage, held down his first team place and deservedly won a Second Division Championship medal. For most of his Derby career, he alternated between right-back and central defence without establishing himself securely in either. Not until 1988-89 was he an automatic first choice, playing in every FL game that season. The following season he fell out of favour, again playing only 19 games and it was very surprising that Norwich City, requiring a replacement for Andy Linighan, who had been sold to the Arsenal, paid their then club record fee for his services in the summer of 1990. Lost his place to John Polston in December 1990 and then vied with Ian Butterworth for the other central defender's slot. He was back in favour at the start of 1991-92 and held his place to January, but was dropped, following a home defeat by Oldham Athletic, in favour of Polston. He thus played little part in the "Canaries' " FA Cup run to the Semi-Final and was not selected again until the last three games of the season. Through no fault of his own, he has struggled to justify his enormous transfer fee, the size of which was more influenced by the £1 million fee paid by Arsenal for Linighan, rather than his true market value.

Clubs	Signing Date	Transfer Fee	APPEARANCES				GOALS			
			Lge	FL Cup	FA Cup	Others	Lge	FL Cup	FA Cup	Others
Derby County	12.82	–	157+9	9+3	12	8+2	1			
Norwich City*	7.90	£700,000	47	8	2	5				

BLAKE Mark Anthony

Born: Nottingham, 16 December 1970

Height: 5'11"

Weight: 12.3

International Honours: E Sch, E Yth, E "U21"-9

Position/Skill Factor: Constructively skilful midfielder who is capable of beating opponents to create chances.

Career History: Joined Villa while still at school, signing associated forms in March 1986, before going on to become a trainee in July 1987. Made his FL debut for the club at Luton Town on 14 October 1989 and was called up for the England Under 21 squad in 1990 after only a handful of first team appearances. Enjoyed an extended run in the team from October 1991, following the departure of Gordon Cowans, to January 1992 and later deputised on two occasions for Dariusz Kubicki at right-back. Seems certain to develop further, but in which position remains to be seen, as he has so far been tried out in central midfield, on the flanks and at full-back.

Clubs	Signing Date	Transfer Fee	APPEARANCES				GOALS			
			Lge	FL Cup	FA Cup	Others	Lge	FL Cup	FA Cup	Others
Aston Villa*	7.89	–	26+4	1+1	2	2	2			
Wolverhampton W.	1.91	Loan	2							

BOARDMAN Craig George

Born: Bradford, 30 November 1970

Height: 6'0" Weight: 11.8

Position/Skill Factor: Central defender with good control who never appears hurried. Always looking to pass the ball, rather than clear his lines.

Career History: Came to Nottingham Forest in October 1985 as an associated schoolboy, before signing on as a trainee in July 1987 and progressing to the professional ranks in the 1989 close season. Although appearing as a substitute in a 4-0 League Cup victory over Bolton Wanderers on 25 September 1991, he has still to make his FL debut.

Clubs	Signing Date	Transfer Fee	APPEARANCES				GOALS			
			Lge	FL Cup	FA Cup	Others	Lge	FL Cup	FA Cup	Others
Nottingham Forest*	5.89	–		0+1						

BODEN Christopher (Chris) Desmond

Born: Wolverhampton, 13 October 1973

Height: 5'9" Weight: 11.0

Position/Skill Factor: Left-back with a very good left foot, he also has a great attitude to the game. Prepared to battle for possession.

Career History: Yet to play League football, he first came to Aston Villa as an associated schoolboy in February 1988, before graduating as a trainee on leaving school in July 1990. Has only been a professional since the end of 1991, but according to a few good judges, he stands a good chance of making the grade.

Clubs	Signing Date	Transfer Fee	APPEARANCES				GOALS			
			Lge	FL Cup	FA Cup	Others	Lge	FL Cup	FA Cup	Others
Aston Villa *	12.91									

BOOTY Martyn James

Born: Kirby Muxloe, 30 May 1971

Height: 5'10" Weight: 11.13

Position/Skill Factor: Adventurous full-back, who likes to get forward and link up with the attack. Reluctant to just clear his lines, he is always looking to pass and is very comfortable on the ball.

Career History: Signed professional forms for Coventry City during the 1989 close season, having been at the club as a trainee since July 1987. Made his first appearance at right-back in the League Cup, versus Arsenal when the "Sky Blues" surprisingly eliminated the "Gunners" from the competition, following up with his FL debut three days later at home to Chelsea on 2 November 1991. Also made two FA Cup appearances as an auxiliary defender to cope with the aerial bombardments of Cambridge United, albeit unsuccessfully, as Coventry were eliminated by a last minute goal in the replay. Further opportunities were restricted by the consistency of Brian Borrows and also the preference of City's management for midfielder Lloyd McGrath as cover for the former.

Clubs	Signing Date	Transfer Fee	APPEARANCES				GOALS			
			Lge	FL Cup	FA Cup	Others	Lge	FL Cup	FA Cup	Others
Coventry City*	6.89	–	2+1	1	2					

BORROWS Brian

Born: Liverpool, 20 December 1960

Height: 5'10"

Weight: 10.12

International Honours: E"B"

Position/Skill Factor: Right-back with a good range of passing skills, both short and long. A very good player, he likes to get forward and is extremely comfortable on the ball.

Career History: Started his career with local club Everton where he was an associated schoolboy (October 1975) and an apprentice (July 1977), before turning pro. After nearly two years in the wings, he made his FL debut at Goodison Park against Stoke City on 13 February 1982. However, unable to establish a regular first team place, he was allowed to join Bolton Wanderers, who were then struggling at the foot of the Second Division. He was too good a player to remain in the Third Division for long and after just over two years at Burnden Park he signed for Coventry City in the 1985 close season. Immediately establishing himself in the number two shirt, he was unfortunate to lose the opportunity of a FA Cup winners medal in 1987, when an injury sustained in the last League game of the season ruled him out of the Final against Tottenham Hotspur. Has since had the consolation of being voted City's "Player of the Year" and has been a model of consistency in six seasons since his arrival at Highfield Road. Remained first choice at right-back in 1991-92 and despite advancing age, should continue to do so in the absence of any obvious challengers.

Clubs	Signing Date	Transfer Fee	APPEARANCES				GOALS			
			Lge	FL Cup	FA Cup	Others	Lge	FL Cup	FA Cup	Others
Everton	4.80	–	27	2						
Bolton Wanderers	3.83	£10,000	95	7	4	4				
Coventry City*	6.85	£80,000	261+2	31	16	10+1	9		1	

BOSNICH Mark John

Born: Sydney, Australia, 13 January 1972

Height: 6'2" Weight: 13.7

Position/Skill Factor: Brave goalkeeper who is not afraid to come for crosses, not as a catcher, but as a puncher. Active between the posts at all times. Good left footed kicker.

Career History: Joined Manchester United as a 17-year-old non-contract player from the Australian side, Sydney Croatia and made three appearances in two years with the "Reds", keeping a clean sheet on his FL debut at home to Wimbledon on 30 April 1990. United were hoping to sign him on contract, but problems in obtaining a work permit forced him to return home to Australia in the summer of 1991. It was therefore something of a surprise and exasperation to Manchester United, when Aston Villa announced his signing, out of the blue, in February 1992; the work permit problem apparently resolved. Made his debut for Villa at Luton in April and with Nigel Spink no longer an automatic first team choice, he has a golden opportunity to claim the 'keeper's jersey for Villa.

Clubs	Signing Date	Transfer Fee	APPEARANCES				GOALS			
			Lge	FL Cup	FA Cup	Others	Lge	FL Cup	FA Cup	Others
Manchester United	6.89	–	3							
Sydney Croatia (Aust)	8.91	–								
Aston Villa*	2.92	–	1							

BOULD Stephen (Steve) Andrew

Born: Stoke, 16 November 1962

Height: 6'2" Weight: 11.13

Position/Skill Factor: Reliable centre-back, who is extremely good in the air and is always likely to pop up with important goals from set pieces. Not afraid to come out of defence with the ball looking to make a constructive pass.

Career History: Came to Stoke City at the age of 15, signing associated schoolboy forms in September 1978, before becoming an apprentice in June 1979. Made his FL debut at Middlesbrough on 26 September 1981 and had a spell on loan with Torquay United while still trying to establish himself with the "Potters". In his first four seasons, he played at right-back, but was converted to central defender with great success, after the departure of Paul Dyson to West Bromwich Albion. Followed former team mate Lee Dixon to Highbury in the Summer of 1988 and was prominent at the heart of Arsenal's defence in their League Championship winning sides of 1988-89 and 1990-91, being ever present in the latter. Surprisingly never considered for international honours, many judges feel he was a key element in Arsenal's impregnable defence of 1990-91, which equalled a Football League record of only 18 goals conceded in 38 games. This judgement appeared to be confirmed in the early months of 1991-92, when in his absence through injury, Arsenal had conceded 18 goals in only 12 games and were falling behind in the Championship race. However, his return in November failed to halt the slump and, perhaps not fully fit, he was rested again. His second comeback heralded a remarkable improvement in the "Gunners'" performances. Unbeaten in their last 16 games, winning ten and drawing six, scoring 41 goals to only 15 against, Arsenal re-established their credentials to be considered the strongest team in the country. Sadly it was not enough to qualify them for European competition.

Clubs	Signing Date	Transfer Fee	APPEARANCES				GOALS			
			Lge	FL Cup	FA Cup	Others	Lge	FL Cup	FA Cup	Others
Stoke City	11.80	–	179+4	13	10	5	6	1		
Torquay United	10.82	Loan	9		2					
Arsenal*	6.89	£390,000	107+5	9	12	1+1	3			

BOUND Matthew Terence

Born: Melksham, 9 November 1972

Height: 6'2" Weight: 14.0

Position/Skill Factor: Centre-back with a great attitude. Attacks the ball both on the ground and in the air. Also a good left footed passer long into the channels.

Career History: First came to Southampton as an associated schoolboy in November 1986, before progressing through the club as a trainee (July 1989) to become a full-time professional during the 1991 close season. Made his FL debut as a substitute in the last home game of the season against Oldham Athletic on 25 April 1992 and should make even more progress in 1992-93.

Clubs	Signing Date	Transfer Fee	APPEARANCES				GOALS			
			Lge	FL Cup	FA Cup	Others	Lge	FL Cup	FA Cup	Others
Southampton*	5.91	–	0+1							

BOWEN Mark Rosslyn

Born: Neath,
7 December 1963

Height: 5'8"

Weight: 11.6

International Honours:
W Sch, W Yth,
W "U21"-3, W-18

Position/Skill Factor: A reliable left-back who favours his right foot. Very dangerous when going forward, especially in playing the ball up front and getting the return of pass within shooting range.

Career History: Came to Tottenham Hotspur while still at school, signing associated schoolboy forms in October 1978 and becoming an apprentice in June 1980. After turning professional he made his FL debut at home to Coventry City on 29 August 1983. However, during his time at White Hart Lane, he could never quite lay claim to a regular place in the side, due to a surfeit of established stars always being available and in the summer of 1987 he signed for Norwich City. Had a short run on the left side of midfield, before making his mark at left-back from where he made a huge contribution to the side during 1988-89, when City topped the First Division for most of the early part of the season, eventually finishing fourth. Likes to get forward and the following season he actually finished as the club's joint leading League goalscorer with seven to his credit. Won his first international cap for Wales in 1986 and has been a regular Welsh squad member since joining Norwich, although until 1991 most of his games were as substitute. He remained first choice left-back in 1991-92, until February, when he surprisingly lost his place to Colin Woodthorpe. He was restored to the team later in the season in a variety of positions and took part in the FA Cup Semi-Final versus Sunderland when the "Canaries" missed a golden opportunity to reach their first ever Final.

Clubs	Signing Date	Transfer Fee	APPEARANCES				GOALS			
			Lge	FL Cup	FA Cup	Others	Lge	FL Cup	FA Cup	Others
Tottenham Hotspur	12.81	–	14+3		3	0+1	2			
Norwich City*	7.87	£90,000	168+2	16	17	11	14	1	1	

BOWRY Robert (Bobby)

Born: Hampstead, 19 May 1971

Height: 5'8" Weight: 10.0

Position: Midfield player.

Career History: Discovered playing non-League football in and around London, he had an unsuccessful trial with Queens Park Rangers earlier in the season, before signing professional with Crystal Palace in April 1992. Has yet to play in the first team.

Clubs	Signing Date	Transfer Fee	APPEARANCES				GOALS			
			Lge	FL Cup	FA Cup	Others	Lge	FL Cup	FA Cup	Others
Crystal Palace*	4.92	–								

BOWYER Gary David

Born: Manchester, 22 June 1971

Height: 6'0" Weight: 12.13

Position/Skill Factor: Very strong left sided midfielder who can also play on the wing. Likes to hustle and tackle.

Career History: The son of Ian, who played for Manchester City, Leyton Orient, Nottingham Forest and Sunderland, before becoming player-manager at Hereford United, he was turning out for the junior side, Westfields, before joining his father at Edgar Street as a non-contract player. Made his FL debut at home to Aldershot on 3 March 1990 and joined a select band of footballers who have appeared in the same match with their father, when Ian brought himself on as a substitute against Scunthorpe United. His father's refusal to sign him on a contract for Hereford was the cause of Ian's dismissal as manager. Thus Nottingham Forest were able to sign him without having to part with a fee. However, with nearly 40 professionals on the Forest books, his chances of a first team game seem slim at present, but with his diverse qualities, when compared to the rest of Forest's midfield players, it will be interesting to watch his progress in 1992-93.

Clubs	Signing Date	Transfer Fee	APPEARANCES				GOALS			
			Lge	FL Cup	FA Cup	Others	Lge	FL Cup	FA Cup	Others
Hereford United	12.89	–	12+2				2			
Nottingham Forest*	9.90	–								

BRADSHAW Carl

Born: Sheffield,
2 October 1968

Height: 6'0"

Weight: 11.0

International Honours:
E Yth

Position/Skill Factor: Quick darting right-winger, cum striker, who uses his pace to unsettle defenders. Roams across the front line with great enthusiasm, often creating chances for others.

Career History: Sheffield born and bred, he started as an associated schoolboy with Sheffield Wednesday in March 1983, graduating to apprentice status in April 1985, before turning pro just before his 18th birthday. Made his FL debut the same month whilst on loan to Barnsley at home to Crystal Palace on 23 August 1986 and despite scoring, the "Tykes" lost 3-2. Played his first game for Wednesday later that year and scored in a 2-2 draw at Queens Park Rangers. Being very much in the shadow of Carl Shutt, his first team chances were limited and at the beginning of the 1988-89 season he moved to Manchester City in exchange for Imre Varadi. Only played one full match while at Maine Road, before returning to Sheffield one year later and signing for United. Settled down immediately, helping the club gain promotion to the First Division as runners-up in his first season. Proved a willing partner for Brian Deane, in the absence of Tony Agana, but his scoring record is unimpressive for a forward, although in fairness it must be noted that most of his appearances for United have been on the flanks rather than in the middle. In and out of the team during 1991-92, he made fewer appearances than the two previous seasons and his future may lie away from Bramall Lane. His brother Darren is a defender with Newcastle United.

Clubs	Signing Date	Transfer Fee	APPEARANCES				GOALS			
			Lge	FL Cup	FA Cup	Others	Lge	FL Cup	FA Cup	Others
Sheffield Wednesday	8.86	-	16+16	2+2	6+1	1	4		3	
Barnsley	8.86	Loan	6				1			
Manchester City	9.88	£50,000	1+4		0+1	0+1				
Sheffield United*	9.89	£50,000	59+16	4+1	10	4	5	1	3	

BRAZIL Derek Michael

Born: Dublin, 14 December 1968

Height: 5'11" Weight: 10.5

International Honours: IR Yth, IR "U21"-3, IR"B"

Position/Skill Factor: Big strong central defender who is good in the air and very quick on the ground.

Career History: Spotted by Manchester United while playing for Rivermount Boys Club in Dublin, he turned pro at Old Trafford and later made his FL debut at home to Everton on 10 May 1989, when coming on as a substitute. Apart from a solitary League appearance made on loan with Oldham Athletic, then in the Second Division, he patiently awaits his first full match in the top flight. He gained valuable experience during a three month loan with Swansea City in 1991-92, playing 12 FL games. However, his chances of a first team place at Old Trafford seem as remote as ever.

Clubs	Signing Date	Transfer Fee	APPEARANCES				GOALS			
			Lge	FL Cup	FA Cup	Others	Lge	FL Cup	FA Cup	Others
Manchester United*	3.86	–	0+2							
Oldham Athletic	11.90	Loan	1			1				
Swansea City	9.91	Loan	12	2		1				

BREITKREUTZ Matthias

Born: Berlin, Germany, 12 May 1971

Height: 5'9"

Weight: 11.3

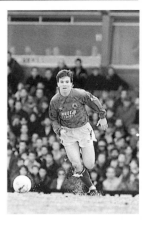

Position/Skill Factor: Highly skilled midfield player with great vision who makes telling early passes. Very dangerous around the box with bending free kicks..

Career History: Signed from Bergmann Borsig, a former East German club based in Berlin, along with Stefan Beinlich for a combined fee of £200,000. Made faster progress than his colleague, being selected for several games at the end of the season, after making his FL debut as a substitute at Villa Park against Sheffield Wednesday on 18 January 1992.

Clubs	Signing Date	Transfer Fee	APPEARANCES				GOALS			
			Lge	FL Cup	FA Cup	Others	Lge	FL Cup	FA Cup	Others
Aston Villa*	10.91	£100,000	7+1							

BRENNAN Mark Robert

Born: Rossendale, 4 October 1965

Height: 5'9"

Weight: 11.1

International Honours: E Yth, E "U21"-5

Position/Skill Factor: Very skillful midfielder with a lovely left foot and good vision, who provides chances for others.

Career History: Although Lancashire born, he was an associated schoolboy (June 1982) and an apprentice (July 1982) with Ipswich Town, before turning pro with the Suffolk club and making his FL debut at home to Arsenal on 12 November 1983. Won a regular midfield place by the end of the season and became a fixture at Portman Road over the next four years. Was transferred to Middlesbrough in the 1988 close season and settled well on Teeside, but after two seasons, which saw the club continually struggling in the lower reaches of the Second Division, he moved on to Manchester City. Has found it difficult to win a regular place in City's midfield. Endured another disappointing season at Maine Road in 1991-92, after being in the starting line-up for the first eight games of the season. Reportedly on trial with French First Division club Metz in March 1992, but was soon back in the City team near the end of the season. Faces stiff competition at Maine Road, following the recent signings of Steve McMahon and Fitzroy Simpson.

Clubs	Signing Date	Transfer Fee	APPEARANCES				GOALS			
			Lge	FL Cup	FA Cup	Others	Lge	FL Cup	FA Cup	Others
Ipswich Town	4.83	–	165+3	21+1	12	11	19	2	3	1
Middlesbrough	7.88	£375,000	61+4	6	4	8	6			1
Manchester City*	7.90	£500,000	25+4	4	1	2	6	1		

BREVETT **Rufus** Emanuel

Born: Derby, 24 September 1969

Height: 5'8" Weight: 11.0

Position/Skill Factor: Strong left footed full-back who is quick into the tackle and defends well. However, when the occasion demands, he can play an overlapping role ending with a telling cross into the penalty area.

Career History: After being released as a junior by his home town club, he joined Doncaster Rovers as an associated schoolboy (July 1987) and a month later he signed trainee forms. Almost immediately made his FL debut at home to Sunderland on 29 August 1987 and appeared a further 15 times that season, before the club were relegated to the Fourth Division. Played an important part in Rovers' outstanding youth team of 1987-88, which amazingly reached the FA Youth Cup Final, knocking out Manchester City, Sheffield Wednesday and "Spurs", before capitulating to Arsenal. After joining the professional ranks he soon earned a regular slot at left back, missing only eight League games from a possible 96, before his transfer to Queens Park Rangers in February 1991. When Kenny Sansom moved to Coventry City, he was given his chance in the side immediately and played in the last 10 games of the season. Although signed by Don Howe as Kenny Sansom's replacement, he apparently did not impress new manager Gerry Francis and lost his place to Clive Wilson soon into the 1991-92 season, languishing in the reserves thereafter.

Clubs	Signing Date	Transfer Fee	APPEARANCES				GOALS			
			Lge	FL Cup	FA Cup	Others	Lge	FL Cup	FA Cup	Others
Doncaster Rovers	6.88	–	106+3	5	4	10+1	3			
Q.P.R.*	2.91	£250,000	16+1	1						

BRIGHT **Mark** Abraham

Born: Stoke, 6 June 1962

Height: 6'0" Weight: 11.0

Position/Skill Factor: Unselfish striker who plays for his team. Very fast with wonderful touch, he controls the ball with all parts of his body, head, chest, thighs and feet and is a good finisher.

Career History: Signed by Port Vale from near neighbours Leek Town of the former Cheshire League, he made his FL debut at home to York City on 1 May 1982 in a 0-0 draw. Although he failed to command a regular place at Vale Park, he did enough to impress Leicester City manager Gordon Milne and moved to Filbert Street, following Port Vale's relegation to Division Four in 1984. However, at Leicester, Mark was very much in the shadows of Alan Smith and Gary Lineker and after only two seasons he was signed by Steve Coppell, the Crystal Palace manager. It proved to be a bargain signing as he formed a lethal striking partnership with Ian Wright, which assisted the club's return to the First Division in 1989 and even more remarkably to the 1990 FA Cup Final when Palace succumbed narrowly in a replay to Manchester United, after a thrilling 3-3 draw in the first game. His partnership with Wright lasted almost five years and only ended when the latter was transferred to Arsenal in September 1991. Although the club have still

to find an effective replacement for Wright, Bright remained one of Palace's most consistent performers in 1991-92 in a rather disappointing season, playing in every game (54 in all competitions) and finishing leading scorer for the third time with 16 FL goals, plus four in cup games.

Clubs	Signing Date	Transfer Fee	APPEARANCES				GOALS			
			Lge	FL Cup	FA Cup	Others	Lge	FL Cup	FA Cup	Others
Port Vale	10.81	–	18+11	1+1	0+1	2	10		1	
Leicester City	7.84	£33,000	26+16	3+1	1		6			
Crystal Palace*	11.86	£75,000	219+3	22	13+1	22	88	11	2	9

BRIGHTWELL David John

Born: Lutterworth,
7 January 1971

Height: 6'2"

Weight: 12.7

Position/Skill Factor: Midfield player who can also play in the centre of the defence. Very good in the air and quick on the ground, he needs to build up his strength for the rigours of First Division football.

Career History: The son of the famous 1964 British Olympic track medalists, Ann Packer and Robbie Brightwell and younger brother of Ian, also at Manchester City, he signed professional forms for the club, immediately after finishing his school education. Later he was loaned out to Third Division Chester City in order to gain experience and made his FL debut at home to Cambridge United on 25 March 1991. After waiting nearly four years for his City FL debut, he finally made the breakthrough with a substitute's appearance at Wimbledon on 22 February 1992, followed by his full debut at home to Aston Villa, the week after, replacing Steve Redmond. It seemed that he might keep his place as Redmond immediately asked for a transfer. Instead both players were then sidelined in favour of Dutch trialist, Michel Vonk.

Clubs	Signing Date	Transfer Fee	APPEARANCES				GOALS			
			Lge	FL Cup	FA Cup	Others	Lge	FL Cup	FA Cup	Others
Manchester City*	4.88	–	3+1							
Chester City	3.91	Loan	6							

BRIGHTWELL Ian Robert

Born: Lutterworth,
9 April 1968

Height: 5'10"

Weight: 11.7

International Honours:
E Sch, E Yth, E "U21"-4

Position/Skill Factor: Midfielder, who often plays at full-back and is a very useful man to have in your team. Has great stamina.

Career History: Son of the famous Olympic athletes, Ann Packer and Robbie Brightwell, Ian has a younger brother David, who is also at Maine Road. Came up through the Manchester City junior ranks as an associated schoolboy (September 1982) and won a FA Youth Cup winners medal before making his FL debut at home to Wimbledon on 23 August 1986. One of a batch of potentially brilliant youngsters who broke into City's first team almost simultaneously during 1987-88, the others being Andy Hinchcliffe, Paul Lake, Steve Redmond, Ian Scott and David White. Initially a midfielder, he was surprisingly discarded midway through the successful 1988-89 promotion campaign, in favour of new signing Gary Megson. In 1989-90, he was an occasional performer in midfield, appearing as substitute as often as first choice, but was given a new role in 1990-91 at right-back, at least until the arrival of Andy Hill from Bury. An infrequent scorer, his equalising goal - a rasping 35 yard drive - against United in the Manchester "derby" game in February 1990 will long remain part of City folklore. Although he re-established himself in midfield in 1991-92, he seemed to be regarded as a utility player, switching to full-back every time Hill or Pointon was unavailable. This chopping and changing has not assisted his career and he has not made the progress once expected of him.

Clubs	Signing Date	Transfer Fee	APPEARANCES				GOALS			
			Lge	FL Cup	FA Cup	Others	Lge	FL Cup	FA Cup	Others
Manchester City*	5.86	–	148+28	10+2	8+4	4+4	15		1	

BROCKLEHURST David

Born: Chesterfield, 7 March 1974

Height: 5'10" Weight: 11.0

International Honours: E Sch

Position: Forward.

Career History: Signed professional forms for Sheffield United during the summer of 1992, having previously been at Bramall Lane as an associated schoolboy (April 1988) and as a trainee (July 1990). No first team experience.

Clubs	Signing Date	Transfer Fee	APPEARANCES				GOALS			
			Lge	FL Cup	FA Cup	Others	Lge	FL Cup	FA Cup	Others
Sheffield United*	6.92	–								

BROWN Richard Anthony

Born: Nottingham,
13 January 1967

Height: 5'10½"

Weight: 12.12

Position/Skill Factor: A full-back who can play on both sides of the park, although basically right footed. Distributes the ball well and will look to pass short and join in.

Career History: An ex-Nottingham Forest associated schoolboy (June 1981), he turned professional with Sheffield Wednesday in December 1984, following a spell with Ilkeston Town. Released without a first team appearance, he found his way back into the Football League with Blackburn Rovers, via non-League clubs, Ilkeston Town, Grantham, Boston United and Kettering Town. Having signed for Rovers early in 1990-91, he was loaned out to Maidstone United in order to gain experience and made his FL debut at Hereford United on 23 February 1991. Finally made his Rovers' debut, one year after signing, on 14 September 1991 at home to Port Vale at right-back and played a few games before being rested. Recalled by new manager Kenny Dalglish in November, he held his place until February, when he gave way to new signing Chris Price. Later had a few outings in midfield, before being recalled for the four vital end of season games in the Second Division from which Rovers grabbed eight price-less points and scraped into the Play-Offs. Surprisingly lost his place to previously out of favour David May in the Play-Offs, as Rovers finally achieved their ambition of Premier League football.

Clubs	Signing Date	Transfer Fee	APPEARANCES				GOALS			
			Lge	FL Cup	FA Cup	Others	Lge	FL Cup	FA Cup	Others
Sheffield Wed.	12.84	£10,000								
Ilkeston Town	7.86	–								
Grantham	1.87	–								
Boston United	7.87	–								
Kettering Town	7.88	£500								
Blackburn Rovers*	9.90	£15,000	24+2		2	1				
Maidstone United	2.91	Loan	3							

BRUCE Stephen (Steve) Roger

Born: Corbridge, 31 December 1960

Height: 6'0" Weight: 12.6

International Honours: E Yth, E"B"

Position/Skill Factor: A very consistent central defender. Good in the air, he competes for everything and has a great approach to the game. Often scores vital goals from corners and penalties.

Career History: Born in Northumberland, he was introduced to League football by Gillingham, first signing apprentice forms in July 1977 before making his FL debut at Blackpool on 18 August 1979. He missed just six matches that season as a midfield player, but soon switched to a defensive role, becoming an outstanding Third Division player. Norwich City then signed him for a record fee (For Gillingham) and it wasn't too long before he and Dave Watson were forming a fine central defensive partnership at Carrow Road. However, at the end of his first season, 1984-85, the club were relegated from Division One, although there was to be some solace in the shape of a League Cup winners medal, following City's 1-0 victory over Sunderland in the Final. The following season, he battled away to help Norwich win the Second Division Championship and became the backbone of the side as they established themselves in the First Division.

Since joining Manchester United, he has missed very few games and over the last two seasons has teamed up well with Gary Pallister at the heart of the defence. Played in the losing League Cup final against Sheffield Wednesday in 1991, but hasn't been short of honours while at United, having won an FA Cup Winners medal in 1990 and a European Cup Winners Cup medal in 1991. Always a dangerous presence at corners and free kicks, he puts some First Division forwards to shame. In 1990-91, he was actually United's leading scorer with 13 FL goals, two League Cup goals and an amazing five goals in the European Cup Winners Cup, including United's opener in the Final against Barcelona (incorrectly credited to Hughes by some sources). A grand total of 20 goals is an astonishing total for a defender, although it should be qualified by noting that over half of them were penalties.

Played a prominent role in United's Championship bid of 1991-92, ultimately unsuccessful, but had the consolation of another League Cup winners medal after a narrow win over Nottingham Forest, making up for the disappointment of a losers medal the previous year.

Clubs	Signing Date	Transfer Fee	APPEARANCES				GOALS			
			Lge	FL Cup	FA Cup	Others	Lge	FL Cup	FA Cup	Others
Gillingham	10.78	–	203+2	15	14		29	6	1	
Norwich City	8.84	£125,000	141	20	9	10	14	5	1	
Manchester United*	12.87	£800,000	161	19	21	16	26	4	1	5

BRYDON Lee

Born: Stockton, 15 November 1974

Height: 5'11³/₄" Weight: 11.4

International Honours: E Sch

Position: Central defender.

Career History: Turned professional for Liverpool during the 1992 close season, having been at the club since first coming to Anfield as an associated schoolboy in January 1991, before progressing through the ranks as a trainee on leaving school in July 1991. No first team experience.

Clubs	Signing Date	Transfer Fee	APPEARANCES				GOALS			
			Lge	FL Cup	FA Cup	Others	Lge	FL Cup	FA Cup	Others
Liverpool*	6.92	–								

BRYSON James Ian Cook

Born: Kilmarnock, 26 November 1962

Height: 5'11"

Weight: 11.11

Position/Skill Factor: Winger who can play on both flanks and is capable of taking defenders on and then beating them. Always a danger around the box, he is very quick off the mark.

Career History: Commenced his career with his home town club Kilmarnock, who signed him in 1981 from local junior team Hurlford, he made 220 appearances and scored 44 goals in seven seasons. He was signed by manager Dave Bassett for Sheffield United, following the club's relegation to Division Three in 1988. A fairly typical Bassett signing, in that he cost a modest fee, he was unknown south of the border before his arrival and performed beyond all reasonable expectations, raising his game as the "Blades" became upwardly mobile. Made his FL debut at Reading on 27 August 1988 and got a flying start with his new club, scoring five goals in his first five matches. His aggressive play was a significant factor in helping United out of the Third Division that term and in 1989-90 he missed just seven matches as the team gained promotion for the second season running as Second Division runners-up. As United struggled to get away from the bottom rungs of the First Division for the most part of 1990-91, he made some vital strikes, including winning goals against Sunderland and Chelsea. Enjoyed another good season in 1991-92, although not always first choice and finished as second top scorer with nine FL goals, most of them match winners or savers, which considerably assisted the "Blades'" remarkable recovery from bottom place in November to ninth position by the end of the season.

Clubs	Signing Date	Transfer Fee	APPEARANCES				GOALS			
			Lge	FL Cup	FA Cup	Others	Lge	FL Cup	FA Cup	Others
Sheffield United*	8.88	£40,000	129+10	10	15+3	7	33	1	4	3

BUDDEN John

Born: Croydon, 17 July 1971

Height: 6'1" **Weight:** 11.9

Position: Defender.

Career History: One of three young locally born players to turn professional with Crystal Palace in the summer of 1992, he was originally an associated schoolboy (February 1986) at the club, but took time out to concentrate on studies, before deciding on a career in football. Has yet to experience first team football.

Clubs	Signing Date	Transfer Fee	APPEARANCES				GOALS			
			Lge	FL Cup	FA Cup	Others	Lge	FL Cup	FA Cup	Others
Crystal Palace*	6.92	–								

BURKE Rafael Edward

Born: Bristol, 3 July 1974

Height: 5'8" **Weight:** 10.7

International Honours: E Yth

Position: Forward.

Career History: Came up from the West Country to join the Manchester United professional staff during the 1992 close season, having previously been at the club as an associated schoolboy (February 1989) and as a trainee (July 1990). No first team experience.

Clubs	Signing Date	Transfer Fee	APPEARANCES				GOALS			
			Lge	FL Cup	FA Cup	Others	Lge	FL Cup	FA Cup	Others
Manchester United*	6.92	–								

BURLEY Craig William

Born: Irvine, 24 September 1971

Height: 6'1"

Weight: 11.7

International Honours: S Sch, S Yth, S."U21"-1

Position/Skill Factor: Nonstop working midfielder who covers a lot of ground. A good passer of the ball, he also has great vision.

Career History: A nephew of George Burley, the former Ipswich star, he joined Chelsea as a trainee in December 1987 and made his FL debut when coming on as a substitute in Chelsea's 7-0 thrashing away to Nottingham Forest on 20 April 1991. After making further substitute appearances in 1991-92, he made his full FL debut at right-back at home to Southampton on 12 February 1992. Remarkably, one week later, he was selected for the Scotland Under 21 match versus Denmark. He completed five further appearances for Chelsea in his more customary midfield role and seems well set to make many more in the Premier League.

Clubs	Signing Date	Transfer Fee	APPEARANCES				GOALS			
			Lge	FL Cup	FA Cup	Others	Lge	FL Cup	FA Cup	Others
Chelsea*	9.89	–	6+3			2				

BURROWS David

Born: Dudley,
25 October 1968

Height: 5'8"

Weight: 11.0

International Honours:
E "U21"-7, E"B", FL Rep

Position/Skill Factor: Hard tackling left-back who can also play in central defence and midfield when called on. Likes nothing more than a 50-50 tackle and doesn't lose many. Has a good left foot and is always on the lookout for shooting opportunities when getting forward down the left flank.

Career History: Started his football career as an associated schoolboy with West Bromwich Albion in January 1983, eventually becoming an apprentice in April 1985. After making his FL debut for Albion at home to Sheffield Wednesday on 22 April 1986, he went on to play a further 36 League matches, before Liverpool recognised his potential and signed him. He quickly laid claim to a regular place at Anfield and played 23 full games in Liverpool's 1989-90 League Championship winning team, alternating with Steve Staunton in the left-back slot, before finally establishing a firm hold on the position in 1990-91. Owing to Liverpool's chronic injury problems in 1991-92, he was often detailed to play in central defence, or midfield, to cover the absence of other players. Less adventurous than previous Liverpool left-backs, he didn't score his first goal for the club until August 1991, when his first minute volley against local rivals, Everton, set the "Reds" up for a 3-1 victory. He finished the season on a high, winning an FA Cup winners medal, playing alongside Mark Wright in the heart of the defence, during Liverpool's 2-0 defeat of Sunderland.

Clubs	Signing Date	Transfer Fee	APPEARANCES				GOALS			
			Lge	FL Cup	FA Cup	Others	Lge	FL Cup	FA Cup	Others
W.B.A.	10.86	–	37+9	3+1	2	1	1			
Liverpool*	10.88	£550,000	103+9	11	16+1	9	1			

BUSST David John

Born: Birmingham, 30 June 1967

Height: 6'1" Weight: 12.7

Position/Skill Factor: Centre-back who is a good competitor and is useful in the air in both penalty boxes.

Career History: Signed by Coventry City from non-league Moor Green early in 1992, he has yet to make his FL debut.

Clubs	Signing Date	Transfer Fee	APPEARANCES				GOALS			
			Lge	FL Cup	FA Cup	Others	Lge	FL Cup	FA Cup	Others
Coventry City*	1.92	–								

BUTTERWORTH Ian Stuart

Born: Crewe,
25 January 1964

Height: 6'1"

Weight: 12.6

International Honours:
E "U21" - 8

Position/Skill Factor: Good footballing centre-back, strong and more than useful in the air, he is an influential figure at the back. Not content to boot the ball out of defence and will look to pass at every opportunity.

Career History: First joined Coventry City as a 14-year-old when signing as an associated schoolboy player in April 1978, before becoming an apprentice in June 1980. Had been a pro for little more than six months when he made his FL debut for the club at Swansea City on 13 March 1982. Quickly won a regular place at the heart of the "Sky Blues'" defence where his form soon attracted considerable attention. After four seasons at Highfield Road, he moved to Nottingham Forest in a £450,000 deal which also included Stuart Pearce. His stay at Forest lasted just 18 months and after spending a month on loan at Norwich City, the deal was made permanent a short while later. Has proved to be an influential figure in the "Canaries'" side and although he suffered from an illness which forced him to miss much of the 1989-90 season, he is now back to his best. A regular choice in central defence in 1991-92, he missed some games in mid-season through injury but returned in February to play a sterling role in the "Canaries'" FA Cup run to the Semi-Final.

Clubs	Signing Date	Transfer Fee	APPEARANCES				GOALS			
			Lge	FL Cup	FA Cup	Others	Lge	FL Cup	FA Cup	Others
Coventry City	8.81	–	80+10	5	5+1		10			
Nottingham Forest	6.85	£250,000	26+1	6	1					
Norwich City	9.86	Loan	4							
Norwich City*	12.86	£160,000	177+3	13+1	22	10+1	3			

BYRNE Raymond

Born: Newry, 4 July 1972

Height: 6'1" Weight: 11.2

Position: Central defender.

Career History: Discovered by Nottingham Forest playing for his hometown side Newry Town, he signed for Brian Clough's side early in 1991. Has yet to make a first team appearance. Spent 1991-92 playing in the centre of the reserve side's defence and with Des Walker and Darren Wassall both transferred during the close season, he will be looking for an early opportunity in 1992-93.

Clubs	Signing Date	Transfer Fee	APPEARANCES				GOALS			
			Lge	FL Cup	FA Cup	Others	Lge	FL Cup	FA Cup	Others
Nottingham Forest*	2.91									

CALDWELL Peter James

Born: Weymouth, 5 June 1972

Height: 6'1" Weight: 11.7

Position/Skill Factor: Goalkeeper with very safe hands who will improve given experience. Good long drop kicks.

Career History: A professional for over two years, he first came to Queens Park Rangers as an associated schoolboy in December 1986, before becoming a trainee in June 1988. During 1991-92 he found himself third in line behind Jan Stejskal and Tony Roberts and has yet to make a first team appearance..

Clubs	Signing Date	Transfer Fee	APPEARANCES				GOALS			
			Lge	FL Cup	FA Cup	Others	Lge	FL Cup	FA Cup	Others
Q.P.R.*	3.90	–								

CAMPBELL Kevin Joseph

Born: Lambeth, 4 February 1970

Height: 6'0"

Weight: 13.1

International Honours: E "U21" -4

Position/Skill Factor: This young striker with strength and pace, two useful feet and who is also good in the air, has every chance of becoming a leading light in the game. He is just as capable of setting up others as well as scoring himself.

Career History: Has been at Highbury since signing on as an associated schoolboy in October 1985. In July 1986 he joined the trainee ranks, before turning pro and making his FL debut for Arsenal at Everton on 7 May 1988, when coming on as a substitute during the last game of the 1987-88 season. This followed his part in Arsenal's FA Youth Cup Final victory over Doncaster Rovers, when his place left opposition defenders for dead in a brilliant first half hat-trick of solo goals in the first leg. With Alan Smith and Paul Merson holding down the two strikers' roles at Highbury, first team opportunities were limited and to provide him with more experience, he had long spells on loan at Leyton Orient in 1988-89 and Leicester City in 1990-91, where he was a consistent scorer. 1990-91 saw him win a Championship medal with Arsenal, when, after several appearances as a substitute, he became a regular on the title run-in, scoring seven valuable goals in 14 full League outings. Despite his splendid form he was still not established in 1991-92, even after Paul Merson was switched to the flank, because manager George Graham then signed Ian Wright from Crystal Palace, who became an instant scoring sensation. Not until the end of the season did he win a regular place at the expense of Alan Smith, following an electrifying performance as a substitute against Sheffield Wednesday when he transformed a pedestrian 1-1 draw into a 7-1 rout. His superb strike in the 70th minute opened the floodgates and inspired his forward colleagues to five more breathtaking goals. Despite starting only 22 games, he finished the season as second top scorer with 13 FL goals. It is statistically interesting to note that in the 31 FL games that he played, Arsenal collected 62 points, whilst in the 11 games that he was not required, Arsenal picked up only ten points. One may only speculate therefore that if he had played in every game the "Gunners" might still be Champions! His place in the Arsenal is surely now established and an England call up only a matter of time.

Clubs	Signing Date	Transfer Fee	APPEARANCES				GOALS			
			Lge	FL Cup	FA Cup	Others	Lge	FL Cup	FA Cup	Others
Arsenal*	2.88	–	45+23	2+4	5+2	5+2	24		1	1
Leyton Orient	1.89	Loan	16				9			
Leicester City	11.89	Loan	11			1	5			1

Eric Cantona

CANTONA Eric

Born: Paris, France, 24 May 1966

Height: 6'1½" Weight: 13.7

International Honours: French Int

Position/Skill Factor: An extremely skilful striker with a good footballing brain. Very quick in possession, he has fast feet and knows where the goal is.

Career History: Mercurial French international forward who joined Leeds United in February 1992, following his voluntary "retirement" from French League football and who added some flair to Leeds's improbable, but well earned, League Championship triumph. Arrived at Elland Road after spells with French First Division Clubs', Auxerre, Bordeaux, Montpellier, Marseille and Nimes Olympique. His record at international level for France is outstanding (14 goals in 20 games), even surpassing his more celebrated partner — Jean Marie Papin of Marseille, but at club level he was not an automatic first choice with Marseille — only 18 games out of 38 in 1990-91 scoring 8 goals — and following his £1 million transfer to newly promoted Nimes in the summer of 1991, he struggled to score in an ultra-defensive set up with, only one goal from 20 games. Saddled with a "bad boy" image in France, following a sending off and a two month suspension after insulting the disciplinary panel, he then announced he would never play for a French club again. His agent arranged an introduction to Sheffield Wednesday, but a "contretemps" in the arrangements caused him to walk out before manager Trevor Francis had seen him in action. He then joined Leeds on loan for a £100,000 initial fee, making his FL debut as a substitute debut at Oldham Athletic on 8 February 1992. Given the background to his signing, it seemed improbable that he would adapt easily to the hurly-burly of English football and it is to his credit that he soon established a "rapport" with the Elland Road faithful with his arrogant and supremely confident forward runs. Manager Howard Wilkinson was unwilling to disturb his existing forward partnership of Chapman and Wallace and most of his appearances were as substitute, but one goal was sufficient to seal the marriage. In the closing minutes of the home game with Chelsea, he collected an airborne pass on his instep, whilst tightly marked by two defenders, flicked the ball between them and wrong footing them in the same movement, smashed the ball on the half volley from an acute angle into the roof of the net. It not only brought the house down, but was rightly selected as "Goal of the Season" by the ITV panel of judges. At the end of the 1991-92 season his transfer from Nimes was finalised for a total fee of £900,000. Notwithstanding his reputation, his conduct both on and off the field has been exemplary and as one of few forwards with genuine "star quality" in the Premier League, it is to be hoped that his stay with Leeds will be long and fruitful. Played in all three games during France's unsuccessful European Championship sojourn in Sweden during the summer.

Clubs	Signing Date	Transfer Fee	APPEARANCES				GOALS			
			Lge	FL Cup	FA Cup	Others	Lge	FL Cup	FA Cup	Others
Leeds United*	2.92	£900,0000	6+9				3			

CAREY Brian Patrick

Born: Cork, 31 May 1968

Height: 6'3" Weight: 11.13

International Honours: 1R-1

Position/Skill Factor: A tall central defender who uses his height to good advantage in both penalty areas.

Career History: Came to Manchester United from Cork City, but before making an appearance for the "Reds", he was loaned out to Wrexham and made his FL debut at Peterborough United on 19 January 1991. He had an even longer (three month) stay with Wrexham in 1991-92, during which, he starred in their historic FA Cup victory over reigning League Champions, Arsenal and the two epic games with West Ham in the Fourth Round. The Welsh club had hoped to sign him permanently, but United manager Alex Ferguson considered he still had a future at Old Trafford and recalled him although he still awaits his First Division debut. However, he was selected for the Irish Republic national squad at the end of the season and made a brief appearance as substitute in the friendly match against the USA.

Clubs	Signing Date	Transfer Fee	APPEARANCES				GOALS			
			Lge	FL Cup	FA Cup	Others	Lge	FL Cup	FA Cup	Others
Manchester United*	9.89									
Wrexham	1.91	Loan	3	.						
Wrexham	12.91	Loan	13		3	3				

CARR Gerard John

Born: Coventry, 23 December 1973

Height: 6'0" Weight: 12.2

Position: Central defender.

Career History: Locally born and bred, he signed professional forms for Coventry City during the 1992 close season, having been at the club first as an associated schoolboy (May 1989), before graduating as a trainee in July 1990. No first team experience.

Clubs	Signing Date	Transfer Fee	APPEARANCES				GOALS			
			Lge	FL Cup	FA Cup	Others	Lge	FL Cup	FA Cup	Others
Coventry City*	6.92	–								

CARRUTHERS Martin George

Born: Nottingham, 7 August 1972

Height: 5'11" Weight: 11.9

Position/Skill Factor: Striker who is very useful in the air and is always looking to get on the end of far-post opportunities.

Career History: Signed trainee forms for Aston Villa in July 1988, before turning professional two years later. His first two appearances in the Villa first team were as substitute in a Zenith Cup game in November 1991 and a FA Cup game at Derby County just before his FL debut at Wimbledon on 8 February 1992. Competition for forward places at Villa Park is likely to be fierce in 1992-93, but unless the players currently ahead of him in experience (Atkinson, Regis and Yorke), show more consistent scoring form than in 1991-92, he may receive another opportunity quite soon.

Clubs	Signing Date	Transfer Fee	APPEARANCES				GOALS			
			Lge	FL Cup	FA Cup	Others	Lge	FL Cup	FA Cup	Others
Aston Villa*	7.90	–	2+1		0+1	0+1				

CARTER James (Jimmy) William Charles

Born: Hammersmith, 9 November 1965

Height: 5'10" Weight: 10.4

Position/Skill Factor: Tricky right-winger who, on his day, is as good as anyone. With a real turn of pace, he will knock the ball past defenders in order to get in telling crosses.

Career History: Signed associated schoolboy forms for Crystal Palace in January 1980, before beginning an apprenticeship with the club in July 1982. After turning pro with the "Eagles" and without getting a game, he was given a free transfer to Queens Park Rangers, where he suffered the same fate before signing for Millwall. Made his FL debut at home to Oldham Athletic on 14 March 1987 and was a regular on the wing for the rest of the season. The following season, he assisted Millwall to the Second Division Championship and became a great crowd favourite at the Den. Nevertheless, he was not always an automatic first choice and it was the cause of great puzzlement when Kenny Dalglish signed him for Liverpool in January 1991 for a massive fee. It was a strange signing since it was unclear which player he was intended to replace and many judges considered that however good he might be in the Second Division, he was hardly Liverpool standard. The question was never answered. After two games for the "Reds", he was replaced by another new signing, David Speedie and one month after he arrived at Anfield, his manager Kenny Dalglish had left mysteriously, thus leaving his two new signings with uncertain futures. It was soon clear that he had no future under new manager Graham Souness in 1991-92 and in any case injury ruled him out of contention for selection. Ironically, had he been fit, he would almost certainly have received another opportunity to show his mettle, such was the injury crisis at Anfield. In the event, once fit again, he was "rescued" from obscurity by Arsenal manager George Graham. Unfortunately, his initial appearances for the "Gunners" coincided with their mid-season slump and he soon found himself in the same position as previously at Anfield — out of contention for a first team place.

Clubs	Signing Date	Transfer Fee	APPEARANCES				GOALS			
			Lge	FL Cup	FA Cup	Others	Lge	FL Cup	FA Cup	Others
Crystal Palace	11.83	–								
Q.P.R.	12.85	–								
Millwall	3.87	£15,000	99+11	3+1	6+1	5+1	11		2	
Liverpool	1.91	£800,000	2+3		2					
Arsenal*	10.91	£500,000	5+1		1					

CASCARINO Anthony (Tony) Guy

Born: Orpington, 1 September 1962

Height: 6'2" Weight: 11.10

International Honours: IR-38

Position/Skill Factor: Striker who is one of the best headers of the ball in the game, using his height to maximum advantage and is very dangerous on crosses. He is not just an aerial player, also having a strong left foot.

Career History: Signed for Gillingham from Kent League side, Crockenhill, in exchange for a team kit and made his FL debut away to Burnley on 2 February 1982. His goalscoring exploits in the Third Division over the next five seasons, during which he consistently topped the "Gills'" scoring lists, earned him his first international cap for the Republic of Ireland against Switzerland on 11 September 1985 and led to Millwall parting with their record transfer fee. In his first term at the Den, he formed a deadly partnership with Teddy Sheringham, where their goals helped Millwall to win the Second Division title and carried the "Lions" into the top flight for the first time in their history. Moved to Aston Villa when Millwall were clearly doomed to relegation, but struggled to make an impact and after only 16 months and 11 FL goals for Villa, he was transferred to Glasgow Celtic in the 1991 close season. He was unable to settle in Glasgow either, not scoring his first Scottish League goal until October and was frequently relegated to substitute. Finally, Celtic manager Liam Brady decided to cut his losses and allowed him to return to London, signing for Chelsea, in February 1992. Despite scoring on his Chelsea debut — a late equaliser against Crystal Palace — he was frequently omitted from the team in the remaining games of the season and netted only once more in 12 games. Since leaving Millwall, his club career has been a personal nightmare,

before graduating as a trainee in August 1990. Yet to make a first team appearance, but looks to be a fine long term prospect.

Clubs	Signing Date	Transfer Fee	APPEARANCES				GOALS			
			Lge	FL Cup	FA Cup	Others	Lge	FL Cup	FA Cup	Others
Tottenham Hotspur*	3.92	–								

CASTLEDINE Stewart Mark

Born: Wandsworth, 22 January 1973

Height: 6'1" Weight: 12.13

Position/Skill Factor: Aggressive midfield player with a tremendous work rate who never gives the opposition a moments peace.

Career History: Made his FL debut for Wimbledon as a substitute in the penultimate game of the 1991-92 season at Norwich City on 25 April 1992, having been a professional since the summer of 1991. First came to Plough Lane as an associated schoolboy in May 1987 and showed enough promise for the "Dons" to sign him on as a trainee in July 1989 when he reached school leaving age.

Clubs	Signing Date	Transfer Fee	APPEARANCES				GOALS			
			Lge	FL Cup	FA Cup	Others	Lge	FL Cup	FA Cup	Others
Wimbledon*	7.91	–	0+2							

CHADWICK Luke

Born: Birmingham, 8 September 1973

Height: 5'11" Weight: 11.12

Position: Right-back.

Career History: A 1992 close season professional signing for Coventry City, he has progressed through the club's junior sides, having been at Highfield Road since joining "Sky Blues" as an associated schoolboy in June 1989. No first team experience as yet.

Clubs	Signing Date	Transfer Fee	APPEARANCES				GOALS			
			Lge	FL Cup	FA Cup	Others	Lge	FL Cup	FA Cup	Others
Coventry City*	6.92	–								

CHAMBERS Leroy Dean

Born: Sheffield, 25 October 1972

Height: 5'8¾" Weight: 11.4

failing to win the acclaim of supporters of his last three clubs. In international football, however, with the Irish Republic, he has looked well capable of holding his own at the highest level.

Clubs	Signing Date	Transfer Fee	APPEARANCES				GOALS			
			Lge	FL Cup	FA Cup	Others	Lge	FL Cup	FA Cup	Others
Gillingham	1.82	–	209+10				78			
Millwall	6.87	£200,000	105				42			
Aston Villa	3.90	£1,500,000	43+3	20+1	17+1	3	11	1		
Glasgow Celtic	7.91	£1,100,00								
Chelsea*	2.92	£750,000	11		2		2			

CASKEY Darren Mark

Born: Basildon, 21 August 1974

Height: 5'8" Weight: 11.9

International Honours: E Sch, E Yth

Position/Skill Factor: Midfield player who is a good competitor and a strong tackler.

Career History: A recent addition to the Tottenham Hotspur professional ranks, he first came to White Hart Lane as an associated schoolboy in December 1988,

Position/Skill Factor: Strong and aggressive striker, who works hard and gets himself into good positions, but needs to find the net more often.

Career History: A promising youngster who has recently turned professional for Sheffield Wednesday, he first came to Hillsborough as an associated schoolboy (November 1986), before progressing to trainee status, on leaving school in July 1989. Yet to make a first team appearance.

Clubs	Signing Date	Transfer Fee	APPEARANCES				GOALS			
			Lge	FL Cup	FA Cup	Others	Lge	FL Cup	FA Cup	Others
Sheffield Wednesday*	6.91	–								

CHANNING Justin Andrew

Born: Reading, 19 November 1968

Height: 5'10" Weight: 11.3

International Honours: E Yth

Position/Skill Factor: A full-back with tremendous pace, he also has the ability to get forward and deliver quality crosses. Very difficult to pass down the flank because of his pace and recuperative powers.

Career History: Another home grown talent at Queens Park Rangers, who began as an associated schoolboy in January 1983 and then signed up as an apprentice in June 1985, before turning professional and making his FL debut at Luton Town on 1 November 1986. Most of his initial appearances were in midfield, but he had a fair run at right-back, from April to November 1989, until displaced when new signing David Bardsley moved into the number two shirt. Since then, he has made only the occasional appearance in midfield. In 1991-92, he made only one first team appearance (Zenith Cup) and after six years at Loftus Road and so few games, his chances seem rather limited.

Clubs	Signing Date	Transfer Fee	APPEARANCES				GOALS			
			Lge	FL Cup	FA Cup	Others	Lge	FL Cup	FA Cup	Others
Q.P.R.*	8.86	–	40+13	3+1	2	5	4			

CHAPMAN Lee Roy

Born: Lincoln, 5 December 1959

Height: 6'2" Weight: 13.0

International Honours: E "U21"-1, E"B"

Position/Skill Factor: An old-fashioned centre-forward, who is one of the best headers in the game today, when the ball is in the penalty area. Also gets in front of defenders to great advantage.

Career History: The son of Roy, who was an inside forward with several Midland clubs in the '50s and '60s, he signed associated schoolboy forms for Stoke City in February, 1977. His FL debut was actually for Plymouth Argyle at home to Watford on 9 December 1978, whilst on loan from the "Potters". Spent three seasons at Stoke before signing for Arsenal, but due to a cartilage operation he was unable to establish a niche at Highbury, finding himself in and out of the side. Moved on to

Sunderland, but it was at his next club, Sheffield Wednesday, where he finally came good, scoring 19 goals in his first season and also was leading scorer in 1986-87 and 1987-88. After four good seasons at Hillsborough, he strangely chose to sign for an obscure Second Division French club, Niort, but the move turned sour when the French club were unable even to honour the modest transfer fee. He was "rescued" by Nottingham Forest, and repaid manager Brian Clough's faith in him with 16 League and cup goals, helping the club into third place in the First Division and a League Cup — Simod Cup double. It was a big surprise when Forest allowed him to join Leeds United in order to reinforce their bid for First Division status. The money was well spent as he scored 12 FL goals, including the winner in the final game at Bournemouth, which clinched the Second Division Championship for the club. Scored 21 goals from 38 First Division matches as United claimed fourth position in 1990-91, and established themselves amongst the elite.

Now playing at the peak of his career, he spearheaded Leeds' successful bid for the 1991-92 League Championship, top scoring once again with 16 FL goals, plus four cup goals, which included two hat-tricks — away to Sheffield Wednesday and at home to Wimbledon.

Clubs	Signing Date	Transfer Fee	APPEARANCES				GOALS			
			Lge	FL Cup	FA Cup	Others	Lge	FL Cup	FA Cup	Others
Stoke City	6.78	–	95+4	5	3		34	3	1	
Plymouth Argyle	12.78	Loan	3+1							
Arsenal	8.82	£500,000	15+8	0+2	0+1	2	4			2
Sunderland	12.83	£200,000	14+1		2		3		1	
Sheffield Wednesday	8.84	£100,000	147+2	17	17+1	2+1	63	6	10	
Niort (France)	6.88	£350,000								
Nottingham Forest	10.88	£350,000	48	12	5	6	15	6	3	3
Leeds United*	1.90	£400,000	97	12	7	4	49	8	3	3

CHARLES Gary Andrew

Born: Newham,
13 April 1970

Height: 5'9"

Weight: 10.11

International Honours:
E "U21"-4, E - 2

Position/Skill Factor: Right-back with lovely balance and great pace. Likes to get forward in order to join up with the attack.

Career History: A Londoner, he originally came to Nottingham Forest as an associated schoolboy (May 1985), before becoming a trainee in July 1986. Then, after turning pro, he made his FL debut at home to Arsenal on 6 November 1988. Apart from a few games on loan with Leicester City, he had to wait until February 1991 for his next opportunity in a Forest shirt, from which point his career went temporarily into orbit. In quick succession he won his second England Under 21 cap, played in the 1991 FA Cup Final — after only ten FL games for Forest — and was called up for the England tour of Australasia, making his England debut against New Zealand and winning a second cap against Malaysia. Although he started 1991-92 as first choice right-back for Forest, he lost his place to Brian Laws in mid-season. He returned to favour long enough to play on the losing side in the 1992 League Cup Final in April, but thereafter Brian Laws was the man in possession of the right-back slot. Hailed in the summer of 1991 as the next England right-back for a generation, his name was not even considered for the European Championship Finals of 1992. Rob Jones of Liverpool had emerged as "their apparent", while Lee Dixon and Gary Stevens were still the first choices. Still has time on his side to make up lost ground, however, and will become a very good player with further experience.

Clubs	Signing Date	Transfer Fee	APPEARANCES				GOALS			
			Lge	FL Cup	FA Cup	Others	Lge	FL Cup	FA Cup	Others
Nottingham Forest*	11.87	–	40+2	8	8+2	4+2	1		1	
Leicester City	3.89	Loan	5+3							

CHARNOCK Philip Anthony

Born: Southport, 14 February 1975

Height: 5'9³/₄" Weight: 11.3

Position: Midfield player.

Career History: Signed professional forms for Liverpool during last summer, having been at the club since leaving school and coming to Anfield at a trainee in July 1991. No first team experience.

Clubs	Signing Date	Transfer Fee	APPEARANCES				GOALS			
			Lge	FL Cup	FA Cup	Others	Lge	FL Cup	FA Cup	Others
Liverpool*	6.92	–								

CHATFIELD Ian Roy

Born: Horley, 10 November 1972

Height: 5'10" Weight: 12.10

Position/Skill Factor: Short for a goalkeeper, but is a good shot stopper and very brave.

Career History: First came to Chelsea as an associated schoolboy (October 1988), before signing as trainee in July 1989, he turned professional in the 1991 close season and has yet to make a first team appearance.

Clubs	Signing Date	Transfer Fee	APPEARANCES				GOALS			
			Lge	FL Cup	FA Cup	Others	Lge	FL Cup	FA Cup	Others
Chelsea*	7.91	–								

CHEREDNIK Alexei

Born: Russia,
12 December 1960

Height: 5'9"

Weight: 11.7

International Honours:
USSR Int

Position/Skill Factor: A very quick right-back who is more suited to playing in the sweeper system. Does very well going forward and is a good passer of the ball.

Career History: Became the first Russian to play in the English First Division when he came off the subs' bench to make his FL debut for Southampton at Liverpool on 31 March 1990. Played at right-back for the remaining seven matches of the season and continued in that position during the early part of the 1990-91 season. Unfortunately, he has since been hit by injuries, after seeming to have adjusted well to the English game. An experienced USSR international player, he was signed from Dnepr of the Russian First Division. Injured at the beginning of the 1991-92 season, he was out for at least two months, following a knee operation. On recovering, he was unable to claim a first team place, but was a regular member of the "Saints'" reserve side that won both the Football Combination and Reserve Team Cup.

Clubs	Signing Date	Transfer Fee	APPEARANCES				GOALS			
			Lge	FL Cup	FA Cup	Others	Lge	FL Cup	FA Cup	Others
Southampton*	2.90	£300,000	19+4	3	1					

CHERRILL Matthew

Born: Sheffield, 10 October 1973

Height: 6'0" Weight: 11.7

Position: Midfield player.

Career History: A local discovery, he signed professional forms for Sheffield United during the summer of 1992, having previously been at Bramall Lane as an associated schoolboy (November 1987) and as a trainee (July 1990). No first team experience.

Clubs	Signing Date	Transfer Fee	APPEARANCES				GOALS			
			Lge	FL Cup	FA Cup	Others	Lge	FL Cup	FA Cup	Others
Sheffield United*	6.92	–								

CHETTLE Stephen (Steve)

Born: Nottingham, 27 September 1968

Height: 6'0"

Weight: 12.0

International Honours: E "U21"-12

Position/Skill Factor: A good reliable central defender who is comfortable on the ball and makes great interceptions.

Career History: A local lad, he signed professional forms for Nottingham Forest after starting out with the club as an associated schoolboy (January 1983) and later graduating to the apprentice ranks (May 1985). Came off the substitute's bench to make his FL debut in a 4-3 defeat at Chelsea on 5 September 1987 and by the end of that season had been given a good run in the right-back position, which he retained until December 1988 when Brian Laws took over. Thereafter, he played in central defence, sharing with Terry Wilson the honour of partnering Des Walker, although by 1990-91 he was an automatic first choice again. Was a member of the Forest sides that won

the League Cup against Luton Town in 1989 and Oldham Athletic the following year. Missing just one game in 1990-91, he formed a formidably solid partnership with Des Walker, but in the last match of the season, the FA Cup Final, it was of no avail as Tottenham Hotspur took the trophy back to London after a 2-1 victory. His position was placed at risk by the summer signing of Carl Tiler, although in the event, Walker's injury allowed him to partner Tiler for two months and when Walker returned it was Tiler who gave way for a few weeks. However, from December onwards, he had few opportunities and seems to be out of favour. The departure of Des Walker to Italy in the summer of 1992 may give him another opportunity to win back a first team place.

Clubs	Signing Date	Transfer Fee	APPEARANCES				GOALS			
			Lge	FL Cup	FA Cup	Others	Lge	FL Cup	FA Cup	Others
Nottingham Forest*	8.86	–	126+13	22+2	26+1	10+2	6	1		1

CLARKE Andrew (Andy)
Weston

Born: Islington, 22 July 1967

Height: 5'10"

Weight: 11.7

International Honours: E semi-pro Int

Position/Skill Factor: Can operate either up front, or as a goalscoring winger. Combines great pace with skill and scores frequently, because he is always looking for shooting positions.

Career History: First made his name when playing for Barnet when they were still members of the Vauxhall Conference. Manager Barry Fry has earned a fortune for the north London club by finding young talent, grooming it in the highly successful Barnet team, and then looking for likely buyers. In 1990-91 alone, he had sold Regis and Harding to Notts County for £65,000 and Gridelet to Barnsley for £175,000, but regarded Clarke as his prize asset, after he scored 17 Conference goals in 35 games. He circulated a video of Clarke's finest moments to various FL clubs, but although many showed an interest, including Manchester United, all shied away from the £300,000 asking fee. Eventually, Barnet accepted Wimbledon's reduced offer of £250,000, a record fee paid to a non-League club. Made his FL debut as a sub at home to Norwich City on 2 March 1991 and after three more similar appearances, he claimed a regular place through to the end of the season. During 1991-92, strangely, having invested so much money, Wimbledon seemed reluctant to try him in partnership with John Fashanu and 21 of his 34 appearances during 1991-92 were as substitute.

Clubs	Signing Date	Transfer Fee	APPEARANCES				GOALS			
			Lge	FL Cup	FA Cup	Others	Lge	FL Cup	FA Cup	Others
Wimbledon*	2.91	£250,000	20+26	1+1	0+1		6	1		

CLARKE Stephen (Steve)

Born: Saltcoats,
29 August 1963

Height: 5'9"

Weight: 11.10

International Honours:
S Yth, S "U21"-8, S-5

Position/Skill Factor: Intelligent full-back, used mainly on the right hand side, who is adept at hitting long passes into "channels". A good defender, he is not afraid to tackle and is also quick to intercept and start up attacks.

Career History: Began in Scottish junior soccer with Beith, before signing for St Mirren and making his debut against Hibernian in September 1982. Transferring south of the border to Chelsea, he had played in more than 150 League games for St Mirren. Made his FL debut as a substitute at Norwich City on 24 January 1987 and had his best season in 1987-88 when making 38 FL appearances. It was also in 1987-88 that he won the first of his full international caps when selected to play for Scotland against Hungary at Hampden Park on 9 September 1987. Since 1989, however, he has had to share the right-back slot with Welsh international, Gareth Hall, but neither player has established a lasting hold on the position. In 1991-92, he started the season as first choice and held his place until December, before making way for Hall. Returned in March for the closing weeks of the campaign.

Clubs	Signing Date	Transfer Fee	APPEARANCES				GOALS			
			Lge	FL Cup	FA Cup	Others	Lge	FL Cup	FA Cup	Others
Chelsea*	1.87	£422,000	161+2	10	8	16	6	1	1	1

CLEMENTS Stephen (Steve)

Born: Slough, 26 September 1972

Height: 5'10" Weight: 11.10

International Honours: E Sch, E Yth

Position/Skill Factor: A useful all-round player who can play at full-back and centre-back, but will probably settle into midfield. A very good passer, he finds an extra gear when defending.

Career History: A promising young midfield player, he signed professional for Arsenal early in 1990-91. First arrived at Highbury as an associated schoolboy in February 1987, before being taken on as a trainee, on leaving school in July 1989, he has since played regularly for the England Youth side. During 1991-92 he made good progress in the reserve side, although he has yet to make a first team appearance. 1992-93 could be his big year.

Clubs	Signing Date	Transfer Fee	APPEARANCES				GOALS			
			Lge	FL Cup	FA Cup	Others	Lge	FL Cup	FA Cup	Others
Arsenal*	11.90	–								

CLOUGH Nigel Howard

Born: Sunderland, 19 March 1966

Height: 5'9" Weight: 11.4

International Honours: E "U21"-15, FL Rep, E"B", E-7

Position/Skill Factor: A deep-lying centre-forward who creates as many goals as he scores with his subtle touches and penetrating passes. His much publicised lack of pace probably hindered his international career, but his unconventional role — half midfield, half forward, is also perhaps difficult to blend with more stereotyped players.

Career History: The son of the famous footballer and manager, Brian Clough, he was playing with Heanor Town in the Northern Counties (East) League and AC Hunters, a Sunday league team in Derby, before joining his father at Nottingham Forest as a non-contract player in 1984. Signed a professional contract a year later, after he had already made his FL debut at home to Ipswich Town on 26 December 1984. He established a regular first team place in his first season as a professional and was leading scorer with 15 goals. Although not a prolific goalscorer, he has topped the Forest charts in most subsequent seasons. Instrumental in helping Forest to win the League Cup in successive years, when scoring twice in the 3-1 victory over Luton Town in 1989 and in laying on the pass for Nigel Jemson to net the only goal of the 1990 Final against Oldham Athletic. Earlier, he had emulated his father, who had played twice for England during 1959-60 and was the club's leading scorer with 14, but although he was a member of the side that reached the FA Cup Final, he was unable to change the course of the match as Tottenham Hotspur won 2-1. Significantly, the FA Cup is the only major trophy that Brian Clough has yet to win, either as a player or manager. 1991-92 was his least productive season for goals (only five FL and three in cup games) and for the first time in his Forest career he suffered the indignity of being dropped from the team. And at the end of the season he even played in central defence to cover for injuries. Despite these upheavals, he was still held in high regard by the England manager and was recalled for the matches against France, Czechoslovakia and the CIS and was also included in the squad of 20 for the European Championships in Sweden, although he didn't get a game.

Clubs	Signing Date	Transfer Fee	APPEARANCES				GOALS			
			Lge	FL Cup	FA Cup	Others	Lge	FL Cup	FA Cup	Others
Nottingham Forest*	9.84	–	265+4	41	24	11+3	91	21	5	1

COCKERILL Glenn

Born: Grimsby, 25 August 1959

Height: 6'0" Weight: 12.4

Nigel Clough

Position/Skill Factor: Hard working midfield player with strong engines, who is always on hand to help team-mates out of a hole. Often makes forward runs, finishing with an accurate shot, he is useful in the air and a good tackler on the ground.

Career History: The son of Ron, who played for Huddersfield Town (1952-58) and Grimsby Town (1958-68), his younger brother, John, is currently at Grimsby. Signed for Lincoln City, having played for non-League Louth United and made his FL debut in an eventful 5-4 win at home to Northampton Town on 5 February 1977. After some good performances, he was transferred to Swindon Town, but when Lincoln decided that they wanted him back 18 months later, in a drive for promotion to the Second Division, they had to part with nearly £30,000 more than they sold him for in the first place, despite the fact that his career had not been advanced to any degree. In all, played over 200 League games during his two spells at City, before transferring to Sheffield United in March 1984, and helping the "Blades" secure promotion to the Second Division. Still utterly dependable, even while United teetered precariously close to the brink, Chris Nicholl made Glenn his first signing when he was appointed manager of Southampton. Soon settled into the side and played a significant part in the "Saints" reaching the FA Cup Semi-Final in 1986. Since then he has missed very few matches, forming a strong midfield partnership with Jimmy Case and Barry Horne and over the past six seasons has been the club's most consistent player. Enjoyed another consistent season in 1991-92, missing only six FL games, as his team struggled to retain a place in the First Division, although sustaining long runs in the three cup competitions, eventually reaching the Final of the Zenith Cup.

Clubs	Signing Date	Transfer Fee	APPEARANCES				GOALS			
			Lge	FL Cup	FA Cup	Others	Lge	FL Cup	FA Cup	Others
Lincoln City	11.76	–	65+6	2	2		10			
Swindon Town	12.79	£11,000	25+3	3			1			
Lincoln City	8.81	£40,000	114+1	16	7	1	25	1		
Sheffield Wednesday	3.84	£125,000	62	6	1		10	1		
Southampton*	10.85	£225,000	239+11	32+1	19+2	12	32	5	2	

COLE Andrew Alexander

Born: Nottingham,
15 October 1971

Height: 5'11"

Weight: 11.2

International Honours:
E Sch, E Yth, E."U21"-3

Position/Skill Factor: A striker with great potential who is quick and elusive with good skills to match.

Career History: First signed for Arsenal as an associated schoolboy in December 1985 and later graduated as a trainee in August 1988. Made his FL debut at Highbury

against Sheffield United on 29 December 1990 when coming on as a replacement for Perry Groves. During 1991-92 he made no further appearances for Arsenal, but gained more FL experience in two extended loan spells with Fulham and Bristol City. He proved to be a sensation at Ashton Gate with eight goals from 12 games, which undoubtedly saved the "Robins" from relegation to Division Three. When he joined City they were lying in 23rd place, but his goals inspired a run of five victories and three draws in eight games, which lifted the team well clear of the bottom four. Naturally, Bristol City would have been delighted to keep him, but his form must also have convinced Arsenal manager George Graham that he had a future at Highbury. His progress was also noted by the England management who called him up for the annual end of season Under 21 tournament in Toulon, France.

Clubs	Signing Date	Transfer Fee	APPEARANCES				GOALS			
			Lge	FL Cup	FA Cup	Others	Lge	FL Cup	FA Cup	Others
Arsenal*	10.89	–	0+1			0+1				
Fulham	9.91	Loan	13			2	3			1
Bristol City	3.92	Loan	12				8			

COLEMAN Christopher (Chris)

Born: Swansea, 10 June 1970

Height: 6'2" Weight: 12.10

International Honours: W Sch, W Yth, W "U21"-3, W-1

Position/Skill Factor: A left-back who is a natural athlete with the perfect build for a defender. Has a lovely left foot, capable of making both short and long passes and loves to get up into attacking positions.

Career History: Started out with Manchester City as an associated schoolboy in November 1984, before becoming a trainee with his hometown club, Swansea City, in June 1987 and signing professional only two months later, such was his promise. Made his FL debut away to Stockport County on 15 August 1987 and played 29 League games that season as the club gained promotion to the Third Division in Play-Off position. Injuries apart, he missed very few games in the "Swans'" number three shirt and was ever present in 1989-90. Transferred to Crystal Palace for a large fee in the summer of 1991, it seemed a strange signing with Paul Bodin and Richard Shaw already contesting the left-back slot. Ironically, it was another defender, Lee Sinnott, who was first choice for the position for much of the season. Made his Palace debut in October and enjoyed a short run at left-back before returning to the reserves. Later, he was recalled for an extended run in the team during March, apparently in midfield and although not previously noted for his scoring prowess, remarkably hit a "purple patch" of four goals in five consecutive games. Not only that, but when called up by Wales manager Terry Yorath for a friendly in Austria, he scored the equaliser on his international debut, after coming on as substitute.

Clubs	Signing Date	Transfer Fee	APPEARANCES				GOALS			
			Lge	FL Cup	FA Cup	Others	Lge	FL Cup	FA Cup	Others
Swansea City	8.87	–	159+1	8	13	15	2		1	
Crystal Palace*	7.91	£275,000	14+4	2+2		2	4			

COLLETT Andrew Alfred

Born: Stockton, 28 October 1973

Height: 5'10½" Weight: 12.7

Position/Skill Factor: On the small side for a goalkeeper, but makes up for any deficiencies in that area with good positional sense. Very quick and alert.

Career History: A recent acquisition to the Middlesbrough professional ranks, he first came to the club as an associated schoolboy in May 1989, before signing as a trainee in July 1990. Yet to make a first team appearance.

Clubs	Signing Date	Transfer Fee	APPEARANCES				GOALS			
			Lge	FL Cup	FA Cup	Others	Lge	FL Cup	FA Cup	Others
Middlesbrough*	3.92	–								

COLLIER Darren James

Born: Stockton, 1 December 1967

Height: 6'0" Weight: 12.6

Position/Skill Factor: Goalkeeper. Very quick off his line and a good shot stopper.

Career History: Turned professional with Blackburn Rovers during 1987-88, having been a non-contract player on Middlesbrough's books and made his FL debut in a 2-0 defeat at Ipswich Town on 13 May 1989, the last match of the season, deputising for Terry Gennoe. Also deputised for Gennoe in 16 FL games in 1989-90 and again at the start of 1990-91, but apparently did not satisfy Rovers' manager, Don Mackay, who then signed Mark Grew on loan from Port Vale and later Bobby Mimms from Tottenham to take over as first choice. Was not selected at all in 1991-92 and since the recent signing of Matt Dickins from Lincoln City, he has been pushed back to third choice 'keeper.

Clubs	Signing Date	Transfer Fee	APPEARANCES				GOALS			
			Lge	FL Cup	FA Cup	Others	Lge	FL Cup	FA Cup	Others
Blackburn Rovers*	12.87	–	27	3		1				

COLLINS Sean Cathal

Born: Belfast, 1 January 1974

Height: 5'8" Weight: 10.10

International Honours: NI Yth

Position: Midfield player.

Career History: Came across the Irish Sea to join the Norwich City professional ranks during the 1992 close season, having previously been at Carrow Road as an associated schoolboy (April 1989) and as a trainee (July 1990). No first team experience.

Clubs	Signing Date	Transfer Fee	APPEARANCES				GOALS			
			Lge	FL Cup	FA Cup	Others	Lge	FL Cup	FA Cup	Others
Norwich City*	6.92	–								

COLLYMORE Stanley (Stan) Victor

Born: 22 January 1971

Height: 6'2"

Weight: 12.2

Position/Skill Factor: A forward who will undoubtedly improve with experience. Has most of the ingredients to make a good attacker and with pace and strength, is also good in the air.

Career History: Signed from Stafford Rangers in the GM Vauxhall Conference, he had previously been a trainee at both Walsall (July 1988) and Wolverhampton Wanderers (March 1989). At the end of his trainee period at Molineux, he stayed on as a non-contract player, while manager Graham Turner pondered over offering him a full contract, but was finally released in October and joined neighbouring Stafford. In 1990-91 he struck a rich vein of form with eight goals in ten consecutive games, which prompted Crystal Palace to pay a large fee for his services. In his first season as a Palace player he was only used as a substitute, making his FL debut at home to Queens Park Rangers on 16 February 1991. Continued to make occasional appearances as substitute in 1991-92, scoring his first goal for Palace, a late equaliser against Queens Park Rangers, but had to wait until March 1992 before making his full FL debut.

Clubs	Signing Date	Transfer Fee	APPEARANCES				GOALS			
			Lge	FL Cup	FA Cup	Others	Lge	FL Cup	FA Cup	Others
Crystal Palace*	12.90	£100,000	4+14	1+2			1	1		

CORK Alan Graham

Born: Derby, 4 March 1959

Height: 6'0"

Weight: 12.0

Position/Skill Factor: Very experienced striker who is one of the cleverest headers of a ball in the game. Always manages to get his head to crosses.

Career History: Came through the Derby County junior ranks, prior to turning pro for the "Rams" in the 1977-78 close season. Never picked for the first team, while at the Baseball Ground, he made his FL debut on loan with Lincoln City at Oxford United on 14 September 1977, before being snapped up on a free transfer by Football League newcomers, Wimbledon. He scored his first goal for his new club in a 3-1 win against Bournemouth and in 14 years at Wimbledon, "Corky" as he is affectionately known has extended the "Dons" goalscoring record to more than 150 in all matches. Top scored in 1978-79 with 22 FL goals, 23 in 1980-81, and 29 in 1983-84 when Wimbledon won promotion to the Second Division. A broken leg sustained in September 1981 kept him sidelined for nearly two years, but he returned as sharp as ever in April 1983, scoring five goals in seven games to assist the "Dons" push for the Fourth Division Championship. Has played in every Division with the club during their climb to First Division status and was also a member of the side that unexpectedly defeated Liverpool 1-0 in the 1988 FA Cup Final. In recent years he has been a valuable squad player, playing in a number of different positions and frequently deployed as substitute. For a player who spent all of his career in the lower divisions, he has adapted well to the First Division and when he was given a free transfer by Wimbledon in February 1992, his former manager Dave Bassett, gave him another opportunity to extend his First Division life with Sheffield United.

Clubs	Signing Date	Transfer Fee	APPEARANCES				GOALS			
			Lge	FL Cup	FA Cup	Others	Lge	FL Cup	FA Cup	Others
Derby County	7.77	–								
Lincoln City	9.77	Loan	5							
Wimbledon	2.78	–	352+78	29+7	25+5	3+4	145	14	8	1
Sheffield United*	3.92	–	7+1				2			

COTON Anthony (Tony) Philip

Born: Tamworth, 19 May 1961

Height: 6'2"

Weight: 13.7

International Honours: E"B"

Position/Skill Factor: One of the best goalkeepers in the country. Has a keen positional sense and marshals his defences well. Brave, with very good hands, he is not afraid to come for crosses.

Career History: Joined Birmingham City from local non-League side, Mile Oak Rovers of Tamworth and made a sensational start in his FL debut at home to Sunderland on 27 December 1980 when he saved a penalty after less

than a minute. Became a regular early in 1982-83 after contesting the goalkeepers jersey, first with Jeff Wealands and then Jim Blyth. Signed for First Division Watford early into the 1984-85 season, when the club having played seven games without a win, had conceded 15 goals. He immediately replaced Steve Sherwood and soon became a big favourite at Vicarage Road, being voted "Player of the Year" on three separate occasions. He was only transferred to Manchester City when the club, needing money desperately, was forced to sell one of its major assets. Only missed four games in his first season at Maine Road, after he replaced Andy Dibble and confidence spread throughout the side as they finished in fifth place for 1990-91. Regarded by some judges as the safest 'keeper in the First Division during 1991-92, following lapses in form by Chris Woods and David Seaman, but despite playing for England manager Graham Taylor during his long reign at Watford, his only international honour to date is as a substitute in an England "B" match in March 1992.

Clubs	Signing Date	Transfer Fee	APPEARANCES				GOALS			
			Lge	FL Cup	FA Cup	Others	Lge	FL Cup	FA Cup	Others
Birmingham City	10.78	–	94	10	10					
Watford	9.84	£300,000	233	18	32	8				
Manchester City*	7.90	£1,000,000	70	8	4	3				

COTTEE Anthony (Tony) Richard

Born: West Ham, 11 July 1965

Height: 5'8" Weight: 11.5

International Honours: E Yth, E "U21"-8, E-7

Position/Skill Factor: Live wire striker with good pace, who hits the ball well. Often capable of losing his marker in the box, he has a knack of getting in on the end of chances.

Career History: Went to West Ham United, signing associated schoolboy forms in November 1979 and later became an apprentice in May 1981. He took the First Division by storm in his FL debut at Upton Park on New

Years Day, 1983, marking the occasion with the opening goal in a 3-0 win over Tottenham Hotspur and followed up with another strike at Luton just three days later. Forming good strike partnerships with Paul Goddard and later with Frank McAvennie, he consistently topped the club's goalscoring charts and on 10 September 1986 his good club form was rewarded when he made his full England debut against Sweden, coming on as a substitute. The following two seasons saw him miss only one League game, while scoring 36 goals and Everton were forced to part with a club record fee when they signed him in the 1988 close season. Despite scoring a hat-trick against Newcastle United in his debut for the "Toffees", he has never established an automatic first team slot even though he has been the club's leading goalscorer every season. 1991-92 followed a similar pattern to his three previous seasons at Goddison Park. In and out of the team, an early hat-trick against Spurs in October was another false dawn. Despite the departure of Mike Newell to Blackburn, his opportunities became fewer and fewer, following the signing of Mo Johnston. Although his goals per game ratio in FL games for Everton is better than most, he is clearly out of favour with manager Howard Kendall and is in need of a fresh challenge.

Clubs	Signing Date	Transfer Fee	APPEARANCES				GOALS			
			Lge	FL Cup	FA Cup	Others	Lge	FL Cup	FA Cup	Others
West Ham United	9.82	–	203+9	19	24	1	92	14	11	1
Everton*	8.88	£2,300,000	97+19	12+3	13+6	10+2	44	6	4	12

COTTERILL Stephen (Steve)
John

Born: Cheltenham, 20 July 1964

Height: 6'1" Weight: 12.5

Position/Skill Factor: A striker who is very useful in the air and moves well off the ball. Often confuses defenders with twists and turns around the box.

Career History: Began with hometown club, Cheltenham Town, before moving on to Alvechurch and then Burton Albion in 1988. Signed by Wimbledon in a joint deal, involving John Gayle, after scoring 30 goals in 1988-89, he made his FL debut as a substitute at Southampton on 22 April 1989. Did not make a full League appearance until 18 November 1989 and celebrated in style by scoring a last minute equaliser against Everton at Goodison Park. During 1991-92 he made no appearances, due to a knee injury which required an operation, but is making good progress and is expected back in time for the start of the new season.

Clubs	Signing Date	Transfer Fee	APPEARANCES				GOALS			
			Lge	FL Cup	FA Cup	Others	Lge	FL Cup	FA Cup	Others
Wimbledon*	2.89	£30,000	6+4	2		1+1	3			

COUSIN Scott

Born: Leeds, 31 January 1975

Height: 5'9" Weight: 12.7

International Honours: E Yth

Position: Goalkeeper.

Career History: Although born in Leeds, he was initially on Norwich City's Books as an associated schoolboy (March 1989). However, on leaving school, he decided against leaving home and joined Leeds United as a trainee in September 1991. Turning professional at Elland Road early in 1992, he has yet to make either a first or reserve appearance, having been out injured for most of the season.

Clubs	Signing Date	Transfer Fee	APPEARANCES				GOALS			
			Lge	FL Cup	FA Cup	Others	Lge	FL Cup	FA Cup	Others
Leeds United*	2.92	–								

COUSINS Anthony (Tony)
James

Born: Dublin, 25 August 1969

Height: 5'9" Weight: 11.10

International Honours: IR "U21"-4

Position: Forward.

Career History: Signed from the League of Ireland side, Dundalk, in 1990-91, he followed in the footsteps of other great Irish "Reds" as a star of the future than of the present. He made no first team appearances during the 1991-92 season.

Clubs	Signing Date	Transfer Fee	APPEARANCES				GOALS			
			Lge	FL Cup	FA Cup	Others	Lge	FL Cup	FA Cup	Others
Liverpool*	10.90	£70,000								

COWAN Thomas (Tom)

Born: Bellshill, 28 August 1969

Height: 5'8½" Weight: 11.6

Position/Skill Factor: A naturally left footed left-back who is a very good passer, both long and short and will make rapid improvement once he adjusts to the English game.

Career History: Joined Sheffield United from Glasgow Rangers for a surprisingly large fee, considering his limited experience. Started his career with Clyde FC who signed him in 1988 from Netherdale Boys Club, he quickly found his way into the "Bully Wee" team. After only seven months and 16 games with Clyde, he was snapped up by Rangers. However, competition for places is always fierce at Ibrox Park and most of his 12 first team appearances in three seasons were as substitute. Made his FL debut for Sheffield United at Norwich City on 17 August 1991 and although creating a good impression with the supporters at Bramall Lane in the first-half of the season, he was dropped in January 1992 in favour of David Barnes, before reappearing at the end of the season.

Clubs	Signing Date	Transfer Fee	APPEARANCES				GOALS			
			Lge	FL Cup	FA Cup	Others	Lge	FL Cup	FA Cup	Others
Sheffield United*	7.91	£350,000	20	2	1	1				

COWANS Gordon Sidney

Born: Cornforth, 27 October 1958

Height: 5'9" Weight: 10.7

International Honours: E Yth, E "U21"-5, E"B",
E-10

Position/Skill Factor: Top class midfield general who can make a side tick. One of the most skilful players in the country, he has good vision and is a great passer, both short and long.

Career History: Known as "Sid" to his friends and colleagues, he first came to Aston Villa as an associated schoolboy in July 1973, before signing as an apprentice on leaving school April 1975. Made his FL debut as a substitute at Manchester City on 7 February 1976, while still an apprentice and by the end of the following season was a regular in a side that finished fourth in the First Division and won the League Cup, defeating Everton 3-2 at the third attempt after two dreary drawn games. Remained an automatic first choice in midfield for the next six years. Indeed, he was ever present in FL games for four seasons from 1979 to 1983 – 168 consecutive matches and a remarkable record for a midfield player which could not be equalled in the increasingly physical environment and tactical switches of the 1980s. Voted "Young Player of the Year" in 1980, he inspired Villa to an improbable League Championship in 1980-81 and an even more amazing European Cup triumph in 1982. After winning England Under 21 caps between 1978 and 1980 and a "B" cap in 1980-81, he graduated to full England honours when he made his debut against Wales on 23 February 1983. Seemed well set to be a regular England selection when he broke his leg in a pre-season game in August 1983 which kept him sidelined for the whole of 1983-84. Returned in 1984-85, but could not recapture his pre-injury form and at the end of the season he moved to Italian First Division club, Bari, along with team-mate Paul Rideout. It seemed to be the swansong of his career, but he made a surprise and brief England comeback in 1985-86 with two more caps against Egypt and the Soviet Union. After three not entirely successful years in Italy (two in the Second Division), he returned to Aston Villa in the summer of 1988. Seemed to be well past his best and when he was dropped at the start of the 1989-90 season the "writing was on the wall". To his and Graham Taylor's credit, he came back with renewed vigour to inspire Villa to second place, their best performance since 1980-81. Ever present, for the fifth time, in 1990-91, he amazingly made a second England comeback when Graham Taylor selected him against the Irish Republic in November 1990. The gamble did not pay off, however, as England failed to come to terms with the Irish tactics and the game passed him by. He finally lost his place in the Villa team in October 1991 and transferred soon afterwards to ambitious Blackburn Rovers whom he assisted to promotion, via the Play-Offs after a roller-coaster season.

COX Neil James

Born: Scunthorpe, 8 October 1971

Height: 5'11" Weight: 13.0:

Position/Skill Factor: Right-back who reads the game well for one so young and has a lovely right foot.

Career History: Came through the Scunthorpe United junior ranks, first as an associated schoolboy (February 1986) and then as a trainee (July 1988), before turning pro with his local side. Soon afterwards he was pushed into the first team, making his FL debut at Halifax Town on 6 October 1990 at right-back, although misleadingly wearing the number seven shirt. After only 17 FL games for the "Irons", he was signed by Aston Villa manager Josef Venglos, on the recommendation of Villa Youth Coach, Richard Money, who knew of Cox's potential, when previously a coach with Scunthorpe. Villa paid an astonishing fee for a player with less than six months FL experience. Obviously signed with a view to the future, than the present, his situation became "cloudy" under new manager Ron Atkinson, who made a point of clearing out nearly all of his two predecessors' purchases. Fortunately Cox was young and untried and survived the purge. Made the breakthrough into Villa's first team away to Notts County on 10 March, and made several more appearances, all in midfield.

Clubs	Signing Date	Transfer Fee	APPEARANCES				GOALS			
			Lge	FL Cup	FA Cup	Others	Lge	FL Cup	FA Cup	Others
Aston Villa	9.76	–	276+10	23+4	19+1	23+1	42	5	3	2
Bari (Italy)	7.85	£500,000								
Aston Villa	7.88	£250,000	114+3	15	9	11+1	7			
Blackburn Rovers*	11.91	£200,000	26		2	3	1			1

Clubs	Signing Date	Transfer Fee	APPEARANCES				GOALS			
			Lge	FL Cup	FA Cup	Others	Lge	FL Cup	FA Cup	Others
Scunthorpe United	3.90	–	17		4	4+1	1			
Aston Villa*	2.91	£400,000	4+3			1				

CREWS Barry William

Born: Stirling, 29 October 1973

Height: 5'6" Weight: 10.0

Position: Midfielder.

Career History: Signed professional forms for Coventry City during the 1992 close season, having come to the club as a trainee in October 1990. No first team experience.

Clubs	Signing Date	Transfer Fee	APPEARANCES				GOALS			
			Lge	FL Cup	FA Cup	Others	Lge	FL Cup	FA Cup	Others
Coventry City*	6.92	–								

CRISP Richard Ian

Born: Wordsley, 23 May 1972

Height: 5'6" Weight: 10.6

Position/Skill Factor: Hard tackling right-back, who can also play in midfield, he is prepared to work and run for the full 90 minutes. Has a wonderful attitude.

Career History: Signed professional in the 1990 close season for Aston Villa, having been on the club's books previously as an associated schoolboy (November 1986) and as a trainee (July 1988). Has yet to make a first team appearance.

Clubs	Signing Date	Transfer Fee	APPEARANCES				GOALS			
			Lge	FL Cup	FA Cup	Others	Lge	FL Cup	FA Cup	Others
Aston Villa*	7.90	–								

CROOK Ian Stuart

Born: Romford,
18 January 1963

Height: 5'8"

Weight: 10.6

International Honours:
E"B"

Position/Skill Factor: Can dictate the game from midfield with his vision, flair and passing ability. Great long passer of the ball, who can unlock a defence when the game is tight.

Career History: Made his FL debut for Tottenham Hotspur at Coventry City on 1 May 1982, after being earlier signed by the club as an associated schoolboy (September 1977) and as an apprentice (May 1979). Unable to win a permanent place at White Hart Lane due to the vast array of talent available, after six seasons he was transferred to Norwich City. Following his arrival he had spells in and out of the side, but soon became a regular as he blossomed while playing in a good footballing side. Once regarded as a key player in the "Canaries'" passing style, he lost his first team place in October 1991 to the more prosaic Jeremy Goss and made only occasional appearances thereafter, playing little part in Norwich's FA Cup run.

Clubs	Signing Date	Transfer Fee	APPEARANCES				GOALS			
			Lge	FL Cup	FA Cup	Others	Lge	FL Cup	FA Cup	Others
Tottenham Hotspur	8.80	–	10+10	1	0+1	1+1	1			
Norwich City*	6.86	£80,000	151+19	14+4	10+4	11+1	11	2		1

CROSBY Gary

Born: Sleaford,
8 May 1964

Height: 5'7"

Weight: 9.11

Position/Skill Factor: A winger who is extremely quick off the mark, enabling him to get well clear of defenders to supply good early crosses. Has a surprisingly long throw for one so small.

Career History: A "fairy tale" example of the old adage "If at first you don't succeed, try and try again". Originally an associated schoolboy (October 1979) and non-contract player with Lincoln City, he was released in 1982 and joined non-League side, Lincoln United. Four years later he was offered another chance by Lincoln City, during a one month trial period, but despite several first team games, after making his FL debut at Cardiff City on 16 September 1986, he was not offered a professional contract. He joined Grantham of the then Southern League (Midland Division) who were managed by Martin O'Neill, the former Nottingham Forest hero. His scintillating form, prompted a recommendation to Forest manager, Brian Clough, who signed him for a modest fee, albeit a record for Grantham. Typically, Mr Clough pitched him into first team action after less than two months at the City Ground and equally typically, he repaid his manager's faith in him, scoring in his first full appearance against Chelsea and then netting the winner against Birmingham City in an FA Cup tie, following some old fashioned direct wing play. In only his ninth first team game and just four months after playing at a very humble level, he destroyed the defence of the all-conquering Liverpool team on Easter Monday, as Forest inflicted the second League defeat of the season on the eventual Champions — a real "rags to riches" story. Made more headlines, scoring a controversial goal against Manchester City in March 1990, when he headed the ball out of the 'keeper's hands and stabbed it into the net. Ended 1989-90 on a high, collecting a League Cup winners medal from the 1-0 win over Oldham Athletic, but was less fortunate in 1990-91 when Forest were beaten 2-1 by Tottenham Hotspur in the FA Cup Final. Has not perhaps developed as much as his early Forest career suggested and has a tendency to waste his brilliant running on the ball with poor quality crosses. Nevertheless, he remains the club's first choice right-winger, enjoying another successful season in 1991-92, as Forest reached two cup finals, winning the Zenith Cup against Southampton, but losing 1-0 to Manchester United in the League Cup Final.

Clubs	Signing Date	Transfer Fee	APPEARANCES				GOALS			
			Lge	FL Cup	FA Cup	Others	Lge	FL Cup	FA Cup	Others
Lincoln City	8.86	–	6+1	2						
Grantham	11.86	–								
Nottingham Forest*	12.87	£20,000	115+8	24+1	17+1	10+1	11	2	3	4

CROSSLEY Mark Geoffrey

Born: Barnsley,
16 June 1969

Height: 6'0"

Weight:13.9

International Honours:
E "U21"-3

Position/Skill Factor: A goalkeeper who presents a very small target to aim at and is at his best in one-to-one situations. Kicks the ball very long from his hands.

Career History: Played in Nottingham Forest's junior side, coming straight from school, before turning pro and making his FL debut as a replacement for the injured Steve Sutton in a 2-1 win at home to Liverpool on 26 October 1988. Three days later, he kept a clean sheet in a 1-0 win over Newcastle United and although he had two short spells in the side the following term, deputising for Sutton, it wasn't until 1990-91 that he claimed a regular place. Emerging from the shadows, he was an ever present, conceded only 50 League goals in a demanding season and played with credit in the 1991 FA Cup Final

against Tottenham Hotspur, which Forest lost, 2-1. Started as first choice 'keeper at the City Ground, in 1991-92, but lost his place to Andy Marriott in March 1992, following a well publicised off the field incident in his home town. Thus, he missed out on both of Forest's Wembley Cup Finals in the Zenith and Rumbelows Cups, although restored to favour by the end of the season.

Clubs	Signing Date	Transfer Fee	APPEARANCES				GOALS			
			Lge	FL Cup	FA Cup	Others	Lge	FL Cup	FA Cup	Others
Nottingham Forest*	7.87	–	84	15	14	8				

CULVERHOUSE David Paul

Born: Harlow, 9 September 1973

Height: 6'0" Weight: 11.6

Position/Skill Factor: Centre-back who is very good in the air. Reads the game well and often comes out of defence with the ball.

Career History: A 1992 close season professional signing for Tottenham Hotspur, having been at the club since first joining as an associated schoolboy in March 1988, before graduating as a trainee in August 1990. No first team experience, but has had a couple of reserve matches. Brother of Ian who plays for Norwich City.

Clubs	Signing Date	Transfer Fee	APPEARANCES				GOALS			
			Lge	FL Cup	FA Cup	Others	Lge	FL Cup	FA Cup	Others
Tottenham Hotspur*	5.92	–								

CULVERHOUSE Ian Brett

Born: Bishops Stortford,
22 September 1964

Height: 5'10"

Weight: 11.2

International Honours:
E Yth

Position/Skill Factor: Skilful right-back, cum sweeper. Good all rounder who reads the game well and intercepts well. A good passer, he loves to get forward and join in attacking play when the time is right.

Career History: Another of the former Tottenham Hotspur connection now at Norwich City, he was an apprentice at White Hart Lane (May 1981), before turning professional and making his FL debut at Notts County as a substitute on 21 February 1984. He had only appeared in one full League game for the "Spurs", but after signing for the "Canaries", he went straight into the first team, playing 18 matches, before he finished on the losing side and ended his first season, 1985-86, with a Second Division Championship medal. At the end of 1990-91 he had played more games for Norwich than any other member of the current squad and was justifiably honoured as City's "Player of the Year". Lost his place through injury in September 1991, but returned in February 1992 to play a part in Norwich's ultimately disappointing FA Cup run. His younger brother David has just turned professional with Tottenham Hotspur.

Clubs	Signing Date	Transfer Fee	APPEARANCES				GOALS			
			Lge	FL Cup	FA Cup	Others	Lge	FL Cup	FA Cup	Others
Tottenham H	9.82	–	1 + 1							
Norwich City*	10.85	£50,000	112 + 1	16	24	17	.			1

CUNDY Jason Victor

Born: Wandsworth,
12 November 1969

Height: 6'1"

Weight: 13.7

International Honours:
E Yth, E "U21"-3

Position/Skill Factor: A powerfully built centre-back and one of the best young defenders in the country. Strong in the air and aggressive, he has a good turn of pace, which is sometimes used to good effect in an attacking role.

Career History: After signing associated schoolboy forms for Chelsea in March 1985, he became a trainee in July 1986. Made his FL debut for the "Blues" in the number five shirt at Queens Park Rangers on 1 September 1990 and showed a lot of early promise. Later that season, he had assured his place in Chelsea's defence, playing alongside Kenneth Monkou and producing some staggering displays in helping to secure a highly suspect defence. Lost his place to new signing Paul Elliott in 1991-92, but returned to first team duty in January 1992 in place of Kenneth Monkou. Somewhat surprisingly, was loaned to Tottenham Hotspur just before the transfer deadline and impressed enough to make the transfer permanent in the summer of 1992.

Clubs	Signing Date	Transfer Fee	APPEARANCES				GOALS			
			Lge	FL Cup	FA Cup	Others	Lge	FL Cup	FA Cup	Others
Chelsea	8.88	–	40 + 1	6	6	4	2			
Tottenham Hotspur*	3.92	£750,000	10							

CURLE Keith

Born: Bristol, 14 November 1963

Height: 6'0" Weight: 12.0

International Honours: E"B", FL Rep, E-3

Position/Skill Factor: Central defender with the skills of a winger. Has great pace and is quite capable of coming out of defence with the ball to set up chances. Reads the game well.

Career History: Has had a tough soccer education, plying his trade around a variety of west country clubs from the lower reaches, before eventually reaching the top level with Wimbledon. Started as an associated schoolboy with Bristol City in December 1977, but then switched his allegiance to Bristol Rovers, firstly as an apprentice (July 1980) and later as a pro. Made his FL debut in a 2-2 draw at home to Chester City on 29 August 1981 and scored the equaliser for a Rovers side that included Gary Mabbutt and the player-manager, Terry Cooper. After failing to command a regular place, he was transferred to Torquay United, but four months later the club doubled their money when Terry Cooper re–signed him for Bristol City. As a midfielder he was unexceptional, despite his tremendous pace, but in October 1984, Cooper switched him to central defence, in which position he gradually excelled. After three seasons, he moved to Reading and although the club were relegated to the Third Division at the end of 1987-88, his outstanding displays in the "Royals'" defence, prompted Wimbledon to sign him. There, he teamed up with Eric Young, to form a formidable defensive partnership and captained the side with distinction. It was still a major surprise when Peter Reid signed him for Manchester City in the summer of 1991, for a massive fee, considering his lack of honours, except at "B" level. On the fringe of international selection, he finally made his

England debut as substitute in April 1992 against the CIS in Mexico, following up with his full debut in Hungary two weeks later. Originally not included in the England squad for the European Championship Finals in Sweden, he was called up as a last minute replacement for the injured Gary Stevens and played at right-back in the 0-0 draw against the eventual Champions, Denmark.

Clubs	Signing Date	Transfer Fee	APPEARANCES				GOALS			
			Lge	FL Cup	FA Cup	Others	Lge	FL Cup	FA Cup	Others
Bristol Rovers	11.81	–	21 + 11	3	1		4			
Torquay United	11.83	£5,000	16		1	1	5		1	
Bristol City	3.84	£10,000	113 + 8	7 + 1	5	14 + 1	1			
Reading	10.87	£150,000	40	8		5				
Wimbledon	10.88	£500,000	91 + 2	7	5	6	3			1
Manchester City*	8.91	£2,500,000	40	4	1	1	5			

CURZON Richard

Born: Mansfield, 6 September 1973

Height: 5'7" **Weight:** 9.6

Position: Left-winger.

Career History: Joined the Sheffield Wednesday professional staff during the 1992 close season, having been at the club as a trainee since July 1990. Has no first team experience.

Clubs	Signing Date	Transfer Fee	APPEARANCES				GOALS			
			Lge	FL Cup	FA Cup	Others	Lge	FL Cup	FA Cup	Others
Sheffield Wednesday*	6.92	–								

DALEY Anthony (Tony) Mark

Born: Birmingham, 18 October 1967

Height: 5'7" **Weight:** 10.8

International Honours: E Yth, E-7

Position/Skill Factor: Predominantly a right-winger, although comfortable on both flanks, he is very quick off the mark, has great pace and leaves defenders trailing when he runs at them. On his day the most exciting winger in the League, but prone to inconsistency and often wastes his superb runs on the ball with weak crosses.

Career History: Signed for Aston Villa as an associated schoolboy in April 1983, later becoming an apprentice in July 1984. Made his FL debut for Aston Villa away at Southampton on 20 April 1985 and was an instant hit with the fans. In 1985-86 he suffered the disappointment of relegation with Villa to the Second Division and the following season injury and loss of form kept him out of the side. However, he eventually won back his place in January 1988, making ten appearances and scoring three

vital goals as Villa went back to the First Division as runners-up. Over the past few seasons he has missed several matches, mainly due to injury and the 1990-91 season saw him play only three more games after being carried off at Manchester United in December 1990, a sad loss for the Villa faithful. 1991-92 was probably his best season to

date, holding down a regular place in the Villa team and winning his first England cap as substitute in the vital European Championship qualifying game in Poland, which England drew 1-1. Later in the season, he made his full international debut in Moscow against the CIS, where his run and cross set up Gary Lineker for England's first goal in a 2-2 draw. He was retained for the subsequent games against Hungary and Brazil, thus earning his selection for the 20 man squad for the 1992 European Championship Finals in Sweden. Used as a substitute in the opening match, a 0-0 draw against Denmark, he later played in what was ultimately the final game for England, against Sweden and had two good chances of scoring. Although he did not score and England went out of the competition, he was a danger to the Swedish defence every time he got the ball wide on the right and proved one of the few successes of a disappointing squad.

Clubs	Signing Date	Transfer Fee	APPEARANCES				GOALS			
			Lge	FL Cup	FA Cup	Others	Lge	FL Cup	FA Cup	Others
Aston Villa*	5.85	–	162+31	17 + 1	13+1	13+2	28	4	2	1

DAVIES Christian (Chris) Alexander Nicholas

Born: Grays, 18 November 1974

Height: 6'0" **Weight:** 12.8

Position/Skill Factor: Goalkeeper. Handles the ball well and is an excellent shot stopper.

Career History: Essex born, he started out as a Charlton Athletic associated schoolboy (July 1989), before signing for Nottingham Forest as a trainee in August 1991, on leaving school. Joined the Forest professional ranks just four months later, but has yet to make an appearance in reserve team.

Clubs	Signing Date	Transfer Fee	APPEARANCES				GOALS			
			Lge	FL Cup	FA Cup	Others	Lge	FL Cup	FA Cup	Others
Nottingham Forest*	12.91	–								

DAVIES Martin Lemuel

Born: Swansea, 28 June 1974

Height: 6'1" Weight: 12.4

Position: Goalkeeper.

Career History: Signed on the dotted line for Coventry City during the summer of 1992, having been at Highfield Road first as an associated schoolboy (November 1988), before graduating as a trainee in July 1990. No first team experience.

Clubs	Signing Date	Transfer Fee	APPEARANCES				GOALS			
			Lge	FL Cup	FA Cup	Others	Lge	FL Cup	FA Cup	Others
Coventry City*	6.92	–								

DAVIES Simon Ithel

Born: Winsford, 23 April 1974

Height: 5'11" Weight: 10.2

Position: Midfield player.

Career History: Joined the Manchester United professional staff during the 1992 close season, having previously been at Old Trafford as an associated schoolboy (June 1988) and as a trainee (July 1990). No first team experience.

Clubs	Signing Date	Transfer Fee	APPEARANCES				GOALS			
			Lge	FL Cup	FA Cup	Others	Lge	FL Cup	FA Cup	Others
Manchester United*	6.92	–								

DAVIS Neil

Born: Bloxwich, 15 August 1973

Height: 5'8" Weight: 11.0

Position/Skill Factor: Striker who is very quick off the mark and can finish strongly.

Career History: Signed from non-League Redditch United in the 1991 close season, he has yet to make a first team appearance for Aston Villa. Is one to watch out for in the future.

Clubs	Signing Date	Transfer Fee	APPEARANCES				GOALS			
			Lge	FL Cup	FA Cup	Others	Lge	FL Cup	FA Cup	Others
Aston Villa*	5.91	£25,000								

DAVIS Paul Vincent

Born: Dulwich, 9 December 1961

Height: 5'8"

Weight: 9.7

International Honours: E "U21"-11, E"B", FL Rep

Position/Skill Factor: Cultured midfielder with a magical left foot. Always appearing to have plenty of time, the sign of a top player, he is a lovely passer of the ball and has great vision.

Career History: Spotted by Arsenal as a 15-year-old, he came to Highbury on associated schoolboy forms in October 1977 and on leaving school he signed as an apprentice (June 1978). Making great progress he turned professional during the 1979 close season and went on to make his FL debut in the 2-1 win over the local rivals, Tottenham, at White Hart Lane on 7 April 1980. Over the next two seasons he battled to establish himself in a talented Arsenal midfield and gained representative honours when doing so. Although winning a League Cup winners medal in 1987 and a runners-up medal the following year, a lengthy suspension imposed early in 1988-89 meant he was unable to regain his place and was forced to spend most of the club's League Championship winning season in the reserves. His suspension for a well publicised off the ball incident, probably cost him an international career and subsequent injury problems left him out in the cold for nearly two years. Made up for that with a League Championship medal in 1990-91, only missing one match in the campaign. However, in 1991-92, after starting the season as first choice, he fell out of favour with manager George Graham following Arsenal's surprise elimination from the European Cup by Benefica, and lost his place to David Hillier.

Clubs	Signing Date	Transfer Fee	APPEARANCES				GOALS			
			Lge	FL Cup	FA Cup	Others	Lge	FL Cup	FA Cup	Others
Arsenal*	7.79	–	301+18	42+3	19+5	9+1	29	4	3	1

DAVISON Robert (Bobby)

Born: South Shields,
17 July 1959

Height: 5'10"

Weight: 11.5

Position/Skill Factor: Striker with a great work rate, who tackles defenders and never gives them time to settle, he always looks for them to make mistakes.

Career History: A former shipyard worker, he was discovered by Huddersfield Town when playing for Seaham Red Star in the Northern League. However, given little chance to shine at Leeds Road and after one season and only one full game, his FL debut at Rotherham United on 30 August 1980, he was transferred to Fourth Division Halifax Town where he soon established a reputation as a reliable marksman and it was not long before Derby County moved in for him. Over the next five seasons, he became the "Rams'" leading goalscorer and in 1983-84 he netted 24, the best tally for a top scorer since 1956-57. In 1985-86 his 17 goals helped Derby to climb out of the Third Division and in 1986-87 he scored 19 times as the club became Second Division Champions. Leeds United were the next to acquire his goalscoring skills in their bid to return to the First Division. This was duly achieved in 1989-90 when the club won the Second Division title, with Davison scoring 11 times in 25 FL outings. Since rejoining the First Division, his first team appearances have been restricted and he played little part in Leeds' League Championship campaign of 1991-92. Early in the season he returned to Derby on loan, scoring nine goals in ten games, which lifted the "Rams" into a promotion challenging position. A permanent move seemed an obvious next step, but neither a transfer fee or personal contract details could be agreed and he returned to Elland Road. Later in the season he joined Sheffield United on loan, scoring twice on his debut in the Sheffield "derby" game at Hillsborough as United completed a remarkable "double" over their more illustrious neighbours.

DAY Mervyn Richard

Born: Chelmsford,
26 June 1955

Height: 6'2"

Weight: 15.1

International Honours:
E Yth, E "U23"-5

Position/Skill Factor: Very experienced goalkeeper with good hands, cool under pressure and sound positional sense.

Career History: Once considered to be a future England keeper, he joined West Ham United as an apprentice in July 1971 and made his FL debut at home to Ipswich Town on 27 August 1973. Played in heavy rain, he let three goals in as the "Hammers" drew. Since coming into League soccer he often had to endure a leaky defence and was delighted to keep a clean sheet at Wembley in the 1975 FA Cup Final as West Ham defeated Fulham, 2-0. However, following the signing of Phil Parkes, he lost confidence and surprisingly moved on to Leyton Orient, then of the Second Division, but who descended to the Third in 1982. His career was rescued by Aston Villa, who signed him as cover for Nigel Spink. When Spink was injured in March 1984, he re-established his First Division credentials and was perhaps unlucky to lose his place when the latter became available again during the next season. Signed for Leeds United as the replacement for David Harvey and after joining was automatic first choice for five years, missing a mere handful of games through injury. In 1989-90 he kept 17 clean sheets as the club won the Second Division title. But since John Lukic made the journey back to Elland Road from Arsenal, he has been relegated to the role of understudy and was not even required to make one solitary appearance in 1990-91. His only FL action in 1991-92 was on loan to struggling Luton Town in March 1992, until he found the travelling from his home too problematic and a solitary appearance in the last game of the season for Sheffield United, when all three of the "Blades'" keepers were unavailable through injury.

Clubs	Signing Date	Transfer Fee	APPEARANCES				GOALS			
			Lge	FL Cup	FA Cup	Others	Lge	FL Cup	FA Cup	Others
Huddersfield Town	7.80	£1,000	1+1							
Halifax Town	8.81	£20,000	63	4	2		29	4		
Derby County	12.82	£90,000	203+3	18	11	4	83	6	7	2
Leeds United*	11.87	£350,000	79+12	4	2+4	7+2	32	1	1	3
Derby County	9.91	Loan	10				9			
Sheffield United	3.92	Loan	6+5				4			

Clubs	Signing Date	Transfer Fee	APPEARANCES				GOALS			
			Lge	FL Cup	FA Cup	Others	Lge	FL Cup	FA Cup	Others
West Ham United	3.73	–	194	14	14	10				
Leyton Orient	7.79	£100,000	170	8	10					
Aston Villa	8.83	£15,000	30	3						
Leeds United*	1.85	£30,000	22.5	14	10	16				
Luton Town	3.92	Loan	4							
Sheffield United	5.92	Loan	1							

DEANE Brian Christopher

Born: Leeds, 7 February 1968

Height: 6'3" Weight: 12.7

International Honours: E"B", E-2

Position/Skill Factor: Powerful striker who leads the line well. Quick off the mark, brave and good in the air, he is always good for 20 plus goals a season.

Career History: Came through the junior ranks at Doncaster Rovers, making his FL debut at home to Swansea City on 4 February 1986 and spent little more than two seasons at the Belle Vue Ground before Dave Bassett, recognising his potential, signed him for Sheffield United in the 1988 close season. It was another typical "coup" by Dave Bassett as his scoring record for Doncaster was unimpressive, yet he was an instant success at Bramall Lane. Scored on his League debut for United, a 3-1 win at Reading in the opening game of the season and immediately formed a lethal striking partnership with Tony Agana as the club gained promotion to the Second Division that term. The following season, hopes were high of a United return to the First Division after a 15 year absence and Deane's 21 League goals played a big part in helping the "Blades" achieve their ambition. Despite his partner being continually dogged by injury, he continued to find the net regularly, even with United struggling at the foot of Division One. His impressive club form was finally translated into international status when he was selected for England's summer tour of 1991 and played twice against New Zealand. Although dogged by injury in the opening months of 1991-92, he returned in November to enjoy another successful season even without a regular partner and once again finished top scorer with 12 FL goals, plus four cup goals, which included a superb 45 yard chip against Liverpool when Grobbelaar was stranded outside the penalty area. Despite his good club form, his nascent international career became still-born with only a substitute appearance in an England "B" match to add to his two caps. Constantly the subject of transfer speculation, he is now valued at £2 million.

Clubs	Signing Date	Transfer Fee	APPEARANCES				GOALS			
			Lge	FL Cup	FA Cup	Others	Lge	FL Cup	FA Cup	Others
Doncaster Rovers	12.85	–	59+7	3	2+1	2+2	12		1	
Sheffield United*	7.88	£30,000	156	12	18	1	68	9	8	2

DEARDEN Kevin Charles

Born: Luton, 8 March 1970

Height: 5'11" Weight: 12.8

Position/Skill Factor: Very agile goalkeeper who is a good shot stopper. Also impresses with his early use of the ball.

Career History: Has been at Tottenham Hotspur since his early teens, first signing as an associated schoolboy in December 1984 and later graduating to trainee in July 1986. However, goalkeeping opportunities at White Hart Lane, with Erik Thorstvedt and Ian Walker on the staff, have been non-existent, apart from an appearance in the League Cup, a 2-1 victory over Hartlepool United in 1990-91. His FL debut came while on loan to Cambridge United at Exeter City on 11 March 1989 and he kept a clean sheet in a 3-0 win. Has since been loaned out to Hartlepool United, Swindon Town, Peterborough United and Hull City as he gains valuable experience, while awaiting the day for a First Division opportunity to present itself. Still awaiting his first team debut for "Spurs", in 1991-92, he seems set to create a FL record for temporary transfers, with further loan spells at Rochdale and Birmingham City. Whilst at St Andrews, he assisted the "Blues" to promotion from the Third Division.

Clubs	Signing Date	Transfer Fee	APPEARANCES				GOALS			
			Lge	FL Cup	FA Cup	Others	Lge	FL Cup	FA Cup	Others
Tottenham Hotspur*	7.88	–		1						
Cambridge United	3.89	Loan	15							
Hartlepool United	8.89	Loan	10							
Swindon Town	3.90	Loan	1							
Peterborough United	8.90	Loan	7							
Hull City	1.91	Loan	3							
Rochdale	8.91	Loan	2							
Birmingham City	3.92	Loan	12							

DEWHURST Robert Matthew

Born: Keighley, 10 September 1971

Height: 6'3" Weight: 13.1

Position/Skill Factor: Central defender with a great attitude, who is good in the air and has a nice left foot.

Career History: Very tall for his age, he signed as a trainee for Blackburn Rovers in February 1989 and made his FL debut in a 2-1 win at Ewood Park against Hull City on 28 August 1990, a month before turning professional. Enjoyed a brief run in central defence and again at right-back, before returning to reserve team football in January 1991. During 1991-92 he didn't even get a "look-in", but had a two month loan spell with Third Division Darlington where he played 12 games in the number 11 shirt as an auxiliary defender.

Clubs	Signing Date	Transfer Fee	APPEARANCES				GOALS			
			Lge	FL Cup	FA Cup	Others	Lge	FL Cup	FA Cup	Others
Blackburn Rovers*	10.90	–	13	1						
Darlington	12.91	Loan	11				1			

Was a regular between the City posts during the following season, but in 1990-91 found himself understudying Tony Cotton and was loaned out to Middlesbrough for a lengthy spell. In 1991-92 was pushed further out to the side lines by manager Peter Reid, but extended loans with Bolton Wanderers and West Bromwich have not as yet led to the permanent transfer from Maine Road that he probably needs to recover his career.

Clubs	Signing Date	Transfer Fee	APPEARANCES				GOALS			
			Lge	FL Cup	FA Cup	Others	Lge	FL Cup	FA Cup	Others
Cardiff	8.82	–	62	4	4					
Luton Town	7.84	£125,000	30	4	1	1				
Sunderland	2.86	Loan	12							
Huddersfield Town	3.87	Loan	5							
Manchester City*	6.88	£240,000	74	6	5	2				
Middlesbrough	2.91	Loan	19			2				
Bolton Wanderers	9.91	Loan	13			1				
West Bromwich	2.92	Loan	9							

DIBBLE Andrew (Andy) Gerald

Born: Cwmbran,
8 May 1965

Height: 6'2"

Weight: 13.7

International Honours:
W Yth, W "U21"-2, W-3

Position/Skill Factor: Good all-round experienced goal-keeper who is strong on crosses and gets his angles right. A sound last line of defence.

Career History: He started his career with Cardiff City as an associated schoolboy in June 1979, before becoming an apprentice in July 1981. Made his FL debut while still an apprentice at home to Crystal Palace on 8 May 1982, at the end of a season which saw the club relegated to the Third Division. The following term, he was one of five goalies used by City, making 20 League appearances and helping the club back to the Second Division at their first attempt, as runners-up. After a further season at Ninian Park, he moved to Luton Town, but unfortunately, for him, he spent most of his time there as understudy to Les Sealey and was loaned out to Sunderland and Huddersfield Town, despite being capped twice by the full Welsh side against Canada in May 1986. However, he played a few games for the "Hatters" at the end of 1987-88, one of which included the League Cup Final against Arsenal. His 70th minute save from Nigel Winterburn's penalty when Luton were reeling at 2-1 down, was the turning point of the match. Amazingly, Luton found fresh legs to come back to win 3-2, thus collecting their first ever major football trophy. Despite this change of fortunes, three months later he was on his way to Manchester City, where he played a part in the club's successful challenge for promotion back to the First Division.

DICKENS Alan William

Born: Plaistow, 3 September 1964

Height: 6'1" Weight: 12.2

International Honours: E Yth, E "U21"-1

Position/Skill Factor: An attacking midfield player, who will always get into the opposition's penalty box. A stylish, good passer of the ball, he is adept at one-twos around the penalty area.

Career History: Came up through West Ham United's junior ranks having been an associated schoolboy (July 1980) and an apprentice (July 1981). Made his FL debut away to Notts County on 18 December 1982 and scored in a 2-1 win. Had an extended run in the side at the end of that season, but didn't command a regular place until 1985-86, when he missed only one FL match in West Ham's finest ever Football League campaign as they amassed 84 points and third place, only four points behind perennial Champions, Liverpool. Remained a first team regular at Upton Park for three more seasons before being signed by Chelsea in an effort to add some craft to their midfield. He settled in well until a run of three heavy defeats led manager Bobby Campbell to rethink his strategy and he found himself out in the cold. Has since struggled to regain his place in the side. Remained on the fringe of first team action in 1991-92, making only occasional appearances. Clearly needs to rekindle his career.

Clubs	Signing Date	Transfer Fee	APPEARANCES				GOALS			
			Lge	FL Cup	FA Cup	Others	Lge	FL Cup	FA Cup	Others
West Ham United	8.82	–	173+19	14+3	19+3	3	23	3	3	1
Chelsea*	8.89	£650,000	39+9	3		4	1			3

153

DICKINS Matthew (Matt) James

Born: Sheffield,
3 September 1970

Height: 6'4"

Weight: 14.0

Position/Skill Factor: Self assured goalkeeper with a good pair of hands who cuts a commanding figure between the posts.

Career History: Started out with his local club, Sheffield United, as an associated schoolboy in October 1986, before progressing as a trainee (July 1987) to professional status in the 1989 close season. After spending 18 months without a first team appearance at Bramall Lane, he received a free transfer and signed for Lincoln City towards the end of 1990-91. Made his FL debut in a 1-1 draw at Darlington on 9 April 1991 and went on to play in the remaining six games of the season, keeping two clean sheets. Created a big impression in 1991-92, despite missing three months of the season to injury, which cost him a move to Burnley. It all worked out well for him, when he was signed by Second Division Blackburn Rovers just before the transfer deadline as a potential replacement for Bobby Mimms. Sadly, for him, a misjudgment in the last minute of his debut game for Rovers at home to Wolverhampton Wanderers on 14 April 1992, allowed a long range shot from Paul Birch to creep into the net and cost his team a vital point. Mimms was recalled for the remaining League games and the Play-Offs. However, he has a good chance of playing Premier League Football this coming season.

Clubs	Signing Date	Transfer Fee	APPEARANCES				GOALS			
			Lge	FL Cup	FA Cup	Others	Lge	FL Cup	FA Cup	Others
Sheffield United	7.89	–								
Lincoln City	2.91	–	27	1	1	2				
Blackburn Rovers*	3.92	£250,000	1							

DICKOV Paul

Born: Livingston, 1 November 1972

Height: 5'5½" Weight: 11.5

International Honours: S Sch, S Yth, S "U21"-1

Position/Skill Factor: A skilful striker who has the ability to go a long way in the game and is a real competitor.

Career History: Came down south at the beginning of 1989 to sign on as a trainee at Arsenal and after making

good progress, he graduated to the professional ranks a year later. Still to make a first team appearance, he represented the Scottish Under 21 side during the summer.

Clubs	Signing Date	Transfer Fee	APPEARANCES				GOALS			
			Lge	FL Cup	FA Cup	Others	Lge	FL Cup	FA Cup	Others
Arsenal*	12.90	–								

DIXON Kerry Michael

Born: Luton, 24 July 1961

Height: 6'0" Weight: 13.10

International Honours: E "U21"-1, E-8

Position/Skill Factor: An old fashioned striker with an outstanding scoring record. Good in the air, strong on the ball with a good turn of pace, he also creates goals from wide positions with early crosses.

Career History: Son of a former pro, Mike, who turned out for Luton Town and Coventry City, he first played in Tottenham Hotspur's youth team as a centre-forward. No doubt to "Spurs'" later embarrassment, he was released after one year and joined Dunstable Town of the Southern League, where he built a reputation as a prolific goalscorer, before joining Reading. Made his FL debut at home to Walsall on 16 August 1980 and finished the campaign as the club's leading goalscorer. The next season, despite Reading being relegated, he still managed to top the Third Division scoring list with 26 League goals. Joining Chelsea, he quickly made his mark with two strikes in his first match and began to form a lethal partnership with David Speedie, notching 28 goals as the club won the Second Division title in 1983-84. Topped the First Division scoring chart in his first season in the top flight with 24 and despite a great start at international level, he was never given an extended run. This, after making his England debut as a sub against Mexico on 9 June 1985 and playing in the next two full internationals against West Germany and the USA and scoring four goals. Unfortunately for him, his arrival on the international scene coincided with that of Gary Lineker, a very similar player. In 1988-89, after just one season in the Second Division, Dixon's 25 goals were a major factor in the club gaining promotion and the Second Division Championship. His long reign as Chelsea's undisputed first choice centre forward seemed to be drawing to a close in 1991-92 as the goals dried up (only five in 34 FL games) and he lost his place in January to Graham Stuart and new signing, Tony Cascarino. Although restored to the team late in the season, the goals continued to elude him and it now seems unlikely that he will break Chelsea's all-time leading scorers record, currently held by Bobby Tambling with 168 FL goals.

Clubs	Signing Date	Transfer Fee	APPEARANCES				GOALS			
			Lge	FL Cup	FA Cup	Others	Lge	FL Cup	FA Cup	Others
Tottenham Hotspur	7.78	–								
Reading	7.80	£20,000	110+6	6+1	2+1		51			
Chelsea*	8.83	£175,000	331+4	40+1	19+2	25	147	24	8	12

DIXON Lee Michael

Born: Manchester, 17 March 1964

Height: 5'9" Weight: 10.12

International Honours: E"B", FL Rep, E-12

Position/Skill Factor: One of the best attacking full-backs in the country, who gets forward and delivers telling crosses. His coolness under pressure has also proved invaluable in his role of penalty taker.

Career History: Broke into League football with Burnley after coming through the club's junior ranks, making his FL debut at home to Queens Park Rangers on 10 May 1983 and played in a handful of games before moving to Chester City. He spent the best part of two seasons at Sealand Road until signing for Bury, but after just one season he was sold to Stoke City. Proved to be a most reliable defender and was soon transferred to Arsenal in return for a healthy profit margin. However, it wasn't until the beginning of 1988-89 that he won a regular place in the "Gunners'" defence at right-back, when he made the position his own and was rewarded for his consistency with a League Championship medal that season. And on 25 April 1990, he realised another ambition when he made his full England debut against Czechoslovakia at Wembley, sharing the spoils of a 4-2 victory. Was an ever present in 1990-91, scoring five penalties, as Arsenal stormed to their second League Championship in three seasons. His form dipped during 1991-92, no doubt unsettled by a spectacular own goal for Coventry City in an early season game. however, he recovered his poise and assisted the "Gunners" to a superb end of season run, following their mid-season slump. He lost his international place first to Rob Jones and then to Gary Stevens and perhaps was relieved to be recalled for the squad of 20 to compete in the 1992 European Championship Finals in

Sweden. Tragically for him, he was then forced to withdraw through injury.

Clubs	Signing Date	Transfer Fee	APPEARANCES				GOALS			
			Lge	FL Cup	FA Cup	Others	Lge	FL Cup	FA Cup	Others
Burnley	7.82	–	4	1						
Chester City	2.84	–	56+1	2	1	3	1			
Bury	7.85	–	45	4	8	1	6		1	
Stoke City	7.86	£40,000	71	6	7	4	5			
Arsenal*	1.88	£400,000	151+2	16	13	8	15		1	

DOBBS Gerald Francis

Born: Lambeth, 24 January 1971

Height: 5'8" Weight: 11.7

Position/Skill Factor: Enthusiastic midfielder. Always gets his foot in, moves about well and has the ability to take on defenders and beat them.

Career History: Came to Wimbledon straight from school as a trainee in September 1989 and following good progress, he signed professional forms during the 1989 close season. After a long wait, he finally made his FL debut on 2 April 1992 at home to Nottingham Forest, appearing three more times before the end of the 1991-92 season.

Clubs	Signing Date	Transfer Fee	APPEARANCES				GOALS			
			Lge	FL Cup	FA Cup	Others	Lge	FL Cup	FA Cup	Others
Wimbledon*	7.89	–	2+2							

DOBSON Anthony (Tony) John

Born: Coventry, 5 February 1969

Height: 6'1" Weight: 12.10

International Honours: E "U21"-4

Position/Skill Factor: Big, strong tackling left-back, or central defender, with a great left foot.

Career History: Locally born and bred, he signed for Coventry City as an apprentice in June 1985, graduating to the professional ranks a year later and after making good progress in the reserve side, he made his FL debut as a substitute at home to Leicester City on 6 December, 1986. Established himself at left-back from February 1989 to the end of the season when he won his four England Under 21 caps. Lost his place in October 1989 and when he returned it was more in central defence than his favoured position of left-back. Eclipsed by Paul Edwards from the start of 1990-91, he only played a handful of games, before deciding to further his career with ambitious Blackburn Rovers. At Ewood Park, he took up a position in central defence and assisted Rovers to stave off relegation in the closing weeks of the season. Dropped after only four games of 1991-92, he took little further part in the club's ultimately successful promotion campaign and will be hoping for a change of luck in 1992-93.

Clubs	Signing Date	Transfer Fee	APPEARANCES				GOALS			
			Lge	FL Cup	FA Cup	Others	Lge	FL Cup	FA Cup	Others
Coventry City	7.86	–	51+3	5+3	1	0+1	1			
Blackburn Rovers*	1.91	£300,000	21+1	2		1				

DODD Jason Robert

Born: Bath,
2 November 1970

Height: 5'10"

Weight: 11.10

International Honours:
E "U21"-8

Position/Skill Factor: Very useful right-back. All-round player who can defend, pass the ball well and is better than average in the air. Often comes forward to join up with the attack.

Career History: Joined Southampton as an 18-year-old from the Beazer Homes League side, Bath City, at the end of 1988-89. Made his FL debut the following season at Queens Park Rangers on 14 October 1989, when the "Saints" won 4-1 and in the next game, his first home appearance, Liverpool were trounced by the same scoreline. Had a good initial season, making 21 League appear-

ances in all, but had to share the number two shirt with Alexei Cherednik during 1990-91. In 1991-92, he seemed to have established himself as the undisputed right-back at The Dell, only to lose his place to Jeff Kenna in the second-half of the season.

Clubs	Signing Date	Transfer Fee	APPEARANCES				GOALS			
			Lge	FL Cup	FA Cup	Others	Lge	FL Cup	FA Cup	Others
Southampton*	3.89	£50,000	63+6	14+1	10	5				

DOHERTY Adrian John

Born: Strabane, 10 June 1973

Height: 5'8" Weight: 10.6

Position/Skill Factor: Midfield player. A good prospect, he is very quick with excellent ball skills.

Career History: A Manchester United associated schoolboy signing in November 1987, he turned professional at Old Trafford on leaving school during the 1990 close season.

Clubs	Signing Date	Transfer Fee	APPEARANCES				GOALS			
			Lge	FL Cup	FA Cup	Others	Lge	FL Cup	FA Cup	Others
Manchester United*	7.90	–								

DONACHIE William (Willie)

Born: Glasgow, 15 October 1951

Height: 5'9" Weight: 11.5

International Honours: S "U23"-2, S-35

Position/Skill Factor: Very experienced left-back, or midfield player. Still shows all his old enthusiasm and hasn't lost his wonderful footballing brain. A good passer of the ball, he has pace and style.

Career History: Signed for Manchester City from Glasgow Amateurs in October 1968, shortly after his 17th birthday. Turning pro, he made his FL debut in midfield at home to Nottingham Forest on 7 February 1970. He became a regular in the side during 1970-71 and was converted to left-back, following the broken leg suffered by Glyn Pardoe. His great displays in the number three shirt did not go unrecognised internationally and he made his debut in the full Scotland team in a 2-0 victory over Peru on 26 April 1972. A regular over the next eight years, he was an ever present in both 1973-74 and 1976-77 and won a League Cup winners medal in 1976 when City defeated Newcastle United, 2-1. After more than 400 appearances for the club, he left to join Portland Timbers in the North American Soccer League, although he came back for a while with Norwich City, before returning to the States. Signed for Burnley in 1982-83 where he was a guiding influence to the youngsters, until given a free transfer in the 1984 close season and joining Oldham Athletic. Prior to 1988-89, he was still a driving force for the "Latics" from midfield, but during the past three seasons he has predominantly played out his career in the reserve side.

Recently appointed club coach at Boundary Park, he didn't make any FL appearances in 1991-92 and in coming up to 40 years of age, his first team days would appear to be behind him.

Clubs	Signing Date	Transfer Fee	APPEARANCES				GOALS			
			Lge	FL Cup	FA Cup	Others	Lge	FL Cup	FA Cup	Others
Manchester City	12.68	–	347+4	40	21		2			
Portland (NASL)	3.80	£200,000								
Norwich City	9.81	£200,000	11	3						
Portland (NASL)	3.82	£200,000								
Burnley	11.82	–	60	4	12	4	3			
Oldham Athletic*	7.84	–	158+11	13+2	5	2	3			

DONAGHY Malachy (Mal) Martin

Born: Belfast, 13 September 1957

Height: 5'10" Weight: 12.7

International Honours: NI "U21"-1, NI-76

Position/Skill Factor: Full-back, cum central defender, who does the job without any fuss. A good positional player, he is not easy to beat and passes the ball simply, but effectively.

Career History: Joined Luton Town from the Irish League side, Larne, in the 1978 close season and made his FL debut at home in a 6-1 thrashing of Oldham Athletic

on 19 August 1978. Settled into the side as a regular and was an ever present in 1979-80, 1980-81, 1981-82, 1984-85, 1985-56 and 1986-87 and during his ten years at Kenilworth Road, he only missed 16 League games, a remarkable record of consistency. Won the first of many international caps when he played for Northern Ireland against Scotland at Windsor Park on 16 May 1980 and shared the spoils of a 1-0 victory. Originally played at left-back, but was switched to central defence in 1981-82, following the transfer of Paul Price to Tottenham. Although not noted as a goalscorer, he scored nine in 1981-82 when the club won the Second Division title. Prior to signing for Manchester United, he also won a League Cup winners medal when Luton beat Arsenal 3-2 in 1988. At United, he initially played alongside Steve Bruce at the centre of the defence, but on the arrival of Gary Pallister he was switched to right-back. Following a lay off through injury in 1989-90, he was loaned back to Luton in an effort to speed up match fitness, before returning to Old Trafford. In 1990-91 he wore five different shirts, although nearly always operating in central defence and was on the bench for the European Cup Winners Cup Final win over Barcelona. Remained a valuable squad player in 1991-92, covering for Steve Bruce and Gary Pallister and for both full-back positions as required. Unlucky to miss out on United's League Cup Final victory over Nottingham Forest, as he had played regularly in the preceding weeks. Instead, manager Alex Ferguson recalled Paul Parker, who was returning after injury.

Clubs	Signing Date	Transfer Fee	APPEARANCES				GOALS			
			Lge	FL Cup	FA Cup	Others	Lge	FL Cup	FA Cup	Others
Luton Town	6.78	£20,000	410	34	36	3	16	2	3	
Manchester United*	10.88	£650,000	76+12	9+5	10	3+3				
Luton Town	12.89	Loan	5							

DONNELLY Darren Charles

Born: Liverpool, 28 December 1971

Height: 5'10" Weight: 11.6

Position/Skill Factor: A skilful striker who leads the line well and can score goals.

Career History: A young player who looks to have a bright future, he first came to Blackburn Rovers as an associated schoolboy in April 1986, before signing as a trainee on leaving school in July 1988. After turning professional during the 1990 close season, he made his FL debut when coming on as substitute at home to Charlton Athletic on 13 April 1990 and was later rewarded with his first full game at Millwall on the last day of the season. He made no further appearances in 1991-92 and with so many forwards on the books at Ewood Park, he may have to tough it out in the reserves for a while.

Clubs	Signing Date	Transfer Fee	APPEARANCES				GOALS			
			Lge	FL Cup	FA Cup	Others	Lge	FL Cup	FA Cup	Others
Blackburn Rovers*	6.90	–	1+1							

DOOLAN John

Born: Liverpool, 7 May 1974

Height: 5'11½" Weight: 12.4

Position: Central defender.

Career History: A local discovery, he joined the Everton professional staff during the 1992 close season, having previously been at Goodison as an associated schoolboy (February 1989) and as a trainee (June 1990).

Clubs	Signing Date	Transfer Fee	APPEARANCES				GOALS			
			Lge	FL Cup	FA Cup	Others	Lge	FL Cup	FA Cup	Others
Everton*	6.92	–								

DORIGO Anthony (Tony) Robert

Born: Melbourne, Australia, 31 December 1965

Height: 5'8" Weight: 10.7

International Honours: E "U21"-11, E"B", E-10

Position/Skill Factor: Attacking left-back with a lovely left foot. Plays like a midfielder when in possession. Likes nothing better than surging upfield with the ball and his deep crosses have created many goal scoring opportunities. Also packs a fierce shot from free-kicks.

Career History: Emigrated from Australia to sign associated schoolboy forms for Aston Villa in January 1982, before being apprenticed in September of the same year. made his FL debut away to Ipswich Town on 12 May 1984 and claimed a regular place over the next two seasons. Joined Chelsea when Villa were relegated from the First Division, but saw his new club suffer the same fate at the end of his first season there. However, the "Blues" bounced straight back as Second Division Champions in 1988-89, with Dorigo's raids down the left flank helping to make goals for both Kerry Dixon and Gordon Durie. Also scored the only goal of the game when Chelsea beat Middlesbrough in the 1989-90 Zenith Data Cup Final at Wembley. Now a regular in the England squad, he made his full international debut against Yugoslavia at Wembley on 6 September 1989, when coming off the sub's bench. Transferred to Leeds in the summer of 1991, his signing perhaps was the final piece of the jigsaw for Howard Wilkinson, in creating a perfectly balanced team with experienced quality players in each position. Reached the zenith of his career to date, playing an outstanding role in Leeds' unexpected, but well merited League Championship triumph. At international level he is unlucky to understudy one of England's (and Europe's) finest players in Stuart Pearce. Nevertheless, he won four more caps in 1991-92 and was included in Graham Taylor's squad of 20 for the 1992 European Championship Finals in Sweden, although he did not make an appearance.

Clubs	Signing Date	Transfer Fee	APPEARANCES				GOALS			
			Lge	FL Cup	FA Cup	Others	Lge	FL Cup	FA Cup	Others
Aston Villa	7.83	–	106+5	14+1	7	2	1			
Chelsea	5.87	£475,000	146	14	4	16	11			1
Leeds United*	5.91	£1,300,000	38	5	1	1	3			

DOWIE Iain

Born: Hatfield, 9 January 1965

Height: 6'1"

Weight: 12.12

International Honours: NI "U21"-1, NI-11

Position/Skill Factor: Big powerful striker who is an excellent header of the ball, particularly at the far post. A good target man, he brings his team-mates into the game with clever flicks and headers.

Career History: Was a relatively late arrival to League football at the age of 23, joining Luton Town from non-League Hendon, having previously played with St Albans City, Hertford Town and Cheshunt. Made his FL debut at Charlton Athletic on 14 January 1989 as a substitute and only played in one full game that season. Finally, won a regular place up front in November 1989, after Roy Wegerle had departed to Queens Park Rangers and his four goals in the final five matches, helped Luton claw themselves away from the foot of the First Division to avoid relegation on goal difference. His good form did not go unnoticed at international level, either and he made his debut as a sub for Northern Ireland against Norway on 27 March 1990 in Belfast. In 1990-91, after scoring twice in the 3-1 win over Liverpool and getting the winner against Nottingham Forest, he was transferred to West Ham United, who were looking to bolster their First Division prospects. Promotion was duly attained, with Iain playing in the final 12 matches and scoring four goals. Surprisingly, in view of the "Hammers'" subsequent inability to score, he was transferred to Southampton in the early weeks of 1991-92 and played a significant role in the "Saints'" ultimately successful struggle against relegation. Whilst goal scoring opportunities were scarce in the club's essentially negative style of play, all of his nine FL goals were either match winners, or point savers.

Clubs	Signing Date	Transfer Fee	APPEARANCES				GOALS			
			Lge	FL Cup	FA Cup	Others	Lge	FL Cup	FA Cup	Others
Luton Town	12.88	£30,000	53+13	3+1	1+2	5	15			
Fulham	9.89	Loan	5				1			
West Ham United	3.91	£480,000	12				4			
Southampton*	9.91	£500,000	25+5	1+3	4	4	9			

DOYLE **Maurice**

Born: Ellesmere Port, 17 October 1969

Height: 5'8" Weight: 10.7

Position/Skill Factor: A midfielder with very good engines who loves to battle for the ball, he has the right ingredients to become a good player, but needs more experience.

Career History: Made his FL debut for Crewe Alexandra, while still a trainee, at Tranmere Rovers on 25 April 1988 in a 2-2 draw. Started life at Gresty Road as an associated schoolboy (December 1985), before becoming a trainee in July 1986 and turning pro with the club in the 1988 close season. Had appeared in only three full League games, although scoring twice, in 1988-89, when Queens Park Rangers signed him as a player for the future. Yet to play for the "Rs", he was back on loan with his old club for a spell in 1990-91. Made no first team appearances during 1991-92 and it now seems unlikely that he will achieve a breakthrough with Q.P.R.

Clubs	Signing Date	Transfer Fee	APPEARANCES				GOALS			
			Lge	FL Cup	FA Cup	Others	Lge	FL Cup	FA Cup	Others
Crewe Alexandra	7.88	–	6+2				2			
Q.P.R.*	4.89	£120,000								
Crewe Alexandra	1.91	Loan	6+1		2		2			

DOZZELL **Jason** Alvin Winans

Born: Ipswich, 19 December 1967

Height: 6'2" Weight: 12.0

International Honours: E Yth, E "U21"-9

Position/Skill Factor: Midfield player with lovely skills, whose first touch gives him both time and space. Good in the air, he is also highly capable of scoring with late runs into the box.

Career History: Local boy who has come through the ranks with Ipswich Town, firstly as an associated schoolboy (February 1982) and then as an apprentice (April 1984), before turning pro. Actually made his FL debut while still an associated schools player, coming on as a sub at home to Coventry City on 4 February 1984 and scoring in a 3-1 victory. At 16 years and 56 days, he is the youngest player ever to have appeared in a League match for Ipswich. In 1985-86 he won a regular place in the side, but it was not enough to save them from relegation to the Second Division. Was ever present in Town's team the following season and yet again in 1989-90, when he was a key team player in midfield. Lost his place at the beginning of 1990-91 and when John Lyall restored him to the first team in November it was in a forward position. He continued in this role during Ipswich's Second Division Championship campaign of 1991-92 in partnership with Chris Kiwomya. Although not a prolific scorer (11 goals in 45 FL games), his deft touches create scoring opportunities for his colleagues. Also scored four goals in five FA Cup games, including one in extra-time at Anfield in a

Fifth Round replay, which seemed certain to give Ipswich a historic victory — never having won there in 25 visits. On this, as on so many other occasions, Liverpool "came back from the dead" to win the tie. Will be a vital player for Town in their bid to establish themselves in the Premier League.

Clubs	Signing Date	Transfer Fee	APPEARANCES				GOALS			
			Lge	FL Cup	FA Cup	Others	Lge	FL Cup	FA Cup	Others
Ipswich Town*	12.84	–	271+20	22+1	18	22	45	3	10	4

Clubs	Signing Date	Transfer Fee	APPEARANCES				GOALS			
			Lge	FL Cup	FA Cup	Others	Lge	FL Cup	FA Cup	Others
Grimsby Town	6.78	–	242+30	20+4	12+3		89	9	5	
Norwich City	8.85	£105,000	121	11	6	12	50	2	2	3
Glasgow Rangers	6.88	£600,000								
Coventry City*	10.89	£800,000	34+7	3+3	4+1	2	5	4		
Birmingham City	10.91	Loan	5+2							

DRINKELL Kevin Smith

Born: Grimsby,
18 June 1960

Height: 5'11"

Weight; 12.6

Position/Skill Factor: Striker, who shields the ball well and. gets a lot of "flick ons" with his head. Capable of bringing teams into the game with effective passes both inside and around the opposition's penalty area.

Career History: Joined his local club, Grimsby Town, as an apprentice in June 1978 and made his FL debut at home to Gillingham on 11 April 1977, while still a junior. He helped Town out of the Fourth Division in 1978-79, before winning a Third Division Championship medal the following season and was a key member as the club settled into Division Two. By 1984-85 he was forming a successful attacking strike-force with Paul Wilkinson, but after declining to sign a new contract at Blundell Park he left to join Norwich City in the 1985 close season. Scoring 22 goals in 41 games during his first season, he was good value for his Second Division Championship medal as Norwich gained promotion. After maintaining that impressive strike rate over the next two years, Graeme Souness added him to Glasgow Rangers' growing list of English exiles and although he was there for little more than a year, he won both Premier Division Championship and League Cup medals. Never settled in Scotland and after losing his place in 1989-90, John Sillett, Coventry City's manager, paid out a club record fee, hoping that he was the man to link up with David Speedie. However, the move was not a great success as he was unfortunately ravaged by injuries, playing only 32 League matches in two season. During 1991-92 it was a costly error in hindsight by Coventry, because two years after signing for the "Sky Blues" he was granted a free transfer. Unfortunately, he was no longer of interest to First Division clubs and few others could match his Coventry salary. Although he played a handful games for Coventry and was also on loan to Birmingham during the season, his career is now "in limbo".

DUFFIELD Peter

Born: Middlesbrough, 4 February 1969

Height: 5'6" Weight: 10.7

Position/Skill Factor: Hard working forward who can also play in midfield when required. Often capable of scoring vital goals.

Career History: Began his career with his home town club, Middlesbrough, where he signed as an associated schoolboy in September 1984 and as a trainee in August 1985, before going pro. He was released at a time when Middlesbrough were facing bankruptcy, cutting and cut their playing staff to a mere 14 and signed for Sheffield United in the summer of 1987. Made his FL debut as a sub at home to Leicester City on 17 October 1987, but after only a handful of games in his first year, he was loaned out to Fourth Division Halifax Town. Had better fortune there and in his first League game, a 2-2 draw against Scunthorpe United, he scored in the opening minute and followed that up with a second goal, 12 minutes later. After scoring at the rate of a goal every two games during the loan period, he arrived back at Bramall Lane and following a run of subs' appearances and with United losing their way in the Third Division promotion battle, he got the chance he had been waiting for. Having taken on the job of penalty king, he helped himself to a dozen goals as United returned to the Second Division as runners-up. Out in the cold again, his first match of the 1989-90 campaign was when he came on as a substitute against Portsmouth to score twice in a 2-1 win. Six weeks later, he suffered a broken leg, sustained while scoring against Swindon Town. Since that injury, he has only managed a few appearances from the bench as he looks to fight his way back into first team reckoning. Following two substitute appearances for the "Blades" early in 1991-92, he fell out of favour and had an unsuccessful spell on trial at St. Mirren during the latter half of the season, before arriving back at Bramall Lane.

Clubs	Signing Date	Transfer Fee	APPEARANCES				GOALS			
			Lge	FL Cup	FA Cup	Others	Lge	FL Cup	FA Cup	Others
Middlesbrough	11.86	–								
Sheffield United*	8.87	–	34+24	2+5	6+2	3	16	2	1	3
Halifax Town	3.88	Loan	12			1	6			
Rotherham United	3.91	Loan	17				5			

DURIE Gordon Scott

Born: Paisley, 6 December 1965

Height: 5'10" Weight: 13.0

International Honours: S "U21"-4, S"B", S-21

Position/Skill Factor: A skilful, strong running striker who is capable of scoring spectacular goals. Has the ability to ghost past defenders and makes good runs off the ball. Always looking to score when inside the box.

Career History: Began his soccer career with Scottish junior side, Hill O'Beath, before signing for East Fife and then Hibernian. After scoring 40 goals in 111 matches, he was soon attracting scouts from south of the border and Chelsea moved in quickly for him. He made his FL debut at Stamford Bridge against Watford on 5 May 1986 in the last game of the 1985-86 season and the "Blues" were beaten 5-1. Found it difficult to win a first team place initially, but once David Speedie had left for Coventry City, he became a regular up front, alongside Kerry Dixon. Although unfortunate to be dogged by injuries, he has still managed to score over 50 League goals for Chelsea, including five in a 7-0 win at Walsall during 1988-89, the season that the "Blues" ran away with the Second Division Championship. Earlier, after winning Under-21 honours, he finally made his debut for the full Scottish side as a substitute in a European Championship qualifying round in Bulgaria on 11 November 1987. Struggled with injuries in 1990-91, but still finished as Chelsea's top scorer with 12 goals from 24 League outings. On the eve of the 1991-92 season, he was transferred to Tottenham Hotspur for a massive fee and by comparison with his

time at Chelsea, he remained relatively injury free in his first season at White Hart Lane, playing in 31 League games. Unfortunately, his scoring touch deserted him, going 17 League games without a goal between September 1991 and late March 1992, before ending his "drought" with a hat-trick against Coventry City. Six FL goals, plus four in cup matches, was hardly the return "Spurs" were expecting on their investment. Despite his disappointing tally at club level, he remained first choice for Scotland's national team and was included in Andy Roxburgh's squad for the European Championship Finals in Sweden where he played against both Holland and Germany with some distinction.

Clubs	Signing Date	Transfer Fee	APPEARANCES				GOALS			
			Lge	FL Cup	FA Cup	Others	Lge	FL Cup	FA Cup	Others
Chelsea	4.86	£380,000	115+8	10	6	12	51	5	1	3
Tottenham Hotspur*	8.91	£2,200,000	31	6	1	8	6	2		3

DURRANT Lee Roger

Born: Great Yarmouth, 18 December 1973

Height: 5'7" Weight: 10.10

International Honours: E Sch

Position: Left sided midfield player.

Career History: Signed professional forms for Ipswich Town during the 1992 close season, having come to Portman Road as a trainee in July 1990. No first team experience.

Clubs	Signing Date	Transfer Fee	APPEARANCES				GOALS			
			Lge	FL Cup	FA Cup	Others	Lge	FL Cup	FA Cup	Others
Ipswich*	6.92	–								

EARLE Robert (Robbie) Gerald

Born: Newcastle-under-Lyme, 27 January 1965

Height: 5'9" Weight: 10.10

Position/Skill Factor: Attacking midfield player with great energy and excellent in the air. Times his runs into the box to score valuable goals with great precision.

Career History: Made his FL debut for Port Vale, after playing in their junior sides, at Swindon Town on 28 August 1982 in a 1-0 defeat. However, it wasn't until 1984-85 that he gained a regular place in the team and was an ever present (including subs' appearances), scoring 15 goals. When he came into soccer with the club, Vale were in the Fourth Division and although promoted shortly after, they were soon relegated. His play was instrumental in raising them to Second Division status by 1988-89 and injuries apart, his appearances were guaranteed. Prior to Vale gaining promotion from the Third Division for the first time since 1953-54, he had formed an effective partnership with Andy Jones. Since Jones' departure to

Charlton Athletic in September 1988, he has played in midfield, but with no perceptible reduction in his strike rate (one goal per 3.4 games) which is probably better than any other regular midfielder in the Football League. It is perhaps surprising that no first Division club had made a move for him before Wimbledon's massive offer in the 1991 close season. Adjusted to First Division football without a tremor, scoring in his first three games for the "Dons" and ending the season as second top scorer with 14 goals from 40 games — clearly a very sound investment.

Clubs	Signing Date	Transfer Fee	APPEARANCES				GOALS			
			Lge	FL Cup	FA Cup	Others	Lge	FL Cup	FA Cup	Others
Port Vale	7.82	–	284+10	21+2	20+1	18+1	77	4	4	5
Wimbledon*	7.91	£775,000	40	2	2	1	14			1

EDGEHILL **Richard** Arlon

Born: Oldham, 23 September 1974

Height: 5'8½" Weight: 11.2

Position: Defender.

Career History: Joined the Manchester City professional staff during the 1992 close season, having previously been at the club as an associated schoolboy (November 1988) and as a trainee (July 1991). No first team experience.

Clubs	Signing Date	Transfer Fee	APPEARANCES				GOALS			
			Lge	FL Cup	FA Cup	Others	Lge	FL Cup	FA Cup	Others
Manchester City*	6.92	–								

EBBRELL **John** Keith

Born: Bromborough,
1 October 1969

Height: 5'7"

Weight: 9.12

International Honours:
E Sch, E Yth,
E "U21"-14, E"B"

Position/Skill Factor: Talented midfielder with two good feet and lovely balance. Sprays passes all over the park and is always looking to create chances for others.

Career History: From the Lilleshall School of Excellence, he joined Everton as an associated schoolboy in November 1983 and graduated to trainee status in July 1986. His FL debut came as a substitute at home to Wimbledon on 4 February 1989 and he had played a further 13 full League matches by the end of the following season. 1990-91 saw him open his scoring account with the club on the very first day against Leeds United and he went on to play in 34 League matches, while proving a major influence in turning Everton's season around, following their dismal start. Played in all but three end of season games for Everton in 1991-92 and will clearly be an integral part of the Everton team for years to come. A mainstay of the England Under 21 team since 1988, he may soon come into contention for his full international debut.

EDINBURGH **Justin** Charles

Born: Brentwood,
18 December 1969

Height: 5'9"

Weight: 11.6

Position/Skill Factor: Full-back with a good left foot, who will join up with the attack at every opportunity.

Career History: Discovered by Southend United, he signed as a trainee in July 1986 before turning pro and making his FL debut at home to Cardiff City on 23 September 1988. Although yet to become a regular at Roots Hall, he had shown such early promise in the number three shirt that London giants, Tottenham Hotspur, were suitably convinced that he was a star of the future and moved for him in the 1990 close season, after taking a close look at him during a loan period at White Hart Lane from January to March 1990. Having played a few games before Christmas during his first term, he was then alternating with Pat van den Hauwe and Mitchell Thomas in either of the full-back positions, right through to the end of the season. His year was complete, when after being selected for the "Spurs'" FA Cup Final team against Nottingham Forest, he received a winners medal following a 2-1 victory. He started 1991-92 in the reserves, regained his place in October, but lost it again in November. Restored to favour in March 1992, he stayed in the side until the end of the season.

Clubs	Signing Date	Transfer Fee	APPEARANCES				GOALS			
			Lge	FL Cup	FA Cup	Others	Lge	FL Cup	FA Cup	Others
Everton*	11.86	–	87+9	9	10	6+2	4	1	2	1

Clubs	Signing Date	Transfer Fee	APPEARANCES				GOALS			
			Lge	FL Cup	FA Cup	Others	Lge	FL Cup	FA Cup	Others
Southend United	7.88	–	36+1	2+1	2	4+1				1
Tottenham Hotspur*	7.90	£150,000	36+3	6+2	5	3	1			

EDWARDS Paul

Born: Birkenhead,
25 December 1963

Height: 5'11"

Weight: 11.0

Position/Skill Factor: Excellent attacking full-back with a cultured left foot. Good passer, who would rather use the ball constructively than kick upfield.

Career History: Signed by Crewe Alexandra from Vauxhall Conference team Altrincham, he made his FL debut when coming on as a sub at Hartlepool United on 27 February 1988. Was soon a regular in the number three shirt and in his first full season, 1988-89, he only missed one match as the club gained promotion from the Fourth Division in third place. Highly rated by his fellow professionals, he was selected as best left-back in the Third Division in the annual PFA awards of 1989-90 and it came as no surprise when Coventry City stepped in and signed him at the tail-end of the season. He went straight into the side and following a sticky start, settled down well after taking over from Greg Downs, although due to injuries he played in only two of the last 17 games of 1990-91. Lost his place to former England international Kenny Sansom and the emerging Lee Hurst and was unable to win it back during 1991-92, making only a few fleeting appearances in the first two months of the season.

Clubs	Signing Date	Transfer Fee	APPEARANCES				GOALS			
			Lge	FL Cup	FA Cup	Others	Lge	FL Cup	FA Cup	Others
Crewe Alexandra	1.88	–	82+4	6	8	7+1	6			1
Coventry City*	3.90	£350,000	32+4	6	2	2				

EDWARDS Russell

Born: Beckenham, 21 December 1973

Height: 6'2" Weight: 12.7

Position: Defender.

Career History: A 1992 close season professional signing for Crystal Palace, having been at the club since joining as an associated schoolboy in March 1988 and graduating

through the club's junior ranks. No first team experience as yet.

Clubs	Signing Date	Transfer Fee	APPEARANCES				GOALS			
			Lge	FL Cup	FA Cup	Others	Lge	FL Cup	FA Cup	Others
Crystal Palace*	6.92	–								

EHIOGU Ugochuku (Ugo)

Born: Hackney,
3 November 1972

Height: 6'1"

Weight: 12.0

International Honours:
E "U21"-4

Position/Skill Factor: A good defender with great pace who is more than capable of man to man marking.

Career History: Came through the West Bromwich Albion junior ranks as a trainee (July 1989) and made his FL debut wearing the number 14 shirt at Hull City on 22 September 1990, appearing once more as a substitute in 1990-91. Normally, clubs with trainees on contract have first option on their services, but before formalities could be completed, Aston Villa stepped in and signed him during 1991-92, creating considerable ill feeling between the two clubs, not assuaged by the modest fee decided upon by the tribunal. Clearly it was a good move for Ugo, who was included in the Villa first team squad from the start of the season, making his debut at right-back at home to Arsenal on 24 August, 1991. Remained on the fringe of the first team all season, making nine further appearances. Called up to the England Under 21 squad, he made his international debut at the end of the season, before participating in the annual Under 21 tournament in Toulon, France.

Clubs	Signing Date	Transfer Fee	APPEARANCES				GOALS			
			Lge	FL Cup	FA Cup	Others	Lge	FL Cup	FA Cup	Others
W.B.A. (Tr)	7.89	–	0+2							
Aston Villa*	7.91	£40,000	4+4		0+1	1				

ELKINS Gary

Born: Wallingford, 4 May 1966

Height: 5'9" Weight: 11.13

International Honours: E Yth

Position/Skill Factor: Attacking full-back with a smart left foot and a good enough range of passes that allow him to play in midfield when required.

Career History: Became a Fulham apprentice in July 1982 and within a year of turning pro he had made his FL debut in a 2-1 win at home against Middlesbrough on 22 September 1984. Unfortunately, just as he was beginning to work his way into the team, he suffered a broken leg in February 1986. Out of the side for over a year, he came back, appearing on and off, mainly in the number three shirt, until transferred to Wimbledon following a loan period at Exeter City. Playing only sporadically in 1990-91, he spent most of his first season at Plough Lane, deputising for Terry Phelan, when required. Whilst still a cover player, he made 17 full appearances in 1991-92, often in midfield and proved a useful man to have in the wings.

Clubs	Signing Date	Transfer Fee	APPEARANCES				GOALS			
			Lge	FL Cup	FA Cup	Others	Lge	FL Cup	FA Cup	Others
Fulham	12.83	–	100+4	6	2+2	7+1	2			
Exeter City	12.89	Loan	5							
Wimbledon*	8.90	£20,000	25+3	1		1+1	1			

ELLIOTT Paul Marcellus

Born: Lewisham,
18 March 1964

Height: 6'2"

Weight: 14.1

International Honours:
E Yth, E "U21"-3

Position/Skill Factor: Centre-back who reads the game well. Dangerous from set pieces, he is very quick and often saves the day with last ditch tackles.

Career History: Was an associated schoolboy with Charlton Athletic (April 1980), before becoming an apprentice a few months later in July 1980. His FL debut was in an away match against Crystal Palace on 12 September 1981 and, injuries apart, stayed in the team until transferred to Luton Town when the club were under severe financial pressures. Had two full seasons at Kenilworth Road before Aston Villa decided that he was the man they needed as a replacement for Brendan Ormsby, who was injured. Was lured to Italy in the summer of 1987, playing with Pisa for two years. At the end of his contract he returned not to England, but to Scotland, signing for Celtic and played for his new club in the Scottish Cup Final against Aberdeen in 1990, collecting a runners-up medal. During 1991-92, after two years with the "Bhoys", he returned to London, signing for Chelsea. Although performing well personally, his defensive partners were constantly changing in a shaky defence, and it was another disappointing season for the "Blues".

Clubs	Signing Date	Transfer Fee	APPEARANCES				GOALS			
			Lge	FL Cup	FA Cup	Others	Lge	FL Cup	FA Cup	Others
Charlton Athletic	3.81	–	61+2	2	1		1			
Luton Town	3.83	£95,000	63+3	5	2		4			
Aston Villa	12.85	£400,000	56+1	7	4	1	7			
Pisa (Italy)	7.87	£400,000								
Glasgow Celtic	6.89	£600,000								
Chelsea*	7.91	£1,400,000	35	2	5	5	3			

EVERINGHAM Nicholas Peter

Born: Hull, 1 December 1973

Height: 5'10" Weight: 10.12

International Honours: E Yth

Position: Midfield player.

Career History: Joined the Oldham Athletic professional ranks during the summer of 1992, having previously been at the club as an associated schoolboy (June 1988) and as a trainee (July 1990). No first team experience.

Clubs	Signing Date	Transfer Fee	APPEARANCES				GOALS			
			Lge	FL Cup	FA Cup	Others	Lge	FL Cup	FA Cup	Others
Oldham Athletic*	6.92	–								

FAIRCLOUGH Courtney (Chris) Huw

Born: Nottingham,
12 April 1964

Height: 5'11"

Weight: 11.2

International Honours:
E "U21"-7, E "B"

Position/Skill Factor: Good, reliable centre-back who clears his lines with the minimum fuss. Does well in the air, sticking his head in even when he is likely to get injured.

Career History: The elder brother of Mansfield Town's Wayne, he was a Nottingham Forest associated schools player (November 1978) and apprentice (July 1980), before making his FL debut at Anfield on 4 September 1982 when Liverpool won 4-3. Played over 100 games at Forest, despite missing the entire 1985-86 season through injury. Joined Tottenham in the summer of 1987 and was an ever present in his first season at White Hart Lane. Leeds signed him just before the March 1989 transfer deadline in order to stiffen their defence and in helping the club to become the Second Division Champions in 1989-90, he formed a solid defensive partnership with Peter Haddock, while also making a valuable contribution at the other end with eight goals. Back in the top flight for 1990-91, his new partner was Chris Whyte and between them they missed only six games all season as the side finished fourth in the table. After dropping out of the team with injury early into 1991-92, he returned in October to resume his partnership with Whyte, which was the bedrock on which Leeds' eventual League Championship triumph was based.

Clubs	Signing Date	Transfer Fee	APPEARANCES				GOALS			
			Lge	FL Cup	FA Cup	Others	Lge	FL Cup	FA Cup	Others
Nottingham Forest	10.81	–	102+5	9+1	6	9+2	1	1		
Tottenham Hotspur	6.87	£387,000	60	7	3		5			
Leeds United*	3.89	£500,000	117+1	11+2	8	8	15	2		

FAIRWEATHER Carlton

Born: Camberwell, 22 September 1961

Height: 5'11" Weight: 11.0

Position/Skill Factor: Left-winger with a cultured left foot who is a good crosser of the ball. He has a good footballing brain and is always trying to create goal scoring chances. Also, excellent in the air.

Career History: Signed for Wimbledon, after attracting considerable attention with some strong performances for Tooting and Mitcham of the then Isthmian (now Diadora League), having previously played for Bromley and Dulwich Hamlet. He made his FL debut at Oldham Athletic on New Year's Day, 1985, scoring the only goal of the game and the following season he helped the "Dons" gain promotion to the First Division. During seven years at Wimbledon, he has yet to win a permanent place in the side, but when called upon he often pops up to score important goals. After playing in the first six games of 1991-92, he was discarded for the remainder of the season, suffering the same fate as Wimbledon's other wingers (Bennett and Anthrobus).

Clubs	Signing Date	Transfer Fee	APPEARANCES				GOALS			
			Lge	FL Cup	FA Cup	Others	Lge	FL Cup	FA Cup	Others
Wimbledon*	12.84	£13,000	118+20	15+1	9+1	7+1	26	1	1	

FALCONER William (Willie) Henry

Born: Aberdeen,
5 April 1966

Height: 6'1"

Weight: 12.10

International Honours:
S Sch, S Yth

Position/Skill Factor: Left sided player who can perform equally well at left-back, or in midfield. Scores goals from dead ball situations where his height makes him a danger to most defences.

Career History: Discovered playing for Lewis United, a Scottish junior side, he joined Aberdeen in 1983, making 77 appearances and scoring 13 goals in five seasons, before moving south of the border to sign for Watford during the 1988 close season. Struggled to hold down a regular place, after making his FL debut at home to Birmingham City on 27 August 1988, playing in several different positions following his arrival at Vicarage Road, he was nevertheless a valuable member of the first team squad. Predominantly a midfielder, he can score important goals and three in the final five matches of 1990-91, including winners against Charlton Athletic and Portsmouth, were just enough to keep the "Hornets" in the Second Division by the skin of their teeth. Signed by new manager Lennie Lawrence for Middlesbrough in the 1991 close season, he made an excellent start with his new club, scoring four goals in his first ten games from midfield, before a serious long term injury suffered in late September, put him out of contention for six months. He returned to the team in March 1992 in time to assist their charge for promotion, playing both in midfield and at left-back. Despite some hiccups, the team finally achieved second place and automatic promotion and no doubt he will be an important cog in the club's efforts to establish itself in the Premier League.

Clubs	Signing Date	Transfer Fee	APPEARANCES				GOALS			
			Lge	FL Cup	FA Cup	Others	Lge	FL Cup	FA Cup	Others
Watford	6.88	£300,000	85+13	5	6	4+3	12		1	
Middlesbrough*	8.91	£200,000	25	1+1			5			

FARRELL David William

Born: Birmingham, 11 November 1971

Height: 5'11" Weight: 11.2

Position/Skill Factor: Left-winger with tremendous pace, he has a good left foot and is a lovely crosser of the ball.

Career History: Signed by Aston Villa from non-League side, Redditch United, early in 1992, he has yet to make a first team appearance and is still very much in the learning stage.

Clubs	Signing Date	Transfer Fee	APPEARANCES				GOALS			
			Lge	FL Cup	FA Cup	Others	Lge	FL Cup	FA Cup	Others
Aston Villa*	1.92	£45,000								

FASHANU John

Born: Kensington, 18 September 1962

Height: 6'1" Weight: 11.2

International Honours: E-2

Position/Skill Factor: A great target man. Dangerous and brave in the air, he can hold the ball up until support is forthcoming. Is an unusual penalty taker, with just two or three steps.

FEAR Peter

Born: Sutton, 10 September 1973

Height: 5'10" Weight: 10.8

Position: Midfield player.

Career History: Signed professional forms for Wimbledon during the 1992 close season, having previously been at the club as an associated schoolboy (November 1987) and as a trainee (July 1990). No first team experience as yet.

Clubs	Signing Date	Transfer Fee	APPEARANCES				GOALS			
			Lge	FL Cup	FA Cup	Others	Lge	FL Cup	FA Cup	Others
Wimbledon*	6.92	–								

FENTON Graham Anthony

Born: Wallsend, 22 May 1974

Height: 5'10" Weight: 11.3

Position/Skill Factor: Can play either up front, or in midfield and for a physical player, he has a good touch.

Career History: Has yet to make a first team appearance for Aston Villa, having only recently signed professional forms. Started out at Villa Park as an associated schoolboy in May 1989, before joining the club as a trainee on leaving school in July 1990 and to date has only progressed as far as the reserves.

Clubs	Signing Date	Transfer Fee	APPEARANCES				GOALS			
			Lge	FL Cup	FA Cup	Others	Lge	FL Cup	FA Cup	Others
Aston Villa*	2.92	–								

FENWICK Terence (Terry) William

Born: Seaham, 17 November 1959

Height: 5'10" Weight: 10.11

International Honours: E Yth, E "U21"-11, E-20

Position/Skill Factor: Very experienced central defender. A good tackler, he is also a quality striker of the ball. Shows great character and is a difficult man to shake off.

Career History: Home grown talent who came up through the Crystal Palace teams as an associated schoolboy (April 1975) and then as an apprentice (May 1976), before joining the professional ranks and making his FL debut at Tottenham Hotspur on 17 December 1977. In 1978-79, he played 20 matches as Palace won the Second Division Championship, but it wasn't until 1980-81 that he settled into the side as a regular performer. His form brought the scouts flocking to Selhurst Park and he moved across London to Queens Park Rangers in exchange for a large fee. Was a key member of the Ranger's side that eventu-

Career History: Nicknamed "Fash the Bash" in honour of his combative style and the younger brother of Justin, who played for Norwich City and Nottingham Forest, during the 1980s, he turned pro with Norwich City, having previously been an associated schoolboy at Cambridge United (February 1979). He had to wait two years to make his FL debut at home to Shrewsbury Town on 17 October 1981, by which time Justin had moved on and after receiving few opportunities in four years at Carrow Road, which included a spell on loan to Crystal Palace, he was transferred to Lincoln City. Made an immediate impact with City, before being signed by Millwall, where he teamed up with Steve Lovell. Their goalscoring partnership was a major factor in the "Lions" attaining promotion to the Second Division and reaching the Quarter-Finals of the FA Cup. The following season, Dave Bassett saw him as the man to seal Wimbledon's promotion to the First Division and four goals from the final nine League matches proved his judgement correct. In 1988, he collected an FA Cup winners medal after Wimbledon defeated Liverpool 1-0 and his sterling displays were rewarded when he was selected to play for England against Chile at Wembley on 23 May 1989. Despite suffering more than his fair share of injuries, he has been the club's leading goalscorer in each of the last six seasons. One of the few remaining members of the 1988 FA Cup Final team, Wimbledon owner Sam Hamman has made great efforts to persuade him to remain with the "Dons", offering him the club presidency and a bonus for each goal scored. Off the field, belying his aggressive image on it, he is charming and articulate with a budding career as a media personality ahead of him, currently as presenter of the TV programme "On The Line".

Clubs	Signing Date	Transfer Fee	APPEARANCES				GOALS			
			Lge	FL Cup	FA Cup	Others	Lge	FL Cup	FA Cup	Others
Norwich City	10.79	–	6+1				1			
Crystal Palace	8.83	Loan	1	1						
Lincoln City	9.83	–	31+5	2	2+1	1	11			
Millwall	11.84	£55,000	50	4	9	2	12	2	4	1
Wimbledon*	3.86	£125,000	209+2	13+1	19	5	88	8	9	2

FERDINAND Leslie (Les)

Born: Acton,
18 December 1966

Height: 5'11"

Weight: 13.5

Position/Skill Factor: Good all-round striker. With his aerial strength and pace to match, he cannot be treated lightly by opposing defences.

Career History: Was snapped up by Queens Park Rangers after he was spotted playing in the Vauxhall-Opel League with Hayes and was immediately given his FL debut, coming on as a sub at Coventry City on 20 April 1987. With opportunities scarce at Loftus Road, he was loaned out to Brentford and then, more exotically, for one year to the Istanbul-based Turkish team, Besiktas, managed by Gordon Milne, the former Leicester City manager. On his return, he still found it difficult to win a regular place and was kept out of the side by the likes of Trevor Francis, Colin Clarke and Mark Falco and more recently, Roy Wegerle. In 1990-91, he finally began to make an impact as injuries depleted the club's ranks and during Q.P.R.'s fight to get away from the bottom of the First Division table he scored some priceless goals, including winners against Luton Town, Southampton, Manchester City and Coventry City. Under new manager Gerry Francis, he started 1991-92 as first choice, but soon lost his place to new signing Garry Thompson. Returned to favour in March and ended the season in impressive style with eight goals from the last 13 games.

Clubs	Signing Date	Transfer Fee	APPEARANCES				GOALS			
			Lge	FL Cup	FA Cup	Others	Lge	FL Cup	FA Cup	Others
Q.P.R.	4.87	£15,000	43+10	2+3	0+1	1	20	2		
Brentford	3.88	Loan	3							
Besiktas (Turkey)	6.88	Loan								

FERGUSON Darren

Born: Glasgow,
9 February 1972

Height: 5'10"

Weight: 10.4

International Honours:
S Yth, S "U21"-3

ally lost to Tottenham Hotspur in the 1982 FA Cup Final, although he did pop up with a late equaliser at Wembley to force a replay. After starring in the Queens Park Rangers side that won the Second Division title in 1982-83 and reaching third place in the First Division the following season, he won his first England cap when playing against Wales in 1984. Became one of Terry Venables initial signings as manager of Tottenham in December 1987 and immediately linked up well with Gary Mabbutt, although the side struggled for lack of goals. After a relatively poor season in 1988-89, a broken leg sustained in a League Cup tie at Old Trafford in October 1989 forced him to miss the remainder of that campaign. On his recovery and in an effort to achieve match fitness, he was loaned out to Leicester City in 1990, but despite temporarily slotting back into a central defensive role on his return until February, he was injured again and did not re-emerge until the last game of the season. Back in favour at the start of 1991-92, he lost his place when jailed for a motoring offence in September — the third such case involving a First Division player in three years. Having served his sentence, however, he was restored to the team in December at full-back, holding his place until March, when Edinburgh was recalled.

Clubs	Signing Date	Transfer Fee	APPEARANCES				GOALS			
			Lge	FL Cup	FA Cup	Others	Lge	FL Cup	FA Cup	Others
Crystal Palace	12.76	–	62+8	4+1	7				1	
Q.P.R.	12.80	£110,000	256	28+1	18	5	33	6	6	
Tottenham Hotspur	12.87	£550,000	87+1	14	7	5	8	2		
Leicester City	10.90	Loan	8			1	1			

Position/Skill Factor: Midfield player. Good passer, both short and long, he comes forward well and should eventually get among the goals.

Career History: Son of the Manchester United manager, Alex, he came through the United ranks after signing as a trainee in July 1988 and made his FL debut at Sheffield United on 26 February 1991. In five appearances, including subs, was not once on the winning side in 1990-91. Selected for the first game of 1991-92, he then went back to tne reserves, before making a couple of appearances in the closing games of the season. Made his debut for the Scotland Under 21 side in February and was called up for the annual end of season tournament in Toulon, France.

·Clubs	Signing Date	Transfer Fee	APPEARANCES				GOALS			
			Lge	FL Cup	FA Cup	Others	Lge	FL Cup	FA Cup	Others
Manchester United*	7.90	–	4+5							

FERGUSON Gary

Born: Belfast, 16 September 1974

Height: 5'11" Weight: 10.11½

International Honours: NI Yth

Position: Central defender.

Career History: After gaining a bit of a "bad-boy" reputation last season as a first year trainee, being sent off several times whilst playing for the Reading youth team, he joined his old boss, Ian Branfoot, when signing professional forms at Southampton in the 1992 close season in return for a small fee. Originally taken on during Branfoot's stewardship at Reading as an associated schoolboy in May 1989, he became a trainee in August 1991 on leaving school and showed signs of making a good player. No first team experience as yet.

Clubs	Signing Date	Transfer Fee	APPEARANCES				GOALS			
			Lge	FL Cup	FA Cup	Others	Lge	FL Cup	FA Cup	Others
Southampton*	6.92	£20,000								

FICKLING Ashley

Born: Sheffield, 15 November 1972

Height: 5'11" Weight: 11.3

International Honours: E Sch

Position/Skill Factor: Full-back who is strong in the tackle and has a tremendous amount of enthusiasm.

Career History: Picked up on Sheffield United's doorstep, he signed as an associated schoolboy in December 1987, before progressing to the club's professional ranks in the 1991 close season. Although he has still to play a League match, he was "blooded" in a League Cup tie at Bramall Lane against Wigan Athletic on 8 October 1991 and is expected to make a breakthrough in 1992-93.

Clubs	Signing Date	Transfer Fee	APPEARANCES				GOALS			
			Lge	FL Cup	FA Cup	Others	Lge	FL Cup	FA Cup	Others
Sheffield United*	7.91	–		1						

FINLEY Darren Jonathan

Born: Belfast, 19 December 1973

Height: 5'4" Weight: 10.0

International Honours: NI Yth

Position: Left-back.

Career History: Signed professional forms for Queens Park Rangers during the 1992 close season, having previously been at Loftus Road as an associated schoolboy (May 1989) and as a trainee (August 1990). No first team experience.

Clubs	Signing Date	Transfer Fee	APPEARANCES				GOALS			
			Lge	FL Cup	FA Cup	Others	Lge	FL Cup	FA Cup	Others
Q.P.R.*	5.92	–								

FITZGERALD Scott Brian

Born: Westminster, 13 August 1969

Height: 6'0" Weight: 12.2

Position/Skill Factor: Very useful centre-back. Can pass long and short, reads the game well, takes up good covering positions and defends well. Is also a good kicker of the ball.

Career History: Starting life at Wimbledon as a trainee in July 1986, he later turned pro and made his FL debut when coming off the subs' bench at Plough Lane against Tottenham Hotspur on 28 April 1990. After four years as a professional with the "Dons" this was his only first team experience and it was therefore a surprise when he started 1991-92 in the first team, replacing the injured Dean Blackwell. To his credit, he grabbed the opportunity with both hands and remained a first team regular throughout the season.

Clubs	Signing Date	Transfer Fee	APPEARANCES				GOALS			
			Lge	FL Cup	FA Cup	Others	Lge	FL Cup	FA Cup	Others
Wimbledon*	7.87	–	34+3	2	2	1	1			

FLATTS Mark Michael

Born: Islington, 14 October 1972

Height: 5'6" Weight: 9.8

International Honours: E Yth

Position/Skill Factor: A wingman, who can tackle, he has terrific pace, two good feet and is a lovely crosser of the ball.

Career History: One for the future, he initially came to Arsenal as an associated schoolboy in January 1987, before signing on as a trainee in July 1989 when he left school. Turned professional at the end of 1990. Still to make a first team appearance, he will look for a breakthrough in 1992-93.

Clubs	Signing Date	Transfer Fee	APPEARANCES				GOALS			
			Lge	FL Cup	FA Cup	Others	Lge	FL Cup	FA Cup	Others
Arsenal*	12.90	–								

FLECK Robert

Born: Glasgow, 11 August 1965

Height: 5'7" Weight: 10.8

International Honours: S Yth, S "U21"-7, S-4

Position/Skill Factor: Stocky, bustling striker, who is a natural goalscorer. Quick and aggressive, he unsettles defenders and when hitting balls early, often catches goal-keepers on the wrong foot.

Career History: Began his soccer career with Glasgow Rangers, but first played in a senior match when on loan to Partick Thistle. Won a Scottish Championship medal with Rangers in 1986-87, scoring 19 times in 40 League matches and halfway through the following term, Norwich paid a then club record fee to bring him south. In all games, whilst at Ibrox, he had made 68 full appearances, 34 substitutions and scored 34 goals. He made his FL debut at Wimbledon on 18 December 1987 and despite being unlucky with injuries has found the net fairly consistently at Carrow Road. His unselfish running was duly rewarded when Scotland selected him for the game against Argentina in March 1990 and he went on to play in the World Cup Finals. After missing several games at the start of 1990-91, he rekindled the form he is more than capable of producing on the big occasion. During 1991-92,

he enjoyed another good season at Carrow Road, top scoring with 11 FL, plus eight cup goals. Unfortunately injured in the bruising FA Cup Quarter-Final replay with Southampton, he was recalled for the Semi-Final against Sunderland, but was subdued and seemed to be less than 100 per cent fit as the "Canaries" succumbed almost tamely to the "Wearsiders". There is little doubt that with Fleck in top gear, it would have been a different game. Surprisingly overlooked by Scotland manager Andy Roxburgh, he did not add to his four caps.

Clubs	Signing Date	Transfer Fee	APPEARANCES				GOALS			
			Lge	FL Cup	FA Cup	Others	Lge	FL Cup	FA Cup	Others
Norwich City*	12.87	£580,000	130+13	13	13+2	7	39	11	11	4

FLEMING Craig

Born: Halifax, 6 October 1971

Height: 6'0"

Weight: 11.7

Position/Skill Factor: Right-back, who can also play in the centre of the defence. A confident player, he is always prepared to have the ball and is very difficult to disposess. Also takes up good positions.

Career History: Made his FL debut for Halifax Town, while still a trainee, at home to Scunthorpe United on 2 January 1989, coming on as a sub. Started out at the Shay as an associated schoolboy (December 1986) and graduated to trainee status in July 1988, before signing pro forms, 18 months later. Established himself in the number five shirt towards the end of 1989-90 and was the club's only ever present the following season, when despite Halifax's struggles, he showed maturity beyond his years. Signed for Oldham Athletic, newly promoted to the First Division, in the 1991 close season and was soon in action, mainly at full-back. Although in and out of the team up to January, he took a firm hold on the right-back slot by the end of the season. Also scored his first ever FL goal at Everton in March, but it was not enough for the "Latics" to avoid defeat. His elder brother Paul, who also started his career with Halifax, is currently a full-back with Mansfield Town

Clubs	Signing Date	Transfer Fee	APPEARANCES				GOALS			
			Lge	FL Cup	FA Cup	Others	Lge	FL Cup	FA Cup	Others
Halifax Town	3.90	–	56+1	4	3	1+2				
Oldham Athletic*	8.91	£80,000	28+4	2+1	2	1	1			

FLEMING Curtis

Born: Manchester,
8 October 1968

Height: 5'10"

Weight: 12.8

Position/Skill Factor: A very promising right-back, who is extremely quick in recovery and uses his pace effectively when going forward.

Career History: After two false starts in English League football, Fleming, who is Irish, notwithstanding his birthplace, finally made a permanent move when signing for Second Division Middlesbrough in the summer of 1991. A defender with St Patricks Athletic in his native Dublin, he had been the target of English club scouts for three years and previously had trials for Swindon Town in March 1989 and Manchester City in August 1990, but on both occasions he returned home within a month, presumably homesick. He immediately joined the first team squad at Ayresome Park and made his FL debut as a substitute at Ipswich Town on 24 August 1991, but as understudy to Gary Parkinson, he had to wait until November before making his first full appearance and held his place for seven matches. Returned to first team duty in March 1992 and remained first choice right-back for the crucial end of season run-in, which saw "Boro" promoted to the new Premier League, in second place.

Clubs	Signing Date	Transfer Fee	APPEARANCES				GOALS			
			Lge	FL Cup	FA Cup	Others	Lge	FL Cup	FA Cup	Others
Middlesbrough*	8.91	£50,000	23+5	2+1		1+1				

FLEMING Terence (Terry) Maurice

Born: Marston Green, 5 January 1973

Height: 5'9" Weight: 11.0

Position/Skill Factor: Very quick, direct right-winger who is a useful crosser of the ball. Also good in the air.

Career History: Graduated through Coventry City's junior ranks as an associated schoolboy (March 1988) and as a trainee (July 1989), before being taken on as a full time pro. Has already had a brief taste of First Division football when coming on for his FL debut as a sub at Wimbledon on 2 February 1991. No further FL appear-

ances in 1991-92, but was on the fringe of the first team at the end of the season.

Clubs	Signing Date	Transfer Fee	APPEARANCES				GOALS			
			Lge	FL Cup	FA Cup	Others	Lge	FL Cup	FA Cup	Others
Coventry City*	7.91	–	0+2							

FLINT Jonathan Andrew

Born: Mansfield, 27 October 1973

Height: 5'11" Weight: 11.4

Position: Central defender.

Career History: Joined the Sheffield Wednesday professional staff during the 1992 close season, having previously been at Hillsborough as an associated schoolboy (April 1989) and as a trainee (July 1990). No first team experience as yet.

Clubs	Signing Date	Transfer Fee	APPEARANCES				GOALS			
			Lge	FL Cup	FA Cup	Others	Lge	FL Cup	FA Cup	Others
Sheffield Wednesday*	6.92	–								

FLITCROFT Gary William

Born: Bolton, 6 November 1972

Height: 6'0" Weight: 11.7

International Honours: E Sch, E Yth

Position: Midfield.

Career History: Initially an associated schoolboy (February 1987) at Maine Road, he joined Manchester City as a trainee in July 1989, on leaving school and progressed to the club's paid ranks by the 1991 close season. As a first year junior professional, he was not called upon by City manager, Peter Reid, but was loaned out to Third Division neighbours, Bury, for experience in late season, making his FL debut at Chester City on 7 March 1992. Although impressing during his 12 match run, playing in both midfield and central defence, he could not help the "Shakers" from sliding back into the Fourth Division.

Clubs	Signing Date	Transfer Fee	APPEARANCES				GOALS			
			Lge	FL Cup	FA Cup	Others	Lge	FL Cup	FA Cup	Others
Manchester City*	7.91	–								
Bury	3.92	Loan	12							

FLOWERS Timothy (Tim) David

Born: Kenilworth,
3 February 1967

Height: 6'2"

Weight: 14.0

International Honours:
E Yth, E "U21"-3

Position/Skill Factor: Very consistent goalkeeper, who comes for crosses with confidence and sweeps up well behind his defence. Kicks very long from his hands.

Career History: The son of Ron, a former Wolverhampton Wanderers and England international wing-half, he followed in his father's footsteps and joined "Wolves" as an associated schoolboy (March 1981) and then as an apprentice (August 1983), before signing pro forms at Molineux. Made his FL debut at home to Sheffield United on 25 August 1984 and though conceding two goals in a 2-2 draw, showed great potential and went on to play 38 League matches that season. The club, however, were relegated to the Third Division and in 1985-86 he shared the goalkeeping duties with Scott Barrett as "Wolves" were relegated yet again, this time to the Fourth Division. Had a spell on loan at Southampton without playing a match, before signing for the "Saints" as Peter Shilton's understudy. He made a less than auspicious start with his new club when on the wrong end of a five goal mauling on his debut and then fractured a cheekbone in his second game. Remained in the shadows of Shilton and then John Burridge, spending a couple of loan periods at Swindon Town, before finally breaking through, following the latter's transfer to Newcastle United in the summer of 1989. Now firmly established as a first choice 'keeper at the club, he has missed only five FL games in the last three seasons. His best moment in 1991-92 came in the FA Cup Fourth Round replay at Old Trafford, when his save from Ryan Gigg's spot-kick in the penalty shoot-out, ensured the "Saints'" further progress in the competition.

Clubs	Signing Date	Transfer Fee	APPEARANCES				GOALS			
			Lge	FL Cup	FA Cup	Others	Lge	FL Cup	FA Cup	Others
Wolverhampton W.	8.84	–	63	5	2	2				
Southampton*	6.86	£70,000	136	21	15	8				
Swindon Town	3.87	Loan	2							
Swindon Town	11.87	Loan	5							

FLYNN Sean Michael

Born: Birmingham, 13 March 1968

Height: 5'7" Weight: 11.2

Position/Skill Factor: Enthusiastic midfielder cum striker, with a great work rate, who will only get better with experience.

Career History: Formerly an associated schoolboy with West Bromwich Albion (May 1982), he established a growing reputation in local West Midlands football with Beazer Homes League teams, Bromsgrove Rovers and Halesowen Town, before joining Coventry City in December 1991, for an initial fee of £20,000, thus following in the footsteps of Tim Clarke and Andy Pearce, who also joined the "Sky Blues" from Halesowen. Most non-league players joining First Division clubs can expect to serve some time in the reserves before graduating to the first team. Instead, manager Terry Butcher pitched him into action almost immediately on the right side of midfield. He made a fairy tale FL debut away to Sheffield United on Boxing Day 1991, scoring a stupendous goal from 30 yards in City's remarkable 3-0 victory. Although it proved to be his only goal to date, he held his place to the end of the season, under new manager Don Howe, and after ten games, Halesowen received an additional £10,000 with more to follow if he makes further progress.

Clubs	Signing Date	Transfer Fee	APPEARANCES				GOALS			
			Lge	FL Cup	FA Cup	Others	Lge	FL Cup	FA Cup	Others
Coventry City*	12.91	£30,000	21+1				2			

FORREST Craig Lorne

Born: Vancouver, Canada,
30 September 1967

Height: 6'4"

Weight: 14.4

International Honours:
Canadian Int

Position/Skill Factor: Goalkeeper who comes for crosses and is very quick off his line to collect balls played in behind his defenders.

Career History: Joined Ipswich Town as an apprentice in September 1984, signing pro forms just under a year later, but when unable to claim a first team place was loaned out to Colchester United and made his FL debut there against Wrexham on 4 March 1988. The following season, he started for Town in the first 22 matches, but after a particularly bad defeat at Chelsea, Ron Fearon displaced him. He eventually got his place back and was an ever present in 1989-90. In 1990-91 he kept eight clean sheets in League games and continued to improve as he reaped the benefit of the club's specialist goalkeeping coaching, provided by Phil Parkes, the former England 'keeper. Played in all 56 League and cup games for Ipswich in 1991-92, which saw the Town carry off the Second Division Championship and earn automatic promotion to the new Premier League. Also selected for the Canadian national team after the season ended.

Clubs	Signing Date	Transfer Fee	APPEARANCES				GOALS			
			Lge	FL Cup	FA Cup	Others	Lge	FL Cup	FA Cup	Others
Ipswich Town*	8.85	–	162	11	8	11				
Colchester United	3.88	Loan	11							

FORREST Cuan Frank

Born: Zimbabwe, 26 March 1974

Height: 5'11" Weight: 11.11

Position: Right-back.

Career History: A professional signing for Nottingham Forest in the 1991 close season, he first came to the City Ground as an associated schoolboy (November 1989), before joining the club as a trainee in July 1990. A Gary Charles look-a-like, he has yet to play first team soccer.

Clubs	Signing Date	Transfer Fee	APPEARANCES				GOALS			
			Lge	FL Cup	FA Cup	Others	Lge	FL Cup	FA Cup	Others
Nottingham Forest*	7.91	–								

FOSTER John Colin

Born: Manchester, 19 September 1973

Height: 5'11" Weight: 11.4

International Honours: E Sch

Position: Right-back.

Career History: Joined the Manchester City professional staff during the 1992 close season, having previously been at Maine Road as an associated schoolboy (February 1988) and as a trainee (July 1990). No first team experience.

Clubs	Signing Date	Transfer Fee	APPEARANCES				GOALS			
			Lge	FL Cup	FA Cup	Others	Lge	FL Cup	FA Cup	Others
Manchester City*	6.92	–								

FOWLER Robert Bernard

Born: Liverpool, 9 April 1975

Height: 5'7³/₄" Weight: 10.3

Position: Centre-forward.

Career History: Signed professional forms for Liverpool during the summer, having previously been at Anfield as an associated schoolboy (November 1990) and as a trainee (July 1991). No first team experience.

Clubs	Signing Date	Transfer Fee	APPEARANCES				GOALS			
			Lge	FL Cup	FA Cup	Others	Lge	FL Cup	FA Cup	Others
Liverpool*	4.92	–								

FOX Ruel Adrian

Born: Ipswich,
14 January 1968

Height: 5'6"

Weight: 10.0

Position/Skill Factor: A winger who is very quick, he favours his right foot, but can go both ways. A real "box of tricks", he loves taking defenders on. Does extremely well in the air for his size.

Career History: Progressing through the Norwich City junior ranks, initially as an associated schoolboy (October 1983) and then as an apprentice (August 1984), he signed pro forms early in 1986. Made his FL debut at Carrow Road against Oxford United on 29 November 1986, but, apart from 1987-88, has found it difficult to hold down a regular place in facing fierce competition from Dale Gordon and Ian Crook. However, he finished 1989-90 on a high note with three goals in as many matches and kept his place at the beginning of the next season, eventually playing 23 League games, as the club yet again put the emphasis on good football. A regular performer for the "Canaries" in 1991-92, he occasionally played as a striking partner for Robert Fleck, but did not score often enough to justify continuation of that role. When Dale Gordon departed to Glasgow Rangers in November 1991, he was at last able to claim the right-wing slot as his own.

Clubs	Signing Date	Transfer Fee	APPEARANCES				GOALS			
			Lge	FL Cup	FA Cup	Others	Lge	FL Cup	FA Cup	Others
Norwich City*	1.86	–	91+22	9+2	7+2	6+3	11	1		

FRANCIS Trevor John

Born: Plymouth, 19 April 1954

Height: 5'10" Weight: 11.7

International Honours: E Yth, E "U23"-5, E-52

Position/Skill Factor: One of the most gifted of strikers since the war, he had nearly everything including pace, acceleration and tremendous skill. A player never loses his ability and he hasn't. Always looking to create chances, he is especially dangerous when getting into wide positions.

Career History: After joining Birmingham City as an apprentice in July 1969, he made his FL debut as the club's youngest ever player at Cardiff City on 5 September 1970. Before the season was over, he had scored 16 League goals, including four against Bolton Wanderers and had become the youngest player ever to score four in

Trevor Francis

a League match. His form was instrumental in City being promoted to the First Division in 1971-72 and in nine seasons at St Andrews, he was the club's top scorer in six and will always be remembered by "Blues'" supporters as their finest post-war player, if not of all-time. Traditionally a dour and struggling team, Birmingham enjoyed perhaps their brightest post-war spell during Francis' stay. However, the team was not strong enough to win trophies and with the "Blues" facing relegation in February 1979, he became Britain's first £1 million footballer, when signing for Nottingham Forest. Almost two years earlier and not before time, he had finally been rewarded with a full international cap, the first of many, when he made his debut for England against Holland at Wembley on 9 February 1977. His stay at Forest was relatively brief and during his time there he was sidelined with injuries for a lengthy spell. But he enjoyed some success, scoring the only goal of the game against Malmo in the 1979 European Cup Final and receiving a League Cup winners medal in 1980, while on the reverse side of the coin, he missed out on a second European Cup winners medal in 1980 through injury. Unfortunately, he never enjoyed a fully harmonious relationship with Forest manager, Brian Clough, who objected violently to his playing summer football in the USA with Detroit Express and he was transferred to Manchester City at the beginning of the 1981-82 season. Had just one term at Maine Road, before joining Italian League Team, Sampdoria of Genoa, where he won Italian Cup winners medal in 1985. As in England, his career in Italy was continually interrupted by injuries, but when available, he delighted the hyper-critical fans with his skills. On completing four seasons with Sampdoria he joined another Italian club, Atalanta of Bergamo for one year, before returning to Britain. When signing for Glasgow Rangers, he quickly won a Skol Cup winners medal, but after just four months at Ibrox he was appointed as player-manager of Queens Park Rangers. He didn't have a smooth ride at Loftus Road and was replaced as the club's manager by Don Howe in November 1989, although it wasn't long before Ron Atkinson invited him to join Sheffield Wednesday. In his first full season at Hillsborough he played 18 League games and made a remarkable 20 appearances from the subs' bench, as a valuable member of the squad that was promoted to the First Division and won the League Cup. Even at the age of 36, his silky touches and ability to conjure up goal chances from nothing soon brought him status as a "folk-hero" at Hillsborough and when Ron Atkinson suddenly walked out in the summer of 1991, Francis was the popular choice to succeed him. He fully justified the directors' and supporters' faith in him by piloting Wednesday to their highest FL placing (third) for 30 years and qualification for the UEFA Cup. Although not starting a game during the season, he brought himself on as a substitute no fewer than 22 times and on several occasions, set up winning goals for the "Owls".

Clubs	Signing Date	Transfer Fee	APPEARANCES				GOALS			
			Lge	FL Cup	FA Cup	Others	Lge	FL Cup	FA Cup	Others
Birmingham City	5.71	–	278+2	18	19		118	3	6	
Nottingham Forest	2.79	£1,000,000	69+1	5	8	9	28		5	4
Manchester City	9.81	£1,200,000	26	1	2		12		2	
Sampdoria (Italy)	9.82	£800,000								
Atalanta (Italy)	7.86									
Glasgow Rangers	9.87	£75,000								
Q.P.R.	3.88	–	30+2	8	1	1	12	3		
Sheffield Wednesday*	2.90	–	28+42	5+2	2+1	1	5	3	1	

FRANK Ian David

Born: Sheffield, 19 September 1973

Height: 5'7" **Weight:** 10.1

Position: Midfield player.

Career History: A local discovery, he signed professional forms for Sheffield Wednesday during the 1992 close season, having previously been at the club as an associated schoolboy (May 1988) and as a trainee (July 1990). No first team experience as yet.

Clubs	Signing Date	Transfer Fee	APPEARANCES				GOALS			
			Lge	FL Cup	FA Cup	Others	Lge	FL Cup	FA Cup	Others
Sheffield Wednesday*	6.92	–								

FREEDMAN Douglas Alan

Born: Glasgow, 21 January 1974

Height: 5'10" **Weight:** 10.7

International Honours: S Sch

Position: Forward.

Career History: Signed professional forms for Queens Park Rangers during the 1992 close season, having been at Loftus Road as a trainee since August 1990. No first team experience.

Clubs	Signing Date	Transfer Fee	APPEARANCES				GOALS			
			Lge	FL Cup	FA Cup	Others	Lge	FL Cup	FA Cup	Others
Q.P.R.*	5.92	–								

FROGGATT Stephen Junior

Born: Lincoln, 9 March 1973

Height: 5'10"

Weight: 11.0

Position/Skill Factor: Exciting young left-winger, who has pace, skill and a lovely left foot. He is capable of both scoring and creating goals. Takes dangerous corner kicks.

Career History: First joined Aston Villa as an associated schoolboy in March 1988 and then as a trainee in July 1989, before turning professional 18 months later. Although, as a first year professional, he was not expecting a first team outing so soon, he made his FL debut as a substitute on Boxing Day 1991 at home to West Ham United and subsequently enjoyed a short run in the first team from February to March. During this spell he scored a spectacular winning goal at Swindon in the Fifth Round of the FA Cup.

Clubs	Signing Date	Transfer Fee	APPEARANCES				GOALS			
			Lge	FL Cup	FA Cup	Others	Lge	FL Cup	FA Cup	Others
Aston Villa*	1.91	–	6+3		2+1				1	

FURLONG Paul Anthony

Born: Wood Green, 1 October 1968

Height: 6'0" **Weight:** 11.8

International Honours: E Semi-Pro Int

Position/Skill Factor: An improving striker with good skills and a nice left foot, who will score goals at any level.

Career History: Signed for Coventry City from Diadora (ex Vauxhall) League club, Enfield, where he came up through the youth team in 1987 and was a consistent scorer for the next four seasons. A move into the Football League had been predicted for some time before Coventry pounced for a substantial fee. He was thrown into first team action immediately and responded with four goals in the first eight games of the season, following his FL debut at home to Manchester City on 17 August 1991. Although remaining a semi-regular performer for the remainder of the season, he scored only once more (in the League Cup).

Clubs	Signing Date	Transfer Fee	APPEARANCES				GOALS			
			Lge	FL Cup	FA Cup	Others	Lge	FL Cup	FA Cup	Others
Coventry City*	7.91	£130,000	27+10	4	1+1	1	4	1		

GAGE Kevin William

Born: Chiswick, 21 April 1964

Height: 5'9" **Weight:** 11.2

International Honours: E Yth

Position/Skill Factor: Strong tackling aggressive full-back who gives his opponent no time to settle on the ball and likes to join up with the attack when the opportunity presents itself.

Career History: Made his FL debut at Plough Lane for Wimbledon as the club's youngest ever player, while still an apprentice, against Bury on 2 May 1981 in the last game of the 1980-81 season and although the "Dons" were beaten 4-2, they were still able to celebrate promotion to the Third Division. Had previously been an associated schoolboy (January 1980) before becoming an apprentice in July 1980. Made 21 appearances the following term as Wimbledon dropped back into the Fourth Division, but from then on it was success all the way as the little south London side marched to the First Division in four seasons. After helping to establish the "Dons" in the "top bracket", he was transferred to Aston Villa and was an ever present in the side that was promoted to the First Division in 1987-88. While Villa became the League Championship runners-up in 1989-90, he struggled to maintain his form and was in and out of the side from then on. He clearly had no future at Villa Park under new manager Ron Atkinson and was rescued from obscurity by his former manager, Dave Bassett, who took him on loan to Sheffield United in November 1991 and then sealed the transfer two months later. He settled in at right-back and had the satisfaction of scoring against his former club at Villa Park in a 1-1 draw late in the season.

Clubs	Signing Date	Transfer Fee	APPEARANCES				GOALS			
			Lge	FL Cup	FA Cup	Others	Lge	FL Cup	FA Cup	Others
Wimbledon	1.82	–	135+33	7+2	8+3	0+1	15	1	1	
Aston Villa	7.87	£100,000	113+2	13	9	8	8	3	1	
Sheffield United*	11.91	£150,000	22		2+2		1			

GALLACHER Kevin William

Born: Clydebank, 23 November 1966

Height: 5'7" **Weight:** 9.11

International Honours: S Yth, S "U21"-7, S-12

Position/Skill Factor: Winger cum striker, with great pace, who can go past defenders to get his crosses in, or can cut inside to score. When playing up front, he is very composed in the box and always looks likely to get a goal.

Career History: Made his name in the Scottish Premier Division with Dundee United, having been signed from Duntocher BC and scored 27 goals in 131 matches before signing for Coventry City. In four seasons at United, the club went to successive losing Scottish Cup Finals against St Mirren (1987) and Celtic (1988) and were runners-up in the UEFA Cup Final against IFK Gothenburg in 1987. First capped by Scotland in a Rous Cup match on 17 May 1988, he came south to Coventry for a club record fee and made his FL debut in a 3-2 home win against Chelsea on 3 February 1990. Topped the club's League goalscoring charts in 1990-91 with 11 from 32 appearances and scored a hat-trick in the Fourth Round of the League Cup against Nottingham Forest, in an astonishing 5-4 victory. Undoubtedly Coventry's most talented player and their only forward capable of scoring consistently, he was switched from the wing to central striker in March 1991, scoring six goals in 13 games. He continued in this role for 1991-92 and his absence through injury from March to April 1992 was a major factor in Coventry's slide into the relegation zone. Although he won three more caps for Scotland during the season, they were all as substitute,

and he seemed likely to miss out on Scotland's European Championship squad, until called up as a last minute replacement for the injured John Robertson of Hearts. Although Scotland went out of the tournament after losing to Holland (1-0) and Germany (2-0), although they beat the CIS (3-0), he enhanced his reputation playing in a side that performed well above expectation.

Clubs	Signing Date	Transfer Fee	APPEARANCES				GOALS			
			Lge	FL Cup	FA Cup	Others	Lge	FL Cup	FA Cup	Others
Coventry City*	1.90	£900,000	80	9	3	2	22	7		

GALLEN Stephen James

Born: Ealing, 21 November 1973

Height: 6'0" Weight: 11.0

Position: Defender.

Career History: Signed professional forms for Queens Park Rangers during the 1992 close season, having been at Loftus Road as a trainee since June 1990. No first team experience.

Clubs	Signing Date	Transfer Fee	APPEARANCES				GOALS			
			Lge	FL Cup	FA Cup	Others	Lge	FL Cup	FA Cup	Others
Q.P.R.*	5.92	–								

GANNON John Spencer

Born: Wimbledon, 18 December 1966

Height: 5'8"

Weight: 10.10

Position/Skill Factor: Creative midfielder who is always involved in the game. A confident player, he has a lovely left foot and some nice touches.

Career History: Signed for Wimbledon as an associated schoolboy in January 1981 and then as an apprentice in July 1983, but before joining the pro ranks, he made his FL debut at Bradford City on 2 May 1981, scoring in a 1-1 draw. Played a couple of times for Wimbledon in the First Division the following term, but found it difficult to win a regular place and was loaned out to Crewe Alexandra for three months. Still unable to establish himself at Plough Lane on his return, he later spent a period on loan to Sheffield United, managed by his old Wimbledon boss, Dave Bassett. Entering the fray as a sub, he scored in a 4-1 win against Blackpool and stayed on to help United gain promotion to the Second Division at the end of that season, 1988-89. The move was made permanent during the close season and he quickly won a regular place in the "Blades'" midfield, missing only seven matches, as the club went back to the First Division as runners-up. Considering his lack of achievement at Wimbledon, his progress at Bramall Lane has been remarkable and typical of Dave Bassett's talent of transforming apparently undistinguished players into First Division stalwarts. Left out at the beginning of 1991-92, he was restored to the first team in late September and played in every game for the "Blades" thereafter, assisting their remarkable rise from bottom position in November to ninth in May.

Clubs	Signing Date	Transfer Fee	APPEARANCES				GOALS			
			Lge	FL Cup	FA Cup	Others	Lge	FL Cup	FA Cup	Others
Wimbledon	12.84	–	13+3	1+1		1	2			
Crewe Alexandra	12.86	Loan	14+1			1				
Sheffield United	2.89	Loan	8+8				1			
Sheffield United*	6.89	–	90+3	7	11	4	4			

GARNER Simon

Born: Boston,
23 November 1959

Height: 5'9"

Weight: 11.12

Position/Skill Factor: A very experienced striker who is a proven goalscorer. Good with his back to the goal, he will hold the ball up and suddenly turn defenders to get a shot in. Also makes intelligent runs off the ball.

Career History: An outstanding club servant, he has been with Blackburn Rovers for 16 years, since signing as an apprentice in August 1976. Turned professional early in 1977-78 and made his FL debut when substituting for John Aston at Newcastle United on 9 September 1978, a few days after turning out in a League Cup match at Exeter City. Originally a midfielder, he displayed a knack for scoring vital goals which persuaded manager Howard Kendall to play him up front from January 1980 and he assisted the club back to Division Two. Took time to show his paces as a consistent goalscorer, with only seven FL goals from 33 games in 1980-81. Despite a lack of goals (Rovers failing to score in 16 out of 42 games), the team amazingly missed promotion by only one place. From 1981-82 onwards, however, he was a consistent scorer, leading the Rovers' goal charts with 14 FL goals in 1981-82, 22 in 1982-83, 19 in 1983-84, 12 in 1985-86, 14 in 1987-88, 20 in 1988-89 and 18 in 1989-90. With such a record, it is surprising, but a relief to Rovers' fans, that no First Division club made a persistent effort to secure his services. In April 1989 he became Rovers' highest all-time goalscorer, beating the previous record of 140 FL goals held by Tommy Briggs since 1958. After losing his place early in 1991-92, his future seemed in doubt when Kenny Dalglish took over in October. However, he responded with four goals in four games and Dalglish was happy to offer him a new two year contract. Subsequently lost his place to new signing Mike Newell, but was restored to the team in February when the latter was injured and Speedie suspended, simultaneously. After three games without a goal, Dalglish lost patience and signed Roy Wegerle from Queens Park Rangers to replace him. From this point, Blackburn's promotion campaign collapsed and although the team recovered in time to reach the Play-Offs and eventual promotion, it is interesting to speculate whether Rovers might have won promotion more easily if Dalglish had shown more patience with his veteran striker. With so many forwards on the books at Ewood Park, he may have little future there, but after so many near misses, no player deserves more, the chance of First Division football, however brief it may be.

Clubs	Signing Date	Transfer Fee	APPEARANCES				GOALS			
			Lge	FL Cup	FA Cup	Others	Lge	FL Cup	FA Cup	Others
Blackburn Rovers*	11.77	–	455+29	32+2	24+5	17+1	168	11	7	6

GAUNT Craig

Born: Sutton-in Ashfield, 31 March 1973

Height: 5'11½" Weight: 12.2

International Honours: E Yth

Position/Skill Factor: Central defender who can play at full-back or in midfield. A useful all-round player, he is a good passer and has an extra gear when defending.

Career History: A recent acquisition to Arsenal's professional ranks, he has yet to receive a first team outing. First came to Highbury as an associated schoolboy in May 1989 and just two months later, he signed as a trainee. Came through the Lilleshall School of Excellence.

Clubs	Signing Date	Transfer Fee	APPEARANCES				GOALS			
			Lge	FL Cup	FA Cup	Others	Lge	FL Cup	FA Cup	Others
Arsenal*	4.91	–								

GAYLE Brian Wilbert

Born: Kingston,
6 March 1965

Height: 6'1"

Weight: 12.7

Position/Skill Factor: Quick and aggressive centre-back who defends well and is good in the air.

Career History: Discovered as a 16-year-old by Wimbledon, he was apprenticed in July 1981, turning pro three years later after having a spell on loan with local Vauxhall League team, Tooting & Mitcham. Made his FL debut in the number five shirt at home to Shrewsbury Town on 27 March 1985 and kept his place for the rest of the season. During 1985-86, the season the "Dons" were promoted to the First Division, he was displaced by Mick Smith during October and didn't regain his position in the side until the following season. Was transferred to Manchester City in the 1988-89 close season, after not being selected for the 1988 Wimbledon FA Cup winning team and immediately helped City back to the First Division, while missing only five games. Dropped when Howard Kendall took over at Maine Road, he signed for Ipswich Town and apart from a short spell in 1990-91, he held down a regular place with the Suffolk club. Signed by his former manager at Wimbledon, Dave Bassett, for Sheffield United soon into the 1991-92 season, his debut was delayed for two weeks as the "Blades'" directors struggled to raise the transfer fee. Made a nervous start with his new club, whose defence was leaking goals in abundance. However, after scoring twice in a 3-2 defeat away to Manchester City, he settled down to form a high-ly effective central defensive partnership with Paul Beesley, which assisted the "Blades" to rise from the foot of the table to a final ninth place. After such a good season, it was ironic that it was his emphatically headed own goal in the penultimate game against Leeds United, that virtually clinched the League Championship for their Yorkshire rivals.

Clubs	Signing Date	Transfer Fee	APPEARANCES				GOALS			
			Lge	FL Cup	FA Cup	Others	Lge	FL Cup	FA Cup	Others
Wimbledon	10.84	–	76+7	7	8	2	3	1	1	
Manchester City	7.88	£325,000	55	8	2	1	3			
Ipswich Town	1.90	£330,000	58	3	0+1		4			
Sheffield United*	9.91	£750,000	33	3	3	1	4		1	1

GAYNOR Thomas (Tommy)

Born: Limerick,
29 January 1963

Height: 6'0"

Weight: 12.9

Position/Skill Factor: Striker with a good touch, who likes the ball on the ground. Very aware of passes and one-twos around the penalty area, he is not a prolific scorer, but has two useful feet.

Career History: Started his FL career with Doncaster Rovers, then of the Third Division, after joining them from League of Ireland team, Limerick, making his FL debut at home to Swindon Town on 21 December 1986 in a 2-2 draw. He quickly impressed at the Belle Vue Ground with his busy beavering displays, but wasn't an automatic first choice and it was a surprise when, after less than one year at Belle Vue, he was snapped up by Nottingham Forest. Almost immediately he came into the side in place of the injured Paul Wilkinson and made quite an impact on the Forest fans when scoring in his first two home games. Set Brian Clough's side on their way to League Cup glory in 1988-89, with a goal in the first-leg against Chester City and then followed up in the second-leg with his first ever hat-trick. Later in the season he collected a winners medal after helping Forest beat Luton 3-1 in the Final. Finding it difficult to make an impact in 1990-91, he had a brief spell on loan to Newcastle United. Has usually performed well when called upon by Brian Clough, but his first team opportunities were very scarce in 1991-92 due to the presence of Teddy Sheringham.

Clubs	Signing Date	Transfer Fee	APPEARANCES				GOALS			
			Lge	FL Cup	FA Cup	Others	Lge	FL Cup	FA Cup	Others
Doncaster Rovers	12.86		28+5	2+1			7	1		
Nottingham Forest*	10.87	£30,000	43+14	10	5+1	3+2	10	8	1	1
Newcastle United	11.90	Loan	4				1			

GELLING Stuart John

Born: Liverpool, 8 September 1973

Height: 5'6" Weight: 9.0

Position: Centre midfield.

Career History: Signed professional forms for Liverpool during last summer, having been at the club since leaving school and coming to Anfield as a trainee in June 1990. No first team experience.

Clubs	Signing Date	Transfer Fee	APPEARANCES				GOALS			
			Lge	FL Cup	FA Cup	Others	Lge	FL Cup	FA Cup	Others
Liverpool*	6.92	–								

GEMMILL Scot

Born: Paisley,
2 January 1971

Height: 5'10"

Weight: 11.0

International Honours:
S "U21"-4

Position/Skill Factor: Looks to be a very good all-round midfield player, having both vision and stamina in abundance. Always looking to play one-twos around the box, he can also score goals.

Career History: Son of the dynamic little Scot, Archie, who masterminded some of Brian Clough's greatest successes, at both Derby County and Nottingham Forest, he became a trainee at Nottingham Forest in March 1988 under the scrutiny of the club coach, his father. Later he turned pro and came into the side in the number eight shirt for his FL debut at Wimbledon on 30 March 1991, playing once more before going back on the subs's bench. Made remarkable progress in 1991-92, yet another example of Brian Clough throwing a young player "in at the deep end" and the gamble succeeding handsomely. Selected to partner Roy Keane in midfield, in preference to the experienced Garry Parker, he held his place for almost the entire season and assisted Forest to two Wembley Cup Finals, being on the winning side for the Zenith Cup Final victory over Southampton, but on the losing side in the League Cup Final against Manchester United. Also called up for the Scottish Under 21 squad, making several appearances. Although not included in the Scotland squad of 20 for the European Championships in

Sweden, he was nevertheless invited to join the touring party for experience, indicating that his full international debut for Scotland may not be long delayed.

Clubs	Signing Date	Transfer Fee	APPEARANCES				GOALS			
			Lge	FL Cup	FA Cup	Others	Lge	FL Cup	FA Cup	Others
Nottingham Forest*	1.90	–	41+2	8+1	4	6	8	2		3

GERRARD Paul William

Born: Heywood, 22 January 1973

Height: 6'2" Weight: 11.2

Position/Skill Factor: Brave young goalkeeper, who cuts a commanding figure and kicks long and hard. Has a brilliant attitude to the game.

Career History: On leaving school, he joined Oldham Athletic as a trainee in August 1989 and had progressed to the club's professional ranks in the 1991 close season. Yet to make the first team, having been held back by a knee operation, he is reckoned to be a bright prospect for the future.

Clubs	Signing Date	Transfer Fee	APPEARANCES				GOALS			
			Lge	FL Cup	FA Cup	Others	Lge	FL Cup	FA Cup	Others
Oldham Athletic*	7.91	–								

GIBSON Terence (Terry) Bradley

Born: Walthamstow, 23 December 1962

Height: 5'5"

Weight: 10.0

International Honours: E Sch, E Yth

Position/Skill Factor: Small and stocky striker. Good mover off the ball, he was once extremely adept at getting into the box and scoring goals. Strong on the ball with good control, he has an excellent awareness.

Career History: At one time considered far too small for First Division football, after being taken on by Tottenham Hotspur as an associated schoolboy in July 1977, he began to grow and eventually signed apprenticeship forms in April 1979. Made his FL debut at White Hart Lane against Stoke City on 29 December 1979, just days before becoming a full-time professional and was sent to play in Sweden during the English summer in a further attempt

to build himself up. Although he managed to put on a few pounds, first team opportunities were limited at "Spurs" and during his time there he mainly played second fiddle to Steve Archibald and Garth Crooks. Eventually, in 1983-84, he jumped at the opportunity to join Coventry City, scoring at Watford on his debut and finishing the season as City's top goalscorer with 19, including a hat-trick in a 4-0 win over Liverpool. After scoring 52 goals in 112 starts in all matches for the "Sky Blues", who remained near the foot of the First Division during his time there, he was sold to Manchester United. His stay at Old Trafford was fairly disastrous, with only occasional first team appearances and only one goal and after a year and a half, he joined Wimbledon for what was then a record transfer fee for the club. Although he failed to command an immediate regular first team place at Wimbledon, a run of three goals in the final three League matches of 1987-88, secured his place in the side to face Liverpool in the FA Cup Final. Duly collected a winners medal following a 1-0 victory, but over the past few seasons he has suffered a spate of injury problems. Since leaving Coventry over six years ago, his career has stalled and in 1991-92 he played only a handful of games for Wimbledon without a goal. Loaned out to Swindon Town at the end of the season, a club managed by his former Spurs colleague, Glenn Hoddle, he made little impact.

Clubs	Signing Date	Transfer Fee	APPEARANCES				GOALS			
			Lge	FL Cup	FA Cup	Others	Lge	FL Cup	FA Cup	Others
Tottenham Hotspur	1.80	–	16+2	1	5	0+2	4	1	1	1
Coventry City	8.83	£100,000	97+1	7	6	2	43	3	5	1
Manchester United	1.86	£650,000	14+9	0+2	1+1		1			
Wimbledon*	8.87	£200,000	74+4	10	10	8	20	6	3	1
Swindon Town	3.92	Loan	8+1				1			

GIGGS Ryan Joseph

Born: Cardiff, 29 November 1973

Height: 5'11" Weight: 9.9

International Honours: W Yth, W "U21"-1, W-3

Position/Skill Factor: Left-winger with lovely skills, who delights in taking defenders on. Has a beautiful left foot and uses it to advantage at set plays. Is also capable of scoring spectacular goals.

Career History: The son of the former Rugby League international, Brian Wilson, he has since taken his mother's name and despite his prodigious talent threatening to break Duncan Edwards' record as the youngest ever Manchester United player, he had to wait until he was 17 years and three months for the honour of playing in the first team. He first came to Old Trafford as an associated schoolboy (February 1988), before graduating to trainee (July 1990) and eventually turning pro following his 17th birthday. Made his FL debut when coming on as a sub at home to Everton on 2 March 1991 and in his first full match, the local "derby" against Manchester City, he scored the only goal of the game. Even before his United

appearances for Forest, he was freed and given a one year contract with Middlesbrough.

Clubs	Signing Date	Transfer Fee	APPEARANCES				GOALS			
			Lge	FL Cup	FA Cup	Others	Lge	FL Cup	FA Cup	Others
Nottingham Forest	12.90	–								
Middlesbrough*	4.92	–								

GITTENS Jonathan (Jon)

Born: Birmingham,
22 January 1964

Height: 5'11"

Weight: 12.6

Position/Skill Factor: Centre-back with tremendous pace and a change of gear which makes him difficult to beat. A strong marker, he is good in the air and uses the ball simply, but well.

Career History: Spotted by Southampton when playing for non-League side, Paget Rangers, he came into the side following injuries to Nick Holmes and Mark Wright and made his FL debut at Birmingham City on 19 April 1986. During his second season there, he had several short spells partnering Wright and alternating with Kevin Bond and Mark Blake, before being allowed to move to Swindon Town in the summer of 1987. Took a while to settle, but eventually he became a regular first choice in central defence and was a member of the Town side that earned promotion to the First Division in the Play-Offs of 1989-90, only to be later deprived of the honour when the club were charged with financial irregularities and demoted to the Third Division, but subsequently reinstated to the Second Division, on appeal, by the FA. Amazingly, he was re-signed by his former club Southampton for a fee ten times greater than he was sold for. The "Saints" had suffered a series of injuries to key defenders at the back-end of the 1990-91 season and were then in desperate need for ready made replacements. However, in 1991-92, under a new manager Ian Branfoot, he found himself in competition with four other central defenders for just two places and lost out. He joined Middlesbrough on loan in February 1992 with a view to a permanent transfer. Although sidelined for much of his loan period, he eventually took over from the injured Alan Kernaghan for the crucial run-in, which lifted "Boro" from seventh to second place and automatic promotion to the new Premier League.

Clubs	Signing Date	Transfer Fee	APPEARANCES				GOALS			
			Lge	FL Cup	FA Cup	Others	Lge	FL Cup	FA Cup	Others
Southampton	10.85	£10,000	18	4	1					
Swindon Town	7.87	£40,000	124+2	15+1	9	13+1	6			1
Southampton*	3.91	£400,000	16+3	4		1				
Middlesbrough	2.92	Loan	9+3							

debut he was tipped as a future football star, but his progress in 1991-92, under the tutelage of the normally ultra-cautious Alex Ferguson, was positively electrifying. Included in the first team squad from the start of the season, his sparkling wing play and supremely confident, audacious goal scoring, soon earned him a regular place and rave reviews in the media. The combination of Giggs on one wing and Kantschelskis on the other, gave the "Reds" a new attacking dimension, missing for years at Old Trafford and for a while it seemed that United would be League Champions with a combination of flair and efficiency. It was not to be, however and although he was a member of the team which brought the League Cup to Old Trafford for the first time, the League Championship prize slipped away in a welter of draws and ultimately, defeats. His contribution to the season's entertainment was recognised by his fellow professionals when he was voted "Young Player of the Year" in the PFA Awards in April — the youngest player ever to receive the accolade. He was also selected by Wales, becoming their youngest full international in October 1991, at 17 years 11 months, but surprisingly perhaps his three caps to date have all been as substitute.

Clubs	Signing Date	Transfer Fee	APPEARANCES				GOALS			
			Lge	FL Cup	FA Cup	Others	Lge	FL Cup	FA Cup	Others
Manchester United*	12.90	–	33+7	6+2	2+1	1	4	3		

GILCHRIST Philip Alexander

Born: Stockton, 25 August 1973

Height: 6'0" Weight: 11.12

Position/Skill Factor: Left-back who can play in the centre of the defence. Strong and quick with a natural left foot.

Career History: A North-East discovery, he signed associated schoolboy forms with Nottingham Forest in March 1988, before joining the club as a trainee in July 1989 after leaving school. Turned professional at the City Ground at the end of 1990, but after 16 months and no first team

GLASS James (Jimmy) Robert

Born: Epsom, 1 August 1973

Height: 6'1" Weight: 11.10

Position/Skill Factor: Goalkeeper. A good shot stopper, he is reliable on crosses and organises his defences well.

Career History: A recent professional signing who has come through Crystal Palace's ranks as an associated schoolboy (December 1988) and as a trainee (July 1989). Yet to appear in first team soccer, he played for Palace's junior side that reached the FA Youth Cup Final last season.

Clubs	Signing Date	Transfer Fee	APPEARANCES				GOALS			
			Lge	FL Cup	FA Cup	Others	Lge	FL Cup	FA Cup	Others
Crystal Palace*	7.91	–								

GLASSER Neil Richard

Born: Johannesburg, South Africa, 17 October 1974

Height: 5'10" Weight: 11.4

Position/Skill Factor: Another good passer in the Nottingham Forest mould, he is also a tenacious ball-winner from midfield.

Career History: South African born youngster who signed as an associated schoolboy player for Nottingham Forest in September 1989, before coming to the City Ground as a trainee in August 1991. Turned professional just two months later and still awaits a first team outing.

Clubs	Signing Date	Transfer Fee	APPEARANCES				GOALS			
			Lge	FL Cup	FA Cup	Others	Lge	FL Cup	FA Cup	Others
Nottingham Forest*	10.91	–								

GLOVER Edward Lee

Born: Kettering, 24 April 1970

Height: 5' 10"

Weight: 12.1

International Honours: S Yth, S "U21"-3

Position/Skill Factor: Striker with a lovely first touch on the ball, who is very good with his back to the goal. Turns defenders in the penalty area to create shooting opportunities.

Career History: A Nottingham Forest associated schoolboy (May 1985) and later a trainee (July 1986), before signing pro forms, he made his FL debut at Charlton Athletic on 15 August 1987. Following an impressive first season when he made 17 appearances and looked set to make an immediate impact, he was not seen again in a Forest shirt for the next three years. His career was knocked back by a serious knee injury sustained in his second game for the Scotland Under 21 team in Norway early in 1988-89 and subsequently a broken leg suffered in a reserve game. Having had spells on loan to Leicester City and Barnsley during 1989-90, he came back with a bang when playing in the first nine games of 1990-91, including the 2-1 League Cup Final defeat at the hands of Tottenham Hotspur. Stayed on the periphery of the Forest first team in 1991-92 and an early season loan to Luton Town proved abortive when he was injured in his first game at Kenilworth Road. For all his promise, he does not score enough goals on his occasional runs in the first team to justify a regular place. However, he did score on important goal during the season, at White Hart Lane in the League Cup Semi-Final, second-leg, which was the launch pad for Forest's well deserved victory and progress to the Final.

Clubs	Signing Date	Transfer Fee	APPEARANCES				GOALS			
			Lge	FL Cup	FA Cup	Others	Lge	FL Cup	FA Cup	Others
Nottingham Forest*	4.87	–	37+7	2+3	7+2	3+1	4	2	1	
Leicester City	9.89	Loan	3+2				1			
Barnsley	1.90	Loan	8		4					
Luton Town	9.91	Loan	1							

GODDARD Paul

Born: Harlington, 12 October 1959

Height: 5'8"

Weight: 11.8

International Honours: E "U21"-8, E-1

Position/Skill Factor: A striker who can hold the ball up, he has an excellent touch and a very good brain. Is at his most dangerous when balls are played into him on the edge of the penalty area.

Career History: First came to Queens Park Rangers as a 15-year-old when he signed associated schoolboy forms in November 1974. Became an apprentice in July 1976, before turning pro in the Summer of 1977 and going on to make his FL debut at home to Arsenal on 11 April 1978, when introduced as a sub. In his first full game he scored against Coventry City and although claiming a regular place shortly afterwards, it was not until 1979-80 that he really came to the fore, scoring 16 League goals in a great partnership with Clive Allen. On the basis of that form, West Ham United parted with a large fee for him to act as the foil for David Cross. In his first season at Upton Park, he won a Second Division Championship medal and reached the League Cup Final and although he scored in the replay, the "Hammers" were beaten 2-1 by Liverpool. Only missed a handful of games for the club prior to 1985-86 and was honoured by England when he came on as a sub against Iceland on 2 June 1982, but suffered a serious injury in August 1985 and when returned to full fitness again, could not dislodge Terry Cottee and Frank McAvennie, languishing in the reserves before being transferred to Newcastle United. Although highly regarded on Tyneside, he and his family were homesick for the south and after topping United's goalscoring charts, he was allowed to move to Derby County in the 1988 close season. Quickly formed a good partnership with Dean Saunders, but with the side going well, Millwall made an offer for the 30-year-old player that Derby could hardly refuse. It was a desperation signing by the "Lions", struggling in vain for First Division survival and a disastrous move for both club and player. New "Lions'" manager Bruce Rioch had no interest in him and one year later Millwall wrote off their over hasty £800,000 investment and granted him a free transfer. His former manager at Upton Park, John Lyall, then signed him for Ipswich Town and he showed a brief glimpse of his previous form with six goals in ten games, before injury ended his season. Bizarrely, he was listed in the "Lions'" programme on 1 January 1990 as turning out for the opposing side, Derby, but overnight he had signed for the home side and played for them instead. In 1991-92, he played only a minor role in Ipswich's Second Division Championship campaign after losing his place in September and when drafted back into the side in late season it was in midfield.

Clubs	Signing Date	Transfer Fee	APPEARANCES				GOALS			
			Lge	FL Cup	FA Cup	Others	Lge	FL Cup	FA Cup	Others
Q.P.R.	7.77	–	63+7	4+1			23			
West Ham United	8.80	£800,000	159+11	26	10+1	6	54	12	3	2
Newcastle United	11.86	£415,000	61	3	6		19	1	3	
Derby County	8.88	£425,000	49	7	1+1	5	15	2		1
Millwall	12.89	£800,000	17+3		4+1		1		1	
Ipswich Town*	1.91	–	37+6	1	0+1	2	10			

GORDON Dean Dwight

Born: Croydon, 10 February 1973

Height: 6'0" Weight: 11.5

Position/Skill Factor: Extremely athletic player who can perform equally well either on the left-wing, at left-back, or in the centre of the defence. Strong in the tackle, he has a good left foot and is adept at hitting long balls behind defenders.

Career History: First joined Crystal Palace as an associated schoolboy in November 1988, before signing on as a trainee in July 1989 and progressing to the club's professional staff during the 1991 close season. Made a few early appearances as a substitute in League Cup and Zenith Cup games in October 1991, prior to his FL debut, also as a substitute, at Selhurst Park against Tottenham Hotspur

on 22 December 1991. At the end of the season, he started in two games for Palace on the left-wing, before being withdrawn at a later stage.

Clubs	Signing Date	Transfer Fee	APPEARANCES				GOALS			
			Lge	FL Cup	FA Cup	Others	Lge	FL Cup	FA Cup	Others
Crystal Palace*	7.91	–	2+2	0+1		0+1				

GOSS Jeremy

Born: Cyprus, 11 May 1965

Height: 5'9"

Weight: 10.9

International Honours: E Yth, W-3

Position/Skill Factor: Non-stop defensive midfield player, who is a real team man. Pressures opponents into mistakes and is good on the ball. Loves to keep the game flowing with quick passing movements.

Career History: A member of Norwich City's FA Youth Cup Final team against Everton in 1983, he joined the club on a manpower work experience scheme, before turning to the pro ranks and making his FL debut as a sub, when coming on for Tony Spearing at Coventry City on 12 May 1984. Was selected for an England Under 19 team in 1984, which for statistical purposes is treated as a youth international. In a remarkable story of patience and perseverance by both player and his club, he had to wait until December 1987 before winning a regular place with the "Canaries". Then a knee injury ruled him out of the reckoning in 1988-89 and a hernia operation in the summer of 1989 reduced his chances in 1989-90. He made a comeback in the latter half of 1990-91 and did enough to prompt Wales' manager Terry Yorath to select him for two games at the end of the season, making his international debut against Iceland in April 1991, thus becoming an oddity of a Cyprus born player (albeit of English parentage) turning out for both England and Wales! Started 1991-92 on the bench, but displaced Ian Crook in October and, more than eight years after signing professional, finally won a regular place, holding it until the end of the season. Also won a further cap for Wales in April 1992.

Clubs	Signing Date	Transfer Fee	APPEARANCES				GOALS			
			Lge	FL Cup	FA Cup	Others	Lge	FL Cup	FA Cup	Others
Norwich City*	3.83	–	68+20	5	9+1	8	4	2		3

GRAY Andrew (Andy) Arthur

Born: Lambeth, 22 February 1964

Height: 5'10" Weight: 10.2

Position/Skill Factor: Tremendously powerful midfielder, always in the heat of the action and a strong tackler. Packing a terrific shot in his right foot, he is also respected by opposing defences for his long throws.

Career History: Before signing for Crystal Palace, he played non-League soccer first for Corinthian Casuals and then with Dulwich Hamlet of the Vauxhall League where he was observed by Palace manager, Steve Coppell. Made his FL debut at home to Cardiff City on 9 December 1984, coming on as a sub in a 1-1 draw at Grimsby Town. He then began to establish himself in the Palace midfield, taking over from Peter Nicholas, who moved to Luton Town. After three years at Selhurst Park, he joined Second Division Aston Villa, helping the club to promotion as runners-up, but soon found himself back in London with Queens Park Rangers, who were struggling in 16th place in the First Division. In helping the club to climb to mid-table respectability, he finished on the losing side only twice in 11 matches. However, his former club, Palace, having just won promotion from the Second Division decided to take him back to Selhurst Park and he started 1989-90 in midfield against his previous club at Loftus Road. He was influential in helping Palace to their first ever FA Cup Final, scoring the late equaliser which took the epic Semi-Final with Liverpool into extra-time. He

Clubs	Signing Date	Transfer Fee	APPEARANCES				GOALS			
			Lge	FL Cup	FA Cup	Others	Lge	FL Cup	FA Cup	Others
Crystal Palace	11.84	£2,000	91+7	9+1	3	0+1	27	2		
Aston Villa	11.87	£150,000	34+3	3	3+1	0+2	4	1	1	
Q.P.R.	2.89	£425,000	11				2			
Crystal Palace	8.89	£500,000	87+3	15	11	14	12	4	2	4
Tottenham Hotspur*	2.92	£900,000	14				1			

was a consistent performer in 1991-92 and was called up, along with club colleague, Geoff Thomas, by England manager Graham Taylor (his boss at Villa) for the vital European Championship qualifier in Poland in November 1991, in which England scraped a 1-1 draw and qualified by the skin of their teeth. Unfortunately, his England debut seemed to turn his head and his attitude so infuriated his manager, Steve Coppell, that he was dropped from the Palace team in January and transfer listed. He was then loaned to Tottenham Hotspur for the remainder of the season with a view to a permanent transfer, now firmed up.

GRAY Stuart

Born: Withernsea,
19 April 1960

Height: 5'10"

Weight: 11.10

Position/Skill Factor: Left sided player who can operate either in midfield or at full-back. A steady passer, with a lovely left foot, he specialises in hitting his front men with the long ball.

Career History: Signed for Nottingham Forest from Withernsea YC as an 18-year-old in 1978, but had to wait until 7 February 1981, before making his FL debut at Manchester City. Despite only missing a few games in 1981-82, he struggled to command a regular place in the following campaign and had a spell on loan at Bolton Wanderers. Signed for Barnsley that summer and played over 100 games for the club prior to his move to Aston Villa during 1987-88. He quickly fitted in to the Villa midfield and scored five valuable goals in 19 appearances as the club gained promotion to the First Division as runners-up. Since then, he played regularly until losing the left-back slot he had occupied since November 1988, in the closing weeks of 1990-91. Out in the cold under new manager Ron Atkinson, he signed for Southampton after two months of 1991-92, appearing first at left-back and then in midfield. He struggled to hold his place, however and following the Fifth Round FA Cup replay against Bolton Wanderers in late February, which the "Saints" all but lost, he played no further part in the campaign.

Clubs	Signing Date	Transfer Fee	APPEARANCES				GOALS			
			Lge	FL Cup	FA Cup	Others	Lge	FL Cup	FA Cup	Others
Nottingham Forest	3.78	–	48+1	5+1	3	1	3			
Bolton Wanderers	3.83	Loan	10							
Barnsley	8.83	£40,000	117+3	7	6+1	2	23	3		1
Aston Villa	11.87	£150,000	102+4	11	5+1	7+2	9	1	3	2
Southampton*	9.91	£200,000	10+2	5	4	1			1	

GREENMAN Christopher (Chris)

Born: Bristol, 22 December 1968

Height: 5'11" Weight: 11.0

International Honours: E Sch

Position/Skill Factor: A young central defender who is strong in the air and on the ground. Will continue to improve with experience.

Career History: Joined Coventry City from school at the unusually advanced age of 19, having earlier been on Bristol Rovers' books as an associated schoolboy (April 1983). Waited over three years to make his FL debut at home to Crystal Palace on 19 October 1991 in the left-back position. Played a few more times during the season, but with Atherton, Pearce and Billing in competition for the central defensive slots at Highfield Road, first team opportunities are fairly scarce.

Clubs	Signing Date	Transfer Fee	APPEARANCES				GOALS			
			Lge	FL Cup	FA Cup	Others	Lge	FL Cup	FA Cup	Others
Coventry City*	7.88	–	4			1				

GREGORY David Spencer

Born: Sudbury, 23 January 1970

Height: 5'11" Weight: 11.6

Position/Skill Factor: Useful midfield player who makes good runs into the opposition's penalty area. Sees passes quickly, he makes them and moves into space for the return ball.

Career History: Has been at Ipswich Town since signing associated schoolboy forms for the club in November 1985. Became a trainee in July 1986 and finally made his FL debut at Chelsea on 22 December 1988, nearly two years after signing professional. Prior to 1990-91, he had made only one full League appearance, but temporarily claimed a place in midfield when David Lowe had a spell out of the side early on in the season. Expected to progress in 1991-92, he fell back, making only fleeting appearances in Ipswich's Second Division Championship triumph and automatic promotion to the new Premier League.

Clubs	Signing Date	Transfer Fee	APPEARANCES				GOALS			
			Lge	FL Cup	FA Cup	Others	Lge	FL Cup	FA Cup	Others
Ipswich Town*	3.87	–	15+13	3+1	1	3+2	1			4

GROBBELAAR Bruce David

Born: Durban, South Africa, 16 October 1957

Height: 6'1" Weight: 13.0

International Honours: Zimbabwe Int

Position/Skill Factor: Highly underrated, perhaps over confident goalkeeper. Comes for crosses anywhere in the box and has superb reflexes. An entertainer, extrovert in the extreme, he loves to leave his box and dribble with the ball and enjoys every minute.

Career History: Served in the Zimbabwean army during the civil war before seeking a football career abroad, firstly with Vancouver Whitecaps, in the North American Soccer League. Had a spell as a non-contract player with Crewe Alexandra in the late 1970s, making his FL debut at Wigan Athletic on 21 December 1979. Became the regular choice, playing on to the end of the season and actually scoring from the penalty spot against York City in his last game for the club before returning to Vancouver. A year later, Bob Paisley, the Liverpool manager, having noted his potential at Crewe brought him to Anfield as understudy to Ray Clemence. Instead, after Clemence's abrupt and mysterious, departure to Tottenham, he found himself first choice 'keeper and made his debut at Wolverhampton Wanderers on the opening day of 1981-82. That first season, he was an ever present as Liverpool completed a League Championship — League Cup "double" and during the last nine seasons he has been an integral part of the Liverpool side that has won a further five League Championships, two FA Cup trophies, two League Cups, the European Cup and the Super Cup. Has been an ever present in six of the ten seasons spent at Anfield, a remarkable record. The 1991-92 season was typical for Bruce, brilliant one moment, fallible the next. His place in the team was under threat all season, both from the reserve Mike Hooper and a much speculated new signing. But he held on, only giving way through injury, or (in the case of the UEFA Cup) the bizarre "foreigners" ruling. Injured late in the season, he was restored to first team duty for the FA Cup final against Sunderland when, doubtless to his chagrin, he had little to do. Bruce's occasional "blunders" became part of soccer folk-lore in the 1980s and prompted some to label him as a "bad" or "unreliable" 'keeper, ignoring his more frequent breathtaking and gravity-defying saves which turn matches. Apparently spring-heeled, he can also reach shots bound for the top corners of the net and is probably the most athletic 'keeper since Chelsea's Peter ("The Cat") Bonetti. Bruce is not a "bad" 'keeper, but an eccentric and highly unorthodox one who seemingly loves to live dangerously on the field.

Clubs	Signing Date	Transfer Fee	APPEARANCES				GOALS			
			Lge	FL Cup	FA Cup	Others	Lge	FL Cup	FA Cup	Others
Crewe Alexandra	12.79	–	24				1			
Vancouver (NASL)	5.80	–								
Liverpool*	3.81	£250,000	406	63	60	53				

GROVES Perry

Born: Bow, 19 April 1965

Height: 5'11"

Weight: 11.12

Bruce Grobbelaar

Position/Skill Factor: A thrusting unselfish winger whose pace and two useful feet make him a constant threat to defences. Capable of getting among the goals when coming in on his right foot.

Career History: The nephew of Vic Groves, who played for Arsenal between 1955 and 1963, he started soccer life as an associated schoolboy (May 1980) at Wolverhampton Wanderers, before becoming an apprentice at Colchester United in September 1981. He made his FL debut at Layer Road against Bournemouth on 10 April 1982, while still an apprentice and spent four good seasons with the Essex club until signing for Arsenal for a surprisingly modest fee at the start of 1986-87. Despite struggling to become a regular in the "Gunners'" line-up, he was frequently employed as a substitute and often popped up to score valuable goals. After coming on as a sub for Arsenal in the 1987 League Cup Final against Liverpool, he set up the winning goal and has since won League Championship medals with the club in 1988-89 and 1990-91. A useful squad player who can cover for both forward and wide positions, his appearances in 1991-92, mainly as substitute, became more sporadic with such a wealth of talent at manager George Graham's disposal and he may feel it is time to seek a more regular team place elsewhere.

Clubs	Signing Date	Transfer Fee	APPEARANCES				GOALS			
			Lge	FL Cup	FA Cup	Others	Lge	FL Cup	FA Cup	Others
Colchester United	6.82	–	142+14	9+1	6	6	26	1	1	2
Arsenal*	9.86	£50,000	91+64	18+8	11+6	2+3	21	5	1	1

GUNN Bryan James

Born: Thurso,
22 December 1963

Height: 6'2"

Weight: 13.13

International Honours:
S Sch, S Yth,
S "U21"-8, S "B", S-1

Position/Skill Factor: Consistent goalkeeper who cuts a commanding figure in the penalty area. Very good when coming for crosses, he gives an air of confidence to the defence. Has a very long drop kick that can turn defence into attack in an instant.

Career History: Was at Aberdeen for six years, after signing from Invergordon BC as understudy to Jim Leighton, but only made 15 appearances. Luckily, when Norwich City were looking for a replacement for Chris Woods, his name sprang readily to mind and he moved south to Carrow Road. Made his FL debut at home to Tottenham Hotspur on 8 November 1986 and his fine performances for the remainder of that season were vital in ensuring the club's fifth place in the First Division. Since joining the "Canaries", he has missed a mere handful of games and his consistency was rewarded at international level when Scotland picked him for a home friendly match with Egypt on 16 May 1990 and included him in their World

Cup squad. It was a well merited call-up, but tragically he committed errors which cost two goals in an all-round feeble Scottish performance, ending in a humiliating 1-3 defeat and has not been considered since. His undisputed hold on the 'keepers jersey at Carrow Road came to an end in January 1992 when he suffered a back injury in a match against Sheffield and was forced to retire at half-time. In his absence, his deputy, Mark Walton, staked a formidable claim to the position.

Clubs	Signing Date	Transfer Fee	APPEARANCES				GOALS			
			Lge	FL Cup	FA Cup	Others	Lge	FL Cup	FA Cup	Others
Norwich City*	10.86	£150,000	200	18	20	15				

GYNN Michael (Micky)

Born: Peterborough,
19 August 1961

Height: 5'3"

Weight: 10.10

Position/Skill Factor: All action midfielder with good pace, who runs his heart out and is in his element when making runs into the opposition's penalty area. Strikes the ball well.

Career History: Began his career as an apprentice (July 1977) with his hometown club, Peterborough United and made his FL debut for them at Lincoln City on 14 April 1979. Became a big hit with the London Road crowd during his four years at the club and despite his distinct lack of size, he showed an ability to score frequently. And in his final season at Peterborough, 1982-83, he topped the club's goalscoring charts with 17 FL goals, an amazing total for a midfielder, before signing for Coventry City during the summer. Soon settled into the City squad, but it wasn't until his goalscoring exploits in the 1987 FA Cup run, culminating in the "Sky Blues'" 3-2 victory over Tottenham Hotspur in the Final, that he claimed much media attention. Had a long spell out with injuries in 1988-89, but has since come back with all his old vim and vigour. In and out of the Coventry team throughout 1991-92, he once again demonstrated the knack of scoring vital goals — in the penultimate game of the season at home to West Ham, his 44th minute strike of a loose ball in the penalty area (Coventry's first goal for six games and 494 minutes of "drought"), was just enough to preserve their status in the Premier League.

Clubs	Signing Date	Transfer Fee	APPEARANCES				GOALS			
			Lge	FL Cup	FA Cup	Others	Lge	FL Cup	FA Cup	Others
Peterborough United	4.79	–	152+4	10	13		33	1	3	
Coventry City*	8.83	£60,000	188+33	22+4	15+2	6	30	6	4	2

HADDOCK Peter Murray

Born: Newcastle,
9 December 1961

Height: 5'11"

Weight: 11.5

Position/Skill Factor: Strong tackling defender and a good header of the ball, who can play equally well either at full-back or centre-back. A valuable squad member.

Career History: A Geordie, he first signed for Newcastle United as an associated schoolboy in October 1976, before becoming an apprentice in June 1978 and eventually graduating to full professional. Made his FL debut at Queens Park Rangers in a 3-0 defeat and he went on to make 30 appearances that season. Afterwards, however, he found it difficult to hold down a place and was loaned to Burnley. Following his return to St James' Park, Billy Bremner signed him for Leeds United, but he had to wait a further year before gaining a regular place at Elland Road. Missed only six matches throughout 1989-90 and well deserved his Second Division Championship medal. Has suffered badly from injuries during his career and made only 10 appearances in 1990-91, being out for long periods as he struggled to reach full fitness. Made no appearances in 1991-92, with younger players providing adequate cover for the defensive positions.

Clubs	Signing Date	Transfer Fee	APPEARANCES				GOALS			
			Lge	FL Cup	FA Cup	Others	Lge	FL Cup	FA Cup	Others
Newcastle United	12.79	–	53+4	5	3					
Burnley	3.86	Loan	7							
Leeds United*	7.86	£45,000	106+12	9+2	5+2	9+1	1			

HALL Gareth David

Born: Croydon,
20 March 1969

Height: 5'8"

Weight: 10.7

International Honours:
E Sch, W "U21"-1, W-9

Position/Skill Factor: Strong tackling right-back who likes to get forward in support of his forwards. Good shooting capability from long range.

Career History: Came up through the Chelsea junior ranks, first as an associated schoolboy (September 1984) and then as an apprentice (July 1985), before turning pro. Made his FL debut at Wimbledon, while still a trainee, on 5 May 1987 and although finding it hard to establish himself in the "Blues'" defence, his performances were good enough for him to be called up to play for Wales, winning his first cap when coming on as a sub against Yugoslavia on 23 March 1988. Was a member of the Chelsea squad that won the Second Division title in 1989-90 and finally earned a regular place towards the end of the following term. Out of contention for a first team place in 1991-92, until January 1992 when he replaced Steve Clarke, he held the right-back slot only until March when the latter returned. His limited first team involvement also hampered his international progress, with only one substitute appearance for Wales to add to his previous caps.

Clubs	Signing Date	Transfer Fee	APPEARANCES				GOALS			
			Lge	FL Cup	FA Cup	Others	Lge	FL Cup	FA Cup	Others
Chelsea*	5.86	–	71+12	7	6	9+3	1			1

HALL David Terence

Born: Manchester, 19 October 1973

Height: 6'1" Weight: 11.10

International Honours: E Sch, E Yth

Position: Central Defender.

Career History: Joined the Oldham Athletic professional staff during the summer of 1992, having previously been at the club as an associated schoolboy (December 1987) and as a trainee (July 1990). No first team experience.

Clubs	Signing Date	Transfer Fee	APPEARANCES				GOALS			
			Lge	FL Cup	FA Cup	Others	Lge	FL Cup	FA Cup	Others
Oldham Athletic*	6.92	–								

HALL Richard Anthony

Born: Ipswich,
14 March 1972

Height: 6'1"

Weight: 13.0

International Honours:
E Yth, "U21"-2

Position/Skill Factor: Big strong central defender who enjoys the physical side of the game, both on the ground and in the air. Also good in the air at set plays.

Career History: Signed as an associated schoolboy (June 1987) for his local club, Ipswich Town, but was allowed to leave without furthering his career. Became a trainee with Scunthorpe United in July 1988 and showed so much promise that he was deemed good enough to make his FL debut at home to Grimsby Town on 26 December 1989, while still a junior. That was his only League appearance during the season, but in 1990-91 he started as a regular first team choice and after only 21 appearances, he was sold to Southampton in the same week as another promising "Irons'" youngster, Neil Cox, was transferred to Aston Villa. Definitely one for the future, the "Saints" gave him a chance to show his paces at the Dell in the last match of the season against Wimbledon, when he came on for Neil Ruddock. He started 1991-92 as a first choice central defender for the "Saints", scoring on his first full appearance and although in and out of the team during the season he can feel pleased with his rapid progress so far. In February he scored two almost identical headers from right-wing corners in the space of four minutes in a Fifth Round FA Cup tie at Bolton — a remarkable occurrence. At the end of the season he was called up for the England Under 21 squad to compete in the annual tournament in Toulon, France, making one appearance.

Clubs	Signing Date	Transfer Fee	APPEARANCES				GOALS			
			Lge	FL Cup	FA Cup	Others	Lge	FL Cup	FA Cup	Others
Scunthorpe United	3.90	–	22	2	3	4	3			
Southampton*	2.91	£200,000	21+6	4+1	5	3	2		2	

HALLE Gunnar

Born: Oslo, Norway,
11 August 1965

Height: 5'11"

Weight: 11.2

International Honours:
Norwegian Int

Position/Skill Factor: Very quick right-back who is a fitness fanatic. A good passer of the ball, he loves getting forward with the attack.

Career History: An established Norwegian international with 28 caps to his credit, he was signed by Joe Royle in February 1991 from Norwegian League side, Lillestrom, with a view to stiffening the "Latics" defence, following a drubbing at Oxford. He immediately replaced Paul Warhurst in the right-back position, making his FL debut in a 2-0 win at home to Port Vale on 16 February 1991. Needed little time to settle into the English game and after just 17 League matches he was the proud owner of a Second Division Championship medal. In 1991-92 he

started the "Latics'" First Division campaign as first choice right-back, but sustained an injury in late September from which he apparently failed to recover full fitness, playing in only two further games to the end of the season.

Clubs	Signing Date	Transfer Fee	APPEARANCES				GOALS			
			Lge	FL Cup	FA Cup	Others	Lge	FL Cup	FA Cup	Others
Oldham Athletic*	2.91	£280,000	27	1						

HALLWORTH Jonathan (Jon) Geoffrey

Born: Stockport,
26 October 1965

Height: 6'2"

Weight: 12.10

Position/Skill Factor: Confident goalkeeper who presents a commanding figure and comes off his line quickly for crosses. He often starts attacks with quick throws and long kicks.

Career History: Developed by Ipswich Town after signing as an associated schoolboy in November 1980, he progressed to an apprenticeship in July 1982, before turning pro. He made his FL debut while on loan to Bristol Rovers at Reading on 26 January 1985, conceding three goals in a 3-2 defeat, before his first game for Ipswich in November 1985. Prior to 1987-88, he spent most of his time at Portman Road deputising for Paul Cooper, but started that season as first choice and played 31 consecutive games, before making way for Ron Fearon and Craig Forrest. Never played again for Town's first team and one year later was transferred to Oldham Athletic where he immediately took over the goalkeeping duties from Andy Rhodes. Lost his place temporarily to Rhodes the following term and when the latter was transferred to Dunfermline Athletic in the 1990 close season, Oldham manager Joe Royle signed John Keeley from Brighton for a large fee, presumably to be the "Latics'" number one 'keeper, with Hallworth as cover. Instead, he started the 1990-91 season as first choice and putting his previous erratic form behind him, performed superbly, appearing in all 46 games of Oldham's Second Division Championship season. In Oldham's first season back in Division One, he was again consistent to a fault, missing only the final game of 1991-92, whilst poor John Keeley languished in the reserves.

Clubs	Signing Date	Transfer Fee	APPEARANCES				GOALS			
			Lge	FL Cup	FA Cup	Others	Lge	FL Cup	FA Cup	Others
Ipswich Town	5.83	–	45	4	1	6				
Bristol Rovers	1.85	Loan	2			1				
Oldham Athletic*	2.89	£75,000	118	12	13	1				

HARKES John Andrew

Born: New Jersey, USA,
8 March 1967

Height: 5'10"

Weight: 11.10

International Honours:
USA Int

Position/Skill Factor: A midfield player who can also play as an attacking right-back. Passes the ball well, is aggressive and a good crosser when getting forward in a wide position.

Career History: Spotted by Second Division Sheffield Wednesday, while playing for the University of North Carolina and the USA national side, he was a bargain signing and despite being a natural midfielder, he took over the number two shirt when Roland Nilsson was injured and filled in admirably. He made his FL debut at Hillsborough against Oldham Athletic on 3 November 1990 and in only his tenth first team game, his run and 30 yard dipping volley in a League Cup Fourth Round replay at Derby, with Peter Shilton in goal, not only sealed his acceptance by "Owls'" fans, but was considered by many to be "goal of the season". He completed his first season, assisting the club to gain promotion to the First Division in third place and also collected a League Cup winners medal for his part in the "Owls'" surprise 1-0 victory over Manchester United. During 1991-92 he provided cover right across midfield and was a frequent performer in several different positions, including right-back and central defence, whilst waiting for a chance to claim a place of his own.

Clubs	Signing Date	Transfer Fee	APPEARANCES				GOALS			
			Lge	FL Cup	FA Cup	Others	Lge	FL Cup	FA Cup	Others
Sheffield Wednesday*	10.90	£70,000	36+16	10	5+1	3	5	1		

HARKIN Sean Christopher

Born: Birmingham, 3 December 1973

Height: 5'6" Weight: 11.0

Position/Skill Factor: Striker with good skills, who needs to find the net more regularly if he is to remain up front.

Career History: Missed by the big Birmingham clubs, he was an associated schoolboy (October 1988), before further progressing through the Manchester City ranks as a trainee (July 1990) to full professional status early in 1991. He has yet to make a first team appearance, having made only one appearance in City's reserve side.

Clubs	Signing Date	Transfer Fee	APPEARANCES				GOALS			
			Lge	FL Cup	FA Cup	Others	Lge	FL Cup	FA Cup	Others
Manchester City*	1.91	–								

HARKNESS Steven (Steve)

Born: Carlisle,
27 August 1971

Height: 5'9"

Weight: 10.11

International Honours:
E Yth

Position/Skill Factor: Strong tackling midfielder with a good left foot. Very aggressive, he can also play at left-back if required.

Career History: Joined his local team Carlisle United as an associated schoolboy in March 1987 and after accepting a trainee contract in September 1987, he made his FL debut at Brunton Park in the 3-0 win over Hereford United on 18 February 1989, shortly before he turned professional. Remaining in the first team until the end of the season, his early development was obviously noted at Anfield and after only four months as a pro at Brunton Park he was signed by Liverpool. Spent his first two season with the "Reds" in the reserve team, although a regular choice for the England youth team. He was called up for his Liverpool debut at right-back early in 1991-92, when Liverpool's injury crisis ruled out five regulars simultaneously, he made occasional appearances throughout the season in both full-back positions. It remains to be seen if he will make the grade at Anfield and earn a regular place, but if he does it is likely to be at left-back.

Clubs	Signing Date	Transfer Fee	APPEARANCES				GOALS			
			Lge	FL Cup	FA Cup	Others	Lge	FL Cup	FA Cup	Others
Carlisle United	3.89	–	12+1							
Liverpool*	7.89	£75,000	7+4	2+1	1	3+1				

HARPER Alan

Born: Liverpool,
1 November 1960

Height: 5'8"

Weight: 10.9

International Honours:
E Yth

Position/Skill Factor: Very experienced utility player who can play in a whole variety of positions, both in defence and midfield. An excellent reader of the game, he is also very constructive when in possession.

Career History: Was an associated schoolboy (October 1975) with Liverpool, before progressing to an apprenticeship in June 1977 and later turning pro with the club. In five years as a professional at Anfield, he was unable to make even a single appearance with Phil Thompson and Alan Hansen holding down the central defenders positions and was eventually allowed to leave for close neighbours, Everton. Made his FL debut at Goodison Park against Stoke City on 27 August 1983 where he proved a valuable acquisition, gaining League Championship medals in 1984-85 and 1986-87, an FA Cup winners medal in 1985 and a European Cup Winners Cup medal in 1985. An infrequent scorer, his rare goals nevertheless tended to be vital ones. Ironically his first ever strike for Everton was against his former club in a Merseyside "derby" and secured a 1-1 draw. His second goal was in the 1986 FA Cup Semi-Final against Sheffield Wednesday after coming on as substitute and helped his team to a 2-1 victory and into the Cup Final. After over 100 appearances for the "Toffees", he moved to Sheffield Wednesday, but during an 18 month spell at Hillsborough, found it difficult to establish a regular place. However, when his former Everton manager, Howard Kendall, by then in charge of Manchester City, brought him to Maine Road as one of his first signings, he found an automatic niche at full-back. In 1990-91 he was back to his customary role as a cover player, operating mostly as a defensive midfielder. Almost predictably, he reunited with Howard Kendall, now back at Everton, for the third time and was a regular member of the 1991-92 team, alternating, as always, between full-back and midfield slots.

Clubs	Signing Date	Transfer Fee	APPEARANCES				GOALS			
			Lge	FL Cup	FA Cup	Others	Lge	FL Cup	FA Cup	Others
Liverpool	4.78	–								
Everton	6.83	£100,000	103+24	17+2	10+8	13+1	4		1	
Sheffield Wednesday	7.88	£275,000	32+3	1+1	1	1				
Manchester City	12.89	£150,000	46+4	3	6	3	1	1		
Everton*	8.91	£200,000	29+4	1+1	1	2				

HARRIOTT Marvin Lee

Born: Dulwich, 20 April 1974

Height: 5'11" **Weight:** 10.11

International Honours: E Sch, E Yth

Position/Skill Factor: Useful right-back who is very quick to get forward.

Career History: Having already gained England youth honours at West Ham United, he was surprisingly released by the club, while still a trainee and was immediately snapped up by Oldham Athletic at the end of 1991-92. Starting out at Upton Park as an associated schoolboy in June 1988, before signing as a trainee in July 1990, on leaving school, he has yet to appear in first team football.

Clubs	Signing Date	Transfer Fee	APPEARANCES				GOALS			
			Lge	FL Cup	FA Cup	Others	Lge	FL Cup	FA Cup	Others
Oldham Athletic*	4.92	–								

HARTFIELD Charles

Born: Lambeth, 4 September 1971

Height: 6'0" **Weight:** 12.0

International Honours: E Yth

Position/Skill Factor: Strong midfield player who loves a tackle. Displaying a lovely left foot, he also has very good technique.

Career History: Joined Arsenal as a trainee in July 1988, having been an associated schoolboy at Aston Villa (July 1986) and turned professional 14 months later. After two years as a professional at Highbury, without a "sniff" of first team action, he was granted a free transfer and Dave Bassett signed him up for Sheffield United in the 1991 close season. Surprisingly , but perhaps typically for Bassett, he was plunged into first team duty almost immediately, making his FL debut away to Crystal Palace on 31 August 1991. Was perhaps unfortunate to be sent off for an apparently innocuous offence in his third match (at Oldham Athletic) when the "Blades" with only nine men on the field, reduced a 2-0 half time deficit to 2-1. After a handful of games in midfield and at full-back he was then rested and played almost no part in the rest of the campaign.

Clubs	Signing Date	Transfer Fee	APPEARANCES				GOALS			
			Lge	FL Cup	FA Cup	Others	Lge	FL Cup	FA Cup	Others
Arsenal	9.89	–								
Sheffield United*	8.91	–	6+1	1						

HAWTHORNE Mark

Born: Glasgow, 31 October 1973

Height: 5'9" **Weight:** 10.12

Position: Midfield Player.

Career History: A 1992 close season professional signing for Crystal Palace, he initially joined the club as a non-contract junior player on leaving school and has graduated through the "Eagles'" youth sides. No first team experience as yet.

Clubs	Signing Date	Transfer Fee	APPEARANCES				GOALS			
			Lge	FL Cup	FA Cup	Others	Lge	FL Cup	FA Cup	Others
Crystal Palace*	6.92	–								

HEANEY Neil Andrew

Born: Middlesbrough, 3 November 1971

Height: 5'9" **Weight:** 11.1

International Honours: E Yth, E. "U21"-4

Position/Skill Factor: Skilful left-winger who can get down the flank and is a lovely crosser of the ball.

Career History: A full time professional player with Arsenal, having come through the junior ranks first as an associated schoolboy (January 1987) and then as a trainee (July 1988). He first played in the Football League, whilst on loan to Fourth Division Hartlepool in 1990-91, making his FL debut when coming on as a sub at home to Chesterfield on 19 January 1991. During the 1991-92 season, he enjoyed a successful two month loan period with Cambridge United from January to March 1992, scoring on his debut and playing a prominent role in the club's ultimately unsuccessful Second Division promotion challenge. After returning to Highbury, he made his Arsenal debut as a sub away to Sheffield United in April. Clearly a player to watch out for in the future, he was a regular in the England youth teams of 1989 and 1990, graduating to the England Under 21 squad for the end of season games in May 1992, playing four times.

Clubs	Signing Date	Transfer Fee	APPEARANCES				GOALS			
			Lge	FL Cup	FA Cup	Others	Lge	FL Cup	FA Cup	Others
Arsenal*	11.89	–	0+1							
Hartlepool United	1.91	Loan	2+1							
Cambridge United	1.92	Loan	9+4		1		2			

HEATH Michael

Born: Hull, 7 February 1974

Height: 5'9" Weight: 12.6

Position/Skill Factor: Agile goalkeeper who is a good shot stopper.

Career History: Signed professional forms for Tottenham Hotspur during the recent summer, having been at the club since leaving school and coming to White Hart Lane as a trainee in August 1990. Yet to make the first team, he was injured for most of the season with a broken toe.

Clubs	Signing Date	Transfer Fee	APPEARANCES				GOALS			
			Lge	FL Cup	FA Cup	Others	Lge	FL Cup	FA Cup	Others
Tottenham Hotspur*	5.92	–								

HENDERSON Damian Michael

Born: Leeds, 12 May 1973

Height: 6'0½" Weight: 13.2

Position/Skill Factor: Big strong striker who is brave and very useful in the air.

Career History: A second year professional who has yet to play first team football, he first came to Leeds United as an associated schoolboy in June 1987, before signing on as a trainee when leaving school in July 1989. A regular in the reserve side.

Clubs	Signing Date	Transfer Fee	APPEARANCES				GOALS			
			Lge	FL Cup	FA Cup	Others	Lge	FL Cup	FA Cup	Others
Leeds United*	7.91	–								

HENDON Ian Michael

Born: Ilford, 5 December 1971

Height: 6'0" Weight: 12.10

International Honours: E Yth, E "U21"-4

Position/Skill Factor: Highly rated defender cum midfielder, who is a lovely striker of the long ball with his right foot. Useful in the air, he makes a very strong defender.

Career History: Signed for Tottenham Hotspur as an associated schoolboy in January 1986, he graduated to trainee status in August 1988, before joining the pro ranks and made his FL debut at Aston Villa on 16 March 1991, when coming on as a sub in a 3-2 defeat. Made further appearances as sub in 1991-92, plus a full game at Swansea in the League Cup when Spurs were surprisingly defeated 1-0 (but easily winning the second leg) and was later farmed out to Portsmouth and Leyton Orient on short loans during the season to increase his experience. Almost certain to be a "Spurs'" defender of the future, he has already played many games for the England Youth team, graduating to the Under 21 squad in May 1992 and making four appearances in central defence.

Clubs	Signing Date	Transfer Fee	APPEARANCES				GOALS			
			Lge	FL Cup	FA Cup	Others	Lge	FL Cup	FA Cup	Others
Tottenham Hotspur*	12.89	–	0+4	1		0+1				
Portsmouth	1.92	Loan	1+3							
Leyton Orient	3.92	Loan	5+1							

HENDRIE John Grattan

Born: Lenoxtown, 24 October 1963

Height: 5'7" Weight: 11.4

International Honours: S Yth

Position/Skill Factor: A crowd pleasing right-winger, who can both run with the ball and shoot with deadly accuracy. Strong and stocky, he has an abundance of pace and is extremely durable. Also, very consistent.

Career History: Joining Coventry City as an apprentice in June 1980, he turned pro at the end of the 1980-81 season and later made his FL debut at West Ham United on 21 November 1981. After spending four years at Highfield Road, having few opportunities to shine and following a period on loan at Hereford United, he was signed on a free transfer by Bradford City in the 1984 close season. Showed outstanding form at Valley Parade and in his first season, 1984-85, as an ever present, he won a Third Division Championship medal as the club climbed up the League. During his time at Bradford, he only missed one match in four seasons (due to a suspension) and after attracting a lot of interest, he signed for Newcastle United. Unfortunately it was a disastrous season for the "Magpies", ending in relegation from the First Division. Hendrie was one of the few successes in the team and became a great crowd favourite, especially after a typical break-away solo goal at Anfield in September which was the springboard for a rare, almost historic, 2-1 victory over Liverpool. However, he was not a favourite with new manager Jim Smith and was sold to Leeds United the following summer. Although he played 22 League matches for Leeds and collected a Second Division Championship medal in 1989-90, he found it difficult to hold down a regular place and was allowed to leave for Middlesbrough during the 1990 close season. Immediately settled into the side, making 40 League appearances as the "Boro" strove to reach the First Division, only to fail at the Play-Off stage. Slightly below par in 1991-92, he lost his place briefly in mid-season, but, after returning to the team in January, he played in every game subsequently in "Boro's" valiant League Cup run up to the Semi-Final, where they succumbed after a great struggle to Manchester United. He was also a driving force during the closing stages of the League campaign when the club rose from seventh to second place and thus gained automatic promotion to the new Premier League.

Clubs	Signing Date	Transfer Fee	APPEARANCES				GOALS			
			Lge	FL Cup	FA Cup	Others	Lge	FL Cup	FA Cup	Others
Coventry City	5.81	–	15+6	2			2			
Hereford United	1.84	Loan	6							
Bradford City	6.84	–	173	17	11	11	46	3	6	4
Newcastle United	6.88	£500,000	34	2	4	3	4	1		
Leeds United	6.89	£600,000	22+5	1	1	2	5			
Middlesbrough*	6.90	£550,000	78+1	13	5+2	2	6	2	1	1

HENDRY Edward Colin James

Born: Keith,
7 December 1965

Height: 6'1"

Weight: 12.2

Position/Skill Factor: Big, imposing central defender, who does well in the air and is useful on the ground. Often pushed up-front to try and snatch a goal when all seems lost.

Career History: Now in his second spell with Blackburn Rovers, he originally came to Ewood Park from the Scottish Premier Division club, Dundee, near the end of 1986-87. Made his FL debut at home to Stoke City on 14 March, 1987 at centre-forward and scored in his next two games, at Derby County and West Bromwich Albion. His fifth game for Rovers was at Wembley in the Final of the then Full Members (now Zenith) Cup and he scored the only goal in their victory over Charlton Athletic. The following season he played exclusively in central defence, struck a remarkable 12 goals from open play and was also ever present. Scored seven goals from 38 games in 1988-89 and in both seasons, Rovers' hopes of promotion were thwarted at the Play-Off stage. Seeking a transfer at the start of 1989-90, he was dropped controversially for a few weeks and soon after his return was transferred to Manchester City. Went straight into the City team and held his place to the end of 1990-91, although his impressive goal scoring ratio was sharply reduced. In 1991-92 he lost his place to new signing Keith Curle at the start of the season and made only a few appearances as substitute (scoring a last minute winner at West Ham in one of them), before returning to Ewood Park two years after he left. Apart from losing his place for one month in January, he played a vital role in Rovers' promotion campaign and the Play-Offs, making a quick return to the top flight.

Clubs	Signing Date	Transfer Fee	APPEARANCES				GOALS			
			Lge	FL Cup	FA Cup	Others	Lge	FL Cup	FA Cup	Others
Blackburn Rovers	3.87	£30,000	99+3	4	3	7	22			1
Manchester City	11.89	£700,000	57+6	4+1	5	4	5	1	2	2
Blackburn Rovers*	11.91	£700,000	24+4		0+1	3	4			

HENDRY John

Born: Glasgow, 6 January 1970

Height: 5'11" Weight: 10.0

International Honours: S "U21"-1

Position/Skill Factor: Striker who has lovely skills and a very good first touch. Is learning all the time, but already has the ability to make something out of nothing.

Career History: Spotted by Scottish League side, Dundee, playing in junior soccer with Hillington YC, he played two games for the club and was loaned out to Forfar Athletic, where he scored six goals in ten matches, before coming south to join Tottenham Hotspur in the 1990 close season. Made his FL debut at Norwich City on 10 April 1991, scoring in a 2-1 defeat and in his only other full game for "Spurs", he got the equaliser in the last game of the season at Manchester United. During 1991-92 he appeared only occasionally as a substitute for "Spurs" and had a spell on loan to Charlton Athletic, late in the season. Made only one full appearance for Athletic, although scoring a late winner against Millwall in one of his four appearances as a sub. Amazingly, this was Charlton's first victory over their near neighbours for 24 years.

Clubs	Signing Date	Transfer Fee	APPEARANCES				GOALS			
			Lge	FL Cup	FA Cup	Others	Lge	FL Cup	FA Cup	Others
Tottenham Hotspur*	7.90	£50,000	3+6	0+1			3			
Charlton Athletic	2.92	Loan	1+4				1			

HENRY Nicholas (Nicky) Ian

Born: Liverpool, 21 February 1969

Height: 5'6" Weight: 9.8

Position/Skill Factor: Keeps things ticking over in midfield. Holds up the ball well, he is a good passer and is always available when team mates get into trouble.

Career History: Slipped through the Liverpool net when signing as an associated schoolboy (January 1985) with Oldham Athletic and later progressing to trainee status (July 1986). Illness and injuries severely restricted his progress at first and it was feared at one time that he would not stand up to the rigours of League soccer. On recovering full fitness, however, he made his FL debut at Hull City on 19 September 1987 and by March 1989 was a regular in midfield after spending the summer and autumn of 1988 with Swedish club Halmstad for top level experience. Since then, has only missed a handful of games. A member of the "Latics'" 1989-90 team which created history by reaching the Semi-Finals of the two major cup competitions and contesting the League Cup Final with Nottingham Forest, before losing narrowly 1-0. In the FA Cup, Oldham knocked out both Aston Villa and Everton, before fighting out a thrilling 3-3 draw with Manchester United in the Semi-Final. At a critical stage of the replay, a fierce 25 yard shot from Henry hit the United bar and bounced down on the goal line. Had it counted as a goal it is probable that Oldham would have contested both Finals. Happily, the disappointments of 1990 were soon forgotten when he won a Second Division Championship medal the following season. During 1991-92 he was ever present in Oldham's first season in the top flight for 69 years and scored six vital FL goals to help the "Latics" stay just clear of the relegation battle and preserve their status in the new Premier League. Unfortunate never to be considered for the England Under 21 squad.

Clubs	Signing Date	Transfer Fee	APPEARANCES				GOALS			
			Lge	FL Cup	FA Cup	Others	Lge	FL Cup	FA Cup	Others
Oldham Athletic*	6.87	–	142+7	16+3	14	4	10	2		

HEPWORTH Richard

Born: Pontefract, 8 January 1974

Height: 5'7" Weight: 10.7

Position: Midfielder.

Career History: A newcomer to the professional ranks of League Champions, Leeds United, he signed on the dotted line during the 1992 close season, having previously been at Elland Road as an associated schoolboy (February 1988) and as a trainee (September 1990). Has no first team experience.

Clubs	Signing Date	Transfer Fee	APPEARANCES				GOALS			
			Lge	FL Cup	FA Cup	Others	Lge	FL Cup	FA Cup	Others
Leeds United*	6.92	–								

HERRERA Roberto

Born: Torquay, 12 June 1970

Height: 5'7" Weight: 10.6

Position/Skill Factor: A full-back with a good left foot. Very quick on his feet in defence, he can get himself out of trouble when the need be. Also, likes to get forward to link up with the attack.

Career History: Signed for Queens Park Rangers as a 16-year-old trainee in June 1986, before progressing to the pro ranks and although getting a run out in the first team as a sub in the League Cup in 1988-89, he had to wait until the end of the following season before he was selected for a League match. His FL debut came at Anfield, against Liverpool on 28 April 1990 and he made three more

appearances in central defence in 1990-91 during an injury crisis at Loftus Road — unfortunately, all three games were lost. The signing of Rufus Brevett in March 1991 reduced his chances of staking a regular claim to the left-back spot at Loftus Road and in 1991-92 he made only a single appearance as a sub for Rangers in a League Cup tie, before joining his home town club, Torquay United, on loan for the closing weeks of the season. Although he played 11 games for the "Gulls" in the Third Division, he could do little to stop their slide back into the Fourth Division.

Clubs	Signing Date	Transfer Fee	APPEARANCES				GOALS			
			Lge	FL Cup	FA Cup	Others	Lge	FL Cup	FA Cup	Others
Q.P.R.*	2.88	–	4+2	1+2		1+1				
Torquay United	3.92	Loan	11							

HILL Andrew (Andy) Rowland

Born: Maltby,
20 January 1965

Height: 5'11"

Weight: 12.0

International Honours:
E Yth

Position/Skill Factor: A very experienced right-back for his age, he looks good when breaking out of defence with the ball. Rarely misses a passing opportunity.

Career History: Started his soccer career at Old Trafford when signing as an associated schoolboy for Manchester United in October 1979, before graduating as an apprentice (May 1981). Turned pro almost two years later, but after a season in the reserve side he was released and signed for Bury and it was here that he blossomed. He made his FL debut in the number two shirt at Darlington on 25 August 1984 and by the end of his first season at Gigg Lane, 1984-85, the club had gained promotion from the Fourth Division in fourth place. Following many outstanding performances with the "Shakers" and being recognised as one of the best defenders outside the First Division, he was later made club captain. Unfortunately, during 1990-91, Bury FC was hit by financial difficulties and in order for the club to balance its books, he signed for Manchester City on the recommendation of Sam Ellis, City's assistant manager, and previously Hill's manager at Bury, following a short loan period. In 1991-92 he established himself as first choice right-back at Maine Road, scoring four vital FL goals from open play, into the bargain, which demonstrates his enthusiasm to get forward.

Clubs	Signing Date	Transfer Fee	APPEARANCES				GOALS			
			Lge	FL Cup	FA Cup	Others	Lge	FL Cup	FA Cup	Others
Manchester United	1.83	–								
Bury	7.84	–	264	22	12	19	10	1		1
Manchester City*	12.90	£200,000	43+1	5		1	5			

HILL Colin Frederick

Born: Uxbridge,
12 November 1963

Height: 5'11"

Weight: 12.2

International Honours:
NI-6

Position/Skill Factor: Very experienced centre-back cum full-back, who intercepts well and will invariably pick out the right pass to make in the circumstances. Has good pace.

Career History: Came to Highbury while still at school, signing associated schoolboy forms for Arsenal in December 1977, before becoming an apprentice in June 1980 on the first rungs to eventual stardom. made his FL debut at Norwich City on 20 April 1983, but apart from 1983-84 when he played 37 League games, he couldn't hold down a regular first team place, following the arrival of Viv Anderson and Tommy Caton and was given a free transfer in 1986. Somewhat surprisingly, he joined CS Maritimo, an obscure Portuguese First Division club, based on the island of Madeira. On his return to England, he had to rebuild his career from the bottom, when signing for Fourth Division Colchester United and in two seasons there, helped the club to avoid the ultimate drop into the Vauxhall Conference. Following that, his luck changed for the better when Dave Bassett gave him the opportunity to climb back up the League with Sheffield United and in 1989-90, his first season at the club, he did just that as the club gained promotion to the First Division as runners-up. His fine displays did not go unnoticed at international level either and he duly won his first cap for Northern Ireland against Norway at Windsor Park on 27 March 1990. In 1991-92 he was a scapegoat for the "Blades'" customary disastrous start to a season and following the signing of Brian Gayle in September, he lost his place in the team, only playing as cover for other defenders when injured. He joined Leicester City on loan, just before the late March transfer deadline, with a view to a permanent move and assisted the "Foxes" to the Second Division Play-Offs, where after thrashing Cambridge United, they lost out to Blackburn Rovers for the third promotion place. He also won two more caps for Northern Ireland.

Clubs	Signing Date	Transfer Fee	APPEARANCES				GOALS			
			Lge	FL Cup	FA Cup	Others	Lge	FL Cup	FA Cup	Others
Arsenal	8.81	–	46	4	1		1			
CS Maritimo (P'tugal)	7.86	–								
Colchester United	10.87	–	64+5	2	7	3+1			2	
Sheffield United*	7.89	£85,000	75+5	5	10+2	3	1			
Leicester City	3.92	Loan	10			3				

HILL Keith John

Born: Bolton,
17 May 1969

Height: 6'0"

Weight: 11.3

Position/Skill Factor: Central defender who can also play at full-back. Good in the air, he attacks the ball well. Will bring the ball out of defence, in preference to clearing his lines.

Career History: Following several outstanding performances for Blackburn Rovers' junior side, he turned professional in the 1987 close season and made his FL debut in a 2-0 defeat at home to Middlesbrough on 26 September 1987, only three days after playing in a 1-1 draw against Liverpool in the League Cup. Deputised for Colin Hendry and David Mail in 15 matches in 1988-89, before winning a regular place at the start of 1989-90. Sadly, an injury in January ruled him out until the final match of the season. In and out during Rovers' troubled 1990-91, he again missed out for the second half of the season. Won his place back in October 1991 and remained a regular first choice, despite fierce competition from Colin Hendry and Kevin Moran, until late in the season. Giving way to Moran, he missed out on the Play-Offs which finally assured Rovers of their dream of promotion to the Premier League.

Clubs	Signing Date	Transfer Fee	APPEARANCES				GOALS			
			Lge	FL Cup	FA Cup	Others	Lge	FL Cup	FA Cup	Others
Blackburn Rovers*	5.87	–	89+6	6	5+1	3+2	4	1		

HILLIER David

Born: Blackheath,
19 December 1969

Height: 5'10"

Weight: 11.6

International Honours:
E "U21"-1

Position/Skill Factor: Impressive midfield player. Has plenty of stamina and is a strong tackler and above all else, he gives everything for the team.

Career History: Began his career with Arsenal as an associated schoolboy in January 1984 and was later upgraded to trainee status in July 1986. He was blooded in the League Cup at Chester City in the number four shirt and just four days later, made his FL debut away to Leeds United on 29 September 1990, when coming on as a sub for Nigel Winterburn. Played in most of the final matches of the 1990-91 season, with Michael Thomas on the sidelines and did not look out of place as the "Gunners" won the League Championship. Also won his first and only England Under 21 cap in April 1991. In 1991-92 he started in the first team line-up, but only won a regular place in the "Gunners'" team after their elimination from the European Cup by Benfica in November. With Paul Davis out of favour, Michael Thomas on his way to Liverpool and Siggi Jonsson retired, Arsenal were almost bereft of midfielders and a lot of responsibility lay on his shoulders. To his credit, he accepted the challenge head on and although Arsenal slumped badly in mid-season, they ended in magnificent style, unbeaten in 16 games with Hilliers' place in the team established beyond doubt.

Clubs	Signing Date	Transfer Fee	APPEARANCES				GOALS			
			Lge	FL Cup	FA Cup	Others	Lge	FL Cup	FA Cup	Others
Arsenal*	2.88	–	36+7	2	3+2	1	1			

HINCHCLIFFE Andrew (Andy) George

Born: Manchester,
5 February 1969

Height: 5'10"

Weight: 12.10

International Honours:
E Yth, E "U21"-1

Position/Skill Factor: Full-back with a wonderful left foot. Can strike 60 yard crossfield passes with ease and loves to get forward to deliver quality crosses to the target men.

Career History: Joined Manchester City as an associated schoolboy in May 1983, before becoming an apprentice in July 1985. Made his FL debut for City in a 2-1 home win over Plymouth Argyle on 15 August 1987 and missed just two matches that first season. Played a prominent part in the club's promotion to the First Division during the following year, scoring five times from the left-back position. And proved consistent in the top flight before injury forced an early end to his season in 1989-90. During the 1990 close season, however, he was transferred to Everton in exchange for Neil Pointon and a large cash adjustment in City's favour, making his debut at Goodison against Leeds United on 25 August 1990, the opening day of 1990-91. Although injured early on, he recovered well

enough to play in 30 matches, including the losing Zenith Data Cup Final against Crystal Palace. It has not proved to be a happy move for him. Once regarded as one of the most promising left-backs in the country, he is now only an occasional performer for Everton. Apparently not highly regarded by manager Howard Kendall, hence his transfer from City, he found his former manager following him to Goodison Park only a few months later. In 1991-92 he had a run in the team at left-back up to December, but following the arrival of Gary Ablett, his only appearances were on the left side of midfield.

Clubs	Signing Date	Transfer Fee	APPEARANCES				GOALS			
			Lge	FL Cup	FA Cup	Others	Lge	FL Cup	FA Cup	Others
Manchester City	6.86	–	107+5	11	12	4	8	1	1	1
Everton*	7.90	£800,000	36+3	5	5	4	1			

HIRST David Eric

Born: Cudworth, 7 December 1967

Height: 5'11" Weight: 12.5

International Honours: E Yth, E "U21"-7, E"B", E-3

Position/Skill Factor: One of that rare breed of strikers who can run with the ball and finish with devastating power and accuracy, normally with a strong left foot shot. Also, brave in the air.

Career History: Started his career with Barnsley as an apprentice in July 1984, making his FL debut, three months prior to turning professional, at Charlton Athletic on 17 August 1985 and by the end of that first season he had scored nine goals in 27 full matches. His first goal for Barnsley, against Leeds United in October 1985, is still recalled with awe by Oakwell regulars — a 50 yard run, followed by a blistering shot — but down the years it has become his trademark. He soon showed that his first FL goal was no fluke, with eight more in a run of ten games, before being rested. Clearly a "Wonderkind", he was snapped up by neighbouring Sheffield Wednesday at the end of his first season as a professional. Somewhat surprisingly, his first three seasons with the "Owls" were comparatively disappointing, considering his meteoric start with Barnsley and he found himself in and out of the side. Eventually began to make his mark at Hillsborough in 1989-90 when scoring 14 goals, but unfortunately for both him and the fans, the club exploded into the Second Division. However, he fairly exploded on the scene in 1990-91, with his 24 goals good enough to see Wednesday promoted back to the First Division at the first time of asking and as the proud possessor of a League Cup winners medal, following the club's thrilling victory over Manchester United. At the end of the season, he was called up by Graham Taylor for the England summer tour of Australasia, making his international debut against Australia and then playing in the New Zealand match. He started the 1991-92 season with a magnificent strike in the third minute of the first match against Aston Villa and continued in similar vein. Despite two short absences through injury, he finished the season once again as leading scorer with 18 FL goals, plus three in cup ties. Selected once more for England against France in February, he was withdrawn at half-time to make way for Gary Lineker. Perhaps unlucky to be excluded from the England squad for the European Championship finals in Sweden, he will surely enjoy further opportunities to advance his international career in the near future.

Clubs	Signing Date	Transfer Fee	APPEARANCES				GOALS			
			Lge	FL Cup	FA Cup	Others	Lge	FL Cup	FA Cup	Others
Barnsley	11.85	–	26+2	1			9			
Sheffield Wednesday*	8.86	£200,000	168+21	8+5	4+2	6	72	7	5	4

HITCHCOCK Kevin Joseph

Born: Canning Town, 5 October 1962

Height: 6'1"

Weight: 12.2

Position/Skill Factor: All action goalkeeper who is very agile and quick off his line. Is also a good kicker, particularly from his hands.

Career History: Nottingham Forest first spotted him playing for Isthmian League team, Barking and moved smartly to sign him. Could not immediately break in to the Forest side and was signed by Mansfield Town in a loan deal and made his FL debut at Colchester United on 10 March 1984. Played out the rest of the season at the Field Mill Ground and during the summer the transfer was made permanent. Missed just three matches over the next three seasons, assisting the "Stags'" promotion run to the Third Division in 1985-86, before John Hollins signed him for Chelsea, with half of the large fee going to Forest, according to the terms of his previous transfer. However, Chelsea were struggling at the wrong end of the First Division at the time and his efforts were not enough to prevent defeat by Middlesbrough over two legs of the Play-Off final. Began the next season as second choice to Roger Freestone and following the signing of Dave Beasant his first team prospects seemed even more remote. After playing just four games in 1990-91, he spent some time on loan at Northampton Town during their vain Third Division promotion bid. After three years at Stamford Bridge with little first team action, he made a breakthrough in 1991-92 as Dave Beasant lost form and Roger Freestone departed to Swansea. Called up for the third game of the season, he alternated with Beasant throughout the season, making 21 FL appearances. However, he ended the season as second choice again.

Clubs	Signing Date	Transfer Fee	APPEARANCES				GOALS			
			Lge	FL Cup	FA Cup	Others	Lge	FL Cup	FA Cup	Others
Nottingham Forest	8.83	£15,000								
Mansfield Town	2.84	Loan	14							
Mansfield Town	6.84	£140,000	168	12	10	20				
Chelsea*	3.88	£250,000	35	2	4	9				
Northampton Town	12.90	Loan	17			1				

HODGE Stephen (Steve) Brian

Born: Nottingham, 25 October 1962

Height: 5'7" Weight: 9.12

International Honours: E "U21"-8, E"B", E-24

Position/Skill Factor: Left footed midfield player who is very quick and can get his foot in when required. Often scores goals with late runs into the opponents penalty box.

Career History: Was first noticed by Nottingham Forest as a 14-year-old and signed on associated schoolboy forms in July 1977. Later became an apprentice (July 1979), before joining the professional ranks and making his FL debut at Ipswich Town on 15 May 1982. He only missed a handful of games over the next three full seasons and figured prominently in Brian Clough's plans. Was surprisingly allowed to join Aston Villa after just two games in 1985-86 and he impressed enough to warrant a full England call up when coming on for Gordon Cowans during a 1-0 win over the USSR on 26 March 1986 in Tbilisi. After replacing the injured Brian Robson for five matches in the World Cup in Mexico that year, another large fee exchanged hands when Tottenham Hotspur signed him as a replacement for Glasgow Rangers bound Graham Roberts. Helped "Spurs" to the losing FA Cup Final against Coventry City that season, but never settled in London and eventually moved back to Nottingham Forest in the summer of 1988. Since being back at the City

Ground, he has won League Cup winners medals in 1989 and 1990 and came on as a sub during the losing 1991 FA Cup Final against his old team, Tottenham. Impatient

with his frequent non-availability through injury, Brian Clough sold him to Leeds United in the summer of 1991 and although not an automatic first team choice, he played enough games to qualify for a League Championship medal, while his seven FL goals were vital to United's cause. It remains to be seen if he can stake a claim to a regular first team place, possibly as the replacement for the ageing, but hitherto tireless Gordon Strachan on the right side of midfield.

Clubs	Signing Date	Transfer Fee	APPEARANCES				GOALS			
			Lge	FL Cup	FA Cup	Others	Lge	FL Cup	FA Cup	Others
Nottingham Forest	10.80	–	122+1	10	6	11	30	2		4
Aston Villa	8.85	£450,000	53	12	4	1	12	3	1	
Tottenham Hotspur	12.86	£650,000	44+1	2	7		7		2	
Nottingham Forest	8.88	£550,000	79+3	20+1	11+1	8	20	6	2	2
Leeds United*	7.91	£900,000	12+11	3+2	1		7			

HODGES Glyn Peter

Born: Streatham, 30 April 1963

Height: 6'0" Weight: 12.3

International Honours: W Yth, W "U21"-5, W-16

Position/Skill Factor: Left-winger with lovely skill. By crossing great early balls, he doesn't need to beat defenders and causes all sorts of problems.

Career History: After starting his career at Wimbledon as an associated schoolboy in February 1979, he showed enough early promise to be taken on as an apprentice (July 1979) just five months later. He then proceeded to make his FL debut, while still an apprentice, at Halifax Town on 27 September 1980, when coming on as a sub. Played 27 full League games that season as the club were promoted to the Third Division in fourth place and although they were relegated the following year, he won a Fourth Division Championships medal in 1982-83 as the "Dons" came straight back. In 1983-84 he played in 39 League matches when Wimbledon moved into the Second Division as runners-up and at the end of the season he won his first full Welsh cap when he came on as a sub against Norway on 6 June 1984. The fairy story was completed in 1985-86 when the little south Londoners marched into the First Division in third place. He had now played in all four divisions with the same club, an amazing feat and having accomplished that, he signed for Newcastle United in the 1987 close season. After only three months and seven games and unable to settle in the north-east, he joined Watford, a team doomed to relegation to the Second Division at the end of that season. Spent almost three years at Vicarage Road, before moving back to south London with Crystal Palace in the 1990 close season. The move was not a success. After making only a handful of appearances, his career was rescued by his former manager at Wimbledon and Watford, Dave Bassett, who signed him for Sheffield United in January 1991. Scored three vital goals in his first four games for

the "Blades" and played a significant role in their remarkable escape from relegation trouble when winning seven consecutive games from January to March. Suffered a rather indifferent season in 1991-92, losing his left-wing slot to the emerging Dane Whitehouse, but reappearing later on the right side of midfield, without making a great impression.

Clubs	Signing Date	Transfer Fee	APPEARANCES				GOALS			
			Lge	FL Cup	FA Cup	Others	Lge	FL Cup	FA Cup	Others
Wimbledon	2.81	–	200+32	14+2	13+2	0+1	49	3	2	
Newcastle United	7.87	£200,000	7							
Watford	10.87	£300,000	82+4	5	8	2+1	15	2	2	1
Crystal Palace	7.90	£410,000	5+2	2+2					1	
Sheffield United*	1.91	£450,000	34+4		3+1		6		1	

HODGES Lee Leslie

Born: Epping, 4 September 1973

Height: 5'9" Weight: 11.6

International Honours: E Yth

Position/Skill Factor: A natural goal scoring forward with a good first touch.

Career History: Another of Tottenham Hotspur's bright youngsters, he first came to White Hart Lane as an associated schoolboy in March 1988, before signing on as a trainee in August 1990. made good progress into the club's professional ranks, but has still to make a first team appearance.

Clubs	Signing Date	Transfer Fee	APPEARANCES				GOALS			
			Lge	FL Cup	FA Cup	Others	Lge	FL Cup	FA Cup	Others
Tottenham Hotspur*	2.92	–								

HOLDEN Ian Andrew (Andy)

Born: Flint, 14 September 1962

Height: 6'1" Weight: 13.0

International Honours: W "U21"-1, W-1

Position/Skill Factor: Strong central defender who is very good in the air and likes to tackle. Very experienced.

Career History: Discovered by Chester City, playing for non-League Rhyl, he made a meteoric start to his full-time soccer career. Following his FL debut on 22 August 1983 against Northampton Town, he played in all but two League matches that season and was later capped by Wales against Israel on 10 June 1984. As the club captain, he had a disappointing season in 1985-86, being out for most of the time with a severe ankle injury, but Chester fared better, gaining promotion to the Third Division as Fourth Division runners-up. After signing for Wigan Athletic early in 1986-87, he struggled through the season with the same old injury and when gradually coming back to peak fitness, he had the terrible misfortune to break a leg at Doncaster Rovers on 2 January 1988. He never played for Wigan again and was transferred to Oldham Athletic where he made his comeback, playing 13 League matches in 1988-89. Injured again in August 1989, he made only three further appearances later in the season, but started 1990-91 as first choice only to suffer injury yet again in the second League match of the season and played no further part in the "Latics'" Second Division Championship campaign. Absent throughout 1991-92, he has recently been declared 100 per cent fit by the club and appointed player-coach.

Clubs	Signing Date	Transfer Fee	APPEARANCES				GOALS			
			Lge	FL Cup	FA Cup	Others	Lge	FL Cup	FA Cup	Others
Chester City	8.83	£3,000	100	8	2	4	17	1	2	2
Wigan Athletic	10.86	£45,000	48+1	3	7	7	4			
Oldham Athletic*	1.89	£130,000	21		2		4			

HOLDEN Richard (Rick) William

Born: Skipton, 9 September 1964

Height: 5'11"

Weight: 12.7

Position/Skill Factor: A lively left-winger who can not only score goals, but creates many others with accurate crosses from either foot. Often he will pick the ball up deep and run at the full-back, giving himself the option of crossing early or going past his rival.

Career History: Spotted by Burnley playing for Carnegie Teachers Training College in Leeds, he made just one subs' appearance for the club, whilst on trial, for his FL debut at Leyton Orient on 3 May 1986. Not offered a contract by the "Clarets", he joined Halifax Town in September 1986 on a non-contract basis and after winning a regular place, he abandoned any ambitions as a teacher and signed a professional contract in January 1987. His impressive play on the left flank soon had the scouts turning up at the Shay, but with Town almost safe from relegation in March 1988, he signed for Watford. Went straight into a side that was doomed for the Second Division and stayed at Vicarage Road until the end of the following season when the club failed at the Play-Off stage to regain its First Division status. Was transferred to Oldham Athletic at the start of the 1989-90 season and sparkled as an ever present in 65 matches as the "Latics" reached the FA Cup Semi-Final and the League Cup Final. 1990-91 was even better and he missed only four League matches and won a Second Division Championship medal as the club attained promotion to the top flight for the first time since 1923. He enjoyed another excellent season for the "Latics", on their return to Division One in 1991-92, playing in every single game, although on four occasions as substitute. Now recognised as one of the most effective left-wingers in the country, it is probably now too late for him to start an international career at the age of 28. An in-depth statistical analysis of First Division goals in 1991-92, revealed that his crosses had "created" no fewer than 19 goals for his team mates, more "assists" than by any other top level player.

Clubs	Signing Date	Transfer Fee	APPEARANCES				GOALS			
			Lge	FL Cup	FA Cup	Others	Lge	FL Cup	FA Cup	Others
Burnley	3.86	–	0+1							
Halifax Town	9.86	–	66+1	2	7	8	12			
Watford	3.88	£125,000	42	2	6	3+1	8			
Oldham Athletic*	8.89	£165,000	125+4	15+1	13	3	19	4	2	1

HOLLOWAY Ian Scott

Born: Kingswood,
12 March 1963

Height: 5'7"

Weight: 9.12

Position/Skill Factor: The ideal midfield type who can also play on the right-wing. Has a good footballing brain and works hard to get into good positions in order to receive the ball. Also, he doesn't give the ball away easily.

Career History: Locally born and bred, he first came to Bristol Rovers as an associated schoolboy in July 1977 and graduated to apprentice status in July 1979. Made his FL debut a month after turning pro at Wrexham on 25 April 1981, but it wasn't until 1983-84 that he began to hold down a regular place. His promising displays alerted Wimbledon, who were looking to tighten up in midfield for their second season in Division Two. He signed for the "Dons" in the 1985 close season, but spent less than a year at Plough Lane, before being on the move across London, to Brentford. had previously had a spell on loan at Griffin Park in March 1986 and this deal was made permanent in time for the new season. However, the move was not wholly successful and he had another period on loan, this time with Torquay United. The prodigal son finally returned home, re-signing for Bristol Rovers and in 1989-90, as an ever present, he enjoyed his best-ever season, winning a Third Division Championship medal into the

bargain. He was ever present yet again in 1990-91 as the club consolidated itself in Division Two and scored winning goals on three separate occasions, albeit two of them being penalties. After ten years playing in the lower divisions, it seemed that any chance of performing at the top level had long since passed him by, but when "Pirates'" manager Gerry Francis moved to Queens Park Rangers in the summer of 1991, one of his first signings for the "R's" was Holloway. He started the season in the first team squad and following Ray Wilkins' injury in the first game, deputised capably in the unfamiliar role of central midfield. On Wilkins' return in November, he switched back to the right-wing, only to move inside again from February until the end of the season in place of Simon Barker.

Clubs	Signing Date	Transfer Fee	APPEARANCES				GOALS			
			Lge	FL Cup	FA Cup	Others	Lge	FL Cup	FA Cup	Others
Bristol Rovers	3.81	–	104+7	10	8	5	14	1	2	
Wimbledon	7.85	£35,000	19	3	1		2			
Brentford	3.86	£25,000	27+3	2	3	0+1	2			
Torquay United	1.87	Loan	5							
Bristol Rovers	8.87	£10,000	179	5		19	26		1	2
Q.P.R.*	8.91	£230,000	34+6	3	1	1+1				

HOLMAN Mark Brett

Born: Croydon, 29 November 1973

Height: 5'11" Weight: 12.4

Position: Midfielder.

Career History: Joined the Crystal Palace professional ranks during the 1992 close season, having previously been at Selhurst Park as an associated schoolboy (February 1988) and as a trainee (July 1990).

Clubs	Signing Date	Transfer Fee	APPEARANCES				GOALS			
			Lge	FL Cup	FA Cup	Others	Lge	FL Cup	FA Cup	Others
Crystal Palace*	6.92	–								

HONEYWOOD Lee Brian

Born: Chelmsford, 3 August 1971

Height: 5'8" Weight: 10.10

International Honours: E Yth

Position/Skill Factor: Young defender who has good ability on the ball. Sees openings quickly and doesn't elaborate when passing.

Career History: Joined Ipswich Town as a trainee on leaving school in July 1987 and progressed to the club's professional staff during the 1989 close season. Yet to make a first team appearance, he patiently awaits an early opportunity, having now been on the professional staff for over three years.

Clubs	Signing Date	Transfer Fee	APPEARANCES				GOALS			
			Lge	FL Cup	FA Cup	Others	Lge	FL Cup	FA Cup	Others
Ipswich Town*	5.89	–								

HOOPER Michael (Mike)
Dudley

Born: Bristol, 10 February 1964

Height: 6'2" Weight: 13.5

Position/Skill Factor: Agile goalkeeper. Very brave in coming for the ball and strong on crosses, he will not be intimidated. Also has good kicking ability.

Career History: Came to Bristol City from non-League side, Mangotsfield, whom he played for while completing his studies at Bristol University. Earlier, he had been on City's books as a 14-year-old associated schoolboy, signing in November 1978. Made his FL debut, his one and only game for the club, at Ashton Gate against Lincoln City on 1 December 1984, before joining Fourth Division Wrexham on a free transfer. He immediately replaced Stuart Parker as the "Robins'" custodian and showed such potential, having appeared in less than 40 League matches, that Liverpool signed him as cover for Bruce Grobbelaar. Playing as the reserve custodian at Anfield is usually a 'keepers' graveyard, as his predecessors, Ian Wardle and Bob Bolder, left the club without making a single first team appearance. He was more fortunate and made his Liverpool debut in the opening game of 1986-87, deputising for seven FL games until Grobbelaar's return, also playing in the last four matches of the season. He later enjoyed an extended first team run of 17 consecutive games in 1988-89, until two errors at Sheffield Wednesday led to him being dropped. Sidelined in 1989-90, he was loaned to Leicester City in September 1990 and although conceding ten goals in his first two games, it was acknowledged at the time, that it was due more to Leicester's defensive disorganisation, than the hapless 'keeper. After returning to Anfield, he played seven more League games in late season during Grobbelaar's absence through injury. Although a less flamboyant 'keeper than Grobbelaar, many shrewd judges considered that he deserved an extended run in the side and when the latter was dropped "officially" for the first time, in October 1991, he received another chance, but after only two games he was injured. Came back to play four matches at the end of the season when Grobbelaar suffered a hand injury, but when the latter was recalled for the 1992 FA Cup Final against Sunderland, he lost all patience and refused to join the squad. His future at Anfield now appears to be in some doubt.

Clubs	Signing Date	Transfer Fee	APPEARANCES				GOALS			
			Lge	FL Cup	FA Cup	Others	Lge	FL Cup	FA Cup	Others
Bristol City	1.84	–	1		1	1				
Wrexham	2.85	–	34	4						
Liverpool*	10.85	£40,000	42	7	3	5+1				
Leicester City	9.90	Loan	14							

HOPE Christopher (Chris)
Jonathan

Born: Sheffield, 14 November 1972

Height: 6'0" Weight: 11.1

Position/Skill Factor: Good footballing central defender, he is also effective in the air. A neat passer who doesn't give the ball away easily.

Career History: Following a spell in the north-east as a junior with Darlington, he signed professional forms for Nottingham Forest in the 1990 close season. Yet to make a first team appearance, he is one for the future, but with Darren Wassell and Des Walker having left during the summer, he will be hoping for an early opportunity in 1992-93.

Clubs	Signing Date	Transfer Fee	APPEARANCES				GOALS			
			Lge	FL Cup	FA Cup	Others	Lge	FL Cup	FA Cup	Others
Nottingham Forest*	8.90	–								

HORNE Barry

Born: St Asaph, 18 May 1962

Height: 5'10" Weight: 11.6

International Honours: W-30

Position/Skill Factor: Competitive, hard tackling midfield player, who keeps his passing simple and is quite capable of scoring spectacular goals.

Career History: A late starter to League football, he completed a chemistry degree at Liverpool University, while playing as a part-timer for Rhyl in the Northern Premier League. On leaving university, he signed for Fourth Division Wrexham and made his FL debut at Swindon Town on 24 August 1984. Showed great promise and consistency during his three years at the Racecourse Ground, missing only two League games and it came as no surprise when he moved to a bigger club, when signing for Portsmouth. Played his first game for "Pompey" at Oxford on the opening day of the 1987-88 season and a month later, made his first appearance for the Welsh national team, coming on as a sub in the 88th minute of a European Championship qualifier against Denmark. Since then he has been an automatic first choice in the Welsh team. Only missed two League matches that season and although the club were relegated to the Second Division, he had firmly established himself in midfield. The following year, Southampton's manager, Chris Nicholl, looking to strengthen his midfield, brought the Welshman to the Dell as the club's most expensive signing. Very quickly settled down in the side and apart from a spell out injured at the end of 1989, very rarely missed a match. While playing a sterling role in the "Saints'" successful battle against relegation in 1991-92, he also became a hero to the club's supporters (if he wasn't before) with two goals in a FA Cup Fifth Round replay at home to Bolton Wanderers in late February. In the 90th minute of the game, Bolton had apparently scored the winner to go 2-1 up, but in the third minute of injury time, Horne received the ball in midfield, carried it forward and seeing no other options available took aim from 35 yards. The shot carried such venom and topspin that it tumbled the hapless Bolton 'keeper backwards into his own net with the ball for an amazing equaliser. He later scored the winner in extra-time.

Clubs	Signing Date	Transfer Fee	APPEARANCES				GOALS			
			Lge	FL Cup	FA Cup	Others	Lge	FL Cup	FA Cup	Others
Wrexham	6.84	–	136	10	7	15	17	1	2	3
Portsmouth	7.87	£60,000	66+4	3	6		7			
Southampton*	3.89	£700,000	111+1	15+2	15	7	6	3	3	1

HOUGHTON Raymond (Ray) James

Born: Glasgow, 9 January 1962

Height: 5'8" Weight: 11.4

International Honours: IR-46

Position/Skill Factor: Industrious midfield player with wonderful vision, who can unlock the best of defences. Can see the whole pitch, instinctively knows where his team mates are and weights his passes perfectly.

Career History: Worked his way through West Ham United's junior ranks, before making his FL debut when coming on as a sub at Arsenal on 1 May 1982. That was to be his only opportunity with the "Hammers" and on being freed, he joined Fulham. Only missed a handful of games in three seasons at Craven Cottage, before signing for Oxford United, newly promoted to the First Division and looking for midfield creativity. In his first season with the club, he collected a League Cup winners medal, scoring the second goal in the 3-0 victory over Queens Park Rangers and was selected for the Republic of Ireland against Wales in Dublin on 26 March 1986. Although born in Scotland, he qualified for the Irish team, by virtue of his father and went on to become one of the cornerstones of Jack Charlton's team. His unanswered goal for Ireland in the seventh minute of the match against England during the 1988 European Championships in Germany, was

the first nail in England's coffin for that competition. Signed by Liverpool in October 1987, he quickly displaced the unfortunate Craig Johnston from the right midfield slot. The move also subtly altered the "Reds'" style of play as Johnston was happy to perform in an orthodox right-wing role, whilst Houghton was preferred in the middle of the pitch. He played 28 FL games in 1987-88, finding the net five times and was good value for his League Championship medal that season. The following term, he played in every game, winning an FA Cup winners medal as Liverpool beat their local rivals, Everton, 3-2 at Wembley, but lost out on another League Championship medal a week later when Arsenal denied the "Reds" in the final minute of the last match. Unfortunately, in 1989-90, he missed half of the season through injury, making only 16 appearances, although enough to qualify him for another League Championship medal. Played consistently during 1990-91 when, after a marvellous start to the season, the "Reds" capsized somewhat, following Kenny Dalglish's dramatic resignation. In

1991-92 he was one of the few Liverpool regulars to avoid serious long term injury and his seven League strikes kept the team afloat at a time when goals were in short supply. Finished the season with an FA Cup winners medal, following Liverpool's 2-0 victory over Sunderland in the Final.

Clubs	Signing Date	Transfer Fee	APPEARANCES				GOALS			
			Lge	FL Cup	FA Cup	Others	Lge	FL Cup	FA Cup	Others
West Ham United	7.79	–	0+1							
Fulham	7.82	–	129	12	4		16	2	3	
Oxford United	9.85	£147,000	83	13	3	6	10	3		1
Liverpool*	10.87	£825,000	147+6	13	26+1	8	28	3	4	3

HOUGHTON Scott Aaron

Born: Hitchin,
22 October 1971

Height: 5'5"

Weight: 11.6

International Honours:
E Sch, E Yth

Position/Skill Factor: Small tricky winger with good pace, who is quite capable of scoring goals. With two good feet, he is a lovely early crosser of the ball.

Career History: A young forward with Tottenham Hotspur, having come through the ranks as an associated schoolboy (June 1986), then a trainee (August 1988), before signing as a professional, he was loaned out to Second Division Ipswich Town in 1990-91 in order to acclimatise him to League football. Made his FL debut at Portman Road against Portsmouth on 2 April 1991, coming on as a sub for Romeo Zondervan and staying until the end of the season. During 1991-92 he frequently appeared as substitute for Tottenham and in one game scored twice (along with a brace from Gary Lineker), after an interruption due to floodlight failure, when "Spurs" overturned a 0-1 deficit to record a remarkable 4-1 victory over Luton Town.

Clubs	Signing Date	Transfer Fee	APPEARANCES				GOALS			
			Lge	FL Cup	FA Cup	Others	Lge	FL Cup	FA Cup	Others
Tottenham Hotspur*	7.90	–	0+10	0+2		0+2	2			
Ipswich Town	3.91	Loan	7+1				1			

HOWE Stephen (Steve) Robert

Born: Cramlington, 6 November 1973

Height: 5'7" Weight: 10.4

International Honours: E Yth

Position/Skill Factor: Skilful midfield player who can pass the ball around.

Career History: Spotted as a 14-year-old playing in the north-east, he signed associated schoolboy forms for Nottingham Forest in June 1988, before coming to the City Ground as a trainee, on leaving school, in July 1990. Making good progress, he turned professional just one month after his 17th birthday. Although he has yet to be given a first team opportunity, the staff at Forest have a very high opinion of his abilities and he could make a breakthrough in 1992-93.

Clubs	Signing Date	Transfer Fee	APPEARANCES				GOALS			
			Lge	FL Cup	FA Cup	Others	Lge	FL Cup	FA Cup	Others
Nottingham Forest*	12.90	–								

HOWELLS David

Born: Guildford,
15 December 1967

Height: 5'11"

Weight: 11.1

International Honours:
E Yth

Position/Skill Factor: Good team player who is very adaptable. Has appeared mainly in midfield, but is capable of man-to-man marking, or playing in an attacking role.

Career History: Joined Tottenham Hotspur in July 1984 on a YTS scheme and signed full professional forms just six months later. Waited over a year for his FL debut, but it was worth waiting for as he scored the winning goal in a 2-1 victory at Sheffield Wednesday on 22 February 1986. One of the best of a good crop of youngsters who have worked their way into the "Spurs'" side over the last few years, he started his career as a forward, but has now settled into the team in a defensive midfield role. Consolidated his position in 1990-91 when making 29 League appearances and collecting an FA Cup winners medal, following the 2-1 victory over Nottingham Forest. His younger brother, Gareth, a goalkeeper, who started his career with "Spurs" without breaking through, is now with Torquay United. Played through most of 1991-92, but tended to be sacrificed whenever "Spurs" changed their tactical formation. Scored only one goal in the season, albeit a vital one which secured a 1-1 draw at Leeds in December.

Clubs	Signing Date	Transfer Fee	APPEARANCES				GOALS			
			Lge	FL Cup	FA Cup	Others	Lge	FL Cup	FA Cup	Others
Tottenham Hotspur*	1.85	–	106+28	11+2	5+2	7	14	1	1	

HOYLAND Jamie William

Born: Sheffield,
23 January 1966

Height: 6'0"

Weight: 12.8

International Honours:
E Yth

Position/Skill Factor: Has all the essential ingredients of the modern midfield player. With plenty of stamina, he makes good forward runs and does well in the air.

Career History: Son of Tommy, a wing-half with Bradford City and Sheffield United between 1949 and 1961, he started his career at Manchester City, first as an associated schoolboy (July 1981), then as an apprentice (July 1982), before signing as a fully fledged pro. Introduced at Maine Road for his FL debut against Derby County on 26 November 1983, he only made one further appearance in two years with City and was released during the 1986 close season. On leaving, found his niche in the Third Division with Bury and was ever present in both 1988-89 and 1989-90, when he finished up as the club's top scorer with 16 goals. The time was right for him to move up a grade, but on signing for Sheffield United, one of his father's old clubs, he found it difficult to immediately adjust to the pressures of the First Division. In a side that struggled for most of the season, he appeared in only 17 League games, as the team was continually chopped and changed. Seemed to establish himself in the "Blades'" midfield in 1991-92, playing in every game until the FA Cup Third Round tie with Luton Town in January when he was withdrawn with an injury. After regaining fitness, he surprisingly played only twice more and then only briefly as substitute, as his place went first to Michael Lake and then to new signing, Paul Rogers.

Clubs	Signing Date	Transfer Fee	APPEARANCES				GOALS			
			Lge	FL Cup	FA Cup	Others	Lge	FL Cup	FA Cup	Others
Manchester City	11.83	–	2	0+1						
Bury	7.86	–	169+3	14+1	6	12	35	5		2
Sheffield United*	7.90	£250,000	40+7	3+1	2	2	4	1		1

HUGHES David Robert

Born: St Albans, 30 December 1972

Height: 5'10½" Weight: 10.9

International Honours: E Sch

Position/Skill Factor: Hard working midfield player who tackles back. Looks confident with the ball and he passes and moves well.

Career History: Signed by Southampton on associated schoolboy terms in March 1991 at the relatively late age of 18, he turned professional during the 1991 close season, on leaving school. Still to play in the first team, he looks a useful prospect for the near future.

Clubs	Signing Date	Transfer Fee	APPEARANCES				GOALS			
			Lge	FL Cup	FA Cup	Others	Lge	FL Cup	FA Cup	Others
Southampton*	7.91	–								

HUGHES Leslie **Mark**

Born: Wrexham, 1 November 1963

Height: 5'8" Weight: 12.5

International Honours: W Sch, W Yth, W "U21"-5, W-42

Position/Skill Factor: Striker who is as strong as an ox, but skillful as well. Brings maximum pressure to bear in opponents' penalty areas, when tackling defenders, he makes chances for others as well as being a proficient goalscorer himself. A lovely volleyer of the ball.

Career History: Came to Manchester United as a 14-year-old, signing as an associated schoolboy in March 1978 and then, on leaving school, becoming an apprentice in June 1980. Turned pro and made his FL debut when coming on as a sub at Old Trafford against Southampton on 21 January 1984. Earlier in the season, however, he had been introduced to the Old Trafford faithful during a League Cup tie against Port Vale and he later played his first full game at Oxford United in the Fourth Round of the competition, marking the occasion with a goal. By the end of 1983-84 he was a regular front runner and his progress was recognised internationally when he was selected to play for Wales against England in May 1984. In a dream debut for his country, he scored the only goal of the game at his hometown ground, Wrexham. In 1984-85, his first full season, he was the club's leading scorer with 24 League goals and was prominent as United triumphed 1-0 in the FA Cup Final against Everton. Although finding goals harder to come by, the following season, he was still the subject of a £2.5 million bid from the Spanish giants, Barcelona, managed by Terry Venables, who eventually signed him to link up with Gary Lineker. However, while Lineker was feted for his goals, the Spanish fans didn't seem to appreciate the Welshman's ability to make space for other players with his unselfish running off the ball. His stay in Spain was less than successful and following a brief spell in Germany on loan with Bayern Munich he returned to Old Trafford in the 1988 close season. More than 46,000 fans welcomed him back for the game against Queens Park Rangers, but the season was generally a disappointing one for both him and United. However, there was consolation in 1989-90 when United beat Crystal Palace 1-0 in a replay to win the FA Cup Final, after the teams had drawn 3-3 in the first match. The six goal thriller had been a personal triumph, when he put United ahead on the hour and then equalised with just seven minutes of extra-time remaining. With that victory, United returned to European competition when the ban on English clubs was finally lifted. After rather nervy progress in the UEFA Cup against inferior opposition, United reached the final in Rotterdam to face Hughes' former club, Barcelona, as marginal "underdogs". In fact, the "Reds" fully deserved their 2-1 victory and his goal, a tremendous shot on the run from a tight angle, clinched the victory. He is also credited by some sources with scoring the first goal, although he only touched Bruce's already goalbound header over the line. A UEFA Cup winners medal was consolation for defeat by Sheffield Wednesday in the League Cup Final three weeks earlier, as was being voted by his fellow professionals as the 1991 PFA "Player of the Year", an award he had previously won in 1989. During 1991-92 he helped United win the League Cup for the first time, but the club failed at the final hurdle to win the League Championship, having promised to do so all season. Unfortunately, although not

Mark Hughes

alone, his personal goal drought from the end of February to the final game of the season, obviously contributed to the failure.

Clubs	Signing Date	Transfer Fee	APPEARANCES				GOALS			
			Lge	FL Cup	FA Cup	Others	Lge	FL Cup	FA Cup	Others
Manchester City*	8.88	–	25+1	5	1	1	1			

Clubs	Signing Date	Transfer Fee	APPEARANCES				GOALS			
			Lge	FL Cup	FA Cup	Others	Lge	FL Cup	FA Cup	Others
Manchester United	11.80	–	85+4	5+1	10	14+2	37	4	4	2
Barcelona (Spain)	7.86	£2,500,000								
Bayern Munich (Germ)	10.87	Loan								
Manchester United*	7.88	£1,500,000	141+4	21	20+1	15+1	47	6	7	5

HUGHES Michael Eamonn

Born: Larne,
2 August 1971

Height: 5'6"

Weight: 10.8

International Honours:
NI Sch, NI Yth, NI
"U21"-1, NI-4

Position/Skill Factor: A potentially brilliant left-winger with great pace and enormous self confidence, he has the ability to beat defenders and get in telling crosses. Possesses a sweet left foot.

Career History: Joined Manchester City as a trainee in July 1988, having been an associated schoolboy since October 1985, but such was his talent he was given a professional contract only one month later following his 17th birthday. Soon afterwards he made his FL debut on the left-wing away to Ipswich on 8 October 1988. He was a vital member of the City youth team which reached the FA Youth Cup Final in 1989, losing narrowly to Watford. It was a surprise to many that he made only one further appearance (as a sub) in the next two seasons. However, in September 1991, he finally broke through into the first team and held his place until February 1992 when he was rested. His mazy and thrilling runs dazzled the City faithful, although prone to inconsistency. Called up by Northern Ireland manager Billy Bingham, he made his international debut in Denmark in November and held his place for the remaining internationals. In only his fourth appearance for Northern Ireland he scored a goal of outstanding quality in a friendly against the World Champions, Germany, in Bremnen in June. Receiving the ball wide on the right he ran clear of the German defence and then, as the defenders ran back to cover, he calmly cut inside them to create space for a shot and rifled the ball high into the net from 25 yards. It was a goal a veteran would have been proud of and it earned Northern Ireland a 1-1 draw, arguably their best ever result. Clearly, Michael Hughes is a star of the future.

HUMPHREY John

Born: Paddington,
31 January 1961

Height: 5'10"

Weight: 11.1

Position/Skill Factor: Very experienced right-back who can both defend and attack with the best of them. Good long accurate kicker with his right foot.

Career History: On leaving school, he signed for Wolverhampton Wanderers as an apprentice in July 1977, before becoming a full-time pro 18 months later. Made his FL debut at Southampton on 7 April 1980, but didn't really earn a regular place until the 1982-83 season, when he was ever present in the side that won promotion back to the First Division. After "Wolves" were relegated in successive seasons to the Third Division, he signed for Charlton Athletic in the summer of 1985. In his first term with the "Valiants", he played 39 League games and was influential in helping the team back to the First Division as runners-up, after a gap of some 30 years. Missed only a handful of matches in five seasons spent at Charlton and was sold to the club's landlords, Crystal Palace, during the 1990 close season, following relegation to the Second Division. He made his Palace debut on the opening day of the 1990-91 season at Luton Town and it wasn't before too long that his impressive displays at right-back had made him just as popular with the other Selhurst Park fans. At the end of the season he was ever present in a Crystal Palace side that reached its highest ever League position, third in the First Division. Started as first choice right-back in 1991-92, but lost his place in October to Gareth Southgate after the Palace defence – so tight the previous season – had leaked an alarming 19 goals in nine games. Won his place back in December and remained unchallenged for the rest of the season.

Clubs	Signing Date	Transfer Fee	APPEARANCES				GOALS			
			Lge	FL Cup	FA Cup	Others	Lge	FL Cup	FA Cup	Others
Wolverhampton W.	1.79	–	149	8	7		3			
Charlton Athletic	7.85	£60,000	194	13	9	15	3			1
Crystal Palace*	6.90	£400,000	74+1	9+2	4	6+1	1			

HURLOCK Terence (Terry) Alan

Born: Hackney, 22 September 1958

Height: 5'9" Weight: 13.2

International Honours: E"B"

Position/Skill Factor: Very under-rated competitive midfield player who loves a tackle and doesn't lose many. He sees passes very quickly and is a good one-touch player.

Career History: Began as an associated schoolboy with West Ham United in October 1974, before signing as an apprentice for the club in April 1975. When his apprenticeship expired he was not offered a professional contract and went into non-League soccer. Was spotted by Third Division Brentford when playing for Leytonstone and Ilford of the then Isthmian League and after signing was pushed straight into the team, making his FL debut at Walsall on 30 August, 1980. Retained his FL place and proved extremely reliable over the next six seasons at Griffin Park, earning a reputation as the best midfield player in the Third Division. When he moved to promotion chasing Reading in February 1986, the transfer fee was a record for both clubs. Although Reading achieved their objective and Hurlock won a Third Division Championship medal, he never lived up to his reputation at Elm Park and after losing his place, within a year of joining the "Royals", he had signed for Second Division rivals, Millwall. The following season his decision to join Millwall was vindicated as he won a Second Division Championship medal and the "Lions" reached the top flight for the first time in their long history. When the club

was relegated at the end of 1989-90, he surprisingly moved north of the border, signing for Scottish League side, Glasgow Rangers. In an outstanding first season at Ibrox, he only missed seven games and won Scottish Championship and Scottish League Cup winners medals. However, with Rangers seeking to reduce their contingent of English players, following the bizarre UEFA ruling on "foreigners", he was sold to Southampton for a profit soon into the 1991-92 season and was an integral part of the "Saints'" team which struggled successfully against relegation and enjoyed good runs in three cup competitions, reaching the Final of the Zenith Cup.

			APPEARANCES				GOALS			
Clubs	Signing Date	Transfer Fee	Lge	FL Cup	FA Cup	Others	Lge	FL Cup	FA Cup	Others
Brentford	8.80	£6,000	220	17	17	9	18	2	4	
Reading	2.86	£82,000	29	3	1	2				
Millwall	2.87	£95,000	103+1	7	5	1+1	8	2		
Glasgow Rangers	8.90	£325,000								
Southampton*	9.91	£400,000	27+2	4	5	6				1

HURST Lee Jason

Born: Nuneaton,
21 September 1970

Height: 6'0"

Weight: 11.9

Position/Skill Factor: Left-back, who can also play on the wing, with good skill and plenty of pace. Has the ability to beat defenders and get in telling crosses.

Career History: Local talent who started with Coventry City as an associated schoolboy (October 1985) and graduated to trainee status in July 1987, before signing as a pro just under two years later. Made his FL debut at Wimbledon on 2 February 1991, following an injury to Paul Edwards and showed promise, playing three more games. Enjoyed a short run at left-back in the "Sky Blues'" team from late October to late December 1991, before giving way to Kenny Sansom, returning after injury. Subsequently appeared briefly on the left side of midfield and at right-back and it remains to be seen in which position he finally settles down in.

			APPEARANCES				GOALS			
Clubs	Signing Date	Transfer Fee	Lge	FL Cup	FA Cup	Others	Lge	FL Cup	FA Cup	Others
Coventry City*	5.89	–	11+3	2+1	1+1					

HUTCHISON Donald (Don)

Born: Gateshead, 9 May 1971

Height: 6'2" Weight: 11.4

Position/Skill Factor: Midfield player who gets forward well and has the ability to score goals.

Career History: Made his FL debut for Hartlepool United, while still a trainee, at home to Scunthorpe United on 7 October 1989 and impressed, scoring twice in his first five League games. First came to the club as a trainee in June 1989 and within seven months of signing pro forms, Hartlepool being desperate for cash, had sold him to Liverpool after videos showing his abilities had been sent to all the leading clubs. With Liverpool's chronic injury crisis in 1991-92, he might have expected to make more progress, but had to wait until late March 1992, before making his Anfield debut as a sub at home to Notts County. Made two further substitute appearances before the end of the season.

Clubs	Signing Date	Transfer Fee	APPEARANCES				GOALS			
			Lge	FL Cup	FA Cup	Others	Lge	FL Cup	FA Cup	Others
Hartlepool United	3.90	–	19+5	1+1	2	1	3			
Liverpool*	11.90	£175,000	0+3							

IMPEY Andrew (Andy) Rodney

Born: Hammersmith, 30 September 1971

Height: 5'8" Weight: 10.6

Position/Skill Factor: Winger with plenty of ability and two good feet. Very pacy, he will take on and beat defenders to get telling crosses in.

Career History: Started his football career as a trainee with Wimbledon in July 1988, but his contract was terminated after only one month and he joined Yeading of the Vauxhall League Division Two South. In 1989-90, Yeading not only won promotion to Division One, as Champions of the League, but they also reached Wembley for the Final of the FA Vase and defeated Bridlington after a replay, with Impey a key player in the team at the age of 18. Soon after the Final, he was signed up by Queens Park Rangers. Had to wait a little time for some first team action, but after three subs' appearances in the League and Zenith Cups in October 1991, he made his FL debut at Coventry City on 11 January 1992, deputising for the injured Andy Sinton. Later, in March, he returned to the team on the right-wing and held his place till the end of the season.

Clubs	Signing Date	Transfer Fee	APPEARANCES				GOALS			
			Lge	FL Cup	FA Cup	Others	Lge	FL Cup	FA Cup	Others
Q.P.R.*	6.90	35,000	13	0+1		0+2				1

HYDE Graham

Born: Doncaster,
10 November 1970

Height: 5'7"

Weight: 11.7

Position: Midfield player.

Career History: Joined Sheffield Wednesday as a trainee in June 1987, having been an associated schoolboy since January 1985 and turned professional one year later. Had to wait over three years for his FL debut, finally turning out in midfield at Manchester City on 14 September 1991, in place of the injured John Sheridan. made further appearances later in the season, once again deputising for Sheridan.

Clubs	Signing Date	Transfer Fee	APPEARANCES				GOALS			
			Lge	FL Cup	FA Cup	Others	Lge	FL Cup	FA Cup	Others
Sheffield Wednesday*	5.88	–	9+4	1	1+1	1				1

INCE Paul Emerson Carlyle

Born: Ilford, 21 October 1967

Height: 5'11" Weight: 11. 6

International Honours: E Yth, E "U21"-2, E"B"

Position/Skill Factor: A midfield bundle of energy, he is both destructive and constructive in breaking up attacks and setting counter-attacks in motion. Capable of scoring spectacular goals.

Career History: Came to West Ham United as a 14-year-old associated schoolboy in December 1981, graduating through the YTS scheme, before signing as a professional during the 1985 close season. Made his FL debut when coming on as a sub at Newcastle United on 30 November 1986 and kept his place for the next match, at Upton Park against Southampton. Although scoring in a 3-1 win, he found himself out of the side a few weeks later. Had a better season in 1987-88, but really came to the fore the following year, during West Ham's run to the League Cup Semi-Finals. He scored two spectacular goals in a 4-1 win over Liverpool and another in a 2-1 victory against Aston Villa. However, it ultimately proved a disappointing season for the club as they slipped into the Second Division. Having declared a wish to leave Upton Park, he finally signed for Manchester United after playing the opening game of the 1989-90 season for West Ham. Made his United debut in a 5-1 win against Millwall and then scored twice in a League Cup tie at Portsmouth for a great start to his new career. Unfortunately, he struggled to settle in after that, with the club showing indifferent League form.

But United's run in the FA Cup offered respite and he won an FA Cup winners medal, following the eventual 1-0 replay win over Crystal Palace in 1990. Played 31 League games in 1990-91 as the team improved to sixth place in the First Division and was in the side that was beaten 1-0 by Sheffield Wednesday in the League Cup Final. But the highlight of the season was reserved for the penultimate game when he won a European Cup Winners Cup medal, following United's great 2-1 victory over Barcelona in Amsterdam. Played in most of the 1991-92 campaign,

earning a League Cup winners medal, after United's 1-0 victory over Nottingham Forest, but missing out on the more coveted League Championship, after the "Reds" had been favourites all season. An infrequent scorer, he tends to collect goals in braces, scoring another couple at Norwich City at a critical stage of the season.

Clubs	Signing Date	Transfer Fee	APPEARANCES				GOALS			
			Lge	FL Cup	FA Cup	Others	Lge	FL Cup	FA Cup	Others
West Ham United	7.85	-	66+6	9	8+2	4	7	3	1	1
Manchester United*	9.89	£1,250,000	87+3	15+1	6+1	11	6	2		

IRONSIDE Ian

Born: Sheffield, 8 March 1964

Height: 6'2" Weight: 13.0

Position/Skill Factor: Goalkeeper with an excellent build, who is extremely capable and has good handling ability.

Career History: Goalkeeping son of Roy, a former Rotherham United and Barnsley custodian, who played League football between 1954 and 1969, he came through the Barnsley junior sides before turning to the pro ranks at the beginning of the 1982-83 season. Was released by the "Tykes" without playing a game and drifted into local non-League soccer. Later, when spotted by Scarborough playing for North Ferriby United, of the Northern Counties (East) League, he came back into League football as cover for Kevin Blackwell, who was injured. Gave such sterling displays, following his FL debut in a 1-0 defeat at Hartlepool United on 26 March 1988, that he eventually took over in 1990-91 as first choice 'keeper, playing 40 League games and keeping 11 clean sheets. Transferred to Second Division Middlesbrough in the summer of 1991, as cover for Steve Pears, he must have been disappointed to find his next FL action was back with Scarborough on loan in March 1992. However, on returning to Ayresome Park, he deputised for the injured Pears in the vital last game of the season at Wolverhampton Wanderers, which "Boro" won 2-1 to clinch promotion. With any luck he will play in the Premier League this coming season — something he probably never even dreamt of while performing in front of crowds of 100 with North Ferriby!

Clubs	Signing Date	Transfer Fee	APPEARANCES				GOALS			
			Lge	FL Cup	FA Cup	Others	Lge	FL Cup	FA Cup	Others
Barnsley	9.82	-								
North Ferriby United	7.84	-								
Scarborough	3.88	-	88	2	2	10				
Middlesbrough*	8.91	£80,000	1							
Scarborough	3.92	Loan	7							

IRWIN Dennis Joseph

Born: Cork,
31 October 1965

Height: 5'7"

Weight: 9.7

International Honours:
IR Sch, IR Yth,
IR "U21"-3, IR-13

Position/Skill Factor: Full-back who can play either side and loves to get forward. A lovely striker of the ball, he takes most of the right sided corners and free-kicks around the penalty area.

Career History: Came to Leeds United from his native Ireland to sign as an apprentice in March 1982 and three months after turning pro, he made his FL debut at Elland Road against Fulham on 21 January 1984. The following season he missed only one League game, but after starting out as a regular in 1985-86, he lost his place to Neil Aspin and at the end of the season was amazingly given a free transfer. Was quickly snapped up by Second Division Oldham Athletic, replacing Willie Donachie in the number two shirt for the opening match of 1986-87 and playing in all but one game during a season that saw the club only miss out on promotion at the Play-Off stage. Stayed four years with the "Latics", the highlights coming in 1989-90, his last season at Boundary Park. Oldham reached the League Cup Final, going down 1-0 to Nottingham Forest and were involved in two thrilling FA Cup Semi-Finals against Manchester United, before losing out to a Mark Robins goal in extra-time. He so impressed Alex Ferguson, the United manager, that during the 1990 close season he moved to Old Trafford in exchange for a large fee. Missed very few matches in 1990-91 and although a member of the side that lost 1-0 to Sheffield Wednesday in the League Cup Final, that experience was well and truly pushed into the background a few weeks later when United beat Barcelona 2-1 to win the European Cup Winners Cup. Certainly a season to remember, for he also won his first full cap for the Republic when playing in the 1-0 victory over Morocco in Dublin on 12 September 1990 and has remained an automatic choice since. Switched to left-back in 1991-92, he played a full part in United's tantalising season, missing only seven games through injury during the campaign. Won a League Cup medal to make up for the disappointments of 1990 and 1991 and may be unique in appearing in three consecutive Finals with two different clubs. On his first return to Boundary Park since leaving Oldham, remarkably (for a full-back) he scored twice in a 6-3 thriller.

Clubs	Signing Date	Transfer Fee	APPEARANCES				GOALS			
			Lge	FL Cup	FA Cup	Others	Lge	FL Cup	FA Cup	Others
Leeds United	10.83	–	72	5	3	2	1			
Oldham Athletic	5.86	–	166+1	19	13	5	4	3		
Manchester United*	6.90	£625,000	70+2	14+1	6	9	4			

JACKSON Matthew Alan

Born: Leeds,
19 October 1971

Height: 6'1"

Weight: 12.12

International Honours:
E Sch Int, E "U21"-4

Position/Skill Factor: Right-back who can play at centreback. Oozing class, he is a lovely striker of the ball. Very confident when the ball is at his feet.

Career History: Played for Luton Town as a junior, signing associated schoolboy forms in November 1986, before turning professional and although making an appearance for the "Hatters" in a Zenith Data Cup match, he was loaned out to Preston North End where he made his FL debut at Deepdale when coming on as a sub against Crewe Alexandra on 30 March 1991. Made his Luton debut as a sub at Arsenal on 27 August 1991 and his first full League game at right-back at home to Southampton

on 4 September. After only 11 first team games for Luton, he was transferred to Everton for a massive fee, considering his limited experience. Settled in easily at Goodison Park in the right-back position and held his place to the end of the season, scoring his first ever senior goal in a televised 1-1 draw with eventual champions, Leeds, in February. Clearly a player with a bright future, he was called into the England Under 21 squad at the end of the season, making four appearances at right-back.

Clubs	Signing Date	Transfer Fee	APPEARANCES				GOALS			
			Lge	FL Cup	FA Cup	Others	Lge	FL Cup	FA Cup	Others
Luton Town	7.90	–	7+2	2		0+1				
Preston North End	3.91	Loan	3+1							
Everton*	10.91	£600,000	30		2	1	1			

JAMES David

Born: Welwyn Garden City, 1 August 1970

Height: 6'4" Weight: 14.7

International Honours: E "U21"-10

Position/Skill Factor: Tall young goalkeeper who will continue to improve with experience. Has good positional sense and is very agile for such a big man.

Career History: A young England Under 21 international goalkeeper who first hit the headlines last season when surrounded by much transfer speculation, he initially joined Watford as an associated schoolboy in November 1984, before graduating from trainee status in July 1986 to the professional ranks during the summer of 1988. He spent two years in the shadow of Tony Cotton, but when the latter moved to Manchester City in the 1990 close season, he got the break that he had been looking for. Made his FL debut at home to Millwall on 25 August 1990 and at the end of 1990-91, except for one Zenith Cup game, he was ever present. His form was so outstanding that he was soon called up to the England Under 21 squad and was regular first choice throughout the season. During 1991-92 he turned out in all but three FL games, conceding a mere 42 goals in 43 appearances and playing a large part in Watford's recovery from a relegation position to mid-table security. His name was constantly linked with Liverpool and other First Division clubs throughout the season and his eventual departure was inevitable, when he indeed joined Liverpool. However, manager Graham Souness indicated that he would have to fight for his place, so he may not start 1992-93 as the "Reds'" first choice 'keeper.

Clubs	Signing Date	Transfer Fee	APPEARANCES				GOALS			
			Lge	FL Cup	FA Cup	Others	Lge	FL Cup	FA Cup	Others
Watford	7.88	–	89	6	2	1				
Liverpool*	6.92	£1,000,000								

JEMSON Nigel Bradley

Born: Preston,
10 August 1969

Height: 5'10"

Weight: 11.10

International Honours:
E "U21"-1

Position/Skill Factor: Striker with a good first touch, who passes and moves well, he will always create scoring chances. Very good at playing one-twos on the edge of the penalty area.

Career History: Started out with his local team Preston North End as an associated schoolboy in August 1984, before signing on as a trainee on leaving school in August 1986. And he was still only a trainee when he made his FL debut at Aldershot on 3 May 1986. Played in just four games the following season and scored in three of them, but didn't really break into the side until 1987-88, his first year as a full professional. Showing a precocious talent for one so young, he was signed by Nottingham Forest, but before making an appearance for the club, he was loaned out to Bolton Wanderers and back to Preston in order to gain more experience. After nearly two years at the City Ground he finally made his Forest debut on Boxing Day, 1989, at Luton Town, replacing Lee Chapman who had moved on to Leeds United and later in the season scored the only goal of the game against Oldham Athletic in the League Cup Final at Wembley. Made a good start to the 1990-91 season, playing in the first 23 matches, but lost his way after being sidelined through injury and was not selected for the FA Cup Final side that lost 2-1 to

Tottenham Hotspur, even though he had earlier scored a hat-trick in the 3-1 Fifth Round replay victory over Southampton. With the signing of Teddy Sheringham in the summer of 1991, his future with Forest seemed bleak and although starting the season wide on the left, he was replaced by another new player, Kingsley Black and transferred shortly afterwards to Sheffield Wednesday. He has struggled to make an impact at Hillsborough so far, despite scoring a brace of goals against Manchester United, when coming on as substitute in an early game for Wednesday. After January he played little part in the "Owls'" impressive season.

Clubs	Signing Date	Transfer Fee	APPEARANCES				GOALS			
			Lge	FL Cup	FA Cup	Others	Lge	FL Cup	FA Cup	Others
Preston North End	6.87	–	28+4		2	5+1	8		1	5
Nottingham Forest	3.88	£150,000	45+2	9	3	1	13	4	3	
Bolton Wanderers	12.88	Loan	4+1							
Preston North End	3.89	Loan	6+3			2	2			1
Sheffield Wednesday*	9.91	£800,000	11+9	1+2	1	1+1	4			1

JENKINS Iain

Born: Prescot, 24 November 1972

Height: 5'10" Weight: 11.6

Position/Skill Factor: A good passer and an excellent reader of the game, this left-back should have an excellent future Very quick off the mark, he is not easily beaten.

Career History: Signed for Everton in May 1987 on associated schoolboy forms, before becoming a trainee in June 1989, he made his FL debut at Queens Park Rangers in the left-back position on 11 May 1991, thus joining an exclusive band of youngsters to have played for the club, prior to turning professional. After joining the paid ranks, he had to wait almost exactly one year for his next first team opportunity, appearing in the last three games of the 1991-92 season.

Clubs	Signing Date	Transfer Fee	APPEARANCES				GOALS			
			Lge	FL Cup	FA Cup	Others	Lge	FL Cup	FA Cup	Others
Everton*	6.91	–	2+2							

JENNINGS Paul

Born: Kensington, 16 June 1974

Height: 5'11" Weight: 12.6

Position: Central Defender.

Career History: Signed as a professional for Wimbledon during the 1992 close season, having initially come to the club as a trainee in July 1990. No first team experience.

Clubs	Signing Date	Transfer Fee	APPEARANCES				GOALS			
			Lge	FL Cup	FA Cup	Others	Lge	FL Cup	FA Cup	Others
Wimbledon*	6.92	–								

JOBSON Richard Ian

Born: Holderness,
9 May 1963

Height: 6'1"

Weight: 12.2

International Honours:
E"B"

Position/Skill Factor: Footballing central defender who has the skill of a midfielder. Has some delightful touches and passes the ball well. Reads situations and likes to bring the ball out of defence, rather than just clear his lines.

Career History: Came out of non-League football with Burton Albion to sign for Watford during 1982-83 and made his FL debut at home to Ipswich Town on 18 December 1982, before playing a further 13 League games as the club gained promotion to the First Division. The following season he made a good start, but soon lost his place to Les Taylor and on getting back to fitness after recovering from a spell out injured, he was transferred to promotion chasing Hull City. Played just six matches that season as the club were promoted to the Second Division in third place, but soon settled into the side first at right-back and later in central defence as one of the more consistent players and was ever present in 1987-88 and 1988-89, while missing only one game in 1989-90. At the beginning of 1990-91, Oldham Athletic, who were aiming to reach Division One after an absence of nearly 70 years, moved quickly for him when Andy Holden was injured in the second game of the season. Apart from one match on the subs' bench, he didn't miss a game and with the club never out of the top three all season, was good value for his Second Division Championship medal. Injured in the third match of the "Latics'" First Division campaign, he returned one month later and remained in the side for the rest of the season. Has probably arrived too late for full international honours, but was rewarded for his consistency with two England "B" games in 1991-92.

Clubs	Signing Date	Transfer Fee	APPEARANCES				GOALS			
			Lge	FL Cup	FA Cup	Others	Lge	FL Cup	FA Cup	Others
Watford	11.82	£22,000	26+2	2	0+1	5+1	4			
Hull City	2.85	£40,000	219+2	18	12	8	17		1	
Oldham Athletic*	9.90	£460,000	79+3	6	4	2	1	1		

JOHNSEN Erland

Born: Fredrikstad, Norway, 5 April 1967

Height: 6'0" Weight: 12.10

International Honours: Norwegian Int

Position/Skill Factor: Very composed centre-back who never looks to be in a hurry. Useful in the air, he is a confident passer of the ball out of defence.

Career History: Signed by Chelsea from Bayern Munich in 1989-90, after winning a Bundesliga Championship medal, he soon established himself in the side when replacing David Lee and making 18 League appearances, following his FL debut at Queens Park Rangers on 9 December 1989. However, on recovering from injuries received at the beginning of the 1990-91 season, he was unable to win back his place in the side after Ken Monkou and young Jason Cundy had struck up such a good understanding at the heart of the Chelsea defence. His first team opportunities were further limited by the signing of Paul Elliott and he made only seven first team appearances in 1991-92. Although time is still on his side, it has not so far proved to be a happy signing for either club or player.

Clubs	Signing Date	Transfer Fee	APPEARANCES				GOALS			
			Lge	FL Cup	FA Cup	Others	Lge	FL Cup	FA Cup	Others
Chelsea*	11.89	£306,000	30+1		1					

JOHNSON Andrew James

Born: Bath, 2 May, 1974

Height: 6'0" Weight: 12.0

Position/Skill Factor: Very quick defender, who can play in midfield, he loves to bring the ball out of defence and link up with the attack. Is a good passer.

Career History: Joined Norwich City as a trainee in July 1990, turning professional in March 1992. One month later, he made his FL debut at Sheffield Wednesday on 20 April 1992 and was promising enough to be selected for the final game of the season against Leeds United.

Clubs	Signing Date	Transfer Fee	APPEARANCES				GOALS			
			Lge	FL Cup	FA Cup	Others	Lge	FL Cup	FA Cup	Others
Norwich City*	3.92	–	2							

JOHNSON David Alan

Born: Dinnington,
29 October 1970

Height: 6'2"

Weight: 13.8

Position/Skill Factor: Strong running striker with a good left foot, he also runs well off the ball.

Career History: From a mining village east of Sheffield, he first joined Wednesday as an associated schoolboy in November 1985, graduating to trainee in June 1987 and to full professional status two years later. After waiting patiently in the reserves for over two years for a first team opportunity, he made his FL debut whilst on loan to Third Division Hartlepool United on 2 October 1991 at Darlington. Impressed sufficiently during his two month loan to be "blooded" by Wednesday soon after his return, away to Aston Villa in January 1992, making occasional appearances thereafter.

Clubs	Signing Date	Transfer Fee	APPEARANCES				GOALS			
			Lge	FL Cup	FA Cup	Others	Lge	FL Cup	FA Cup	Others
Sheffield Wednesday*	7.89	–	5+1							
Hartlepool United	10.91	Loan	7		2		2			1

JOHNSON Gavin

Born: Eye,
10 October 1970

Height: 6'0"

Weight: 11.1

Position/Skill Factor: Hard working midfielder who can fill any position down the left hand side of the field. With a nice left foot and good skill, he creates chances for others.

Career History: Locally born and bred player who first came to Ipswich Town as an associated schoolboy in March 1985, before graduating to trainee status in July 1987. Was given his chance in 1988-89, making his FL debut at Portman Road in the number three shirt against Barnsley on 21 February 1989, just a few days after signing professional. Played only sporadically over the next two seasons, but performed well when required. Finally came to the fore in 1991-92, appearing in most of the games during Ipswich's Second Division Championship campaign. Originally a central defender, where his chances were limited by Brian Gayle and David Linighan, he was switched to the left side of midfield, although, confusingly wearing the number two shirt. The highlight of his career to date was scoring at Anfield in a FA Cup Fifth Round replay against Liverpool — an equaliser which extended the match to extra time when Town lost narrowly by 3-2. Also scored goals in the last two games of the season which clinched the Championship for Ipswich.

Clubs	Signing Date	Transfer Fee	APPEARANCES				GOALS			
			Lge	FL Cup	FA Cup	Others	Lge	FL Cup	FA Cup	Others
Ipswich Town*	2.89	–	45+14	1+1	5	3+1	5		1	1

JOHNSTON Maurice (Mo)

Born: Glasgow, 30 April 1963

Height: 5'9" Weight: 10.6

International Honours: S "U21"-3, S-38

Position/Skill Factor: A striker with good control who has the ability to turn either way to get his shots in. Always scores goals and is never far away when crosses come in.

Career History: Started out with junior side, Milton Battlefield, before being snapped up by Scottish First Division team, Partick Thistle, in July 1980 and scoring 41 goals from 85 games in just over three years. He proved to be an inspired signing by Watford, following the departure of their leading marksman, Luther Blissett, to AC Milan. Prior to him joining Watford, the club had only won two matches out of 15 played. Made his FL debut at Manchester United on 19 November 1983 and quickly made his mark on the scoresheet in his third game when he scored a hat-trick against Wolverhampton Wanderers at Molineux in only eight minutes. At the end of the League programme his tally was 20 goals from 29 matches and the team had surged up the table to 11th place and had reached the FA Cup Final for the first time in the club's history. Although there was to be no fairy tale ending for Watford as they lost 2-0 against Everton, Mo had already had the satisfaction of winning his first full cap for Scotland, when coming on against Wales on 28 February 1984. However, he was unable to settle in the south and during the summer requested a transfer. After playing in Watford's first nine League games in 1984-85, he had his wishes granted when allowed to return home with Glasgow Celtic. Scored 52 goals in 99 games and winning Scottish Premier League (1985-86) and Scottish Cup

(1985) medals in three seasons at Celtic, before signing for the French club, Nantes. Returning to Britain two years later, he made headline news when becoming the first Catholic player to play for Glasgow Rangers, after turning down a move to Celtic. In two seasons at Ibrox, he played 65 League games, while scoring 26 goals and won two Scottish Cup medals and a Scottish Premier League Championship medal in 1989-90. From 1985 to 1990, he was a regular selection for Scotland and his six goals from eight games in the qualifying group were a major factor in Scotland reaching the 1990 World Cup Finals in Italy. Sadly, an embarrassing defeat by Costa Rica in their first game, effectively put an end to any further progress and some unfavourable post match publicity prompted Johnston to announce his premature retirement from international football. After one year out, however, he was persuaded to revoke his decision. In another surprising twist to his career, he joined Everton in November 1991. It seemed like a shrewd move to boost the "Toffees'" declining fortunes, but sadly he was unable to provide any spark to the team who finished a disappointing 12th. During the season, he announced his retirement from international football for the second time and it is unlikely that Andy Roxburgh will waste any time trying to change his mind again.

Clubs	Signing Date	Transfer Fee	APPEARANCES				GOALS			
			Lge	FL Cup	FA Cup	Others	Lge	FL Cup	FA Cup	Others
Watford	11.83	£200,000	37+1	1	7		23		3	
Glasgow Celtic	10.84	£400,000								
Nantes (France)	6.87	£1,000,000								
Glasgow Rangers	7.89	£1,500,000								
Everton*	11.91	£1,500,000	21	1	1	1	7			

JONES Philip Lee

Born: Wrexham, 29 May, 1973

Height: 5'8" Weight: 9.7

International Honours: W Yth, W "U21"

Position/Skill Factor: Very quick striker with a good goal scoring record who will improve greatly with further experience.

Career History: Very few 17-year-olds make their first team debut watched by a television audience of millions, but this is what happened to Lee who, due to the UEFA "foreigners" rule, was selected by Wrexham manager Brian Flynn for a second-leg European Cup Winners Cup tie at home to Manchester United on 7 November 1990. What is more, apparently unabashed by the enormity of the occasion, he embarrassed the United defence at least twice with his forward runs. Having earlier signed for the club in July 1990, he made his FL debut two days later as a sub at Northampton Town on 9 November 1990. By the end of the 1990-91 season, he had almost become a regular in the side and had shown tremendous promise of things to come, signing professional forms in the summer. Started the 1991-92 season in Wrexham's first team, but lost his place in September when goals eluded him. He didn't take part in the club's historic FA Cup Third Round victory over League Champions, Arsenal, but in the Fourth Round tie against West Ham at Upton Park, he came on as substitute and in the 80th minute latched on to Gareth Owen's through ball, took it forward and despite the intimidating presence of West Ham keeper

Ludo Miklosko rushing towards him, managed to toe-poke the ball past him and over the line for Wrexham's amazing second equaliser in a 2-2 draw. Sadly, there were to be no more heroics in the replay, but Lee won his place back and shortly after a scoring burst of six goals in six games, he was signed by Liverpool manager Graham Souness for £300,000 with an equivalent amount to follow if he makes the grade. Although yet to make his Liverpool debut, it may come very soon if the injury crisis and goal drought which afflicted the "Reds" in 1991-92, continues into the new season. Liverpool fans will be hoping that he turns into the "new" Ian Rush!

Clubs	Signing Date	Transfer Fee	APPEARANCES				GOALS			
			Lge	FL Cup	FA Cup	Others	Lge	FL Cup	FA Cup	Others
Wrexham	7.91	–	24+15	2	1+2	2	9		1	2
Liverpool*	3.92	£300,000								

JONES Robert (Rob) Marc

Born: Wrexham, 5 November 1971

Height: 5'11" Weight: 11.0

International Honours: W Sch, E Yth, E-1

Position/Skill Factor: He is the complete full-back, decisive in the tackle and winning balls cleanly without fouling. His passing is quick and accurate over both short and long distances and he is not afraid to race down the wing like a traditional winger and cross decisively. He can also play on either flank. In addition to his natural ability his coolness and composure under pressure is astonishing in one so young.

Career History: The grandson of Billy Jones who played left-half for Liverpool when they lost 2-0 to Arsenal in the 1950 FA Cup Final, he started as an associated schoolboy with Crewe Alexandra in September 1987 and actually made his FL debut at Gresty Road against Darlington on 9 April 1988, before signing as a trainee in July 1988. The following season, he played 12 times as the club gained promotion to the Third Division in third place, but it wasn't until 1990-91 that he regularly began to hold down the right-back spot and although the club were relegated, his performances were often outstanding. In September 1991, he was simply one of a number of promising youngsters with Crewe. By the end of the season he was undisputed first choice right-back for Liverpool with a FA Cup Winners medal and his first cap for England under his belt and was being hailed as England's future right-back for the next generation — a "fairy tale" almost without parallel in the modern game. When Graham Souness signed him in early October, it was surely intended to bring him on slowly. Instead, because of Liverpool's injury crisis, he was introduced to the first team immediately, in traditionally the toughest game of the season, away to Manchester United at Old Trafford and faced by United's teenage prodigy Ryan Giggs. Rob passed his initial test with flying colours, not putting a foot wrong and except for injuries and cup disqualifications, remained part of the Liverpool team for the rest of the season. In February, England manager Graham Taylor took an enormous gamble by selecting him for the friendly game with France, but as ever he rose to the occasion. Unafraid to go forward, he had a goal chance after only ten minutes, but blasted wide. Otherwise his performance in England's 2-0 victory was impeccable, showing touches and a composure worthy of a veteran. Because of injury and then Liverpool's FA Cup commitments, he was not selected for England's squad for the European Championship Finals in Sweden. Sadly, shortly after the FA Cup Final, it was revealed that he needed to rest over the summer with shin splint problems. Provided that he gets over his injury problem, he appears to have a glittering future ahead of him.

| | | | APPEARANCES | | | | GOALS | | | |
Clubs	Signing Date	Transfer Fee	Lge	FL Cup	FA Cup	Others	Lge	FL Cup	FA Cup	Others
Crewe Alexandra	12.88	–	60+16	9	0+3	3	2			
Liverpool*	10.91	£300,000	28		9	2+1				

JONES Ryan Anthony

Born: Sheffield, 23 July 1973

Height: 6'1¼" Weight: 12.5

Position/Skill Factor: At present playing either in midfield or at left-back, he is very strong and athletic and has a sweet left foot.

Career History: A local discovery, he first joined Sheffield Wednesday as an associated schoolboy in September 1987. Signed as a trainee in July 1989, on leaving school and progressed to the professional ranks in the 1991 close season. Observed by a few good judges to have an excellent chance of making the grade, he has yet to be given a first team opportunity.

| | | | APPEARANCES | | | | GOALS | | | |
Clubs	Signing Date	Transfer Fee	Lge	FL Cup	FA Cup	Others	Lge	FL Cup	FA Cup	Others
Sheffield Wednesday*	6.91	–								

JONES Vincent (Vinny) Peter

Born: Watford: 5 January 1965

Height: 5'11" Weight: 11.10

Position/Skill Factor: Midfielder who is a great motivator on the field and hates to lose, always giving 100 per cent Infamous for his intimidatory style, he is perhaps a better player than given credit for and is dangerous from set pieces and his long throws.

Career History: One of the most remarkable rises to fame in Football League history. Jones was a bricklayer playing part-time football for Wealdstone of the then Gola League (now Vauxhall Conference), when Dave Bassett signed him for Wimbledon. Unknown and unrated in non-League football, he had played only 28 games in two seasons (1984-86) and none at all in 1986-87 for Wealdstone before the move. Yet Bassett plunged him straight into the First Division, making his FL debut at Nottingham Forest on 22 November 1986 and scoring the winning goal against Manchester United in only his second game and scoring again in his third, fourth and eighth games. Four First Division goals in eight games, all from midfield and yet two months earlier he could not get a game with Wealdstone! Although making only 24 League appearances the following season and sharing the number four shirt with Vaughan Ryan, he played in all the FA Cup rounds, culminating in the 1-0 win over Liverpool in the Final. Continuously dogged by disciplinary problems, he couldn't manage a full set of appearances in 1988-89, but it was still something of a shock when Bobby Gould, the new manager at Wimbledon, allowed him to depart in the close season to Leeds United. Played in all but the club's first three League matches and won a Second Division Championship medal as Leeds pipped Sheffield United for the title in 1989-90, his first season at Elland Road. However, having reached Division One, manager Howard Wilkinson decided to replace midfield muscle with midfield finesse, by signing Gary McAllister from Leicester City and he made only one more appearance for Leeds, before his former Wimbledon manager, Dave Bassett, signed him for Sheffield United in a bid to arrest the club's poor start in the First Division. In order to secure his services, United had to part with a club record fee and he was immediately appointed team captain, a move which surprised many, but was sound, as the "Blades" gradually proved their mettle and moved up the table away from the danger zone. Since he was both successful and popular at Bramall Lane, it was puzzling that Bassett agreed to sell him at a financial loss to Chelsea, in the second week of 1991–92. As with his previous clubs, he quickly became an integral part of the Chelsea team in a disappointing season for the "Blues". In the Fifth Round of the FA Cup against his former club, he created what is presumably a world record by getting booked for a foul committed immediately following the kick-off!

| | | | APPEARANCES | | | | GOALS | | | |
Clubs	Signing Date	Transfer Fee	Lge	FL Cup	FA Cup	Others	Lge	FL Cup	FA Cup	Others
Wimbledon	11.86	£10,000	77	6+2	2+2	3	9		1	
Leeds United	6.89	£650,000	44+2	2	1	4	5			
Sheffield United	9.90	£700,000	35	4	1	1	2			
Chelsea*	8.91	£575,000	35	1	4	5	3		1	2

JOSEPH Roger Anthony

Born: Paddington, 24 December 1965

Height: 5'11" Weight: 11.13

International Honours: E"B"

Position/Skill Factor: Right-back with tremendous pace, he has a great build for a defender and is lean and hungry. Good at striking long passes in behind the opposing full-back.

Career History: Starting in non-League football with Southall, before joining Brentford in 1984-85, he made his FL debut at Griffin Park against Millwall on 19 May 1985 and by the end of the following term had established himself in the right-back position. Had four years with the "Bees", before Wimbledon, who had carefully been noting his progress, signed him in time for the start of 1988-89 and he went straight into the team, only missing a handful of games in the middle of the season due to injury. After a difficult season in 1989-90, again disrupted by injury, he finally settled down in 1990-91 as an ever present and had his best season yet. His elder brother Francis, now retired from League football, also played for Wimbledon and Brentford in a career which embraced ten different clubs. Injuries again plagued him in 1991-92 and although performing regularly in the first half of the season, he only played in five more games after the New Year.

Clubs	Signing Date	Transfer Fee	APPEARANCES				GOALS			
			Lge	FL Cup	FA Cup	Others	Lge	FL Cup	FA Cup	Others
Brentford	10.84	–	103+1	7	1	8	2			
Wimbledon*	8.88	£150,000	108+6	12	5+1	6				

KAMINSKY Jason Mario George

Born: Leicester, 3 December, 1973

Height: 6'0" Weight: 12.4

Position/Skill Factor: Left footed striker who is an out and out front man. Always looking for the goal.

Career History: First came to Nottingham Forest as an associated schoolboy in December 1989, before signing on as a trainee in July 1990. Had progressed to the professional ranks a year later and made his FL debut at Luton Town on 14 April 1992. Not in the Nigel Clough, Tommy Gaynor or Lee Glover mould at Forest, but has so far scored at every level and looks to repeat the dose in First Division football.

Clubs	Signing Date	Transfer Fee	APPEARANCES				GOALS			
			Lge	FL Cup	FA Cup	Others	Lge	FL Cup	FA Cup	Others
Nottingham Forest*	7.91	–	0+1							

KANTCHELSKIS Andrei

Born: Kirovograd, USSR, 23 January 1969

Height: 5'10" Weight: 12.4

International Honours: USSR Int

Position/Skill Factor: Very direct right-winger, he uses his pace to go past defenders. Presents goal scoring opportunities for his strike-force with good early crosses.

Career History: A Soviet Union international before the disintegration of that country, he came to Britain in order to advance his career. Signed for Manchester United as a non-contract player from top Russian side, Shakhtyor Donetsk and made his FL debut at Crystal Palace on 11 May 1991. Alex Ferguson was sufficiently impressed to offer him a contract in the summer of 1991 and in the first game of the new season and his first at Old Trafford, at home to Notts County, he was an instant sensation on the right-wing with United's fans. Although he remained part of the first team scene throughout the season, he was not an automatic first choice and was frequently demoted to substitute, partly because the manager seemed reluctant to play with two orthodox wingers in every match. He scored several vital goals during the season, most of them spectacular and won his first honour when he was a member of the United team which defeated Nottingham Forest 1-0 in the League Cup Final. Played in all three matches for the CIS as the Soviets were "bombed" out of the European Championships by Scotland.

Clubs	Signing Date	Transfer Fee	APPEARANCES				GOALS			
			Lge	FL Cup	FA Cup	Others	Lge	FL Cup	FA Cup	Others
Manchester United*	3.91	£650,000	29+6	4	2	1	5	2	1	

KAVANAGH Graham Anthony

Born: Dublin, 12 December 1973

Height: 5'10" Weight: 12.4

International Honours: IR Yth

Position/Skill Factor: A young midfield player with good control who can take on and beat opponents.

Career History: Signed by Middlesbrough from League of Ireland side, Home Farm, during the 1991 close season, he has yet to make a first team appearance for the "Teesiders".

Clubs	Signing Date	Transfer Fee	APPEARANCES				GOALS			
			Lge	FL Cup	FA Cup	Others	Lge	FL Cup	FA Cup	Others
Middlesbrough*	8.91									

KEANE Roy Maurice

Born: Cork, 10 August 1971

Height: 5'10" Weight: 11.3

International Honours: IR "U21", IR-7

Position/Skill Factor: A midfield player with plenty of stamina, who comes from deep positions to score valuable goals. Always prepared to play his way out of trouble, he is a good passer of the ball.

Career History: Turned out to be one of the finds of 1990-91 after being signed by Nottingham Forest from Cobh Ramblers, in the Republic of Ireland, during the 1990 close season. Typically, Brian Clough plunged him straight into first team action and against the then League Champions! He made his FL debut at Liverpool on 28 August 1990 and finished the season playing in the FA Cup Final side that lost 2-1 to Tottenham Hotspur. In a season where it was generally expected that he would initially have difficulties getting into Forest's reserve side, he made 35 League appearances and was also recognised fully at international level when playing for the Irish Republic against Chile on 22 May 1991 in Dublin. He confirmed the progress made in his initial term with another excellent season in 1991–92 when Forest reached the Finals for two cup competitions, defeating Southampton 3-2 in the Zenith Cup Final, but falling to Manchester United in the League Cup Final. His goal in extra-time of the second-leg of the Semi-Final at White Hart Lane against "Spurs", clinched Forest's place at Wembley. He also established himself in the Irish national team.

Clubs	Signing Date	Transfer Fee	APPEARANCES				GOALS			
			Lge	FL Cup	FA Cup	Others	Lge	FL Cup	FA Cup	Others
Nottingham Forest*	5.90	£10,000	74	12	14	5	16	5	2	2

KEARTON Jason Brett

Born: Ipswich, Australia, 9 July 1969

Height: 6'1" Weight: 11.10

Position/Skill Factor: Very consistent young goalkeeper. A good stopper, he also comes out well for crosses.

Career History: Came to England in 1988 seeking to further his football career, after gaining experience in his native country with Brisbane Lions. Signed by Everton, he started as third choice behind Neville Southall and Mike Stowell, but following the latter's departure to "Wolves" in the summer of 1990, he became reserve 'keeper. However, one year later, he was back to third choice when Everton signed Irish international Gerry Peyton as cover for Southall. He was able to advance his career with two extended three month loans, in 1991-92, firstly with Stoke City, where he made his FL debut at Bradford City on 17 August 1991 and later with Blackpool, who won promotion to the Third Division through the Play Offs, after he returned to Goodison Park.

Clubs	Signing Date	Transfer Fee	APPEARANCES				GOALS			
			Lge	FL Cup	FA Cup	Others	Lge	FL Cup	FA Cup	Others
Everton	10.88	–								
Stoke City	8.91	Loan	16							
Blackpool*	1.92	Loan	12							

KEELEY John Henry

Born: Plaistow, 27 July 1961

Height: 6'1" Weight: 14.2

Position/Skill Factor: Very consistent goalkeeper, not showy, but reliable. Takes up good positions to make a save look easy.

Career History: Signed as an apprentice for Southend United in June 1977, before progressing to the professional ranks and making his FL debut at Roots Hall against Colchester United on 12 October 1979. Played first team football only sporadically and spent most of his time at the club as deputy to Mervyn Cawston. In November 1984, his FL career seemed over when he "walked out" of the club following three heavy defeats and a disagreement and spent the remainder of the season with Maldon Town of the Essex Senior League. However, it was at Chelmsford City that Brighton & Hove Albion discovered him a year later, when they required a deputy for Perry Digweed. Made a handful of appearances during his first season at the club, but it was in 1987-88 that he finally broke through as an ever present in the Albion side that gained promotion to the Second Division at the first time of asking, as runners-up. During the 1990 close season, he moved to Oldham Athletic for a large fee, presumably as first choice but, in the event was not called upon, as John Hallworth played in every game throughout the "Latics'" Second Division title winning campaign. His "dream move" turned into more of a nightmare in 1991-92. Once again, shut out of the first team 'keeper's jersey by Hallworth, he was loaned out to Oxford United and Reading for some FL action. Finally, after nearly two years at Boundary Park, manager Joe Royle selected him for the final game of the season at home to Manchester City. Sadly for Keeley, the "Latics" were thrashed 5-2 by their near neighbours.

Clubs	Signing Date	Transfer Fee	APPEARANCES				GOALS			
			Lge	FL Cup	FA Cup	Others	Lge	FL Cup	FA Cup	Others
Southend United	7.79	–	63	4	5	3				
Maldon Town	11.84	–								
Chelmsford City	7.85	–	–							
Brighton & H.A.	8.86	£5,000	138	6	9	7				
Oldham Athletic*	8.90	£240,000	1			1				
Oxford United	11.91	Loan	6							
Reading	2.92	Loan	6							

KELLY Garry

Born: Drogheda, 9 July, 1974

Height: 5'9" Weight: 10.0

International Honours: IR-"U21"

Position/Skill Factor: Skilful winger with two good feet, he has some lovely touches and can produce measured crosses.

Career History: A young Irish forward who joined Leeds United as a professional soon after his 17th birthday. Amazingly, given the competition for places at Elland Road, he made a first team appearance only one month after joining the club, as a substitute in a League Cup-tie against Scunthorpe and made his FL debut, again as a substitute, away to Nottingham Forest on 22 December

1991. For a 17-year-old player to be included in the first team squad, clearly indicates a lot of potential for the future.

Clubs	Signing Date	Transfer Fee	APPEARANCES				GOALS			
			Lge	FL Cup	FA Cup	Others	Lge	FL Cup	FA Cup	Others
Leeds United*	9.91	–	0+2	0+1						

KENNA Jeffrey (Jeff) Jude

Born: Dublin, 27 August 1970

Height: 5'11" Weight: 11.9

International Honours: IR "U21"-3

Position/Skill Factor: Favours his right foot, but can play in both full-back positions. Gets his foot in well and is not afraid to move up field with the ball.

Career History: Irish born full-back who joined Southampton as a trainee in June 1987, turning professional two years later. He had to wait another two years for his FL debut, turning out as a substitute in the penultimate game of 1990-91, away to Derby County on 4 May 1991 and made his full debut at right-back one week later. Before his "Saints'" debut, he had already been selected three times for the Irish Republic Under 21 team. In 1991-92 he played second fiddle to Jason Dodd until January, but once in the team he held his place, apart from one brief hiatus, until the end of the season and was a member of the "Saints'" team which lost 2-3 to Nottingham Forest in the Zenith Cup Final.

Clubs	Signing Date	Transfer Fee	APPEARANCES				GOALS			
			Lge	FL Cup	FA Cup	Others	Lge	FL Cup	FA Cup	Others
Southampton*	4.89	–	15+1		3+1	3				

KENNY Marc Vincent

Born: Dublin, 17 September 1973

Height: 5'11" Weight: 11.10

Position/Skill Factor: Creative midfield player with good control who is an excellent passer of the ball.

Career History: Young Irish player who signed for Liverpool on his 17th birthday from the League of Ireland side, Home Farm and has yet to play first team football.

Clubs	Signing Date	Transfer Fee	APPEARANCES				GOALS			
			Lge	FL Cup	FA Cup	Others	Lge	FL Cup	FA Cup	Others
Liverpool*	9.90	–								

KENNY William

Born: Liverpool, 19 September 1973

Height: 5'10" Weight: 12.0

Position: Midfielder.

Career History: Joined the Everton professional staff during the 1992 close season, having previously been at Goodison as an associated schoolboy (November 1989) and as a trainee (June 1990). No first team experience.

Clubs	Signing Date	Transfer Fee	APPEARANCES				GOALS			
			Lge	FL Cup	FA Cup	Others	Lge	FL Cup	FA Cup	Others
Everton*	6.92	–								

KENT Shane

Born: New Zealand, 30 August 1974

Height: 5'9" Weight: 10.4

International Honours: NI Yth

Position: Right-Back

Career History: Signed professional forms for Sheffield United during the summer of 1992, having first come to the club as a trainee in July 1990. No first team experience.

Clubs	Signing Date	Transfer Fee	APPEARANCES				GOALS			
			Lge	FL Cup	FA Cup	Others	Lge	FL Cup	FA Cup	Others
Sheffield United*	6.92	–								

KEOWN Martin Raymond

Born: Oxford, 24 July 1966

Height: 6'1" Weight: 12.4

International Honours: E Yth, E "U21"-8, E-9

Position/Skill Factor: Commanding centre-back who reads situations well. A very good defender with plenty of pace, he is a strong tackler and dominant in the air.

Career History: Came to Arsenal as a 14-year-old, signing as an associated schoolboy in October 1980 and moving up to apprentice in June 1982, before turning professional. However, chances were limited at Highbury and he made his FL debut for Brighton & Hove Albion at Manchester City on 23 February 1985, whilst on loan. He remained at the Goldstone Ground on loan for the opening weeks of 1985-86, but after returning to Arsenal, he finally won a place at the heart of the defence, playing through the latter half of the season. During the summer break, though, Aston Villa signed him and after starting out in the number two shirt, he reverted to a more central role, but although he played well, the club were relegated to the Second Division at the end of the season. Was a major influence for Villa during 1987-88 as they regained their First Division status at the first attempt, but once their position had been secured at the end of the following season, he moved on to Everton. Initially, it seemed as if he would be used as cover for Dave Watson and Kevin Ratcliffe, but when both players suffered injuries during the season, he got an extended run in the side, which has continued into 1990-91, with him being used as a full-back and third central defender. He was firmly established in the heart of Everton's defence in 1991–92 as Kevin Ratcliffe's long reign came to an end and missed only three games through injury. At the age of 25 it seemed that an international career had passed him by. However, his Everton form was so impressive that England manager Graham Taylor gave him a chance in the friendly against France in February 1992. He quickly developed an understanding with Des Walker and was retained for the remainder of England's programme, with the bonus of scoring a goal in his second match against Czechoslovakia. By May he had become an automatic selection for the European Championship Finals and played in all three games as England were ultimately sunk without trace by the host nation, Sweden.

Clubs	Signing Date	Transfer Fee	APPEARANCES				GOALS			
			Lge	FL Cup	FA Cup	Others	Lge	FL Cup	FA Cup	Others
Arsenal	1.84	–	22		5					
Brighton & H.A.	2.85	Loan	21+2	2		2	1	1		1
Aston Villa	6.86	£200,000	109+3	12+1	6	2	3			
Everton*	6.89	£750,000	79+4	7	10	6				

KERNAGHAN Alan Nigel

Born: Otley,
25 April 1967

Height: 6'2"

Weight: 12.12

International Honours:
NI Sch

Position/Skill Factor: Central defender, who can also play up front when required. He is strong in the tackle, has a good right foot and is more than useful in the air.

Career History: Began with Middlesbrough as an associated schoolboy player in September 1981, before graduating through the apprenticeship scheme (July 1983) to full professional status. Made his FL debut at Ayresome Park against Notts County on 27 February 1985, but although playing 24 League matches in 1987-88, he wasn't given another extended run until 1989-90, during a season when the club only escaped relegation to the Third Division by a whisker. As a forward he had never shown any propensity for scoring goals and at the start of 1989-90 he was switched to a central defensive role. It was ironic therefore that when restored to his original position to cover for injuries to other forwards in November 1989, he scored a hat-trick at Blackburn. The die was already cast, however and he soon resumed his defensive role. In 1990-91 he played in all games to the end of November, but after losing his place to Simon Coleman he was loaned out to Charlton Athletic and on his return came back into the side for the last few games of the season. Comically, Charlton manager Lennie Lawrence tried to persuade him to join the London club during the summer of 1991. However, after Lawrence was appointed manager of "Boro", he changed tack and had to persuade him to remain at Ayresome Park! With the departure of Simon Coleman and later Tony Mowbray, his place in the heart of "Boro's" defence was at last assured and he was a regular performer in 1991-92 until injured at Tranmere Rovers in April. Thus, he was absent for the crucial end of season games which raised the side to second place and automatic promotion to the Premier League.

Clubs	Signing Date	Transfer Fee	APPEARANCES				GOALS			
			Lge	FL Cup	FA Cup	Others	Lge	FL Cup	FA Cup	Others
Middlesbrough*	3.85	–	144+40	18+7	7+4	14+2	13	1	3	2
Charlton Athletic	1.91	Loan	13							

KERR David William

Born: Dumfries, 6 September 1974

Height: 5'11" Weight: 11.4

Position/Skill Factor: Strong tackling midfield player who covers every blade of grass.

Career History: Came down from Scotland on leaving school to sign as a trainee for Manchester City in September 1990 and a year later had progressed to the club's professional ranks. Yet to make a first team appearance, he has only recently turned out for City's reserves.

Clubs	Signing Date	Transfer Fee	APPEARANCES				GOALS			
			Lge	FL Cup	FA Cup	Others	Lge	FL Cup	FA Cup	Others
Manchester City*	9.91	–								

KERR Dylan

Born: Valetta, Malta, 14 January 1967

Height: 5'11" Weight: 12.5

Position: Full-back.

Career History: Started his football career as a junior at Sheffield Wednesday in September 1983, before turning over to the professional ranks a year later. Released on a free transfer in the summer of 1985, he joined a group of English players who went to South Africa to play for Pretoria based Arcadia Shepherds. On his return to England, in autumn 1988, he linked up briefly with Frickley Athletic of the Northern Premier League, before being offered a trial by his former manager at Hillsborough, Howard Wilkinson, by then in charge of Leeds United. He was then awarded a contract and made his FL debut at Elland Road when coming on as a sub against Brighton & Hove Albion on 15 April 1989. Deputised twice for the injured Michael Whitlow during the club's Second Division Championship winning season of 1989-90, but was not required during the following term. Played no part in Leeds' League Championship campaign of 1991-92, but had further FL experience on loan to Doncaster Rovers at the beginning of the season and three months with Blackpool from January to March 1992.

Clubs	Signing Date	Transfer Fee	APPEARANCES				GOALS			
			Lge	FL Cup	FA Cup	Others	Lge	FL Cup	FA Cup	Others
Sheffield Wednesday	9.84	–								
Arcadia S'herds (SA)	7.85	–								
Frickley Athletic	8.88	–								
Leeds United*	1.89	–	3+5		1	0+4				
Doncaster Rovers	8.91	Loan	7				1			
Blackpool	12.91	Loan	12				1			

KEY Lance

Born: Kettering, 13 May 1968

Height: 6'2" **Weight:** 14.6

Position/Skill Factor: Goalkeeper. Good shot stopper, he is both agile and brave.

Career History: Joined Sheffield Wednesday at the tail-end of 1989-90 from non-Leaguers, Histon, only to find himself fourth choice behind England's Chris Woods, Chris Turner and Kevin Pressman. Still to make a first team appearance for Wednesday, he was loaned out to York City in April 1992 and looked sure to make his FL debut at Bootham Crescent, until picking up an injury which unluckily put him out of action for the rest of the season.

Clubs	Signing Date	Transfer Fee	APPEARANCES				GOALS			
			Lge	FL Cup	FA Cup	Others	Lge	FL Cup	FA Cup	Others
Sheffield Wednesday*	4.90	–								

KILFORD Ian Anthony

Born: Bristol, 6 October 1973

Height: 5'10" **Weight:** 10.5

Position/Skill Factor: Constructive midfield player who is always looking to make a telling pass.

Career History: Came to Nottingham Forest as an associated schoolboy in April 1988, before graduating as a trainee in July 1990 and to the club's professional ranks at the end of 1990-91. A first year professional, he was on the fringe of the Forest reserve side in 1991-92 and hopes for better luck in 1992–93.

Clubs	Signing Date	Transfer Fee	APPEARANCES				GOALS			
			Lge	FL Cup	FA Cup	Others	Lge	FL Cup	FA Cup	Others
Nottingham Forest*	4.91	–								

KING Philip (Phil) Geoffrey

Born: Bristol,
28 December 1967

Height: 5'10"

Weight: 12.0

International Honours:
E"B"

Position/Skill Factor: As an attacking left-back, he can often be used as an extra forward when the occasion demands. Has a superb left foot and is capable of delivering quality passes and crosses.

Career History: Joined Exeter City as an associated schoolboy in February 1982 and on leaving school, became an apprentice in May 1984. Within a month of turning professional, he had made his FL debut at St James' Park against Halifax Town on 23 February 1985. Created a good impression when in the side, but remained in the shadow of the long serving Keith Viney and was allowed to join Torquay United in the 1986 close season. Slotting into the number three shirt immediately, he showed such promise that Third Division Swindon Town moved for him in mid-season to bolster their promotion hopes. Second Division status was duly attained and he continued to star for the "Robins", being ever present in 1987-88 and very rarely missing a game. It was only a matter of time before he joined the "elite" and it came as no surprise when he signed for Sheffield Wednesday during 1989-90. Sadly for him, Wednesday were relegated at the end of his first season at Hillsborough, but the following term he missed only three League games as the club responded magnificently to the challenge and returned to the First Division at the first time of asking, in third place. He also had the added bonus of receiving a League Cup winners medal, following the great 1-0 victory over Manchester United at Wembley. An unsung hero of the Wednesday team, he played in all but four games of the 1991-92 campaign when the "Owls" achieved their highest placing (third) for 31 years and qualified for the 1992-93 UEFA Cup. He also scored his first goal for Wednesday, albeit it was only a consolation effort in a 3-1 defeat to local rivals, United. At the end of the season he was amazed and gratified to be voted the Supporters' "Player of the Year", ahead of such notables as David Hirst, Carlton Palmer and Roland Nilsson.

Clubs	Signing Date	Transfer Fee	APPEARANCES				GOALS			
			Lge	FL Cup	FA Cup	Others	Lge	FL Cup	FA Cup	Others
Exeter City	1.85	–	24+3	1		1+2				
Torquay United	7.86	£3,000	24	2	1	2	3			
Swindon Town	2.87	£155,000	112+4	11	5	13	4			
Sheffield Wednesday*	11.89	£400,000	106+1	13	8	4	1			

KITE Philip (Phil) David

Born: Bristol,
26 October 1962

Height: 6'1"

Weight: 14.7

International Honours:
E Sch, E Yth

Position/Skill Factor: A very strong and fit goalkeeper, he comes out well for crosses. He is a good shot stopper and extremely agile for such a big man.

Career History: Locally born and bred, he signed for Bristol Rovers as an associated schoolboy in January 1978, before taking out a football apprenticeship on leaving school in July 1979. Made his FL debut at Derby County on 10 January 1981, where a Don Gillies own goal was the deciding factor in a 2-1 defeat. In 1982-83 he gained a regular place in the side and was ever present and the following season, impressed Southampton enough to sign him as cover for Peter Shilton. The move, however, was not a great success and he was loaned out to both Middlesbrough and Gillingham. When freed by the "Saints", during the 1987 close season, he remained without a club for eight months, while he recovered from an injury. Eventually, he signed for Gillingham, alternating with the long serving Ron Hillyard, who held the most appearances record for the club. After little more than two years with the "Gills", he moved to Bournemouth to understudy the Eire international, Gerry Peyton. After one year at Dean Court, he was signed by Dave Bassett for Sheffield United as cover for Simon Tracey and received an immediate first team opportunity when the latter was injured during the "Blades'" first game back in Division One. He performed well, despite United's disastrous start to the season, but had to give way to Tracey when fit again towards the end of October. After coming into the side for eight games early in 1991-92, he spent an extended three month loan with Fourth Division Mansfield Town, but was unlucky to be injured in March, when Tracey was also absent, forcing Dave Bassett to sign a third 'keeper, Mel Rees.

Clubs	Signing Date	Transfer Fee	APPEARANCES				GOALS			
			Lge	FL Cup	FA Cup	Others	Lge	FL Cup	FA Cup	Others
Bristol Rovers	10.80	–	96	12	8	2				
Southampton	8.84	£50,000	4			1				
Middlesbrough	3.86	Loan	2							
Gillingham	2.87	–	70	5	4	10				
Bournemouth	6.89	£20,000	7	1						
Sheffield United*	8.90	£25,000	11	5	1	1				
Mansfield Town	11.91	Loan	11			1				

KIWOMYA Christopher (Chris) Mark

Born: Huddersfield,
2 December 1969

Height: 5'10"

Weight: 10.5

Position/Skill Factor: Athletic striker with great pace. Runs at defenders and twists and turns, making him a difficult player to mark.

Career History: Followed his brother Andy, the former Barnsley player, into League soccer, when he joined Ipswich Town as a trainee in July 1986. On turning professional, he had to wait a further 19 months before making his FL debut as a sub at Portman Road against Bradford City on 24 September 1988. Showed early promise, but didn't really become a regular until 1990-91 when he played 34 matches and topped the club's goal scoring charts. Originally a winger, he was converted by Town manager John Lyall into a central striker and responded brilliantly with a burst of seven goals from eight games at the end of the season. Surprisingly overlooked for England Youth and Under 21 honours, he was a regular performer in 1991-92, as Ipswich won the Second Division Championship, leading the way with 16 FL goals, plus three cup goals.

Clubs	Signing Date	Transfer Fee	APPEARANCES				GOALS			
			Lge	FL Cup	FA Cup	Others	Lge	FL Cup	FA Cup	Others
Ipswich Town*	3.87	–	112+23	6	8	5+1	32	1	1	3

KOZMA Istvan

Born: Pazto, Hungary,
3 December 1964

Height: 6'0"

Weight: 12.6

International Honours:
Hungarian Int

Position/Skill Factor: A typically skilful continental midfield player who passes and moves well.

Career History: A Hungarian International, who first

came to these shores in September 1989 when he joined Scottish Premier Division club Dunfermline Athletic from the famous French club, Girondins de Bordeaux. After nearly three seasons at East End Park as a first team regular, he was signed by Liverpool manager Graham Souness in February 1992 to bolster a first team squad ravaged by injuries. He made his FL debut away to Norwich City on 22 February 1992 and made occasional appearances subsequently, although not in the reckoning for a FA Cup Final place. It remains to be seen if he has a future at Anfield or whether he will move on when the injury crisis eases.

Clubs	Signing Date	Transfer Fee	APPEARANCES				GOALS			
			Lge	FL Cup	FA Cup	Others	Lge	FL Cup	FA Cup	Others
Liverpool*	2.92	£300,000	3+2		0+2					

KRUSZYNSKI Zbigniew (Detzi)

Born: Divschav, Poland, 14 October 1961

Height: 6'0" Weight: 12.12

Position/Skill Factor: A tough midfielder who sees the picture quickly and holds the ball up well. A good passer, he is more of a "setter up", than a creator of chances.

Career History: Snapped up by the then Wimbledon manager, Bobby Gould, at the tail end of 1988, from the West German side FC 08 Homburg, he made his FL debut as a sub at West Ham United on 2 January 1989. Proved to be a capable deputy for Vinny Jones over a three match spell later that term, his performances earning him a regular place alongside the latter in the "Dons'" midfield for the rest of the season. Following the departure of Jones to Leeds United during the 1989 close season, he was outstanding as the team's anchor man, but after appearing in the first 33 games of 1990-91, he fell out of favour, losing his place to Lawrie Sanchez. Made only one appearance for the "Dons" in 1991-92 and finished the season on loan to Third Division Brentford, assisting them to the Third Division Championship and automatic promotion to the new First Division.

Clubs	Signing Date	Transfer Fee	APPEARANCES				GOALS			
			Lge	FL Cup	FA Cup	Others	Lge	FL Cup	FA Cup	Others
Wimbledon*	12.88	£100,000	65+6	4+1	6	3+2	4			
Brentford	3.92	Loan	8							

KUBICKI Dariusz

Born: Warsaw, Poland, 6 June 1963

Height: 5'10" Weight: 11.7

International Honours: Polish Int

Position/Skill Factor: Right-back. A very good defender who is not easily beaten, he also has a constructive side and is an excellent passer of the ball.

Career History: Polish international full-back who signed for Aston Villa at the start of the 1991-92 season from Legia Warsaw and made his FL debut at Southampton on 31 August 1991. An automatic first choice at right-back until February 1992, he lost his place to new signing Earl Barrett and took little part in the remaining proceedings.

Clubs	Signing Date	Transfer Fee	APPEARANCES				GOALS			
			Lge	FL Cup	FA Cup	Others	Lge	FL Cup	FA Cup	Others
Aston Villa*	8.91	£200,000	23	2	4+1	1				

LAKE Michael Charles

Born: Denton,
15 November 1966

Height: 6'1"

Weight: 13.7

Position/Skill Factor: Big strong midfield player who is capable of scoring spectacular goals with long range shooting.

Career History: Older brother of Paul, who plays for Manchester City, he was discovered by Sheffield United while turning out for non-League Macclesfield Town. Previously with Curzon Ashton, after being a junior at Manchester City, he made his FL debut away to Newcastle United on 25 November 1989, but was plagued by injuries, playing only a handful of games up to the end of 1990-91. After remaining on the periphery of the first team, with several appearances as substitute in the early months of 1991-92, he burst into prominence with a series of cracking goals in the New Year against Southampton, Nottingham Forest and Manchester City, which launched United's surge up the First Division table. After two years on the sidelines, he seemed at last to have staked a claim to a regular first team slot, only to be struck down again by injury, losing his place to new signing Paul Rogers.

Clubs	Signing Date	Transfer Fee	APPEARANCES				GOALS			
			Lge	FL Cup	FA Cup	Others	Lge	FL Cup	FA Cup	Others
Sheffield United*	10.89	£60,000	13+16	3+2	5	0+1	4		1	

LAKE Paul Andrew

Born: Denton,
28 October 1968

Height: 6'0"

Weight: 12.2

International Honours:
E "U21"-5, E"B"

Position/Skill Factor: Hard working midfield player with good passing techniques, who can also play at full-back.

Career History: It was only natural that he would sign for Manchester City as an associated schoolboy (February 1983) and later as an apprentice (July 1985). Made his FL debut at Wimbledon on 24 January 1987, while still a trainee and the following season he had become a regular, playing in 37 League matches, as City were promoted to the First Division as runners-up. Originally a midfielder, he was switched to right-back during 1988-89 by manager Mel Machin and alternated between the two positions in 1989-90. Being treated as a utility player did not do much to advance his career and 1990-91 turned into a nightmare for him when he was carried off with a serious knee injury during the third match against Aston Villa. And following an operation to rectify the problem, he didn't play again that season. Once regarded as the most talented of City's crop of brilliant youngsters in the late 1980s, his future career must be in doubt after two years on the sidelines.

Clubs	Signing Date	Transfer Fee	APPEARANCES				GOALS			
			Lge	FL Cup	FA Cup	Others	Lge	FL Cup	FA Cup	Others
Manchester City*	5.87	–	104+4	10	9	5	7	1	2	1

LAKE Robert Matthew

Born: Stockton, 13 October 1971

Height: 5'11½" Weight: 12.0

Position/Skill Factor: Slim midfielder with a constructive attitude to the game.

Career History: Has progressed through the ranks at Middlesbrough as an associated schoolboy (November 1985), trainee (July 1988) and a full professional (October 1989). A star of "Boro's" FA Youth Cup side of 1989-90, he was quickly expected to breakthrough into the first team. Unfortunate to be injured during 1990–91, he has now been sidelined for the past 18 months.

Clubs	Signing Date	Transfer Fee	APPEARANCES				GOALS			
			Lge	FL Cup	FA Cup	Others	Lge	FL Cup	FA Cup	Others
Middlesbrough*	10.89	–								

LANGTON Edward

Born: Liverpool, 30 July 1974

Height: 5'10" Weight: 12.2

Position: Central Defender.

Career History: A locally born player, he joined the Everton professional staff during the 1992 close season, having previously been at Goodison as an associated schoolboy (December 1988) and as a trainee (June 1990).

Clubs	Signing Date	Transfer Fee	APPEARANCES				GOALS			
			Lge	FL Cup	FA Cup	Others	Lge	FL Cup	FA Cup	Others
Everton*	6.92	–								

LAW Brian John

Born: Merthyr Tydfil, 1 January 1970

Height: 6'2" Weight: 11.10

International Honours: W Sch, W Yth, W "U21"-2, W-1

Position/Skill Factor: Central defender who is both strong on the ground and in the air. Has a good left foot and is capable of hitting the front men with lovely long passes.

Career History: First came to Queens Park Rangers as an associated schoolboy in January 1986, before signing up as a trainee in May 1986. Graduated to the pro ranks and made his FL debut at Loftus Road against Sheffield Wednesday on 23 April 1988, when coming on as a substitute. Since then, he proved so capable when standing in for the more established stars like Danny Maddix and Alan McDonald at the centre of Rangers' defence, that Wales selected him for a full international against Sweden in Stockholm on 25 April 1990. Out injured for the whole of 1991-92, he has yet to get back to full fitness.

Clubs	Signing Date	Transfer Fee	APPEARANCES				GOALS			
			Lge	FL Cup	FA Cup	Others	Lge	FL Cup	FA Cup	Others
Q.P.R.*	8.87	–	19+1	2+1	3	1				

LAWS Brian

Born: Wallsend, 14 October 1961

Height: 5'10"

Weight: 11.5

International Honours: E"B", FL rep

Position/Skill Factor: Good all-round right-back. He can pass, both short and long, will get forward and join up in the attack when the opportunity presents itself and is not easily beaten when defending.

Career History: Another north-easterner who made the trek to Turf Moor for a start in League football with Burnley, signing as an associated schoolboy in November 1976, before progressing to a football apprenticeship in June 1978. Turning pro early in 1979-80, he didn't make his FL debut until the final game of the season at Watford on 3 May 1980, but 16 games without a win sealed the club's fate and following the final whistle, they were relegated to the Third Division. He spent a further three years at Burnley, winning a Third Division Championship medal in 1981-82, before crossing the Pennines in the 1983 close season, bound for Huddersfield Town. It was a fairly uneventful time at Leeds Road and some 18 months later he was sold to Middlesbrough, then struggling at the foot of the Second Division. In a roller coaster period at Ayresome Park, he played in the side relegated to the Third Division in 1985-86 and then, although out injured from February 1987, he was a member of the squad that won promotion back to the Second Division at the first attempt as runners-up. A right-back for nearly all his career, he was switched by "Boro" manager Bruce Rioch to midfield in 1986-87 with great success. The following season, 1987-88, he was in the team that won promotion back to the Second Division, via the Play-Offs, but instead of playing in the upper bracket with the "Teesiders", he opted to join Nottingham Forest. Waited some months for his Forest debut, coming on as a sub in a cracking 3-3 draw at West Ham United on 12 November 1988 and then took over the right-back position from Steve Chettle for the rest of the season. Was unfortunate to put through his own goal in the 3-1 FA Cup Semi-Final defeat by Liverpool that season, but gained compensation in the shape of a League Cup winners medal in the 3-1 defeat of Luton Town. The following season he was ever present in the Forest rearguard and won a second League Cup winners medal, this time at the expense of Oldham Athletic, who went down 1-0. Although playing 38 League matches in 1990-91, he was surprisingly left out of the FA Cup Final side due to play Tottenham Hotspur, in favour of Gary Charles. Forest lost 2-1 on the day, but in coming on for Lee Glover, he at least got another run out on the famous Wembley turf. Played second fiddle to Gary Charles for most of 1991–92, but won his place back in January 1992, following the former's loss of form. Once again lost his place to Charles for the League Cup final, but came on as a substitute and was first choice for the final games of the season.

Clubs	Signing Date	Transfer Fee	APPEARANCES				GOALS			
			Lge	FL Cup	FA Cup	Others	Lge	FL Cup	FA Cup	Others
Burnley	10.79	–	125	14	15		12	2	1	
Huddersfield Town	8.83	£10,000	56	7	3		1			
Middlesbrough	3.85	£30,000	103+5	6+1	8+1	6+1	12	2		
Nottingham Forest*	7.88	£120,000	98+9	22+3	12+2	9+1	4		1	

LAWTON Craig Thomas

Born: Hawarden, 5 January 1972

Height: 5'7" Weight: 10.3

International Honours: W Sch, W Yth, W "U21"-1

Position/Skill Factor: Midfield player, cum striker, he is a good goal scorer. Has a lovely left foot, can both pass and move and is also a strong tackler.

Career History: First came to Manchester United as an associated schoolboy player in September 1987 and on leaving school he joined the club as a trainee in July 1988. Had progressed to the professional ranks by the 1990 close season, but with nearly 40 full-time pros at Old Trafford, competition for places was fierce and an early first team opportunity was not forthcoming. Plagued with injuries during 1991-92, but made the Welsh Under 21 team.

Clubs	Signing Date	Transfer Fee	APPEARANCES				GOALS			
			Lge	FL Cup	FA Cup	Others	Lge	FL Cup	FA Cup	Others
Manchester United*	7.90	–								

LEE David John

Born: Kingswood, 26 November 1969

Height: 6'3" Weight: 14.0

International Honours: E Yth, E "U21"-9

Position/Skill Factor: Can play at centre-back and in midfield and has lovely skill for such a big man. Has two good feet and a footballing brain. Brings the ball out of defence and is quite capable of scoring goals.

Career History: From the Bristol area, he began his career at Chelsea as an associated schoolboy in March 1984, progressing to the professional ranks as a trainee and made his FL debut at Stamford Bridge against Leicester City on 1 October 1988. He came on as a sub and scored in a 2-1 victory and went on to make 20 appearances that first season, mostly in central defence including eight as a substitute as Chelsea won promotion back to the First Division at their first attempt, as Champions. Played in the first 23 games of 1989-90, before injury restricted him to a handful of subs' appearances for the remainder of the season and found it difficult to re-establish himself in the side during 1990-91. In 1991-92 with his future at Stamford Bridge uncertain, he was loaned out to Third Division Reading and Second Division Plymouth Argyle. For Reading he scored a remarkable five goals in five appearances, apparently from central defence! With Plymouth he saw out the season, but was unable to prevent their slide to relegation.

Clubs	Signing Date	Transfer Fee	APPEARANCES				GOALS			
			Lge	FL Cup	FA Cup	Others	Lge	FL Cup	FA Cup	Others
Chelsea*	6.88	–	53+19	6+1	1+3	5+1	6	1		1
Reading	1.92	Loan	5				5			
Plymouth Argyle	3.92	Loan	9				1			

LEE David (Dave)

Born: Blackburn,
5 November 1967

Height: 5'8"

Weight: 10.2

Position/Skill Factor: Small nippy right-winger with good acceleration. Can go past defenders with skill and pace and is an accurate crosser.

Career History: Joined Bury as an apprentice in July 1984 and made his FL debut as a substitute at Chesterfield on 17 August 1985, a year before turning professional. Gained a regular place in the side during the middle of the following term and his exciting play, along with that of other young players, gave rise to the hope that Bury could climb out of the Third Division. Twice the club failed at the Play-Off stage, in 1989-90 and 1990-91, but his performances during this period were one of the major reasons for the "Shakers" being involved in the chase for a promotion place. Only missed three League games since 1988-89 and in 1990-91, he was the club's leading marksman with 16 in all games. It was no great surprise when he was given a chance in the First Division by Southampton just after 1991-92 began. Unfortunately, it proved to be a case of the wrong club at the wrong time. After only a few games as first choice, he was demoted first to substitute and then disappeared from view in the second half of the season. In a team struggling against relegation and committed to obdurate defence, there was no room for two attacking wingers (Le Tissier was the other).

Clubs	Signing Date	Transfer Fee	APPEARANCES				GOALS			
			Lge	FL Cup	FA Cup	Others	Lge	FL Cup	FA Cup	Others
Bury	8.86	–	203+5	15	6	19+1	35	1		4
Southampton*	8.91	£350,000	11+8		0+1	1+1				

LEE **Justin** David

Born: Hereford, 19 September 1973

Height: 5'6½" Weight: 11.5

International Honours: E Yth

Position/Skill Factor: Midfielder cum full-back, who has a good left foot and a wide range of passing skills.

Career History: A recent Arsenal professional signing, he first came to the club as an associated schoolboy in March 1988, before graduating to trainee status in July 1990.

Clubs	Signing Date	Transfer Fee	APPEARANCES				GOALS			
			Lge	FL Cup	FA Cup	Others	Lge	FL Cup	FA Cup	Others
Arsenal*	10.91	–								

LE SAUX **Graeme** Pierre

Born: Jersey, 17 October 1968

Height: 5'10"

Weight: 11.2

International Honours: E "U21"-4, E"B"

Position/Skill Factor: Left-back or midfield player who is capable of playing anywhere on the left side. Skilful, very quick and a good crosser of the ball, he creates chances wherever he plays.

Career History: Spotted by Chelsea when playing for a local Jersey side, St Pauls, he signed professional forms without any further ado and within 18 months had made his FL debut as a sub at Portsmouth on 13 May 1989, the "Blues" having already been confirmed as the 1988-89 Second Division Champions. Had to wait until Boxing Day, 1989, to make his second appearance, again as a sub, but he scored to earn Chelsea a 2-2 draw at Selhurst Park. Even though the club shelled out £3 million for Andy Townsend and Dennis Wise at the start of the 1990-91 season, it did not unduly hinder his progress in the first team as he made 24 League appearances and proved to be one of the most exciting young players in the country. Won a regular place in 1991-92 mostly on the flank, but occasionally at left-back and was one of the few successes in a disappointing season.

Clubs	Signing Date	Transfer Fee	APPEARANCES				GOALS			
			Lge	FL Cup	FA Cup	Others	Lge	FL Cup	FA Cup	Others
Chelsea*	12.87	–	67+9	6+3	6+1	8+1	8	1		

LE TISSIER **Matthew** Paul

Born: Guernsey, 14 October 1968

Height: 6'0" Weight: 11.6

International Honours: E Yth, E"B"

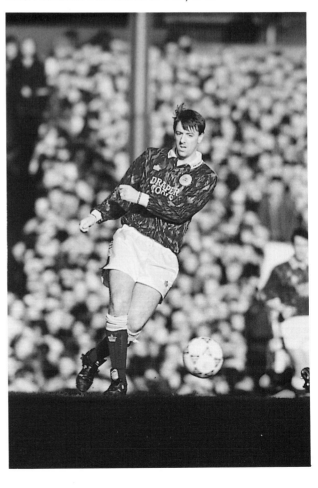

Position/Skill Factor: Winger cum striker, with pace, who is brilliant with the ball at his feet, often beating defenders for fun. Can both score and create and opens the door when others can't find the key.

Career History: First came to Southampton as an associated schoolboy in September 1984, before graduating as an apprentice in July 1985 and scoring 56 goals for the "Saints'" team that coming season. made his FL debut as a sub at Norwich City on 30 August 1986, two months prior to turning professional and during that first season he scored eight League and cup goals, including a hat-trick in a 4-0 win over Leicester City. The youngest player ever to score a hat-trick for the Club, he was taken along slowly and didn't become a regular until 1989-90, although he had netted nine goals in 21 starts in the previous campaign. Twenty strikes in 35 League matches that term was further testimony to his ability as he linked up well with two more of the club's young stars, Rod Wallace and Alan Shearer. Topping the Southampton scoring charts again in 1990-91 with 27 in all games and netting the winning goal on five separate occasions, he had earlier declined an offer to become part of the French international set-up, preferring to take his chances with England. One of the most exciting young players of his generation, it is astonishing that he was never played at Under 21 level. By comparison with the two previous season, 1991-92 was rather mundane as Southampton changed their playing style under new manager Ian Branfoot and goals became very scarce in their struggle against relegation. Scored only six FL goals, of which two were penalties, but netted nine in the various cup competitions (Rumbelows, Zenith and FA) in all of which the "Saints" enjoyed a long run. He played (and scored) in the Zenith Cup Final his first Wembley appearance, but was on the losing side against Nottingham Forest.

Clubs	Signing Date	Transfer Fee	APPEARANCES				GOALS			
			Lge	FL Cup	FA Cup	Others	Lge	FL Cup	FA Cup	Others
Southampton*	10.86	–	143+30	20+6	15+1	11+1	60	11	5	9

LIMBER Nicholas (Nicky)

Born: Doncaster, 23 January 1974

Height: 5'10" Weight: 11.2

Position/Skill Factor: A full-back with two useful feet and a nice feel for the ball. Good long thrower.

Career History: One of the many promising young players discovered by Doncaster Rovers in recent years, he signed as an associated schoolboy for the club in June 1988, before becoming a trainee on leaving school in July 1990. Made his FL debut at Gillingham on 11 May 1991, the last day of the 1990-91 season, still eight months short of the 18th birthday. Selected for the first match of the new season, he was then rested until October. On his return to the team he scored a brilliant 88th minute equaliser against Gillingham in only his fourth game. Only three weeks after signing professional for Doncaster, he was transferred to Manchester City, as the Fourth Division club were forced to sell their most promising players for modest fees simply to stay in business. At least in Limber's case there may be further payments to a maximum of £300,000, if he makes the grade with City.

Clubs	Signing Date	Transfer Fee	APPEARANCES				GOALS			
			Lge	FL Cup	FA Cup	Others	Lge	FL Cup	FA Cup	Others
Doncaster Rovers	1.92	–	13			1+1	1			1
Manchester City*	1.92	£75,000								

LIMPAR Anders

Born: Sweden, 24 August 1965

Height: 5'8" Weight: 11.5

International Honours: Swedish Int

Position/Skill Factor: Left-winger with wonderful natural ability. Has great balance, with two good feet and can wrong foot defenders with ease. Capable of both scoring and creating goals.

Career History: Signed by Arsenal from the Italian club, Cremonese, following his exciting performances for Sweden in the 1990 World Cup Finals, he added a new dimension to the "Gunners'" attack during 1990-91. Following his FL debut at Wimbledon on 25 August 1990, the club was rarely out of the top two all season and he celebrated winning a League Championship medal by scoring a hat-trick in the last match, a 6-1 victory at Highbury over Coventry City. Earlier in the season, he had scored the only goal of the infamous game against Manchester United at Old Trafford when 21 players were booked and both teams heavily fined for bringing the game into disrepute. Finished his first season in English football with a tally of 11 League goals, several of them match winners and delighted the Highbury legions as he showed the art of popping up in the penalty area to pounce on half chances. Prior to his spell in Italy, he played for a leading Swiss team, Young Boys of Berne. His second season at Highbury was a strange affair. In and out of the team throughout, he only started 23 FL games, yet at the end of 1991-92 was credited with 15 goal "assists", more than all but two First Division players, who both played the full season. In addition, he scored a remarkable goal with a 50 yard chip against Liverpool late in the season. In view of his vital contributions to the team it is puzzling that he was not an automatic first choice. Ended his disappointing English season with strangely subdued performances for Sweden in the European Championships. He played in all four matches as the host country finally went out 3-2 to Germany in the Semi-Final.

			APPEARANCES				GOALS			
Clubs	Signing Date	Transfer Fee	Lge	FL Cup	FA Cup	Others	Lge	FL Cup	FA Cup	Others
Arsenal*	7.90	£1,000,000	55+8	3	5	3	16		2	1

LINDSAY Scott William

Born: Preston, 15 November 1973

Height: 5'7" Weight: 9.12

Position: Left-winger.

Career History: Came through Blackburn Rovers' junior ranks to sign professional forms during the 1992 close season, having been at Ewood Park as an associated schoolboy (November 1988) and as a trainee (July 1990). No first team experience as yet.

			APPEARANCES				GOALS			
Clubs	Signing Date	Transfer Fee	Lge	FL Cup	FA Cup	Others	Lge	FL Cup	FA Cup	Others
Blackburn Rovers*	6.92	–								

LINIGHAN Andrew (Andy)

Born: Hartlepool, 18 June 1962

Height: 6'3"

Weight: 12.6

International Honours: E"B"

Position/Skill Factor: Tough tackling, consistent centre-back who is very good in the air and more than adaptable on the ground. Very good at hitting long diagonal balls to the front men.

Career History: Elder brother of David, currently of Ipswich Town and the son of Brian, who played a single game for Darlington back in 1958, he began his career with Hartlepool United after coming out of local junior football with Smiths Dock and made his FL debut at home to Stockport County on 28 March 1981. Went on to make over 100 appearances for the "Pool", before moving on to Leeds United in the 1984 close season and was ever present for them until transferring to Oldham Athletic some 18 months later. Quickly established himself at the heart of the "Latics'"defence, where his consistency was noted by several First Division clubs. Norwich City won the race for his signature as they bid to become a force to be reckoned with and he went straight into the side as the replacement for Steve Bruce, who had been transferred to Manchester United four months earlier. he proved as reliable as ever as City made an unprecedented push for the League title in 1988-89, only to falter on the run-in to finish in fourth place, their highest position ever. During a two year spell at Carrow Road, he missed just two games, but was on the move again in the 1990 close season as Arsenal, seeking to strengthen their squad, made the "Canaries" an offer they couldn't refuse. Proved a capable deputy in the absence of club skipper, Tony Adams, but with such a strong squad available at Highbury, he played very few games as the League Championship came back to north London. It was strange that Arsenal should pay such a large fee for a player who only provided cover for Adams and Bould. With Bould injured for the first three months of the 1991-92 season he had the chance to establish himself, but although he played on and off until the New Year, once both Adams and Bould were fit he played no further part in the campaign.

			APPEARANCES				GOALS			
Clubs	Signing Date	Transfer Fee	Lge	FL Cup	FA Cup	Others	Lge	FL Cup	FA Cup	Others
Hartlepool United	9.80	–	110	7+1	8	1	4	1		1
Leeds United	5.84	£200,000	66	6	2	2	3	1		
Oldham Athletic	1.86	£65,000	87	8	3	4	6	2		
Norwich City	3.88	£350,000	86	6	10	4	8			
Arsenal*	6.90	£1,250,000	22+5	1+1	3+1	2				1

LINIGHAN Brian

Born: Hartlepool, 2 November 1973

Height: 6'0" Weight: 10.3

Position: Right-back.

Career History: With his twin brother, John, he is the latest of the Linighan family to turn professional. Their father, Brian snr, played for Darlington in the 1950s, while brothers Andy and David are currently defenders with Arsenal and Ipswich Town, respectively. Having been at the club as an associated schoolboy since June 1988 and a trainee since July 1990, he signed on the dotted line during the 1992 season. Has no first team experience.

			APPEARANCES				GOALS			
Clubs	Signing Date	Transfer Fee	Lge	FL Cup	FA Cup	Others	Lge	FL Cup	FA Cup	Others
Sheffield Wednesday*	6.92	–								

LINIGHAN David

Born: Hartlepool,
9 January 1965

Height: 6'2"

Weight: 10.12

Position/Skill Factor: Strong central defender who is very good in the air and is especially dangerous at set plays. With his excellent left foot, he is adept at hitting long balls in behind the opposing full-backs.

Career History: Son of Brian, who played for Darlington in 1958 and like his brother Andy, who also joined Hartlepool United from Smiths Dock, he made his FL debut at home to Bradford City on 27 March 1982. Played mainly in the shadow of Andy for a long while and it wasn't until 1985-86 that he finally held down a regular place, missing just eight matches throughout the campaign. Impressed Arthur Cox enough for Derby County to move for him during the summer, but after just four months and no first team appearances, he was transferred to Shrewsbury Town. Finally getting a chance to prove his worth in League football, he missed only three matches in 18 months at Gay Meadow and alerted Ipswich Town, who were looking to replace Ian Cranson, following his move to Sheffield Wednesday. In three seasons at Portman Road, since signing for the "Town", he has become a fixture in central defence and in 1990-91 he had an outstanding season as the club captain, which was recognised by the fans when he picked up their "Player of the Year" award. Played a sterling role in Ipswich's Second Division Championship campaign in 1991-92, at least until the end of March when an injury sustained in the home game against Barnsley ruled him out for the rest of the season. However, the hard work had already been done, with Ipswich coasting home to promotion.

Clubs	Signing Date	Transfer Fee	APPEARANCES				GOALS			
			Lge	FL Cup	FA Cup	Others	Lge	FL Cup	FA Cup	Others
Hatlepool United	3.82	–	84+7	3+1	4	2	5	1		
Derby County	8.86									
Shrewsbury Town	12.86	£30,000	65	5	3	1	2			
Ipswich Town*	6.88	£300,000	162+1	9	9	10	8			

LINIGHAN John

Born: Hartlepool, 2 November 1973

Height: 5'8³/₄" Weight: 8.9

Position: Central defender.

Career History: Signed professional forms for Sheffield Wednesday during the summer, along with his twin brother Brian, having previously been at Hillsborough as an associated schoolboy (June 1988) and as a trainee (July 1990). Father Brian (Darlington) and brothers Andy and David, currently playing, have all made FL appearances and both he and his brother will obviously hope to join them in the not too distant future.

Clubs	Signing Date	Transfer Fee	APPEARANCES				GOALS			
			Lge	FL Cup	FA Cup	Others	Lge	FL Cup	FA Cup	Others
Sheffield Wednesday*	6.92	–								

LITTLEJOHN Adrian Sylvester

Born: Wolverhampton, 26 September 1970

Height: 5'10" Weight: 10.4

International Honours: E Yth

Position/Skill Factor: Very quick winger, with a natural left foot, who goes past defenders looking to hit the front men.

Career History: On being released by West Bromwich Albion during the 1989 close season, after a period at the Hawthorns as an associated schoolboy (November 1984) and later as a trainee (July 1987), he signed for nearby Walsall. Made his FL debut at Huddersfield Town on 13 January 1990 and proved a useful player to have around, both in midfield or on the subs' bench. A graduate from the FA School of Excellence. During the 1991 close season, after two years at Fellows Park, he was given a free transfer and was surprisingly picked up by Dave Bassett for Sheffield United — a curious reversal of the usual trend for First Division free transfers to sign for lower division clubs. made his debut for the "Blades" in the third match as substitute and his full debut in the fifth game of the season. Was not selected again until December when he was given a short run as Brian Deane's forward partner, but without success and he played no further part in the campaign.

Clubs	Signing Date	Transfer Fee	APPEARANCES				GOALS			
			Lge	FL Cup	FA Cup	Others	Lge	FL Cup	FA Cup	Others
Walsall	5.89	–	26+18	2+1	1	4	1			
Sheffield United*	8.91	–	5+2			1				

LIVINGSTONE Glen

Born: Birmingham, 13 October 1972

Height: 6'2" Weight: 14.1

International Honours: E Sch, E Yth

Position/Skill Factor: Reliable goalkeeper who commands the penalty area well and is extremely agile for a big man.

Career History: Local discovery, he came through the Birmingham schools sides to sign associated schoolboy forms for Aston Villa in February 1988. On leaving school, he joined Villa as a trainee in July 1989, before turning professional early in 1991 and was a regular selection for the England Youth team in 1990-91. Still awaiting his first team debut for Villa which may be further delayed by the arrival of Australian, Mark Bosnich, as reserve to Nigel Spink, he played three games in the Vauxhall Conference in January 1992, whilst on loan to Cheltenham Town and eleven in Villa reserves during 1991-92.

Clubs	Signing Date	Transfer Fee	APPEARANCES				GOALS			
			Lge	FL Cup	FA Cup	Others	Lge	FL Cup	FA Cup	Others
Aston Villa*	1.91	–								

LIVINGSTONE Stephen (Steve)

Born: Middlesbrough,
8 September 1968

Height: 6'1"

Weight: 12.7

Position/Skill Factor: Big striker. Acting as a target man, he is strong in possession and holds the ball up well. Extremely dangerous at the far post with his aerial power.

Career History: The son of Joe, who played for Middlesbrough, Carlisle United and Hartlepool United between 1960-1967, he joined Coventry City on a YTS scheme in August 1985, before turning professional just under a year later. After making his FL debut as a substitute at Luton Town on 18 April 1987, he made his full debut in the last match of the season at home to Southampton. Hardly got a look-in for the next two seasons, but caused a sensation in 1989-90 when standing in for Kevin Drinkell in January 1990. In a team which could not even average a goal a game, he scored four in a Fifth Round League Cup replay against Sunderland, who were thrashed 5-0. He then scored three times in the next two League games, plus another in the League Cup Semi-Final against Nottingham Forest, although it was not enough to avoid defeat. Eight goals in four consecutive games, then he was inexplicably dropped from the team, being accused of lacking pace by the Coventry management. Scored twice in an early season game in 1990-91, but clearly his face did not fit at Highfield Road and he was transferred to Blackburn Rovers midway through the term. Made a good start at Ewood Park with seven goals in his first ten games and his final tally of nine was second only to Frank Stapleton with ten. Surprisingly passed over for selection in 1991-92, both by Don Mackay and subsequently by Kenny Dalglish, even when Rovers suffered simultaneous injuries to their main strikers Mike Newell and Dave Speedie.

Clubs	Signing Date	Transfer Fee	APPEARANCES				GOALS			
			Lge	FL Cup	FA Cup	Others	Lge	FL Cup	FA Cup	Others
Coventry City	7.86	–	17+14	8+2		0+1	5	10		
Blackburn Rovers*	1.91	£450,000	24+4	1			10			

LOMAS Stephen (Steve) Martin

Born: Hanover, Germany, 18 January 1974

Height: 6'0" Weight: 11.7

International Honours: NI Yth

Position/Skill Factor: Midfield player. Good passer with a lovely touch, he is adept at making long runs upfield into the opposing penalty area.

Career History: Turned professional for Manchester City on his 17th birthday, having been at Maine Road, first as an associated schoolboy (May 1988) and then as a trainee (July 1990). Yet to make his FL debut, he is a useful looking prospect who will obviously be hoping for a first team opportunity during 1992-93.

Clubs	Signing Date	Transfer Fee	APPEARANCES				GOALS			
			Lge	FL Cup	FA Cup	Others	Lge	FL Cup	FA Cup	Others
Manchester City*	1.91	–								

LOWE David Anthony

Born: Liverpool, 30 August 1965

Height: 5'11" Weight: 11.0

International Honours: E Yth, E "U21"-2

Position/Skill Factor: Skilful right-winger who has good ability with his back to the goal. Often feints to pass the ball, then drags it past surprised defenders.

Career History: Joined Wigan Athletic as an apprentice in August 1982 and made his FL debut at Reading on 23 October 1982, eight months before he would turn professional and by the end of the season he was holding down a regular place in the side. Was ever present in 1985-86 as the "Latics" narrowly failed to gain promotion to the Second Division and joint top scorer with 16 FL goals the following term, before signing for Ipswich Town during the summer of 1987. Enjoyed an outstanding first season with Ipswich, missing only three games and top scoring with 17 FL goals, as well as being selected as an over-age player for the England Under 21 team. In his second and third season he was absent through injury for long spells, but still managed to lead the scoring lists with 13 FL goals in 1989-90. Unfortunately, he seemed unable to shake off the injury jinx and played little part in the 1990-91 campaign. Apart from a short spell early in the season, when he made seven League appearances, he wasn't a key player in the Second Division Championship season of 1991-92. Indeed, while his team mates were clinching the title, he was out on loan to Port Vale, unable to prevent the Potteries team sinking back into the Third Division.

Clubs	Signing Date	Transfer Fee	APPEARANCES				GOALS			
			Lge	FL Cup	FA Cup	Others	Lge	FL Cup	FA Cup	Others
Wigan Athletic	6.83	–	179+9	8	16+1	18	40		4	9
Ipswich Town*	6.87	£80,000	121+13	10	3	10+2	37	2		6
Port Vale	3.92	Loan	8+1				2			

LUCAS Richard

Born: Chapeltown, 22 September 1970

Height: 5'10" Weight: 11.4

Position/Skill Factor: Left-back who can play in central defence and is a good man-for-man marker and a strong tackler.

Career History: Joined Sheffield United as an associated schoolboy in June 1985 and on leaving school signed on as a trainee in July 1987. Turning professional two years later, he made his FL debut at Aston Villa on 1 December 1990, deputising for the injured David Barnes and made a promising enough start to be given further opportunities before the season was over. Did not progress as expected in 1991-92 and only added a single subs' appearance (in September) to his record.

Clubs	Signing Date	Transfer Fee	APPEARANCES				GOALS			
			Lge	FL Cup	FA Cup	Others	Lge	FL Cup	FA Cup	Others
Sheffield United*	7.89	–	8+2		1					

LUKIC Jovan (John)

Born: Chesterfield, 11 December 1960

Height: 6'4" Weight: 13.7

International Honours: E Yth, E "U21"-7, E"B"

Position/Skill Factor: Like many goalkeepers, he improves with age, being very consistent and making few mistakes. Extremely agile for a big man, he has safe hands and deals well with crosses. Also, has great kicking ability.

Career History: First started out as an associated schoolboy at Leeds United in October 1975 under the watchful eye of David Harvey, before signing as an apprentice in May 1977, on leaving school and later turning pro. Actually played his opening senior match against Valletta in the UEFA Cup and ten days later made his FL debut at Brighton & Hove Albion on 13 October 1979, keeping clean sheets in both games. Went on to play 146 successive League matches for United, a club record, but after asking for a transfer, he was dropped and missed the second half of the 1982-83 season. Transferred to Arsenal, as cover for Pat Jennings in the 1983 close season, he eventually took over the number one jersey at Highbury in 1985 and was soon recognised as one of the top 'keepers in Britain. And in 1986-87 he collected his first club honour when Arsenal beat Liverpool 2-1 to take the League Cup. Later, as an ever present in 1988-89, he won a League Championship medal, when conceding only 36 goals all season, as the "Gunners" stormed to the title. But at the end of the following term, he moved back to Leeds, after Arsenal purchased David Seaman from Queens Park Rangers. With United finishing in fourth place on their return to the First Division, he was a major influence in organising their defence into one of the best in the country. Ever present in Leeds' League Championship triumph of 1991-92, he conceded only 37 goals in 42 games and confirmed his reputation as one of the top 'keepers in the country, being unlucky never to be considered for full international honours.

Clubs	Signing Date	Transfer Fee	APPEARANCES				GOALS			
			Lge	FL Cup	FA Cup	Others	Lge	FL Cup	FA Cup	Others
Leeds United	12.78	–	146	7	9	3				
Arsenal	7.83	£75,000	223	32	21	4				
Leeds United*	6.90	£1,000,000	80	11	7	5				

LYDERSON Pal

Born: Norway, 10 September 1965

Height: 6'0½" Weight: 14.1

International Honours: Norwegian Int

Position/Skill Factor: A right-footed full-back. Very much a passer, he prefers to play the ball out of defence, rather than to simply clear it.

Career History: A Norwegian international, he was signed by Arsenal early in the 1991-92 season from Norwegian club IK Start of Kristiansand. With Lee Dixon and Nigel Winterburn holding firm to the full-back slots at Highbury, first team opportunities were slow in coming. However, he enjoyed a little run at the end of the season, making his FL debut at Norwich City on 8 April 1992 in place of Winterburn and then deputising for Dixon in the next three games.

Clubs	Signing Date	Transfer Fee	APPEARANCES				GOALS			
			Lge	FL Cup	FA Cup	Others	Lge	FL Cup	FA Cup	Others
Arsenal*	9.91	£500,000	5+2							

MABBUTT Gary Vincent

Born: Bristol, 23 August 1961

Height: 5'9" Weight: 10.10

International Honours: E Yth, E "U21"-7, E"B", E-16

Position/Skill Factor: Cool commanding central defender with a tremendous attitude and a captain who leads by example. A great enthusiast, he has a good football brain and despite a lack of inches, is excellent in the air.

Career History: One of a footballing family, his father Ray turned out for Bristol Rovers and Newport County between 1956-71 and elder brother Kevin played first team soccer at Bristol City and Crystal Palace between 1976-85. He followed in his father's footsteps when signing as an associated schoolboy at Bristol Rovers in October 1976, later becoming an apprentice in July 1977, before taking the plunge in the professional ranks. Actually made his FL debut at Burnley, while still an apprentice, on 16 December 1978 and during his four years at Eastville showed his character as well as his great ability, when managing to keep his much discussed diabetes condition under control. Signed for Tottenham Hotspur and made his debut in midfield in the opening game of the 1982-83 season at Luton Town, marking the event with a goal and eventually finished the season as the club's second highest League goal scorer, with ten to his credit. Made his first full England appearance against West Germany on 13 October 1982 at Wembley in the right-back slot, later playing for his country, just like his

club, in a variety of positions. Won a UEFA Cup winners medal in 1984, following Tottenham's penalty victory over Anderlecht and as club captain, led "Spurs" to the FA Cup Final against Coventry City in 1987, when after putting his side 2-1 up in the first half, he then deflected a speculative cross from Lloyd McGrath into his own goal for Coventry's winner. Four years later in 1991, he again led Tottenham out at Wembley for an FA Cup Final, against Nottingham Forest, this time he ended a winners medal, following "Spurs'" 2-1 victory. As consistent as ever in 1991-92, he missed only three games in "Spurs'" disappointing campaign. Also made a surprise comeback to the international scene when Graham Taylor found himself short of available central defenders. But although winning three more caps, he was not included in the squad for the European Championship Finals.

Clubs	Signing Date	Transfer Fee	APPEARANCES				GOALS			
			Lge	FL Cup	FA Cup	Others	Lge	FL Cup	FA Cup	Others
Bristol Rovers	1.79	–	122+9	10	5+1		10	1	1	
Tottenham Hotspur*	8.82	£105,000	326+13	49+2	28+2	29+4	25	2	4	4

McALLISTER Brian

Born: Glasgow, 30 November 1970

Height: 5'11" Weight: 12.5

Position/Skill Factor: Central defender. Good in the air and with a strong left foot, he is capable at hitting wonderful long passes behind the opposing team's full-backs.

Career History: Came to Wimbledon as a trainee in September 1987 and later, on turning pro, had to wait almost a year to make a first team appearance. After playing in a Zenith Data Cup match against Portsmouth, he made his FL debut at home to Arsenal on 13 January 1990 and in order to gain further experience, was loaned out to Plymouth Argyle for a short spell in 1990-91. Increased his experience with nine more FL appearances for the "Dons" in the second half of the 1991-92 season, mostly in central defence.

Clubs	Signing Date	Transfer Fee	APPEARANCES				GOALS			
			Lge	FL Cup	FA Cup	Others	Lge	FL Cup	FA Cup	Others
Wimbledon*	2.89	–	10+3			1				
Plymouth Argyle	12.90	Loan	7+1							

McALLISTER GARY

Born: Motherwell, 25 December 1964

Height: 5'10" Weight: 9.6

International Honours: S "U21"-1, S"B", S-17

Position/Skill Factor: One of the best midfield players in the country. Capable of scoring goals, he has good vision and is able to switch play with long diagonal passes. Very dangerous at free-kicks.

Career History: Started out with Fir Park BC, before signing for his home town side, Motherwell. After playing 52 League games and winning a Scottish First Division Championship medal in 1984-85, he came south to join Leicester City during the 1985 close season. Easily adjusting to the pace of the English First Division, he made his FL debut at home to Ipswich Town on 28 September 1985 and marked his first term at Filbert Street with seven League goals. Unfortunately, his nine goals the following season, when only Alan Smith scored more, couldn't prevent City from making the drop into Division Two. Over the next three seasons, he was Leicester's leading goal scorer twice and his brilliant form was eventually recognised when he was capped by Scotland, making his full international debut against East Germany on 25 April 1990 in Glasgow. It was inevitable that a bigger club would make a move for him and during the 1990 close season, Leeds United, seeking more craft in their midfield on their return to the First Division, forked out a large fee to bring him to Elland Road. Made an immediate impact in midfield and was ever present throughout the 1990-91 campaign as the club finished in fourth position. Played a major role in Leeds' League Championship triumph of 1991-92, vindicating Howard Wilkinson's decision to sign him. Also a vital member of the Scottish national team and an automatic selection for the squad for the 1992 European Championship Finals in Sweden where he performed with distinction, scoring in the 3-0 win over CIS.

Clubs	Signing Date	Transfer Fee	APPEARANCES				GOALS			
			Lge	FL Cup	FA Cup	Others	Lge	FL Cup	FA Cup	Others
Leicester City	8.85	£125,000	199+2	14+1	5	4	46	3	2	
Leeds United*	6.90	£1,000,000	79+1	11	7	4	7	2	1	1

McAREE Rodney Joseph

Born: Dungannon, 19 August 1974

Height: 5'7½" **Weight:** 10.0

International Honours: NI Yth

Position/Skill Factor: An attacking midfielder who likes to be involved, he is very constructive when in possession.

Career History: Signed as a Liverpool professional during the 1991 close season, having been with the club as a trainee since June 1990, he has yet to make a first team appearance.

Clubs	Signing Date	Transfer Fee	APPEARANCES				GOALS			
			Lge	FL Cup	FA Cup	Others	Lge	FL Cup	FA Cup	Others
Liverpool*	8.91	–								

McCARTHY Alan James

Born: Wandsworth, 11 January 1972

Height: 5'11" **Weight:** 12.10

International Honours: E Yth

Position/Skill Factor: Central defender who reads situations well enough to stop attacks before they properly develop. Never appearing hurried, he has a good left foot and uses the ball well.

Career History: Joined Queens Park Rangers as an associated schoolboy in February 1986, before progressing to trainee status in June 1988 and later turning professional. Made his FL debut at Loftus Road against Arsenal on 24 November 1990, during an injury crisis when Rangers lost both first choice central defenders and three days after playing in a Zenith Data Cup match at Southampton. Played three games for Rangers in November and December 1991 as a third central defender in the number seven shirt, from which the "Rs" collected seven points. With seven central defenders competing for two first team slots at Loftus Road, some rationalisation will be necessary if he is to make a breakthrough.

Clubs	Signing Date	Transfer Fee	APPEARANCES				GOALS			
			Lge	FL Cup	FA Cup	Others	Lge	FL Cup	FA Cup	Others
Q.P.R.*	12.89	–	4+1		0+1	2				

McCLAIR Brian John

Born: Bellshill, 8 December 1963

Height: 5'9" **Weight:** 12.2

International Honours: S "U21"-8, S"B", S-25

Position/Skill Factor: Striker. A wonderful team player who always makes himself available. Timing his forward runs to perfection, he gets into the penalty area to score many goals on the blind side of defenders.

Career History: Came down south to sign as an apprentice with Aston Villa in July 1980, but was not offered a professional contract and returned to Scotland to join his local club Motherwell when just 18. On getting into the "Bairns'" first team at the beginning of 1981-82, four goals in 11 games helped the club into the Premier Division and the following season a further 11 strikes, prompted Billy McNeill to sign him for Celtic in July 1983. His first season at Celtic Park saw him find the net 23 times in 35 League matches and in a total of 175 games for the club, he scored 121 goals. Also won a Scottish Cup medal in 1985 and a Premier Division Championship medal in 1985-86 and his fine club performances were finally recognised at international level, when he was picked to play for Scotland against Luxembourg at Hampden Park in November 1986. Desperate to re-establish themselves at the forefront of English soccer and to replace Mark Hughes, Manchester United signed him during the 1987 close season. Made his FL debut at Southampton on 15 August 1987 and became the first United player since George Best in 1967-68 to notch up more than 20 FL goals in a season, with a remarkable haul of 24 League goals, including a hat-trick in a 4-1 victory over Derby County. The following season, his goal ratio dropped as he linked up with the returning Mark Hughes, but eventually the partnership began to bear fruit in terms of club

honours, culminating in an FA Cup Final victory over Crystal Palace in 1990. A disappointed member of the side that lost 1-0 in the 1991 League Cup Final to Sheffield Wednesday, his sorrow was short lived when three weeks later he won a European Cup Winners Cup medal, following United's 2-1 defeat of Barcelona. Has shown remarkable consistency during four seasons at Old Trafford, only missing five League matches and in manager Alex Ferguson's frequent tactical manoeuvres, often played in a wide midfield role, leaving Hughes as a lone

striker. Ever present in 1991-92, he enjoyed his best season since his initial one at Old Trafford, top scoring with 18 FL goals, plus six cup goals, including the winner in the League Cup Final against Nottingham Forest which brought the trophy to Old Trafford for the first time. For much of the season he appeared certain to add a League Championship medal to his collection of trophies, but a goal drought from his striking partner, Hughes (amongst other things), saw United's challenge collapse in the closing week. A regular member of the Scottish national team and included in the squad for the 1992 European Championship Finals in Sweden and after failing to score for Scotland after 23 games, he broke his "duck" with a goal in the 3-0 demolition of CIS. Unfortunately, despite that great win, Scotland went out of the tournament after earlier losing to Holland and Germany.

Clubs	Signing Date	Transfer Fee	APPEARANCES				GOALS			
			Lge	FL Cup	FA Cup	Others	Lge	FL Cup	FA Cup	Others
Manchester United*	7.87	£850,000	190+3	28	24	14	70	14	11	6

McDONALD Alan

Born: Belfast, 12 October 1963

Height: 6'2" Weight: 12.7

International Honours: NI Sch, NI Yth, NI-33

Position/Skill Factor: A rugged and uncompromising, strong tackling central defender, who is difficult to get the better of. Very good in the air, he is extremely dangerous in the opposing box from dead ball situations.

Career History: An associated schoolboy (March 1980) and an apprentice (July 1980), before turning professional with Queens Park Rangers, he actually made his FL debut, whilst on loan to Charlton Athletic at the Valley against Crystal Palace on 4 April 1983. Played his first League game for Rangers the following season in a 4-0 win at Wolverhampton Wanderers and scored his first goal for the club two games later, in a resounding League Cup win over Crewe Alexandra. Made way for Steve Wicks during the latter half of the campaign, but over the next few seasons, he established himself as one of the best central defenders in the First Division. In October 1985, he won the first of many international caps when he played for Northern Ireland in a 1-0 win over Romania in Bucharest and a month later was one of the stars of a brave performance against England at Wembley, a 0-0 draw sealing Northern Ireland's place in the 1986 World Cup Finals. That season, he was a key player as Queens Park Rangers reached the League Cup Final against Oxford United, but a winners medal eluded him as Rangers went down 3-0. Very consistent over several years, he struggled with injuries during 1990-91 and missed a large part of the club's programme as they hovered at the bottom of the First Division, before climbing to safety during the last two months of the season. With a surfeit of central defenders at Loftus Road, he played second fiddle to Danny Maddix and Darren Peacock in the first three months of 1991-92. However, after displacing Maddix in November, he held his place till the end of the season and assisted the "Rs" to climb from 21st place to mid-table, following an impressive run of 19 FL games with only one defeat.

Clubs	Signing Date	Transfer Fee	APPEARANCES				GOALS			
			Lge	FL Cup	FA Cup	Others	Lge	FL Cup	FA Cup	Others
Q.P.R.*	9.81	–	242+5	28	22	5	8	2	1	
Charlton Athletic	3.83	Loan	9							

MacDONALD Callum

Born: Stirling, 21 September 1973

Height: 5'8" Weight: 11.1

Position/Skill Factor: Striker with skill on the ball, who twists and turns and is capable of beating defenders.

Career History: Came down south to sign for Southampton as a trainee in October 1990, before progressing to the club's professional ranks during the 1991 close season. Has yet to make a first team appearance.

Clubs	Signing Date	Transfer Fee	APPEARANCES				GOALS			
			Lge	FL Cup	FA Cup	Others	Lge	FL Cup	FA Cup	Others
Southampton*	7.91	–								

McDONALD David Hugh

Born: Dublin, 2 January 1971

Height: 5'10" Weight: 11.0

Position/Skill Factor: Strong tackling right-back who uses the ball well from deep positions with long passes into the front players.

Career History: After leaving school, he joined Tottenham Hotspur as a trainee in May 1987, before turning professional in the 1988 close season. Yet to appear for "Spurs", he was loaned out to Fourth Division Gillingham for a two month spell in 1990-91 and made his FL debut wearing the number two shirt at York City on 29 September 1990. After four seasons as a professional at White Hart Lane without a first team game, 1992-93 will probably be his last chance of a breakthrough.

Clubs	Signing Date	Transfer Fee	APPEARANCES				GOALS			
			Lge	FL Cup	FA Cup	Others	Lge	FL Cup	FA Cup	Others
Tottenham Hotspur*	7.88	–								
Gillingham	9.90	Loan	10			2				

McDONALD Neil Raymond

Born: Wallsend,
2 November 1965

Height: 5'11"

Weight: 11.4

International Honours:
E Sch, E Yth, E "U21"-5

Position/Skill Factor: Can play equally well at right-back or in midfield. A great striker of the ball with his right foot, he can hit long crossfield passes with ease. Always looks threatening when he goes forward and is a good crosser of the ball.

Career History: On leaving school and having already won English schoolboy honours, he signed as an apprentice for Newcastle United in July 1982 and made his FL debut at St James' Park against Barnsley on 25 September 1982, while still too young to turn professional. Won a permanent place by the end of the season, teaming up in midfield with ex-England star, Terry McDermott, in a side that also included Kevin Keegan and Chris Waddle. Injury restricted his contribution to just 12 matches the following season as United won promotion to the First Division, but he made his mark in the top flight by continuing to churn out consistent performances. Transferred to Everton in the 1988 close season, he was introduced at Goodison Park in the opening match of 1988-89, a 4-0 win over Newcastle, playing in what was a new look, expensive side. Figured most of the season in the right-back position, although missing three months earlier through injury and played in the 3-2 FA Cup Final defeat by near neighbours, Liverpool. Proved a valuable asset to Everton, being able to play in a variety of positions, as the team struggled to find the right balance. Out of favour at the start of 1991-92, he was transferred to newly promoted Oldham Athletic for a large fee. Surprisingly, he was unable to claim a regular place either at right-back, where there was a vacancy to be filled, or in midfield and so far has only been utilised as a cover player.

Clubs	Signing Date	Transfer Fee	APPEARANCES				GOALS			
			Lge	FL Cup	FA Cup	Others	Lge	FL Cup	FA Cup	Others
Newcastle United	2.83	–	163+17	12	10+1	3	24	3	1	
Everton	8.88	£525,000	76+14	7	17	9+1	4	3		
Oldham Athletic*	10.91	£500,000	14+3	2			1			

McENROE David John

Born: Dublin, 19 August 1972

Height: 5'8" Weight: 10.10

Position/Skill Factor: Hard working midfield player with the ability to pass the ball about.

Career History: A two year professional with Queens Park Rangers, he first came to Loftus Road as a trainee in June 1989 and has yet to be given a chance of first team football.

Clubs	Signing Date	Transfer Fee	APPEARANCES				GOALS			
			Lge	FL Cup	FA Cup	Others	Lge	FL Cup	FA Cup	Others
Q.P.R.*	8.90	–								

McGARRY Ian John

Born: Darwen, 13 February 1974

Height: 5'7" Weight: 10.0

Position: Right-winger.

Career History: Turned professional for Blackburn Rovers during the 1992 close season, having been at Ewood Park as an associated schoolboy (April 1988) and as a trainee (July 1990). No first team experience as yet.

Clubs	Signing Date	Transfer Fee	APPEARANCES				GOALS			
			Lge	FL Cup	FA Cup	Others	Lge	FL Cup	FA Cup	Others
Blackburn Rovers*	6.92	–								

McGEE Paul

Born: Dublin, 17 May 1968

Height: 5'6" Weight: 9.10

International Honours: IR "U21"-3

Position/Skill Factor: A live wire winger. Good ability with the ball, with twists and turns, he is well capable of beating defenders. Crosses the ball well with both feet.

Career History: Joined Colchester United from the League of Ireland side, Bohemians, early in 1989 and made his FL debut at Layer Road in a 2-2 draw against Burnley on 10 February 1989. After just three games for United, who appeared doomed to relegation to the Vauxhall Conference, but later saved themselves, he was

sold to Wimbledon for a massive profit of £85,000. He had to wait until the final game of the season before making his bow for the "Dons", against Championship chasing Arsenal at Highbury and his goal in a 2-2 draw seemed at the time to strike a mortal blow to the "Gunners'" title hopes. Struggled to make an impact after the 1989 summer break, playing just 11 games without finding the net, but regained his place in 1990-91, following a two goal burst away to Crystal Palace in October. In common with the "Dons'" other wingers (Anthrobus, Bennett and Fairweather), he had a hard time in 1991-92, but at least, unlike the others, he broke back into the first team on five occasions for a total of 15 FL games.

Clubs	Signing Date	Transfer Fee	APPEARANCES				GOALS			
			Lge	FL Cup	FA Cup	Others	Lge	FL Cup	FA Cup	Others
Colchester United	2.89	£35,000	3			1				
Wimbledon*	3.89	£120,000	53+4	1+1	5	2	9	1		

McGOLDRICK Edward (Eddie) John Paul

Born: Islington, 30 April 1965

Height: 5'10" Weight: 12.0

International Honours: IR-3

Position/Skill Factor: Originally a winger, he is more than useful as an attacking midfielder, where his pace takes him past defenders. Good early crosser of the ball.

Career History: While still at school, he signed associated schoolboy forms with Peterborough United in December 1979, but was allowed to drift away from London Road and joined non-League Kettering Town. Moved on to Gola League rivals, Nuneaton Borough and it was from there that he came into the League with Northampton Town during the 1986 close season, signed by Graham Carr, his former manager at Nuneaton. Made his FL debut at Scunthorpe United on 23 August 1986 and at the end of his first season had won a Fourth Division Championship medal, with his skilful play being a major contributory factor in the club's success. After two season's at the County Ground, he signed for Second Division Crystal Palace early in 1989 and in his first season at the club he was a member of the team that was promoted to the top flight, via the Play-Offs. Despite being a regular during the early part of 1989-90, he found himself among the long term injured and did not regain his place in time for the FA Cup Final against Manchester United. Eventually won back a place in the team during 1990-91, this time in the number 11 shirt when he made way for John Salako on the right as Palace achieved their highest ever League position, third in the First Division. Played in 36 FL games in 1991-92, all in the number 11 shirt, although his role is primarily defensive these days. Ironically, he scored his first FL goal for Palace after nearly three years "drought". Won his first cap for the Irish Republic against Switzerland in March 1992 and played twice more for the Irish team before the summer break.

Clubs	Signing Date	Transfer Fee	APPEARANCES				GOALS			
			Lge	FL Cup	FA Cup	Others	Lge	FL Cup	FA Cup	Others
Northampton Town	8.86	£10,000	97+10	9	6+1	7	9		1	1
Crystal Palace*	1.89	£200,000	97+8	13+1	4	13+1	3			3

McGRATH Lloyd Anthony

Born: Birmingham, 24 February 1965

Height: 5'9"

Weight: 10.6

International Honours: E Yth, E"U21"-1

Position/Skill Factor: As a brave, tough tackling, 90 minute midfield player, he is known for his man-to-man marking ability. Always shows great enthusiasm and is useful in the air.

Career History: Came up through the Coventry City ranks as an associated schoolboy (January 1980), before signing as an apprentice in June 1981. However, after turning professional, he had to wait more than 18 months to make his first appearance in a "Sky Blue" shirt. Unfortunately, his FL debut at Southampton on 28 April 1984, turned out to be a far from happy occasion as City were thrashed 8-2, their biggest defeat since the war. However, his industry earned him a regular place the following term, even after he had endured another disaster while wearing the number five shirt, a 6-2 defeat at Chelsea. One of the heroes of the Coventry 3-2 FA Cup Final win over Tottenham Hotspur in 1987, he performed an effective marking job on Glenn Hoddle and provided the cross which was deflected by Gary Mabbutt into his own net for the winning goal. Although serious injuries forced him to miss much of the League programme during the last three seasons, he continued to battle away. After nearly ten years at Highfield Road, he finally won a regular place in 1991-92 and was absent for only two games — a remarkable achievement for a utility player who operated in a variety of different positions during the season, playing in both full-back and all four midfield slots.

Clubs	Signing Date	Transfer Fee	APPEARANCES				GOALS			
			Lge	FL Cup	FA Cup	Others	Lge	FL Cup	FA Cup	Others
Coventry City*	12.82	–	170+8	19	15	6	4	1		

McGRATH Paul

Born: Ealing, 4 December 1959

Height: 6'0" Weight: 13.2

International Honours: IR-55

Position/Skill Factor: Good all-round player, now settled in central defence after playing in many positions. Strong, good in the air, he has a knack of reading dangerous situations almost before they occur.

Career History: Although born in England, he was discovered by Manchester United while playing for St Patricks Athletic in the League of Ireland. Came into the side for his FL debut at Old Trafford against Tottenham Hotspur on 13 November 1982, when deputising for Kevin Moran and eventually gained a regular place. Won an FA Cup winners medal in 1985, following United's 1-0 victory over Everton and earlier that season he had made his international debut for the Republic of Ireland in Dublin, coming on as a substitute against Italy on 5 February 1985. In 1985-86, he was runner-up to Gary Lineker as the PFA "Player of the Year", testament to his outstanding performances and to the fact that he only missed two League matches that season. Spent a long spell out injured in 1987-88, but recovered well and in the summer months, starred in the Irish midfield during the European Championships. Only played 18 League games in 1988-89, as injuries again took their toll and during the close season he was allowed to leave for Aston Villa. Proved an inspired signing as the club rocketed from 17th place the previous term, to First Division runners-up and while they slipped somewhat in 1990-91, he continued to shine as the defensive lynch pin the Villa team depends on. One of the Irish Republic's all-time great players, his performances both in midfield and central defence are perhaps the single most important factor in the establishment of Jack Charlton's team as one of the strongest in Europe and one which qualified for the 1990 World Cup Finals in Italy, the first time ever for the Republic. Another excellent season

Paul McGrath

personally during 1991-92, although a disappointing one for his team. Only missed one FL game and his central defensive partnership with Shaun Teale made the Villa defence one of the tightest in the First Division.

Clubs	Signing Date	Transfer Fee	APPEARANCES				GOALS			
			Lge	FL Cup	FA Cup	Others	Lge	FL Cup	FA Cup	Others
Manchester United	4.82	£30,000	159+4	13	15+2	9	12	2	2	
Aston Villa*	7.89	£400,000	111	9	12	7	2			

McGREGOR Paul Anthony

Born: Liverpool, 17 December 1974

Height: 5'11" Weight: 10.10

Position: Forward.

Career History: A Liverpudlian, he signed associated schoolboy forms with Nottingham Forest in March 1989 and on leaving school joined the club as a trainee in August 1991. Turned professional on his 17th birthday and with keen competition for first team places at the City Ground, he may have to take his place in the queue.

Clubs	Signing Date	Transfer Fee	APPEARANCES				GOALS			
			Lge	FL Cup	FA Cup	Others	Lge	FL Cup	FA Cup	Others
Nottingham Forest*	12.91	–								

McKEE Colin

Born: Glasgow, 22 August 1973

Height: 5'10" Weight: 10.11

International Honours: S Sch

Skill Factor: Striker. Very good on the ball, he is quick, skilful and a dangerous finisher.

Career History: Signed professional forms for Manchester United in the 1991 close season, having been at Old Trafford as a trainee since June 1989. No appearances in 1991-92, but played a starring role in United's successful youth squad which defeated Crystal Palace 6-3 on aggregate in the FA Youth Cup Final.

Clubs	Signing Date	Transfer Fee	APPEARANCES				GOALS			
			Lge	FL Cup	FA Cup	Others	Lge	FL Cup	FA Cup	Others
Manchester United*	6.91	–								

McKILLIGAN Neil

Born: Falkirk, 2 January 1974

Height: 5'9" Weight: 10.8

Skill Factor: Midfielder who can also play at right-back.

Career History: Signed as a professional for Southampton during the summer of 1992, having first come to the club as a trainee in September 1990. No first team experience.

Clubs	Signing Date	Transfer Fee	APPEARANCES				GOALS			
			Lge	FL Cup	FA Cup	Others	Lge	FL Cup	FA Cup	Others
Southampton*	6.92	–								

McKINNON Raymond (Ray)

Born: Dundee, 5 August 1970

Height: 5'8" Weight: 9.11

International Honours: S Sch, S "U21"-5

Position: Midfield player.

Career History: A 22-year-old Scot, who made rapid strides as a midfield player with Dundee Untied in 1991-92, having been with the club as a professional since August 1987. After winning five Scottish Under 21 caps, Nottingham Forest recognised his talent and moved quickly to sign him during the 1992 close season. Made 46 full and seven substitute appearances and scored six goals in Scottish League matches during his time at Dens Park.

Clubs	Signing Date	Transfer Fee	APPEARANCES				GOALS			
			Lge	FL Cup	FA Cup	Others	Lge	FL Cup	FA Cup	Others
Nottingham Forest*	6.92	£750,000								

McMAHON Gerard

Born: Belfast, 29 December, 1973

Height: 5'11½" Weight: 11.0

International Honours: NI Yth

Position: Forward.

Career History: After showing exciting form for Glenavon in the Irish League last season, Tottenham Hotspur moved quickly to sign him during the summer of 1992 and expect great things from this young man in the near future.

Clubs	Signing Date	Transfer Fee	APPEARANCES				GOALS			
			Lge	FL Cup	FA Cup	Others	Lge	FL Cup	FA Cup	Others
Tottenham Hotspur*	6.92	£30,000								

McMAHON Stephen (Steve)

Born: Liverpool, 20 August 1961

Height: 5'9" Weight: 11.8

International Honours: E "U21"-6, FL Rep, E"B", E-17

Position/Skill Factor: All-purpose midfielder with a

wealth of experience. A strong tackler, who is very competitive, he also has a powerful shot. Shows great vision in picking out telling passes.

Career History: Began his soccer career on the Everton side of Stanley Park when becoming an apprentice with the "Toffees" in December 1977 and after turning to the professional ranks, he had to wait a further year before appearing in the first team. Made his FL debut at Sunderland on 16 August 1980 and played for most of the season until an injury slowed him down. A great competitor, it was a surprise when he was allowed to move to Aston Villa and in two full seasons at Villa Park, he showed his worth, albeit that the club was not very successful. Then, just two weeks into the 1985-86 season, with Villa having conceded eight goals in three games and Liverpool looking to add extra bite to their midfield, he transferred his allegiances to Anfield. At the end of his first season with the "Reds", the club had done the "double", only the fifth side to do so and although he wasn't selected for the FA Cup Final side, he picked up a League Championship medal as his share of the spoils. From then on it was success all the way; two more League Championship medals in 1987-88 and 1989-90 and an FA Cup winners medal in 1989, following the 3-2 victory over local rivals, Everton. Recognition at full international level had to come and it was no surprise when he picked up his first England cap in Tel Aviv in a 0-0 draw against Israel on 17 February 1988. Suffered several injury problems in 1990-91 and following the Fifth Round FA Cup tie at Anfield against Everton, he came off the field, not to play again for the rest of the season. The loss of both McMahon and Whelan dealt a fatal blow to Liverpool's title hopes that season. Played the best football of his career in his first three seasons at Anfield. Suffered a serious knee injury in the second game of the 1988-89 and

although he recovered and returned to the team he was not quite as effective as before, although still a very committed player. Started his international career at the relatively late age of 26 and probably just after he had passed his peak and as with Peter Reid, his path to the national team was blocked by Bryan Robson. After the appointment of Graham Souness as Liverpool manager, it was soon clear that his days at Anfield were numbered. Nevertheless, the timing of his departure was a surprise, with Liverpool in the middle of an injury crisis. However, the fee was one Liverpool could hardly refuse for a 30-year-old player. Ironically, his last match for Liverpool was against the club about to sign him — Manchester City. It was assumed that McMahon was signed to replace his new manager Peter Reid in the team, but in fact the two played together for a while, with disappointing results. To his credit, McMahon recovered from his ineffective start and was back to his best, scheming the downfall of Champions-to-be, Leeds United, in an amazing 4-0 victory and assisting City to finish 1991-92 in fine style and a final placing of fifth.

Clubs	Signing Date	Transfer Fee	APPEARANCES				GOALS			
			Lge	FL Cup	FA Cup	Others	Lge	FL Cup	FA Cup	Others
Everton	8.79	–	99+1	11	9		11	3		
Aston Villa	5.83	£175,000	74+1	9	3	4	7			
Liverpool	9.85	£375,000	202+2	27	30	16	28	13	7	1
Manchester City*	12.91	£900,000	18		1					

McMANAMAN Steven (Steve)

Born: Bootle, 11 February 1972

Height: 5'11" Weight: 10.2

International Honours: E Yth, E "U21"-2

Position/Skill Factor: An old-fashioned winger who has the ability to deceive and "ghost" past defenders. A good dribbler with close control and great balance, he can stop quickly and then in the same breath, accelerate.

Career History: A local discovery who first came to Liverpool as an associated schoolboy in February 1987, he graduated through the club as a trainee (May 1988) to professional status. Introduced as a substitute in front of the Anfield faithful on three occasions in 1990-91, making his FL debut against Sheffield United on 15 December 1990, he impressed many sound judges with his play. Such was his talent that he was chosen to play for the England Under 21 team against Wales on 5 December, even before his FL debut. He was expected to make only occasional appearances in 1991-92, but because of the injury crisis at Anfield, he was retained for most of the season. After appearing in a number of positions, including central striker where, despite his confident running, he was fairly ineffectual, he found himself on the right-wing and was devastating in becoming a key player throughout Liverpool's tortuous, but ultimately successful FA Cup run. Prior to the Quarter-Final, he scored in every round, twice critically, but when he was injured by a clumsy tackle in the Semi-Final against Portsmouth, his season appeared over until fate took a hand. He only regained fitness during Cup Final week and was not even considered to be match fit, but when John Barnes was ruled out of the Final, Graeme Souness decided to replace him with

FL debut when coming on as a sub at Tottenham Hotspur on 25 October 1988 and in his first two full games during 1988-89, he scored a goal apiece. That form should have accelerated his progress, but he has since remained in the shadows and was still waiting for a breakthrough in 1991-92, making only a handful of appearances in the closing weeks of the campaign.

Clubs	Signing Date	Transfer Fee	APPEARANCES				GOALS			
			Lge	FL Cup	FA Cup	Others	Lge	FL Cup	FA Cup	Others
Southampton*	4.88	–	8+9	0+2	0+3	1	2			

MADDIX Daniel (Danny) Shawn

Born: Ashford, Kent, 11 October 1967

Height: 5'11"

Weight: 11.0

Position/Skill Factor: Strong tackling central defender who is good in the air and one of the best man-for-man markers around. He sticks like glue to his opponents.

Career History: On failing to make an impression at senior level, having been an associated schoolboy (July 1982) and an apprentice (April 1984), before signing professional, he was freed by Tottenham Hotspur in the 1987 close season. This followed a period on loan at Southend United, where he had made his FL debut at Roots Hall against Scunthorpe United on 4 November 1986. Immediately snapped up by west London rivals, Queens Park Rangers, he was introduced to the Rangers' first team as a sub in a 3-1 defeat at Sheffield Wednesday in November 1987, but had to wait until the end of the season for further games. Originally a midfielder, he was converted to central defender by Rangers in 1988-89 with great success and by 1990-91, as an integral part of the Rangers' side, had fitted comfortably into a three man central defence alongside Alan McDonald and Paul Parker. In December 1990, Rangers' manager Don Howe signed two central defenders, Darren Peacock and Andy Tillson, following an injury crisis at Loftus Road. Thereafter, competition for the central defensive slots was intense, especially when new manager Gerry Francis reverted to a conventional flat "back-four". He started 1991-92 as first choice with Peacock, but after losing his place to McDonald in November 1991, played little part in the remainder of the campaign.

Clubs	Signing Date	Transfer Fee	APPEARANCES				GOALS			
			Lge	FL Cup	FA Cup	Others	Lge	FL Cup	FA Cup	Others
Tottenham Hotspur	7.85	–								
Southend United	10.86	Loan	2							
Q.P.R.*	7.87	–	113+12	14	13	2+3	6	2	1	

McManaman. It was a gamble, but proved to be an inspired decision. After an ineffective 40 minutes on the left wing, he was switched to the right side and immediately caused havoc in Sunderland's defence. Early in the second-half, a mazy dribble took him past three defenders, before he released the ball inside to Michael Thomas, who hit a rising volley into the roof of the net. It was the turning point of the match as Liverpool cruised to a 2-0 victory and it was also justice that McManaman, having played a major role in the "Reds'" progress to Wembley, should play such a leading part in its dénouement.

Clubs	Signing Date	Transfer Fee	APPEARANCES				GOALS			
			Lge	FL Cup	FA Cup	Others	Lge	FL Cup	FA Cup	Others
Liverpool*	2.90	–	26+6	5	8+1	8	5	3	3	

MADDISON Neil Stanley

Born: Darlington, 2 October 1969

Height: 5'9" Weight: 11.8

Position/Skill Factor: Midfield player who can also play up front. Makes good runs off the ball and gets into the penalty box to score goals. Keeps his passing simple, but effective.

Career History: Another north-easterner on Southampton's books, he signed as a 14-year-old associated schoolboy in October 1983, before becoming a trainee, on leaving school, in July 1986. Turned professional and made his

MAHORN Paul Gladstone

Born: Leyton, 13 August 1973

Height: 5'8" Weight: 11.6

Position/Skill Factor: Young central defender who is very useful in the air and has great speed off the mark.

Career History: Signed professional forms for Tottenham Hotspur early in 1992, having been a trainee since May 1990, he shows great promise, but has yet to make a first team appearance.

Clubs	Signing Date	Transfer Fee	APPEARANCES				GOALS			
			Lge	FL Cup	FA Cup	Others	Lge	FL Cup	FA Cup	Others
Tottenham Hotspur*	1.92	–								

MAIORANA Giuliano

Born: Cambridge, 18 April 1969

Height: 5'9" Weight: 11.8

Position/Skill Factor: Very quick left-winger who looks to get down the line and get his crosses over. Possesses a super left foot.

Career History: A "fairy tale" story with, as yet, no happy ending. Of Italian parentage he was playing for obscure Histon of the Jewson Eastern Counties League when "spotted" by Manchester United scouts and following a successful trial he was offered a four year contract. Made his FL debut, coming on as a sub against Millwall, at Old Trafford on 14 January 1989, within two months of turning professional, but has yet to be given a run in the side. In the last two seasons he has been totally eclipsed by the emergence of Lee Sharpe and Ryan Giggs and although offered a fresh contract by United in the 1992 close season, he will have difficulty in advancing his career at Old Trafford.

Clubs	Signing Date	Transfer Fee	APPEARANCES				GOALS			
			Lge	FL Cup	FA Cup	Others	Lge	FL Cup	FA Cup	Others
Manchester United*	11.88	£30,000	2+5	0+1						

MAKEL Lee

Born: Sunderland, 11 January 1973

Height: 5'10" Weight: 9.10

Position: Midfield player.

Career History: Joined Newcastle United as a trainee in June 1989, having been at St James' Park since February 1987 as an associated schoolboy and played in a Zenith Cup tie in November 1990, before turning professional in February 1991. Made his FL debut as a substitute at West Bromwich Albion on 4 May 1991 and his full debut three days later — one of a deluge of promising youngsters

blooded by Ossie Ardiles in 1990-91. Played only a handful of games in 1991-92, mostly in December, for the struggling Tynesiders and he was not selected again, following the arrival of new manager, Kevin Keegan. Clearly unimpressed, Keegan sold him to Blackburn Rovers during the summer of 1992 and stands to be proved wrong.

Clubs	Signing Date	Transfer Fee	APPEARANCES				GOALS			
			Lge	FL Cup	FA Cup	Others	Lge	FL Cup	FA Cup	Others
Newcastle United	2.91	–	6+6	1		0+1	1			
Blackburn Rovers*	6.92	£160,000								

MAKIN Christopher (Chris)

Born: Manchester, 8 May 1973

Height: 5'11" Weight: 11.0

International Honours: E Yth

Position/Skill Factor: Midfield player with plenty of stamina who pressures opponents well and has two great feet.

Career History: Spotted by Oldham Athletic playing in Manchester schools' football, he came to Boundary Park as an associated schoolboy in June 1987. Signed for the club as a trainee in August 1989 and progressed to the professional ranks during the 1991 close season. No first team appearances in 1991-92, but has an excellent chance of making a very good player according to local knowledge.

Clubs	Signing Date	Transfer Fee	APPEARANCES				GOALS			
			Lge	FL Cup	FA Cup	Others	Lge	FL Cup	FA Cup	Others
Oldham Athletic*	7.91	–								

MARGETSON Martyn Walter

Born: Neath,
8 September 1971

Height: 6'0"

Weight: 13.10

International Honours:
W Sch, W Yth,
W "U21"-1

Position: Goalkeeper.

Career History: After joining Manchester City as an associated schoolboy in February 1987, he progressed to trainee status on leaving school in July 1988, before turning professional in the 1990 close season. Made his FL debut in the penultimate game of the 1990-91 season away to Manchester United on 4 May 1991. Standing in for the injured Tony Coton, he was not disgraced when United's

Ryan Giggs scored the only goal of the game and a week later turned out against Sunderland. Was regarded as City's number two 'keeper, despite the presence of Andy Dibble, and deputised for Coton in the opening game of 1991-92 and then on three subsequent occasions. If he makes the grade with City, he is likely to be the long term successor to Neville Southall in the Welsh national team.

Clubs	Signing Date	Transfer Fee	APPEARANCES				GOALS			
			Lge	FL Cup	FA Cup	Others	Lge	FL Cup	FA Cup	Others
Manchester City*	7.90	–	5	1		1				

MARLOWE Andrew Daniel

Born: Birmingham, 25 September 1973

Height: 5'7" Weight: 11.2

International Honours: E Yth

Position/Skill Factor: Very quick and useful when going forward which makes it possible for him to play either wide on the right-wing, or at right-back.

Career History: First joining Tottenham Hotspur as an associated schoolboy in November 1987, on leaving school, he came to the club as a trainee in August 1990, turning professional early in 1992 and has yet to make a first team appearance.

Clubs	Signing Date	Transfer Fee	APPEARANCES				GOALS			
			Lge	FL Cup	FA Cup	Others	Lge	FL Cup	FA Cup	Others
Tottenham Hotspur*	2.92	–								

MARRIOTT Andrew

Born: Sutton-in-Ashfield, 11 October 1970

Height: 6'0"

Weight: 12.7

International Honours: E Sch, E Yth, E "U21"-1

Position/Skill Factor: A young agile goalkeeper who is not afraid to come for crosses and is a very good shot stopper.

Career History: Went to Arsenal as a 15-year-old associated schoolboy in October 1985 and progressed to a trainee in July 1987, before signing professional forms at Highbury. However, Arsenal also had another talented young 'keeper in Alan Miller and allowed Marriott to leave Highbury and link up with Nottingham Forest. In order to gain experience he was loaned out for most of

1989-90. Made his FL debut for West Bromwich Albion in a 3-1 win at Leicester City on 9 September 1989 and later in the season had loan spells with Blackburn Rovers and Fourth Division Colchester United. Played in the last ten games of the season for the Essex club, who were eventually demoted to the Vauxhall Conference. Spent the first three months of 1991-92 on loan to eventual Fourth Division Champions, Burnley. The "Clarets" wanted to sign him permanently, but Brian Clough knew he still had a future with Forest. His opportunity came in March just after Steve Sutton had moved to Derby County, leaving Marriott as undisputed number two 'keeper. He made his FL debut for Forest at home to Manchester United on 18 March 1992 when Crossley was dropped as a disciplinary measure and held his place up to the League Cup Final when Forest lost 1-0 to Manchester United, before returning to the reserves for the closing weeks of the campaign. Made his debut for the England Under 21 squad in the end of season tournament in Toulon, France.

Clubs	Signing Date	Transfer Fee	APPEARANCES				GOALS			
			Lge	FL Cup	FA Cup	Others	Lge	FL Cup	FA Cup	Others
Arsenal	10.88	–								
Nottingham Forest*	6.89	£50,000	6	1		1				
W.B.A.	9.89	Loan	3							
Blackburn Rovers	12.89	Loan	2							
Colchester United	3.90	Loan	10							
Burnley	8.91	Loan	15			2				

MARSH Michael (Mike) Andrew

Born: Liverpool, 21 July 1969

Height: 5'8"

Weight: 11.0

Position/Skill Factor: Midfield player who strikes the ball well. His use of the ball is good and he is always looking for the chance of a shot at goal.

Career History: Signed from Kirkby Town of the North West Counties League during the 1987 close season, he made his FL debut when coming on for Jan Molby at Anfield against Charlton Athletic on 1 March 1989. He made a breakthrough in 1991-92, largely as a result of Liverpool's chronic injury crisis and remained a useful member of the first team squad throughout the season, playing mostly on the right side of midfield, although occasionally at full-back. He was on the bench, but not required for the 1992 FA Cup Final against Sunderland. Scored a vital goal against Auxerre in the UEFA Cup Second Round second-leg at Anfield which helped the "Reds" to overturn a 2-0 first leg deficit. It remains to be seen however, whether he can win a regular place, if and when Liverpool have a fully fit squad of players.

Clubs	Signing Date	Transfer Fee	APPEARANCES				GOALS			
			Lge	FL Cup	FA Cup	Others	Lge	FL Cup	FA Cup	Others
Liverpool*	8.87	–	20+19	4+1	4+2	7+1				1

MARSHALL Ian Paul

Born: Liverpool, 20 March 1966

Height: 6'1" Weight: 12.12

Position/Skill Factor: Plays equally well either as a central defender or as a striker. As an attacker, he is a chaser of lost causes and his strength and deceptive pace, gives defenders a tough time. He is also a good striker of the ball.

Career History: Began with Everton as an associated schoolboy (April 1980), before becoming an apprentice on leaving school in July 1982 and later progressing to the professional ranks. made his FL debut when deputising for the injured Derek Mountfield against West Bromwich Albion at Goodison Park on 20 August 1985, but first team chances were few with Kevin Ratcliffe and Dave Watson holding down the central defensive positions for Everton and he was allowed to sign permanently for Oldham Athletic in March 1987, after just two weeks of a loan period, as a replacement for Andy Linighan. Very consistent at the heart of the Oldham defence in 1988-89, but ever since he'd arrived at Boundary Park he had tried to convince manager Joe Royle that there was a frustrated centre-forward in him trying to get out and when he lost his place to Earl Barrett, Royle did indeed try him up front during Oldham's great twin cup runs of 1989-90 with some success. But after scoring in the first FA Cup Semi-Final against Manchester United in 1990, he was again injured and missed selection for the League Cup final side to play Nottingham Forest. In the opening match of the 1990-91 season away to Wolves he scored a superb hat-trick in a 3-2 victory, including two goals in the last five minutes which turned the game upside down. Afterwards Royle commented ruefully "There'll be no living with him after this"!. Indeed, he proved he could be a natural forward and despite being plagued by injuries, finished the season as top scorer with 17 FL goals from only 26 games as Oldham stormed to the Second Division Championship. He proved he could do it at First Division level as well, by scoring six goals in his first eight games of 1991-92. Thereafter, however, the goals dried up and following a FA Cup disaster away to Leyton Orient when the "Latics" went down 4-2 after extra-time, Royle switched him back to central defence, which became permanent after Earl Barrett's departure to Aston Villa. Not to be denied his moments of glory, however, he came up to score an 86th minute winner with a 30 yard "daisy cutter" in a 4-3 thriller with Notts County – a result which virtually sealed Oldham's First Division survival.

Clubs	Signing Date	Transfer Fee	APPEARANCES				GOALS			
			Lge	FL Cup	FA Cup	Others	Lge	FL Cup	FA Cup	Others
Everton	3.84	–	9+6	1+1		7	1			
Oldham Athletic*	3.88	£100,000	139+4	14	13	2+1	34		3	1

MARSHALL Scott Roderick

Born: Edinburgh, 1 May 1973

Height: 6'1½" Weight: 12.5

International Honours: S Sch, S Yth

Position/Skill Factor: Central defender. Very good in the air, he reads the game well and will come out of defence looking to pass the ball, rather than just clear his lines.

Career History: Signed professional forms for Arsenal at the end of the 1990-91 season, having been at Highbury as a trainee since July 1989. No first team appearances in 1991-92, he has yet to make his FL debut.

Clubs	Signing Date	Transfer Fee	APPEARANCES				GOALS			
			Lge	FL Cup	FA Cup	Others	Lge	FL Cup	FA Cup	Others
Arsenal*	3.91	–								

MARTIN Lee Andrew

Born: Hyde, 5 February 1968

Height: 5'11"

Weight: 11.5

International Honours: E "U21"-2

Position/Skill Factor: A very reliable left-back who can also play in the centre of the defence, he is good in the air and not easy to beat. Never misses an opportunity of coming out of defence with the ball to link up with the attack.

Career History: First came to Manchester United as an associated schoolboy in February 1982, before joining the YTS scheme on leaving school in June 1985. Turned professional during the 1986 close season and made his FL debut at Old Trafford against Wimbledon on 9 May 1988, when coming on for Remi Moses. Got his chance of a regular first team football in 1988-89, with Viv Anderson injured and made 20 League appearances. But it was during the following season that he really made his mark, as he began to establish himself on the left-hand side of the United defence. His form was such that he was selected for the 1990 FA Cup Final side to play Crystal Palace and he shot to fame in the replay when latching on to a Neil Webb pass to rifle in the only goal of the game. After all the glamour of the previous season, he lost his place in the team at the beginning of 1990-91 and spent most of the time in the shadow of the more experienced Clayton Blackmore. Still recovering from injury, he made only one appearance as sub in the League, plus four other appearances in cup matches during 1991-92.

Clubs	Signing Date	Transfer Fee	APPEARANCES				GOALS			
			Lge	FL Cup	FA Cup	Others	Lge	FL Cup	FA Cup	Others
Manchester United*	5.86	–	55+17	4+2	13+1	4+3	1		1	

MARTYN Anthony **Nigel**

Born: St Austell, 11 August 1966

Height: 6'2" Weight: 14.0

International Honours: E "U21"-11, E"B", E-3

Position/Skill Factor: A commanding goalkeeper. Very agile for a big man, he is difficult to beat and always presents an imposing figure to the opposition. Also has a very long kick.

Career History: Bristol Rovers spotted him playing for the Cornish based South-Western League club, St Blazey, from where they signed him at the start of 1987-88. He went straight into the Rovers' side, making his FL debut at Twerton Park in a 3-1 win over Rotherham United on 15 August 1987 and was an almost instant success, holding his place for most of the season. The following term, he was ever present as the club lost out on promotion in the Third Division Play-Offs and soon after starting the 1989-90 season, he became the first £1million British goalkeeper when signing for Crystal Palace. The Palace manager, Steve Coppell, made his move within three months of the club's return to the First Division, having seen his defence leak an alarming number of goals. Settling down immediately, his presence in the Palace goal brought some stability at the back and was a solid platform in their bid for FA

Cup glory as well as safeguarding their League status. Prior to the Semi-Finals of the FA Cup, he had only conceded one goal, but the thriller against Liverpool saw Palace win sensationally 4-3, while the Final against Manchester United produced three goals apiece, before the "Eagles" lost the replay 1-0. Ever present in 1990-91, only beaten 41 times during the League programme, he was outstanding as the club rose to their highest ever place, third in the First Division. Missed only three games in 1991-92, although Palace's defences were crumbling somewhat in the first half of the season when 40 goals were conceded. After numerous England Under 21 appearances and some England "B" games, his international prospects seemed to have dimmed until some well-publicised lapses by England's number two 'keeper, David Seaman, persuaded Graham Taylor to look at him again. After coming on as second-half substitute against the CIS in Moscow on 29 April 1992, he made a full appearance against Hungary two weeks later and did enough to justify his selection as reserve to Chris Woods in the England squad for Sweden, although he was not called upon.

Clubs	Signing Date	Transfer Fee	APPEARANCES				GOALS			
			Lge	FL Cup	FA Cup	Others	Lge	FL Cup	FA Cup	Others
Bristol Rovers	8.87	–	101	6	6	11				
Crystal Palace*	11.89	£1,000,000	101	13	11	14				

MARWOOD **Brian**

Born: Seaham,
5 February 1960

Height: 5'7"

Weight: 11.6

International Honours:
E-1

Position/Skill Factor: Skilful right-winger with zip and pace and at his best a frequent scorer. More effective in a wide position where he can get past defenders to either cross the ball accurately for those better placed or to cut inside and shoot.

Career History: Came through the ranks at Hull City, first as an associated schoolboy (February 1976) and later, on leaving school, as an apprentice (June 1976). After turning professional, he waited almost two years before making his FL debut at Boothferry Park against Mansfield Town on 12 January 1980. Had a good goal scoring record at Hull and was soon attracting the attention of the bigger clubs. On signing for Sheffield Wednesday during the 1984 close season, he proved to be an excellent acquisition and quickly made his mark in the First Division. Had a spell out of action during the 1986-87 season, which coincided with a lean time for the "Owls", but came back and was just beginning to find his feet when he found himself on his way to Arsenal as part of George Graham's rebuilding process. In just over two seasons at Highbury, he gained his one and only England cap when coming on as a sub against Saudi Arabia on 16 November 1988 and at the end of that same season, celebrated with a League Championship medal, albeit missing the last five games. Found himself in and out of the side as the manager tried various permutations during 1989-90 and then, following the signing of Anders Limpar, was left out in the cold. It was time to move on again and Sheffield United, without a win to their name, came for him at the beginning of 1990-91, in the hope that he could supply the ammunition for Brian Deane and Tony Agana to explode. Although he only made 17 League appearances, he was a valued member of the squad that clawed its way up the First Division table to safety and at the same time successfully managed to combine his football career with his tireless work on behalf of the PFA. Made even fewer appearances in 1991-92 after he had been elected Chairman of the PFA and seemed set to return to his native north-east when he joined Middlesbrough on loan in October 1991, but no permanent deal was arranged.

Clubs	Signing Date	Transfer Fee	APPEARANCES				GOALS			
			Lge	FL Cup	FA Cup	Others	Lge	FL Cup	FA Cup	Others
Hull City	2.78	–	154+4	4+1	16	5	51		1	
Sheffield Wednesday	8.84	£115,000	125+3	13	19	0+1	27	5	3	
Arsenal	3.88	£600,000	52	6	2	3+1	16	1		2
Sheffield United*	9.90	£350,000	14+8	3	0+2		3			
Middlesbrough	10.91	Loan	3	1		1				

MATTEO Dominic

Born: Dumfries, 28 April 1974

Height: 6'0½" Weight: 11.0

Position: Central Defender.

Career History: A recent professional signing for Liverpool, having been at the club since first coming to Anfield as an associated schoolboy in September 1989, he later progressed through the ranks as a trainee in June 1990. No first team experience.

Clubs	Signing Date	Transfer Fee	APPEARANCES				GOALS			
			Lge	FL Cup	FA Cup	Others	Lge	FL Cup	FA Cup	Others
Liverpool*	6.92	–								

MATTHEW Damian

Born: Islington, 23 September 1970

Height: 5'11"

Weight: 10.10

International Honours: E "U21"-6

Position/Skill Factor: A creative midfield player with great stamina, who passes and moves, always making angles for his team-mates.

Career History: Another in a long line of good Chelsea discoveries, he came through as an associated schoolboy (May 1986) and then as a trainee, on leaving school in August 1987. Turned professional during the 1989 close season, making his FL debut at Stamford Bridge against Crystal Palace on 16 April 1990 and followed up with a useful spell in the side during 1990-91 as he tendered his claim for a regular first team place. Expected to make progress in 1991-92, in fact he only made a handful of first team appearances mostly as substitute, although it is a thankless task to understudy Andy Townsend. Seemingly more highly rated by the England management than Chelsea's, at one time he had more England Under 21 caps than FL appearances for the "Blues".

Clubs	Signing Date	Transfer Fee	APPEARANCES				GOALS			
			Lge	FL Cup	FA Cup	Others	Lge	FL Cup	FA Cup	Others
Chelsea*	6.89	–	10+7	5		1				

MAY David

Born: Oldham, 24 June 1970

Height: 6'0" Weight: 12.0

Position/Skill Factor: Very quick and strong central defender with sound positional sense who is very good in the air and a useful passer of the ball.

Career History: Started his soccer career as an associated schoolboy at Blackburn Rovers in October 1984, becoming a trainee in July 1986, on leaving school and eventually graduating to the club's professional ranks in the summer of 1988. Making his FL debut at Swindon Town on 1 April 1989, he had a good run in the side in central defence at the beginning of 1989-90, before sustaining an injury that put him out of first team action until the following November. Once back to full match fitness, he wrested the number five shirt from Andy Hill, only missing one game in 19, until being forced to stand down for three matches near the end of the season. Enjoyed another long run in the first team at the beginning of 1991-92 before making way for Kevin Moran in October. Only played two more Second Division games to the end of the season — one at Cambridge when manager Kenny Dalglish deployed no fewer than four central defenders to counter the "up and under" tactics of their opponents. The strategy backfired when poor May scored an own goal to put United 2-0 ahead. Amazingly, was recalled at right-back for the three end of season Play-Off games against Derby County and Leicester City, a ploy justified by the outcome of Premier League football this coming season.

Clubs	Signing Date	Transfer Fee	APPEARANCES				GOALS			
			Lge	FL Cup	FA Cup	Others	Lge	FL Cup	FA Cup	Others
Blackburn Rovers*	6.88	–	49	3	3	4	1			

MEAKER Michael John

Born: Greenford, 18 August 1971

Height: 5'11" Weight: 11.5

Position/Skill Factor: Left-winger who runs well with the ball at his feet and is very quick off the mark. Favours his right foot and loves coming inside the full-back, looking to shoot for goal.

Career History: Came to Queens Park Rangers straight from school as a trainee in November 1988 and signed as a professional at the end of 1989. made his FL debut at Manchester City when he came on for Dominic Iorfa on 1 December 1990 and over the remainder of the 1990-91 season appeared a further seven times as a substitute. Only one further selection, again as substitute, for Rangers in 1991-92, but made five full appearances on loan to Plymouth Argyle, in mid season.

Clubs	Signing Date	Transfer Fee	APPEARANCES				GOALS			
			Lge	FL Cup	FA Cup	Others	Lge	FL Cup	FA Cup	Others
Q.P.R.	12.89	–	0+9			0+1				
Plymouth Argyle*	11.91	Loan	4			1				

MEGSON Gary John

Born: Manchester,
2 May 1959

Height: 5'10"

Weight: 11.6

Position/Skill Factor: Midfield player who has matured with age and has become a great team man. Always making himself available, he has plenty of stamina which allows him to work all over the pitch.

Career History: Started his soccer apprenticeship at Plymouth Argyle in August 1975, with the blessing of his father, Don, the former Sheffield Wednesday and Bristol Rovers full-back (1959-1971) and had progressed to the club's professional ranks by the 1977 close season. Made his FL debut at Home Park against Portsmouth on 29 October 1977 and quickly adjusted to League soccer, showing great verve and spirit. Spent two seasons with the club, before making the giant leap up to the First Division with Everton, for a six figure sum that broke Plymouth's transfer record. Got off to a fair start with the "Toffees", but lost his place to Gary Stanley in 1980-81 and at the end of the season was transferred to his father's former club, Sheffield Wednesday. Missed only three League matches in three years at Hillsborough and after helping Wednesday to promotion to the First Division in 1983-84,

he moved down the road to Nottingham Forest. But when suffering the same fate as Asa Harford before him and John Sheridan afterwards, in being rejected by Brian Clough almost as soon as he had signed and after three months without a game, he was sold on to Newcastle United. Unfortunately, his first team chances were also restricted at St James' Park and he only stayed a little over a year before Sheffield Wednesday secured his return to the club for a knock down sum. In his second spell with the "Owls", he again stayed three years and was very consistent, but was allowed to join Manchester City in January 1989 and marked his debut with the only goal of the game at Oldham Athletic. A key figure in midfield as the side won promotion that season, he found himself out in the cold when City found it hard to adjust to the rigours of life in the First Division. However, a change in fortune for the club, coincided with his return to first team duty and in 1990-91 City rose to fifth place in the top flight, as he formed the backbone of the side, playing alongside player-manager, Peter Reid. Started 1991-92 in City's first team and played until October, but only intermittently afterwards, following the arrival of Steve McMahon and Fitzroy Simpson.

Clubs	Signing Date	Transfer Fee	APPEARANCES				GOALS			
			Lge	FL Cup	FA Cup	Others	Lge	FL Cup	FA Cup	Others
Plymouth Argyle	5.77	–	78	9	5		10			
Everton	12.79	£250,000	20+2		3		2		1	
Sheffield Wednesday	8.81	£130,000	123	13	12		13	2	5	
Nottingham Forest	8.84	£175,000								
Newcastle United	11.84	£130,000	21+3	1+1	2		1		1	
Sheffield Wednesday	12.85	£60,000	107+3	10	15	3	12		1	
Manchester City*	1.89	£250,000	78+4	5	7+1	2	2			

MENDONCA Clive Paul

Born: Islington, 9 September 1968

Height: 5'10" Weight: 11.7

Position/Skill Factor: Natural goal scoring striker with quick feet. Moves very well off the ball and takes up good positions in the penalty area.

Career History: London born, but from the Sunderland area, he came out as a professional with Sheffield United at the start of 1986-87, having been an apprentice at the club since July 1985. Made his FL debut at Brighton & Hove Albion on 2 May 1987 and played a handful of games during the following season, before being loaned out to Doncaster Rovers. On coming back to Bramall Lane, he was promptly sold to nearby Rotherham United and almost immediately found himself a member of the side that was relegated to the Fourth Division at the end of the 1987-88 season. Found it difficult to hold down a place, playing only five League games, as the "Millers" came back to the Third Division as Champions at the first time of asking. He had better fortune in 1989-90, scoring 14 goals from 32 FL games, but was always more popular with the fans than the management and frequently lost his place for short periods. It was the same story in 1990-91 and although he was top scorer, it was with only ten FL goals as the team slumped back into the Fourth Division. It was a major surprise, therefore, when Dave Bassett re-signed him for Sheffield United in the summer of 1991 for a considerably larger fee than when he left Bramall Lane.

It was not an inspired signing, unusually for Bassett, although in fairness, Mendonca was given few opportunities, mostly as substitute, to prove his worth. he made no further appearances for the "Blades" after December, but had two separate loan periods with Grimsby Town in the New Year.

Clubs	Signing Date	Transfer Fee	APPEARANCES				GOALS			
			Lge	FL Cup	FA Cup	Others	Lge	FL Cup	FA Cup	Others
Sheffield United	9.86	–	8+5	0+1		1	4			
Doncaster Rovers	2.88	Loan	2							
Rotherham United	3.88	£35,000	71+13	5+2	4+1	3+2	27	1	2	1
Sheffield United*	7.91	£110,000	4+6	0+2		0+1	1			
Grimsby Town	1.92	Loan	10				3			

MERSON Paul Charles

Born: Harlesden, 20 March 1968

Height: 5'10" Weight: 11.9

International Honours: E Yth, E "U21"-4, E"B", E-6

Position/Skill Factor: Top class winger, or forward, who has close control and runs well with the ball. Favours his right foot and will regularly come off the left flank looking for a crack at goal. An exciting player with explosive finishing potential.

Career History: Came up through the Arsenal youth system, first as an associated schoolboy (May 1982) and later, on leaving school in July 1984, as an apprentice. Graduated to the professional ranks and made his FL debut at Highbury when coming on for Niall Quinn against Manchester City on 22 November 1986. Marked his first full senior game with a goal in a 2-1 win at Brentford towards the end of that season, following a brief loan period at Brentford and served notice that it would not be long before he challenged for a regular place in the Arsenal side. Getting his chance in 1988-89, he took it excellently, playing 37 League matches and scoring ten goals, in partnership with Alan Smith, as Arsenal pipped Liverpool in the last game of the season to become League Champions. His progress was acknowledged by his peers when voted the PFA "Young Player of the Year" in 1989. After a disappointing 1989-90, by their high standards, the "Gunners"again went for broke in 1990-91 and he missed only two games when winning his second League Championship medal in three years. His natural combativeness could be explained away by the fact that between 1951-53, his uncle Stan had 13 fights as a professional boxer. With the emergence of Kevin Campbell and the arrival of Ian Wright in 1991-92, he was switched by manager George Graham to a wide role on either flank. It was a very successful move as he not only scored 12 FL goals (including a first ever senior hat-trick against Crystal Palace), but was also credited with 15 assists and played in every game. His form was noted by England manager Graham Taylor who selected his as a substitute for the early season game against Germany, and played him three more times at the end of the season. He did enough to justify inclusion for the 1992 European Championship Finals and came on for Andy Sinton as England went out of the competition to the host nation, Sweden, following a 2-1 defeat.

Clubs	Signing Date	Transfer Fee	APPEARANCES				GOALS			
			Lge	FL Cup	FA Cup	Others	Lge	FL Cup	FA Cup	Others
Arsenal*	11.85	–	139+28	13+2	13+2	7+1	49	5	3	
Brentford	1.87	Loan	6+1			1+1				

MIDDLETON Craig

Born: Nuneaton, 10 September 1970

Height: 5'9"

Weight: 11.0

Position/Skill Factor: Useful attacking midfield player who makes intelligent runs into the opposition's penalty area and is a good provider for others.

Career History: The twin brother of Lee, who has just been released from the Coventry City playing staff, he first joined "Sky Blues" as an associated schoolboy in January 1987, before signing on as a trainee in July 1987

246

and graduating to the club's professional ranks in the summer of 1989. Made his FL debut at Tottenham Hotspur on 14 April 1990 when he came on for Micky Gynn in a 3-2 defeat. Spent 1991-92 mainly with City's reserves, but when making two first team appearances, his form suggested that he might not be too far away from holding down a regular place in the side.

Clubs	Signing Date	Transfer Fee	APPEARANCES				GOALS			
			Lge	FL Cup	FA Cup	Others	Lge	FL Cup	FA Cup	Others
Coventry City*	5.89	–	1+1	1						

MIKE Adrian Roosevelt

Born: Manchester, 16 November 1973

Height: 6'0" Weight: 11.8

International Honours: E Sch

Position: Forward.

Career History: An exciting young star of the future, he made his FL debut for Manchester City, while still a trainee, at home to Notts County on 25 April 1992 and in the next match, the last game of the season at Oldham Athletic, he scored the first goal in a 5-2 victory. A recent summer professional signing, he first came to Maine Road as an associated schoolboy in January 1988, before joining the trainee ranks in July 1990.

Clubs	Signing Date	Transfer Fee	APPEARANCES				GOALS			
			Lge	FL Cup	FA Cup	Others	Lge	FL Cup	FA Cup	Others
Manchester City*	6.92	–	2				1			

MILLER Alan John

Born: Epping,
29 March 1970

Height: 6'2"

Weight: 13.8

International Honours:
E Yth, E "U21"-4

Position/Skill Factor: Good all-round goalkeeper from the FA School of Excellence at Lilleshall. Possessing a safe pair of hands, he inspires confidence. Is also recognised for his kicking ability.

Career History: Started his football life at Highbury as an associated schoolboy in July 1984, becoming a trainee in July 1986. Yet to play for Arsenal's first team since turning professional, mainly due to the consistency of John Lukic and then David Seaman, he was loaned out to Plymouth Argyle in 1988-89 and made his FL debut at Home Park against Oldham Athletic, keeping a clean sheet in a 3-0 win on 26 November 1988. Amazingly made his England Under 21 debut just after signing professional forms and before appearing in the League. Unfortunate to be understudy to David Seaman, as he would probably be a first choice at most clubs, he gained further FL experience on loan with West Bromwich Albion and Birmingham City during 1991-92, spending three months at St Andrews assisting the "Blues'" drive to promotion.

Clubs	Signing Date	Transfer Fee	APPEARANCES				GOALS			
			Lge	FL Cup	FA Cup	Others	Lge	FL Cup	FA Cup	Others
Arsenal*	5.88	–								
Plymouth Argyle	11.88	Loan	13		2					
W.B.A.	8.91	Loan	3							
Birmingham City	12.91	Loan	15			1				

MILLER Paul Anthony

Born: Woking, 31 January 1968

Height: 6'0" Weight: 11.0

Position/Skill Factor: A good runner off the ball, he also does well in the air and always looks to score goals.

Career History: Started his soccer career as a Wimbledon associated schoolboy in March 1982, before leaving to play for non-League sides, Wealdstone and Yeovil Town. After coming back to the club as a professional during the summer of 1987, he made his FL debut at Watford on 15 August 1987, but only managed a couple more games during the season and was loaned out for a short while to Newport County. The following season he was given a concerted run in the side, which extended into 1989-90 and although interspersed with another spell on loan, this time to Bristol City, he appeared to be making good progress. Unfortunate to be injured during the first match of 1990-91, against Arsenal, he was unable to play again for the rest of the season. Remained sidelined for 16 months, not returning to first team duty until December 1991. Appropriately his first goal after his return was an equaliser against Arsenal at Highbury. A regular team member in the second half of the season, goals eluded him, however.

Clubs	Signing Date	Transfer Fee	APPEARANCES				GOALS			
			Lge	FL Cup	FA Cup	Others	Lge	FL Cup	FA Cup	Others
Wimbledon*	8.87	–	54+7	2+2	2	1	9			
Newport County	10.87	Loan	6				2			
Bristol City	1.90	Loan	0+3			2				

MILLER Robert James

Born: Manchester, 3 November 1972

Height: 6'0" Weight: 11.1

247

Position/Skill Factor: Full-back with a very good left foot, who is also a smart passer of the ball when under pressure.

Career History: An Oldham Athletic professional since the 1991 close season, having been a trainee since August 1989, he struggled with injuries all last season and has yet to make his FL debut.

Clubs	Signing Date	Transfer Fee	APPEARANCES				GOALS			
			Lge	FL Cup	FA Cup	Others	Lge	FL Cup	FA Cup	Others
Oldham Athletic	2.85	–	161+1	19+1	12	4	17	1	1	
Everton	8.90	£1,000,000	16+1	0+1	1	4	1			1
Oldham Athletic*	7.91	£600,000	36	4		1	3	1		1

Clubs	Signing Date	Transfer Fee	APPEARANCES				GOALS			
			Lge	FL Cup	FA Cup	Others	Lge	FL Cup	FA Cup	Others
Oldham Athletic*	7.91	–								

MILLIGAN Michael (Mike) Joseph

Born: Manchester,
20 February 1967

Height: 5'8"

Weight: 11.0

International Honours:
IR "U21"-1, IR"B", IR-1

Position/Skill Factor: All-action midfield general who is a good competitor and a reliable team player. A tenacious performer, he is a useful man to have on your side, especially in breaking down the oppositions rhythm.

Career History: Although starting out as a Manchester City associated schoolboy (April 1981), he was not offered terms by the club when leaving school and joined Oldham Athletic on a YTS scheme in December 1984. After progressing to the club's professional ranks early in 1985, he had to wait a further year before making his FL debut at Sheffield United on 12 April 1986. Very consistent over the next four season, he was inspirational to a side seeking to attain First Division status, but the nearest he came during his time with the "Latics" was when reaching the Play-Offs in 1986-87. Played a significant role in Oldham's wonderful cup runs of 1989-90, winning through to the Semi-Final of the FA Cup, before succumbing in a replay to Manchester United and the Final of the League Cup, losing to Nottingham Forest. Moved to Everton in the 1990 close season, as an aspiring First Division midfield general, but did not fit in at Goodison Park and struggled to win a regular place. His older brother Terry was with Crewe Alexandra in 1986-87, having previously been at Manchester City and Oldham, without getting a game. Returned to Oldham at a knock-down price in the summer of 1991 and played a leading role in consolidating the "Latics'" newly won First Division status. After a long wait, he finally broke into the Irish Republic team in April 1992, although only as substitute in a low priority friendly against the USA team.

MILTON Simon Charles

Born: Fulham,
23 August 1963

Height: 5'9"

Weight: 11.9

Position/Skill Factor: Right-winger who is capable of scoring explosive goals after bursting through from midfield. Produces good early crosses and is a sweet striker of the ball.

Career History: Joined Ipswich Town from local Eastern Counties League club, Bury Town, in the 1987 close season and made his FL debut while on loan with Exeter City at home to Stockport County on 21 November 1987, scoring two goals, plus another in their next League game at Darlington. He was soon back at Portman Road for a run out and following another spell on loan at Torquay United, he played in Ipswich's last six League games of 1987-88. In the final match of the season, a 3-2 victory over Bradford City, he scored the winner, which lifted Town from 11th to eighth place in the Second Division. Has worked hard to establish himself during the last three season, only missing five League matches in 1989-90, but lost his way temporarily in 1990-91 as he struggled to find his true form. Out of favour at the start of 1991-92, he fought his way back into the first team in October and held his place for the remainder of the season as Town climbed up the table to finish as Second Division Champions with a superb run in the New Year. He played mainly on the right side of midfield, but also deputised for Chris Kiwomya up front on occasions and can also operate in the middle of the park — a useful utility player, with a good scoring ratio.

Clubs	Signing Date	Transfer Fee	APPEARANCES				GOALS			
			Lge	FL Cup	FA Cup	Others	Lge	FL Cup	FA Cup	Others
Ipswich Town*	7.87	£5,500	131+18	8+2	8	10+1	35	1	1	3
Exeter City	11.87	Loan	2			1	3			
Torquay United	3.88	Loan	4			0+1	1			

MIMMS Robert (Bobby) Andrew

Born: York,
12 October 1963

Height: 6'2"

Weight: 12.13

International Honours:
E "U21"-3

Position/Skill Factor: Very experienced goalkeeper. Extremely agile for such a big man, he commands his lines well. Sets up attacks with good quick throws to his full-backs and kicks long and accurately from his hands.

Career History: An associated schoolboy (October 1979) and then an apprentice (April 1980) with Halifax Town, he graduated as a professional in the 1981 close season. With John Kilner and Lee Smelt barring his way at the Shay, he was transferred to Rotherham United after only three months as a professional and eventually made his FL debut at home to Blackburn Rovers on 8 May 1982. Understudy to Ray Mountford and then Alan Stevenson, he became first choice 'keeper at Millmoor from March 1984 and was ever present the following season, when he won two England Under 21 caps, both times as substitute. Transferred to Everton in the summer of 1985 to act as deputy to Neville Southall, he made his debut for the "Toffees" in late October and was hurriedly recalled from a loan spell with Notts County late in the season when the latter was injured. Played in the last nine League games of 1985-86, during which Everton lost the League Championship to Liverpool. No blame can be attached to Mimms, however, who kept a clean sheet in the first six of those games! Also played in the 1986 FA Cup Final, but was powerless to prevent Liverpool overturning a half-time deficit to run out 3-1 winners and complete the "Double". Although getting some first team action in each of his three seasons at Goodison Park, he was frequently loaned out to other clubs to keep in trim. Finally, he welcomed the chance of regular first team football when he was signed by Tottenham Hotspur late in 1987-88. Sadly for him, his reign as first team 'keeper at White Hart Lane lasted slightly less than one year as "Spurs" then signed Norwegian Erik Thorstvedt in January 1989. After two years of understudying Thorstvedt and a short period on loan to Aberdeen, he was sold to Blackburn Rovers. Immediately replaced Mark Grew, who had been on loan from Port Vale and played in the last 22 games of the season, with relegation to the Third Division being averted in the penultimate match, a 1-1 draw at home to Wolverhampton Wanderers. Since joining the Lancashire club, he has missed only one game in 18 months and in a season that was fraught with tension he kept 14 clean sheets as Rovers won their way back to the First Division after an absence of 26 years, despite scraping into the Play-Offs in sixth position.

Clubs	Signing Date	Transfer Fee	APPEARANCES				GOALS			
			Lge	FL Cup	FA Cup	Others	Lge	FL Cup	FA Cup	Others
Halifax Town	8.81	–								
Rotherham United	11.81	£15,000	83	7	3	1				
Everton	6.85	£150,000	29	2	2	4				
Notts County	3.86	Loan	2			1				
Sunderland	12.86	Loan	4							
Blackburn Rovers	1.87	Loan	6							
Manchester City	9.87	Loan	3							
Tottenham Hotspur	2.88	£325,000	37	5	2					
Aberdeen	2.90	Loan								
Blackburn Rovers*	12.90	£250,000	67	2	4	4				

MINETT Jason

Born: Peterborough, 12 August, 1971

Height: 5'10" Weight: 10.2

Position/Skill Factor: Left-back who can play in midfield. Typical of the Norwich City tradition, he is a good passer and is always taking up good positions to receive the return ball.

Career History: Discovered by Norwich City as a 14-year-old, he signed associated schoolboy forms in June 1986 and on leaving school in August 1987, became a trainee. Turned professional in the 1989 close season and was introduced to the first team for his FL debut at Leeds United on 1 September 1990. Both of his substitute appearances in 1990-91 saw him come off the bench and both times City suffered 3-0 defeats. No further appearances in 1991-92, but offered a new contract during the summer.

Clubs	Signing Date	Transfer Fee	APPEARANCES				GOALS			
			Lge	FL Cup	FA Cup	Others	Lge	FL Cup	FA Cup	Others
Norwich City*	7.89	–	0+2							

MINTON Jeffrey Simon Thompson

Born: Hackney, 28 December 1973

Height: 5'5" Weight: 11.7

Position/Skill Factor: Skilful midfielder with a lovely touch and good vision. Has much awareness around the box and can make telling passes.

Career History: Turned professional with Tottenham Hotspur early in 1992, having first come through the ranks at White Hart Lane as an associated schoolboy (March 1988), before becoming a trainee in August 1990. Soon after signing professional forms, he made his FL debut for "Spurs" in an end of season game at home to Everton on 25 April 1992 and scored in a 3-3 draw.

Clubs	Signing Date	Transfer Fee	APPEARANCES				GOALS			
			Lge	FL Cup	FA Cup	Others	Lge	FL Cup	FA Cup	Others
Tottenham Hotspur*	1.92	–	2				1			

Jan Molby

MOHAN Nicholas (Nicky)

Born: Middlesbrough,
6 October 1970

Height: 6'2"

Weight: 12.0

Position/Skill Factor: A central defender who began his League career at full-back. Great strength and an excellent physique makes him dominant in the air.

Career History: Although locally born and bred, he signed professional forms for Middlesbrough after coming to the club from Charlton Athletic where he had been on trial. Made his FL debut at Southampton on 14 January 1989 at right-back and the following season he began to make his presence felt in both full-back positions. However, in 1990-91, he was unavailable for selection, due to injuries and suspension. Made a comeback in November 1991, taking the place of Tony Mowbray in central defence, after the latter's departure to Celtic. Formed a sound partnership with Alan Kernaghan in assisting "Boro" to two fine cup runs (reaching the Semi-Final of the League Cup and the Fifth Round of the FA Cup) and at the end of the season climbing to second place and automatic promotion to the new Premier League.

Clubs	Signing Date	Transfer Fee	APPEARANCES				GOALS			
			Lge	FL Cup	FA Cup	Others	Lge	FL Cup	FA Cup	Others
Middlesbrough*	11.87	–	53+2	7	4+1	5	2			

MOLBY Jan

Born: Jutland, Denmark, 4 July 1963

Height: 6'1" Weight: 14.7

International Honours: Danish Int

Position/Skill Factor: Midfield player with a wonderful touch and possessing quick feet for such a big man. Great strength in possession and a lovely striker of the ball, he is possibly the best long ball passer in the modern game. Dangerous at free-kicks with a powerful shot and Liverpool's first choice penalty taker.

Career History: Signed for Liverpool in the 1984 close season, following a successful stay with the Dutch side, Ajax of Amsterdam and made his FL debut at Norwich City on 25 August 1984. His great influence in midfield minimised the loss of Graeme Souness to Italian soccer, although later, Kenny Dalglish would often use him as a "sweeper". Played 39 League games in 1985-86, as Liverpool did the "double", winning the League

Championship and defeating local rivals, Everton 3-1 in the FA Cup Final. But it could have been so different. After Gary Lineker had given Everton the lead at Wembley, it was only Jan's tremendous passing ability that turned the game around as he picked out Ian Rush for the equaliser and Craig Johnston for the second "Reds'" goal. In the following season, almost a failure by Liverpool's standards, he was a key member of the side that finished second in the First Division and were beaten 2-1 by Arsenal in the League Cup Final. Suffered from injury in 1987-88, making only one full League appearance, although coming on as a sub in the losing FA Cup Final against Wimbledon and was absent for a large tract of the following season after being jailed for three months on a drink-driving conviction. Although winning a second League Championship medal in 1989-90, he only made 12 appearances and in recent years lost his way somewhat, with weight and injury problems and had to play second fiddle to Ronnie Whelan and Steve McMahon in Liverpool's midfield. Injured at the start of 1991-92, he returned to the side in October 1991 and was a fairly regular selection for the remainder of the season. Because of his weight problems and his lack of mobility, he is sometimes caught in possession, although he has the strength to shove off most challenges. Given time and space he can direct operations as he showed in the 1992 FA Cup Final against Sunderland when he orchestrated nearly all of Liverpool's second-half offensive, seemingly without moving from the centre circle! Out of favour with the present manager of the Danish national team, he was not considered for the squad when Denmark was called up at the last minute for the European Championship in Sweden.

Clubs	Signing Date	Transfer Fee	APPEARANCES				GOALS			
			Lge	FL Cup	FA Cup	Others	Lge	FL Cup	FA Cup	Others
Liverpool*	8.84	£575,000	164+19	20+3	24+4	14+2	37	8	4	4

MONKOU Kenneth (Ken) John

Born: Necare, Surinam,
29 November 1964

Height: 6'0"

Weight: 12.9

International Honours:
Dutch "U21" Int

Position/Skill Factor: Central defender who is strong in the air and powerful in the tackle, he is also a good athlete. Has good skills on the ball and is capable of hitting quality long balls behind opposing defences.

Career History: After being signed by Chelsea from the Dutch club, Feyenoord, at the back end of 1988-89, he was refused permission to play in a match for his former club shortly afterwards and the plane that he would have been travelling on, crashed, killing many of his old teammates. Made his FL debut at Stamford Bridge in Chelsea's Second Division title winning side against Stoke

City on 1 May 1989, coming on for Joe McLaughlin, who was shortly to leave the club. Soon established himself at the heart of the Chelsea defence, missing just four games in his first full season as the club consolidated its position in the First Division, finishing in the fifth place. In 1990-91, although the "Blues" fared less well than expected, one of the bonuses of a disappointing season was his partnership with promising young Jason Cundy, which augured well for the future. Partnered new signing Paul Elliott for the first half of 1991-92, until losing his place to Cundy in January, but returned to the Chelsea team in March, following the latter's departure to Tottenham Hotspur.

Clubs	Signing Date	Transfer Fee	APPEARANCES				GOALS			
			Lge	FL Cup	FA Cup	Others	Lge	FL Cup	FA Cup	Others
Chelsea*	3.89	£100,000	92+2	12	3	10	2			

MOODY Paul

Born: Portsmouth, 13 June 1967

Height: 6'3" Weight: 13.12

Position/Skill Factor: Tall striker who is obviously a handful in the air and has a strong shot. Pulls away to the far post well when team-mates get into crossing positions.

Career History: Signed in the summer of 1991 by Southampton from local Beazer Homes League club, Waterlooville, for whom he was top scorer with 25 goals in 1990-91. Prior to 1988, he played for Fareham Town in the same league. Made his FL debut in the first game of the season at home to Tottenham Hotspur on 17 August 1991 as a substitute and made his full debut two weeks later at home to Aston Villa. Thereafter, first team opportunities were extremely scarce with Iain Dowie and Alan Shearer holding down the strikers' slots at The Dell.

Clubs	Signing Date	Transfer Fee	APPEARANCES				GOALS			
			Lge	FL Cup	FA Cup	Others	Lge	FL Cup	FA Cup	Others
Southampton*	7.91	£50,000	2+2		0+1					

MOORE Alan

Born: Dublin, 25 November 1974

Height: 5'9½" Weight: 10.10

Position/Skill Factor: Left sided midfield player with a good touch. Impresses with his ability to both see and deliver telling passes with his left foot.

Career History: Joined Middlesbrough as a trainee in July 1991, turning professional just after his 17th birthday. No first team appearances to date, but was selected as a substitute in three games in 1991-92 without being called on to the field.

Clubs	Signing Date	Transfer Fee	APPEARANCES				GOALS			
			Lge	FL Cup	FA Cup	Others	Lge	FL Cup	FA Cup	Others
Middlesbrough*	12.91	–								

MOORE Thomas Kevin

Born: Grimsby, 29 April 1958

Height: 5'11"

Weight: 12.2

International Honours: E Sch

Position/Skill Factor: Commanding central defender who is a wonderful professional. Strong in the air, a good defender, with a smashing left foot and a useful scorer of goals from set plays.

Career History: One of three footballing sons of Norman, who was a centre-forward with Grimsby Town, Hull City, Blackburn Rovers and Bury between 1946-1952. His younger brothers, Andy and David, also played for Grimsby, among other teams, as did his uncle Roy, soon after the war. Signed as a professional for Grimsby straight from school and after working his way through the junior sides, he made his FL debut at Bury on 21 August 1976. In more than ten seasons at Blundell Park, he was an automatic choice, starting out at left-back, before moving to the centre of the defence and winning a Third Division Championship medal in 1979-80. Joined promotion chasing Oldham Athletic during 1986-87 when his chances of playing in the top flight with Town had all but evaporated and then saw his First Division prospects with his new club disappear at the Play-Off stage. However, got his chance in the First Division when his old team-mate Chris Nicholl, then managing Southampton, brought him to the Dell as a replacement for the outgoing Mark Wright. Settled into the side well as a regular choice for a couple of seasons, but more recently has had to share the central defensive duties with Russell Osman and Neil Ruddock. Released on a free transfer in the summer of 1991, he was subsequently re-signed for one more year by incoming "Saints'" manager, Ian Branfoot. With five other central defenders on the books it seemed a strange decision, especially when he was scarcely used in the first-half of the season. However, after returning to The Dell from a successful loan period with Bristol Rovers, he was restored to the "Saints'" first team in place of Richard Hall and held his place for the remainder of the season. As a result he was offered another contract for 1992-93.

Clubs	Signing Date	Transfer Fee	APPEARANCES				GOALS			
			Lge	FL Cup	FA Cup	Others	Lge	FL Cup	FA Cup	Others
Grimsby Town	7.76	–	397+3	41	25	2	28	3	3	
Oldham Athletic	2.87	£100,000	13			2	1			
Southampton*	7.87	£125,000	112+4	15	12	5	8	1		1
Bristol Rovers	1.92	Loan	7							

MOORE Neil

Born: Liverpool, 21 September, 1972

Height: 6'0½" Weight: 11.13

Position/Skill Factor: A good all-round central defender who is very aggressive and strong in the air.

Career History: Came to Everton straight from school as an associated schoolboy in February 1988, before signing on as a trainee in June 1989. Turning professional during the 1991 close season, he has yet to make a first team appearance and has just had a leg operation. Hopes to be fully fit for 1992-93.

Clubs	Signing Date	Transfer Fee	APPEARANCES				GOALS			
			Lge	FL Cup	FA Cup	Others	Lge	FL Cup	FA Cup	Others
Everton*	6.91	–								

MORAH Olisa (Ollie) Henry

Born: Islington, 30 September 1972

Height: 5'11" Weight: 13.5

International Honours: E Sch, E Yth

Position/Skill Factor: Striker who runs well with the ball and has an electric turn of pace which takes him away from defenders.

Career History: Signed trainee forms for Tottenham Hotspur in July 1989, having been an associated schoolboy (November 1986) and turned professional two years later. Loaned out to Fourth Division Hereford United for experience, it seemed a pointless exercise for both club and player, as he made only two brief appearances as a substitute. The first, his FL debut, being at Carlisle United on 23 November 1991. With a large playing staff at White Hart Lane, he will have to be patient for his "Spurs'" debut.

Clubs	Signing Date	Transfer Fee	APPEARANCES				GOALS			
			Lge	FL Cup	FA Cup	Others	Lge	FL Cup	FA Cup	Others
Tottenham Hotspur*	7.91	–								
Hereford United	11.91	Loan	0+2							

MORALEE Jamie David

Born: Wandsworth, 2 December 1971

Height: 6'1" Weight: 11.1

Position/Skill Factor: Striker with good control who moves about well and has a keen eye for goal.

Career History: Joined Crystal Palace as a trainee in July 1988, turning professional two years later. Had to wait 18 months for his FL debut at home to Coventry City on 1 February 1992, when he came on as substitute and a further month for his full debut away to Southampton. Made a few more appearances, mostly as substitute, before the end of the season.

Clubs	Signing Date	Transfer Fee	APPEARANCES				GOALS			
			Lge	FL Cup	FA Cup	Others	Lge	FL Cup	FA Cup	Others
Crystal Palace*	7.90	–	2+4							

MORAN Kevin Bernard

Born: Dublin, 29 April 1956

Height: 5'11" Weight: 12.9

International Honours: IR-62

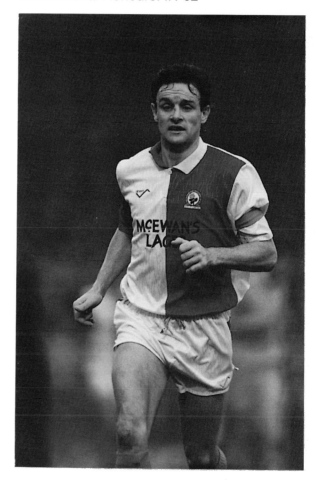

Position/Skill Factor: Very experienced, tough tackling, never-say-die central defender, who will not be beaten. He is never afraid to tackle and has picked up many injuries for his pains.

Career History: A former Irish Gaelic footballer with the Pegasus club of Dublin, he signed for Manchester United early in 1978, with only limited experience of soccer. After making his FL debut in a 1-1 draw at Southampton on 30 April 1979, he became a first team regular in 1980-81, replacing Gordon McQueen, having already won his first Republic of Ireland cap against Switzerland on 30 April 1980. won his first major club honour in 1983 when United defeated Brighton & Hove Albion 4-0 in the FA Cup Final replay, after a 2-2 draw. Two years later he again appeared in the FA Cup Final and created a record he would rather forget by becoming the first player in the history of the competition to be sent off. Whilst it was a crude foul on Peter Reid, it was a professional foul and not a vicious one and although the referee was technically correct in his decision, it must be said that worse fouls in previous and subsequent Finals have gone unpunished. Despite his absence, United went on to win 1-0 in extra-time and happily, but belatedly, he eventually received his winners medal. Plagued by injury throughout his United career, he only once came close to completing a full season — in 1983-84. After ten years at Old Trafford, he decided to see out his career overseas, joining Sporting Gijon of the Spanish First Division. However, after 16 months out of the limelight, he returned to League football with Second Division Blackburn Rovers, turning down an offer by Ron Atkinson, who would not guarantee him first team football with Sheffield Wednesday. A mainstay of the Irish Republic team since his debut, the highlight of his international career was undoubtedly playing in all five games in the World Cup Finals in 1990. Remarkably, at the age of 35, he played in no fewer than 41 FL games of Blackburn's tortuous, but ultimately successful promotion campaign of 1991-92, plus the three vital Play-Off games. Although surely close to retirement, he will be looking forward to one last chance of top flight football next season.

Clubs	Signing Date	Transfer Fee	APPEARANCES				GOALS			
			Lge	FL Cup	FA Cup	Others	Lge	FL Cup	FA Cup	Others
Manchester United	2.78	–	228+3	24+1	18	15+1	21	2	1	
Sporting Gijon (Spain)	8.88	–								
Blackburn Rovers*	1.90	–	88+4	5	4	5	5			1

MORAN Paul

Born: Enfield, 22 May 1968

Height: 5'10" Weight: 10.0

Position/Skill Factor: Speedy winger who likes to run at defenders in order to commit them. A good striker of the ball, he is always looking for a shooting opportunity in and around the penalty area.

Career History: Came to Tottenham Hotspur on the YTS scheme on leaving school in July 1984 and two years after signing professional forms, made his FL debut at Everton on 11 May 1987. Has only played sporadically for the "Spurs" since then, having been loaned out to three different teams, Portsmouth (1988-89), Leicester City (1989-90) and Newcastle United (1990-91), while he awaits his chance of a prolonged run at White Hart Lane. Looked to be a potentially brilliant player in a televised game at Derby in December 1987, when after coming on as a second-half substitute, his runs and crosses turned the match in "Spurs'" favour. Since 1989, his career has been at a standstill and his only first team appearance in 1991-92 was as a substitute in an early season European Cup Winners Cup game against Stockerau of Austria.

Clubs	Signing Date	Transfer Fee	APPEARANCES				GOALS			
			Lge	FL Cup	FA Cup	Others	Lge	FL Cup	FA Cup	Others
Tottenham Hotspur*	7.85	–	14+13	1+5	3+1		2			
Portsmouth	1.89	Loan	3							
Leicester City	11.89	Loan	10				2			
Newcastle United	2.91	Loan	1							
Southend United	3.91	Loan	1							

MORROW Stephen (Steve) Joseph

Born: Bangor, N.I., 2 July 1970

Height: 6'0" Weight: 11.3

International Honours: NI Sch, NI Yth, NI "U21"-1, NI-6

Position/Skill Factor: A full-back with an educated left foot, he also has a penchant for linking up with the attack.

Career History: First spotted by Arsenal as a 14-year-old in Northern Ireland, he signed associated schoolboy forms in May 1985, before coming to Highbury as a trainee on leaving school in July 1987. Although still to play for the "Gunners", his ability was recognised at full international level when he came on as a sub for Northern Ireland against Uruguay in Belfast on 18 May 1990. Has continued to play for Northern Ireland and has also had a spell on loan at Reading where he made his FL debut against Exeter City on 19 January 1991. With his path to the Arsenal first team blocked by Nigel Winterburn, he had three loan periods in 1991-92, with Watford (for two months), Reading (two weeks) and Barnet where he puzzlingly played only one game. Finally called up to the "Gunners'" first team squad in April 1992, he made two appearances as substitute, but found another full-back blocking his way — the Norwegian, Pal Lyderson. Happily, his lack of first team experience at Highbury has not prevented him continuing an international career with Northern Ireland.

Clubs	Signing Date	Transfer Fee	APPEARANCES				GOALS			
			Lge	FL Cup	FA Cup	Others	Lge	FL Cup	FA Cup	Others
Arsenal*	5.88	–	0+2							
Reading	1.91	Loan	10							
Watford	8.91	Loan	7+1		1					
Reading	10.91	Loan	3							
Barnet	3.92	Loan	1							

MORTIMER Paul Henry

Born: Kensington, 8 May 1968

Height: 5'11"

Weight: 11.3

International Honours: E "U21"-2

Position/Skill Factor: Athletic midfielder with a great left foot, he has the ability to produce very long passes and has a good shot. Also useful in the air.

Career History: Was an apprentice at Fulham (July 1984), before drifting into non-League soccer with Farnborough Town of the then Vauxhall League, when not offered a professional contract. Signed professional for Charlton Athletic, making his FL debut at home to Norwich City on 7 November 1987 and played a number of games that season when Garth Crooks was out injured. Gained a regular place the following season, 1988-89, when Charlton were relegated to the Second Division. His run of good form was interrupted, however, when he was injured at Bristol Rovers early in 1990-91, but he returned in November, missing only one of the last 33 matches, while assisting his team to safety. Transferred to Aston Villa in the summer of 1991 for a remarkably modest fee in view of his talent and experience. However, he couldn't find his best form at Villa Park and after only three months he abruptly returned to London to join Crystal Palace, this time for a more appropriate fee (but of little consolation to Charlton!). Although returning to the scene of his former glories with Charlton, at Selhurst Park, he has so far been unable to settle into the Palace team, being in and out since the New Year.

Clubs	Signing Date	Transfer Fee	APPEARANCES				GOALS			
			Lge	FL Cup	FA Cup	Others	Lge	FL Cup	FA Cup	Others
Charlton Athletic	9.87	–	108+5	4+1	8	3+1	17			
Aston Villa	7.91	£350,000	10+2	2			1			
Crystal Palace*	10.91	£500,000	17+4		1	3	2			

MOULDEN Paul Anthony

Born: Farnworth,
6 September 1967

Height: 5'10"

Weight: 11.0

International Honours:
E Yth

Position/Skill Factor: Striker who twists and turns well around the edge of the penalty area and "sniffs" out goal scoring chances well.

Career History: After scoring hundreds of goals at schoolboy level, allegedly a record total recognised in the "Guinness Book of Records", he signed associated schoolboy forms for Manchester City in December 1981, before progressing through the club, first as an apprentice (June 1984) and later as a professional. Made his FL debut at Aston Villa on 1 January 1986 and didn't get a run in the side until 1988-89, when City were promoted to the First Division as runners-up. As the club's leading scorer with 13 goals to his credit, he was surprisingly transferred the following summer to Bournemouth when

City signed Clive Allen. In his second game for the "Cherries", he scored his first ever League hat-trick, in a 5-4 victory over Hull City after Bournemouth had lead 4-1 at half-time. Later in the season, with the club already doomed for the Third Division, he returned to Lancashire with Oldham Athletic. Since joining the "Latics", he has provided cover for Ian Marshall and Andy Ritchie, without winning a regular place, but played enough games in 1990-91 to win a Second Division Championship medal. Played virtually no part in Oldham's first campaign at the top level for 69 years in 1991-92 and was possibly unavailable because of injury. His only two appearances were as substitute at the end of the season and will spend the close season playing in Norway.

Clubs	Signing Date	Transfer Fee	APPEARANCES				GOALS			
			Lge	FL Cup	FA Cup	Others	Lge	FL Cup	FA Cup	Others
Manchester City	9.84	–	48+16	5+1	2+3	3+1	18	4	1	3
Bournemouth	7.87	£160,000	32	4	0+1	1	13			
Oldham Athletic*	3.90	£225,000	16+18	2+1			4	1		

MUNRO Stuart

Born: Falkirk, 15 September 1962

Height: 5'11" Weight: 11.10

International Honours: S"B"

Position/Skill Factor: Good attacking left-back with a nice touch on the ball.

Career History: A big money signing by Blackburn Rovers from Glasgow Rangers in the 1991 close season, he made his FL debut at home to the eventual Second Division Champions, Ipswich Town, on 31 August 1991, but following a succession of injuries, did not make any further first team appearances during 1991-92. Started his top level career with St Mirren, whom he joined from Bo'ness United in 1980. Made his debut at left-back in October 1980, but with no further appearances to his name he was released at the end of 1981-82 to join Scottish Second Division club, Alloa Athletic, where he stayed for 19 months, mainly playing on the left-wing. Picked up by Glasgow Rangers in February 1984, he soon made his debut for them, but had to wait until 1985-86 to win a regular place. Stayed seven years at Ibrox Park and despite fierce competition for places was almost ever-present at left-back in 1986-87 and 1989-90. Won four Scottish League Championship medals in 1986-87, 1988-89, 1989-90 and 1990-91, plus three Skol Cup medals, before moving south of the border. Even when fit, his future at Ewood Park must be doubtful with Alan Wright in total command of the left-back slot.

Clubs	Signing Date	Transfer Fee	APPEARANCES				GOALS			
			Lge	FL Cup	FA Cup	Others	Lge	FL Cup	FA Cup	Others
Blackburn Rovers*	7.91	£350,000	1							

MUSTOE Robin (Robbie)

Born: Witney,
28 August 1968

Height: 5'10"

Weight: 10.8

Position/Skill Factor: An athletic midfielder who can run all day. Loves a challenge, he is always looking to get into the opposition's penalty area.

Career History: Born locally, he came through Oxford United's junior and reserve team ranks, before signing professional forms in the 1986 close season. Called up for first team duty, he made his FL debut when coming on as a sub at Norwich City on 29 November 1986, but it was not until late 1987-88 that he began to play fairly regularly, as the club sought to find the right midfield blend. Unfortunately, United were relegated to the Second Division at the end of the season, but over the following two terms he had improved to such a degree that Middlesbrough, after just escaping relegation to the Third Division and wishing to tighten up in midfield, signed him during the summer of 1990. The move proved to be an unqualified success as he recorded 41 League appearances, but for the club, the season ended in disappointment in the Play-Offs. Played a major part in "Boro's" fine season in 1991-92, assisting the team to the Semi-Final of the League Cup and the Fifth Round of the FA Cup. Sadly, his season came to a premature end when injured in the League Cup Semi-Final second leg against Manchester United, which "Boro" lost only after extra time. He played no further part in the promotion campaign as the club climbed up the table to second place and automatic promotion.

Clubs	Signing Date	Transfer Fee	APPEARANCES				GOALS			
			Lge	FL Cup	FA Cup	Others	Lge	FL Cup	FA Cup	Others
Oxford United	7.86	–	78+13	2	2	3	10			
Middlesbrough*	7.90	£375,000	67+4	13+1	6	5+1	6	4		

MYERS Andrew (Andy) John

Born: Hounslow,
3 November 1973

Height: 5'9"

Weight: 12.6

International Honours:
E Yth

Position/Skill Factor: Can play at left-back or along the left side of midfield. A very good competitor, he has great pace and ability.

Career History: Only with Chelsea as a trainee since July 1990, he made his FL debut at Stamford Bridge when coming on as a sub for Damian Matthew against Luton Town on 6 April 1991, two months before signing professional forms. The youngest Chelsea debutant since Tommy Langley in 1974, before being superceded by Ian Pearce just over a month later, he was a regular choice for the England Youth team in 1990-91. Made his first full appearance for Chelsea, in place of Dennis Wise, against Liverpool in October 1991 and scored their second goal in a 2-2 draw. Later in the season, enjoyed two short runs at left-back and seems certain to be Chelsea's first choice in years to come.

Clubs	Signing Date	Transfer Fee	APPEARANCES				GOALS			
			Lge	FL Cup	FA Cup	Others	Lge	FL Cup	FA Cup	Others
Chelsea*	6.91	–	9+5	0+1	2	1	1			

NAYIM Mohamed Ali Amar

Born: Ceuta, Morocco,
5 November 1966

Height: 5'8"

Weight: 11.4

International Honours:
Moroccan Int

Position/Skill Factor: Very skilful left sided midfield player with an excellent first touch. Sees passes early and delivers good crosses for oncoming forwards. Clever creator of chances.

Career History: A reserve team player for Spanish League club, Barcelona, under Terry Venables before following his former manager to Tottenham Hotspur early in 1988-89. After leaving the Spanish giants, Venables had returned to England to manage "Spurs", but when negotiating the transfer of Gary Lineker, he also persuaded Nayim to come to England, initially on a loan basis. Made his FL debut at White Hart Lane against Norwich City on 21 February 1989 and scored in his second match, a 2-0 win at Southampton. The move was made permanent in the summer of 1989, when the transfer of Lineker was also secured. Found it hard to adjust to life in the Football League at first and spent his early months in and out of the side, but in the latter half of 1989-90, his improved form finally warranted a regular first team place. Made 32 League appearances in 1990-91 and won an FA Cup winners medal after coming on as a sub in Tottenham's 2-1 victory over Nottingham Forest. A regular first team performer in the first half of "Spurs'" disappointing 1991-92 campaign, his appearances became more intermittent after the turn of the year. Perhaps he has still to realise the full potential Terry Venables saw in him at Barcelona.

Clubs	Signing Date	Transfer Fee	APPEARANCES				GOALS			
			Lge	FL Cup	FA Cup	Others	Lge	FL Cup	FA Cup	Others
Tottenham Hotspur*	11.88	£250,000	80+14	9+6	3+3	7	8	3	1	

NDLOVU Peter

Born: Bulawayo,
Zimbabwe,
25 February 1973

Height: 5'8"

Weight: 10.12

International Honours:
Zimbabwe Int

Position/Skill Factor: A forward with great pace, he shows real skill on the ball and looks to be an exciting player when in full flow.

Career History: A Zimbabwe international from the age of 15, he was first noted by Coventry City during their summer tour of that country in 1990. Invited for a trial, he signed a contract the following summer. Soon given a first team opportunity, making his FL debut away to Queens Park Rangers on 24 August 1991, as a substitute. In his fifth game, also as substitute, away to League Champions, Arsenal, he scored a superb breakaway solo goal to clinch the points for Coventry — a remarkable entry to big time football. Scored another spectacular goal — the winner — against Aston Villa a few weeks later. Apart from these highlights he struggled, as did all of Coventry's forwards in 1991-92 and he was rested after December, not returning to first team duty until the closing weeks. With stronger support he could prove to be an excellent acquisition and a star of the future.

Clubs	Signing Date	Transfer Fee	APPEARANCES				GOALS			
			Lge	FL Cup	FA Cup	Others	Lge	FL Cup	FA Cup	Others
Coventry City*	7.91	£10,000	9+14	2		0+1	2			

NETHERCOTT Stuart

Born: Ilford, 21 March 1973

Height: 5'9" Weight: 12.4

Position/Skill Factor: Extremely competitive central defender who is strong both in the air and on the ground. Specialises in kicking long balls into the areas behind the opposing full-backs.

Career History: Joined Tottenham Hotspur as a trainee in July 1989, turning professional two years later. Not expected to make an appearance in "Spurs'" first team for a year or two, he nevertheless had an early baptism in the Football League on loan to Fourth Division Maidstone United, making his FL debut on 7 September 1991 at Scunthorpe United. He remained with the Kent club for three months before returning to White Hart Lane and later had a shorter loan spell with Fourth Division newcomers, Barnet.

Clubs	Signing Date	Transfer Fee	APPEARANCES				GOALS			
			Lge	FL Cup	FA Cup	Others	Lge	FL Cup	FA Cup	Others
Tottenham Hotspur*	7.91	–								
Maidstone United	9.91	Loan	13			1	1			
Barnet	2.92	Loan	3							

NEVIN Patrick (Pat) Kevin
Francis Michael

Born: Glasgow, 6 September 1963

Height: 5'6" Weight: 10.0

International Honours: S Yth, S "U21"-5, S"B", S-14

Position/Skill Factor: An old fashioned winger and a bundle of tricks, who creates chances for others with his mazy runs. One of the game's real entertainers and at his best, reminiscent of Charlie Cooke, Chelsea's wizard of the dribble in the 1960s.

Career History: Signed from Scottish junior side, Gartcosh United, he made several appearances for Clyde from the subs' bench, before playing his first full game against Cowdenbeath in November 1981. His good form in two season with Clyde alerted Chelsea and they moved quickly for him in the 1983 close season, to provide ammunition for a new strike force of Kerry Dixon and David Speedie. Made his FL debut at Sheffield Wednesday on 17 September 1983 and immediately settled into the side, playing 38 League games and scoring 14 goals and winning a Second Division Championship medal, as Chelsea cruised into the top bracket. During his five years in London, he became the idol of the crowd at Stamford Bridge and his great talent was finally rewarded at full international level when Scotland introduced him from the subs' bench against Romania on 26 March 1986. Following the "Blues'" relegation to the Second Division in 1987-89, he was sold to big spenders, Everton and lined up alongside another big money signing, Tony Cottee, in a 4-0 win against Newcastle United on the opening day of the 1988-89 season. A knee injury sustained in his third game for Everton ruled him out until Christmas and he made only 20 full League appearances that season, although he did play in the 3-2 defeat at the hands of the club's local rivals, Liverpool, in the FA Cup Final. Again battled against injury during the following season and it wasn't until 1990-91 that the Everton fans saw him at his best. It was not enough, however, for Everton manager Howard Kendall, who signed Robert Warzycha and then Mark Ward to replace him and he spent most of the 1991-92 on the sidelines, the majority of his limited appearances being as substitute, before being loaned to Merseyside neighbours, Tranmere Rovers. Although not good enough for Everton, he was included in the Scotland squad competing in the European Championship Finals in Sweden and made two substitute appearances against Germany and the CIS as the side showed impressive form, before going out of the tournament.

Clubs	Signing Date	Transfer Fee	APPEARANCES				GOALS			
			Lge	FL Cup	FA Cup	Others	Lge	FL Cup	FA Cup	Others
Chelsea	7.83	£95,000	190+3	25+1	8+1	13	36	5	1	4
Everton*	7.88	£925,000	81+28	10+1	12+5	8+3	16	2	2	1
Tranmere Rovers	3.92	Loan	8							

NEWELL Michael (Mike) Colin

Born: Liverpool,
27 January 1965

Height: 6'0"

Weight: 11.0

International Honours:
E "U21"-4, E"B"

Position/Skill Factor: Strong running striker. Good in the air, he competes well on the ground and holds the ball up until others are at hand.

Career History: Formerly a Liverpool junior, he was not offered terms at Anfield and made his FL debut, whilst on trial with Crewe Alexandra, at home to Swindon Town on 8 October 1983. Surprisingly, in view of his subsequent progress, he did not impress the "Alex" manager, Dario Gradi, who has probably developed more young talent than any manager in the game today and he moved on for another trial with Wigan Athletic. Did enough to earn a contract, but despite winning a regular place in 1984-85, was not a consistent scorer until 1985-86 when he netted 16 FL goals in 24 games — form which persuaded Luton Town to sign him in mid-season. Took the leap from Third to First Division football in his stride and in 1986-87 he was ever present to joint top score with 12 FL goals. Soon after, he was signed by David Pleat for Second Division Leicester City and scarcely missed a match in his two seasons at Filbert Street, top scoring with 13 FL goals in 1988-89. By this time he was being talked of as a future England player, although his modest scoring ratio belied his reputation. Returned to the First Division and his native city, in the summer of 1989, when he joined Everton for a massive fee. Although he went straight into the "Toffees'" team at the expense of Tony Cottee, lack of goals resulted in him losing his place to the latter later in the season. 1990-91 also proved to be another "in and out" season for him as manager Howard Kendall alternated between Cottee and Newell, without getting the best from either of them. Returned to the team in September 1991, but without showing any improvement in his scoring form and Everton decided to recoup their investment when Kenny Dalglish made an offer to take him to Blackburn Rovers for the same valuation as when Everton first signed him. Scored on his debut for Rovers and was showing some useful form when injured in February, prompting Dalglish to sign two more strikers, Roy Wegerle and Duncan Shearer. Returned to first team duty in April to assist Rovers through the critical end of season games and the Play-Offs. Scored a vital goal to level the scores in the first-leg match against Derby (which Rovers eventually won 4-2) and in the Play-Off Final against Leicester, he struck the only goal from the penalty spot, to bring top level football back to Ewood Park for the first time since 1966.

Clubs	Signing Date	Transfer Fee	APPEARANCES				GOALS			
			Lge	FL Cup	FA Cup	Others	Lge	FL Cup	FA Cup	Others
Crewe Alexandra	9.83	–	3							
Wigan Athletic	10.83	–	64+8	6	8	5+1	25	1	6	3
Luton Town	1.86		62+1		5		18		1	
Leicester City	9.87	£350,000	81	9	2	4	21	5		
Everton	6.89	£1,100,000	48+20	7+3	6+2	6	15	4		2
Blackburn Rovers*	11.91	£1,100,000								

NEWHOUSE Aiden Robert

Born: Wallasey, 23 May 1972

Height: 6'0" Weight: 12.0

International Honours: E Sch, E Yth

Position/Skill Factor: Striker with two useful feet and good ability on the ball. Brings his team-mates into the game with astute passes. Is at his best when he can get into wide positions.

Career History: Joined Chester City on associated schoolboy forms in October 1986, prior to starring for the

England boy's team. Became the club's youngest ever player when he made his FL debut at Bury on 7 May 1988, two months before signing as a trainee on leaving school in July 1988. Something of a sensation in 1988-89, he was a regular member of Chester's first team squad at the age of 16. Turned professional after his 17th birthday and was an automatic selection in the first two months of 1989-90, until rested as his team struggled at the foot of the table. Ironically, he was not in the first team when First Division Wimbledon signed him, although his potential was obvious. Since joining the London side, he has continued to be used sparingly, mainly in a subs' capacity, but is still young and is undoubtedly one of the players that Wimbledon will be pinning their hopes on in the near future.

Clubs	Signing Date	Transfer Fee	APPEARANCES				GOALS			
			Lge	FL Cup	FA Cup	Others	Lge	FL Cup	FA Cup	Others
Chester City	7.89	–	29+15	5+1	0+2	2+3	6			1
Wimbledon*	2.90	£100,000	7+15	0+1	2		2			

NEWMAN Richard (Ricky) Adrian

Born: Guildford, 5 August 1970

Height: 5'10" Weight: 11.0

Position: Midfielder.

Career History: Signed professional for Crystal Palace in January 1988 directly from school, although not previously registered with the club on associated forms. Waiting patiently for over four years at Selhurst Park, he has yet to receive a first team call up. However, he finally made his FL debut when on loan to Maidstone United at Northampton Town on 3 March 1992 and impressed sufficiently for Palace to offer him a new contract in the summer of 1992.

Clubs	Signing Date	Transfer Fee	APPEARANCES				GOALS			
			Lge	FL Cup	FA Cup	Others	Lge	FL Cup	FA Cup	Others
Crystal Palace*	1.88	–								
Maidstone United	2.92	Loan	9+1				1			

NEWMAN Robert (Rob) Nigel

Born: Bradford-on-Avon, 13 December 1963

Height: 6'2"

Weight: 12.0

Position/Skill Factor: Utility player who can play in midfield, centre-back or at full-back. Good in the air and is always dangerous at set plays. Also, a direct free-kick specialist.

Career History: Came up through the ranks at Bristol City, first as an associated schoolboy (October 1979) and then as an apprentice (June 1980), before becoming a professional. Made his FL debut at Ashton Gate against Fulham on 6 February 1982, following the departure of eight experienced players whose long term contracts on First Division salaries were threatening the very existence of a club about to drop into the Fourth Division. He immediately settled down as a regular and proved his versatility, playing in five different positions during 1983-84, as the club gained promotion to the Third Division in fourth place. An ever present in 1988-89 and again the following season as the "Robins" moved into the Second Division as runners-up, he increased his reputation for scoring vital goals. At the end of 1990-91, a season that consolidated City's Second Division status, he had played 147 consecutive League games and was by far and away the club's longest serving player. Signed for First Division Norwich City, in the summer of 1991 and although it was a disappointing one for the "Canaries", he enjoyed an excellent first season personally, playing in all but one of his club's 54 match programme and scoring several vital goals from midfield.

Clubs	Signing Date	Transfer Fee	APPEARANCES				GOALS			
			Lge	FL Cup	FA Cup	Others	Lge	FL Cup	FA Cup	Others
Bristol City	10.81	–	382+12	29+1	27	33	52	2	2	5
Norwich City*	7.91	£600,000	41	5	6	1	7	1	1	

NEWSOME Jonathan (Jon)

Born: Sheffield, 6 September 1970

Height: 6'2"

Weight: 13.11

Position/Skill Factor: A good all-round full-back. Although capable of using the ball well and supporting the attack, as a defender he is not easy to pass, having a quick recovery rate and being an excellent and decisive tackler.

Career History: Home grown talent, he started at Sheffield Wednesday as an associated schoolboy in June 1985 and on leaving school in July 1987, he joined the staff as a trainee, before turning professional. made his FL debut at Arsenal on 9 September 1989, when he was introduced as a sub during a 5-0 drubbing and then had a short run in the number two shirt before the club signed Roland Nilsson. With John Harkes, Viv Anderson and Nilsson all vying for the right-back slot, he made only one

League appearance in 1990-91. Surprisingly allowed to leave Hillsborough in the summer of 1991, along with another talented "Owls'" youngster, David Wetherall; they signed for former Wednesday manager Howard Wilkinson at Leeds United as investments for the future. He played little part in United's Championship challenge until March, when he deputised for the injured Mel Sterland. With brilliant last-ditch and scrupulous tackling, he saved his team on several occasions and his headed goal from a free-kick in the vital penultimate fixture away to Sheffield United were a major factor in Leeds' unlikely Championship triumph. His ten FL appearances in 1991-92 were one short of qualification for a Championship medal, but Wilkinson appealed to the Football League and, happily, they agreed that he had richly earned one.

Clubs	Signing Date	Transfer Fee	APPEARANCES				GOALS			
			Lge	FL Cup	FA Cup	Others	Lge	FL Cup	FA Cup	Others
Sheffield Wednesday	7.81	–	6+1	3						
Leeds United*	6.91	£150,000	7+3			1	2			

NEWTON Edward (Eddie) John Ikem

Born: Hammersmith, 13 December 1971

Height: 5'11" Weight: 11.2

International Honours: E Yth

Position/Skill Factor: A midfielder who has already played in a number of different positions, he can use both feet and passes well.

Career History: Joined Chelsea as a trainee in August 1988, having been an associated schoolboy since November 1986 and turned professional two years later. Played in a variety of positions in the "Blues'" youth and reserve teams, including central defence, midfield and up front. Loaned out to Fourth Division Cardiff City in January 1992, he made his FL debut at home to Chesterfield on 25 January 1992 and played a major role in launching the "Bluebirds'" challenge for promotion with his dynamic midfield performances, plus four crucial goals. Sadly, it was not quite enough, as the Welsh club finished three points short of a Play-Off place. At the end of his three month loan period he returned to Stamford Bridge and was rewarded with his first call up to the Chelsea team in the last game of the season away to Everton. Coming on as a second-half substitute, he beat Neville Southall with a stunning 35 yard cross shot to reduce the deficit to 2-1. Clearly a player with an exciting future ahead of him.

Clubs	Signing Date	Transfer Fee	APPEARANCES				GOALS			
			Lge	FL Cup	FA Cup	Others	Lge	FL Cup	FA Cup	Others
Chelsea*	5.90	–	0+1				1			
Cardiff City	1.92	Loan	16				4			

NICHOLLS Ryan Rhys

Born: Cardiff, 10 May 1973

Height: 5'10" Weight: 11.0

International Honours: W Sch

Position/Skill Factor: Midfielder with good ability. A lovely passer of the ball, he can beat defenders to set up goal scoring chances for others.

Career History: Former Welsh schoolboy international who first joined Leeds United on associated forms in January 1989, before signing on as a trainee in September 1990. After turning professional during the 1991 close season, he was out injured for most of 1991-92.

Clubs	Signing Date	Transfer Fee	APPEARANCES				GOALS			
			Lge	FL Cup	FA Cup	Others	Lge	FL Cup	FA Cup	Others
Leeds United*	7.91	–								

NICOL Stephen (Steve)

Born: Irvine, 11 December 1961

Height: 5'10" Weight: 12.0

International Honours: S "U21"-14, S-27

Position/Skill Factor: A versatile player who never lets the side down, whether at full-back, centre-back or in midfield. Very competitive, he is a good passer, both short and long and also likes to get up in support of the attack.

Career History: A stalwart of the Liverpool team since 1984, although his career has been punctuated by injuries, particularly in 1986-87 and 1989-90, he has played a full part in the "Reds'" almost unbroken run of success over the last ten years, winning four League Championship medals in 1983-84, 1985-86, 1987-88 and 1989-90, and three FA Cup winners medals in 1986, 1989 and 1992, plus a losers medal in 1988. Before coming south to join Liverpool early in 1981-82, he spent just over two seasons with Ayr United, having impressed at full-back after signing from a local boy's club. Had to wait nearly 12 months for his FL debut at Birmingham City on 31 August 1982 and made only three more appearances, two of them as a substitute, until earning a more permanent place in midfield the following year. Came into the side in 1983-84 when Craig Johnston was injured and ended the season with League Championship and European Cup winners medals. Fortunately for him, his miss in the penalty "shoot out" against Roma did not prove disastrous, as Liverpool won 4-2 to bring the trophy back to England. Played on the right side of midfield until taking over the right-back position from Phil Neal in October 1985, but following the signing of Barry Venison, he alternated between full-back and midfield and scored his first and only senior "hat-trick" away to Newcastle United in September 1987. In 1988-89, he was switched to central defence, following injuries to Gary Gillespie and Alan Hansen and performed so well in this emergency role that he was voted the Football Writers' Association Footballer of the Year in 1989. Made his international debut for Scotland on 12 September 1984 against Yugoslavia at Hampden Park (a remarkable 6-1 victory for the Scots) and has been a fairly regular selection since playing in the 1986 World Cup Finals in Mexico. One of the few senior players at Anfield to escape long-term injury in 1991-92, he appeared in a variety of positions. Starting out at right-back, he switched to midfield after the emergence of Rob Jones and then to central defence to cover the absence of Nicky Tanner, but had reverted to full-back when winning another FA Cup winners medal at the end of the season. An innocent victim of a constant "club versus country" tug of war between Liverpool and Scotland, he made what was probably his last Scottish appearance against Switzerland in September 1991.

Clubs	Signing Date	Transfer Fee	APPEARANCES				GOALS			
			Lge	FL Cup	FA Cup	Others	Lge	FL Cup	FA Cup	Others
Liverpool*	10.81	£300,000	265+11	22	45	30+2	35	4	3	3

NILSSON Nils Lennart Roland

Born: Helsingborg, Sweden, 27 November 1963

Height: 6'0" Weight: 11.6

International Honours: Swedish Int

Position/Skill Factor: Right-back. Typical continental defender who passes forward and is confident enough to join up with the attack, whether in-field or wide. Great passer of the ball.

Career History: Swedish international full-back who was signed by Sheffield Wednesday from IFK Gothenburg to fill the right-back position that had remained unfilled since Mel Sterland joined Glasgow Rangers in February 1989. Made his FL debut at Hillsborough against Luton Town on 9 December 1989 and apart from missing just one match, held his place for the remainder of the season. However, his presence was not enough to save the club from being relegated to the Second Division, following a run of five defeats in the last six games. With the club unbeaten for the first 14 games of 1990-91, he was injured during the next game at Millwall when the "Owls" were leading 2-0. Wednesday were unable to reorganise defensively after his departure and lost 4-2 and the injury was serious enough to keep him out of the team until the following April. Played in ten of the last 11 matches as Wednesday made sure of promotion back to the First Division at the first time of asking and as an added bonus, won a League Cup winners medal, when starring in the "Owls'" 1-0 victory over Manchester United at Wembley. Played in all but five of Wednesday's excellent 1991-92 campaign when they finished in third place and qualified for the UEFA Cup. Starred for Sweden in the European Championship Finals in 1992, appearing in all four matches, as the host nation went out in the Semi-Finals to Germany after earlier beating England.

Clubs	Signing Date	Transfer Fee	APPEARANCES				GOALS			
			Lge	FL Cup	FA Cup	Others	Lge	FL Cup	FA Cup	Others
Sheffield Wednesday*	11.89	£375,000	81	5	4	2	1			

OAKES Michael Christian

Born: Northwich, 30 October 1973

Height: 6'1" Weight: 12.7

Position: Goalkeeper.

Career History: Son of Alan, the former Manchester City wing-half and record appearance holder, he joined Aston Villa as an associated schoolboy in February 1991, before signing as a professional early in 1992. Started as an outfield player until being converted to goalkeeper. Still very much in the learning stage, he has yet to appear in the reserve side.

Clubs	Signing Date	Transfer Fee	APPEARANCES				GOALS			
			Lge	FL Cup	FA Cup	Others	Lge	FL Cup	FA Cup	Others
Aston VIlla*	2.92	–								

O'CONNELL Patrick Joseph

Born: Dublin, 7 October 1973

Height: 5'9" Weight: 11.12

Position/Skill Factor: Young striker with good ability on the ball.

Career History: A promising young player who has yet to make the first team, he was signed by Leeds United during the 1991 close season from Home Farm of the League of Ireland.

Clubs	Signing Date	Transfer Fee	APPEARANCES				GOALS			
			Lge	FL Cup	FA Cup	Others	Lge	FL Cup	FA Cup	Others
Leeds United*	7.91	£3,000								

O'CONNOR Martyn

Born: Walsall, 10 December 1967

Height: 5'9" Weight: 11.2

Position/Skill Factor: Midfield player with two good feet, who can pass both short and long and looks to score from long range free-kicks.

Career History: Another non-League discovery by Crystal Palace's Steve Coppell, he was signed in the 1992 close season after starring for the 1991-92 Beazer Homes League Champions, Bromsgrove Rovers, having previously played for Bloxwich Town.

Clubs	Signing Date	Transfer Fee	APPEARANCES				GOALS			
			Lge	FL Cup	FA Cup	Others	Lge	FL Cup	FA Cup	Others
Crystal Palace*	6.92	£25,000								

OGRIZOVIC (Steve) Steven

Born: Mansfield,
12 September 1957

Height: 6'3"

Weight: 14.7

Position/Skill Factor: Commanding goalkeeper with good positional sense, who seems to fill the goal. Big and brave, with safe hands, he is not afraid to come for crosses. Can volley-kick the ball into the opponents' box.

Career History: The son of an immigrant Yugoslav miner, he was a police cadet playing in a local Mansfield league, before signing professional forms with Chesterfield in the 1977 close season. Made his FL debut in 3-1 win at Port Vale on 20 August 1977 and appeared in the opening 16 matches that season, keeping six clean sheets. His potential was such that he was quickly snapped up by Liverpool to understudy Ray Clemence, but unfortunately, his first game for the club resulted in a 4-2 defeat at Derby County. After only four games in five years at Anfield, he was involved in a straight swap for Bob Wardle, the Shrewsbury Town goalkeeper. Spent two seasons between the posts at Gay Meadow as an ever present and impressed enough for Coventry City to pay a relatively modest sum for his services during the summer of 1984. He made the news on 25 October 1986, as the first City goalkeeper to score a League goal, when his long punt upfield cleared Martin Hodge in the Sheffield Wednesday goal. And it was his grand display in the "Sky Blues'" goal, especially in the first-half, that helped Coventry win the FA Cup for the first time in their history when they beat Tottenham Hotspur 3-2 in 1987. Recognised for his consistency over the years, it was only an injury suffered at Millwall in October 1989 that brought to an end a run of 320 consecutive matches and in eight seasons at Highfield Road he has only been absent on six occasions.

Clubs	Signing Date	Transfer Fee	APPEARANCES				GOALS			
			Lge	FL Cup	FA Cup	Others	Lge	FL Cup	FA Cup	Others
Chesterfield	7.77	–	16	2						
Liverpool	11.77	£70,000	4			1				
Shrewsbury Town	8.82	£70,000	84	7	5					
Coventry City*	6.84	£72,000	316	32	19	11	1			

O'LEARY David Anthony

Born: Stoke Newington, 2 May 1958

Height: 6'1" Weight: 13.2

International Honours: IR-66

Position/Skill Factor: Cool, reliable central defender who makes few mistakes. Very consistent, he takes up good positions when defending, does well in the air and rarely gives the ball away.

Career History: First came to Highbury as an apprentice in May 1973 and within a month of turning professional had made his FL debut for Arsenal at Burnley on 16 August 1975. His talents were soon rewarded with the first of more than 50 international caps for Eire, coming against England on 8 September 1976 at Wembley. In 1979, he won his first club honour as a member of the "Gunners'" side that won the FA Cup when beating Manchester United, 3-2, a result that made up for the 1-0 defeat at the hands of Ipswich Town in the Final, the previous year. 1979-80 was less successful as far as trophies were concerned, as Arsenal's European Cup Winners Cup Final team were beaten on penalties by Spain's Valencia only four days after losing 1-0 to West Ham United in the FA Cup Final. But on a personal front, he had played in three successive FA Cup Finals at Wembley. Lost his place in the Irish team for reasons unknown, for two seasons (1986-88) after Jack Charlton's appointment, but was restored to favour in 1988-89. Surprisingly, he had to wait a further eight years for his next club honour as Arsenal almost swept all before them. A 2-1 victory over Liverpool brought him a League Cup winners medal in 1987 and the following season, although missing a large chunk of it due to injury, he won a League Championship medal, after one of the closest finishes for many a day. Although he made only one substitute appearance less than the 11 full games he played in during 1990-91, at the end of the season he won another League Championship medal when Arsenal regained the title that they had lost to Liverpool in 1989-90. Has now passed George Armstrong's record of 500 League appearances for Arsenal and at 34 he is still an important member of George Graham's squad, often playing a sweeper role, or as the third central defender behind Tony Adams and Steve Bould. Still a regular performer for the Republic of Ireland.

Clubs	Signing Date	Transfer Fee	APPEARANCES				GOALS			
			Lge	FL Cup	FA Cup	Others	Lge	FL Cup	FA Cup	Others
Arsenal*	7.75	–	517+30	66+2	65	26	11	2	3	

OLNEY Ian Douglas

Born: Luton, 17 December 1969

Height: 6'1" Weight: 11.3

International Honours: E Yth, E "U21"-9

Position/Skill Factor: Striker. Good in the air, he pulls away to the far post when team-mates are in crossing positions. Always looking to bring the midfield players into the game.

Career History: First joined Aston Villa as an associated schoolboy in March 1985 and eventually became a trainee on leaving school in July 1986. Made his FL debut at Charlton Athletic on 15 October 1988, three months after signing professional forms and didn't get a proper run in the side until the end of that season. Won a regular place in the side in 1989-90 and finished second in the Villa scoring lists with nine League goals, as the club achieved a magnificent second place in the First Division. However, with keen competition for places in the Villa forward line under Jozef Venglos, he found it difficult to hold down a regular slot in 1990-91. Made only 14 full appearances under the new manager, Ron Atkinson in 1991-92 and was transferred to Oldham Athletic during the summer.

Clubs	Signing Date	Transfer Fee	APPEARANCES				GOALS			
			Lge	FL Cup	FA Cup	Others	Lge	FL Cup	FA Cup	Others
Aston Villa	7.88	–	52+26	17+2	8+1	13+3	16	4	2	1
Oldham Athletic*	5.92	£700,000								

ORLYGSSON Thorvaldur (Toddy)

Born: Odense, Denmark, 2 August 1966

Height: 5'11"

Weight: 10.8

International Honours: Iceland Int

Position/Skill Factor: An outside-right with good control and plenty of pace.

Career History: An Icelandic international winger, notwithstanding his country of birth, he was signed from Icelandic side, KA Akureyri, making his FL debut almost immediately for Nottingham Forest at home to Southampton on 17 December 1989 and held his place for 11 consecutive League games. Taken off during the game against Coventry City on 10 March 1990, he did not reappear again that season and failed to be give any further chances in 1990-91. Apparently completely forgotten by Brian Clough for two years, he made a surprise return to the first team in April 1992, playing five games at the end of the season, when Forest were missing several players through injury. Obviously hoping that this is a prelude to more opportunities in 1992-93.

Clubs	Signing Date	Transfer Fee	APPEARANCES				GOALS			
			Lge	FL Cup	FA Cup	Others	Lge	FL Cup	FA Cup	Others
Nottingham Forest*	11.89	£175,000	16+1	3	1	0+1	1	1		

OSBORN Simon Edward

Born: Croydon, 19 January 1972

Height: 5'10"

Weight: 11.4

Position/Skill Factor: Has all the essential ingredients required of a good midfield player, with great stamina and is always looking to make an early pass.

Career History: Came to Crystal Palace as a trainee on leaving school in July 1988 and had progressed to the professional ranks by early 1990. Showed enough promise in a Zenith Data Cup game to warrant his FL debut at Selhurst Park, when coming on as a sub during the 1-0 win over Tottenham Hotspur on 17 April 1991. Made good progress in 1991-92 with three separate first team runs in September, December and February, but has still to claim an automatic first team place. With the departure of Andy Gray and Alan Pardew, his big chance should come this season and if allowed to develop, he could become a very good player.

Clubs	Signing Date	Transfer Fee	APPEARANCES				GOALS			
			Lge	FL Cup	FA Cup	Others	Lge	FL Cup	FA Cup	Others
Crystal Palace*	1.90	–	15+3	4		1+3	2			

O'SHAUGHNESSY Brendan

Born: Bury, 20 September 1973

Height: 5'9" Weight: 10.10

Position: Left-back.

Career History: A recent professional signing for Blackburn Rovers during the 1992 close season, having previously been at Ewood Park as an associated schoolboy (June 1988) and as a trainee (July 1990). No first team experience as yet.

Clubs	Signing Date	Transfer Fee	APPEARANCES				GOALS			
			Lge	FL Cup	FA Cup	Others	Lge	FL Cup	FA Cup	Others
Blackburn Rovers*	6.92	–								

PALLISTER Gary Andrew

Born: Ramsgate, 30 June 1965

Height: 6'4" Weight: 13.0

International Honours: FL Rep, E"B", E-5

Position/Skill Factor: Central defender who is a tower of strength in the air and has good pace. A good passer for such a big man, he is comfortable when bringing the ball out of defence and is dangerous at set plays.

Career History: Signed by Middlesbrough at the age of 19, after impressing with his performances for Northern League side, Billingham Town. However, he was not introduced to the League side until the beginning of the following season when he made his FL debut at Wimbledon on 17 August 1985. A 3-0 defeat was hardly an auspicious start for an aspiring youngster, especially when "Boro" were beaten 2-0 by Mansfield Town, four days later and he was loaned out to Darlington for a short spell. Middlesbrough were relegated from the Second Division at the end of that season, but bounced straight back again as runners-up in 1986-87. By now a regular, he was a rock at the heart of the defence, making 44 League appearances. The following season, he was again influential as an ever present in helping the club back to the First Division, via the Play-Offs and was rewarded by England with a full international cap against Hungary in Budapest on 27 April 1988. Unfortunately, his consistent performances couldn't prevent an immediate return to the Second Division and after playing in the first three games of the 1989-90 season for "Boro", he was signed by Manchester United for what was a record transfer fee between two Football League teams and remains one for

a defender. With such a large fee and great expectations surrounding him, he took time to settle down with United and his Old Trafford debut was an anti-climax when he conceded a penalty as United went down 2-0 to Norwich City. However, he began to forge a strong partnership with Steve Bruce and was a key player in the "Red Devils'" march to the FA Cup Final and an eventual 1-0 victory over Crystal Palace in 1990. He finished the campaign as United's "Player of the Year" and 1990-91 brought more success, for after being in the side that lost

1-0 in the League Cup Final to Sheffield Wednesday, he won a European Cup Winners Cup medal, following United's 2-1 victory over Barcelona. A mainstay of United's successful, although ultimately disappointing 1991-92 season, he won League Cup Winners medal, but missed out on League Championship honours. Voted "Player of the Year" by his fellow professionals in the PFA Awards of 1992, he was recalled to the England squad and played in England's first game of 1991-92 against West Germany, which was lost to a "free header" from a corner. Significantly, neither Pallister nor his United colleague, Paul Parker, have been selected since.

Clubs	Signing Date	Transfer Fee	APPEARANCES				GOALS			
			Lge	FL Cup	FA Cup	Others	Lge	FL Cup	FA Cup	Others
Middlesbrough	11.84	–	156	10	10	13	5		1	
Darlington	10.85	Loan	7							
Manchester United*	8.89	£2,300,000	108+3	20	14	13+1	4			1

PALMER Carlton Lloyd

Born: Rowley Regis, 5 December 1965

Height: 6'2" Weight: 11.10

International Honours: E "U21"-7, E"B", E-7

Position/Skill Factor: Can play equally as well either at full-back, in central defence or in midfield. His long legs make him a difficult opponent to pass and at the same time, he can run all day. Often produces tremendous runs from midfield into the penalty area.

Career History: Came to West Bromwich Albion on a YTS scheme in August 1983, after leaving school and turned professional just before Christmas in 1984. Made

his FL debut at Newcastle United on 16 September, 1985, when coming on for Robbie Dennison in a 4-1 defeat. But when Steve Hunt left the club in March 1986, Carlton stepped into his shirt, only to face the prospect of Second Division soccer the following season as Albion found themselves relegated. He continued to hold down a regular place in a struggling side, until signed by his former manager Ron Atkinson for Sheffield Wednesday in February 1989. After settling down well in his first full season, the club, having appeared to have preserved its status, faltered at the last hurdle, losing five of its last six games and were relegated to the Second Division. He only missed two matches during 1990-91 as the "Owls" came back to the First Division at the first time of asking, in third place, but tragically was injured and thus unavailable for Wednesday's surprise League Cup Final victory over Manchester United. At the Hawthorns, he alternated between full-back, central defence and midfield. At Hillsborough, however, he immediately settled into central midfield, forming a partnership with John Sheridan which transformed Wednesday from a typically prosaic and uninspiring First Division side into one of the "classiest" passing teams in the Football League. Confident and composed on the ball, he is not afraid to carry it forward to create penalty box scoring opportunities for his colleagues. An infrequent scorer himself, he caused a sensation in an early season game in 1991-92 by scoring a first-half hat-trick of goals from open play against Queens Park Rangers. It was merely the prelude to his finest season to date, playing in every single game of Wednesday's highly successful season, which was suitably rewarded by a call up to the England squad at the end of the season. Made his international debut against the CIS in Moscow and then played in three subsequent games, performing both in midfield and the unfamiliar role of "sweeper". Included in the England squad for the European Championship Finals, he was one of the few genuine successes of England's generally lack-lustre performances, despite the unjustified and inexplicable denigration and belittling of his talents by some sections of the media.

| Clubs | Signing Date | Transfer Fee | APPEARANCES | | | | GOALS | | | |
			Lge	FL Cup	FA Cup	Others	Lge	FL Cup	FA Cup	Others
W.B.A.	12.84	–	114+7	7+1	4	6	4	1		
Sheffield Wednesday*	2.89	£750,000	134	15	8	5	8			1

PALMER Roger Neil

Born: Manchester, 30 January 1959

Height: 5'10"

Weight: 11.0

Position/Skill Factor: Striker, who can also star in midfield. An excellent worker, he can play in most attacking positions and will always give a sound performance.

Career History: Not only Oldham's all time record goal

scorer, he is one of their greatest ever players, playing a major role in their rise from a struggling unfashionable Second Division outfit to one of the most impressive footballing teams in the country. Manchester City first spotted his potential in local schools soccer and signed him on associated schoolboy forms in January 1974. Following a football apprenticeship (May 1975), he turned professional and just under a year later made his FL debut at Middlesbrough on 27 December 1977. Despite showing his ability to score at the top level, he was given little opportunity at Maine Road and during 1980-81, signed for Oldham Athletic, who were seeking a replacement for Simon Stainrod. He proved extremely consistent as Athletic strove for promotion to the First Division throughout the 1980s and during 1989-90 he broke Eric Gemmill's long standing club goal scoring record of 110 League goals. After a marvellous 1989-90, when the club went so close to cup glory, losing in the FA Cup Semi-Final to Manchester United after a replay and then reaching Wembley only to be beaten in the League Cup Final by Nottingham Forest, promotion success was just around the corner. Although he was injured during the West Ham United game at Boundary Park on 29 March 1991 and was not fit enough to play again in 1990-91, he won a Second Division Championship medal as the "Latics" finally made it to the top flight after a wait of nearly 70 years. His goal scoring ratio of one in every three games, is truly remarkable considering that for most of his Boundary Park career he has been deployed not as an "out and out" striker, but on the right flank. After ten years out of the top flight, he richly deserved the opportunity to play there again and happily regained fitness and returned to first team action in October 1991, although no longer an automatic first team choice in view of his advancing years. Playing on the right flank, he continued to demonstrate his ability to score vital goals.

| Clubs | Signing Date | Transfer Fee | APPEARANCES | | | | GOALS | | | |
			Lge	FL Cup	FA Cup	Others	Lge	FL Cup	FA Cup	Others
Manchester City	1.77	–	22+9	3+3		4	9	1		1
Oldham Athletic*	11.80	£70,000	413+28	34+2	19+4	5+2	141	10	5	1

PALMER Stephen (Steve) Leonard

Born: Brighton, 31 March 1968

Height: 6'1" Weight: 12.7

Position/Skill Factor: Midfielder who can also play in central defence. Strong and willing, he is an ideal anchor man. He can run all day long, tackles well and wins more than his fair share of balls in the air.

Career History: One of very few footballers who have come into professional soccer from Cambridge University. Signed for Ipswich Town in the 1989 close season, following an impressive display in the Varsity match and made his FL debut at Oxford United, ironically, on 23 September 1989. By a strange coincidence, one of his opponents in the 1989 Varsity match, New Zealander Ceri Evans, also signed professional forms — for Oxford United. Only played two more matches that season, but in 1990-91, after a long period on the bench, he finally got a run from December 1990 until April 1991, firstly deputising for Brian Gayle in central defence and later in midfield. Still not a regular in 1991-92, although he did play a part in Ipswich's Second Division Championship campaign with another first team opportunity from November 1991 through to March 1992, before giving way to Paul Goddard.

Clubs	Signing Date	Transfer Fee	APPEARANCES				GOALS			
			Lge	FL Cup	FA Cup	Others	Lge	FL Cup	FA Cup	Others
Ipswich Town*	8.89	–	37+14	2	6	3+2	1			

Clubs	Signing Date	Transfer Fee	APPEARANCES				GOALS			
			Lge	FL Cup	FA Cup	Others	Lge	FL Cup	FA Cup	Others
Luton Town	5.83	–	31+11	1+3	6+2		3	1		
Hull City	2.86	£72,000	82+2	5	4	2	8			1
Nottingham Forest	3.88	£260,000	99+4	22+1	16	8	17	4	5	3
Aston Villa*	11.91	£650,000	25		5		1		1	

PARKER Garry Stuart

Born: Oxford,
7 September 1965

Height: 5'10"

Weight: 11.0

International Honours:
E Yth, E "U21"-6, E"B"

Position/Skill Factor: Midfield player, who will not be hurried and hates to give the ball away. A quality passer, he has a lovely touch and is a great striker of the ball.

Career History: Was an associated schoolboy with Queens Park Rangers (September 1980), before signing for Luton Town as an apprentice in June 1982, on leaving school. Turned professional for the "Hatters" and immediately made his FL debut at Manchester United on 9 May 1983, but was never able to win a regular place in the Town's midfield. Looking to play first team football, he joined Second Division Hull City in 1985-86 and missed very few games for the "Tigers" in two years at Boothferry Park, during which time he also won the first of his England Under 21 caps. With the bigger clubs now watching him, he signed for Nottingham Forest at the tail end of 1987-88 and made just one League appearance that term, before breaking into the team midway through 1988-89. After securing a first team place on the left side of midfield, as the club maintained third place in the League, he also won a League Cup winners medal, following the 3-1 victory over his old club, Luton Town. Only missed two games as Neil Webb's replacement in central midfield during 1989-90 and picked up a second successive League Cup winners medal when playing in the Forest team that defeated Oldham Athletic, 1-0. But in 1990-91, as a member of the side that lost 2-1 to Tottenham Hotspur in the FA Cup Final, it proved to be third time unlucky on the famous Wembley turf. In terms of consistency, he was absent on just five occasions from the Forest team during the last 100 League matches through to the end of the 1990-91 season, a record bettered only by Nigel Clough over the same period. Lost his place to Scot Gemmill at the start of 1991-92, but returned to first team duty in September. After losing his place again, however, he was transferred to Aston Villa in November. Although he became a regular first choice with Villa, he had a quiet first season at Villa Park and his team a disappointing one, suffering from a goal drought.

PARKER Paul Andrew

Born: West Ham, 4 April 1964

Height: 5'7" Weight: 10.9

International Honours: E Yth, E "U21"-8, E"B", E-17

Position/Skill Factor: Right-back, or central defender, who climbs very well in the air for his size. With plenty of pace, he has a very fast recovery rate and is difficult to beat. Reads the game well and always appears to have plenty of time on the ball.

Career History: Crossed London to sign associated schoolboy forms with Fulham in June 1978 and on leaving school he became an apprentice (May 1980). Progressing through the club's youth side, he made his FL debut at Craven Cottage against Reading on 25 April 1981, following his 17th birthday and while still an apprentice. He duly turned professional a year later and it wasn't until 1983-84 that he began to hold down a regular place in the side. At the end of 1985-86, however, Fulham were relegated to the Third Division and although he remained at the club during the following season, it was patently obvious that he deserved a higher class of football. Neighbours, Queens Park Rangers, finally gave him that opportunity in the 1987 close season and he made an impressive debut for them on the opening day of the 1987-88 campaign in a 3-0 win at West Ham United. Ever present throughout his first season at Loftus Road, he was rewarded the following year by England for continued consistent club displays with his first full cap, when coming on as a sub against Albania. Had an impressive World Cup in 1990, but although scoring his first goal for Rangers after 140 appearances, his 1990-91 season was disrupted by injury problems and he made only 13 League appearances. Transferred to Manchester United in the 1991 close season, he established a niche at right-back. Again troubled by injuries in the second half of the season, he made a comeback for the League Cup Final, leaving with a winners medal after a 1-0 victory over Nottingham Forest. Subsequent injuries ruled him out of United's critical last four games of the season, in which three defeats cost them the Championship. They also ruled him out of contention for the England squad to the European Championship Finals.

Clubs	Signing Date	Transfer Fee	APPEARANCES				GOALS			
			Lge	FL Cup	FA Cup	Others	Lge	FL Cup	FA Cup	Others
Fulham	4.82	–	140+13	16	11	2	2	1		
Q.P.R.	6.87	£300,000	121+4	14	16	5	1			
Manchester United*	8.91	£2,000,000	24+2	6	3	2				

PARKINSON Gary Anthony

Born: Thornaby, 10 January 1968

Height: 5'10" Weight: 11.11

Position/Skill Factor: Right-back who is a good all-round defender. A strong tackler with two useful feet, he uses the ball well into the front players.

Career History: Although from the north-east, he started as an associated schoolboy at Everton (October 1982) and on leaving school in June 1984, he joined the club on a YTS scheme. However, he didn't stay at Goodison for long and came home to sign professional forms for Middlesbrough, making his FL debut against Port Vale on 23 August 1986 on Hartlepool's Victoria Ground (Ayresome Park being closed by the receivers). Ever present in his first season, a rare and remarkable achievement, playing at right-back, as Middlesbrough were promoted to the Second Division as runners-up, he was a key figure in the club's success. Quickly off the mark in 1987-88, as the "Boro" were immediately promoted into the First Division, through the Play-Offs, he made 35 League appearances after regaining his place following a suspension period. Although he continued to perform most consistently, the club fared less well and by the end of the following season, were back in the Second Division. After losing his place in the side towards the end of 1989-90, to Colin Cooper, who was switched from left-back, he was not selected again, until standing in for the latter towards the end of the season. Back in favour for the start of 1991-92, following the departure of Cooper to Millwall, he lost his place to Curtis Fleming in March and played little part in the closing weeks of the campaign when "Boro" clinched promotion to the Premier League.

Clubs	Signing Date	Transfer Fee	APPEARANCES				GOALS			
			Lge	FL Cup	FA Cup	Others	Lge	FL Cup	FA Cup	Others
Middlesbrough*	1.86	–	190+8	20	17	19	5	1	1	

PARLOUR Raymond (Ray)

Born: Romford, 7 March 1973

Height: 5'10½" Weight: 11.12

International Honours: E "U21"-4

Position/Skill Factor: Clever midfield player with an impressive range of passing skills.

Career History: Joined Arsenal as a trainee in July 1989, having been an associated schoolboy since January 1988 and turned professional in March 1991. Not expected to make a breakthrough in 1991-92, he benefited from a sudden shortage of midfield players at Highbury and was "thrown in at the deep end" by George Graham when selected to make his FL debut at Anfield, away to Liverpool on 29 January 1992. Impressive in the first-half, he unfortunately conceded a penalty in the second session as the "Gunners" went down 2-0. In his second full game away to Wimbledon he scored in the first minute. Selected for the England Under 21 squad at the end of the season.

Clubs	Signing Date	Transfer Fee	APPEARANCES				GOALS			
			Lge	FL Cup	FA Cup	Others	Lge	FL Cup	FA Cup	Others
Arsenal*	3.91	–	2+4				1			

PARROTT Mark Andrew

Born: Cheltenham, 14 March 1971

Height: 5'11" Weight: 11.0

International Honours: E Sch, E Yth

Position: Left-winger.

Career History: Patiently awaits a first team call-up at Aston Villa after three years in the club's professional ranks, having been at Villa Park first as an associated schoolboy (June 1985), before signing as a trainee on leaving school in July 1987.

Clubs	Signing Date	Transfer Fee	APPEARANCES				GOALS			
			Lge	FL Cup	FA Cup	Others	Lge	FL Cup	FA Cup	Others
Aston Villa*	7.89	–								

PATES Colin George

Born: Carshalton, 10 August 1961

Height: 5'11"

Weight: 11.0

International Honours: E Yth

Position/Skill Factor: Classy central defender with a smart left foot. A good passer, he can bring the ball out of defence and release it into midfield.

Career History: Came through the Chelsea junior teams as an apprentice (August 1977), before joining the club's professional ranks and quickly establishing himself in the side. After making his FL debut in a 7-3 "Blues'" victory at Leyton Orient on 10 November 1979, the next major milestone in his career came in 1983-84 when he was an ever present in the Chelsea side that became Second Division Champions. Although forming a very strong defensive partnership with Joe McLaughlin, as the team consolidated its status in the top flight, he lost his place to Steve Wicks during 1987-88 and following a fair start to the season, Chelsea faltered badly and were relegated after losing in the Play-Offs. When Wicks retired through injury, he started 1988-89 as a regular, but was surprisingly transferred to Charlton Athletic in October. The following season, Charlton were relegated to the Second Division, but during the summer they purchased Joe McLaughlin from Chelsea and the two linked up once again. However, the partnership only lasted five months as the club sold him to Arsenal, who were looking for central defensive cover. Has rarely been required at Highbury and was loaned out to Brighton & Hove Albion for a spell during 1990-91. With so many experienced central defenders at Arsenal, his first team opportunities have been few, but he was given a brief run in the team from October to November in 1991-92.

Clubs	Signing Date	Transfer Fee	APPEARANCES				GOALS			
			Lge	FL Cup	FA Cup	Others	Lge	FL Cup	FA Cup	Others
Chelsea	7.79	–	280+1	32	20	13	10			
Charlton Athletic	10.88	£430,000	37+1	3	3					
Arsenal	1.90	£500,000	10+4	2		2				1
Brighton & H.A.*	3.91	Loan	17			3				

PATERSON Scott

Born: Aberdeen, 13 May 1972

Height: 6'1" Weight: 11.9½

Position/Skill Factor: A constructive midfield player with skill on the ball and good passing ability.

Career History: Young Scottish player signed by Liverpool from Aberdeen-based Highland League club, Cove Rangers in March 1992. Only 20 years of age, he is one for the future.

Clubs	Signing Date	Transfer Fee	APPEARANCES				GOALS			
			Lge	FL Cup	FA Cup	Others	Lge	FL Cup	FA Cup	Others
Liverpool*	3.92	£15,000								

PATTERSON Darren James

Born: Belfast, 15 October 1969

Height: 6'1" Weight: 12.0

Position/Skill Factor: Full-back who can play in midfield. A steady, reliable defender, he kicks lovely long balls into the channels and is useful in the air.

Career History: After starting his career with West Bromwich Albion as an associated schoolboy in November 1985, he progressed to trainee status in July 1986 and to the professional ranks in the summer of 1988. Freed towards the end of the 1988-89 season without a first team outing, he signed for Third Division Wigan Athletic and made his FL debut as a substitute at Leyton Orient on 16 September 1989. Briefly stood in for transferred Paul Beesley in October 1989, but lost his place to promising "Latics'" youngster Alan Johnson in December and was mainly deployed as substitute thereafter, coming on no fewer than 17 times. A useful squad player in 1990-91, he provided cover in central defence, at right-back and in midfield. Won a regular place in central defence at the start of 1991-92, following the departure of Peter Atherton to Coventry, but lost his place to Peter Skipper in February. Returned to finish the season in the right-back slot, but wearing the number 11 shirt! A surprise signing by Crystal Palace during the summer.

Clubs	Signing Date	Transfer Fee	APPEARANCES				GOALS			
			Lge	FL Cup	FA Cup	Others	Lge	FL Cup	FA Cup	Others
W.B.A.	7.88	–								
Wigan Athletic	4.89	–	69+28	7+1	5+4	5	6	3	1	
Crystal Palace*	6.92	£225,000								

PAYNE Grant

Born: Chertsey, 25 December 1973

Height: 5'10" Weight: 12.5

Position: Forward.

Career History: Signed professional forms for Wimbledon during the 1992 close season, having previously been at the club as an associated schoolboy (March 1988) and as a trainee (July 1990). No first team experience as yet.

Clubs	Signing Date	Transfer Fee	APPEARANCES				GOALS			
			Lge	FL Cup	FA Cup	Others	Lge	FL Cup	FA Cup	Others
Wimbledon*	6.92	–								

PAYTON Andrew (Andy) Paul

Born: Whalley,
3 October 1967

Height: 5'9"

Weight: 10.6

Position/Skill Factor: Sharp shooting striker, who is very quick and will always score goals as he ferrets for chances in and around the box.

Career History: Joined Hull City through the YTS scheme in June 1984 and after making good progress, he signed professional forms during the 1986 close season. Made his FL debut at Stoke City on 4 April 1987, coming on for the injured Garry Parker, but had to wait a further ten months for a full game, scoring the opening goal in a 3-1 victory against Leeds United. Following the departure of Keith Edwards, he at last established a regular place in 1989-90 when he topped the club's goal scoring charts with 17 League goals, which included four penalties. He maintained his progress in 1990-91 as the Second Division's third highest scorer after Teddy Sheringham and Steve Bull, but unfortunately, his 25 League goals were not enough to save the "Tigers" from relegation. By now the subject of constant transfer speculation, he scored seven goals in ten FL games in 1991-92, before being picked up by Middlesbrough for a large fee. His subsequent experience was curious to say the least. After netting in the third minute of his debut for "Boro", he was dropped for the next three matches and in fact only started seven more FL games until the end of the season, appearing more frequently as substitute and scoring winning goals against eventual champions, Ipswich Town and against Oxford United. The sparing used of their most expensive asset by "Boro" is difficult to explain, as the team struggled to score throughout the season and their 58 goals from 46 games was one of the lowest goal tallies ever recorded by a promoted team.

Clubs	Signing Date	Transfer Fee	APPEARANCES				GOALS			
			Lge	FL Cup	FA Cup	Others	Lge	FL Cup	FA Cup	Others
Hull City	5.86	–	116+27	7+2	7	3	53	2		
Middlesbrough*	11.91	£750,000	8+11		1+3		3			

PEACOCK Darren

Born: Bristol,
3 February 1968

Height: 6'2"

Weight: 12.6

Position/Skill Factor: A central defender, who is both strong in the air and on the ground. Aggressive, but fair, when he tackles he means business.

Career History: Was on Bristol Rover's books as an associated schoolboy (September 1983) until leaving school, but joined Newport County on a YTS scheme in August 1984. Made his FL debut, as a substitute at Plymouth Argyle on 14 September 1985 and before turning professional the following February, he already had eight full League appearances to his credit. Suffered a serious injury in October 1986 and did not return to FL action until April 1988, by which time Newport were already doomed to demotion from the Football League. Continued playing with the Welsh club in the Vauxhall

Conference in 1988-89. At this stage his FL career seemed over, but he was rescued from obscurity by Hereford United and soon won a regular place in their team. In the opening months of 1989-90, he was actually deployed as a striker with some success, but eventually settled down in central defence. His career took another twist in 1990-91 when he was elevated to the First Division by Queens Park Rangers, who signed him in an emergency following injuries to all their central defenders, along with Andy Tillson from Grimsby Town, with whom he formed a highly effective partnership which assisted Rangers to First Division safety. Held his place in 1991-92, despite the return to fitness of Danny Maddix and Alan McDonald. Considering his humble origins and misfortunes of his early career, his rapid adjustment to top level football has been remarkable and serves as an inspiration to all lower division footballers.

Clubs	Signing Date	Transfer Fee	APPEARANCES				GOALS			
			Lge	FL Cup	FA Cup	Others	Lge	FL Cup	FA Cup	Others
Newport County	2.86	–	24+4	2	1	1+1				
Hereford United	3.89	–	56+7	6	6	6	5		1	
Q.P.R.*	12.90	£200,000	58	4	1	2	1			

PEAKE Andrew (Andy) Michael

Born: Market Harborough,
1 November 1961

Height: 5'10"

Weight: 12.0

International Honours:
E Yth, E "U21"-1

Position/Skill Factor: Skilful midfielder with a good first touch and an accurate passer of the long ball. Capable of scoring from distance.

Career History: First joined Leicester City as an associated schoolboy (September 1976) and on leaving school, signed as an apprentice in July 1987. Made his Fl debut on becoming a professional against Oldham Athletic at Filbert Street on 1 January 1979 and held his place for the remainder of the season. The following term, he won a Second Division Championship medal, playing in a side that included a young Gary Lineker. But perhaps the team was too inexperienced and were relegated first time round. In 1982-83, injuries kept his appearances down to just four as City returned to the First Division in third place. Although coming back to play 21 League games in 1984-85, he was never quite able to hold down a regular first team spot at Filbert Street and was transferred to Grimsby Town in the 1985 close season. Slotted straight into the "Mariners'" midfield and apart from a six match spell halfway through the season, he established himself in the side. However, after three games in 1986-87, he was on his way back to the First Division with Charlton Athletic. Having consistently battled against the elements, the club were finally relegated at the end of 1989-90, but in 1990-91 he had his most consistent season in League football, when making 45 appearances as the captain and assisting Athletic to safety, following a disastrous start to the season. After three months of the 1991-92 season as an ever present in the Charlton team, he followed his former manager, Lennie Lawrence, to Middlesbrough and although not an automatic selection in "Boro's" midfield, he played his part in their late season climb up the table to second place and automatic promotion to the new Premier League.

Clubs	Signing Date	Transfer Fee	APPEARANCES				GOALS			
			Lge	FL Cup	FA Cup	Others	Lge	FL Cup	FA Cup	Others
Leicester City	1.79	–	141+6	5+1	9		13			
Grimsby Town	8.85	£110,000	39	5	1	1	4		1	
Charlton Athletic	9.86	£75,000	174+3	12	8	14+1	5	1		
Middlesbrough*	11.91	£150,000	20+3		4					

PEARCE Andrew (Andy) John

Born: Bradford-on-Avon, 20 April 1966

Height: 6'4"

Weight: 13.0

Position/Skill Factor: Central defender who is very strong in the air and a good distributor of long passes.

Career History: Came to Coventry City from Beazer Homes League team, Halesowen Town, during the 1990 close season after previous experience with West Midland's non-League teams, Wednesbury and Stourbridge. One of three players City have signed from Halesowen, the others being Tim Clarke (now with Huddersfield Town) and Sean Flynn. Made his FL debut deputising for the injured Brian Kilcline at Leeds United on 9 March 1991 and settled in well, keeping his place for the remainder of the season and scoring the winning goal in only his second game at home to Luton Town. Following the departures of Brian Kilcline and Trevor Peake, he established a regular place in 1991-92 at the heart of one of the "meanest" defences in the First Division, partnering Peter Atherton.

Clubs	Signing Date	Transfer Fee	APPEARANCES				GOALS			
			Lge	FL Cup	FA Cup	Others	Lge	FL Cup	FA Cup	Others
Coventry City*	5.90	£15,000	47	4	2	1	3			

PEARCE Ian Anthony

Born: Bury St Edmunds, 7 May 1974

Height: 6'3" Weight: 14.0

Position/Skill Factor: Yet to settle in a fixed position, he can play anywhere; full-back, central defender or striker. A strong header of the ball and also skilful on the ground.

Career History: Joined Chelsea as a 14-year-old associated schoolboy in November 1988 and signed professional forms after leaving school in the 1991 close season. Prior to that, however, he made his FL debut when coming off the bench four days after his 17th birthday, during a 2-2 draw at Aston Villa on 11 May 1991, the last game of the 1990-91 season. Made three further first team appearances as a substitute in October and November 1991 and still awaits his first full game.

Clubs	Signing Date	Transfer Fee	APPEARANCES				GOALS			
			Lge	FL Cup	FA Cup	Others	Lge	FL Cup	FA Cup	Others
Chelsea*	8.91	–	0+3			0+1				

PEARCE Stuart

Born: Hammersmith, 24 April 1962

Height: 5'10" Weight: 12.9

International Honours: E "U21"-1, E-50

Position/Skill Factor: The best left-back in the country, he has great strength and power, which enables him to burst through to score vital goals. Also a free-kick and penalty-kick specialist. A very determined tackler, he never gives way and gives much stability to the team as club captain.

Career History: Started his football career with Wealdstone as a youth player in 1978 and graduated to the first team when his club were founder members of the Alliance Premier League (now Vauxhall Conference). Amazingly, in view of his subsequent career, it was several years before his potential was spotted and he was signed by Coventry City in October 1983. Almost immediately he was selected to play at left-back for his FL debut at Highfield Road against Queens Park Rangers on 12 November 1983 and except for injuries, was a regular choice during his 20 months with the club. Surprisingly sold to Nottingham Forest in the 1985 close season, in a £450,000 double deal involving Ian Butterworth, he was valued at £50,000 less than his team-mate. Going straight into the Forest first team, his all action performances soon brought him to the attention of the England manager and he won his first full cap against Brazil at Wembley on 19 May 1987. By now he was captaining Forest and in 1988 had become the regular choice for England, replacing Kenny Sansom. An automatic choice in the England squad for the World Cup Finals in Italy 1990, it was ironic that the most reliable dead-ball kicker in the England team should fail with his penalty in the Semi-Final "shoot out" against West Germany, but this should not be allowed to overshadow his superb performances throughout the tournament. A frequent visitor to Wembley Stadium, both for club and country. He led Forest to two consecutive League Cup victories over Luton Town (1989) and Oldham Athletic (1990) and returned in 1991 for the FA Cup Final against Tottenham Hotspur. His typical blistering free-kick gave Forest the lead in the 15th minute, but his inexperienced team tired and "Spurs" prevailed after extra-time. Indisputably the finest left-back in England, if not in all Europe, he is not only an accomplished defender, but a very dangerous attacker. In 1990-91 he scored an astonishing total, for a full-back, of 16

Stuart Pearce

goals for Forest (11 FL, plus five cup), some from his unstoppable free kicks, but several from open play. In 1992 he returned yet again for the Zenith Cup Final against Southampton, which Forest won 3-2, but during the game sustained an injury which ruled him out for the remainder of the campaign, including the League Cup Final where his inspiration was sorely missed as Forest succumbed 1-0 to Manchester United. He regained fitness in the nick of time to join the England squad for the European Championship Finals in Sweden, but his leadership was not enough, as the side stumbled out of the tournament along with France at the bottom of their group.

Clubs	Signing Date	Transfer Fee	APPEARANCES				GOALS			
			Lge	FL Cup	FA Cup	Others	Lge	FL Cup	FA Cup	Others
Coventry City	10.83	£25,000	52		2		4			
Nottingham Forest*	6.85	£200,000	236	43	25	15	39	7	7	6

place, mid-way through 1989-90, but after 51 consecutive appearances he was injured in February 1991 and did not appear again that season. Restored to fitness in the summer of 1991, he played in all but one of "Boro's" 59 games in League and cup competitions in a highly successful 1991-92 season under new manager Lennie Lawrence, which saw the club reach the Semi-Final of the League Cup and clinch promotion to the Premier League. His consistency so impressed England manager Graham Taylor that he was called into the England squad at the end of the season, but sadly had to withdraw due to a leg injury sustained in the penultimate game of the season.

Clubs	Signing Date	Transfer Fee	APPEARANCES				GOALS			
			Lge	FL Cup	FA Cup	Others	Lge	FL Cup	FA Cup	Others
Manchester United	1.79	–	4	1						
Middlesbrough	11.83	Loan	12		2					
Middlesbrough*	7.85	£80,000	250	26	18	24				

PEARS Stephen (Steve)

Born: Brandon,
22 January 1962

Height: 6'0"

Weight: 12.11

Position/Skill Factor: Goalkeeper with very safe hands, who is as steady as a rock and makes very few mistakes. Noted for his long kicks.

Career History: Although he had junior trials at Ayresome Park, he eventually signed associated schoolboy forms for Manchester United in October 1976. On leaving school, he became an apprentice (July 1978), before progressing to the professional ranks early in 1979. Actually made his FL debut while on loan to Middlesbrough, at home to Cardiff City on 5 November 1983 and he kept a clean sheet in a 2-0 win. Had two separate loan spells that season, while deputising for Kelham O'Hanlon and only conceded eight goals in 12 appearances. United required £80,000 to make the loan permanent, but despite an appeal to supporters, the club failed to raise the fee and he returned to Old Trafford. He finally made his debut for United, when Gary Bailey broke a finger in January 1985, but it was not a lasting opportunity. In the summer of 1985 he was happy to rejoin Middlesbrough on a permanent basis, after they were at last able to meet the asking fee. Unfortunately, while he showed great ability between the sticks, many others didn't play to their true potential and the club were relegated to the Third Division at the end of his first season. But, missing only one game in the next two seasons, he assisted the club to two consecutive promotion efforts, enabling Middlesbrough to regain First Division status in 1987-88. Loss of form during 1988-89, saw him lose his place in the side to Kevin Poole and the club relegated back to the Second Division. Came back well to regain his

PEARSON Nigel Graham

Born: Nottingham, 21 August 1963

Height: 6'1" Weight: 13.7

Position/Skill Factor: Strong central defender, brave in the air and uncompromising on the ground. A good steady player, he rarely ever gets caught out of position. Inspires by example.

Career History: Came out of non-League football with Heanor Town of the Midland Counties League, when he signed for Shrewsbury Town in 1981-82 and had to wait nine months before being selected for the "Shrews'" first team. Eventually made his FL debut at Oldham Athletic on 28 August 1982 and settled down into the side on a regular basis, until being injured towards the end of 1983-84. Out for well over 12 months, he made a great recovery, establishing himself as one of the best centre-backs in the Second Division. Ever present in 1986-87, he so impressed Sheffield Wednesday after playing against them in the Second Round of the League Cup the following season, that they immediately moved for him. Signed to add a touch of steel to the heart of Wednesday's defence, he rarely missed a game, but in 1989-90 the club dropped into the Second Division when, after appearing to be safe, they lost five of the last six games. As club skipper, however, come the end of the 1990-91 season, he had led the side to an historic 1-0 League Cup Final victory over Manchester United and back to the First Division at the first time of asking, scoring no fewer than 12 goals (six FL, plus six cup) mostly from free-kicks and corners. Although frequently rested or absent through injury in 1991-92, he still played a prominent part in the "Owls'" highly successful season as they finished in third place and qualified for the UEFA Cup.

Clubs	Signing Date	Transfer Fee	APPEARANCES				GOALS			
			Lge	FL Cup	FA Cup	Others	Lge	FL Cup	FA Cup	Others
Shrewsbury Town	11.81	£5,000	153	19	6	3	5			
Sheffield Wednesday*	10.87	£250,000	159	14	9	7	13	5	1	

PEEL Nathan James

Born: Blackburn,17 May 1972

Height: 6'1" Weight: 12.7

Position/Skill Factor: Big striker with two good feet who is also useful in the air. Has a lovely first touch for a big man.

Career History: Joined Preston North End as an associated schoolboy (September 1987) and on leaving school signed on for the club as a trainee in September 1988. Made his FL debut at Deepdale, a month after turning professional, against Grimsby Town on 25 August 1990, when coming off the bench to replace Steve Harper. Scored at Reading, the only time he played for the full 90 minutes during 1990-91. With so little FL experience under his belt, it was a surprise when Dave Bassett signed him for Sheffield United in the summer of 1991. Only made one appearance (as a substitute away to Tottenham Hotspur in November) in 1991-92, but is clearly an investment for the future.

Clubs	Signing Date	Transfer Fee	APPEARANCES				GOALS			
			Lge	FL Cup	FA Cup	Others	Lge	FL Cup	FA Cup	Others
Preston North End	7.90	–	1+9	1		1+1	1			
Sheffield United*	7.91	£50,000	0+1							

PEMBERTON John Matthew

Born: Oldham, 18 November 1964

Height: 5'11"

Weight: 12.3

Position/Skill Factor: Very experienced right-back who links up well with the attack to deliver useful crosses and is a good passer of the ball. Also a long throw specialist.

Career History: Lancashire born defender who was playing with local North West Counties League club Chadderton, when given his FL debut as a trialist for Rochdale at Spotland against Aldershot on 2 October 1984. Following that solitary appearance he continued to play for Chadderton, but towards the end of the season Crewe Alexandra stepped in for him and he immediately went into their League side. He made such good progress that, after three years and over 100 games at Gresty Road, he moved from the Fourth to the Second Division when he signed for Crystal Palace in March 1988. Held down the right-back slot at Selhurst Park throughout the 1988-89 campaign, missing just four games, as Palace gained promotion to the First Division in third place. In 1990, he played a major part in Palace's great FA Cup run and in particular the epic Semi-Final against Liverpool which was won 4-3 after extra-time. His run and cross to set up Mark Bright for Palace's initial goal, first revealed the vulnerability in the heart of the "Reds'" defence, which the "Eagles" exploited to the full. After Manchester United beat Palace 1-0 in the replayed Final, he signed for newly promoted Sheffield United, who were looking to strengthen their squad for an assault on the First Division. He quickly settled into the right-back berth, but injuries interrupted his season as the "Blades" struggled near the foot of the table, before pulling clear to safety. With United having another inconsistent season in 1991-92, he was in and out of the team up to December, but after losing his place to Kevin Gage, he was not selected again until the closing weeks of the campaign.

Clubs	Signing Date	Transfer Fee	APPEARANCES				GOALS			
			Lge	FL Cup	FA Cup	Others	Lge	FL Cup	FA Cup	Others
Rochdale	9.84	–	1							
Crewe Alexandra	3.85	–	116+5	7	3	7	1	1		
Crystal Palace	3.88	£80,000	76+2	6+1	8	12	2			
Sheffield United*	7.90	£300,000	40+1	3		1				

PENNOCK Adrian Barry

Born: Ipswich, 27 March 1971

Height: 6'0" Weight: 12.4

Position/Skill Factor: Promising central defender. Useful in the air, while on the ground, he will come out of defence and look to pass the ball.

Career History: Joined Norwich City in November 1986 as an associated schoolboy, before progressing, first as a trainee (July 1987) and then into the club's professional ranks in the 1989 close season. Made his FL debut in the centre of the defence at Southampton on 27 February 1990 in a 4-1 defeat and showed enough potential to warrant further opportunities.

Clubs	Signing Date	Transfer Fee	APPEARANCES				GOALS			
			Lge	FL Cup	FA Cup	Others	Lge	FL Cup	FA Cup	Others
Norwich City*	7.89	–	1							

PENNYFATHER Glenn Julian

Born: Billericay, 11 February 1963

Height: 5'8" Weight: 10.10

Position/Skill Factor: Hard working, experienced midfielder. A good strong tackler with plenty of stamina, he releases the ball with accurate, but simple passes.

Career History: Came through Southend United's junior sides as an apprentice (July 1979), before turning professional during 1980-81 and making his FL debut at Roots Hall against Doncaster Rovers on 27 February 1981. However, it wasn't until the following season that he played again and settled down as a regular first choice. Unfortunately, Southend were relegated to the Fourth

Division in 1983-84 and it took another three years for the club to regain their Third Division status, as the third placed team in 1986-87. He was an instrumental figure in that success, scoring ten goals from midfield and soon the bigger clubs were taking due note. Second Division Crystal Palace were the first club to make an acceptable offer in November 1987 and he quickly fitted into their midfield. But in 1988-89, the season that the club won promotion to the First Division, he was eclipsed in midfield by Alan Pardew and Geoff Thomas and made only 13 appearances. The following season his chances of a first team recall were further reduced by the return of Andy Gray and he left Selhurst Park without making an appearance in the First Division, signing for struggling Second Division Ipswich Town towards the end of October 1989. His arrival coincided with an upturn in Town's fortunes, although he played very little part in the revival, having spent most of the time in the treatment room. After remaining absent from the 1990-91 League programme, he made a mere handful of appearances in 1991-92, but otherwise played no part in Ipswich's Second Division Championship campaign.

Clubs	Signing Date	Transfer Fee	APPEARANCES				GOALS			
			Lge	FL Cup	FA Cup	Others	Lge	FL Cup	FA Cup	Others
Southend United	2.81	–	231+7	12+1	14+3	5+1	36	2	1	3
Crystal Palace	11.87	£150,000	31+3		1+1	4+2	1			
Ipswich Town*	10.89	£80,000	9+2		0+1	0+1	1			

PENRICE Gary Kenneth

Born: Bristol,
23 March 1964

Height: 5'7"

Weight: 10.0

Position/Skill Factor: A striker who is always on the move, making angles for team-mates in possession. An extremely unselfish player, with good vision.

Career History: Became a Bristol Rovers' associated schoolboy player in April 1978, before crossing town on leaving school to sign as an apprentice at Bristol City in June 1980. On being released, he developed his skills with local Western League club, Mangotsfield and impressed Bristol Rovers, one of the clubs who had rejected him as a youngster. Duly signed professional forms for Rovers and made his FL debut when coming on as a sub at Eastville against Leyton Orient on 27 April 1985. He was soon holding down a regular place and as an ever present in 1987-88, he topped the club's scoring charts for the first time with 18 League goals. The following season he scored 20 and in November 1989, Watford, who were lacking in firepower, brought him to Vicarage Road where his 12 goals from 29 League matches proved vital in preserving their Second Division status. Unfortunately, in

1990-91, he suffered from a string of injury problems and only managed to play 13 times for the "Hornets", prior to March. However, once fully fit, Watford doubled their money when they transferred him to Aston Villa as a potential replacement for David Platt, who was due to leave for Italian football during the coming summer. Although playing a few games at the start of 1991-92 under new manager Ron Atkinson, as a signing of previous Czech manager, Josef Venglos, his cards were marked and he soon rejoined his former manager, Gerry Francis, by now installed at Queens Park Rangers. Since joining Rangers, however, he has struggled to score, apart from two late goals which saved a point at Coventry and had lost his place by the end of the season.

Clubs	Signing Date	Transfer Fee	APPEARANCES				GOALS			
			Lge	FL Cup	FA Cup	Others	Lge	FL Cup	FA Cup	Others
Bristol Rovers	11.84	–	186+2	11	11	13+2	53	3	7	2
Watford	11.89	£500,000	41+2		4	1	17			1
Aston Villa	3.91	£1,000,000	14+6				1			
Q.P.R.*	10.91	£625,000	13+6	1	0+1	1	3	1		

PERRY Christopher (Chris) John

Born: Sutton, 26 April 1973

Height: 5'10" Weight: 10.2

Position/Skill Factor: A central defender with plenty of pace. Reads situations well for one so young and is a good competitive tackler.

Career History: First came to Wimbledon as an associated schoolboy in December 1987, graduating to trainee status in July 1989 and then to the professional ranks during the 1991 close season. Yet to receive a first team call-up, he is highly thought of at the club.

Clubs	Signing Date	Transfer Fee	APPEARANCES				GOALS			
			Lge	FL Cup	FA Cup	Others	Lge	FL Cup	FA Cup	Others
Wimbledon*	7.91	–								

PEVERELL Nicholas (Nick) John

Born: Middlesbrough, 28 April 1973

Height: 5'10" Weight: 11.0

Position: Striker.

Career History: First came to Middlesbrough as an associated schoolboy in April 1988, before signing as a trainee on leaving school in July 1989. A prolific scorer in "Boro's" youth team in 1990-91 and later with the reserves, he turned professional during the 1991 close season and although he played four games on loan to Gateshead in the Vauxhall Conference during November 1991, he missed much of last season through injury.

Clubs	Signing Date	Transfer Fee	APPEARANCES				GOALS			
			Lge	FL Cup	FA Cup	Others	Lge	FL Cup	FA Cup	Others
Middlesbrough*	7.91	–								

Clubs	Signing Date	Transfer Fee	APPEARANCES				GOALS			
			Lge	FL Cup	FA Cup	Others	Lge	FL Cup	FA Cup	Others
Burnley	5.75	–	30	1	1					
Fulham	12.76	£40,000	345	26	20	2				
Southend United	9.83	Loan	10							
Bournemouth	7.86	–	202	15	13	8				
Everton*	7.91	£80,000								
Bolton Wanderers	2.92	Loan	1							

PEYTON Gerald (Gerry) Joseph

Born: Birmingham,
20 May 1956

Height: 6'2"

Weight: 13.9

International Honours:
IR-33

Position/Skill Factor: Very experienced goalkeeper, who has good positional and handling skills. Makes difficult saves look easy. Also, a good long kicker.

Career History: On leaving school he joined Aston Villa as an apprentice (February 1973), before being released in 1974 and going into non-League football with Atherstone Town of the Southern League for one year. He was signed by Burnley, who were looking for a deputy for Alan Stevenson and on making his FL debut at Turf Moor against Liverpool on 6 December 1975, he kept a clean sheet. At the same time, he replaced Stevenson and although the club were relegated to the Second Division at the end of 1975-76, he did so well that he retained his place in the team until October 1976. Following an injury to Peter Mellor, Fulham, who had noted his steady progress, moved in for him and in just under ten years at Craven Cottage he became the all-time third ranking "Cottagers'" goalkeeper, in terms of appearances. During that period, Fulham fluctuated between the Second and Third Divisions, but his form was such, apart from the odd match and a spell on loan at Southend United, that he was regularly chosen to represent the Irish Republic, on his parents' birthright, after winning his first cap against Spain in Dublin on 9 February 1977. Freed at the end of 1985-86, following a long service testimonial, he joined Bournemouth during the summer and won a Third Division Championship medal as an ever present in his first season with the club. Had very few serious threats to his dominance between the posts, despite Bournemouth suffering relegation to the Third Division in 1989-90, still proving to be a reliable goalkeeper. It was a surprise, nevertheless, when Everton signed him in the summer of 1991 as cover for Neville Southall. However, there was to be no dramatic return to the First Division as the Welsh international 'keeper did not miss a game all season. Instead, Peyton spent the closing months of the season on loan to Bolton Wanderers and Norwich City, but only as cover. He did, however, add four more international caps to his tally, playing in an end of season tournament in the USA.

PHELAN Michael (Mike) Christopher

Born: Nelson,
24 September 1962

Height: 5'11"

Weight: 12.3

International Honours:
E Yth, E-1

Position/Skill Factor: Steady and reliable midfielder who can also play at full-back. Holds the ball up well and keeps his passing simple. Difficult to pass, he invariably gets a foot in and is ideal for a man-for-man marking exercise.

Career History: Joined nearby Burnley on associated schoolboy forms in July 1977, before becoming an apprentice on leaving school in July 1979. Turned professional in the 1980 close season and made his FL debut as a substitute at Chesterfield on 31 January 1981. Won a Third Division Championship medal in 1981-82, but in the very next season, as an ever present, he experienced the misery of relegation as the team slid back into Division Three. And when Burnley descended into Division four at the end of 1984-85, he was obviously too talented to be playing at that level and was transferred to Norwich City in the summer. In his first season at Carrow Road, 1985-86, he was present throughout the campaign, winning a Second Division Championship medal as the club moved into the top flight. Rarely missing a game for the "Canaries" over four seasons, he was never better than when captaining the side to fourth place in the First Division in 1988-89, Norwich's highest ever League position. His consistency attracted the attention of bigger clubs and during the 1989 close season, he followed his former club colleague, Steve Bruce, to Manchester United. Made his debut alongside another big money signing, Neil Webb, against Arsenal at Old Trafford on the opening day of 1989-90 and expectancy was high for the club to mount a challenge for the elusive League Championship that season, after a 4-1 win. However, as the side's League form faltered, it was fortunate that United had a good FA Cup run which ended successfully when Crystal Palace were beaten 1-0 in the Final, following a replay. But the season was memorable for other reasons as well, most of all when winning his first England cap, coming on as a sub against Italy on 15 November

1989 at Wembley. And despite the disappointment of finishing on the losing side in the League Cup Final against Sheffield Wednesday in 1991, he climaxed 1990-91 with a European Cup Winners Cup medal, following United's 2-1 victory over Barcelona. With stiff competition for midfield slots at Old Trafford he has become more of a utility player, often playing at right-back. In 1991-92 he took a back seat for most of the season but was recalled for out of favour Neil Webb in the closing months, winning a League Cup winners medal, following the 1-0 victory over Nottingham Forest. But, in the absence of Webb and Robson, could not provide the missing "spark" that United needed to win the Championship.

Clubs	Signing Date	Transfer Fee	APPEARANCES				GOALS			
			Lge	FL Cup	FA Cup	Others	Lge	FL Cup	FA Cup	Others
Burnley	7.80	–	166+2	16	16	8	9	2		2
Norwich City	7.85	£60,000	155+1	14	11	13	9		1	
Manchester United*	6.89	£750,000	82+7	12+2	8	13	2			

PHELAN Terence (Terry)

Born: Manchester, 16 March 1967

Height: 5'8" Weight: 10.0

International Honours: IR Yth, IR "U21"-1, IR-8

Position/Skill Factor: Competitive left-back with electric pace and a good left foot. Loves to run at defenders with the ball.

Career History: Started at Leeds United as an associated schoolboy in March 1982, before progressing to the professional ranks, via the YTS scheme (August 1983). Made his FL debut at Shrewsbury Town on 7 September 1985 and although having a good run of ten games in the side, was freed at the end of the season, along with right-back Dennis Irwin, who also went on to fame and fortune with Oldham Athletic, Manchester United and the Irish Republic. Joining Swansea City during the 1986 close season, he missed just one game during 1986-87, before becoming one of Bobby Gould's first signings for Wimbledon. Apart from a period out, due to injury in the middle of 1987-88, he kept his place throughout the campaign and won an FA Cup winners medal, following the "Dons'" surprise 1-0 victory over Liverpool at Wembley. Continuing to make good progress, he was as consistent as ever in 1991-92, missing only five games through injury during the season. Also made his international debut for the Irish Republic on 11 September 1991, reuniting with his former Leeds colleague, Irwin and remained a regular choice throughout the season.

PHILLIPS David Owen

Born: Wegberg, West Germany, 29 July 1963

Height: 5'10"

Weight: 11.2

International Honours: W Yth, W "U21"-3, W-38

Position/Skill Factor: Left sided midfielder, who is also comfortable at full-back. Has two good feet and is a lovely striker of the ball, especially when around the box. Known for his diagonal passing.

Career History: Born in West Germany, where his father was serving in the RAF, his career started at Plymouth Argyle as an apprentice in August 1979 and on turning professional at the beginning of 1981-82, he made his FL debut at Home Park against Oxford United on 29 August 1981. Appearing sporadically at first, he gained a regular place in the side in 1983-84 and helped Argyle to the FA Cup Semi-Finals, as the first Third Division club to reach that stage of the competition since the early 1960s, scoring the goal that won the Quarter-Final tie against Derby County, direct from a corner in injury time. His good form did not go unnoticed at international level, being selected for Wales at right-back against England at Wrexham on 2 May 1984. Manchester City were impressed by his skills and a few months after his international debut, he was on his way to Maine Road. Was ever present in his first season at City, scoring 12 goals as the club were promoted to the First Division as the third placed side and missed only a handful of matches the following year, before moving to Coventry City in part exchange for goalkeeper Perry Suckling in the summer of 1986. In his first season at Highfield Road, he won an FA Cup winners medal, following Coventry's great 3-2 victory over Tottenham Hotspur at Wembley. After three seasons at Highfield Road he was transferred to Norwich City in the 1989 close season, for a fee that was fixed by a tribunal and marked his debut with a goal in a 2-0 win at Sheffield Wednesday on the opening day of 1989-90. Ever present during 1989-90 and 1990-91, he formed a good left-wing partnership with Mark Bowen as the club looked to improve. In 1991-92, he was switched early in the season to right-back to cover for the absence of Ian Culverhouse. Reverted to his usual position in February, but lost his place in the closing stages of the season. He remained a stalwart of the Welsh team, however.

Clubs	Signing Date	Transfer Fee	APPEARANCES				GOALS			
			Lge	FL Cup	FA Cup	Others	Lge	FL Cup	FA Cup	Others
Leeds United	8.84	–	12+2	3		2				
Swansea City	7.86	–	45	4	5	3				
Wimbledon*	7.87	£100,000	156+4	13+2	11	6	1		2	

Clubs	Signing Date	Transfer Fee	APPEARANCES				GOALS			
			Lge	FL Cup	FA Cup	Others	Lge	FL Cup	FA Cup	Others
Plymouth Argyle	8.81	–	65+8	2+1	12+1	4	15			1
Manchester City	8.84	£65,000	81	8	5	5	13			3
Coventry City	6.86	£150,000	93+7	8	9	5+1	8		1	2
Norwich City*	6.89	£525,000	110	10	12	8	9		1	1

PHILLIPS James (Jimmy) Neil

Born: Bolton,
8 February 1966

Height: 6'0"

Weight: 12.7

Position/Skill Factor: Very skilful left-back, who makes good use of his cultured left foot at set plays, especially with inswinging corners. Loves to get involved in the attack.

Career History: Signed associated schoolboy forms for Bolton Wanderers in August 1981, while playing for the Bolton schools' side and progressed through the club's junior teams as an apprentice (September 1982), before turning professional in the 1983 close season. Made his FL debut at Burnden Park when coming on as a sub against Gillingham on 7 April 1984 and the following season he made the left-back position his own. Towards the end of 1986-87, Glasgow Rangers moved for him and in just over a year at Ibrox, he played in 25 Scottish League games and in four European Cup matches, but spent the second half of 1987-88 playing mainly in the reserves, before coming south to sign for Oxford United. During 18 months at the Manor Ground he was remarkably consistent, missing only two games, but when Middlesbrough made an offer for him that United couldn't afford to turn down, he was on his way to the north-east in order to help a struggling side who were desperate for Second Division survival. Relegation was ultimately staved off and he missed only two games in a 1990-91 turn around as "Boro" only failed to gain promotion to the First Division after falling at the Play-Off stage. One year later promotion was achieved without recourse to the Play-Offs and he played a full part, missing only three games in "Boro's" 59 match programme.

Clubs	Signing Date	Transfer Fee	APPEARANCES				GOALS			
			Lge	FL Cup	FA Cup	Others	Lge	FL Cup	FA Cup	Others
Bolton Wanderers	8.83	–	103+5	8	7	14	2			
Glasgow Rangers	3.87	£95,000								
Oxford United	8.88	£110,000	79	3	4	2	6			1
Middlesbrough*	3.90	£250,000	99	14	7	5	4			2

PICKUP Jonathan James

Born: Sydney, Australia, 24 August 1974

Height: 6'0" Weight: 11.6

Position: Central defender.

Career History: Australian born, he signed professional

forms for Blackburn Rovers during the 1992 close season, having previously been at Ewood Park as an associated schoolboy (October 1988) and as a trainee (July 1990). No first team experience as yet.

Clubs	Signing Date	Transfer Fee	APPEARANCES				GOALS			
			Lge	FL Cup	FA Cup	Others	Lge	FL Cup	FA Cup	Others
Blackburn Rovers*	6.92	–								

PILKINGTON Kevin

Born: Hitchin, 8 March 1974

Height: 6'0" Weight: 12.6

Position: Goalkeeper.

Career History: A summer professional signing for Manchester United, he came to Old Trafford straight from school and will have to take his place in the queue behind Peter Schmeichel, Gary Walsh and Ian Wilkinson.

Clubs	Signing Date	Transfer Fee	APPEARANCES				GOALS			
			Lge	FL Cup	FA Cup	Others	Lge	FL Cup	FA Cup	Others
Manchester United*	6.92	–								

POINTON Neil Geoffrey

Born: Warsop,
28 November 1964

Height: 5'10"

Weight: 11.0

Position/Skill Factor: Very experienced left-back, he is a real professional. Has a good left foot and pushes forward at every opportunity to deliver accurate crosses, whilst sound in defence.

Career History: Although he signed associated schoolboy forms with Nottingham Forest in June 1979, on leaving school, he became an apprentice with Scunthorpe United in June 1981, before turning to the professional ranks with the "Irons" just over a year later. Prior to that he had made his FL debut in a 2-0 home defeat at the Old Show Ground against Torquay United on 6 February 1982 and the following season as an every present he was an integral member of the side that fought its way out of the Fourth Division in fourth place. That success was short lived, however, as the club were immediately relegated, but he was making his mark in the game and in November 1985, League Champions, Everton, swooped to take him to Goodison Park, following early season injuries that had forced them to move Pat van den Hauwe from left-back to the centre of the defence. Slotted straight into the side, but after 14 games, injury brought a premature end to his season and ruled him out of the FA Cup Final team to play Liverpool. Although he won a League Championship medal in 1986-87, the emergence of Pat van den Hauwe and Neil McDonald, made further opportunities in five years at the club hard to come by and he eventually moved to Manchester City in the 1990 close season as part of the deal which took Andy Hinchcliffe to Everton. Quickly making the left-back position his own as City progressed to fifth place in the First Division, he even got on to the score sheet when scoring a late winner at Aston Villa in his second appearance at Maine Road. It is ironic, that although Pointon was the lesser valued of the two left-backs, he has gone from strength to strength with City, whilst poor Hinchcliffe languishes in Everton's reserve team. Pointon played probably the best football of his career in 1991-92 in a rapidly improving City team which achieved a highly creditable fifth place and is now regarded as one of the best left-backs in the country.

Clubs	Signing Date	Transfer Fee	APPEARANCES				GOALS			
			Lge	FL Cup	FA Cup	Others	Lge	FL Cup	FA Cup	Others
Scunthorpe United	8.82	–	159	9	13	4	2	1		
Everton	11.85	£75,000	95+7	6+2	16+2	9+3	5			
Manchester City*	7.90	£600,000	74	8	4	4	2			

POLLOCK Jamie

Born: Stockton,
16 February 1974

Height: 5'11"

Weight: 12.9

Position/Skill Factor: Strong, competitive midfielder, who is a good tackler.

Career History: First came to Middlesbrough as a 14-year-old associated schoolboy in October 1988 and on leaving school, he signed up as a trainee in July 1990. Made his FL debut at Ayresome Park as a substitute in a 2-0 victory over Wolverhampton Wanderers on 27 April 1991. A regular member of the first team squad from October 1991 onwards, he made several more first team appearances before signing professional in December and later in the season scored his first goal for "Boro" — a spectacular 30 yard volley at Leicester in April — although it was not enough·to prevent a 2-1 defeat. Clearly, a player with a bright future.

Clubs	Signing Date	Transfer Fee	APPEARANCES				GOALS			
			Lge	FL Cup	FA Cup	Others	Lge	FL Cup	FA Cup	Others
Middlesbrough*	12.91	–	21+6	6+1	4	2	1			

POLSTON John David

Born: Walthamstow,
10 June 1968

Height: 5'11"

Weight: 11.0

International Honours:
E Yth

Position/Skill Factor: Centre-back who is strong both on the ground and in the air. First and foremost, he is a useful defender.

Career History: Elder brother of Andy, who also played for Tottenham Hotspur, he stepped out with "Spurs" as an apprentice in June 1984, before joining the club's professional ranks a year later. Made his FL debut in a 1-0 win at White Hart Lane against Coventry City on 15 November 1986, but in four seasons he made very few appearances as competition for places was intense. Followed in the footsteps of former "Spurs", Mark Bowen, Ian Crook and Ian Culverhouse, when he joined Norwich City in the 1990 close season. Settled in immediately at the heart of the "Canaries'" defence as a replacement for Andy Linighan, using his natural ability to make up for what he lacked in height and weight. Out of favour for the first half of 1991-92, he returned to the first team in January 1992 in place of Paul Blades and held his position till the end of the season, playing his part in the "Canaries'" FA Cup run which ended so disappointingly at the Semi-Final stage.

Clubs	Signing Date	Transfer Fee	APPEARANCES				GOALS			
			Lge	FL Cup	FA Cup	Others	Lge	FL Cup	FA Cup	Others
Tottenham Hotspur	7.85	–	17+7	3+1			1			
Norwich City*	7.90	£250,000	43+3	0+1	9+1	5	5			

POTTS Anthony John

Born: Bexley, 24 October 1972

Height: 5'8" Weight: 11.9

Position/Skill Factor: Cultured midfielder with good passing technique.

Career History: Was out of action with a ligament injury for most of his first season as a professional at Tottenham Hotspur and only played in a handful of reserve matches. Initially coming to White Hart Lane as an associated schoolboy in January 1989, he impressed enough to be offered trainee terms seven months later in August 1989.

Clubs	Signing Date	Transfer Fee	APPEARANCES				GOALS			
			Lge	FL Cup	FA Cup	Others	Lge	FL Cup	FA Cup	Others
Tottenham Hotspur*	7.91	–								

POWELL Lee

Born: Caerleon, 2 June 1973

Height: 5'5" Weight: 8.10

International Honours: W "U21"-2

Position/Skill Factor: Nippy little winger who can play on either flank. Favouring his right foot, he has quick feet and the ability to unbalance defenders.

Career History: Joined Southampton as a trainee in July 1989, having been on associated schoolboy forms since December 1987. Turning professional at the end of 1990-91, he won a Welsh Under 21 cap, as a substitute, in Poland. Made an early first team appearance from the bench in a League Cup, Second Round tie, at home to Rochdale in October, but had to wait until the end of the season to make his FL debut as a substitute at the Dell against Luton Town on 21 March 1992.

Clubs	Signing Date	Transfer Fee	APPEARANCES				GOALS			
			Lge	FL Cup	FA Cup	Others	Lge	FL Cup	FA Cup	Others
Southampton*	5.91	–	1+3							

POWER Lee Michael

Born: Lewisham, 30 June 1972

Height: 5'11" Weight: 11.2

International Honours: IR "U21"-2

Position/Skill Factor: Striker who spells danger around the box, he is a natural goal scorer and shields the ball well.

Career History: A Londoner, he signed associated schoolboy forms with Norwich City in November 1986 and on leaving school he joined the club as a trainee (July 1988), before graduating to their professional ranks two years later. Prior to that, however, he had already made his FL debut at Aston Villa, when substituting for Robert Fleck in a 3-3 thriller on 28 April 1990. Had a couple of runs in the side during 1990-91 and impressed when scoring Norwich's first two goals in a 3-1 victory over Queens Park Rangers at Loftus Road. In 1991-92, he was somewhat eclipsed by the emergence of Chris Sutton, but returned to make a handful of appearances at the end of the season.

Clubs	Signing Date	Transfer Fee	APPEARANCES				GOALS			
			Lge	FL Cup	FA Cup	Others	Lge	FL Cup	FA Cup	Others
Norwich City*	7.90	–	15+6	1			4			

PRESSMAN Kevin Paul

Born: Fareham,
6 November 1967

Height: 6'1"

Weight: 13.0

International Honours:
E Sch, E Yth, E"U21"-1

Position/Skill Factor: Quick off his line for a big man, he doesn't commit himself too often and excels in one-to-one situations. Kicks very long with his left foot.

Career History: Born in Hampshire, he was spotted by Sheffield Wednesday playing for England schools and signed associated schoolboy forms in December 1981. He became an apprentice with the club on leaving school in June 1984, joining the paid ranks some 18 months later and made his Fl debut in a 1-1 draw at Southampton, incidentally, only a few miles from his birthplace, on 5 September 1987. Took over from Martin Hodge, who had been sold to Leicester City, towards the end of 1987-88 and did well until the last game of the season when Liverpool exploded five past him at Hillsborough in a 5-1 defeat. He was replaced by the returning Chris Turner and made only five first team appearances the following term. However, on regaining his place in 1989-90, he was unfortunately injured during the home game against Manchester City and was carried off, not to play again in a season that ended with the club being relegated to the Second Division. After recovering and playing in the first 22 matches of 1990-91, he was again replaced by Turner between the posts. Although returning to the side for the final match, with the club already assured of promotion back to the top flight, he missed selection for one of Wednesday's finest ever moments, the 1-0 League Cup Final victory over Manchester United. Highly regarded by the "Owls'" supporters, he was shut out of the Wednesday first team in 1991-92, except for one game, by the arrival of Chris Woods, the England 'keeper and was loaned to Stoke City for a short spell near the end of the season. Too good a 'keeper to remain in reserve team football, indefinitely.

Clubs	Signing Date	Transfer Fee	APPEARANCES				GOALS			
			Lge	FL Cup	FA Cup	Others	Lge	FL Cup	FA Cup	Others
Sheffield Wednesday	11.85	–	59	6		3				
Stoke City*	3.92	Loan	4			2				

PRICE Christopher (Chris) John

Born: Hereford,
30 March 1960

Height: 5'7"

Weight: 10.2

Position/Skill Factor: A great attacking right-back, almost a second winger, who passes well down the flank and follows up, looking to get into the action. Always buzzing.

Career History: After signing as an apprentice with his local club, Hereford United, in June 1976, he made his FL debut at Notts County on 1 April 1977, having just turned 17 and still not a professional. A magnificent club servant to Hereford, he stayed ten years and after winning a regular place at right-back in 1978-79, he never played less than 37 FL games in any of the next seven season. Showed his attacking instincts with ten goals from open play in 1981-82 and was always looking to get on the scoresheet. In the summer of 1986 he was sold to Blackburn Rovers for a surprisingly modest fee, leaving behind a FL appearances record for Hereford which would stand for many years. Still only 26 years of age, he quickly adjusted to Second Division football, missing only two games in his first season and only one in 1987-88 when he again scored an amazing ten goals from open play. Missed out on promotion to Division One with Rovers in the Play-Offs, but still reached the pinnacle of his career when Graham Taylor signed him for Aston Villa. Again had no difficulty adjusting to the highest level, missing just two games in 1988-89, four in 1989-90 and being ever present in 1990-91. Perhaps persuaded to curb his attacking instincts, he notched only two goals in three seasons. With the arrival of Ron Atkinson as manager he had no future at Villa Park, but had to wait for most of 1991-92 to pass before getting a transfer, back to Blackburn Rovers. After three years of holding back, it was almost predictable that he should score on his return debut for Rovers as early as the fifth minute and he scored again in his second match. However, he lost his place to Kevin Moran as Rovers' promotion campaign disintegrated in March. Recalled for the Play-Offs, but on the right-wing as Rovers finally achieved their goal the hard way.

Clubs	Signing Date	Transfer Fee	APPEARANCES				GOALS			
			Lge	FL Cup	FA Cup	Others	Lge	FL Cup	FA Cup	Others
Hereford United	1.78	–	327+3	17	19	7+1	27	1	1	
Blackburn Rovers	7.86	£25,000	83	6	2	7	11			
Aston Villa	5.88	£125,000	109+2	14	7	11+2	2			
Blackburn Rovers*	2.92	£150,000	11+2			2	3			

PRIEST Christopher

Born: Leigh, 18 October 1973

Height: 5'10" Weight: 10.10½

Position: Midfielder.

Career History: Joined the Everton professional staff during the 1992 close season, having previously been at Goodison as an associated schoolboy (July 1988) and as a trainee (June 1990).

Clubs	Signing Date	Transfer Fee	APPEARANCES				GOALS			
			Lge	FL Cup	FA Cup	Others	Lge	FL Cup	FA Cup	Others
Everton*	6.92	–								

PROCTOR Mark Gerard

Born: Middlesbrough, 30 January 1961

Height: 5'10" Weight: 12.8

International Honours: E Yth, E "U21"-4

Position/Skill Factor: Dedicated midfield player who is a professional through and through. Known within the football industry as a control and pass man.

Career History: Locally born and bred, it was hardly surprising that he should join Middlesbrough, first as an associated schoolboy (October 1975) and later as an apprentice in June 1977. Made his FL debut, a month before signing professional forms, at Birmingham City on 22 August 1978 and by the end of the season was a regular. After impressing as an England Under 21 star, he was transferred to Nottingham Forest during the 1981 close season and was first team choice until the advent of Terry Wilson. Had a spell on loan with Sunderland towards the end of 1982-83 and on his return he played just once more for Forest, before going back to Roker Park on a more permanent basis. Settled into the side immediately, but was unfortunate to suffer a bad injury on New Years Day 1985 which kept him out of the game until the following December. Came back strongly and scored the first goal (a penalty) in the final game of 1985-86, a 2-0 victory over Stoke City, which ensured that Second Division football remained at Roker Park in the following season. It was only a short-lived reprieve, however, as Sunderland were relegated to the Third Division for the first time ever, at the end of the following season and an indication of their problems was that Proctor was joint top scorer with only eight goals (of which five were penalties). However, soon into the 1987-88 season, he jumped from the Third Division back into the First with Sheffield Wednesday. Held down a regular place in the "Owls'" midfield until his old club, Middlesbrough, struggling at the foot of the First Division, came for him in March 1989. Unfortunately, he was unable to help "Boro" avoid the drop and only a 4-1 win at Ayresome Park in the final game of 1989-90 saved the club from relegation in successive seasons to the Third Division. Suffered from injuries and a loss of form in 1990-91, although he came back well for the remaining 11 matches, including the losing promotion Play-Off games against Notts County. A regular performer for "Boro" in the first half of 1991-92, he lost his place to Jamie Pollock in the New Year and played only a peripheral role in the climax to the season as the club reached the Semi-Final of the League Cup and clinched promotion to the Premier League in the last match.

Clubs	Signing Date	Transfer Fee	APPEARANCES				GOALS			
			Lge	FL Cup	FA Cup	Others	Lge	FL Cup	FA Cup	Others
Middlesbrough	9.78	–	107+2	6	10		12	1	1	
Nottingham Forest	8.81	£440,000	60+4	10	2		5	3	1	
Sunderland	3.83	£115,000	115+2	13	6	2	19	2		2
Sheffield Wednesday	9.87	£275,000	59	1	6	3	4		1	
Middlesbrough*	3.89	£300,000	95+14	7+2	4+2	11+1	6			

QUIGLEY Michael (Mike) Anthony

Born: Manchester, 2 October 1970

Height: 5'6"

Weight: 9.4

Position/Skill Factor: Hard working midfield player, who sees passes early and constantly puts opponents under pressure. Great team man.

Career History: Joined Manchester City as a trainee in July 1987 and turned professional two years later. Has had to show extreme patience for a first team opportunity, which finally arrived in a Zenith Cup tie away to Sheffield Wednesday on 23 October 1991 in the unfamiliar position of right-back. A few weeks later he made his FL debut as a substitute away to Aston Villa on 7 December 1991 and made a few more appearances from the bench before the end of the season.

Clubs	Signing Date	Transfer Fee	APPEARANCES				GOALS			
			Lge	FL Cup	FA Cup	Others	Lge	FL Cup	FA Cup	Others
Manchester City*	7.89	–	0+5			1				

QUINLAN Philip (Phil) Edward

Born: Southport, 17 April 1971

Height: 5'7" Weight: 11.0

International Honours: E Yth

Position/Skill Factor: Young striker with a big heart and plenty of pace.

Career History: Came through Everton's junior ranks as an associated schoolboy (July 1985), before he left school and signed on as a trainee in July 1987. A professional since the 1989 close season, he made his FL debut, while on loan to Huddersfield Town, at Leeds Road against Shrewsbury Town on 12 March 1991. Loaned out for the final eight games of 1990-91, he came off the bench for that one, but then scored twice in his first two full matches for the club. Still awaits his first team debut at Goodison Park.

Clubs	Signing Date	Transfer Fee	APPEARANCES				GOALS			
			Lge	FL Cup	FA Cup	Others	Lge	FL Cup	FA Cup	Others
Everton	7.89	–								
Huddersfield Town*	3.91	Loan	7+1				2			

QUINN Niall John

Born: Dublin, 6 October 1966

Height: 6'4" Weight: 12.4

International Honours: IR Yth, IR "U21"-1, IR-30

Position/Skill Factor: An old fashioned centre-forward who is one of the finest headers in the game. A rare phenomenon as not only is he a "target man", knocking down high balls for his colleagues, but is also a consistent goal scorer himself, with a devastating shot in addition to his aerial power.

Career History: Spotted by Arsenal playing junior football in the Republic with Manortown United, he first came to Highbury on leaving school and played with the juniors until signing as a professional towards the end of 1983. Had to wait a further two years for a chance in the first team, before making his FL debut against Liverpool on 14 December 1985 and he celebrated with a goal in a 2-0 home win. Established himself during the next season, as George Graham's young side began to take shape, but after heading the table for a long period, the "Gunners" faded to finish fourth. But compensation came earlier in the form of selection as a sub for the Irish Republic's full international side in Iceland on 25 May 1986 and later, a League Cup winners medal, following Arsenal's 2-1 victory over Liverpool in 1987. However, after the club had signed Alan Smith in the summer of 1987, opportunities became less frequent and he found himself languishing in the reserves. He played just two games during Arsenal's Championship winning season in 1988-89 and made only a handful of appearances in 1989-90, before he was rescued from obscurity when signing for Manchester City in March 1990. Marked his debut at Maine Road with a goal in a 1-1 draw against Chelsea and three more strikes by the end of the season, secured his place in the Irish World Cup squad for Italy. Only missed one game in 1990-91 as City climbed to fifth place in the First Division and he scored freely, with 20 in the League, as well as laying on chances for others. Enjoyed another excellent season in 1991-92, with 12 FL goals from 36 games, plus two goals in cup competitions, but was overshadowed by his striking partner David White, who scored 22 goals. Remains a regular choice for the Republic of Ireland team.

Clubs	Signing Date	Transfer Fee	APPEARANCES				GOALS			
			Lge	FL Cup	FA Cup	Others	Lge	FL Cup	FA Cup	Others
Arsenal	11.83	–	59+8	14+2	8+2	0+1	44	4	2	
Manchester City*	3.90	£800,000	82	7	3	3	36	2	1	1

READ Paul Colin

Born: Harlow, 25 September 1973

Height: 5'11" **Weight:** 12.6

International Honours: E Sch

Position/Skill Factor: A young striker who appears to have the knack of being in the right position at the right time.

Career History: Snapped up by Arsenal while still at school, he signed associated schoolboy forms in December 1987, before progressing as a trainee (July 1990) to professional status in October 1991. Although he still awaits a first team call-up, he proved his ability in the "Gunners'" youth team, when breaking all previous goal scoring records.

Clubs	Signing Date	Transfer Fee	APPEARANCES				GOALS			
			Lge	FL Cup	FA Cup	Others	Lge	FL Cup	FA Cup	Others
Arsenal*	10.91	–								

READY Karl

Born: Neath, 14 August 1972

Height: 6'1" **Weight:** 12.0

International Honours: W Sch, W "U21"-1

Position/Skill Factor: Full-back or central defender, who is good in the air. A steady player, he passes the ball simply and effectively.

Career History: After joining Queens Park Rangers as a trainee in May 1989, having been on the club's books as an associated schoolboy since March 1988, he turned professional on his 18th birthday. His first team debut came in a League Cup tie at home to Hull City on 9 October 1991 when he was used as a substitute. Later in the season made his FL debut at home to Wimbledon on 1 February 1992, deputising for David Bardsley at right-back. Also won selection for the Welsh Under 21 team.

Clubs	Signing Date	Transfer Fee	APPEARANCES				GOALS			
			Lge	FL Cup	FA Cup	Others	Lge	FL Cup	FA Cup	Others
Q.P.R.*	8.90	–	1	0+1						

REDKNAPP Jamie Frank

Born: Barton-on-Sea, 25 June 1973

Height: 5'11"

Weight: 11.8

International Honours: E Sch, E Yth

Position/Skill Factor: Midfielder with all-round ability. Has excellent close control and is a very good passer of the ball.

Career History: The son of Harry, the former West Ham United, Brentford and Bournemouth player between 1964 and 1983, he was courted by Tottenham Hotspur as an associated schoolboy (September 1987). However, on leaving school, he joined his father who was then managing Bournemouth, as a trainee in September 1989 and made his FL debut at Hull City on 13 January 1990 at the age of 16 years and six months and was called up for his full debut later on in the season, before turning professional in the summer on his 17th birthday. Clearly a player of great potential, his name was already being mentioned as a target for bigger clubs and although not a first team regular in 1990-91, he was picked up by Liverpool in January as an investment for the future, one of Kenny Dalglish's last signings before his shock departure from Anfield. He received a first team opportunity earlier than expected due to Liverpool's long injury list and actually made his debut in a critical UEFA Cup tie away to Auxerre of France on 23 October which Liverpool lost 2-0, although overturning the deficit in the second leg. His Liverpool League debut came at Southampton on 7 December when he scored the equaliser after coming on as a substitute. Further opportunities came his way later in the season, but he played no part in the later stages of the "Reds'" FA Cup run.

Clubs	Signing Date	Transfer Fee	APPEARANCES				GOALS			
			Lge	FL Cup	FA Cup	Others	Lge	FL Cup	FA Cup	Others
Bournemouth	6.90	–	6+7	3	3	2				
Liverpool*	1.91	£350,000	5+1		2	1+1	1			

REDMOND Stephen (Steve)

Born: Liverpool,
2 November 1967

Height: 5'11"

Weight: 12.13

International Honours:
E Yth, E "U21"-14

Position/Skill Factor: A very experienced central defender for one so young, he reads situations well at the back and is a good striker of the ball.

Career History: Although born on Merseyside, he signed as an associated schoolboy player with Manchester City (October 1982), before becoming an apprentice in July 1984, when leaving school. After turning professional he had to wait over 12 months for a chance of first team soccer and while he was learning his trade, he was captaining the City youth side to victory over local rivals Manchester United in the Final of the 1986 FA Youth Cup. By then, he had already made his FL debut at Maine Road against Queens Park Rangers on 8 February 1986 and soon began to hold down a regular place in the side. Played 28 times in the League as City were relegated to the Second Division at the end of 1986-87, but was ever present the following season as the team looked for a quick return and his form and popularity was such, that the fans named him as their "Player of the Year". As the club captain, he led the team back to the First Division as runners-up in 1988-89. A run of 138 consecutive League games was halted at the beginning of 1990-91, but he soon re-established himself and his experience was vital to a side who were challenging for a top three position for most of the season. After playing in all but one of City's first 30 games in 1991-92, he was suddenly dropped in late February, in favour of first David Brightwell and then Dutchman Michel Vonk and demanded a transfer. However, he is surely good enough to win back his place in the City team before too long.

Clubs	Signing Date	Transfer Fee	APPEARANCES				GOALS			
			Lge	FL Cup	FA Cup	Others	Lge	FL Cup	FA Cup	Others
Manchester City*	12.84	–	231+15	24	17	11	6			

REED John Paul

Born: Rotherham, 27 August 1972

Height: 5'6" Weight: 8.11

Position/Skill Factor: Right-winger with good skills and a lot of pace who gets past defenders. A good crosser of the ball, he can also score goals.

Career History: First signing as an associated schoolboy (October 1987) and then as a trainee (July 1988), on graduating he turned professional for Sheffield United during the 1990 close season. Yet to play for United, he was loaned out to Fourth Division Scarborough, in order to gain playing experience and made his FL debut at Chesterfield on 12 January 1991. He did very well with five goals in 14 games, including a brace in a 2-0 win at Northampton Town and a late equaliser at Stockport County. He returned to Scarborough for another loan period in 1991-92, before finally making an appearance for the "Blades" as a substitute in their last match of the season away to Wimbledon on 2 May 1992. Will be hoping to make a breakthrough this coming year.

Clubs	Signing Date	Transfer Fee	APPEARANCES				GOALS			
			Lge	FL Cup	FA Cup	Others	Lge	FL Cup	FA Cup	Others
Sheffield United*	7.90	–	0+1							
Scarborough	1.91	Loan	14				5			
Scarborough	9.91	Loan	5+1							

REES Melvin (Mel) John

Born: Cardiff,
25 January 1967

Height: 6'2"

Weight: 12.12

International Honours:
W Yth

Position: Goalkeeper.

Career History: Joined Cardiff City as an apprentice in August 1983 and on signing as a professional during the 1984 close season, immediately made his FL debut, deputising for Lee Smelt, at Ninian Park against Brighton & Hove Albion on 8 September 1984. After letting in four goals in a 4-2 defeat, he didn't play in the first team again that season, but came back the following term in a side that were doomed to the Fourth Division and conceded 22 goals in nine matches. Eventually gaining a regular place towards the end of 1986-87, he impressed enough to be signed by Watford during the close season, as understudy to Tony Coton. With Coton only missing the odd game, he had spells on loan with Crewe Alexandra and Leyton Orient and when West Bromwich Albion came for him at the beginning of 1990-91, albeit as cover for Stuart Naylor, he jumped at the opportunity. Unfortunately, standing in for the injured Naylor, his first game coincided with the worst result in Albion's history, a 4-2 defeat at home in the Third Round of the FA Cup to non-League Woking. Although he went on to make 18 consecutive League appearances, before making way for Naylor, the club won only four of those games and it came as no surprise when they were relegated to the Third Division for the first time in the club's history at the end of 1990-91. A player whose career has been dogged by misfortune, he was relegated to third choice at the Hawthorns by manager Bobby Gould in 1991-92 and was about to sign on for a second loan period with Norwich City when his former manager, Dave Bassett, made him the offer of a full contract with Sheffield United, desperately needing a 'keeper in the absence of Simon Tracey and Phil Kite. His debut for the "Blades" against Liverpool was nothing short of sensational, keeping out everything the "Reds" could throw at him and helping his side to a 2-0 victory, despite being overrun. He proved it was no fluke with a succession of outstanding saves in the next six games, in which he let in only three goals. From Third Division reject to First Division hero in a matter of weeks, he was rewarded with a call up to the Welsh national squad as understudy to Nevill Southall. Tragically, the jinx that has followed him around, struck again, when he sustained a leg injury in the penultimate game at home to Leeds United. his injury was a major factor in the "Blades'" 2-3 defeat and also forced his withdrawal from the Welsh squad. Since the end of the season, he has undergone a serious operation and is expected to be out of the game for at least 12 months.

Clubs	Signing Date	Transfer Fee	APPEARANCES				GOALS			
			Lge	FL Cup	FA Cup	Others	Lge	FL Cup	FA Cup	Others
Cardiff City	9.84	–	31	3	3					
Watford	7.87	£60,000	3		1	1				
Crewe Alexandra	8.87	Loan	6							
Leyton Orient	1.90	Loan	9			1				
W.B.A.	9.90	£55,000	18		1					
Sheffield United*	3.92	£25,000	8							

REGIS Cyrille

Born: Mariapousoula, French Guyana, 9 February 1958

Height: 6'0" Weight: 13.6

International Honours: E "U21"-6, E"B", E-5

Position/Skill Factor: Powerful striker, with a footballing brain, who is a handful for any defence and is never easy to mark as he pulls away from defenders well. Still very good in the air, he is always a threat at set plays.

Career History: The older brother of David, who currently plays for Plymouth Argyle, he was signed by First Division West Bromwich Albion in the 1977 close season, after impressing with the London based Isthmian League club, Hayes. Prior to that, he had played for Molesey. Scored an outstanding solo-goal in a 2-1 win on his FL debut at the Hawthorns against Middlesbrough on 3 September 1977 and netted 18 times in all games in his first season as a professional, as well as helping Albion to

the Semi-Finals of the FA Cup. His form was such, that international recognition was just around the corner and he won his first full England cap when he came on as substitute for Tevor Francis against Northern Ireland at Wembley on 23 February 1982. With his ever growing reputation, there was much competition when he became available for transfer early in 1984-85 and following lengthy negotiations, he finally signed for Coventry City. Although he found League goals hard to come by in his first two seasons as City struggled at the bottom of the First Division, he did manage to equal a club record when he hammered in five against lowly Chester City in the Second Round of the League Cup on 9 October 1985. 1986-87 brought both him and the club a change of fortune as his partnership with Dave Bennett on the wing bore fruit. As City moved up the table they also reached the FA Cup Final for the first time in their history and at the end of extra-time the "Sky Blues'" fans at last had something to cheer, following a thrilling 3-2 victory over Tottenham Hotspur. Over the last three seasons, although playing regularly, he failed to reach double figures in the League and while he often looked dangerous around the box, his value to the "Sky Blues" was more in his ability to provide chances for others, rather than that of goal scorer. Released on a "free" in the summer of 1991, he joined neighbouring Aston Villa on a one year contract. Expected to be used sparingly, he in fact played throughout the season, missing only three FL games and was Villa's only consistent forward, scoring 11 goals — his best haul for five years.

Clubs	Signing Date	Transfer Fee	APPEARANCES				GOALS			
			Lge	FL Cup	FA Cup	Others	Lge	FL Cup	FA Cup	Others
W.B.A.	5.77	£5,000	233+4	27+1	25	10	82	16	10	4
Coventry City	10.84	£250,000	231+7	24	15+1	4	47	12	3	
Aston Villa*	7.91	–	39	2	5		11			

284

REID Nicholas (Nicky) Scott

Born: Urmston, 30 October 1960

Height: 5'10" Weight: 12.4

International Honours: E "U21"-6

Position/Skill Factor: Experienced midfield dynamo, or full-back, who keeps the team ticking over. A good tackler and passer of the ball, he has a good attitude to the game. Always to be found in the thick of things.

Career History: A product of the excellent Manchester City youth team, he first came to Maine Road as an apprentice in May 1977. After graduating to the professional ranks in October 1978, he appeared twice for the club in UEFA Cup matches against Borussia Moenchengladbach, before making his FL debut away to Ipswich Town on 31 March 1979. Most of his early appearances were at full-back, but in 1980-81 he won a regular slot in midfield, playing in both matches of the replayed 1981 FA Cup Final when City lost 2-3 to Tottenham Hotspur. Remained a regular performer, barring injury, to 1985-86 when he reverted to right-back again, City having no specialist for the position. Lost his way and his place, in 1986-87 when City were relegated and was surprisingly granted a fee transfer at the end of the season. A bargain signing for Blackburn Rovers, he proved he was still a most effective player when appearing in every game in 1987-88 and most matches in 1988-89 when Rovers missed promotion to the First Division in both seasons at the Play-Off stage, as they did again in 1989-90. After three seasons as an automatic first choice, his position came under threat from Lee Richardson in 1990-91. Lost his place early in 1991-92 and for the remainder most of his appearances were as substitute. Played no part in the end of season drama or the Play-Offs and will doubtless be looking to fight his way back into first team contention in 1992-93.

Clubs	Signing Date	Transfer Fee	APPEARANCES				GOALS			
			Lge	FL Cup	FA Cup	Others	Lge	FL Cup	FA Cup	Others
Manchester City	10.78	–	211+5	20	17	6	2			
Blackburn Rovers*	7.87	–	160+14	13	6+2	12+1	9			1

REID Peter

Born: Huyton, 20 June 1956

Height: 5'8" Weight: 10.7

International Honours: E "U21"-6, E-13

Position/Skill Factor: Indomitable midfield battler who never shirks a tackle and is constructive when in possession. Knows the game inside out, with a great footballing brain, he leads by example. Courage is another hallmark of this gritty player.

Career History: Probably the most vital ingredient of Everton's formidable team of the mid 1980s, which won two League Championships in 1984-85 and 1986-87, the FA Cup in 1984 and made three other Cup Final appearances in 1985, 1986 and 1989, he joined Bolton Wanderers straight from school, signing as an apprentice in July 1971, before turning professional three years later. Made his FL debut at Burnden Park when coming on as a substitute against Leyton Orient on 9 October 1974 and by the end of 1974-75 he was holding down a regular place in the side. He missed only three games during the next three seasons and won a Second Division Championship medal as the "Trotters" re-joined the top flight at the end of 1977-78. Suffering an injury at the start of the club's First Division campaign, he recovered to play 14 games, before breaking a leg on New Year's Day 1979 at snowbound Burnden Park, following a collision with George Wood, the Everton goalie, in a League match that was later abandoned. Out for over a year, he came back into a side that would be relegated at the end of the season. He played very few games in 1980-81, mainly due to contractual problems and returning to the team at the beginning of the next season, after just two matches, he had the incredible misfortune to break his right leg again during a League game at Barnsley. On recovering, Everton snapped him up at a basement bargain fee in December 1982, nearly three years after the "Toffees" had originally offered to pay Bolton £600,000 for his services! Injured almost before he got started at Goodison Park, he missed very few games in 1983-84 and won an FA Cup winners medal, following Everton's 2-0 victory over Watford. A member of the side that lost 1-0 to Manchester United in the 1985 FA Cup Final, he was out injured for a large chunk of 1985-86, but was back in time to play in Everton's third successive FA Cup Final, a 3-1 defeat against local rivals, Liverpool. Prior to that, his sterling club displays were finally translated into full international terms, when he was selected to play for England against West Germany in Mexico on 12 June 1985 and another honour followed as the PFA voted him as their "Player of the Year". Injuries were still a major factor in his career and he made only 15 League appearances as Everton won the League title in 1986-87. There was still plenty of spark

left when he was allowed a free transfer to Queens Park Rangers during 1988-89 and when Howard Kendall was appointed manager of Manchester City, one of his first tasks was to bring him to Maine Road as player-coach. As inspirational as ever, he played 28 League matches for City in 1990-91, was appointed player-manager, on Kendall's departure in November 1990 and lifted the club into fifth place in the First Division. Continued to play First Division football in 1991-92 at the age of 35, but following the signings of Steve McMahon and Fitzroy Simpson during the season, he will probably now take a back seat. Has a younger brother, Shaun, recently released by York City.

Clubs	Signing Date	Transfer Fee	APPEARANCES				GOALS			
			Lge	FL Cup	FA Cup	Others	Lge	FL Cup	FA Cup	Others
Bolton Wanderers	5.74	–	222+3	18+1	17		23	1	1	
Everton	12.82	£60,000	155+4	23+2	35	15	8	1	3	1
Q.P.R.	2.89	–	29	2+1			1			
Manchester City*	12.89	–	75+4	2	5		1		1	

RICHARDSON Kevin

Born: Newcastle,
4 December 1962

Height: 5'10"

Weight: 10.12

Position/Skill Factor: Very experienced underrated midfielder. Great competitor and a decisive tackler, he has the ability to swerve the ball and takes a lot of free kicks and corners.

Career History: Hailing from the north-east, he first came to Everton on associated schoolboy forms (July 1978) and on leaving school, a year later, he signed as an apprentice (May 1979). After turning professional, he had to wait nearly 12 months before making his FL debut at Goodison against Sunderland on 21 November 1981, but by the end of 1981-82 he had settled nicely into the number six shirt. The following season he appeared for Everton in both the League Cup and FA Cup Finals. The club were defeated 1-0 by Liverpool in the former, but the "Toffees'" 2-0 victory over Watford in the latter, was recompense enough when collecting an FA Cup winners medal. Never an automatic first choice at Goodison with Paul Bracewell and Peter Reid dictating operations in central midfield, most of his appearances were on the left side of midfield, deputising capably for Kevin Sheedy and scoring several vital goals, but 14 League appearances in 1984-85 assured him of a League Championship medal, as Everton took the title. At the beginning of 1986-87, he moved to Watford and as an influential member of their successful side, his performance in the 3-1 victory over Arsenal in the Sixth Round of the FA Cup that season, impressed the "Gunners" so much that they signed him

during the summer. Proving what a versatile player he could be, he replaced the injured Graham Rix and immediately became an important cog in the side that broke the club record with 14 consecutive wins. And following an incredible victory over Liverpool in the last match of 1988-89, having made 32 appearances for Arsenal, he added another League Championship medal to his list of honours. After playing in Arsenal's first 38 games in 1989-90, he suffered an injury towards the end of the season and, on recovering, he signed for the Spanish team Real Sociedad of San Sebastion, linking up with John Aldridge and Dalian Atkinson during the 1990 close season. Ironically, when John Toshack was reappointed manager of the Spanish club, he decided he only wanted native players in his team and the three expatriates returned to England, Richardson joining Dalian Atkinson at Aston Villa. Played in every one of Villa's 51 match programme without being substituted — a remarkable achievement in today's competitive environment, where few players escape injury during a season.

Clubs	Signing Date	Transfer Fee	APPEARANCES				GOALS			
			Lge	FL Cup	FA Cup	Others	Lge	FL Cup	FA Cup	Others
Everton	12.80	–	95+14	10+3	13	4+1	16	3	1	
Watford	9.86	£225,000	39	3	7	1	2			
Arsenal	8.87	£200,000	88+8	13+3	9	2	5	2	1	
Real Soceidad (Spain)	6.90	£750,000								
Aston Villa*	8.91	£450,000	42	2	5	2	6			

RICHARDSON Lee James

Born: Halifax, 12 March 1969

Height: 5'11" Weight: 11.0

Position/Skill Factor: Midfield player who passes the ball well, both short and long and makes forward runs into the opposition's penalty area to good effect.

Career History: A player who started in the lower reaches of the Football League with Halifax Town, he first joined the club as an associated schoolboy in April 1985, before signing on as a trainee in March 1986. Made his FL debut at Rochdale on 4 May 1987 and by the end of the following term, he was almost a regular in the side, having turned professional during the 1987 close season. After playing in all but one of the first 26 games of 1988-89, he was transferred to Watford for a record fee (for Halifax), thus following in the footsteps of Rick Holden. Went straight into the "Hornets'" team, but lost his place just nine games later. Although playing in more than half of Watford's games in 1989-90, he was "in-and-out" of the side without establishing himself. Perhaps homesick, he returned north to join Blackburn Rovers in the summer of 1990. Seemingly inconsistent, he could not always be sure of his place at Ewood Park, even though he played in all but eight games during 1990-91. Started last season as first choice, but lost his place to Gordon Cowans in November and did not reappear until the end of the season. However, he took part in the five last vital matches of the Second Division campaign and the three Play-Off games, appearing mainly as a substitute.

			APPEARANCES				GOALS			
Clubs	Signing Date	Transfer Fee	Lge	FL Cup	FA Cup	Others	Lge	FL Cup	FA Cup	Others
Halifax Town	7.87	–	43+13	4	4+2	6	2			
Watford	2.89	£175,000	40+1	1+1	1		1			
Blackburn Rovers*	8.90	£250,000	50+12	1+1		2+2	3			

RIPLEY Stuart Edward

Born: Middlesbrough, 20 November 1967

Height: 5'11"

Weight: 12.6

International Honours: E Yth, E "U21"-8

Position/Skill Factor: A left-winger who is good on the ball and has the ability to go past defenders when using his pace to good effect. Always looking to get into scoring positions.

Career History: A member of the local schoolboy team that won the FA schools trophy, it was not surprising that he joined Middlesbrough, first as an associated schoolboy (March 1983), then later as an apprentice (August 1984), before signing professional during 1985-86. Prior to turning professional, however, he had made his FL debut at Ayresome Park when coming on as a substitute against Oldham Athletic on 5 February 1985. After a short loan spell with Bolton, he played a few matches at the tail end of 1986-87 when "Boro" were relegated to the Third Division and became a regular the following season as the side returned to the Second Division as runners-up. Enjoyed an excellent season in 1987-88, playing 40 League games and scoring eight goals, including a hat-trick in a 6-0 home defeat of Sheffield United, which assisted Middlesbrough back into the First Division following the Play-Offs. But after only one season, the club was relegated, only recording one victory in their last 17 matches. Having just escaped further relegation in 1989-90, the "Boro" could consider themselves fortunate to reach the First Division Play-Off stage in 1990-91, before losing to Notts County. But when available for selection, he was one of their few stars in an ultimately disappointing season, scoring in each of the club's last four victories. Played in most of "Boro's" successful 1991-92 campaign, with long runs in the two major cup competitions, before clinching automatic promotion to the Premier League in the last match of the season. Scored only four goals during the season, but one of them, a brilliant run finished by an equally brilliant curling 30 yard shot in a Fifth Round League Cup replay against Peterborough, took "Boro" into the Semi-Final to face Manchester United.

			APPEARANCES				GOALS			
Clubs	Signing Date	Transfer Fee	Lge	FL Cup	FA Cup	Others	Lge	FL Cup	FA Cup	Others
Middlesbrough*	11.85	–	210+39	21+2	17+1	20+1	26	3	1	1
Bolton Wanderers	2.86	Loan	5			0+1	1			

RITCHIE Andrew (Andy) Timothy

Born: Manchester, 28 November 1960

Height: 5'9" Weight: 11.11

International Honours: E Sch, E Yth, E "U21"-1

Position/Skill Factor: A striker who has improved with age and experience. With good skill and a lovely touch, he pulls away from defenders well and gets into excellent scoring positions. Also makes great runs off the ball.

Career History: One of the most accomplished forwards in the Football League, he is a major factor in Oldham Athletic's rise to fame. It is interesting to speculate whether, if Manchester United had shown as much faith in him as their expensive imports, he would now enjoy a similar stature in the game to Gary Lineker and Ian Rush. First went to Manchester United as an associated schoolboy in October 1975 and on leaving school, he signed as an apprentice in September 1977. Less than three months later, on turning professional, he made his FL debut in a 6-2 win at Everton on 26 December 1977 and held his place for three more games until Stuart Pearson was fit enough to return to the side. The following season, he got an extended run, playing 16 times and scoring ten goals, including a hat-trick in the League against Leeds United. Not given many more opportunities to shine, although he scored another hat-trick against Tottenham Hotspur in 1979-80, he was allowed to leave for Brighton & Hove Albion early in the 1980-81 season. Never found his best form on the south coast, although as the club's top scorer

32, he was exchanged for
Second Division Leeds
-83. Spent four full seasons
he showed glimpses of his
quite hit it off. Contractual
lem and he was on a week-
r before finally getting away
letic during the 1987 close
games due to injury in his
k, he delighted the fans with
ling the net, alongside Roger
Palmer and   he had a glorious season in
1989-90, scoring 12 times in cup matches as the club
reached the League Cup Final, losing 1-0 to Nottingham
Forest and the FA Cup Semi-Final, before going out to
Manchester United. But the heartaches of the previous
season were forgotten in 1990-91, as he won a Second
Division Championship medal and could look forward to
playing again in the top flight, after an absence of eight
years. Plagued by injury in 1991-92, he made only a handful of appearances in the First Division, although showing
that his scoring touch had not deserted with four goals in
an early season 7-1 thrashing of Torquay in the League
Cup.

Clubs	Signing Date	Transfer Fee	APPEARANCES				GOALS			
			Lge	FL Cup	FA Cup	Others	Lge	FL Cup	FA Cup	Others
Manchester United	12.77	–	26+7	3+2	3+1		13			
Brighton & H.A.	10.80	£500,000	82+7	3+1	9		23	1	2	
Leeds United	3.83	£150,000	127+9	11	9	2+1	40	3	1	
Oldham Athletic*	8.87	£50,000	139+11	15	6	3	67	17	3	

ROAST Stephen

Born: Bexley, 19 September 1972

Height: 5'6" Weight: 9.4

Position/Skill Factor: A very busy little midfielder who
excels at playing balls into his front men.

Career History: Having signed professional forms for
Southampton during the 1991 close season, after being on
the club's books as an associated schoolboy (October
1986) and as a trainee (July 1989), his immediate task is to
establish himself in the "Saints'" reserve side.

Clubs	Signing Date	Transfer Fee	APPEARANCES				GOALS			
			Lge	FL Cup	FA Cup	Others	Lge	FL Cup	FA Cup	Others
Southampton*	5.91	–								

ROBERTS Anthony (Tony)
Mark

Born: Holyhead, 4 August 1969

Height: 6'0" Weight: 12.0

International Honours: W Yth, W "U21"-3

Position/Skill Factor: A good shot stopper, he is a goalkeeper who never stops giving instructions to his defenders. Very good kicker from his hands.

Career History: Came to Queens Park Rangers as a
trainee in November 1986 and after impressing in the
juniors, he was taken on the professional staff during the
1987 close season. Made his FL debut at Loftus Road
against Coventry City on 18 December 1987, when
deputising for David Seaman and was unfortunate to let
in two very late goals during a 2-1 defeat. Stood in for
Seaman in 1989-90, keeping two clean sheets in five
League games and in 1990-91, after starting the season as
first choice, following the England goalie's departure to
Arsenal, he was later replaced by the club's new signing,
Jan Stejskal. With the consistent Stejskal showing such
commanding form in 1991-92, he only made two first team
appearances, versus Tottenham Hotspur in the League
and Crystal Palace in the Zenith Cup.

Clubs	Signing Date	Transfer Fee	APPEARANCES				GOALS			
			Lge	FL Cup	FA Cup	Others	Lge	FL Cup	FA Cup	Others
Q.P.R.*	7.87	–	19	3		2				

ROBINS Mark Gordon

Born: Ashton-under-Lyne,
22 December 1969

Height: 5'7"

Weight: 10.1

International Honours:
E "U21"-6

Position/Skill Factor: Very skilful striker who does well
with his back to goal, twisting and turning to get his shots
in. Always looking to play his team-mates into goal scoring positions.

Career History: Came to Manchester United as a trainee
on leaving school in July 1986 after being on the club's
books as an associated schoolboy player (February 1984).
Joined the professional ranks at the end of 1986, but had
to wait nearly two years, before coming off the bench for
his FL debut at Wimbledon on 22 October 1988. It was
during United's FA Cup run in 1990 that he really came
to the fore. He netted the only goal of the Third Round
tie at Nottingham Forest and then the one that put the
club on their way to a 3-2 win at Newcastle United in the
Fifth Round. In the Semi-Final, he came on as a substitute
to score the winner in the spectacular tie with Oldham
Athletic, a goal that finally broke the resistance of the
Second Division side. That goal was one of six he scored
in six consecutive games. Finished the season with ten
League and FA Cup goals and an FA Cup winners medal,
following United's 1-0 win over Crystal Palace in the
replayed Final. Remained in the shadows of Brian
McClair and Mark Hughes in 1990-91, making just 19
appearances, 12 of them from the bench. Almost totally
ignored in 1991-92, despite the fact that a shortage of
goals in the second half of the season cost United the
Championship. In one of his rare outings he scored two

goals against Portsmouth in a League Cup tie, after coming on as a substitute.

Clubs	Signing Date	Transfer Fee	APPEARANCES				GOALS			
			Lge	FL Cup	FA Cup	Others	Lge	FL Cup	FA Cup	Others
Manchester United*	12.86	–	19+29	0+7	4+4	4+3	11	2	3	1

ROBINSON Paul

Born: Scarborough, 2 January 1974

Height: 5'9" Weight: 12.2

Position: Goalkeeper.

Career History: Signed professional forms for Sheffield Wednesday during the 1992 close season, having previously been at Hillsborough as an associated schoolboy (July 1988) and as a trainee (July 1990). No first team experience as yet.

Clubs	Signing Date	Transfer Fee	APPEARANCES				GOALS			
			Lge	FL Cup	FA Cup	Others	Lge	FL Cup	FA Cup	Others
Sheffield Wednesday*	6.92	–								

ROBSON Bryan

Born: Witton Gilbert, 11 January 1957

Height: 5'11" Weight: 11.12

International Honours: E Yth, E "U21"-7 E"B", FL Rep, E-90

Position/Skill Factor: Inspirational midfield player who has all the right ingredients. A strong tackler, he passes the ball well when in possession and is always looking to break into the opposition's penalty area to score vital goals. A great captain, he leads by example.

Career History: The outstanding midfield player of his generation, he became an England "icon", whose international displays were, if anything, greater than his club performances and his ability to snatch priceless goals out of nothing helped England to victory on many occasions and on others saved his team from humiliating defeat. His 26 goals from 90 England games, ranks him as England's sixth highest all-time scorer — an astonishing record for a player whose role in the team was as much defensive as attacking. A major influence in every game he plays, his career has been a catalogue of triumphs, mixed with long periods on the sidelines through injury. It is a tribute to his character that he has always come back strongly from each setback. A native of the north-east, he ventured south on leaving school, joining West Bromwich Albion as an apprentice in September 1972, before signing on as a professional in the 1974 close season. He made his FL debut at York City on 12 April 1975 and in his next two games, scored a goal apiece. The following season, he played in 14 League matches as Albion were promoted to the First Division, behind Sunderland and Bristol City, but his progress was hindered when he suffered two broken legs during 1976-77. However, he returned to win his first full England cap against Republic of Ireland at Wembley on 6 February 1980 and in October 1981, he became Britain's costliest player when he signed for Manchester United in a deal that included his team-mate, Remi Moses. He made his United debut in the heat of a Manchester "derby", a goalless draw in front of more than 52,000 fans at Maine Road. Immediately struck up a daunting partnership with Ray Wilkins in United's midfield, showing what a versatile player he was and it came as no surprise when he was appointed club captain and later captain of the England team. Although the League title has always eluded the "Reds" during his time with them, he has been more fortunate in the FA Cup and in a hat-trick of Wembley appearances, he has never been on the losing side. In 1983, he scored two goals in the 4-0 defeat of Brighton & Hove Albion, in a replay and later led United to victory in 1-0 wins over Everton (1984) and Crystal Palace (1990), a match which also required a replay to settle the result. In both 1989-90 and 1990-91, he spent long periods out of the game and was sometimes used as a sweeper in order to prolong his career. Although only playing 15 League games in 1990-91, after missing the early part of the season, he came back to win a European Cup Winners Cup medal at the end of a pulsating 2-1 victory over Barcelona, following the disappointment of the 1-0 League Cup defeat at the hands of Sheffield Wednesday, just three weeks earlier. Skippered England in the 1982 and 1986 World Cups, although on both occasion, his personal involvement was interrupted by injury and his opening goal after only 27 seconds in England's first game of the 1982 World Cup against France is still the fastest goal ever scored in the tourna-

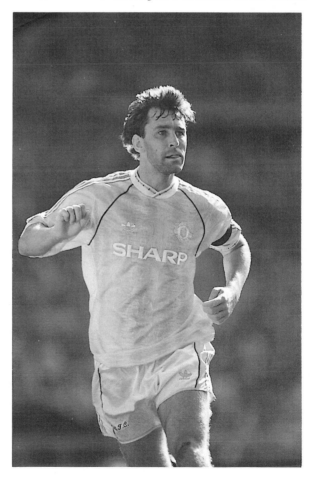

ment. Although a regular member of United's team for the first-half of 1991-92, his absence through injury for much of the second-half of the season was considered to be a major factor in the club's failure to land the League Championship, which appeared to be theirs for the taking

Bryan Robson

until the closing weeks of the campaign. After a disappointing performance against Turkey, he announced his retirement from the international scene — a pity since a fit Robson would surely have inspired a better effort than England put up in the European Championships. Bryan's younger brother, Gary, currently plays for West Bromwich Albion.

Clubs	Signing Date	Transfer Fee	APPEARANCES				GOALS			
			Lge	FL Cup	FA Cup	Others	Lge	FL Cup	FA Cup	Others
W.B.A.	8.74	–	194+4	17+1	10+2	12	39	2	2	3
Manchester United*	10.81	£1,500,000	311+5	44+1	32	25	72	5	9	10

ROBSON Stewart Ian

Born: Billericay,
6 November 1964

Height: 5'11"

Weight: 11.13

International Honours:
E Yth, E "U21"-8

Position/Skill Factor: Midfielder with a great attitude to the game, having to overcome terrible injury problems. A tenacious player, who likes to get forward for a shooting opportunity, he is also a good passer of the ball.

Career History: One of the few players to come into the professional game after a Public School education, he was discovered by Arsenal while playing at Brentwood and signed associated schoolboy forms in December 1978. On leaving school in May 1981, he joined the club as an apprentice and turned over to the paid ranks just seven months later. At the same time, he made his FL debut at West Ham United on 5 December 1981 and within a couple of months had settled into the Arsenal midfield. Unfortunately for him, the club were not among the honours during his time with them, but he impressed the fans well enough to become the "Gunners'" "Player of the Year" in 1985. After losing his place in the side to Steve Williams early in 1986-87, he was eventually transferred to West Ham United and immediately slotted into midfield, alongside his old team-mate, Liam Brady. Injured for most of 1988-89, he was powerless to assist the "Hammers" as they struggled against ultimate relegation and on top of that he was then sidelined for most of the following season, managing only seven League games. On returning, midway through 1990-91, for the FA Cup match against Aldershot, he couldn't finish the match and a few weeks later was loaned out to Coventry City, who signed him on a free transfer at the end of the season. Thought by many to be "finished" at the top level, he proved to be one of the "Sky Blues'" few successes in a dismal season, missing only five FL games during the 1991-92 and scoring three goals (worth seven points to his team), which in the final analysis helped the club to avoid relegation by the skin of their teeth. He was justly voted the supporters "Player of the Year".

Clubs	Signing Date	Transfer Fee	APPEARANCES				GOALS			
			Lge	FL Cup	FA Cup	Others	Lge	FL Cup	FA Cup	Others
Arsenal	11.81	–	150+1	20	13	2	16	3	1	1
West Ham United	1.87	£700,000	68+1	8	6	1	4	1	1	
Coventry City*	3.91	–	40+1	2	1	1	3			

ROCASTLE David Carlyle

Born: Lewisham, 2 May 1967

Height: 5'9" Weight: 11.12

International Honours: E "U21"-14, E"B", E-14

Position/Skill Factor: Skilful right-sided midfield player with good vision and quick feet, who always manages to find space. Is capable of scoring spectacular goals.

Career History: First came to Arsenal as an associated schoolboy in May 1982 and on leaving school, signed as an apprentice in August 1983. Made his FL debut, nine months after turning over to the paid ranks, at Highbury, against Newcastle United on 28 September 1985. Soon became a regular on the "Gunners'" right flank, missing only a handful of games during the next couple of seasons and won a League Cup winners medal, following Arsenal's 2-1 victory over Liverpool in 1987. Ever present in 1988-89, as the club won the League Championship, he was rewarded at full international level with an England cap against Denmark on 7 June 1989. The following season saw the club slip to fourth place in the League and this coincided with him suffering a loss of form. Worse

was to follow in 1990-91, when after playing in the first ten League games, he lost his place in the side and only made another three appearances as Arsenal won the League Championship for the second time in three years. Made a highly creditable comeback in 1991-92 in a new role in central midfield, playing in all but three games of the campaign and scoring one of the goals of the season in a 1-1 draw away to League leaders, Manchester United in October — a magnificent 30 yard lob which hit the bar and bounced into the net off the back of the United 'keeper. Also won a recall to the England squad, playing three times, but apparently not impressing enough to be included in the squad for the European Championship Finals.

Clubs	Signing Date	Transfer Fee	APPEARANCES				GOALS			
			Lge	FL Cup	FA Cup	Others	Lge	FL Cup	FA Cup	Others
Arsenal*	12.84	–	204+14	32+1	18+2	9	24	6	4	

RODGER Simon Lee

Born: Shoreham, 3 October 1971

Height: 5'9" Weight: 11.7

Position/Skill Factor: hard working midfield player with a sweet left foot who is capable of running with the ball, while looking to create goal scoring chances.

Career History: Born on the Sussex coast, he joined nearby Vauxhall League team Bognor Regis Town in 1988. The club had close links with Crystal Palace and after one year with them, he went to Selhurst Park as a trainee in July 1989, turning professional 12 months later. Made remarkable progress in 1991-92 after his FL debut away to Sheffield Wednesday on 5 October 1991. He replaced Paul Mortimer in midfield from December and held his place almost to the end of the season.

Clubs	Signing Date	Transfer Fee	APPEARANCES				GOALS			
			Lge	FL Cup	FA Cup	Others	Lge	FL Cup	FA Cup	Others
Crystal Palace*	7.90	–	20+2	6	0+1	0+1				

ROGERS Paul Anthony

Born: Portsmouth, 21 March 1965

Height: 6'0"

Weight: 11.13

International Honours: E Semi-Pro Int

Position/Skill Factor: All-round midfield player who can both pass and defend well.

Career History: An England semi-professional international from 1989 to 1991 and a stockbroker by profession, he had played nine years for Sutton United in the Isthmian League, Vauxhall-Opel League and Vauxhall Conference when, "out of the blue", Dave Bassett persuaded him to give up his lucrative career and sign professional for Sheffield United at the age of 26. As with many of Bassett's signings it seemed crazy, but it worked! After making his FL debut in midfield away to Luton Town on 22 February 1992 in place of the injured Michael Lake, he took the leap from the Vauxhall League to the First Division in his stride and held his place till the end of the season, helping the "Blades" to rise from 18th place (on his debut) to a final place of ninth.

Clubs	Signing Date	Transfer Fee	APPEARANCES				GOALS			
			Lge	FL Cup	FA Cup	Others	Lge	FL Cup	FA Cup	Others
Sheffield United*	1.92	£35,000	13							

ROSARIO Robert Michael

Born: Hammersmith, 4 March 1966

Height: 6'3" Weight: 12.

International Honours: E "U21"-4

Position/Skill Factor: Striker with a very good left foot, who is also strong in the air. Dangerous at set plays, he shields the ball well and brings his midfield players into shooting positions.

Career History: On Norwich City's books as an associated schoolboy from October 1982, he played several games for non-League Hillingdon Borough, before signing professional forms for the "Canaries", just over a year later. made his FL debut at Carrow Road in a 6-1 victory over Watford on 7 April 1984, without getting his name on the scoresheet, but rectified that little matter with a goal against Stoke City two games later. Did not play in City's first team for another year and was loaned out to Wolverhampton Wanderers for a short spell. In 1985-86, he played eight League games as Norwich won the Second Division Championship and finally began to hold down a regular place the following season, playing in the last 25 matches. Lost his first team place to Wayne Biggins and then to Robert Fleck in 1987-88, but eventually settled down to balance height with speed in an effective partnership with the latter, during 1989-90. An infrequent scorer, he scored the ITV "goal of the season" during 1989-90 with a 35 yard volley against Southampton in a 4-4 draw early in the season. Out of the "Canaries'" team for most of 1990-91 and without a League goal to his name, he was signed by Coventry City in March 1991 as a replacement for the soon to be released Cyrille Regis. It was ironic that a team with a perennial problem in scoring goals should sign a forward with the lowest scoring ratio (one goal for every seven FL games) in the First Division. Despite a good start in 1991-92 with two strikes in his first four games, he unsurprisingly failed to end the club's (and his own personal) drought, scoring only four FL goals in 29 games.

Clubs	Signing Date	Transfer Fee	APPEARANCES				GOALS			
			Lge	FL Cup	FA Cup	Others	Lge	FL Cup	FA Cup	Others
Norwich City	12.83	–	115+11	11	11+1	8+1	18	3	3	5
Wolverhampton W.	12.85	Loan	2			2	1			
Coventry City*	3.91	£600,000	26+5	2+1	2	1	4	2		

ROSENTHAL Ronny

Born: Haifa, Israel, 4 October 1963

Height: 5'10" Weight: 11.12

International Honours: Israeli Int.

Position/Skill Factor: Excellent striker with pace, skill and a terrific left foot. Always looking to get shots in, he is very quick over the vital first ten yards.

Career History: Starting out in his native Israel with Maccabi, Tel Aviv, he came to Liverpool in March 1990, following experience with leading Belgian teams, FC Brugge and Standard Liege. Initially at Anfield on loan, the move became permanent during the 1990 close season after he had made a sensational start in English soccer. Came off the bench for his FL debut, in front of the Kop against Southampton on 31 March 1990. Two weeks later, when deputising for the injured Ian Rush at Charlton Athletic, he made a dream start, scoring a remarkable hat-trick, consisting of two breakaway solo goals and a bullet header. He followed that up with a goal in his next match against Nottingham Forest, scoring another against Chelsea and two more in the final game of the season at Coventry City, with Liverpool having already been crowned League Champions. Rosenthal's introduction, galvanised Liverpool's end of season flourish to their 18th League Championship when it appeared to be ending in anti-climax after the "Reds'" shock defeat by Crystal Palace in the FA Cup Semi-Final. An instant hero with Liverpool supporters because of his direct approach, wherever he receives the ball, he has only one thought in mind — to put his head down and charge towards goal until he can get in a shot. Unfortunately, this style is inimical to Liverpool's passing game and in 1991-92 he was used by the management more as a substitute to save games slipping away from Liverpool's grasp, rather than as an integral member of the team. In fairness, it must be said that he usually appears more dangerous as a second-half substitute than over 90 minutes. Nevertheless, it is a tragedy to see such an exciting player used so sparingly.

Clubs	Signing Date	Transfer Fee	APPEARANCES				GOALS			
			Lge	FL Cup	FA Cup	Others	Lge	FL Cup	FA Cup	Others
Liverpool*	3.90	£1,000,000	16+28	0+6	4+2	1+1	15			

ROWE Ezekiel (Zeke) Bartholomew

Born: Stoke Newington, 30 October 1973

Height: 6'0" Weight: 12.8

Position: Forward.

Career History: A new professional signing for Chelsea, he first came to Stamford Bridge as an associated school-boy in April 1989, before advancing as a trainee in July 1990.

Clubs	Signing Date	Transfer Fee	APPEARANCES				GOALS			
			Lge	FL Cup	FA Cup	Others	Lge	FL Cup	FA Cup	Others
Chelsea*	6.92	–								

ROWNTREE Michael Clive

Born: Hartlepool, 18 November 1973

Height: 5'6" Weight: 10.1

Position: Winger.

Career History: Signed professional forms for Sheffield Wednesday during the 1992 close season, having previously been at Hillsborough as an associated schoolboy (October 1988) and as a trainee (July 1990). No first team experience as yet.

Clubs	Signing Date	Transfer Fee	APPEARANCES				GOALS			
			Lge	FL Cup	FA Cup	Others	Lge	FL Cup	FA Cup	Others
Sheffield Wednesday	6.92	–								

RUDDOCK Neil

Born: Wandsworth, 9 May 1968

Height: 6'2"

Weight: 12.6

International Honours: E Yth, E "U21"-4

Position/Skill Factor: Very strong central defender, who attacks the ball well in the air and heads bravely. Has a great left foot and can hit 50 yard diagonal balls with no difficulty.

Career History: Came through the Millwall junior academy, first as an associated schoolboy (October 1983) and then as an apprentice (June 1984), before turning profes-

Ian Rush

sional in March 1986. Transferred to Tottenham Hotspur one month later, without a single League appearance at the Den, he made his FL debut at White Hart Lane against Charlton Athletic on 18 April 1987 and played three more times that season. At the end of 1987-88, after just three more full appearances, he returned to his former club, Millwall, who had recently been promoted to the First Division, for a fee six times the original amount. Even stranger, in view of the large transfer fee, was the fact that he spent eight months at Millwall without getting a full 90 minutes on the park in a League match. He was then on the move yet again, this time to Southampton. Replacing Kevin Moore at the heart of the defence, he came into a side that was hovering dangerously close to the bottom of the First Division, having gone 13 games without a win. Played 13 matches in 1988-89, as the "Saints" finished outside the danger zone and apart from a short spell out of the side in 1989-90, he settled down as a regular. An exemplar of Southampton's physical approach, he played for most of the 1991-92 season when not suspended. He was sent off twice and booked in every other game up to Christmas, but seemed to "clean up his act" in the New Year. In another bizarre twist to his career, he returned to Tottenham Hotspur soon after the end of the season and will be hoping for more opportunities than during his first stay.

Clubs	Signing Date	Transfer Fee	APPEARANCES				GOALS			
			Lge	FL Cup	FA Cup	Others	Lge	FL Cup	FA Cup	Others
Millwall	3.86	–				3+1				1
Tottenham Hotspur	4.86	£50,000	7+2		1+1				1	
Millwall	6.88	£300,000	0+2	2		1+1	1	3		
Southampton	2.89	£250,000	100+7	14+1	10	6	9	1	3	
Tottenham Hotspur*	5.92	£750,000								

RUSH Ian James

Born: St Asaph, 20 October 1961

Height: 6'0" Weight: 12.6

International Honours: W Sch, W "U21"-2, W-54

Position/Skill Factor: Striker with phenomenal work rate, who puts defenders under pressure and then picks up the pieces. A snapper up of half chances, he is very quick and scores many goals from good near post runs.

Career History: After representing Wales at schoolboy level, he joined Chester City, first as an associated schoolboy (March 1977) and then as an apprentice (August 1978), before signing as a professional at the beginning of 1979-80. Prior to that, he had already made his FL debut at home to Sheffield Wednesday on 28 April 1979 and the following season, he was the club's leading goal scorer with 14. At the tail-end of 1979-80, Liverpool, having noted his potential, moved in to sign him and before he even kicked a ball for the "Reds", he received the first of many Welsh caps when coming on as a substitute during a 1-0 defeat at Hampden Park against Scotland on 21 May 1980. Made no impact in his first season at Anfield, failing to score in seven end of season games. Out of favour at the start of 1981-82, he went to see Bob Paisley about his future at the club and was given the tart answer, "just score goals". Deputising for the injured David Johnson that October, he netted twice in a 3-0 victory over Leeds United and the rest, so to speak, is history, as he simply

burst on the First Division scene with 17 League goals in 32 matches, ending the season with a League Cup winners medal after scoring the third goal in a 3-1 win over Tottenham Hotspur. The next five seasons were honours all the way, except for 1984-85, when the cupboard remained strangely bare, with three League Cup wins (1983 and 1984), a European Cup winners medal (1983-84) and an FA Cup winners medal (1986), after he had scored twice in a 3-1 victory over Everton. It was during this time that his partnership with Kenny Dalglish became legendary and when the latter took over the manager's seat, it was feared that his goal scoring opportunities would suffer, but luckily, Jan Molby also proved to be an expert provider. However, after repeated overtures from the top Italian side, Juventus, he was transferred for a new English record transfer fee during the 1987 close season. He had been the "Reds'" leading scorer in five of his six full seasons at Anfield and seemed to be almost impossible to replace after striking 207 goals in 331 matches (a ratio of one in every 1.6 games, only equalled by Gary Lineker in recent times). Unfortunately, his time at Juventus was not a happy one as the club coach expected him to forage alone. Nevertheless, although he scored eight goals in 29 games, a respectable total for the Italian League, he made no effort to acclimatise and Juventus allowed him to rejoin Liverpool in the summer of 1988. His first term back in England was plagued by injury problems, but he came back with a bang in the FA Cup Final against Everton when, as a substitute, he scored two of Liverpool's goals in a 3-2 extra-time win over their Mersey rivals. In winning his fifth League Championship medal in 1989-90, he found the net 18 times and in 1990-91, he once again headed the club's scoring charts with 16. Endured a miserable time in 1991-92, being absent through injury much of the time. Missing from action at the beginning of the season, he did not appear match fit when returning in September, scoring only four goals in 15 games and apart from playing just three times during February, he was out until late March. As Liverpool tried to work off a heavy backlog of games, he appeared to lack sharpness and with his contract up for renewal in the summer, there were doubts about his future at Anfield. Happily, three goals in the closing four games against Nottingham Forest, Manchester United (his first in 24 attempts against the men from Old Trafford) and Sunderland in the FA Cup Final (his fifth in three Finals), demonstrated that he has not lost the "killer instinct".

Clubs	Signing Date	Transfer Fee	APPEARANCES				GOALS			
			Lge	FL Cup	FA Cup	Others	Lge	FL Cup	FA Cup	Others
Chester City	7.79	–	33+1		5		14		3	
Liverpool	4.80	£300,000	224	47	24	31+1	139	25	19	17
Juventus (Italy)	6.87	£3,200,000								
Liverpool*	8.88	£2,800,000	105+10	13	20+2	9	45	9	15	1

RYAN Vaughan William

Born: Westminster, 2 September 1968

Height: 5'8" Weight: 10.12

Position/Skill Factor: The ideal midfield player with good stamina, he is also a good long kicker of the ball, but can pass it short, equally as well.

Career History: Came through Wimbledon's junior ranks, first as an associated schoolboy (November 1982) and then as an apprentice (July 1985), before signing professional forms during the 1986 close season. Had to wait nearly 12 months for his FL debut, a 2-2 draw at Plough Lane against Tottenham Hotspur on 22 April 1987, but by the following season he was showing much promise. While only playing sporadically in 1988-89, he was loaned out to Sheffield United, managed by his old boss, Dave Bassett, for a short spell and he obviously benefitted from the experience, when he held down a regular spot in the "Dons'" midfield during 1989-90. Unfortunately, injuries sidelined him somewhat during 1990-91 and he didn't get back into first team action until the season was virtually over. Although he started the 1991-92 season in the "Dons'" first team, he lost his place in October and made only occasional appearances over the remainder of the season. It may be that his future lies in a defensive role.

Clubs	Signing Date	Transfer Fee	APPEARANCES				GOALS			
			Lge	FL Cup	FA Cup	Others	Lge	FL Cup	FA Cup	Others
Wimbledon*	8.86	–	67+15	7	1	7+1	3			
Sheffield United	1.89	Loan	2+1			1				

SALAKO John Akin

Born: Nigeria, 11 February 1969

Height: 5'9" Weight: 11.0

International Honours: E-5

Position/Skill Factor: A left-winger with great pace and skill, he is a known dribbler who is more than capable of unlocking the tightest of defences.

Career History: Has been at Crystal Palace since coming to the club as an associated schoolboy in May 1984. On leaving school, he signed on as an apprentice in July 1985, before graduating as a full-time professional during 1986-87 and making his FL debut as a substitute just two months later against Barnsley at Selhurst Park on 24 January 1987. After winning a regular place on the wing at the beginning of 1987-88, he was rested to make way for Phil Barber and was forced to bide his time on the bench. He later assisted Palace to promotion in 1988-89, although used more as a substitute than as first choice. While the "Eagles" acclimatised to their newly won First Division status, he was on loan to Third Division Swansea City for more experience and after returning to Selhurst Park, he played in all of Palace's FA Cup matches in 1989-90. His performance on the left-wing in the 1990 Final against Manchester United first brought him national attention, especially when setting up one of Ian Wright's goals in the 3-3 draw. He finally came into his own during 1990-91, making 35 League appearances and helping the club into third place in the First Division, their highest ever FL position. Now on his way to becoming a star, an example of his quick thinking and coolness came in the dying seconds of the 1991 FA Cup Third Round replay at Nottingham Forest, when he picked up a hurried clearance from the home side's 'keeper, Mark Crossley, just inside the opposing half and promptly lobbed it back over the goalie's head for the equaliser. At the end of the season, he was recognised at full international level when selected for England's tour of Australasia, winning his first cap against Australia on 1 June 1991. After winning another England cap in the early season international against Germany, his blossoming career was brought cruelly to a halt by a serious knee injury sustained against Leeds United in October 1991 and he has not played since. His brother Andrew is currently a full-back with Charlton Athletic.

Clubs	Signing Date	Transfer Fee	APPEARANCES				GOALS			
			Lge	FL Cup	FA Cup	Others	Lge	FL Cup	FA Cup	Others
Crystal Palace*	11.86	–	87+38	9+2	11	11+2	11	2	2	2
Swansea City	8.87	Loan	13			2	3			1

SAMWAYS Vincent (Vinny)

Born: Bethnal Green, 27 October 1968

Height: 5'8"

Weight: 9.0

International Honours: E Yth, E "U21"-5

Position/Skill Factor: Midfielder with superb vision. Has a lovely touch and controls the ball with ease. Rarely giving anything away, he is also an outstanding passer.

Career History: After a period on Tottenham Hotspur's books as an associated schoolboy, beginning in November 1982, he left school in April 1985 to sign on with the club as an apprentice. Turned professional in 1985-86, but didn't make his FL debut until 2 May 1987, as a substitute during a 2-0 defeat at Nottingham Forest. Made rapid strides during 1987-88, with 21 League appearances, but, although a valuable member of the first team squad, he found it hard to hold down a permanent place. However, with Paul Gascoigne often absent through injury in 1990-91, he was given the chance to exert some influence in "Spurs'" midfield and earned his first club honour when he won an FA Cup winners medal, following Tottenham's 2-1 victory over Nottingham Forest. With Gascoigne out of action during 1991-92, he was at last able to stake a regular claim to a first team slot. Unfortunately, he seemed to be made a "scapegoat" for "Spurs'" disappointing season and was dropped in February 1992, manager Peter Shreeves explaining that the "boggy" White Hart Lane pitch was inimical to his passing game. This did not explain, however, why he was not suitable for away games or why he disappeared from the first team squad for the remainder of the season. During the summer, the unsettled Samways was taken off the transfer list for the third time in a year at his own request and looks for a new start in 1992-93.

Clubs	Signing Date	Transfer Fee	APPEARANCES				GOALS			
			Lge	FL Cup	FA Cup	Others	Lge	FL Cup	FA Cup	Others
Tottenham Hotspur*	10.85	–	92+28	18+4	7+1	7+1	8	3		

SANCHEZ Lawrence (Lawrie)
Philip

Born: Lambeth,
22 October 1959

Height: 5'11"

Weight: 11.7

International Honours:
E Sch, NI-3

Position/Skill Factor: Midfield player who has a good football brain. Very confident with the ball, he never seems to be hurried and is always looking to create scoring opportunities.

Career History: The son of John Sanchez, who played for Arsenal and Watford between 1957-1961, he started his career as an associated schoolboy at Reading in September 1977 and made his FL debut in a 2-2 draw at Elm Park, ironically, against Wimbledon on 1 October 1977. Turned professional a year later and spent eight years with the "Royals", winning a Fourth Division Championship medal in 1978-79, making 34 League appearances. Suffered the disappointment of relegation in 1982-83, before experiencing the euphoria of helping the club back to the Third Division at the first time of asking, in third place. During the winter of 1984, he was snapped up by Wimbledon manager, Dave Bassett, as another

piece in the jigsaw which would be completed when the "Dons" reached the First Division and then went on to capture the FA Cup. Made his bow at Plough Lane against Notts County on Boxing Day 1984 and the following season, as an ever present, he helped Bassett achieve his objective of First Division football, when the club finished in third place behind Norwich City and Charlton Athletic. His performances for Wimbledon earned him an international call-up for Northern Ireland in November 1986, when he came on as a sub during a European Championship qualifying match in Turkey and he won two more caps in 1988-89. However, the highlight of his career came in the 1988 FA Cup Final against mighty Liverpool, when he headed in Denis Wise's free-kick for the only goal of the game and set up a result that confounded the critics. Still a force to be reckoned with, although the past two seasons have often seen him struggling with injuries and loss of form, before he re-established himself. Out of contention for the first half of 1991-92, he was recalled to the first team in January when the "Dons" were struggling near the foot of the table and his experience enabled the team to finish in its customary mid-table position.

Clubs	Signing Date	Transfer Fee	APPEARANCES				GOALS			
			Lge	FL Cup	FA Cup	Others	Lge	FL Cup	FA Cup	Others
Reading	9.78	–	249+13	20+1	14	1	28		1	
Wimbledon*	12.84	£29,000	216+12	17	18+1	7	27		2	

SANSOM Kenneth (Kenny)
Graham

Born: Camberwell, 26 September 1958

Height: 5'6" Weight: 11.8

International Honours: E Sch, E Yth, E "U21"-8, E-86

Position/Skill Factor: Very experienced left-back with a cultured left foot and good passing ability, both short and long.

Career History: Started his soccer career as an apprentice at Crystal Palace in April 1975, after winning England schoolboy international honours. Even before turning professional, he had made his FL debut at Tranmere Rovers on 7 May 1975 at the age of 16 years and eight months as Palace's youngest ever debutant and in 1976-77, at the age of 18, he was ever present as Palace won promotion to the Second Division. In 1978-79, he was again ever present, winning a Second Division Championship medal and at the end of the season, received the first of many full international caps when he played for England against Wales at Wembley on 23 May 1979. Had a successful first season in the top flight and following his return from the European Championships in the summer of 1980, he became the game's most expensive full-back, as part of an exchange deal which took him to Arsenal and Clive Allen and Paul Barron in the opposite direction. Made his debut for the "Gunners" in a 1-0 win at West Bromwich Albion on the opening day of the 1980-81 season and firmly established himself as a hugely influential figure in the Arsenal rearguard for over eight years, hardly missing a game, apart from a groin injury at the end of 1986-87. Captain of the team that played in two consecutive League Cup Finals, he received a winners medal, following the 2-1 defeat of Liverpool in 1987, but was not so lucky in 1988, as Luton Town won 3-2 in a last gasp finish. Made his final England appearance against the USSR in the disastrous European Championships of 1988 and on his retirement from international football, was England's most capped full-back. During the 1988 close season,. he fell out with the Arsenal manager,

George Graham and never played for the side again, being transferred to Newcastle United, who were desperately trying to halt the inexorable slide towards the Second Division. It was an unhappy experience, far from home and after spending just six months on Tyneside, he was on his way back to London to sign for his ex-Arsenal and England coach, Don Howe, at Queens Park Rangers. Kicked off 1989-90 against his old club, Crystal Palace and only missed two League games all season as the club recovered well, following a bad start. Then, after appearing in every possible game for Rangers in 1990-91, he was surprisingly sold in March 1991 to a Coventry City side, who were also fighting to stave off relegation and sorely needed a replacement for the injured Paul Edwards. His first game at Highfield Road brought a much needed victory, a 3-1 win over Manchester City and while the club's status ultimately remained intact, City suffered a crushing 6-1 defeat at the hands of his old team, Arsenal, who had already been crowned League Champions, on the last day of a depressing season. Absent through injury in the first half of the 1991-92 season, he returned to first team action in December and remained in the team for the rest of the season as the "Sky Blues" just staved off relegation.

Clubs	Signing Date	Transfer Fee	APPEARANCES				GOALS			
			Lge	FL Cup	FA Cup	Others	Lge	FL Cup	FA Cup	Others
Crystal Palace	12.75	–	172	11	17		3		1	
Arsenal	8.80	£955,000	314	48	26	6	6			
Newcastle United	12.88	£300,000	20		4					
Q.P.R.	6.87	£300,000	64	7	10	1			2	
Coventry City*	3.91	£100,000	30		2					

SAUNDERS Dean Nicholas

Born: Swansea, 21 June 1964

Height: 5'8" Weight: 10.6

International Honours: W-33

Position/Skill Factor: Quicksilver striker who often chases lost causes. Loves balls in behind defenders when he can use his pace to maximum effect and is useful in the air for his size.

Career History: The son of Roy, who played for Liverpool and Swansea City between 1948-1963, he came into League football with Swansea City as an apprentice in November 1980, before graduating to the professional ranks in the 1982 close season. After waiting nearly 18 months for an opportunity, he made his FL debut as a substitute in a 2-2 draw at Charlton Athletic on 22 October 1983. Not highly regarded by Swansea manager John Bond, he was released on a free transfer, following a spell on loan at Cardiff City and signed for Brighton & Hove Albion during the summer of 1985. Immediately impressing the "Seagulls" with 15 League goals in 1985-86, he was recognised by the Welsh manager and made his international debut against the Irish Republic on 26 March 1986 in Dublin, when coming on as a sub. Towards the end of the following season he was sold to Oxford United, who were struggling at the foot of the First Division and he made an immediate impact, scoring six times in 12 games, including two at Luton Town which effectively safeguarded United's status. However, at the end of 1987-88, Oxford were relegated to the Second Division and despite much bitterness towards the club's directors, which ultimately cost manager Mark Lawrenson

his job, he was sold to Derby County in October 1988. The "Rams" received an immediate return on their investment when he hit a brace in a 4-1 win home win over Wimbledon and in three seasons at the Baseball Ground, was the club's leading scorer. His 17 goals from a total of 37 scored in 1990-91, was a remarkable achievement for a team doomed to relegation almost from the start of the season. Scored a hat-trick against relegation companions Sunderland, but even that could only bring a 3-3 draw. Sold to Liverpool during the summer of 1991, for a record transfer fee between two English clubs, along with Mark Wright, he struggled to make an impact at Anfield, despite finishing as the club's leading scorer with 23 goals in all competitions. A breakdown of his goals tally reveals the reason why — nine in the UEFA Cup, including four against Kuusysi Lahti of Finland, two in the League Cup, two in the FA Cup, but only ten from 36 First Division games. The suspicion remains that while Saunders may be deadly against weak opposition, his limitations are shown up by stronger teams. It may be unfair to pass judgement after one season when the usual service from midfield was lacking, but he missed too many easy chances during the season to be yet considered as a striker of the highest class, or worth his enormous transfer fee.

Clubs	Signing Date	Transfer Fee	APPEARANCES				GOALS			
			Lge	FL Cup	FA Cup	Others	Lge	FL Cup	FA Cup	Others
Swansea City	6.82	–	42+7	2+1	1	1+1	12			
Cardiff City	3.85	Loan	3+1							
Brighton & H. A.	8.85	–	66+6	4	7	3	20		5	
Oxford United	3.87	£60,000	57+2	9+1	2	2	22	8	2	1
Derby County	10.88	£1,000,000	106	12	4	5	42	1		5
Liverpool*	7.91	£2,900,000	36	5	8	5	10	2	2	9

SCALES John Robert

Born: Harrogate,
4 July 1966

Height: 6'0"

Weight: 12.2

Position/Skill Factor: Pacey central defender with an athletic build. Can play in most defensive positions, is powerful in the air, has two good feet and is very dangerous at set plays.

Career History: Signed for Leeds United on a YTS scheme in August 1984, but was freed during the 1985 close season and joined Bristol Rovers as a professional. Made his FL debut in a 3-0 defeat at Newport County on 7 September 1985 and by the end of the season he was holding down a permanent place at a club that had been forced to part with many of its leading players due to a financial crisis. Spent two years at Rovers, but when Bobby Gould was given the Wimbledon job in the summer of 1987, he was among his former manager's first

signings. Turning out for the "Dons" in both full-back positions in 1987-88, he settled down well to make 23 League appearances and won an FA Cup winners medal after coming on for Terry Gibson during the 1-0 victory over Liverpool. Since switching to a more central role to replace Eric Young, he has proved to be one of the club's most consistent players, often scoring invaluable goals, as Wimbledon continue to make their presence felt on the First Division scene. Nearly ever present in 1991-92, he was unfortunate to miss the last match of the season through injury.

Clubs	Signing Date	Transfer Fee	APPEARANCES				GOALS			
			Lge	FL Cup	FA Cup	Others	Lge	FL Cup	FA Cup	Others
Bristol Rovers	7.85	–	68+4	3	6	3+1	2			
Wimbledon*	7.87	£70,000	163+5	11+1	11+1	7+1	10			3

SCHMEICHEL Peter Boleslaw

Born: Denmark, 18 November 1968

Height: 6'4" Weight: 14.0

International Honours: Denmark Int

Position/Skill Factor: Top class goalkeeper with great presence. Extremely agile and very fast off his line, he gives the attacker little to aim at. Sets up attacks with accurate throws.

Career History: Danish international goalkeeper who signed for Manchester United from Danish League champions, Brondby IF of Copenhagen. He played in all but

four games of United's 57 match programme in 1991-92, following his FL debut at Old Trafford against Notts County on 17 August 1991, winning a League Cup medal, but missing out on a League Championship medal in the closing weeks of the campaign. Apart from occasional lapses in concentration, he proved to be the answer to a problem position for United since Jim Leighton's fall from grace, conceding only 32 goals in 40 FL games, the best statistics in the First Division. Played for Denmark in the 1992 European Championship Finals in Sweden, as last minute participants, following the expulsion of Yugoslavia. Despite being unprepared for the tournament, the Danes confounded everyone by defeating France and the Netherlands to beat Germany in the Final. Quite apart from keeping superbly throughout the tournament, he became a national hero by saving Marco van Basten's penalty in the Semi-Final "shoot-out" against the Dutch, which enabled Denmark to win 5-4 on penalties after a gripping 2-2 draw.

Clubs	Signing Date	Transfer Fee	APPEARANCES				GOALS			
			Lge	FL Cup	FA Cup	Others	Lge	FL Cup	FA Cup	Others
Manchester United*	8.91	£550,000	40	6	3	3				

SCOTT John Alan

Born: Aberdeen, 9 March 1975

Height: 5'7¼" Weight: 10.13

International Honours: S Sch

Position: Left-back.

Career History: Turned professional for Liverpool during last summer, having been at the club since coming to Anfield as a trainee in August 1991. No first team experience.

Clubs	Signing Date	Transfer Fee	APPEARANCES				GOALS			
			Lge	FL Cup	FA Cup	Others	Lge	FL Cup	FA Cup	Others
Liverpool*	6.92	–								

SEALEY Leslie (Les) Jesse

Born: Bethnal Green, 29 September 1957

Height: 6'1"

Weight: 12.8

Position/Skill Factor: Brave and agile goalkeeper who makes saves that are worth points. Known in the game as a great talker, he never stops shouting instructions and advice to his defenders.

Career History: A great character, he hails from a footballing family, being a cousin of Alan who was prominent for Leyton Orient and West Ham United between 1959-1967. London born, he joined Coventry City as an apprentice in April 1974, before turning professional and making his FL debut at Queens Park Rangers in a 1-1 draw on 11 April 1977. Shared the goalkeeping duties with Jim Blyth until 1982-83, when he only missed three games, but at the end of the season he signed for Luton Town, for whom he was ever present throughout 1983-84. Lost his place to Andy Dibble early in 1984-85, after suffering injury problems and on recovering, he spent some time on loan with Plymouth Argyle. He soon won back a regular place in the "Hatters'" goal and was extremely unlucky in missing the club's 1988 League Cup Final triumph over Arsenal, because of injury. But following the 3-1 League Cup Final defeat at the hands of Nottingham Forest in 1989, he lost his place to Alec Chamberlain. Alex Ferguson took him to Manchester United for two short loan periods, one in December 1989, when he didn't make an appearance and the second time in March 1990 when he played in two League matches. And after United's 3-3 FA Cup Final draw against Crystal Palace, he was called up to replace the unfortunate Jim Leighton for the replay. Returning to the scene of his cousin Alan's 1965 triumph, he made some important saves to ensure a 1-0 victory and was rewarded with a one year contract. Had mixed fortunes in 1990-91. After being left helpless by John Sheridan's strike in the League Cup Final, as United lost 1-0 to Sheffield Wednesday, less than a month later he won a European Cup Winners Cup medal, following the "Red Devils'" brilliant 2-1 victory over Barcelona. Following the signing of Danish 'keeper Peter Schmeichel, he was allowed to leave Old Trafford on a free transfer, signing for Aston Villa as cover for Nigel Spink. From October 1991 to late February 1992, he was actually first choice 'keeper at Villa Park until Spink won his place back. Towards the end of the season he was loaned out to his old club, Coventry City, who had Steve Ogrizovic incapacitated and played two games until the latter was fit to resume.

Clubs	Signing Date	Transfer Fee	APPEARANCES				GOALS			
			Lge	FL Cup	FA Cup	Others	Lge	FL Cup	FA Cup	Others
Coventry City	3.76	–	158	11	9					
Luton Town	8.83	£100,000	207	21	28	3				
Plymouth Argyle	10.84	Loan	6							
Manchester United	3.90	Loan	2		1					
Manchester United	6.90	–	31	8	3	9				
Aston Villa*	7.91	–	18		4	2				
Coventry City	3.92	Loan	2							

SEAMAN David Andrew

Born: Rotherham, 19 September 1963

Height: 6'3" Weight: 13.0

International Honours: E "U21"-10, E"B", E-9

Position/Skill Factor: Confident, unspectacular, yet agile goalkeeper, who is always on his toes. Strong hands are his passport. A good kicker, he will run the ball out to gain extra distance.

Career History: It seems hard to realise that Leeds United released him before he could make an appearance. He had gone to Elland Road as an apprentice in March 1980 and had graduated to the professional ranks early in 1981-82, but with an abundance of goalies available, including John Lukic, United let him go. Fourth Division Peterborough United snapped him up and he soon established himself as the first team choice at London Road, after making his FL debut at Stockport County on 28 August 1982 in a 1-1 draw. In October 1984, Birmingham City, having just sold Tony Coton to Watford, moved in for him as a replacement and he came straight into the side, keeping 13 clean sheets in 33 League matches to assist the "Blues'" promotion to the First Division behind the Champions, Oxford United. Although ever present, City were relegated first time round and in order to continue playing in the top flight, he signed for Queens Park Rangers in time for 1986-87. Ironically, the only game he missed in his first season at Rangers was a 7-1 defeat at Sheffield Wednesday and his consistency was finally rewarded at international level on 16 November 1988 when he kept goal for England against Saudi Arabia in a 1-1 draw. Rarely absent during the four years he spent at Loftus Road, his transfer to Arsenal created something of a stir during the 1990 close season when George Graham decided to release John Lukic and parted with the highest transfer fee ever paid for a goalkeeper. He proved superb value for money, making a solid Arsenal defence even more watertight and won his first League Championship medal as the "Gunners" celebrated their second title win in three years. His League statistics as an ever present in 1990-91, which include 24 clean sheets, 540 minutes without a goal being scored against him and just 18 goals conceded, speak for themselves. Ever present in 1991-92, it was not such a good season for Arsenal's defence, which conceded 46 goals. Regarded by Graham Taylor as England's number two, his occasional international appearances were often the subject of unfair media criticism. After a mistake in the game against Czechoslovakia in March, he was dropped so that Taylor could take a look at Nigel Martyn of Crystal Palace. In the event, it was Martyn and not Seaman, who travelled to Sweden as understudy to Chris Woods for the European Championship Finals.

Clubs	Signing Date	Transfer Fee	APPEARANCES				GOALS			
			Lge	FL Cup	FA Cup	Others	Lge	FL Cup	FA Cup	Others
Leeds United	9.81	–								
Peterborough United	8.82	£4,000	91	10	5					
Birmingham City	10.84	£100,000	75	4	5					
Q.P.R.	8.86	£225,000	141	13	17	4				
Arsenal*	5.90	£1,300,000	80	7	9	5				

SEDGLEY Stephen (Steve) Philip

Born: Enfield, 26 May 1968

Height: 6'1"

Weight: 12.6

International Honours: E "U21"-11

Position/Skill Factor: A central defender, he is a true competitor, who is aggressive and makes decisive tackles. Has an excellent left foot and can hit good diagonal passes. Useful in the air at set pieces.

Career History: A Londoner by birth, he signed as an associated schoolboy for Coventry City in February 1984 and on leaving school, he joined the ground staff as an apprentice in June 1984. Made his FL debut in the "Sky Blues'" midfield, three months after turning professional, at Highfield Road against Arsenal on 26 August 1986. Although he appeared in 25 League matches that season, he was considered too inexperienced to be included in the club's 1987 FA Cup Final team which defeated Tottenham Hotspur 3-2. After three years of steady progress at Coventry, he found himself the subject of a substantial offer made by North London's Tottenham Hotspur and during the 1989 close season he joined the club, who four years earlier could have signed him for free. Immediately fitting into the middle of the back four, alongside Gary Mabbutt, he helped "Spurs" overcome a sticky start to finish third in the League. By now a big favourite with the home fans, he missed a handful of matches through niggling injuries early in 1990-91, but recovered well enough to win an FA Cup winners medal, following the 2-1 victory over Nottingham Forest. In and out of the team during the disappointing 1991-92 campaign, he was usually selected as a substitute when not a first choice and lost his place to on-loan Jason Cundy at the end of the season. With the signing of both Cundy and Neil Ruddock, competition for central defensive roles will be intense.

Clubs	Signing Date	Transfer Fee	APPEARANCES				GOALS			
			Lge	FL Cup	FA Cup	Others	Lge	FL Cup	FA Cup	Others
Coventry City	5.86	–	81+3	9	2+2	5+1	3	2		
Tottenham Hotspur*	7.89	£750,000	85+15	13+1	7+2	5+3		1		

SEGERS Johannes (Hans)

Born: Eindhoven,
Holland,
30 October 1961

Height: 5'11"

Weight: 12.7

Position/Skill Factor: Not very big for a goalkeeper, but extremely agile and not easy to beat. A very good kicker, he uses the ball well with early throws.

Career History: Dutch goalkeeper who played for PSV Eindhoven, before joining Nottingham Forest in the 1984 close season, in part-exchange for the Dutch international 'keeper, Hans van Breukelen. Made his FL debut in a 3-1 win at Coventry City on 17 November 1984, when replacing Steve Sutton in the Forest goal and kept his place for the rest of the season. Sutton regained the goalkeeping duties during the following term and over the next couple of seasons, he had spells on loan at Stoke City, Sheffield United and Dunfermline Athletic to keep in trim for first team football. After Dave Beasant's surprise move to Newcastle United in the summer of 1988, Wimbledon manager, Bobby Gould, moved to sign him as a replacement, following a run of five defeats at the beginning of 1988-89. He made his debut for the "Dons" in a 2-1 win at Everton and at the end of 1990-91, had missed only one match, being very consistent and remarkably injury free. Kept 14 clean sheets in 1991-92 as the "Dons" found themselves near the bottom of the First Division table nearly all season and yet again showed great consistency when missing only one match throughout the duration.

Clubs	Signing Date	Transfer Fee	APPEARANCES				GOALS			
			Lge	FL Cup	FA Cup	Others	Lge	FL Cup	FA Cup	Others
Nottingham Forest	8.84	£50,000	58	4	5					
Stoke City	2.87	Loan	1							
Sheffield United	11.87	Loan	10			1				
Dunfermline Athletic	3.88	Loan								
Wimbledon*	9.88	£180,000	149	13	10	7				

SELLARS Scott

Born: Sheffield,
27 November 1965

Height: 5'7"

Weight: 9.10

International Honours:
E "U21"-3

Position/Skill Factor: Very skilful winger with a good brain. Always creating chances for others, he will make things happen around the opposition's penalty area.

Career History: Missed by the two big Sheffield clubs, he joined Leeds United as an associated schoolboy in December 1981 and on leaving school in July 1982, he had impressed enough for the club to take him on as an apprentice. Just before turning professional, he was given an early first team opportunity, making his FL debut at Shrewsbury Town on 7 May 1983. Enjoyed a good run in midfield the following season, from December 1983 to April 1984 and fully established himself in 1984-85 when he missed only three games. However, he fell out of favour after Leeds' poor start to 1985-86 and was allowed to join Blackburn Rovers for a surprisingly modest fee in the 1986 close season. He started his Rovers' career in midfield, but was switched late in the season to the left-wing to devastating effect. During the next three seasons, he established a reputation as the most dynamic, exciting left-winger in the Second Division. Ever present in 1988-89 and second top scorer with 14 FL goals in 1989-90, injuries unfortunately curtailed his appearances in 1990-91 to a minimum. Having been strangely out of favour with Rovers' manager, Don Mackay, at the start of 1991-92, the new manager, Kenny Dalglish, immediately restored him to the team as a substitute and after coming on in the 39th minute, he inspired Rovers to a 5-2 victory over Plymouth in October. Although prone to inconsistency and not always sure of his place, Rovers' best displays usually coincided with a Sellars' "special performance". In the penultimate game of the Second Division campaign, he scored a vital 86th minute equaliser against Sunderland to secure a crucial point and in the first Play-Off game against Derby, he struck Rovers' first goal from a free-kick to set up a thrilling comeback to 4-2 after his team had gone 2-0 down inside the first 14 minutes.

Clubs	Signing Date	Transfer Fee	APPEARANCES				GOALS			
			Lge	FL Cup	FA Cup	Others	Lge	FL Cup	FA Cup	Others
Leeds United	7.83	–	72+4	4	4	2	12	1		1
Blackburn Rovers*	7.86	£20,000	194+8	12	11	20	35	3	1	2

SELLEY Ian

Born: Chertsey, 14 June 1974

Height: 5'9" Weight: 10.1

International Honours: E Yth

Position: Midfielder.

Career History: Signed professional forms for Arsenal during the 1992 close season, having been at Highbury as an associated schoolboy since October 1988, before graduating to the trainee ranks in July 1990. No first team experience.

Clubs	Signing Date	Transfer Fee	APPEARANCES				GOALS			
			Lge	FL Cup	FA Cup	Others	Lge	FL Cup	FA Cup	Others
Arsenal*	5.92	–								

SHARP Graeme Marshall

Born: Glasgow,
16 October 1960

Height: 6'1"

Weight: 11.8

International Honours:
S "U21"-1, S-12

Clubs	Signing Date	Transfer Fee	APPEARANCES				GOALS			
			Lge	FL Cup	FA Cup	Others	Lge	FL Cup	FA Cup	Others
Everton	4.80	£125,000	306+16	46+2	52+2	21+1	110	15	20	11
Oldham Athletic*	7.91	£500,000	42	4	2	1	12	2	1	

Position/Skill Factor: Tall, powerful striker who is very good in the air and is a difficult opponent to get the better of. Shields the ball excellently and brings his team-mates into the game.

Career History: A product of Scottish junior side, Eastercraigs, Dumbarton introduced him as a raw 19-year-old, in a 6-3 victory at Airdrie in November 1978 and less than 18 months later he was on his way to Everton, after scoring 17 times in 40 matches for the Scottish Second Division side. Made his FL debut at Brighton & Hove Albion on 3 May 1980 and following a "settling-in" season, he established himself during 1981-82, finishing as the club's leading goal scorer with 15. In 1983-84, Everton reached both the League Cup and FA Cup Finals. After losing 1-0 against Liverpool in the former, the "Toffees" returned triumphantly to Wembley to defeat Watford in the FA Cup Final, Graeme scoring the opening goal in a 2-0 win. His 21 goals during the next season went a long way to ensuring a League Championship medal, but the club were not so fortunate in the FA Cup this time round, losing 1-0 in the 1985 Final against Manchester United. Scored the "goal of a lifetime" in a rare "Mersyside Derby" victory over eternal rivals, Liverpool, in October 1984. A Grobbelaar goal-kick was played back from the Everton half to Sharp, who received the ball and turned Alan Hansen in one movement, then hit a dipping volley over the goalkeeper from 30 yards. No more than four seconds had elapsed between Grobbelaar's kick into the safety zone and the ball nestling in the Liverpool net! However, consolation for the FA Cup Final defeat at the hands of Manchester United came in the shape of a European Cup Winners Cup medal, following a 3-1 win over Rapid Vienna. When playing alongside Gary Lineker in 1985-86, their partnership brought 49 goals, but after losing out to Liverpool in the League title race, Everton, in their third consecutive FA Cup Final, succumbed 3-1 to the same team, after an inspired second-half display by the men from Anfield. Absent for a lengthy period in 1986-87, he came back to win another League Championship medal, although his goal rate had dried up somewhat and in the 1989 FA Cup Final, Everton's fourth appearance in six years, he remained goalless as Liverpool won 3-2. Between 1988-89 and 1990-91, he scored only 15 League goals, as his value to the team became more as a provider, than a taker of chances. Won the first of his dozen full Scottish caps in Iceland in May 1985, but has not been selected for several years now. Transferred to newly promoted Oldham Athletic in the summer of 1991, he took on a new lease of life, playing in every single game of 1991-92 and leading the "Latics'" scoring charts with 15 goals, including four in an end of season fixture against Luton Town.

SHARPE Lee Stuart

Born: Halesowen, 27 May 1971

Height: 5'11" Weight: 11.4

International Honours: E "U21"-8, E"B", E-1

Position/Skill Factor: A very skilful player with pace, who is adept either on the left-wing, or at left-back. He is very good when taking defenders on and giving himself the option of shooting or crossing. Strong on the ball.

Career History: An associated schoolboy with Birmingham City (July 1986), on leaving school, however, he signed as a trainee with Torquay United in April 1987 and became their youngest ever player when making his FL debut as a sub at Exeter City on 3 October 1987. Four days later, he impressed a television audience with his impudent and confident skills against "Spurs" in a League Cup tie at White Hart Lane, after coming on as a substitute. He signed professional at the end of 1987-88 and was almost immediately transferred to Manchester United, as the impoverished Fourth Division side cashed in their investment. Made his United debut against West Ham United at Old Trafford in September and proved a reliable squad player, filling in mainly at left-back. After making a good start in 1989-90 on the left-wing, he was injured on New Year's Day against Queens Park Rangers

and didn't play again that season, thus missing out on United's FA Cup triumph. Came to prominence in 1990-91 with a hat-trick against Arsenal in an amazing Third Round League Cup 6-2 defeat of Arsenal at Highbury, but despite scoring in both legs of the Semi-Final, there was no happy ending as United lost 1-0 at Wembley against Second Division, Sheffield Wednesday. However, it was a different story in Europe as he won a European Cup Winners Cup medal, following United's great 2-1 victory over Barcelona. Earlier, on 27 March 1991, he had made his England debut in the European Championships, when coming on for Tony Adams in a 1-1 draw against Eire at Wembley and at just 20 years of age, he could well consider himself as having arrived. He was also voted "Young Player of the Year" in the PFA Awards. After all the excitement of the previous season, 1991-92 was a terrible anti-climax. Absent through injury in the first-half of the season, when fit again in December, he found another teenage prodigy, Ryan Giggs, had taken his place on the left-wing. He could not force his way back on a regular basis and was only a substitute in the League Cup Final victory over Sheffield Wednesday. Since it will be difficult for Alex Ferguson to pick both Giggs and Sharpe for left-wing duties, it may be that Sharpe's future with the club lies at left-back.

Clubs	Signing Date	Transfer Fee	APPEARANCES				GOALS			
			Lge	FL Cup	FA Cup	Others	Lge	FL Cup	FA Cup	Others
Torquay United	5.88	–	9+5			2+3	3			
Manchester United*	5.88	£185,000	60+17	11+4	8+2	8+2	3	7		1

SHAW Paul

Born: Burnham, 4 September 1973

Height: 5'11" Weight: 12.4

Position/Skill Factor: A striker who can also play in midfield, he has a lovely first touch and is always looking for the chance of a long range shot.

Career History: First signing for Arsenal as an associated schoolboy in March 1988, he came to Highbury as a trainee in July 1990 and had progressed to the professional ranks a year later. A very enthusiastic youngster, who has yet to play in the first team, he will look to establish himself in the reserve side during 1992-93.

Clubs	Signing Date	Transfer Fee	APPEARANCES				GOALS			
			Lge	FL Cup	FA Cup	Others	Lge	FL Cup	FA Cup	Others
Arsenal*	9.91	–								

SHAW Richard Edward

Born: Brentford, 11 September 1968

Height: 5'9" Weight: 11.8

Position/Skill Factor: Very good defensive player who can perform equally well at full-back, or in central defence. He can mark man-for-man, if required, but is also comfortable with the ball at his feet and is an excellent passer.

Career History: Came through the Crystal Palace junior network, after signing as an apprentice in July 1985 and

made his FL debut as a substitute at Reading on 19 September 1987, a year after joining the paid ranks. The following season he appeared in the League side 14 times (eight as a substitute) as Palace climbed out of the Second Division, via the Play-Offs. Returning from a spell on loan at Hull City, he took over the number three shirt from David Burke and held it throughout the 1990 FA Cup run, which ended at Wembley, following a 1-0 replay defeat at the hands of Manchester United. Only missed two League matches in 1990-91, as he helped the club to third place in the First Division, their highest ever placing. Suffered a setback in 1991-92, losing his place in September as the Palace defence was leaking goals and played only three more times (in March) to the end of the season. Ironically, although his left-back slot was under threat from new signings, Paul Bodin and Chris Coleman, it was in fact a central defender, Lee Sinnott, who took over the position.

Clubs	Signing Date	Transfer Fee	APPEARANCES				GOALS			
			Lge	FL Cup	FA Cup	Others	Lge	FL Cup	FA Cup	Others
Crystal Palace*	9.86	–	75+9	8+2	8	10+1	1			
Hull City	12.87	Loan	4							

SHEARER Alan

Born: Newcastle, 13 August 1970

Height: 5'11" Weight: 11.3

International Honours: E Yth, E "U21"-11, E"B", E-3

Position/Skill Factor: One of the best strikers in the country, he has all the right attributes. Brave, strong on the ball, he shields it well and is useful in the air.

Career History: Although born in Newcastle, he signed for Southampton, first as an associated schoolboy in September 1984 and then, on leaving school, as a trainee in July 1986. Made his FL debut at Chelsea on 26 March 1988, as a substitute, a month before turning professional. In his first full League game, he caused a sensation, netting a hat-trick in a 4-2 win over Arsenal and becoming the youngest player to score three times in a First Division match. Hit by injuries in 1988-89, he didn't get a run, but by the following season he was beginning to force his way into the side, although he only scored three goals in 19 full League outings. Missed just four games in 1990-91, as he, Matthew le Tissier and Rod Wallace made the "Saints" into one of the most entertaining teams in the First Division. Remarkably, he scored only four goals in 36 FL games, but netted eight times in ten cup games! In 1991-92, incoming manager, Ian Branfoot, changed the "Saints'" style to a physical ultra-defensive one, despite possessing two of the most exciting young forwards in the game and goal chances were at a premium. Nevertheless, he finished as leading scorer with 13 FL goals, plus six in cup games and missed only one match in the club's heavy programme of 60 matches, which included long runs in the League Cup and FA Cup, plus an appearance in the Zenith Cup Final, where the "Saints" were defeated 2-3 by Nottingham Forest after extra-time. Although he has often found goals hard to come by for the "Saints", at international level his record is sensational. 13 goals in 11

Position/Skill Factor: One of the most prolific goalscorers in the Football League, he has a tremendous shot and will take aim the moment he gets sight of goal. And he is easy for his team-mates to find, always making space for himself.

Career History: The brother of David, who played in the Football League between 1978-1988 for a variety of clubs, he joined Chelsea from the Scottish Highland League side, Inverness Clachnacuddin and after more than two years wait he made his FL debut in a 2-2 draw at Stamford Bridge against Leicester City on 1 February 1986, scoring the equaliser. Curiously, after one more appearance, he was transferred to Second Division Huddersfield Town for a modest fee on the March transfer deadline, just seven weeks after his Chelsea debut. Announced his arrival in spectacular fashion, scoring a hat-trick in a "local derby" away to Barnsley on his full debut for the "Terriers" and collecting a brace in his next game, finishing the season with seven goals from just eight appearances. The following season (1986-87), he was ever present and top scored with 21 FL goals, which included four in one match against Bradford City and Chelsea's decision to release him so quickly was looking foolish. In 1987-88, however, he lost form and his place, scoring only ten FL goals as Huddersfield collapsed into Division Three. At the end of the season he was transferred to Swindon Town at a massive profit for the Yorkshire club and ended his first term at the County Ground as top scorer with 14 FL goals, although the team lost out on promotion in the Play-Offs. Once again Swindon reached the Play-Offs in 1989-90, with Shearer top scoring with 20 FL, plus five cup goals. This time Swindon earned the right to compete in the First Division by defeating Middlesbrough in the Play-Off Final, but were denied promotion by a Football League edict which demoted them to the Third Division for financial irregularities perpetrated several years earlier. Fortunately commonsense prevailed and Swindon were at least reinstated to Division Two, on appeal to the FA. The 1990-91 season was an anti-climax as the club only just avoided relegation, despite another 22 FL goals from Shearer. Under new manager Glenn Hoddle in 1991-92, Swindon recaptured the form of two years earlier, with Shearer in devastating form, scoring 22 FL goals (including all four in a 4-0 victory at Plymouth) from 38 games, plus ten cup goals (all in doubles) from 11 games. He was on target for 40 goals in the season when he was signed on the transfer deadline as a desperation measure by Kenny Dalglish for Blackburn Rovers, whose promotion campaign was falling apart with injuries to key strikers. Unfortunately, despite scoring on his debut for Rovers, he was unable to provide the necessary lift and after only six games was dropped and played little part in the final games of the Play Offs.

England Under 21 games was a prelude to his full international debut against France in February 1992, in which he scored the first and set up the second for Nigel Clough and Gary Lineker in England's 2-0 victory. Included in the England squad for the European Championship Finals in Sweden, he played in one match (again versus France), but in common with his team mates, failed to advance his burgeoning reputation. Nevertheless, he would appear to be the logical "heir apparent" to Gary Lineker.

Clubs	Signing Date	Transfer Fee	APPEARANCES				GOALS			
			Lge	FL Cup	FA Cup	Others	Lge	FL Cup	FA Cup	Others
Southampton*	4.88	–	105+13	16+2	11+3	8	23	11	4	5

SHEARER Duncan Nichol

Born: Fort William, 28 August 1962

Height: 5'10"

Weight: 10.9

Clubs	Signing Date	Transfer Fee	APPEARANCES				GOALS			
			Lge	FL Cup	FA Cup	Others	Lge	FL Cup	FA Cup	Others
Chelsea	11.83	£10,000	2				1			
Huddersfield Town	3.86	£10,000	80+3	6	5	2	38	6	3	1
Swindon Town	6.88	£250,000	156+3	19	11	11+1	78	11	7	2
Blackburn Rovers*	3.92	£800,000	5+1			0+1	1			

SHEPSTONE Paul Thomas

Born: Coventry, 8 November 1970

Height: 5'8" Weight: 10.6

International Honours: E Yth

Position/Skill Factor: Very busy, hard working midfielder, with good passing skills.

Career History: A former graduate of the FA School of Excellence at Lilleshall and locally born and bred, he signed for his hometown club, Coventry City, first as an associated schoolboy (April 1985) and then as a trainee (July 1987), before joining the "Sky Blues'" professional ranks in 1987-88. Although good enough to have been capped by England at youth level, with first team opportunities scarce at Highfield Road, he received a free transfer during the 1989 close season and signed for Birmingham City. Unfortunately, things didn't work out there either and he moved into non-League football as a non-contract player with Atherstone United in March 1990. Rescued from obscurity, he joined Blackburn Rovers at the end of the 1989-90 close season and made his FL debut in the first game of 1990-91 at Bristol City on 25 August 1990. Towards the end of the season he became a regular member of the first team squad and seemed on the verge of a breakthrough. Sadly, it was not to be. After only two early season games in 1991-92, he was dropped from the squad by Don Mackay and totally overlooked by new manager Kenny Dalglish for the rest of the season, playing two games on loan to York City in March.

Clubs	Signing Date	Transfer Fee	APPEARANCES				GOALS			
			Lge	FL Cup	FA Cup	Others	Lge	FL Cup	FA Cup	Others
Coventry City	11.87	–								
Birmingham City	7.89	–								
Atherstone United	3.90	–								
Blackburn Rovers*	5.90	–	16+10	1	0+1		1			
York City	3.92	Loan	2							

SHERIDAN Anthony Joseph

Born: Dublin, 21 October 1974

Height: 6'0" Weight: 12.4

International Honours: IR Yth

Position/Skill Factor: Very skilful left-winger with a lovely left foot who can really play.

Career History: On leaving school in the summer of 1991, he came across the Irish Sea to join Coventry City and after signing as a professional on his 17th birthday, immediately began to impress as a member of the "Sky Blues'" youth team. Unfortunately, he became homesick towards the end of the season and returned to Dublin, although it is to he hoped that he will come back refreshed in time for the start of 1992-93.

Clubs	Signing Date	Transfer Fee	APPEARANCES				GOALS			
			Lge	FL Cup	FA Cup	Others	Lge	FL Cup	FA Cup	Others
Coventry City*	10.91	–								

SHERIDAN John Joseph

Born: Manchester, 1 October 1964

Height: 5'9" Weight: 10.8

International Honours: IR Yth, IR "U21"-1, IR-14

Position/Skill Factor: Midfield player who oozes confidence. Always prepared to have the ball and always looking to create goal scoring chances for others. Has a great range of passing skills.

Career History: Started his football career as an associated schoolboy in November 1978 with Manchester City, but was released and snapped up by Leeds United. Made his FL debut at Elland Road on 20 November 1982 against Middlesbrough and remained in the side until the end of the season. After adjusting so quickly to Second Division football, he had the misfortune to suffer a broken leg at Barnsley in October 1983, but on recovering, he came back brilliantly as an ever present in 1984-85. His form didn't go unnoticed by Jack Charlton and he made his debut for the Irish Republic, through parental qualification, against Romania on 23 March 1988. After seven seasons of Second Division football at Elland Road, he seemed to realise his ambition of playing in the First Division when Brian Clough signed him for Nottingham Forest in the summer of 1989. As with Asa Hartford and Gary Megson in previous season, however, once signed he was totally ignored by Clough until rescued by Ron Atkinson for Sheffield Wednesday after four months at the City ground without a FL appearance to his name. When he arrived at Hillsborough, the "Owls" were bottom of the First Division with only one victory and two goals from 11 games. He immediately formed a midfield partnership with Carlton Palmer, which not only stabilised Wednesday and lifted them to mid-table, but also transformed them into a stylish passing outfit, until a tragic late season collapse condemned the team to relegation. He only missed one game in 1990-91, scoring ten goals, including five penalties, as the club returned to the First Division at the first time of asking, but the goal everybody will remember him for came after 38 minutes of the 1991 League Cup Final against the strong favourites, Manchester United. His powerful shot sped into the net to ultimately give Wednesday a shock 1-0 victory and enabled

him to pocket a coveted FA Cup winners medal. Although troubled by injuries in 1991-92, he played a part in Wednesday's best League campaign for 30 years, as they finished in third place and qualified for the 1992-93 UEFA Cup. Selected for the Irish Republic's first match of the season, he was surprisingly overlooked for the remaining games, even when fit.

Clubs	Signing Date	Transfer Fee	APPEARANCES				GOALS			
			Lge	FL Cup	FA Cup	Others	Lge	FL Cup	FA Cup	Others
Leeds United	3.82	–	225+5	14	11+1	11	47	3	1	1
Nottingham Forest	7.89	£650,000		1						
Sheffield Wednesday*	11.89	£500,000	96+1	11	7	3	18	1	2	1

SHERINGHAM Edward (Teddy) Paul

Born: Walthamstow,
2 April 1966

Height: 5'11"

Weight: 12.4

International Honours:
E Yth, E "U21"-1, E"B"

Position/Skill Factor: Striker with nice ball skills who is always looking for a shooting opportunity. Good in the air, on the ground he keeps his passing simple, but effective.

Career History: Joined Millwall as an apprentice in June 1982, before graduating through the club's junior sides and making his FL debut at the Den against Brentford on 15 January 1984, after turning professional. Following a spell on loan at Aldershot and the occasional game for the "Lions", he was finally given a run in 1986–87 when he was ever present, scoring 18 goals. He missed only one game in 1987–88 and in Tony Cascarino, he found the perfect foil to support his ability on the ground. Between them, they scored 42 League goals as the "Lions" roared their way into the top flight for the first time in their history as Second Division Champions. During the club's two seasons in the First Division, it was obvious that goals would be more difficult to come by, although in 1988–89, Millwall amazed the critics by finishing tenth in the table. However, after making a good start in 1989–90, at the end of the season the club were relegated with only five wins to their credit. But back in the Second Division, it was a different story for both the club and Teddy. Although the "Lions" failed at the Play-Off stage, he had a quite magnificent season, scoring 33 League goals, including four in a 4-1 win over Plymouth Argyle and three further hat-tricks. He ended the season as the highest goal scorer in the club's history with 111 and his 38 in all games equalled Richard Parker's and Peter Burridge's records set in 1926-27 and 1960-61, respectively. As Millwall lost out on promotion, it was perhaps inevitable that a First Division club should snap him up, but at least the "Lions" were able to extract a massive fee (for a non-international player) from Nottingham Forest for his services. Not an unqualified

success in his first season at the City Ground, despite playing in all but three games of Forest's 60 match programme and topping the scoring lists with 12 FL goals and nine cup goals. The highlights of his season were a hat-trick against Crystal Palace in a Fifth Round League Cup tie in February and his first two appearances at Wembley, first as a winner in the Zenith Cup Final against Southampton and then as a loser in the League Cup Final against Manchester United.

Clubs	Signing Date	Transfer Fee	APPEARANCES				GOALS			
			Lge	FL Cup	FA Cup	Others	Lge	FL Cup	FA Cup	Others
Millwall	1.84	–	205+15	16+1	12	11+2	94	8	4	5
Aldershot	2.85	Loan	4+1			1				
Nottingham Forest*	7.91	£2,000,000	39	10	4	6	13	5	2	2

SHERON Michael (Mike) Nigel

Born: Liverpool,
11 January 1972

Height: 5'9"

Weight: 11.3

International Honours:
E "U21"-2

Position/Skill Factor: A striker, who can also play in midfield, he has good vision with plenty of skill and looks to have the makings of a top-class player.

Career History: Came through Manchester City's junior ranks, after signing on as a trainee in July 1988, to turn professional during the 1990 close season. Loaned out to Third Division Bury at the end of 1990-91, he made his FL debut at Preston North End on 6 April 1991. Scored the winning goal at Tranmere Rovers in his only full League game, which sent the "Shakers" into the Play-Offs, but was unable to find the net again as Bolton Wanderers ultimately ended Bury's vain hopes of promotion. Made rapid strides in 1991-92, after making his debut for City as a substitute at home to Everton on 17 September. A permanent member of the first team squad thereafter, he established a regular slot on the right side of midfield in the last two months of the campaign, although previously a free scoring striker in City's youth and reserve teams. Called up for the England Under 21 squad at the end of the season.

Clubs	Signing Date	Transfer Fee	APPEARANCES				GOALS			
			Lge	FL Cup	FA Cup	Others	Lge	FL Cup	FA Cup	Others
Manchester City*	7.90	–	20+9	2+1	0+1	1	6	1		
Bury	3.91	Loan	1+4			4	1			

SHERWOOD Timothy (Tim) Alan

Born: St Albans,
2 February 1969

Height: 6'1"

Weight: 11.4

International Honours:
E "U21"-4

Position/Skill Factor: An attacking midfielder who likes to get forward to join up in the attack. A very determined competitor, he uses the ball constructively.

Career History: Signed for nearby Watford as an apprentice in February 1986, having been at the club as a junior since the summer of 1985. After turning professional, he made his FL debut as a substitute at Sheffield Wednesday on 12 September 1987 and made nine full appearances in midfield during a season that ultimately saw the "Hornets" relegated to the Second Division. Had a brief run in the first team in mid-1988-89, but then played little further part in Watford's ultimately unsuccessful promotion drive. With so little experience under his belt, it was a surprise when First Division Norwich signed him for a handsome fee in the summer of 1989, but it proved to be a shrewd signing. He soon won a place in the "Canaries'" team and proved to be a valuable utility player, turning out at right-back, in midfield and central defence and winning selection for the England Under 21 squad. In 1990-91 he firmly established himself in midfield, replacing the departed Andy Townsend and playing in every FL game, bar the last of the season. At this point his career seemed set fair, but it was set back at the start of 1991-92 when he was fined and suspended for a breach of club discipline. Consequently, he lost his place and although making a brief "comeback" in November and December he was eventually transferred, for a large profit, to ambitious Blackburn Rovers. Yet to settle in Lancashire, he soon lost his place in the Rovers' team and played almost no part in the vital end of season games or the Play-Offs.

Clubs	Signing Date	Transfer Fee	APPEARANCES				GOALS			
			Lge	FL Cup	FA Cup	Others	Lge	FL Cup	FA Cup	Others
Watford	2.87	–	23+7	4+1	9	4+1	2			
Norwich City	7.87	£175,000	66+5	7	4	5+1	10	1		2
Blackburn Rovers*	2.92	£500,000	7+4							

SHIRTLIFF Peter Andrew

Born: Hoyland,
6 April 1961

Height: 6'2"

Weight: 13.4

Position/Skill Factor: Very brave central defender, who rarely loses out in the air and is a strong tackler on the ground. Normally clears his lines, but passes the ball well when not under pressure.

Career History: The older brother of Paul, who played for Sheffield Wednesday and Northampton Town between 1980-1985, he signed for the "Owls" as an associated schoolboy in October 1975, before graduating as an apprentice in June 1977. He actually made his FL debut for Sheffield Wednesday, two months prior to turning professional, at Peterborough United on 19 August 1978. But it wasn't until the following season that he began to make his mark, although often having to alternate with Mike Pickering. Only missed six games in 1983-84 as Wednesday were promoted to the First Division, behind Chelsea, but later, with much competition for places, he signed for Charlton Athletic in the summer of 1986. In his first season in London, drama unfolded, as Athletic, by dint of their lowly First Division placing, were forced to play-off against Second Division Leeds United to decide which side would compete in the top flight during 1987-88. One nil down in extra-time, with seven minutes to go, he scored the equaliser and with just four minutes left on the clock, he dived in for the winner. Nothing else in his career could ever match that for excitement, but he was very sound and reliable during his three years at the club and was only ever absent, when injured. However, when Sheffield Wednesday manager Ron Atkinson came for him in the 1989 close season, he returned to Hillsborough for a then club record fee. In his first season, the team, after seeming to secure its First Division status, faltered badly in their last seven matches and were relegated. Promotion was duly attained at the first time of asking in 1990-91, as Wednesday went up behind Oldham Athletic and West Ham United and although he missed the last four games of the season through injury, he was very much present when winning a League Cup winners medal as a result of the "Owls'" splendid 1-0 victory over Manchester United. Out of favour in 1991-92, following the signing of Paul Warhurst, he did not get a game until the New Year, but played a more significant role in the second-half of the season as Wednesday achieved a highly creditable third place.

Clubs	Signing Date	Transfer Fee	APPEARANCES				GOALS			
			Lge	FL Cup	FA Cup	Others	Lge	FL Cup	FA Cup	Others
Sheffield Wednesday	10.78	–	188	17+1	17+1		4		1	
Charlton Athletic	7.86	£125,000	102+1	10	5	7	7			2
Sheffield Wednesday*	7.89	£500,000	84	13	6	3	4	1	2	

SHUTT Carl Steven

Born: Sheffield,
10 October 1961

Height: 5'10"

Weight: 11.10

Position/Skill Factor: A striker whose pace takes him away from defenders. Very dangerous in the penalty area, he has the ability to pounce on any mistakes.

Career History: Sheffield Wednesday introduced him to League football, having snapped him up from Spalding United, of the Northern Counties (East) League, at the end of 1984-85. Ironically, he was previously signed by Wednesday as an associated schoolboy player in April 1978, but had been released. Made his FL debut as a substitute at Oxford United on 31 August 1985 and in his first full League appearance, he struck the equaliser at Hillsborough against Coventry City. Scored nine times in 17 games in his first season. A hero of Wednesday's fine FA Cup run of 1985-86, he netted twice against Derby County in a Fifth Round replay, scored the winner against West Ham United in the Quarter-Final and the first goal in the Semi-Final against Everton, when the "Toffees" came back to win in extra-time. Despite scoring five times in his first ten FL games of 1986-87, he strangely lost his place and thereafter played second fiddle to David Hirst. Therefore it was not too surprising when he was allowed to leave for Bristol City in October 1987. Netted twice in his first game for the "Robins", a 4-2 reversal at Blackpool and scored all four goals in a 4-0 home victory over Fulham, a few weeks later. In 1988-89, however, his scoring rate ground to a halt and he was transferred back to his native Yorkshire, rejoining his former manager, Howard Wilkinson, at Leeds United. Remarkably, he scored a hat-trick against Bournemouth on his Leeds debut and struck again in his second game, but it was not enough to guarantee him a first team place. Due to a glut of forwards at Elland Road, he found it difficult to make his mark during his first term, but had some solace in the shape of a Second Division Championship medal as United once again rejoined the top flight. From November 1990 onwards, he had a good run in a side that eventually finished fourth in the First Division and in settling down alongside Lee Chapman, the pair scored 31 goals between them. Out of favour again in 1991-92, following the signing of Rod Wallace, he made only occasional appearances, but his 14 FL games (eight as a substitute) were enough for him to qualify for a League Championship medal when United won the title.

Clubs	Signing Date	Transfer Fee	APPEARANCES				GOALS			
			Lge	FL Cup	FA Cup	Others	Lge	FL Cup	FA Cup	Others
Sheffield Wednesday	5.85	–	36+4	3	4+1		16	1	4	
Bristol City	10.87	£55,000	39+7	5+2	7+1	10+1	10	4	4	4
Leeds United*	3.89	£50,000	40+25	5+2	6	4+2	17	1		3

SIMPSON Fitzroy

Born: Bradford-on-Avon,
26 February 1970

Height: 5'8"

Weight: 10.7

Position/Skill Factor: Powerful left-winger with an excellent left foot, who will often shoot on sight of goal and is not afraid to take defenders on.

Career History: Signed as a professional for Swindon Town in the 1988 close season, having been a trainee at the club since July 1987 and made his FL debut as a substitute during the home game against Barnsley on 14 January 1989. Given a couple of good runs in 1989-90, he gradually settled into a side that won the First Division Play-Off place at the end of the season, only to be denied by the League's ruling that the club be demoted due to financial irregularities. The following season saw Swindon avoid the drop into Division Three by a narrow margin, but he did well in a team that only won three of its last 17 League matches. A first team regular on the Town left-wing in 1991-92, he played in nearly every game up to the time of his transfer to Manchester City in March 1992. Slotted in immediately at Maine Road, replacing Michael Hughes on the left-wing, although in the long run his future may lie in central midfield.

Clubs	Signing Date	Transfer Fee	APPEARANCES				GOALS			
			Lge	FL Cup	FA Cup	Others	Lge	FL Cup	FA Cup	Others
Swindon Town	7.88	–	78+26	9+1	2+1	3+2	9	1		
Manchester City*	3.92	£500,000	9+2				1			

SIMPSON Ronald James

Born: Easington, 12 March 1974

Height: 5'8" Weight: 11.3

Position: Midfield player.

Career History: Joined the Sheffield Wednesday professional ranks during the 1992 close season, having previously been at Hillsborough as an associated schoolboy (October 1988) and as a trainee (July 1990). No first team experience as yet.

Clubs	Signing Date	Transfer Fee	APPEARANCES				GOALS			
			Lge	FL Cup	FA Cup	Others	Lge	FL Cup	FA Cup	Others
Sheffield Wednesday*	6.92	–								

SINCLAIR Frank Mohammed

Born: Lambeth, 3 December 1971

Height: 5'8" **Weight:** 11.2

Position/Skill Factor: Can play either at full-back or central defence and is very good in the air for his size. Enthusiasm and great pace are his major assets.

Career History: Came to Chelsea from the same school that produced Alan Hudson, when signing associated schoolboy forms in January 1986. Became a trainee in July 1988 and turned professional during the 1990 close season, after some impressive displays in the juniors. He was given a taste of big-time soccer at the end of 1990-91, when he stood in at left-back for England's Tony Dorigo and made his FL debut in a 3-3 draw at Stamford Bridge against Luton Town on 6 April 1991. Made an early appearance in 1991-92 as a fifth defender away to Oldham Athletic, to no avail, as Chelsea crashed 3-0. His next FL action was on loan to West Bromwich Albion at Christmas time where he achieved unwanted notoriety for being sent off in a game at Exeter for assaulting a referee — a charge he denied — and was suspended for nine games. Returned to the Chelsea team at left-back late in the season and is considered a bright prospect for the future.

Clubs	Signing Date	Transfer Fee	APPEARANCES				GOALS			
			Lge	FL Cup	FA Cup	Others	Lge	FL Cup	FA Cup	Others
Chelsea*	5.90	–	12		1					
W.B.A.	12.91	Loan	6				1			

SINNOTT Lee

Born: Pelsall,
12 July 1965

Height: 6'1"

Weight: 12.7

International Honours:
E Yth, E "U21"-1

Position/Skill Factor: Central defender who attacks the ball well in the air and is excellent in both boxes. Very good at hitting long passes into the channels.

Career History: Starting with Walsall as an apprentice in September 1981, he made his FL debut at Portsmouth on 6 March 1982 and by the time he turned professional in November 1982, was a regular in the side. He made 32 League appearances in 1982-83, wearing the number five shirt and his form quickly alerted Watford manager, Graham Taylor, who signed him at the beginning of the following season. Took a while to settle down at Vicarage Road, but by the end of his first season he had strung some impressive performances together and had played at Wembley in Watford's FA Cup Final side that was defeat-

ed 2-0 by Everton. However, by 1985-86, he had ceased to be an automatic first team choice, due to a mixture of injuries and loss of form and was transferred to Bradford City during the 1987 close season. Still only 23 years of age, he made a great start at Valley Parade, missing only two League games and being a tower of strength in a side that only failed to reach the First Division for the first time in their history, at the Play-Off stage. Unfortunately, City were relegated to the Third Division at the end of 1989-90 and while the club did reasonably well in 1990-91, his consistency over the past four seasons, just nine League matches missed, coupled with his ability, deserved a higher grade of football. Not surprisingly, a further chance to play First Division football came his way in the summer of 1991 when he signed for Crystal Palace. Although he started the season in central defence, he was soon switched by manager Steve Coppell to plug a problem slot at left-back, where he remained for most of the season.

Clubs	Signing Date	Transfer Fee	APPEARANCES				GOALS			
			Lge	FL Cup	FA Cup	Others	Lge	FL Cup	FA Cup	Others
Walsall	11.82	–	40	3	4		2			
Watford	9.83	£100,000	71+7	6	11		2			
Bradford City	7.87	£130,000	173	19	9	12	6			1
Crystal Palace*	8.91	£300,000	35+1	5	1	1				

SINTON Andrew (Andy)

Born: Newcastle, 19 March 1966

Height: 5'7" **Weight:** 10.7

International Honours: E Sch, E"B", E-6

Position/Skill Factor: Left-winger with a tremendous work rate, who is the ideal wide player. Has a good footballing brain and will often play the ball early, aiming to get it back.

Career History: An England schoolboy international, he joined Cambridge United as an associated schoolboy in September 1980, before signing as an apprentice on leaving school in August 1982. Became United's youngest ever player when he made his FL debut at the Abbey Stadium against Wolverhampton Wanderers on 2 November 1982 and on signing professional forms, towards the end of the season, he was already holding down a regular place. In four seasons at the club, he played over 100 first team games before the age of 20, while United dropped from the Second to Fourth Division. With Cambridge strapped for cash, he signed for Brentford in 1985-86 and in three and a half years at Griffin Park, barely missed a match for the Third Division outfit. His ability and consistency were noted by Brentford's close neighbours, Queens Park Rangers and in March 1989 he made the jump from Third to First Division football. Started by netting the winner against Aston Villa on his home debut and finished the campaign with three goals. Ever present in 1989-90 and 1990-91, he is a player who fits in well to the modern system and one who Rangers can build around in the future. As consistent as ever in 1991-92, he missed only four FL games and was rewarded with a full international call-up for the vital match in Poland which England drew 1-1 to qualify for the European Championship Finals. In his second international against the CIS in Moscow, he played in the unfamiliar position of left-back and appeared twice more before the Finals. Although not included in the original squad for Sweden, he was called up a late replacement for the injured John Barnes. Played twice in the Finals, once at right-back, but like his colleagues, was unable to provide any inspiration in England's disappointing showing.

Clubs	Signing Date	Transfer Fee	APPEARANCES				GOALS			
			Lge	FL Cup	FA Cup	Others	Lge	FL Cup	FA Cup	Others
Cambridge United	4.83	–	90+3	6	3	2	13	1		1
Brentford	12.85	£25,000	149	8	11	14	28	3	1	2
Q.P.R.*	3.89	£350,000	124	10	11	3	15		2	1

SKINNER Craig Richard

Born: Heywood, 21 October 1970

Height: 5'10" Weight: 11.0

Position/Skill Factor: Right-winger who is a good all-round player with plenty of pace and skill and a good crosser of the ball.

Career History: A local discovery, he first signed for Blackburn Rovers as an associated schoolboy in October 1985, before graduating to the trainee ranks in July 1987. Progressing through the club's junior sides, he turned professional during the 1989 close season and eventually stepped out for his FL debut as a substitute at Ewood Park against Bristol City on 15 December 1990, making a handful of further appearances before returning to the reserves. Enjoyed a brief run in the team early in 1991-92, but hardly got a "look in" following the arrival of new manager, Kenny Dalglish.

Clubs	Signing Date	Transfer Fee	APPEARANCES				GOALS			
			Lge	FL Cup	FA Cup	Others	Lge	FL Cup	FA Cup	Others
Blackburn Rovers*	6.89	–	11+5	0+1	1	2				

SKINNER Justin James

Born: Dorking, 17 September 1972

Height: 5'6" Weight: 11.5

Position/Skill Factor: Enthusiastic left-back who is a strong tackler. And with an excellent left foot, he is well capable of hitting good long diagonal passes.

Career History: Signing professional for Wimbledon during the 1991 close season, he first came to the club as a trainee in July 1989 and has yet to make a first team appearance.

Clubs	Signing Date	Transfer Fee	APPEARANCES				GOALS			
			Lge	FL Cup	FA Cup	Others	Lge	FL Cup	FA Cup	Others
Wimbledon*	7.91	–								

SLAVEN Bernard (Bernie) Joseph

Born: Paisley, 13 November 1960

Height: 5'11"

Weight: 10.10

International Honours: IR-6

Position/Skill Factor: A natural goal scorer, he has great skill and presence and almost "strokes" the ball into the net. Rarely found wanting in the penalty area.

Career History: A goal scoring legend on Teeside, he was signed by Middlesbrough as a basement bargain from Scottish Second Division team, Albion Rovers, at the beginning of 1985-86, following a letter he had written to every big club in England, seeking a trial. Previously, he had played for Morton, Airdrie and Queen of the South, but had only shown goal scoring form with the Coatbridge club, for whom he scored 27 goals in 42 games. Made his FL debut at Leeds United on 12 October 1985 and then scored in his first home match, a 1-1 draw against Bradford City. In a season that saw the club relegated to Division Three, he kicked off with just eight goals, but in 1986-87, his 17 from 46 appearances, playing alongside Archie Stephens, ensured promotion at the first time of asking, behind Bournemouth. He stood head and shoulders above the other forwards in 1987-88, with 21 League goals, as the club were promoted to the First Division, following Play-Off victories over Bradford City and Chelsea. Despite scoring 15 in his first ever season in the top flight, the club were relegated, winning only one of their last 17 League games. Ever present in 1989-90, his scoring rate, with little support, increased to 21 and without him "Boro", who only just saved their Second Division status, would surely have been relegated. They recovered in 1990-91 and only failed to reach the First Division at the Play-Off stage. He found some support up front in the shape of Ian Baird and between them they scored 30 League goals. As the club's leading scorer in every season since 1986-87, he was finally recognised at international level, when selected on parental qualification to play for the Republic of Ireland against Wales on 28 March 1990 in Dublin. Leading scorer yet again in 1991-92 with 17 FL goals from 38 games (ten as substitute), he outscored his new forward partner, Paul Wilkinson, who started every game. Despite his excellent scoring ratio, he was often dropped by new manager Lennie Lawrence, for no apparent reason. It was only fitting, however, that when recalled for the final game of the season at Wolverhampton, he should score the equaliser midway through the second-half which helped "Boro" to overturn a 1-0 deficit and go on to clinch automatic promotion to the Premier League.

Clubs	Signing Date	Transfer Fee	APPEARANCES				GOALS			
			Lge	FL Cup	FA Cup	Others	Lge	FL Cup	FA Cup	Others
Middlesbrough*	9.85	£25,000	273+16	25+1	16+1	27	115	7	7	14

SLINEY Gary Sean

Born: Dublin, 2 September 1973

Height: 5'10" Weight: 12.3

International Honours: IR Yth, IR "U21"

Position/Skill Factor: Very competitive right-back with good distribution who likes to join up in the attack when the opportunity allows.

Career History: After joining Manchester City as a trainee in August 1990, he signed professional forms just a month later on his 17th birthday. Has yet to make a first team appearance.

Clubs	Signing Date	Transfer Fee	APPEARANCES				GOALS			
			Lge	FL Cup	FA Cup	Others	Lge	FL Cup	FA Cup	Others
Manchester City*	9.90	–								

SMALL Bryan

Born: Birmingham, 15 November 1971

Height: 5'9" Weight: 11.8

International Honours: E Yth

Position/Skill Factor: Left-back, or midfielder, he is very strong on the ball and is difficult to dispossess. Has a good left foot and is always keen to get forward.

Career History: Joined Aston Villa as a trainee in July 1988, having been at the club as an associated schoolboy since January 1986, he turned professional two years later. Made his FL debut wearing the number three shirt on 19

October 1991 away to Everton and had a number of further games both at left-back and in midfield during the season, usually standing in for Steve Staunton.

Clubs	Signing Date	Transfer Fee	APPEARANCES				GOALS			
			Lge	FL Cup	FA Cup	Others	Lge	FL Cup	FA Cup	Others
Aston Villa*	7.90	–	8		2+1	2				

SMITH Alan Martin

Born: Bromsgrove, 21 November 1962

Height: 6'3" Weight: 12.10

International Honours: E Semi Pro Int, E"B", FL Rep, E-13

Position/Skill Factor: Unselfish striker and a wonderful team player, who often acts as a foil for others. Has a good touch and runs well off the ball. He also uses his height and skill in the air to good effect.

Career History: Before signing as a professional with Leicester City, he played with Southern League team, Alvechurch and while at the club, he represented the English semi-pro international side. He made his FL debut at Filbert Street against Charlton Athletic on 28 August 1982 and went on to play 39 games that first season, with his 13 League goals playing a major part in City's promotion to the First Division in third place, a remarkable achievement for a first year professional. Partnering the up-and-coming Gary Lineker, he was the perfect decoy, but after the latter's transfer to Everton in the summer of 1985, he assumed the mantle of the club's leading scorer for the next two years. However, his 17 FL goals in 1986-87 were not enough to save Leicester from relegation back to the Second Division and at the end of the season, he signed for Arsenal. In his first term at Highbury he netted 11 goals, including a hat-trick in his fourth game, a 6-0 victory over Portsmouth, to top the "Gunners'" charts and he also scored in the League Cup Final against Luton Town, but couldn't prevent Arsenal going down 3-2 in a thrilling finish. The following season,

1988-89, he won a League Championship medal, striking 23 times in 36 games and opened the scoring in the final game, the 2-0 victory at Liverpool, which decided the title. During the season his club form was finally recognised by Bobby Robson, who selected him to play as a substitute in England's 1-1 draw against Saudi Arabia on 16 November 1988, which also gave him the opportunity to renew his old partnership with Gary Lineker. The goals dried up somewhat in 1989-90, as Arsenal fell away in the League, but he still headed the club's goal charts with just ten. Arsenal were never out of the top two during 1990-91 and at the end of an eventful season, he had won a second League Championship medal. And at the same time he had yet again proved to be a vital cog in the Highbury machine in scoring 22 League goals and laying on several chances for others. He started 1991-92 in lethal form, with seven goals in the first nine FL games and a personal landmark of four in one match (all scored in the space of 16 minutes) against Austria Vienna in the First Round of the European Cup. Thereafter, the goals dried up as Arsenal went into a mid-season slump and he scored only six more to the end of the season, losing his place to the rapidly developing Kevin Campbell. Curiously, despite his loss of form at club level and playing little part in England's "warm-up" games at the end of the season, he was included in the squad for the European Championship Finals in Sweden, but in common with his colleagues made little impact in the two games in which he appeared.

Clubs	Signing Date	Transfer Fee	APPEARANCES				GOALS			
			Lge	FL Cup	FA Cup	Others	Lge	FL Cup	FA Cup	Others
Leicester City	6.82	£22,000	190+10	8+1	8		76	4	4	
Arsenal*	5.87	£800,000	177+12	22+1	16	9	77	12	4	4

SMITH David

Born: Stonehouse, Gloucs, 29 March 1968

Height: 5'8"

Weight: 10.2

International Honours: E "U21"-10

Position/Skill Factor: Left-winger who hugs the touchline and likes nothing better than taking his opponents on. Has good pace and a lovely left foot, which produce telling crosses.

Career History: Came through Coventry City's junior sides, first as an associated schoolboy (December 1983) and then as an apprentice (June 1984), before turning over to the paid ranks in the summer of 1986. Made his FL debut when coming off the bench in a 1-0 defeat at Manchester United on 6 February 1988 and by the end of that first season he was holding down a regular first team place. Rarely missing a game, he has been very consistent since the day he came into the side and has proved to be one of the most promising of City's homegrown players of

recent years. Suffered a disappointing 1991-92, being dropped several times and in and out of the team all season, although fortunately for him, no other player laid claim to the left-wing slot.

Clubs	Signing Date	Transfer Fee	APPEARANCES				GOALS			
			Lge	FL Cup	FA Cup	Others	Lge	FL Cup	FA Cup	Others
Coventry City*	7.86	–	138+10	16	6	4+1	18			

SMITH David Christopher

Born: Liverpool, 26 December 1970

Height: 5'9"

Weight: 11.12

Position/Skill Factor: Small, compact midfield man, who passes well and takes up good positions in order to receive the return ball.

Career History: Liverpool born, he came to Norwich City as a trainee in November 1987 and progressed enough to be taken on as a professional in the summer of 1989. Made his FL debut as a substitute at Derby County on 21 April 1990, but apart from a handful of games in 1990-91, he was still looking forward to a proper run in the side. Again made little headway in 1991-92, with only an end of season appearance to add to his record.

Clubs	Signing Date	Transfer Fee	APPEARANCES				GOALS			
			Lge	FL Cup	FA Cup	Others	Lge	FL Cup	FA Cup	Others
Norwich City*	7.89	–	3+2		2	1+1				

SMITH Mark Alan

Born: Birmingham, 2 January 1973

Height: 6'1" Weight: 13.9

Position: Goalkeeper.

Career History: Joined Nottingham Forest as a trainee in July 1989 and turned professional early in 1991. As one of five 'keepers on the club's books it is no surprise that he has yet to make a first team appearance and he was loaned out to non-League sides, Grantham and Eastwood Town, during 1991-92, in order to gain experience.

Clubs	Signing Date	Transfer Fee	APPEARANCES				GOALS			
			Lge	FL Cup	FA Cup	Others	Lge	FL Cup	FA Cup	Others
Nottingham Forest*	2.91	–								

SMITH Richard (Ricky)

Born: Bristol, 2 September 1973

Height: 5'9" **Weight:** 10.12

Position: Left-back.

Career History: Joined Coventry City during the summer of 1992 as a professional, having been at Highfield Road first as an associated schoolboy (September 1989), before graduating as a trainee in July 1990. No first team experience.

Clubs	Signing Date	Transfer Fee	APPEARANCES				GOALS			
			Lge	FL Cup	FA Cup	Others	Lge	FL Cup	FA Cup	Others
Coventry City*	6.92	–								

SNODIN Ian

Born: Rotherham, 15 August 1963

Height: 5'7"

Weight: 8.12

International Honours: E Yth, E "U21"-4, E"B"

Position/Skill Factor: Accomplished midfield player who looks comfortable either defending or further forward. A good competitor, he passes the ball effectively.

Career History: Younger brother of Glynn, he followed in his footsteps by joining Doncaster Rovers as an associated schoolboy in February 1989, before becoming an apprentice with the club, in August 1979. Made his FL debut at the Belle Vue Ground as a substitute against Bournemouth on 29 March 1980 and scored a few weeks later at Aldershot, before turning professional during the summer. Spent six years at Rovers as they yo-yoed between the Third and Fourth Divisions, making over 200 appearances, before being transferred to the club's more illustrious Yorkshire neighbours, Leeds United, during the 1985 close season. Immediately appointed as club captain, he was at Elland Road for less than two years before the Everton manager, Howard Kendall, added him to his title chasing side in January 1987. Thrown straight into the "Toffees'" midfield, he played throughout the final four months of the season, making 11 League appearances and winning a League Championship medal, after helping his new club to regain the title they had won two years earlier. Despite keen competition for places at Goodison, injuries apart, he would be a regular first team choice. Unfortunately, an injury received in a League match against Sheffield Wednesday in March 1989, kept him out of both selection for England against Albania and the Everton side that lost 3-2 to Liverpool in the FA Cup Final. Eventually recovering to play 25 League games in 1989-90, he yet again succumbed to injury and made only one appearance in 1990-91. Due to injuries, he has not played first team football since November 1990 and his future in the game is now in considerable doubt.

Clubs	Signing Date	Transfer Fee	APPEARANCES				GOALS			
			Lge	FL Cup	FA Cup	Others	Lge	FL Cup	FA Cup	Others
Doncaster Rovers	8.80	–	181+7	9	11+1	3	25	1	1	
Leeds United	5.85	£200,000	51	3	1		6	2		
Everton*	1.87	£840,000	93+3	15+1	22	3	2	1	2	

SOUTHALL Neville

Born: Llandudno, 16 September 1958

Height: 6'1" **Weight:** 12.1

International Honours: W-60

Position/Skill Factor: Very consistent goalkeeper. Never easy to beat, he makes stunning saves when all seems lost. Has tremendous reflexes and is as brave as a lion.

Career History: Now regarded by many good judges to be the best goalkeeper in Europe, if not the world, he had a humble beginning to his football career when joining Fourth Division Bury from non-League Winsford United in the summer of 1980. Made his FL debut in a 2-1 defeat at Wigan Athletic on 29 March 1980 and on keeping his place in the side, immediately impressed several top clubs, including Everton, who signed him during the 1981 close season. After taking over the goalkeeper's jersey on a regular basis half-way into 1981-82, he was called up to replace Dai Davies in the Welsh goal for the match against Northern Ireland at Wrexham on 27 May 1982. Keeping a clean sheet in a 3-0 win, was a great experience, but the harsh reality of First Division football lay just around the corner when he was replaced by the experienced Jim Arnold, following a 5-0 home defeat by Liverpool in November 1982. After losing his place, he was loaned out to Port Vale where he finished on the losing side just once, before returning to Goodison. Showing great character, he went on to regain his place in the side and became the mainstay in the most successful period of the club's history between 1984-1987, when they won two League Championship medals, the FA Cup and the European Cup Winners Cup. His brilliant displays in 1984-85, when Everton won both the League Championship and the European Cup Winners Cup were personally rewarded by the Football Writers' Association when they named him as their "Footballer of the Year". Since those heady days, he has suffered the pain of a losing FA Cup Final at the hands of deadly rivals, Liverpool and the lengthy rebuilding of a side that has yet to threaten the best. However, he remains a model of consistency, having played in every single League game for Everton since October 1987, an unbroken run of 184 matches. Played an outstanding part in Wales' valiant, but ultimately unsuccessful bid to qualify for the 1992 European Championship Finals, during which they defeated the World Champions, Germany, in Cardiff, only to be eliminated in their final group match in the return game.

Clubs	Signing Date	Transfer Fee	APPEARANCES				GOALS			
			Lge	FL Cup	FA Cup	Others	Lge	FL Cup	FA Cup	Others
Bury	6.80	£6,000	39			5				
Everton*	7.81	£150,000	371	48	55	32				
Port Vale	1.83	Loan	9							

Neville Southall

SOUTHGATE Gareth

Born: Watford,
3 September 1970

Height: 5'10"

Weight: 11.12

Position/Skill Factor: An athletic full-back with two good feet who can also play in midfield. A good distributor of the ball himself, he is always ready to support his teammates when they need a passing option.

Career History: First came to Crystal Palace as an associated schoolboy in October 1986, before signing on as a trainee in July 1987 and progressing to the professional ranks at the beginning of 1989. Waited over two years to make his FL debut and when it came, in the most daunting of venues, Anfield, Palace went down 3-0 to Liverpool on 23 April 1991 with a team considerably weakened by injuries. Made considerable progress in 1991-92 and was a regular member of the first team, playing at right-back from October until the New Year, then a few games in central defence, before ending the season in midfield — a true utility player.

Clubs	Signing Date	Transfer Fee	APPEARANCES				GOALS			
			Lge	FL Cup	FA Cup	Others	Lge	FL Cup	FA Cup	Others
Crystal Palace*	1.89	–	27+4	6+1		4				

SPEED Gary Andrew

Born: Hawarden,
8 September 1969

Height: 5'9"

Weight: 10.6

International Honours:
W Yth, W "U21"-3, W-13

Position/Skill Factor: Left-winger with a cultured left foot. Can also play in defence, where he is capable of creating and defending well. Also, very powerful in the air.

Career History: Promising young player who came through the Leeds United youth system, first as an associated schoolboy (January 1985) and then as a trainee (July 1986), before progressing into the paid ranks in the 1988 close season. Made his FL debut in the penultimate game of 1988-89, a 0-0 draw at Elland Road against Oldham Athletic on 6 May 1989. In 1989-90, he found himself regularly on the subs' bench during the early stages of Leeds' Second Division Championship winning season, before getting a run in the side in March and seizing the opportunity in brilliant style. His form earned him a full Welsh cap against Costa Rica on 20 May 1990 and he went on to make United's left-wing slot his own in 1990-91, missing only three League games as the club consolidated its First Division status. Played in all but one of Leeds' victorious League Championship campaign in 1991-92 and scored several vital goals. Towards the end of the season, he deputised effectively for Tony Dorigo at left-back and for Mel Sterland at right-back. Also, he became an automatic selection for the Welsh national team.

Clubs	Signing Date	Transfer Fee	APPEARANCES				GOALS			
			Lge	FL Cup	FA Cup	Others	Lge	FL Cup	FA Cup	Others
Leeds United*	6.88	–	89+16	11+1	7	4+3	17	6		

SPEEDIE David Robert

Born: Glenrothes, 20 February 1960

Height: 5'7" Weight: 11.0

International Honours: S "U21"-1, S-10

Position/Skill Factor: A striker who is as aggressive as they come. Very competitive, he will tackle forwards and defenders alike. His skill on the ball, coupled to his speed off the mark, spells danger to any defence and he is brilliant in the air, especially inside the six yard box.

Career History: While working as a coalminer, he came through Barnsley's junior side to turn professional and immediately made his FL debut at home to Wigan Athletic on 21 October 1978. After two seasons as a professional with Barnsley, without a significant breakthrough, he was released to join Fourth Division Darlington. In two seasons at Feethams, he missed only four FL games and in his second term, scored a remarkable 17 FL goals, all from midfield. Such form persuaded Chelsea to sign him in the summer of 1982. Converted to striker, he had a quiet first season at Stamford Bridge as Chelsea only just avoided relegation to the Third Division, but in 1983-84 he formed a deadly partnership with Kerry Dixon, which spearheaded Chelsea to the Second Division Championship. The following season he made his international debut for Scotland against England on 25 May 1985, a few months after gaining his only Under 21 cap as an over-age player. Winning four more caps in 1985-86, surprisingly, he was not included in the Scotland squad for the World Cup finals in Mexico 1986. Never a prolific scorer for Chelsea, his best season was 1985-86 when he netted 14 FL goals and scored a hat-trick in his team's amazing 5-4 victory over Manchester City in the Final of the Full Members (now Zenith) Cup. After a disappointing 1986-87 season, he started a new career with Coventry City, who signed him for a club record fee. Despite scoring only six goals in 36 games in his first season at Highfield Road, he was immensely popular with the "Sky Blues'" fans for his energy and commitment. In 1988-89, he was switched to midfield and ended the season as top scorer with 14 FL goals and on 1 October he played possibly the match of his life at home to

Middlesbrough, scoring a magnificent hat-trick of headers, only narrowly missing the target with two other efforts. Unbelievably, his team, with one of the meanest defences in the First Division, lost the match 3-4! He scored another hat-trick later in the season against Sheffield Wednesday, but this time Coventry obliged with a 5-0 victory. Recalled to the Scotland squad, he won five more caps before bowing out, or being possibly discarded for disciplinary reasons. His "short fuse" temper was notorious and responsible for many bookings and sendings off. Things came to a head in 1990-91, when an off the field incident with a club vice-president and a sending-off at Crystal Palace, prompted new manager, Terry Butcher, to sell him. He was on the point of joining Aston Villa, when Kenny Dalglish stepped in and signed him for Liverpool. It was a strange signing as Liverpool needed a young midfield player and a commanding central defender, not a striker! Criticism was stifled when Speedie scored an equaliser away to Manchester United on his debut and two goals in three minutes to "kill off" Everton 3-1 in his second game. It seemed Dalglish was a magician, but unfortunately, ten days later, he left the club mysteriously. Sold to Blackburn Rovers in the summer, having scored six goals in eight full appearances, like good wine, he simply improved with age. Despite missing ten games through suspension or "resting", he led the Rovers'

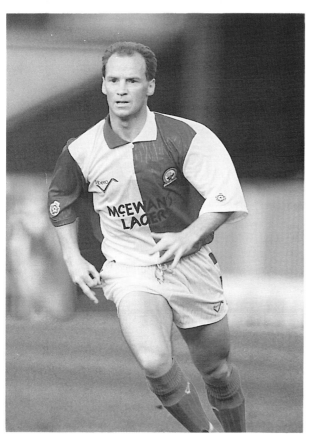

scoring charts by a mile with 23 FL goals in only 36 games. After plundering a hat-trick against Newcastle in February, he was suspended and with his striking partner Mike Newell, seriously injured in the same game, Rovers' manager, Kenny Dalglish, with limitless funds at his disposal, signed Roy Wegerle and later Duncan Shearer to fill the holes in his forward line. Unfortunately, neither settled in quickly and Rovers' promotion effort began to collapse, forcing Dalglish to recall both Speedie and Newell for the vital end of season games. On the last Saturday of the season, Rovers needed three points at Plymouth to reach the Play-Offs against a team needing

three points to avoid relegation. It was a tall order, especially when Argyle took an early lead, but two goals in two minutes from Speedie just before half-time, turned the match on its head and he went on to complete his hat-trick in the second-half to usher Rovers to a 3-1 victory and into the Play-Offs. As if such heroism was not enough for one season, he scored the third and fourth goals of the first-leg Play-Off Semi-Final against Derby, as Rovers overturned an early 0-2 deficit to win 4-2. And in the Play-Off final against Leicester, it was his run into the area that created the penalty converted by Mike Newell, which took Rovers into the Premier League.

Clubs	Signing Date	Transfer Fee	APPEARANCES				GOALS			
			Lge	FL Cup	FA Cup	Others	Lge	FL Cup	FA Cup	Others
Barnsley	10.78	–	10+13							
Darlington	6.80	£5000	88	4	3		21		1	
Chelsea	6.82	£70,000	155+7	23+1	12	7	47	7	5	5
Coventry City	7.87	£780,000	121+1	15	3+1	4	31	3		1
Liverpool	2.91	£675,000	8+4		1+1		6			
Blackburn Rovers*	8.91	£450,000	34+2	2	2	3	23		1	2

SPINK Nigel Philip

Born: Chelmsford,
8 August 1958

Height: 6'1" Weight: 14.6

International Honours:
E"B", FL Rep, E-1

Position/Skill Factor: Commanding goalkeeper, whose huge build helps him dominate his goal area. Confidently comes for crosses and quickly turns defence into attack with a throw or a long kick.

Career History: Joined Aston Villa from his local club, Chelmsford City, in 1976-77, but had to wait nearly three years before making his FL debut at Nottingham Forest on 26 December 1979. Incredibly, his next first team appearance was in the 1982 European Cup Final in Rotterdam, when he came on as a substitute for the injured Jimmy Rimmer after only eight minutes of the game. He played superbly to deny the Bayern Munich forwards, while a Peter Withe goal at the other end won the trophy for Villa. Although he found himself immediately back in the reserves, in 1982-83, he at last usurped Rimmer in December 1982 and grabbed the opportunity with both hands, holding his place for the remainder of the season and impressing enough to be selected for the England trip to Australia in the summer of 1983. It was there that he won his only international cap, coming on at half-time for Peter Shilton during a 0-0 draw on 11 June 1983. Starting 1983-84 as the number one choice for Villa, he had fully established himself when injury struck in a League game at Coventry City in March 1984. He missed the remainder of the season and failed to reclaim his place from Mervyn Day until December 1984. Injuries yet again interrupted his career in each of the next two campaigns, but he was back as an ever present in 1987-88 as Villa were promoted to the First Division, behind Millwall, at the first attempt. And he only missed one League game as Villa became First Division runners-up to Liverpool in 1989-90, when conceding just 38 goals. Automatic first choice 'keeper at Villa Park since 1985, he lost his first team jersey to Les Sealey in October 1991 and his future seemed uncertain. To his credit, he won his place back in March 1992 and held it for the remainder of the season.

Clubs	Signing Date	Transfer Fee	APPEARANCES				GOALS			
			Lge	FL Cup	FA Cup	Others	Lge	FL Cup	FA Cup	Others
Liverpool	9.86	£20,000	55+10	6+2	14+2	1		4	1	1
Bradford City	11.87	Loan	7+1	2		1				
Aston Villa*	8.91	£1,100,000	37	2	4		4			

STEJSKAL Jan

Born: Czechoslovakia, 15 January 1962

Height: 6'3"

Weight: 12.0

International Honours: Czech Int

Position/Skill Factor: Quality goalkeeper who is a good shot stopper and has no fear of coming for crosses. Also a very long kicker with his left foot.

Career History: Initially signed by Queens Park Rangers from Sparta Prague in the 1991 close season, as the replacement for David Seaman, he was not released by the Czech side until their elimination from European competition in mid-October 1990. Made his FL debut in a 3-2 win at Leeds United on 20 October 1990, but after conceding 11 goals in his first four matches, he was rested in order for him to re-adjust to the English game. Justifying his reputation, he came back with renewed vigour to play in the last 22 League games of the season, being beaten only 21 times in assisting Rangers to climb from the foot of the First Division to mid-table security. Unfortunately, lost his Czech international place to his great rival, Ludek Miklosko of West Ham United, however. Once again proved to be one of the safest 'keepers in the League during 1991-92, conceding only 45 goals in 41 games and again helping his club to recover from a dreadful start to the season to finish in mid-table.

Clubs	Signing Date	Transfer Fee	APPEARANCES				GOALS			
			Lge	FL Cup	FA Cup	Others	Lge	FL Cup	FA Cup	Others
Q.P.R.*	10.90	£600,000	67	4	2	2				

STEPHENSON Michael James

Born: Coventry, 6 October 1973

Height: 5'9" Weight: 11.7

Position: Striker.

Career History: Discovered locally, he signed professional forms for Coventry City during the summer of 1992, having been at Highfield Road first as an associated schoolboy (May 1989), before graduating as a trainee in July 1990. No first team experience.

STAUNTON Stephen (Steve)

Born: Drogheda, 19 January 1969

Height: 5'11"

Weight: 11.2

International Honours: IR "U21"-2, IR-34

Position/Skill Factor: Left-back, or left sided midfielder, he likes to push forward and is a good crosser of the ball. Also an excellent passer, who always seems to have plenty of time.

Career History: Joined Liverpool from the League of Ireland side, Dundalk, early in 1986-87 and after spending his first 14 months at Anfield without first team football, he was loaned out to Bradford City and made his FL debut at Valley Parade against Sheffield United on 14 November 1987. He finally broke into the Liverpool squad in 1988-89, making his debut as a second-half substitute at home to Tottenham Hotspur on 17 September 1988. Eventually wresting the left-back slot in the face of stiff competition from David Burrows, he won an FA Cup winners medal at the end of the season, following Liverpool's 3-2 victory over Everton. His performances also brought him international recognition for the Republic of Ireland and during the season he won his first cap against Tunisia on 19 October 1988. An automatic choice for his country, he found it more difficult to hold down a regular place at Anfield during 1989-90, although his 18 League appearances, mainly in midfield, still entitled him to a League Championship medal when Liverpool won the title for a record breaking 18 times. It was the same story in 1990-91 as he competed in the "Reds'" midfield, wearing at least six different shirt numbers, while making 20 League appearances as Liverpool finished as runners-up to Arsenal in the Championship. Transferred to Aston Villa for a massive fee in the summer of 1991, he made a dream debut for his new club, scoring the winner in an amazing 3-2 turnaround away to Sheffield Wednesday in the first match of the season. He remained Villa's first choice left-back for the bulk of a largely disappointing season for the Birmingham club.

Clubs	Signing Date	Transfer Fee	APPEARANCES				GOALS			
			Lge	FL Cup	FA Cup	Others	Lge	FL Cup	FA Cup	Others
Aston Villa*	1.77	£4,000	306	39	24	19+1				

Clubs	Signing Date	Transfer Fee	APPEARANCES				GOALS			
			Lge	FL Cup	FA Cup	Others	Lge	FL Cup	FA Cup	Others
Coventry City*	6.92	–								

STERLAND Melvyn (Mel)

Born: Sheffield,
1 October 1961

Height: 5'10"

Weight: 12.10

International Honours:
E "U21"-7, FL Rep,
E"B", E-1

Position/Skill Factor: Brilliant attacking right-back who likes to get forward in order to pick his forwards out with wonderful crosses. Very dangerous with free-kicks around the box.

Career History: Came to Sheffield Wednesday as an apprentice in June 1978 and made his FL debut as a substitute at Hillsborough against Blackpool on 17 May 1979, prior to signing as a professional. In his very next game, his first full appearance, he scored against Hull City. After gaining a regular place in the side in 1980-81, he soon earned the nickname of "Zico" because of his tremendous ability at dead ball situations. Originally a midfielder, he was converted successfully to right-back in 1981-82. He made 39 League appearances when the "Owls" gained promotion to the First Division in 1983-84 and by this time had become the club's penalty taker, scoring five that season. Niggling injuries prevented him from completing any season at Hillsborough as an ever present, but he had a good recovery rate and was never absent for long. Eventually recognised by the international selectors, he won his one and only full cap for England against Saudi Arabia on 16 November 1988. He would probably have remained at Hillsborough for the duration of his career, but for an inexplicable decision in late 1988 to relieve him of the captaincy, which unsettled him and he requested a transfer, joining the large contingent of English players at Glasgow Rangers. In his brief stay at Ibrox Park, he scored three goals and assisted Rangers to the Scottish Championship, but, presumably homesick, he was surpisingly allowed to leave in the summer to reunite with his former manager, Howard Wilkinson, at Leeds United. Immediately slotting into a side who were desperate to rekindle former glories, with a blend of youth and experience, he won a Second Division Championship medal as United booked their return to the top flight. Back in the First Division for the first time in eight years, Leeds surprised many when finishing fourth, but for him, 1990-91, was memorable as his first season in League football as an ever present. Won his first major honour in English football in 1991-92 as a member of the team which captured the Football League Championship. Once again, his prodigious free-kicks and penalties were a vital factor in that success, although he was sadly forced to sit out the closing weeks of the campaign with injury.

Clubs	Signing Date	Transfer Fee	APPEARANCES				GOALS			
			Lge	FL Cup	FA Cup	Others	Lge	FL Cup	FA Cup	Others
Sheffield Wednesday	10.79	–	271+8	30	34+1	3	37	7	5	
Glasgow Rangers	3.89	£800,000								
Leeds United*	7.89	£600,000	108+3	13	8	9	16	1	1	2

STEWART Paul Andrew

Born: Manchester, 7 October 1964

Height: 5'11" Weight: 11.10

International Honours: E Yth, E "U21"-1, E"B", E-3

Position/Skill Factor: A bustling ex-striker who has been recently converted to midfield. Tackles strongly and powerful in the air, he still scores important goals from good forward runs.

Career History: Joined Blackpool as an apprentice in April 1981, after being on associated schoolboy forms since December 1978 and turned professional early in 1981-82. A few months later, he made his FL debut at Bloomfield Road as a substitute against Rochdale on 10 February 1982. He soon established a regular first team place and was a key player when the "Seasiders" were promoted to the Third Division as runners-up in 1984-85. After making rapid progress in 1986-87 as an out-and-out front man and scoring 21 goals in 32 League games, he signed for Manchester City, who were struggling at the foot of the First Division. Arrived too late to prevent a goal shy team from sliding into the Second Division, but was able to rectify the situation in 1987-88. He hit the target 25 times in 40 League games, including two hat-tricks, before Tottenham Hotspur signed him during the 1988 close season, giving City a profit of £1.5 million in just over one year. An injury delayed his "Spurs'" debut until 1 October and he finally appeared as a substitute at White Hart Lane against Manchester United. And with the score standing at 2-2, he had the misfortune of hitting the bar with a late penalty. Recovering his composure, he ended the season with 12 League strikes and despite a patchy 1989-90, when he shared goal scoring duties with Paul Walsh, he still managed to notch some vital goals. However, it was not until 1990-91, when Terry Venables tried him out in the middle of the park, did he meet with lasting success. He ended the season with an FA Cup winners medal, after starting Tottenham's FA Cup run with the only goal of the game against his old club, Blackpool, in the Third Round. And he all but finished it in the Final, when scoring the equaliser against Nottingham Forest, with "Spurs" winning the FA Cup in extra-time. One of the club's few consistent players in a disappointing 1991-92 campaign, he played in all but four FL games and was called up for the England squad for the first time. Made three international appearances, all as a substitute, but was not included in the squad for the European Championship Finals.

Clubs	Signing Date	Transfer Fee	APPEARANCES				GOALS			
			Lge	FL Cup	FA Cup	Others	Lge	FL Cup	FA Cup	Others
Blackpool	10.81	–	188+13	11	7	6	56	3	2	1
Manchester City	3.87	£200,000	51	6	4	2	27	2	1	1
Tottenham Hotspur*	6.88	£1,700,000	126+5	23	9	9	28	7	2	

STEWART Simon

Born: Leeds, 1 November 1973

Height: 6'1" Weight: 12.4

Position: Central defender.

Career History: After impressing in the club's junior side, he joined the Sheffield Wednesday professional staff last summer, having been at Hillsborough as a trainee since July 1990. Has no first team experience.

Clubs	Signing Date	Transfer Fee	APPEARANCES				GOALS			
			Lge	FL Cup	FA Cup	Others	Lge	FL Cup	FA Cup	Others
Sheffield Wednesday*	6.92	–								

STOCKWELL Michael (Mike) Thomas

Born: Chelmsford, 14 February 1965

Height: 5'6" Weight: 10.2

Position/Skill Factor: A versatile player who can play at right-back, central midfield and on the flanks, with equal efficiency. Quick tackling, quick thinking and never easily beaten, he passes and moves well.

Career History: After coming to Ipswich Town as an apprentice in June 1981, he graduated to the professional ranks during 1982-83 and then waited three years before making his FL debut in a 1-0 win at Coventry City on 26 December 1985. Played a few more times that season, mainly as a substitute, as the team slid into the Second Division. On winning a regular place on the left side of midfield in 1987-88, he was injured during a match at Walsall in January 1989 and did not win his place back, this time at right-back, until October. In 1990-91, he slotted into Town's midfield and played in all but two FL games in the number four shirt. However, the number on his back is not a reliable guide to the position he takes up in any particular game. Ever present in 1991-92 as Ipswich swept to the Second Division Championship and automatic promotion to the new Premier League.

Clubs	Signing Date	Transfer Fee	APPEARANCES				GOALS			
			Lge	FL Cup	FA Cup	Others	Lge	FL Cup	FA Cup	Others
Ipswich Town*	12.82	–	205+14	15+2	10+3	16+2	15	2		1

STONE Steven Brian

Born: Gateshead, 20 August 1971

Height: 5'9" Weight: 11.3

Position/Skill Factor: Hard working central midfield player with plenty of stamina.

Career History: Spotted playing in the north-east, he signed for Nottingham Forest as an associated schoolboy in June 1986, before coming on board as a trainee in July 1987. After turning professional in the 1989 close season, a highly promising career was put on hold for over two years as a thrice broken leg threatened to put him out of the game. Showed great courage in fighting back to full fitness and was rewarded in 1991-92 when he made his FL debut as a substitute in the last match of the season, away to relegated West Ham United on 2 May 1992.

Clubs	Signing Date	Transfer Fee	APPEARANCES				GOALS			
			Lge	FL Cup	FA Cup	Others	Lge	FL Cup	FA Cup	Others
Nottingham Forest*	5.89	–	0+1							

STRACHAN Gordon David

Born: Edinburgh, 9 February 1957

Height: 5'6" Weight: 10.3

International Honours: S Yth, S "U21"-1, S-50

Position/Skill Factor: Fiery right-sided midfielder with a brilliant footballing brain. A tireless goal scoring player, he sees openings quickly and creates goal scoring chances from nothing. Rarely ever gives the ball away, he displays a steely determination and the will to win at all times.

Career History: He started his illustrious career with Dundee, after joining them straight from school and kicked off in the Scottish League as a 19-year-old in 1976. After 60 appearances at Dens Park, he moved to Aberdeen for a fee of £50,000 in November 1977 and it

Gordon Strachan

was there, during a purple spell, that he would eventually win just about every honour possible; two Premier Division Championship medals in 1979-80 and 1983-84, a hat-trick of Scottish Cup winners medals between 1982 and 1984 and a European Cup Winners Cup medal in 1983. His form was such that at the end of that first successful season with the "Dons" he won a full Scottish cap, the first of many, when selected to play against Northern Ireland on 16 May 1980. Having scored 55 goals in 183 League games for Aberdeen, he signed for Manchester United in the 1984 close season, along with Jesper Olsen. After making his FL debut at Old Trafford against Watford on 28 August 1984, by the end of the season he had won an FA Cup winners medal, following the 1-0 extra-time win over Everton. In nearly five years at United, he had been an automatic choice, injuries apart, so it came as something of a surprise when he was sold to Leeds United just before the transfer deadline in 1989. Showing renewed vigour, on being appointed captain for the coming season, he immediately led Leeds, by example, to the Second Division Championship, as an ever present and as the club's top scorer with 16 League goals, including seven penalties and was honoured as "Footballer of the Year" for 1991. Always inspirational, he missed very few games in 1990-91, while Leeds consolidated their First Division status, in fourth place. Remained a mainstay of the team in 1991-92 as Leeds progressed further to win the League Championship in a remarkable end of season twist of fortune. As enthusiastic as ever, he also held his place in the Scotland team and in a low key international against Northern Ireland in February his effervescent performance at the age of 35 put the other 19 younger outfield players to shame. Sadly, his next international appearance — his 50th cap — was probably his last, as at the end of the season, he announced his unavailabilty through injury for the European Championship Finals.

Clubs	Signing Date	Transfer Fee	APPEARANCES				GOALS			
			Lge	FL Cup	FA Cup	Others	Lge	FL Cup	FA Cup	Others
Manchester United	8.84	£500,000	155+5	12+1	22	10+2	33	1	2	3
Leeds United*	3.89	£300,000	126+1	13	7	9	30	2	1	2

STUART Graham Charles

Born: Tooting,
24 October 1970

Height: 5'8"

Weight: 11.6

International Honours:
E Yth, E "U21"-5

Position/Skill Factor: Striker or winger, with good ability on the ball. Having both strength and pace, he can beat defenders to get his shots or crosses in.

Career History: First came to Chelsea as a 15-year-old associated schoolboy in March 1985 and on leaving school

he joined the club as a trainee in August 1987, before graduating to the professional ranks via the FA School of Excellence in the 1989 close season. Made his FL debut at the end of that season at Stamford Bridge against Crystal Palace on 16 April 1990 and scored the final goal in a 3-0 win. Received further opportunities to shine in 1990-91, making 19 League appearances, including two as a substitute and impressed when scoring against two of the top three sides, Arsenal and Crystal Palace. Out of contention at the start of 1991-92, he came into the first team squad in November and was a regular performer for the rest of the season, sometimes on the flanks and sometimes inside, in place of Kerry Dixon. Surprisingly, scored only one goal, but it was one to remember, the winner in the FA Cup Fifth Round tie against Sheffield United. Receiving the ball wide on the right some 40 yards from goal, he cut inside, beating two defenders and slotted the ball underneath the diving 'keeper. Another Chelsea youngster with a bright future.

Clubs	Signing Date	Transfer Fee	APPEARANCES				GOALS			
			Lge	FL Cup	FA Cup	Others	Lge	FL Cup	FA Cup	Others
Chelsea*	6.89	–	39+9	5	4+1	3+1	5	1	1	1

SULLEY Christopher (Chris) Stephen

Born: Camberwell, 3 December 1959

Height: 5'8" Weight: 10.0

Position/Skill Factor: A very experienced, attacking left-back. With good skills and a lovely left foot, he plays the ball around well.

Career History: Given a free transfer by Chelsea in March 1981, having been an apprentice (July 1976) and a professional since December 1977 and without ever playing in the first team, he signed for Bournemouth, immediately making his FL debut as a substitute at home to Darlington on 14 March 1981. The following week he made his full debut on the left-wing. From April 1981 to December 1984 he played in 160 consecutive FL games, almost entirely at left-back, being ever present in 1981-82 (when he assisted the "Cherries" to promotion out of Division Four), 1982-83 and 1983-84. In the summer of 1986 he was, rather strangely, transferred to Scottish Premier League club, Dundee United, but was unable to break into their team on a regular basis and returned south before the end of the season to join Blackburn Rovers. Quickly established a regular slot at Ewood Park in the left-back position and remained first choice, but for injuries, until 1990-91. First choice at the start of 1991-92, he was injured in a game at Leicester City on 21 September and played no further part in Rovers' successful promotion campaign. With Alan Wright now firmly established in the left-back berth, he seems unlikely to stage a permanent "comeback".

Clubs	Signing Date	Transfer Fee	APPEARANCES				GOALS			
			Lge	FL Cup	FA Cup	Others	Lge	FL Cup	FA Cup	Others
Chelsea	12.77	–								
Bournemouth	3.81	–	205+1	14	18	10	3			
Dundee United	7.86	–								
Blackburn Rovers*	3.87	£15,000	134	6	6	9	3			

SULLIVAN Neil

Born: Sutton, 24 February 1970

Height: 6'0" Weight: 12.1

Position/Skill Factor: Brave young goalkeeper who is not afraid to come for crosses. Agile and alert to the dangers of through balls into the penalty area, he is also an excellent long kicker.

Career History: After coming to Wimbledon straight from school to sign as a trainee in July 1986, having been on the club's books as an associated schoolboy player since May 1985, he joined the professional ranks in the 1988 close season. Made his FL debut in a 2-1 win at Aston Villa on 20 April 1991 and with the wonderfully consistent Hans Segers missing just one game in three years, he remained in the wings. Continued to wait patiently as understudy to Segers, for his second first team outing, coming by coincidence, exactly one year later at home to Southampton. Then, with Nigel Martyn indisposed and Crystal Palace desperate for a replacement, he signed on a loan transfer and made his debut for the "Eagles" in the last game of the season, a 1-0 defeat at Queens Park Rangers.

Clubs	Signing Date	Transfer Fee	APPEARANCES				GOALS			
			Lge	FL Cup	FA Cup	Others	Lge	FL Cup	FA Cup	Others
Wimbledon*	7.88	–	2							
Crystal Palace	5.92	Loan	1							

SUTCH Daryl

Born: Beccles, 11 September 1971

Height: 6'0"

Weight: 12.0

International Honours: E Yth, E "U21"-3

Position/Skill Factor: An attacking midfield player and a good passer of the ball, he likes to join in the play in order to create opportunities for others.

Career History: Another good young local player, he first came to Norwich City as an associated schoolboy (January 1986), before joining the club as a trainee in July 1988 and progressing into the paid ranks during the summer of 1990. Made his FL debut, substituting for Lee Power, at Manchester United on 26 December 1990 and sadly his four appearances (two subs) coincided with the "Canaries'" heaviest defeats of the season. He was recalled to the first team squad in January 1992 and made a handful of appearances before the end of season. In view of his limited experience, his end of season call-up to the England Under 21 squad to play in the annual tournament in France was a little surprising, but presumably is a beneficiary of the policy to ensure continuity from the England Youth set-up to full international level.

Clubs	Signing Date	Transfer Fee	APPEARANCES				GOALS			
			Lge	FL Cup	FA Cup	Others	Lge	FL Cup	FA Cup	Others
Norwich City*	7.90	–	7+6	0+1	0+1	1				

SUTTON Christopher (Chris) Roy

Born: Nottingham, 10 March 1973

Height: 6'2"

Weight: 11.12

Position/Skill Factor: A tall centre-forward, or central defender, he is strong, direct and more than useful in the air.

Career History: The son of the former Norwich City, Chester City and Carlisle United footballer, Mike, who played between 1962-1972, he signed for Norwich City as a trainee in July 1989 on the recommendation of his father, before graduating to the club's paid ranks in the 1991 close season. Prior to that, however, he had already made his FL debut at Carrow Road against Queens Park Rangers on 4 May 1991, when coming off the bench to replace Ian Crook. Made good progress in 1991-92. In his second first team game at home to Coventry City he scored an injury time winner in a 3-2 victory, after coming on as substitute. He then had a two month run in central defence in place of the injured Ian Butterworth, before being switched to the attack where he became an FA Cup hero. Scored twice in the "Canaries'" 3-0 Fifth Round victory over Notts County and headed the winner in extra-time against Southampton in a Sixth Round replay — a goal he knew little about as a ricochet bounced off his head and looped into the net over the dumbfounded "Saints'" 'keeper! Unfortunately, his "lucky mascot" tag failed to work in the Semi-Final, when Norwich went out limply to Sunderland.

Clubs	Signing Date	Transfer Fee	APPEARANCES				GOALS			
			Lge	FL Cup	FA Cup	Others	Lge	FL Cup	FA Cup	Others
Norwich City*	7.91	–	16+7	2	6		2		3	

SWITZER George

Born: Salford, 13 October 1973

Height: 5'6" Weight: 9.10

Position: Forward.

Career History: Joined the Manchester United professional staff during the 1992 close season, having previously been at the club as an associated schoolboy (July 1988) and as a trainee (July 1990). No first team experience.

Clubs	Signing Date	Transfer Fee	APPEARANCES				GOALS			
			Lge	FL Cup	FA Cup	Others	Lge	FL Cup	FA Cup	Others
Manchester United*	6.92	–								

TALBOYS Steven John

Born: Bristol, 18 September 1966

Height: 5'11" Weight: 11.1

Position/Skill Factor: Winger with plenty of stamina who can get into shooting positions and is good in the air.

Career History: Signed by Wimbledon from Beazer Homes League club Gloucester City halfway through the 1991-92 season, but has yet to be given a first team opportunity. Started his career as an associated schoolboy with Bristol Rovers in March 1981, before being released and drifting into non-League soccer with Mangotsfield, Bath City and Trowbridge, prior to joining Gloucester City in November 1987.

Clubs	Signing Date	Transfer Fee	APPEARANCES				GOALS			
			Lge	FL Cup	FA Cup	Others	Lge	FL Cup	FA Cup	Others
Wimbledon*	9.92	£10,000								

TALLON Gary Thomas

Born: Drogheda, 5 September 1973

Height: 5'10" Weight: 11.7

Position/Skill Factor: Naturally left footed left-winger and a lovely crosser of the ball, he is a very skilful player.

Career History: Signed from League of Ireland side Drogheda United towards the end of 1991, he has yet to make his first team bow, having played solely in the club's youth team during 1991-92 and looks to be a fair prospect for the not too distant future.

Clubs	Signing Date	Transfer Fee	APPEARANCES				GOALS			
			Lge	FL Cup	FA Cup	Others	Lge	FL Cup	FA Cup	Others
Blackburn Rovers*	11.91									

TANNER Adam David

Born: Maldon, 25 October 1973

Height: 6'0" Weight: 11.12

Position: Central midfield player.

Career History: Signed professional forms for Ipswich Town during the 1992 summer, having first come to the club as a trainee in July 1990. No first team experience.

Clubs	Signing Date	Transfer Fee	APPEARANCES				GOALS			
			Lge	FL Cup	FA Cup	Others	Lge	FL Cup	FA Cup	Others
Ipswich Town*	6.92	–								

TANNER Nicholas (Nicky)

Born: Kingswood, Bristol, 24 May 1965

Height: 6'1"

Weight: 13.10

Position/Skill Factor: Central defender who is both strong in the air and on the ground. A good tackler, he rarely comes away without the ball.

Career History: After playing with the local Western League side, Mangotsfield, he was signed by Bristol Rovers during the summer of 1985 and made his FL debut in a 3-3 draw on the opening day of the 1985-86 season at Darlington on 18 August 1985. A regular first team player in his first two seasons with the "Pirates", he operated in a number of different positions – in midfield, on the flanks and in both full-back positions. At the end of his third season, it was decided to release him for a modest fee and he was faced with a strange choice – regular first team football with Fourth Division strugglers, Torquay United, or as cover for First Division Champions, Liverpool! He elected to join the "Reds", but unsurprisingly found the first team opportunities hard to come by, playing in the reserves as a central defender, a role he had rarely played for Rovers. His first appearance for Liverpool came in December 1989 as substitute, but although he played three more games in 1989-90 it was not enough to qualify for a Championship medal. He then had two loan spells with Norwich City and Swindon Town, respectively, in 1990, but no permanent transfer resulted. After three years at Anfield with only four first team games to his name, it seemed unlikely he would ever break through to regular first team action, but patience is a virtue and when new signing Mark Wright was injured in the second match of 1991-92, Tanner took his place. He grabbed the opportunity splendidly and was a tower of strength in

Liverpool's injury-riddled team. So much so, that he held his place when Wright returned to first team duty and in January 1992 manager Graham Souness offered him an improved contract up to 1995. Tragically, after 26 consecutive FL games, he himself was victim of the injury jinx that cursed Liverpool through the season and although he returned to the first team action before the end of the season, he was no longer first choice and missed the FA Cup Final.

Clubs	Signing Date	Transfer Fee	APPEARANCES				GOALS			
			Lge	FL Cup	FA Cup	Others	Lge	FL Cup	FA Cup	Others
Bristol Rovers	6.85	–	104+3	5	10	5	3			
Liverpool*	7.88	£20,000	34+3	5	2	5+1				
Norwich City	3.90	Loan	6							
Swindon Town	9.90	Loan	7							

TEALE Shaun

Born: Southport,
10 March 1964

Height: 6'0"

Weight: 13.7

International Honours:
E Semi-Pro Int

Position/Skill Factor: Combative central defender, who is aggressive both in the air and on the ground and there are no free headers to be had when he is about. Very dangerous at set plays, he has a good left foot.

Career History: Discarded by Everton, following a period spent as an associated schoolboy (December 1979) and as an apprentice (June 1980) at Goodison, he played for a number of non-League clubs, including Southport, Ellesmere Port, Northwich Victoria and Burscough, before joining Bournemouth from Weymouth in January 1989. Whilst with Weymouth he was selected for a Semi-Professional international against Wales in 1988. Made his FL debut for the "Cherries" as a substitute at home to West Bromwich on 4 February 1989 and immediately settled into the team in central defence in place of Kevin Bond. Ever present in 1989-90, until injured in March, his absence was a major factor in Bournemouth slipping from 14th to 22nd place and relegation back to Division Three. Recognised as one of the most accomplished central defenders in the lower divisions, he was ever present in 1990-91 and realised an ambition he must have thought had long since passed him by, when he was signed by Aston Villa in the summer of 1991. Went straight into Villa's first team, forming a defensive partnership with Paul McGrath as solid as any in the First Division. Although a disappointing season for Villa, he enjoyed an excellent first year at the top level, missing only one game throughout and contributing greatly to a defence which conceded only 44 FL goals.

Clubs	Signing Date	Transfer Fee	APPEARANCES				GOALS			
			Lge	FL Cup	FA Cup	Others	Lge	FL Cup	FA Cup	Others
Bournemouth	1.89	£50,000	99+1	8	5	3	4		1	
Aston Villa*	7.91	£300,000	42	2	5	2		1		

THOMAS Geoffrey (Geoff) Robert

Born: Manchester, 5 August 1964

Height: 5'10" Weight: 10.7

International Honours: E"B", E-9

Position/Skill Factor: A midfield player with great stamina, he also has a good left foot and is capable of striking spectacular goals.

Career History: Started his career at Rochdale, progressing through the club's junior ranks to become a non-contract professional and made his FL debut when coming on as a substitute at Hereford United on 30 October 1982. Rather oddly, he was never offered a professional contract by Rochdale, even when he broke into their first team in February 1984, so had little hesitation in accepting such an offer from Crewe Alexandra. Soon established himself in their midfield and after three years at Gresty Road he was signed by Crystal Palace, then in the Second Division. Immediately settled in at Selhurst Park, missing only three games in 1987-88 through injury and the following season played in the first 22 matches, before suffering a serious injury at home to Walsall in the first match of 1989 – thus missing out on Palace's late season

run which carried them to third place and promotion to Division One, through the end of season Play-Offs. Back to fitness in 1989-90, he helped Palace to First Division stability after an early disaster at Anfield where they were slaughtered 9-0, only to turn the tables later in the season when defeating the "Reds" 4-3 in extra-time of the FA Cup Semi-Final. Played in both games of the 1990 Cup Final which was lost 1-0 in a replay, after a thrilling 3-3 draw in the first match. His career touched new heights in 1990-91 when ever present for Palace as they attained their highest ever FL placing, third and he became an England regular after making his international debut against Turkey at the end of the season. Suffered several setbacks in 1991-92, however, as his club appearances were restricted by three short term injuries, whilst his international career was brought to a halt following the match against France.

Clubs	Signing Date	Transfer Fee	APPEARANCES				GOALS			
			Lge	FL Cup	FA Cup	Others	Lge	FL Cup	FA Cup	Others
Rochdale (N/C)	8.82	–	10+1			0+1	1			
Crewe Alexandra	3.84	–	120+5	8	2	2+1	21			
Crystal Palace*	6.87	£50,000	164+2	20	12+1	15+1	24	3	2	4

THOMAS Martin

Born: Lymington, 12 September 1973

Height: 5'8" Weight: 10.8

Position: Midfield player.

Career History: Turned professional for Southampton during the 1992 close season, having previously been at the Dell as an associated schoolboy (December 1987) and as a trainee (August 1990). No first team experience.

Clubs	Signing Date	Transfer Fee	APPEARANCES				GOALS			
			Lge	FL Cup	FA Cup	Others	Lge	FL Cup	FA Cup	Others
Southampton*	6.92	–								

THOMAS Michael Lauriston

Born: Lambeth, 24 August 1967

Height: 5'10" Weight: 12.4

International Honours: E Sch, E Yth, E "U21"-12, E"B", E-2

Position/Skill Factor: Midfield player with wonderful stamina. Makes great runs, both on and off the ball and has the knack of turning up in the opponent's penalty area and scoring at vital moments.

Career History: A schoolboy international, he signed associated schoolboy forms with Arsenal in July 1982, before progressing through the ranks as an apprentice (August 1983) to become a professional at the end of 1984. Had to wait for over two years for his FL debut and

when the opportunity finally came, it was whilst on loan to Portsmouth on New Years Day 1987 at home to Reading at left-back. Soon after returning to Highbury, he made his Arsenal debut in February and remained part of the first team squad till the end of the season, playing in both full-back positions and in midfield. He firmly established himself at right-back in 1987-88, only to be switched to midfield in February 1988 in place of the suspended Steve Williams. He also showed his talent for scoring unexpected goals – his total of nine in the League, plus

two cup goals, made him second highest scorer for Arsenal that season. Made his first Wembley appearance in the 1988 League Cup Final, but the "Gunners" surprisingly went down to Luton by 3-2. Reached the apex of his career in 1988-89, missing only one game in Arsenal's campaign and winning his first England cap against Saudia Arabia in November. However, the best was saved till last. At one point in the season, Arsenal were runaway leaders of Division One and 19 points ahead of Liverpool, but with one game to go, the Merseysiders, already FA Cup winners, were three points clear with a superior goals difference. By a remarkable twist of fate, Arsenal's last match was at Anfield against their rivals and a 2-0 victory would give them the Championship by the narrowest of margins – equal points, equal goal difference, but superior on goals scored. It is now history that Arsenal achieved this seemingly impossible objective with a goal in the very last minute (if not injury time) by Michael Thomas. Running on to a through ball, he survived an attempted interception by Steve Nicol and went on to steer the ball coolly past Grobbelaar – the most amazing climax to a League Championship in FL history. After this, everything was an anti-climax, although the following season he played in all but two games of a disappointing time for the "Gunners", by their high standards and won a second

England cap against Yugoslavia. In 1990-91 he played a large part in Arsenal's stupendous League Championship campaign (losing only once and conceding only 18 goals), but fell out of favour with George Graham, losing his place to David Hillier in the closing weeks of the campaign. No longer an automatic first choice in 1991-92, he was transferred to the scene of his former triumph when Liverpool signed him apparently as a replacement for Steve McMahon. It was a strange signing in many ways, because Thomas is not a ball-winner, which Liverpool, in the absence of McMahon and Whelan, desperately needed. However, he made a promising start at Anfield, helping the team to climb to third place after a slow start, before falling victim to the injury jinx which plagued the "Reds" throughout the season. On his return to the team for the vital Fifth Round FA Cup match against Aston Villa, along with three other long term casualties (Barnes, Whelan and Venison), he scored the winning goal after being put clear by Barnes. For the remainder of the season he looked hesitant, unconfident and frequently caught in possession and was perhaps fortunate to be included in the FA Cup Final team against Sunderland, following Ronnie Whelan's withdrawal. All was forgiven and forgotten, however, immediately after half-time when the ball came to him on the corner of the penalty area, after a wonderful run by Steve McManaman and without waiting for it to drop, he smashed a rising volley into the roof of the net. Liverpool then took control of the game and Thomas also had a part in the second goal, teeing up the ball for Ian Rush to steer into the net. The FA Cup Final, aside, it remains to be seen if he can solve the problems in Liverpool's midfield.

Clubs	Signing Date	Transfer Fee	APPEARANCES				GOALS			
			Lge	FL Cup	FA Cup	Others	Lge	FL Cup	FA Cup	Others
Arsenal	12.84	–	149+14	22+2	14+3	5+2	24	5		1
Portsmouth	12.86	Loan	3							
Liverpool*	12.91	£1,500,000	16+1		5		3		2	

THOMAS Scott Lee

Born: Bury, 30 October 1974

Height: 5'11" Weight: 11.0

Position: Midfield player.

Career History: A recent acquisition to the Manchester City professional ranks, he was first signed on associated schoolboy forms in December 1988, prior to becoming a trainee in July 1991 and has yet to make a first team appearance.

Clubs	Signing Date	Transfer Fee	APPEARANCES				GOALS			
			Lge	FL Cup	FA Cup	Others	Lge	FL Cup	FA Cup	Others
Manchester City*	3.92	–								

THOMPSON Garry Lindsay

Born: Birmingham, 7 October 1959

Height: 6'1" Weight: 14.0

International Honours: E "U21"-6

Position/Skill Factor: Big, strong old fashioned striker, who puts himself about and is a constant worry to defenders taking too long on the ball. Also, very good in the air.

Career History: One of football's travellers, he has done the rounds since signing professional with Coventry City in the 1977 close season, having earlier been on the club's books as an associated schoolboy (February 1975) and as an apprentice (July 1976). Had a tough baptism when making his FL debut at Highfield Road in a 3-2 defeat against Aston Villa on 21 March 1978, but showed enough to hold his place for the rest of the term. Enjoyed five good seasons at Highfield Road, before losing his place to Jim Melrose in November 1982 and three months later moving to West Bromwich Albion. Played the best football of his career for the "Baggies", top scoring with 13 FL goals in 1983-84 and 19 in 1984-85, which included a hat-trick against Nottingham Forest. To the horror of Albion fans he was transferred to Sheffield Wednesday in the summer of 1985. It was a bad move for both club and player – Albion scored only 35 goals in 1985-86 and were doomed to relegation long before the end of the season, while Thompson struggled to find the net with the "Owls" and returned to the Midlands the following summer to join Aston Villa. The goals continued to elude him at Villa Park and the club sank into Division Two without a fight. Absent through injury in the first half of 1987-88, he was recalled to the first team by new manager Graham Taylor and responded with five goals in his first three games back in the team. After helping Villa back to Division One at the first attempt, he lost his place to new "superstar" Allan McInally at the start of 1988-89 and was eventually transferred to Second Division Watford, whom he assisted to fourth place and the end of season Play-Offs where they lost out to Blackburn Rovers. Out of favour in 1989-90, he was rescued from obscurity by Crystal Palace manager, Steve Coppell, who urgently required a replacement for the injured Ian Wright. Sadly, he was ineligible for the 1990 FA Cup Final after playing (only briefly) for Watford earlier in the competition and in 1990-91 he had to play third fiddle to Mark Bright and Ian Wright. To further his career, he moved to Queens Park Rangers (in a joint deal with Tony Witter) in the first week of 1991-92 and although he soon won a place, his goal scoring touch had completely deserted him and he was dropped in November, playing virtually no part in the remainder of the campaign. Sad to relate, his career has plummeted since leaving West Bromwich in 1985 – as has that of his former club.

Clubs	Signing Date	Transfer Fee	APPEARANCES				GOALS			
			Lge	FL Cup	FA Cup	Others	Lge	FL Cup	FA Cup	Others
Coventry City	6.77	–	127+7	12+1	11		38	7	4	
W.B.A.	2.83	£225,000	91	9	5		39	5	1	
Sheffield Wednesday	3.85	£450,000	35+1	2+1	5		7	1	1	
Aston Villa	6.86	£450,000	56+4	6	4	3	17	2		
Watford	12.88	£325,000	24+10	0+1	7+1		8			
Crystal Palace	3.90	£200,000	17+3	0+1			3	1		
Q.P.R.*	8.91	£125,000	10+5	3		1	1	3		

THOMPSON Gary McDonald

Born: Ipswich, 7 September 1972

Height: 6'0" Weight: 11.4

International Honours: E Sch, E Yth

Position/Skill Factor: Brave young striker, who is very quick, especially in the penalty area and is good in the air.

Career History: Locally born and bred, he has been with Ipswich Town since first signing as an associated schoolboy in October 1986 and progressing through the England schools and youth sides to full professional status during the 1990 close season. Has yet to make a first team appearance, after breaking a leg in his first season, but is now fully recovered and has performed well in the reserves.

Clubs	Signing Date	Transfer Fee	APPEARANCES				GOALS			
			Lge	FL Cup	FA Cup	Others	Lge	FL Cup	FA Cup	Others
Ipswich Town*	7.90	–								

THOMPSON Neil

Born: Beverley,
2 October 1963

Height: 6'0"

Weight: 13.7

Position/Skill Factor: Strong tackling left-back. Supports his forwards well, packs a good shot in his left foot and is very dangerous at set plays. Also, a long throw specialist.

Career History: A player who is in the second phase of his career, having begun in the Football League, before dropping out and making his reputation in non-League football. Started out with Nottingham Forest as an associated schoolboy (January 1979) and later as an apprentice (July 1980). On not being offered professional terms by Forest, he joined Fourth Division Hull City early in 1981-82 and made his FL debut at Tranmere Rovers on 13 February 1982 at left-back, holding his place for the rest of the season. In 1982-83, he was plagued by injury, making only a handful of appearances in Hull's promotion campaign. Released at the end of the season, he joined Scarborough of the Alliance Premier League. At this point his FL career seemed to be over and so it proved, at least for four years. However, in 1986-87, Scarborough won the Championship of the re-titled Vauxhall Conference and became the first team to be "promoted" (rather than elected) to the Football League. Back in the League, he missed only five FL games in 1987-88 and was ever present in 1988-89, scoring nine FL goals and assisting his

team to the Promotion Play-Offs. After being defeated by Leyton Orient, any disappointment for him was short lived, as he moved up the League to join Ipswich Town in the Second Division. In his first season at Portman Road, he played in all but one game in his customary position of left-back and although he lost his place for a while early in 1990-91, he won it back in December. As consistent as ever in 1991-92, he realised an ambition which he must have thought had long since passed him by, as Ipswich swept to the Second Division Championship and with it automatic promotion to the new Premier League.

Clubs	Signing Date	Transfer Fee	APPEARANCES				GOALS			
			Lge	FL Cup	FA Cup	Others	Lge	FL Cup	FA Cup	Others
Hull City	11.81	–	29+2							
Scarborough	8.83	–	87	8	4	9	15	1		1
Ipswich Town*	6.89	£100,000	122+6	4+1	8	8	15			1

THOMPSON Niall

Born: Birmingham, 16 April 1974

Height: 5'11" Weight: 11.0

Position: Forward.

Career History: Turned professional in the 1992 close season with Crystal Palace, having originally joined the club as a non-contract junior player and has yet to experience first team football.

Clubs	Signing Date	Transfer Fee	APPEARANCES				GOALS			
			Lge	FL Cup	FA Cup	Others	Lge	FL Cup	FA Cup	Others
Crystal Palace*	6.92	–								

THORN Andrew (Andy) Charles

Born: Carshalton,
12 November 1966

Height: 6'0"

Weight: 11.5

International Honours:
E "U21"-5

Position/Skill Factor: Dogged central defender who enjoys a battle. Very consistent, he makes few mistakes and is strong in the air in both penalty areas.

Career History: First signed for Wimbledon as an associated schoolboy in June 1982, before progressing to the club's professional ranks early in 1984-85. Made his FL debut at Notts County on 6 April 1985 in midfield and did well enough to keep his place for the remaining nine League games of the season. He started the 1985-86 season on the left side of midfield, until surprisingly switched to central defence in November with great success. Although absent through injury for the second half of the season, he returned in time to join the celebrations as the "Dons" won promotion to Division One for the first time. Enjoyed two good seasons in the top flight, winning five England Under 21 caps in 1987-88 and playing a large part in the club's FA Cup run of 1988, which ended in a shock 1-0 victory over Liverpool. Along with his colleague Dave Beasant, he joined Newcastle United in the summer of 1988, but it was a miserable time for both players as the "Magpies" slid towards relegation without a fight. So desperate were the Tyneside club, that he ended the season as an emergency forward, but to no avail. After losing his place to Bjorn Kristensen early in 1989-90, he was rescued from obscurity by Crystal Palace manager, Steve Coppell, arriving back in London and the First Division. At the end of the season he returned to Wembley for his second FA Cup Final in three years, but this time it ended in disappointment as Palace lost 1-0 in a replay after a 3-3 draw. Has remained an automatic first choice in central defence since his arrival at Selhurst Park.

Clubs	Signing Date	Transfer Fee	APPEARANCES				GOALS			
			Lge	FL Cup	FA Cup	Others	Lge	FL Cup	FA Cup	Others
Wimbledon	11.84	–	106+1	7	9	1	2			
Newcastle United	8.88	£850,000	36	4		3	2	1		
Crystal Palace*	12.89	£650,000	84	12	10	11	2	2		

THORNE Peter Lee

Born: Manchester, 21 June 1973

Height: 6'0" Weight: 12.2

Position/Skill Factor: Athletic striker with a lovely build. Holds the ball up well in and around the penalty area and looks set to find the net regularly.

Career History: A young player who has yet to turn out for the first team, he first signed for Blackburn Rovers as a trainee in July 1989, before progressing to the club's professional ranks in the 1991 close season.

Clubs	Signing Date	Transfer Fee	APPEARANCES				GOALS			
			Lge	FL Cup	FA Cup	Others	Lge	FL Cup	FA Cup	Others
Blackburn Rovers*	6.91	–								

THORSTVEDT Erik

Born: Stavanger, Norway, 28 October 1962

Height: 6'3" Weight: 14.4

International Honours: Norwegian Int

Position/Skill Factor: Agile goalkeeper with a wonderful build who seems to fill the goal. A good shot stopper, he is also safe on crosses. Sets up attacks with long drop kicks.

Career History: Had trials for Tottenham Hotspur as long ago as December 1984 and also with Queens Park Rangers, Arsenal and Borussia Moechengladbach, during his time playing with EIK Tonsberg and Viking Stavanger in his native Norway. After joining the Swedish side IFK Gothenburg, he went for a second trial with "Spurs" in the summer of 1987 and later signed on at White Hart Lane in 1988-89. His English career got off to a less than auspicious start when he conceded a "soft" goal during his FL debut at home to Nottingham Forest on 15 January 1989, a 2-1 defeat that was televised live throughout Europe. Despite this disappointing start, he proved to be a safe and reliable 'keeper and an automatic first choice up to the end of 1990-91 when he won an FA Cup winners medal as "Spurs" defeated Nottingham Forest 2-1 after extra-time. Lost his place to promising youngster Ian Walker, soon into the 1991-92 season, but won it back in October. However, after a shaky performance against Coventry City in late March, he once again gave way to Walker. There appears to be little to choose between the two 'keepers and it will be interesting to see who comes out on top in 1992-93.

Clubs	Signing Date	Transfer Fee	APPEARANCES				GOALS			
			Lge	FL Cup	FA Cup	Others	Lge	FL Cup	FA Cup	Others
Tottenham Hotspur*	12.88	£400,000	113	18	8	7				

TILER Carl

Born: Sheffield,
11 February 1970

Height: 6'2"

Weight: 13.0

International Honours:
E "U21"-13

Position/Skill Factor: A tall central defender who uses his height to good advantage in both penalty areas. Reliably left footed in defence.

Career History: Stepped out with Barnsley as a trainee in September 1987 and made his FL debut as a substitute in the last match of the 1987-88 season at West Bromwich Albion on 7 May 1988, three months before he turned professional with the "Tykes". After occasional appearances at full-back and in central defence in 1988-89 and 1989-90, he enjoyed a run of games from March 1990 to the end of the season, winning the first of many England Under 21 caps. Highly rated from his early days, he became a tower of strength in the Barnsley defence in 1990-91, playing in every match, bar one. During the 1991 close season, he was signed by Nottingham Forest, who were seeking a new partner for Des Walker. Unfortunately, the partnership did not prove to be as effective as hoped for and after January 1992 he lost his place to Darren Wassall and made only occasional first team appearances, missing out on both of Forest's two Wembley visits for the Zenith and League Cup Finals. With the departure of Des Walker to Italy and Wassall to Derby, the way is now clear for Tiler to establish himself in the heart of Forest's defence.

Clubs	Signing Date	Transfer Fee	APPEARANCES				GOALS			
			Lge	FL Cup	FA Cup	Others	Lge	FL Cup	FA Cup	Others
Barnsley	7.88	–	67+4	4	4+1	3+1	4			
Nottingham Forest*	6.91	£1,400,000	24+2	5+1	1	1	2			

TILLSON Andrew (Andy)

Born: Huntingdon,
30 June 1966

Height: 6'2"

Weight: 12.7

Position/Skill Factor: Tall, commanding central defender who is both calm and confident on the ball. A good passer and although a competent tackler, he shines more as an interceptor.

Career History: Discovered by Vauxhall Conference League side, Kettering Town, in December 1987, he followed his manager, Alan Buckley, to Grimsby Town in the 1988 close season. As a non-contract player at Kettering, the "Mariners" were extremely fortunate to obtain the services of such a talented youngster for free and he made his FL debut in the opening game of 1988-89 as a substitute at Cambridge United on 27 August 1988. Apart from the final match that season, he played throughout the campaign and the following term, missed just four League matches as he helped the club gain promotion to the Third Division as runners-up to Exeter City. Ever present in 1990-91 until December and his surprise transfer to Queens Park Rangers, who were in disarray, following simultaneous injuries to their three main defenders, Alan McDonald, Danny Maddix and Paul Parker. Immediately formed an effective partnership with another new signing, Darren Peacock, which assisted Rangers to climb from the foot of Division One to mid-table security. With all their defenders fit again, competition for the central defensive slots at Loftus Road was intense in 1991-92 and he took a back seat, apart from a short first team run in October when manager Gerry Francis experimented with three central defenders, before reverting to a "flat" back four. For most of the second half of the season he was on the bench as a non-playing substitute, not required because the Rangers' defence was so efficient.

Clubs	Signing Date	Transfer Fee	APPEARANCES				GOALS			
			Lge	FL Cup	FA Cup	Others	Lge	FL Cup	FA Cup	Others
Grimsby Town	7.88	–	104+1	8	10	5	6			
Q.P.R.*	12.90	£400,000	27+2	2		1	2			

TINKLER Mark Roland

Born: Bishop Auckland, 24 October 1974

Height: 5'11½" Weight: 11.4

International Honours: E Sch, E Yth

Position/Skill Factor: Midfield player with very quick feet who runs well with the ball. Also, useful in the air.

Career History: Yet to make his FL debut, he signed professional forms for Leeds United towards the end of 1991, having been on the club's books as an associated schoolboy, since January 1991 and as a trainee from August 1991. A regular in Leeds' reserve side during 1991-92.

Clubs	Signing Date	Transfer Fee	APPEARANCES				GOALS			
			Lge	FL Cup	FA Cup	Others	Lge	FL Cup	FA Cup	Others
Leeds United*	11.91	–								

TISDALE Paul Robert

Born: Malta, 14 January 1973

Height: 5'8" Weight: 10.12

International Honours: E Sch

Position/Skill Factor: Midfielder who can also play at right-back. A good footballer, he likes to pass the ball around and is very creative.

Career History: An England junior international, he joined Southampton on associated schoolboy forms in February 1987, before progressing to the club's professional ranks in the 1991 close season. Yet to make his FL debut, he is one to watch out for in the near future.

Clubs	Signing Date	Transfer Fee	APPEARANCES				GOALS			
			Lge	FL Cup	FA Cup	Others	Lge	FL Cup	FA Cup	Others
Southampton*	6.91	–								

TOAL Kieran Michael

Born: Manchester, 14 December 1971

Height: 5'8" Weight: 11.1

International Honours: IR "U21"

Position/Skill Factor: Left-winger who links defence and attack and when getting forward is adept at arriving late in the opponent's penalty area.

Career History: Born of Irish parents, he signed associated schoolboy forms for Manchester United in September 1987, before becoming a trainee at Old Trafford in July 1988, after leaving school. Turned professional during the 1990 close season and although still to make his FL debut, he has already been capped at Under 21 level for the Republic of Ireland.

Clubs	Signing Date	Transfer Fee	APPEARANCES				GOALS			
			Lge	FL Cup	FA Cup	Others	Lge	FL Cup	FA Cup	Others
Manchester Uunited*	7.90	–								

TODD Andrew (Andy) John James

Born: Derby, 21 September 1974

Height: 5'10½" Weight: 11.8

Position/Skill Factor: Promising youngster who can play either as a sweeper, or in the right-back position and is a sweet passer of the ball.

Career History: The son of former England international star, Colin, who played for Sunderland, Derby County, Everton, Birmingham City, Nottingham Forest, Oxford

United and Luton Town, in a career that stretched from 1966 to 1985, he first joined Middlesbrough as an associated schoolboy in March 1991. The "Boro" were managed by his father at the time and on leaving school, he progressed through the club's ranks, first as a trainee in July 1991 and eight months later, as a professional. Has yet to make a first team appearance and struggled with injuries during 1991–92.

Clubs	Signing Date	Transfer Fee	APPEARANCES				GOALS			
			Lge	FL Cup	FA Cup	Others	Lge	FL Cup	FA Cup	Others
Middlesbrough*	3.92	–								

TOLSON Neil

Born: Wordsley, 25 October 1973

Height: 6'2" Weight: 11.5

Position/Skill Factor: Aggressive striker who is extremely quick off the mark. Very good in the air, he is likely to score goals at the higher level and will benefit from added experience.

Career History: Joined Walsall as a trainee in July 1990, having been an associated schoolboy since September 1989 and was one of a crop of talented youngsters that manager Kenny Hibbitt introduced to FL action in 1991-92. Made a dramatic entrance as a substitute in a First Round FA Cup tie away to Yeovil Town on 16 November 1991, scoring a late equaliser to force a replay at Bescot – all to no avail as the "Saddlers" eventually lost! He made his FL debut, again as substitute, the following week, at Rotherham United on 22 November 1991, shortly before signing a professional contract. Further substitute appearances followed, before his first full game away to Doncaster in late February. No sooner had "Saddlers" fans caught a glimpse of their budding "star", however, than he was whipped away from them by Oldham Athletic! Clearly an investment for the future, it would be surprising if he broke into the "Latics'" first team immediately.

Clubs	Signing Date	Transfer Fee	APPEARANCES				GOALS			
			Lge	FL Cup	FA Cup	Others	Lge	FL Cup	FA Cup	Others
Walsall	12.91		3+6		0+1	1+2	1		1	
Oldham Athletic*	3.92	£150,000								

TOWNSEND Andrew (Andy) David

Born: Maidstone, 23 July 1963

Height: 5'11" Weight: 12.7

International Honours: IR 31

Position/Skill Factor: Hard working midfield player who covers both ends of the park. Very creative, he also is highly capable of scoring spectacular goals with his left foot.

Career History: Now recognised as one of the best midfield players around, he followed his father Don, who played for Charlton Athletic and Crystal Palace between 1959–1965, into League soccer, after starting his career in non-League football with Welling United in the Southern League.. In the summer of 1984 he joined Weymouth, along with team mate Tony Agana (currently with Notts County), thus stepping up one grade to the Gola League (now Vauxhall Conference). After only half a season with the Dorset club, for whom he made 29 appearances and scored 10 goals, his performances attracted the attention of Southampton who signed him in January 1985. He did not make an immediate impact in the First Division, however and had to wait until the end of the season before making his FL debut as a left-back, when deputising for Mark Dennis, at the Dell against Aston Villa on 20 April 1985. In 1985-86 he played 27 games, alternating between left-back and midfield, but missed the first half of 1986-87 through injury, before establishing himself as a commanding midfielder in 1987-88. Surprisingly sold to Norwich City in the summer of 1988, he helped to establish the "Canaries'" reputation as a classy passing team which achieved its highest ever FL placing (fourth) and reached the FA Cup Semi-Final. He also won international recognition with the Republic of Ireland, making his debut against France in February 1989 and has remained a regular choice every since. After one more season at Carrow Road he was transferred to Chelsea for a fee the "Canaries" could hardly refuse and immediately confirmed his reputation as one of the leading midfield operators in the top flight, despite the "Blues'" inability to recapture their former glories. Despite only missing seven

FL games in 1991-92, he was never really at his best, carrying a groin strain for much of the season and if Chelsea are going to make an impression on the new Premier League in 1992-93, it is imperative that their key player is at full fitness.

TRACEY Simon Peter

Born: Woolwich,
9 December 1967

Height: 6'0"

Weight: 13.0

Position/Skill Factor: An extremely agile goalkeeper who is a good shot stopper. One of the growing band of 'keepers who dribble out of their penalty area in a bid to obtain extra distance on their kicks.

Career History: Believed to be the only player to make his first team debut at Wembley – the 1988 FA Charity Shield match against Liverpool on 20 August. Currently recognised among the top flight of goalkeepers, he joined Wimbledon on the YTS scheme in August 1985, but made such excellent progress that he was offered professional terms just six months later. As understudy to the remarkably consistent Dave Beasant, he had to wait two and a half years to make his FL debut against Arsenal at Plough Lane on 27 August 1988, after the latter was transferred to Newcastle United. Tragically, it proved to be a nightmare debut as the "Gunners" fired five goals past him in a 5-1 defeat. He was immediately dropped and after the "Dons" signed Hans Segers in October, he was allowed to rejoin his former manager Dave Bassett at Sheffield United for a modest fee. Signed as cover for Graham Benstead, he had to wait until near the end of 1988-89 to make his debut for the "Blades", playing the last six matches of their Third Division promotion season. Quickly established himself as first choice at Bramall Lane and was ever present in his second season as the club raced through Division Two to their second consecutive promotion. Unluckily injured in a collision with Ian Rush in their first game back in the top flight at home to Liverpool, he returned to October 1990 to assist United to recover from a dreadful start to the season. It was a similar story in 1991-92. Returning from injury in November with the "Blades" anchored to the foot of the table, he brought some defensive stability back to the team, which pulled off another remarkable recovery. Touted as the best 'keeper in the country by "Blades'" supporters and the Sheffield press, it is believed that his tendency to roam far and wide from his goal area has not endeared him to England manager Graham Taylor. Ironically, when Taylor relented and included him in an England squad in April 1992, he was already injured during a game at Chelsea in March and thus unavailable for duty!

Clubs	Signing Date	Transfer Fee	APPEARANCES				GOALS			
			Lge	FL Cup	FA Cup	Others	Lge	FL Cup	FA Cup	Others
Southampton	1.85	£35,000	77+6	7+1	2+3	3+2	5			
Norwich City	8.88	£300,000	66+5	3+1	10	3	8			2
Chelsea*	7.90	£1,200,000	67	11	6	4	8	4		

Clubs	Signing Date	Transfer Fee	APPEARANCES				GOALS			
			Lge	FL Cup	FA Cup	Others	Lge	FL Cup	FA Cup	Others
Wimbledon	2.86	–	1			1				
Sheffield United*	10.88	£7,500	113	4	10	5				

TURNER Andrew Peter

Born: Woolwich, 23 March 1975

Height: 5'9" Weight: 11.0

International Honours: E Sch, E Yth

Position/Skill Factor: Very quick and skilful left-winger who has a great left foot and is a lovely crosser of the ball.

Career History: A 1992 close season professional signing for Tottenham Hotspur, having been at the club since first joining as an associated schoolboy in July 1990, before graduating as a trainee in August 1991. No first team experience, he has yet to break into the reserves.

Clubs	Signing Date	Transfer Fee	APPEARANCES				GOALS			
			Lge	FL Cup	FA Cup	Others	Lge	FL Cup	FA Cup	Others
Tottenham Hotspur*	4.92	–								

TUTTLE David Philip

Born: Reading, 6 February 1972

Height: 6'1"

Weight: 12.10

International Honours: E Yth

Position/Skill Factor: Strong tackling central defender who has the perfect build for the job in hand and loses little in the air. On the ground, he is a lovely striker of the ball with his right foot.

Career History: A young player with a promising future, he joined Tottenham Hotspur as an associated schoolboy in April 1986, before signing on as a trainee on leaving school in August 1988. Turned professional early in 1990 and following a substitute appearance in the League Cup, he made his FL debut at Chelsea on 1 December 1990 in a 3-2 defeat, playing a few more times towards the end of the season. Broke back into the "Spurs'" team in October 1991 and in his second game of 1991-92, scored a vital early goal against Hajduk Split in the European Cup Winners Cup, in helping his team to a 2-1 aggregate victory. Tragically, he suffered a serious injury in his fourth match, a League Cup tie against Swansea City, which ruled him out for the remainder of the season.

Clubs	Signing Date	Transfer Fee	APPEARANCES				GOALS			
			Lge	FL Cup	FA Cup	Others	Lge	FL Cup	FA Cup	Others
Tottenham Hotspur*	2.90	–	6+2	1+1		1				1

ULLATHORNE Robert

Born: Wakefield, 11 October 1971

Height: 5'7"

Weight: 10.7

International Honours: E Yth

Position/Skill Factor: Left-back who can play anywhere down the left side. Not very big, but full of enthusiasm, he has the ability to beat defenders and get telling crosses over with a lovely left foot.

Career History: Born in Yorkshire, he joined Norwich City, first as an associated schoolboy (October 1986) and later on leaving school, as a trainee in July 1988. Making good progress, he turned professional during the 1990 close season and made his FL debut in a 5-0 defeat at Nottingham Forest on 24 April 1991, when he replaced Mark Bowen. Began to establish himself in 1991-92, when called up to the first team in September and held down a regular place in midfield until rested in February. Returned to make three more appearances late in the season.

Clubs	Signing Date	Transfer Fee	APPEARANCES				GOALS			
			Lge	FL Cup	FA Cup	Others	Lge	FL Cup	FA Cup	Others
Norwich City*	7.90	–	22	4	2		3			

UNSWORTH David

Born: Chorley, 16 October 1973

Height: 6'0" Weight: 13.0

International Honours: E Yth

Position/Skill Factor: Left-back who can also play in central defence. A well balanced player, he has a lovely left foot and a great first touch of the ball.

Career History: An extremely promising youngster, he made his FL debut for Everton, while still a trainee, at Tottenham Hotspur on 25 April 1992 and although substituting at left-back for Andy Hinchcliffe, he scored a stunning equalising goal with a first touch volley from a corner in a 3-3 thriller. Only recently turned professional, having been at Goodison as an associated schoolboy since December 1987 and as a trainee since May 1990, he seems certain to be challenging for a regular first team place in 1992-93.

Clubs	Signing Date	Transfer Fee	APPEARANCES				GOALS			
			Lge	FL Cup	FA Cup	Others	Lge	FL Cup	FA Cup	Others
Everton*	5.92	–	1+1				1			

VAN DEN HAUWE Patrick
(Pat) William Roger

Born: Dendermonde,
Belgium,
16 December 1960

Height: 6'0"

Weight: 10.8

International Honours:
W 13

Clubs	Signing Date	Transfer Fee	APPEARANCES				GOALS			
			Lge	FL Cup	FA Cup	Others	Lge	FL Cup	FA Cup	Others
Birmingham City	8.78	–	119+4	12	5		1			
Everton	9.84	£100,000	134+1	20	30	15+1	2		1	
Tottenham Hotspur*	8.89	£575,000	97+1	14	8	7		1		

Position/Skill Factor: Strong tackling full-back who loves the physical side of the game. Basically right footed, he can play either side. A ball winner, he leaves others to provide the finesse.

Career History: The son of a Belgian professional goalkeeper, Rene, he moved to England at an early age, before signing as an apprentice for Birmingham City in June 1977. Turning to the paid ranks just over a year later, he made his FL debut at St Andrews against Manchester City on 7 October 1978 and although he did reasonably well, it took him a further three years to win a permanent place in the "Blues'" line-up. A versatile defender, he alternated between both full-back slots and central defence, until settling down at left-back in 1983-84 as an ever present – a season in which the "Blues" were relegated, although enjoying long runs in the League Cup and FA Cup. Not long into 1984-85, he returned to the First Division, signing for Everton and shared in the "Toffees'" impressive run of success with a League Championship medal and a European Cup Winners Cup medal in his first season, an FA Cup Final runners-up medal in 1986 and another League Championship medal in 1986-87. Despite missing most of that season through injury, his 11 end of season games were just enough to qualify him for a medal. Disqualified from playing for his native country, by opting out of National Service, he was "adopted" by Wales, making his international debut against Spain in Wrexham in April 1985. From 1987 to 1989 he shared the left-back slot with Neil Pointon and also filled in at right-back and central defence when required. His last game for Everton was in the 1989 FA Cup Final against Liverpool, when once again he finished on the losing side. Soon afterwards his international career was brought to an end by Welsh manager Terry Yorath when he failed to show up for a match without prior warning. Transferred to Tottenham Hotspur in the second week of the 1989-90 season, he has been a regular choice at left-back (or right-back when paired with Justin Edinburgh) since arriving at White Hart Lane. Returned to Wembley again for a FA Cup Final in 1991 and was "third time lucky", as "Spurs" prevailed 2-1 over Nottingham Forest. Apart from injuries, was once again a regular in the "Spurs'" rearguard during 1991-92, making 35 FL appearances and even scoring, an unusual occurrence for him, in a 3-0 Third Round League Cup tie victory at Grimsby Town.

VARADI Imre

Born: Paddington,
8 July 1959

Height: 5'8"

Weight: 11.1

Position/Skill Factor: A well travelled, veteran striker, who still has plenty of pace and is a very good runner off the ball. Often takes opponents away to make space for others.

Career History: Formerly a chef in Hertfordshire, he was signed by Sheffield United, then in the Second Division, just before the end of 1977-78, after he was discovered playing for the Isthmian League side, Letchworth Garden City. Made his FL debut early in the new season at Bramall Lane against Crystal Palace on 2 September 1978. Curiously, after apparently establishing himself in the team with four goals in six games in December 1978, he was dropped and later in the season sold to Everton. Had to wait nearly two years for a run in the Everton team, but after playing in every game from December 1980 to the end of the season, he was transferred again to Newcastle United in the Second Division. A great crowd favourite at St James' Park, he was ever present and top scorer with 18 FL goals in 1981-82 and shared the leading scorer's role with Kevin Keegan in 1982-83 – both with 21 FL goals. Once again, it was not enough for the management and he moved back to Sheffield – this time with Wednesday. In his first season at Hillsborough, he was the spearhead of the "Owls'" return to Division One after a long exile of 11 years, top scoring with 17 FL goals. Again the club's leading goalscorer with 16 FL goals, the following season, he moved on to West Bromwich in the summer of 1985. For the first time he failed to meet with success as the "Baggies" slid to relegation without a whimper, although he was still top scorer with nine FL goals. Discarded in 1986-87, he moved on to Manchester City and suffered the same fate as the previous season, top scoring (with nine goals) in a relegated team. Although not an automatic first choice in 1987-88, he still scored 17 FL goals from 32 games. Later usurped by Trevor Morley, he moved back to Sheffield Wednesday soon into the 1988-89 season, but by now his goal touch was drying up and he found himself in and out of the team. After only two substitute appearances in 1989-90, he reunited with former "Owls'" manager, Howard Wilkinson, at Leeds, assisting them over the final stretch to the Second Division Championship and promotion back to Division One. For the past two seasons he has provided cover for strikers' positions at Elland Road, but was hardly called upon during Leeds' League Championship triumph of 1991-92. Towards the end of the season he was loaned to Luton Town, but although scoring on his debut in a 2-1 victory over Wimbledon, he was unable to provide any more inspiration to prevent the "Hatters'" relegation.

Clubs	Signing Date	Transfer Fee	APPEARANCES				GOALS			
			Lge	FL Cup	FA Cup	Others	Lge	FL Cup	FA Cup	Others
Sheffield United	4.78	–	6+4		2		4			
Everton	3.79	£80,000	22+4		7		6		1	
Newcastle United	8.81	£100,000	81	4	5		39	1	2	
Sheffield Wednesday	8.83	£150,000	72+4	12	7		33	2	5	
W.B.A.	7.85	£285,000	30+2	5	2	2	9	4		
Manchester City	10.86	£50,000	56+9	4	6	2	26			2
Sheffield Wednesday	9.88	£50,000	14+8	1+1	2	1	3	1	2	
Leeds United*	2.90	£50,000	19+3	1		1+1	4			
Luton Town	3.92	Loan	5+1				1			

VENISON Barry

Born: Consett,
16 August 1964

Height: 5'10"

Weight: 11.9

International Honours:
E Yth, E "U21"-10

Position/Skill Factor: Versatile right-back who links well with midfield and is a good passer of the ball.

Career History: First came to Sunderland as a 14-year-old associated schoolboy (June 1979), before signing on as an apprentice in July 1980, after leaving school. Made his FL debut, while still a junior, at Notts County on 10 October 1981 and by the time he had turned professional, he had already totted up a further nine League appearances for the club. In his eleventh first team game, he scored a superlative goal to win a close 3-2 encounter with Manchester City after coming on as substitute. His first two seasons as a pro at Roker Park, saw him alternate between right-back and midfield, but from 1983 to 1985, he was firmly established at right-back, missing only four FL games in two years and also becoming a regular choice for the England Under 21 team. Sadly for him, the "Rokermen" were relegated to the Second Division at the end of 1984-85. After one season in Division Two, during which he again switched positions between full-back and midfield, he was transferred to First Division Champions, Liverpool, ostensibly as a replacement for Phil Neal. In six seasons at Anfield, he never truly established himself either in the team, or in the hearts of the supporters. He shared the right-back slot with Steve Nicol, but tended to be selected only when Nicol was required for other duties. Nevertheless, he shared in the apparently never-ending Liverpool success story, winning League Championship medals in 1987-88 and 1989-90, plus an FA Cup Winners medal (as substitute) against Everton in 1989. In 1991-92

he was struck down by injury and by the time he regained fitness a new challenger had claimed the right-back slot in the shape of Rob Jones. Returned to the first team in the vital sixth Round FA Cup tie against Aston Villa in March and played several more games to the end of the season, but was not selected for the Cup Final squad against Sunderland. Scored his first two goals in serious competition for Liverpool, but neither were vital, coming at the end of easy 4-0 victories over Tirol in the UEFA Cup and Notts County in the League.

Clubs	Signing Date	Transfer Fee	APPEARANCES				GOALS			
			Lge	FL Cup	FA Cup	Others	Lge	FL Cup	FA Cup	Others
Sunderland	1.82	–	169+4	21	7+1	3	2			1
Liverpool*	7.86	£200,000	103+7	14+3	16+5	6+3	1			2

VONK Michel Christian

Born: Netherlands, 28 October 1968

Height: 6'2" Weight: 11.10

Position/Skill Factor: A good solid central defender, who is excellent in the air and excels as a man-to-man marker.

Career History: Signed on trial by Manchester City from Dutch First Division club, SVV Dordrecht, towards the end of the 1991-92 season, he immediately made his FL debut, as a substitute at Nottingham Forest on 21 March 1992 and quickly settled into the side, replacing Steve Redmond in central defence. Impressed sufficiently to be offered a contract in the summer.

Clubs	Signing Date	Transfer Fee	APPEARANCES				GOALS			
			Lge	FL Cup	FA Cup	Others	Lge	FL Cup	FA Cup	Others
Manchester City*	3.92	£500,000	8+1							

Chris Waddle

WADDLE Christopher (Chris) Roland

Born: Felling, 14 December 1960

Height: 6'0" Weight: 11.5

International Honours: E "U21"-1, E-62

Position/Skill Factor: One of the most skilful of modern day players, he has the ability to leave defenders trailing in his wake. His superb ball control and deceptive pace are ideal for a wide attacking role, but he is equally adept in midfield.

Career History: One of the most exciting players of the last decade, he started his career with Newcastle United who picked him up from local Northern League club, Tow Law Town, in the 1980 close season, having been previously rejected by Sunderland. Quickly found his way into the team after making his FL debut at St James' against Shrewsbury Town on 22 October 1980 as a forward and later in the season he enjoyed a run on the left-wing. Ever present in 1981-82 and missing only five FL games in 1982-83, he was part of perhaps the most star-studded forward line the "Magpies" have ever produced when they won promotion back to Division One in 1983-84 with Waddle scoring 18 FL goals from the left-wing to complement Peter Beardsley's 20 and Kevin Keegan's 27. Called up the same season for his first England cap against the Irish Republic on 26 March 1985, he remained a regular member of the squad for the next six seasons. Following the retirement of Keegan, he reverted to twin striker with Beardsley for Newcastle's first season back in the top flight, scoring 13 goals in a fairly anti-climatic campaign. After a well publicised dispute with "Magpies'" manager, Jack Charlton, he was transferred to Tottenham Hotspur in the summer of 1985 for what appeared, in retrospect, to be a "give away" fee. Accompanied the England squad to the 1986 World Cup Finals, but was dropped in favour of Steve Hodge after the two disappointing opening games against Portugal and Morocco. Enjoyed an excellent second season at White Hart Lane, playing 39 FL games in a campaign when "Spurs" finished third in Division One and reached the 1987 FA Cup Final, only to lose unexpectedly to Coventry City. Plagued by injury and loss of form in 1987-88, he came back strongly the following season in a new creative midfield role to be ever present and top scorer with 14 FL goals, assisting "Spurs" to finish in sixth place, after finding themselves at the foot of the table in November. With "Spurs" facing mounting financial problems, he was sold to French League Champions, Olimpique de Marseille, for a new record fee for an English player. In three seasons with the French club, he won three League Championship honours and reached the Final of the 1991 European Cup when Marseille lost on penalties to Red Star Belgrade after a dreadful 0-0 draw. Cruelly and unjustly derided for his performance in that game, he was the one player on either side actually trying to create and score a goal, narrowly missing the target on two occasions. After speculation linking his name with Newcastle and Leeds United he signed for Sheffield Wednesday in the summer of 1992. Following a series of disputes with the England manager concerning his availability, he played probably his last game for the national side against Turkey in October 1991. In truth, he only showed glimpses of his true ability in an England shirt, frequently wasting good approach work with poor crosses and scoring not one single goal in his 62 international appearances. While always disappointing on the big occasions such as the 1986 and 1990 World Cup final tournaments and the 1988 European Championships, he remains, like John Barnes and Glenn Hoddle, an enigma doomed never to reproduced his club form at the highest international level.

Clubs	Signing Date	Transfer Fee	APPEARANCES				GOALS			
			Lge	FL Cup	FA Cup	Others	Lge	FL Cup	FA Cup	Others
Newcastle United	7.80	£1,000	169+1	8	12		46	2	4	
Tottenham Hotspur	6.85	£590,000	137+1	21	14	4	33	4	5	
Marseille (France)	7.89	£4,250,000								
Sheffield Wednesday*	6.92	£1,000,000								

WADDOCK Gary Patrick

Born: Kingsbury, 17 March 1962

Height: 5'9" Weight: 11.0

International Honours: IR "U21"-1, IR "B", IR-20

Position/Skill Factor: Very experienced strong tackling midfielder, who made an amazing comeback after his career seemed to be prematurely ended by serious injury.

Career History: First came to Queens Park Rangers as a 14-year-old associated schoolboy (November 1976), before progressing through the ranks as an apprentice (July 1978) and later as a professional. Made his FL debut when coming on as a substitute at Swansea City on 15 September 1979 and by the end of the following season he had settled into the side as a first team regular in midfield. For the next five seasons, he was an automatic first choice and a member of the Second Division team which reached the FA Cup Final in 1982 (losing to "Spurs" only after a replay) and won the Second Division Championship in 1982-83. He made his international debut for the Republic of Ireland against Switzerland on 30 April 1980 and remained a regular squad member until November 1985, when a serious injury sustained in a match against Sheffield Wednesday all but ended his career. Made two unsuccessful comebacks in 1986-87, but by December 1987 he was told that his FL career was over, collected his insurance money and had seemingly retired from the game. However, he was determined not to give up easily and accepted the offer of a trial with Belgian club, RSC Charleroi, which proved successful. So successful in fact, that Jack Charlton recalled him to the Irish Republic squad where he met Tony Cascarino who recommended him to Millwall manager, John Docherty. Over two years after his last FL appearance for Queens Park Rangers, he made his come back with Millwall in 1989-90, although not as a regular. Even more surprisingly, perhaps, he won two more Irish caps at the end of the season and the following the "Lions'" relegation from Division One, he played a full part in the 1990-91 campaign. Mysteriously released in September 1991, he was re-signed by his first club Queens Park Rangers after three months in limbo, but did not make the first team, spending the last month of season on loan to Swindon Town.

Clubs	Signing Date	Transfer Fee	APPEARANCES				GOALS			
			Lge	FL Cup	FA Cup	Others	Lge	FL Cup	FA Cup	Others
Q.P.R.	7.79	–	191+12	21+1	14	1	8	2		
RSC Charleroi (Bel.)	2.88	–								
Millwall	8.89	£130,000	51+7	5+1	5	3	2			1
Q.P.R.*	12.91	–								
Swindon Town	3.92	Loan	5+1							

WALKER Ian Michael

Born: Watford,
31 October 1971

Height: 6'1"

Weight: 11.9

International Honours:
E Yth, E "U21"-4

Position/Skill Factor: Very agile goalkeeper who looks confident in everything he does. Has good hands, comes for crosses and uses the ball well. Is also a good drop kicker.

Career History: Son of the new Norwich City manager, Mike, who used to play in goal for Reading, Shrewsbury Town, York City, Watford, Charlton Athletic and Colchester United between 1963-1983, he aspires to surpass his father at the top level. Started his career at Tottenham Hotspur where he had the advantage of first-hand tutelage from the former England Star, Ray Clemence, first as an associated schoolboy (June 1987) and then as a trainee (August 1988), before turning professional at the end of 1989. Unable to get a game at "Spurs", due to the consistency of Erik Thorstvedt, he was loaned out to Oxford United and made his FL debut in a 1-1 draw at the Manor Ground against Wolverhampton Wanderers on 29 September 1990. Such was his talent, that he made his debut for the England Under 21 team against Wales in December before his "Spurs" debut in an end of season game at Norwich in April 1991. Displaced "Spurs'" 'keeper Erik Thorstvedt after three games of the 1991-92 season, but was rested in October. However, he was restored to the team in April 1992 and ended as first choice. Clearly a potential future England player, it will be interesting to see who wins the battle for supremacy between "Spurs'" two 'keepers in 1992-93.

Clubs	Signing Date	Transfer Fee	APPEARANCES				GOALS			
			Lge	FL Cup	FA Cup	Others	Lge	FL Cup	FA Cup	Others
Tottenham Hotspur*	12.89	–	19	1		2				
Oxford United	9.90	Loan	2	1						

WALLACE David (Danny) Lloyd

Born: Greenwich, 21 January 1964

Height: 5'4" Weight: 10.6

International Honours: E Yth, E "U21"-14, E-1

Position/Skill Factor: Winger with two good feet who is very quick off the mark. Extremely direct, he runs straight at defenders in order to commit them and is an excellent crosser from the flanks.

Career History: At 16 years, 313 days of age, he became Southampton's youngest ever player when he made his FL debut while still an apprentice in a 1-1 draw at Manchester United on 29 November 1980. Elder brother of twins, Raymond and Rodney, who currently play for Leeds United, he joined the "Saints" as an associated schoolboy in February 1978, before becoming an apprentice, on leaving school, in July 1980. He then went on to show such exciting form in the junior and reserve sides that he was "blooded" in the cauldron of Old Trafford, as a deputy for the injured Kevin Keegan, 15 months before he signed professional forms for the "Saints". Won a regular place in the team on the left-wing from October 1982 and finished the season as top scorer with 12 FL goals. In 1983-84 he missed only one game, as the club achieved their highest ever placing (second – only three points behind Champions, Liverpool). First choice on the "Saints'" left-wing for the next five seasons, he never reached the heights once predicted for him and despite 14 England Under 21 caps between 1982 and 1985, he made only one full international appearance in England's first ever international against Egypt in Cairo on 29 January 1986. He scored once in a 4-0 victory, but was never selected again. By 1988-89, his last full season at the Dell, he was overshadowed by the exploits of his younger brother Rod on the right-wing and when Manchester United signed him early the next season, some cynics suggested that Alex Ferguson had signed the wrong brother!

It has not proved a happy move for either player, or club. Although a regular in United's team in 1989-90, he failed to provide a spark to their goal shy attack which recorded only 46 FL goals. However, he had the consolation of receiving an FA Cup Winners medal when United defeated Crystal Palace after a replay. After being upstaged by the brilliance of Lee Sharpe and playing only a peripheral role in 1990-91, he was left completely in the cold in 1991-92, making only two appearances (both in the European Cup Winners Cup). Clearly needs to rethink his future at Old Trafford with both Giggs and Sharpe available.

Clubs	Signing Date	Transfer Fee	APPEARANCES				GOALS			
			Lge	FL Cup	FA Cup	Others	Lge	FL Cup	FA Cup	Others
Southampton	1.82	–	240+15	36	21+1	10+2	64	6	4	5
Manchester United*	9-89	£1,200,000	36+9	3+3	6+2	4+2	6	2	2	

WALLACE Michael

Born: Farnworth, 5 October 1970

Height: 5'8" Weight: 10.2

International Honours: E Yth

Position/Skill Factor: Very skilful left-winger with plenty of pace, who often appears to "walk" past opposing defenders.

Career History: Started out at Manchester City as an associated schoolboy in October 1985, before leaving school and signing on as a trainee in July 1987. Although he has been a professional at Maine Road since the summer of 1989 and has won England youth caps, he has yet to make his FL debut.

Clubs	Signing Date	Transfer Fee	APPEARANCES				GOALS			
			Lge	FL Cup	FA Cup	Others	Lge	FL Cup	FA Cup	Others
Manchester City*	7.89	–								

WALLACE Raymond (Ray)
George

Born: Greenwich,
2 October 1969

Height: 5'6"

Weight: 10.2

International Honours:
E "U21"-4

Position/Skill Factor: A right-back with great pace, who is extremely difficult to go past. He is also a very aggressive tackler.

Career History: Brother of Danny and twin of Rodney, he first joined Southampton as an associated schoolboy in December 1983, before signing as a trainee in July 1986 and later turning professional at the tail end of 1987-88. The following season he made his FL debut in the right-back position at the Dell against Sheffield Wednesday on 22 October 1988, playing alongside his two brothers in a 2-1 defeat and held his place for most of the season. Started the first eight games of 1989-90, but lost his place to Jason Dodd in October and never appeared in first team football for Southampton again, apart from one substitute appearance. Up to that point he was keeping pace with his twin brother Rod, both in the "Saints'" team and the England Under 21 squad. After spending all of 1990-91 in the reserves, he was transferred to Leeds United in a joint deal, more it seems to keep his brother company than because the club needed another right-back. His only FL action in 1991-92 was at the end of the season on loan to Swansea City, but even this turned sour. After two games for the "Swans", it was discovered that his registration forms were not received by FL headquarters before the March transfer deadline. Swansea were fined for the administrative error and Wallace returned sadly to Elland Road.

Clubs	Signing Date	Transfer Fee	APPEARANCES				GOALS			
			Lge	FL Cup	FA Cup	Others	Lge	FL Cup	FA Cup	Others
Southampton	4.88	–	33+2	8	2					
Leeds United*	5.91	£100,000								
Swansea City	3.92	Loan	2							

WALLACE Rodney (Rod)
Seymour

Born: Greenwich,
2 October 1969

Height: 5'7"

Weight: 10.1

International Honours:
E "U21"-11

Position/Skill Factor: Winger with tremendous pace over the first vital ten yards, which takes him away from defenders and gets him into shooting, or crossing positions.

Career History: Brother of Danny, currently with Manchester United, he joined Southampton as an associated schoolboy in December 1983, along with his twin, Ray and on leaving school, both of them signed as trainees in July 1986. Made his FL debut, while still a trainee, when coming on as a substitute at Newcastle United on 26 September 1987 and later celebrated his new professional status with a goal in his second full appearance – a late equaliser against Liverpool at Anfield, a scorching cross shot taken with the aplomb of a veteran. In his first full season, mostly on the right-wing, he was ever present and top scorer with 12 FL goals. At this stage he was arguably a more exciting prospect than his elder brother Danny at the same age. In 1989-90 he enjoyed another superb season and the "Saints'" three "pronged" attack of Wallace, Le Tissier and Shearer, made the team one of the most entertaining in the League. Remarkably, of his 18 FL goals, 14 were scored in "braces" – that is to say, in seven games he scored twice. The following season was more of a struggle for his team, but he still achieved 14 FL goals, second only to Le Tissier. It was inevitable perhaps, but sad, that he should move on to a bigger club and shortly after the end of 1991-92 he joined Leeds United, along with twin brother, Ray. After a slow start at Elland Road, he was dropped from the United team, but on his return in October, a burst of six goals in five games, established him as a crowd favourite and maintained his team's momentum towards the League Championship. In the vital penultimate game of the season away to Sheffield United, he scored (if that is the right word!) the most bizarre goal of the season. A clearance by a United defender cannoned sideways off Gary Speed and ricocheted into the net off Wallace's thigh. It was a vital goal as Leeds went on to win 3-2 and virtually clinch the Championship. In the final game at home to Norwich, he scored a more typical goal to win the game – a dash from the halfway line with a clinical finish. If he can fully recapture the form he showed in three seasons at The Dell, Leeds United will be a joy to watch and full international honours will surely be just around the corner.

Clubs	Signing Date	Transfer Fee	APPEARANCES				GOALS			
			Lge	FL Cup	FA Cup	Others	Lge	FL Cup	FA Cup	Others
Southampton	4.88	–	111+17	18+1	10	3+1	44	6	3	2
Leeds United*	5.91	£1,600,000	34	3	1	0+1	11	2		1

WALSH Gary

Born: Wigan,
21 March 1968

Height: 6'1"

Weight: 12.12

International Honours:
E "U21"-2

Position/Skill factor: Tall and commanding goalkeeper with good safe hands.

Career History: A Manchester United associated schoolboy signing in June 1983, he joined the professional ranks at Old Trafford at the rear end of 1984-85, but due to the form of Gary Bailey and Chris Turner he had to wait until 13 December 1986, before making his FL debut in a 3-3 draw at Aston Villa. By the end of the 1986-87 season he was first choice 'keeper and remained so for the first three months of 1987-88, until Turner returned in December 1987. During this first team run, he won two England Under 21 caps, but then had to wait over three years until February 1991 for his next game with United, whilst understudying Jim Leighton and Les Sealey. In 1991–2

found himself as deputy to Peter Schmeichel, making only four first team appearances and with arguably the world's finest 'keeper firmly entrenched at Old Trafford, he may feel it is time to move on.

Clubs	Signing Date	Transfer Fee	APPEARANCES				GOALS			
			Lge	FL Cup	FA Cup	Others	Lge	FL Cup	FA Cup	Others
Manchester United*	4.85	–	37	3		2				
Airdrieonians	8.88	Loan								

WALTERS Mark Everton

Born: Birmingham, 2 June 1964

Height: 5'9" Weight: 11.5

International Honours: E Sch, E Yth, E "U21"-9, E "B", E-1

Position/Skill factor: Skilful, speedy left-winger with good balance, who can go both ways. Favours his left side, but commits defenders by running at them.

Career History: Aston Villa signed him as a 14-year-old associated schoolboy in July 1978, following exciting displays in local schools football that would lead him to an England junior cap later that year. On leaving school, he signed as an apprentice in July 1980 and progressed to the paid ranks during the 1982 close season, after being a key member of the club's FA Youth Cup winning side. His FL debut came on 28 April 1982 at home to Leeds United when he substituted for Tony Morley – a few days before turning professional. In 1982-83 he shared the left-wing

slot with Morley, but fully established himself in 1983-84 when he emerged as one of the most exciting attacking wingers in the country, winning the first of his England Under 21 caps. He continued to thrill the Villa Park faithful for the next two years, scoring several outstanding goals, until it all went sour in 1986-87. Villa were relegated, hardly putting up serious resistance and under new manager, Billy McNeill, he found himself in-and-out of the team. Incensed at his treatment, he demanded a transfer and although his third manager, Graham Taylor, restored him to favour and tried to persuade him to stay, he left halfway through Villa's Second Division promotion campaign to join the large English contingent at Glasgow Rangers. The first black player to sign for the Scottish giants, he had to face the taunts of the bigoted minority, but quickly won over the discerning fans with his thrilling wing play and played a full part in the "Gers'" three consecutive Scottish League Championships from 1988 to 1991, plus winning two Skol League Cup medals in 1988 and 1990. In the summer of 1991, he followed manager Graham Souness to Liverpool, after making his long overdue England debut against New Zealand on the summer tour of Australasia. So far, he has proved to be Souness' most disappointing signing. Handed a glorious opportunity to "win his spurs" by the long term injury to John Barnes early in the season, he proved to be a pale shadow of the player that once transfixed Villa and Ibrox Parks. Hesitant, unconfident and seemingly not match fit, he lost his place in November and and appeared only occasionally thereafter. Enjoyed only two moments of glory during the season. With Barnes unavailable for much of next season, he has another chance to prove himself in 1992-93 and it is to be hoped that this time he shows his undoubted talents.

Clubs	Signing Date	Transfer Fee	APPEARANCES				GOALS			
			Lge	FL Cup	FA Cup	Others	Lge	FL Cup	FA Cup	Others
Aston Villa	5.82	–	168+13	21+1	11+1	5+3	39	6	1	2
Glasgow Rangers	12.87	£500,000								
Liverpool*	8.91	£1,250,000	18+7	4	2+1	4+1	3	2		1

WALTON David Lee

Born: Ashington, 10 April 1973

Height: 6'2" Weight: 13.4

Position: Defender.

Career History: Discovered by Sheffield United while playing non-League football for his hometown club, Ashington, he signed professional forms for the "Blades" during the 1992 close season, thus being given the opportunity of joining many famous former footballing heroes from the town, including Jackie Milburn and Bobby Charlton, who made it to the top.

Clubs	Signing Date	Transfer Fee	APPEARANCES				GOALS			
			Lge	FL Cup	FA Cup	Others	Lge	FL Cup	FA Cup	Others
Sheffield United*	5.92	–								

WALTON Mark Andrew

Born: Merthyr Tydfil, 1 June 1969

Height: 6'2"

Weight: 13.13

International Honours:
W "U21"-1

Position/Skill factor: An all-action goalkeeper who is always issuing instructions to his defence. Very strong when coming out for crosses, he also sets up attacks with great left footed drop kicks.

Career History: The son of Ron, who had a varied career as a winger between 1963-1977 in the lower reaches and currently coaches at Swansea City, he joined Luton Town early in 1987, having been a junior on Swansea City's books. Due to the presence of Les Sealey and Alec Chamberlain at Kenilworth Road, first team opportunities were nil and it wasn't long before he signed for Colchester United at first on loan and then permanently. Made his FL debut at Layer Road against Wolverhampton Wanderers on 21 November 1987 and played in 17 League games during 1987-88. Missed half of the 1988-89 season through injury and somewhat surprisingly moved to First Division Norwich City in the summer of 1989 on the recommendation of his former manager at Layer Road, Mike Walker. Signed as cover for Bryan Gunn, he made his First Division debut in April 1990 away to Aston Villa. In deputising for Gunn, when the latter was injured at Bramall Lane in mid-January 1992, he performed so well that he held his place to the end of the season even after his rival was declared fit.

Clubs	Signing Date	Transfer Fee	APPEARANCES				GOALS			
			Lge	FL Cup	FA Cup	Others	Lge	FL Cup	FA Cup	Others
Luton Town	2.87	–								
Colchester United	11.87	£15,000	40	3	8	5				
Norwich City*	8.89	£75,000	22		5					

WARD Mark William

Born: Huyton
10 October 1962

Height: 5'6"

Weight: 9.12

International Honours:
E Semi-Pro Int

Position/Skill factor: Tiny winger who is a lovely striker of the ball and quite capable of scoring from long range free-kicks. Very competitive, he will tackle full-backs with relish.

Career History: A player who has come the full cycle in football terms, having initially been with Everton as an associated schoolboy (September 1977), an apprentice (June 1979) and a professional (September 1980), before being released in the summer of 1981. He didn't let the experience get him down for too long, however, joining Northwich Victoria of the Alliance Premier League and representing the England Semi-Pro side, before Oldham Athletic recognised his potential and gave him another chance of League soccer. Made his FL debut on the opening day of the 1983-84 season and scored the only goal of the game against Brighton and Hove Albion on 27 August 1983 at Boundary Park. In two seasons with the "Latics", playing on the right-wing, he did not miss a single game – a remarkable record of consistency for a young pro – and it was perhaps not surprising he was snapped up by a First Division club, West Ham United. He was again ever present in his first season at Upton Park, assisting the "Hammers" to their highest ever FL placing (third) and in total he played 131 consecutive games from his FL debut, before being absent, which if not a FL record, must be close to one. He stayed over four years at Upton Park, hardly missing a game until injured in November 1988. However, disciplinary problems started to interrupt his appearances and his form and following the "Hammers'" relegation to Division Two in 1989-90, he moved back north in mid-season to join Manchester City. His arrival at Maine Road allowed David White to move inside and become one of the most deadly strikers in the country and in 20 months with City, he missed only two games. In the 1991 close season, he was surprisingly allowed to leave and rejoin the club that discarded him ten years earlier and made a great start at Goodison Park, scoring twice against League Champions Arsenal in his second game. But like most of his team mates, he was generally inconsistent and disappointing. Curiously, Everton found themselves with a surplus of wingers, but only one "natural" midfielder and in the second-half of 1991-92, he was tried in the middle of the park, without ever suggesting he was the long term solution to the problem.

Clubs	Signing Date	Transfer Fee	APPEARANCES				GOALS			
			Lge	FL Cup	FA Cup	Others	Lge	FL Cup	FA Cup	Others
Everton	9.80	–								
Northwich Victoria	8.81	–								
Oldham Athletic	7.83	£10,000	84	5	3		12			
West Ham United	8.85	£250,000	163+2	20+1	17	6	12	2		
Manchester City	12.89	£1,000,000	54	3	6	3	14			2
Everton*	8.91	£1,100,000	37	2	2	1	4			

WARD Mitchum (Mitch) David

Born: Sheffield, 19 June 1971

Height: 5'8" Weight: 10.7

Position/Skill factor: Right-winger with two good feet who is an excellent striker of the ball.

Career History: Sheffield born and bred, he first joined Sheffield United as an associated schoolboy (July 1985), before progressing through the club as a trainee (July 1987) to professional status in the 1989 close season. With few opportunities available, he had to wait over a year

before making his FL debut in a 1-1 draw at home to Manchester City on 8 September 1990. Retained his place the following week at Southampton, before a spell on loan at Crewe Alexandra and two more end of season games. Remained on the fringe of first team action in 1991-92 and scored twice in six occasional FL outings.

Clubs	Signing Date	Transfer Fee	APPEARANCES				GOALS			
			Lge	FL Cup	FA Cup	Others	Lge	FL Cup	FA Cup	Others
Sheffield United*	7.89	–	7+3	0+1	1	0+1	2			
Crewe Alexandra	11.90	Loan	4		1	2	1		1	

WARHURST Paul

Born: Stockport,
26 September 1969

Height: 6'1"

Weight: 14.0

International Honours:
E "U21"-8

Position/Skill factor: Athletic central defender, or full-back, with good recovery. Reads situations well at the back and breaks up attacks with timely interceptions. Comes out of defence with the ball, looking to pass, rather than clearing his lines.

Career History: Followed in his father Roy's footsteps when he joined Manchester City as an associated schoolboy in November 1983. Roy Warhurst was a tough, uncompromising wing-half, who joined Sheffield United during the last war and went on to play for Birmingham City, Manchester City, Crewe Alexandra and Oldham Athletic, before hanging his boots up in 1961. On leaving school, the younger Warhurst signed on as a trainee at Maine Road in July 1986 and eventually joined the City professional ranks in the 1988 close season. But after only four months and without a chance to prove himself, he was amazingly transferred to Oldham Athletic for a modest fee. Made his FL debut in a 1-1 draw at Portsmouth on 29 October 1988, but spent the rest of the season in the reserves, apart from three other FL outings. Established himself strongly in 1989-90 in central defence, after standing in for the injured Andy Holden, his pace impressed many observers during Oldham's historic double cup runs, when they reached the Final of the League Cup and the Semi-Final of the FA Cup. In 1990-91, he was switched to right-back with great success and became a regular member of the England Under 21 squad. However, he fell out of favour with manager, Joe Royle, following a heavy defeat at Oxford and lost his place to Norwegian, Gunnar Halle. He returned to the team late in the season in the unfamiliar role of striker as the "Latics" stormed to the Second Division Championship and promotion to Division One. He did not stay long enough to see First Division football return to Boundary Park, however, as he was sold for an enormous profit to Sheffield Wednesday in the 1991 close season. Soon established a place in central defence at Hillsborough in 1991-92, but had a mixed season, looking impressive in the first four months, but in-and-out over the second-half.

Clubs	Signing Date	Transfer Fee	APPEARANCES				GOALS			
			Lge	FL Cup	FA Cup	Others	Lge	FL Cup	FA Cup	Others
Manchester City	6.88	–								
Oldham Athletic	10.88	£10,000	60+7	8	5+4	2	2			
Sheffield Wednesday*	7.91	£750,000	31+2	2	1	1				

WARK John

Born: Glasgow, 4 August 1957

Height: 5'10" Weight: 11.7

International Honours: S "U21"-8, S-29

Position/Skill factor: A very experienced player, who is now playing as a central defender and reads situations like the back of his hand, having seen it all before. Still very good in the air, he is also dangerous at set plays.

Career History: A player who has just completed his 17th season of competitive League football and is now back with Ipswich Town, the club with whom he first started out as an apprentice in September 1973. After turning professional with Ipswich during the 1974 close season, he made his FL debut at Portman Road against Leicester City on 29 March 1975, but it was not until 1976-77 that he became a regular in Town's midfield and gave early warning of his goalscoring prowess with ten FL goals from 33 games. In 1977-78 he was absent, injured for the first-half of the season, but returned in January to assist his team to the FA Cup Final against Arsenal. After a wretched League campaign, in which relegation was narrowly averted, Ipswich were definite underdogs, yet they totally out-played the "Gunners". Paul Mariner headed against the crossbar and Wark hit two tremendous shots against the post. Just when it seemed that the Gods had pre-determined that the FA Cup must go to Highbury, Roger Osborne at last scored the winner that Ipswich so richly deserved. Made his international debut for Scotland against Wales on 19 May 1979 and remained a regular selection until 1984, accompanying the squad to the 1982 World Cup finals in Spain, playing in all three games. In total he scored seven goals in his 29 international appearances. In three consecutive seasons from 1979 to 1982,

Town came close to winning the League Championship, without clinching it and his goals (12, 18 and 18, respectively) were instrumental in keeping his team at or near the top. Consolation for these near misses was found in their UEFA Cup victory of 1980-81, in which his contribution was astounding. Four goals against Aris Salonika in the First Round, a hat-trick against Widzew Lodz in the Third Round, goals in both legs of the Fourth Round against St. Etienne, a goal in the Semi-Final against Cologne and goals in each leg of the Final against Dutch team, AZ67 of Alkmaar, which Ipswich won narrowly, 5-4 on aggregate. In total, he scored 14 goals from midfield in 12 games of the competition – a record surely without parallel. In 1982-83 he was top scorer with 20 FL goals, but by then Bobby Robson's team was in decline and he became disaffected and moved to Liverpool in March 1984, in time to share in their League Championship triumph, if not to qualify for a medal. Liverpool's top scorer in 1984-85, with 18 FL goals from 40 games, ahead of Ian Rush, who missed one third of the season with injuries, he continued his remarkable record in European competition with five goals in nine European Cup games, including a hat-trick against Lech-Poznan. But the campaign ended in the disaster of Brussels, when Liverpool lost a meaningless Final to Juventus. Plagued by injury in 1985-86, he again missed out on a League Championship medal and never won his place back at Anfield. After four years at Liverpool, mostly out of the team, he moved back to Ipswich and proved he had not lost his goalscoring touch with 13 FL goals in 1988-89 and ten in 1989-90. Surprisingly, he moved to Middlesbrough for the 1990-91 season and held his place until March, although his goal output dropped sharply. In 1991-92 after being released by "Boro", he returned to Ipswich for the third time, as a non-contract player, apparently to help on the coaching side, rather than as a first team player. Remarkably, he returned to the team in October in a new role, as central defender and held his place to the end of the season as Town swept to the Second Division Championship. It remains to be seen if, at the age of 35, he can continue playing in the Premier League, but whatever his future, he will remain a legend at Portman Road.

Clubs	Signing Date	Transfer Fee	APPEARANCES				GOALS			
			Lge	FL Cup	FA Cup	Others	Lge	FL Cup	FA Cup	Others
Ipswich Town	8.74	–	295+1	24+1	36+1	25	94	12	10	18
Liverpool	3.84	£450,000	64+6	6+4	11+2	13+2	28	3	6	5
Ipswich Town	1.88	£100,000	87+2	4	3	7	23			2
Middlesbrough	8.90	£50,000	31+1	5	2	1	3			
Ipswich Town (N/C)*	8.91	–	36+1	1	5	3	3			

WARNER Vance

Born: Leeds, 3 September 1974

Height: 6'0½" Weight: 11.7

Position/Skill factor: Big, strong central defender who is good in the air and quick into the tackle.

Career History: Yet to make a first team appearance for Nottingham Forest, he came through the club's ranks first as an associated schoolboy (February 1989) and then as a trainee in August 1991, before signing professional forms just one month later. A promising young defender, he was selected as a substitute for an end of season FL match, after only a handful of appearances in the Forest reserve side, but was not called upon.

Clubs	Signing Date	Transfer Fee	APPEARANCES				GOALS			
			Lge	FL Cup	FA Cup	Others	Lge	FL Cup	FA Cup	Others
Nottingham Forest*	9.91	–								

WARZYCHA Robert

Born: Wielun, Poland,
20 August 1963

Height: 5'9"

Weight: 11.9

International Honours:
Polish Int

Position/Skill factor: Very fast right-winger, with two good feet, who likes to take full-backs on and looks to get in early crosses or shots at goal.

Career History: A 27-year-old Polish international, he signed for Everton from Gornik Zabre and immediately went into the first team, making his FL debut at Goodison against Nottingham Forest on 23 March 1991. Quickly became a favourite of the crowd, playing in 11 of the last 13 end of season games and scoring both goals in a 2-2 draw at Aston Villa. A regular member of the first team squad in 1991-92, but not an automatic first choice, sharing right-wing duties with Mark Ward and Pat Nevin. Nevertheless, he played 26 full FL games, scoring the winner at Luton Town in one of his 11 substitute appearances.

Clubs	Signing Date	Transfer Fee	APPEARANCES				GOALS			
			Lge	FL Cup	FA Cup	Others	Lge	FL Cup	FA Cup	Others
Everton*	3.91	£300,000	33+12	1+1	1+1	4	5			2

WATSON David (Dave)

Born: Liverpool, 20 November 1961

Height: 6'0" Weight: 11.12

International Honours: E "U21"-7, E-12

Position/Skill factor: Very good central defender, who is strong in the air and aggressive in the tackle. Always dangerous from corner kicks, where he plunders many vital goals.

Career History: The elder brother of Alex, who also played for Liverpool but is currently with Bournemouth, he started his career at Anfield as an associated schoolboy in October 1976, before turning professional during the summer of 1979. Released by Liverpool 18 months later, without a first team appearance, he joined Norwich City for a six figure sum and went straight into action, making his FL debut at Ipswich Town on 26 December 1980. An instant success at Carrow Road, he became a fixture in the heart of the "Canaries'" defence for the next six years, missing a mere handful of games during that time. After winning Under 21 caps in 1983-84, he was a surprise selection for England's summer tour of South America in 1984,

making his full international debut in the historic 2-0 victory over Brazil in the Maracana Stadium on 10 June. One of the successes of the tour, he remained a semi-regular England performer until 1987-88. In the summer of 1986 he returned to his native city, joining his former club's great rivals, Everton. Formed a very effective central defensive partnership with Kevin Ratcliffe, which lasted until 1991 when Ratcliffe gave way to Martin Keown. In his first season at Goodison Park he assisted the "Toffees" to their second League Championship in three years and also won an FA Cup Finalists medal in 1989, when Everton went down to Liverpool. In 1991-92 he played in every game, until injured in March. Still one of the country's leading central defenders, he should form a redoubtable partnership with the new England cap, Martin Keown, in 1992-93.

Clubs	Signing Date	Transfer Fee	APPEARANCES				GOALS			
			Lge	FL Cup	FA Cup	Others	Lge	FL Cup	FA Cup	Others
Liverpool	5.79	–								
Norwich City	11.80	£100,000	212	21	18		11	3	1	
Everton*	8.86	£900,000	199+1	23	30	15	16	2	3	3

WATSON Gordon William George

Born: Sidcup,
20 March 1971

Height: 6'0"

Weight: 12.0

International Honours:
E "U21"-2

Position/Skill factor: Hard working centre-forward, who tackles defenders as he chases lost causes. Useful in the air, he is a good target man.

Career History: A local discovery, he came through the Charlton Athletic junior ranks as an associated schoolboy (June 1985) and as a trainee (July 1987), before graduating as a professional towards the end of 1988-89. He was soon into first team action, making his FL debut on the opening day of the following season as a substitute at home to Derby County on 19 August 1989, but spent much of 1989-90 sitting on the bench awaiting further opportunities. Forced his way into the Charlton team early in 1990-91 and was a great success, netting seven goals in 15 games, although his team was struggling at the foot of the table. Rested in December, he was signed by Ron Atkinson in February for Sheffield Wednesday as an investment for the future. Made just one full appearance, plus four from the bench for the "Owls" and at the end of the season was called up for the England Under 21 squad to compete in the annual tournament in France. Made a handful of appearances in 1991-92, but the last of them, at home to Leeds in January, may have jeopardised his career when he took a blatant "dive" in the penalty area to "earn" the "Owls" a penalty. It so incensed the Leeds' team that they went on to record a crushing 6-1 victory and as the game was televised, his "card will undoubtedly be marked" by players and referees alike.

Clubs	Signing Date	Transfer Fee	APPEARANCES				GOALS			
			Lge	FL Cup	FA Cup	Others	Lge	FL Cup	FA Cup	Others
Charlton Athletic	4.89	–	20+11	2	0+1	1+1	7	1		
Sheffield Wednesday*	2.91	£250,000	5+4	1	1	0+1				

WATSON Kevin Edward

Born: Hackney, 3 January 1974

Height: 5'9" Weight: 12.6

Position/Skill factor: Skilful midfield player with a lovely touch on the ball. Very creative, passing is his forté.

Career History: Recently turned professional for Tottenham Hotspur, after being at the club since signing as an associated schoolboy in March 1988 and graduating as a trainee in August 1990. No first team experience, having played only a few reserve games to date.

Clubs	Signing Date	Transfer Fee	APPEARANCES				GOALS			
			Lge	FL Cup	FA Cup	Others	Lge	FL Cup	FA Cup	Others
Tottenham Hotspur*	5.92	–								

WATTS Grant

Born: Croydon, 5 November 1973

Height: 6'0" Weight: 11.0

Position: Forward.

Career History: Locally born and bred, he joined the Crystal Palace professional ranks during the 1992 close season, having previously been at Selhurst Park as an associated schoolboy (February 1990) and as a trainee (July 1990).

Clubs	Signing Date	Transfer Fee	APPEARANCES				GOALS			
			Lge	FL Cup	FA Cup	Others	Lge	FL Cup	FA Cup	Others
Crystal Palace*	6.92	–								

WATTS Julian

Born: Sheffield, 17 March 1971

Height: 6'3" Weight: 12.1

Position: Central defender.

Career History: Signed by Rotherham United from local Northern Counties (East) League team, Frecheville CA, during the 1990 close season, he was soon "blooded", making his FL debut in a 3-1 defeat at Millmoor against Huddersfield Town on 13 October 1990. Held his place in central defence until December before being rested, but returned for two end of season games. Included in the first team squad at the beginning of 1991-92, he seemed to be establishing himself, until he was dropped from the team in late November. Apparently out of favour at Millmoor, it was something of a surprise when neighbours Sheffield Wednesday swooped for him just before the March transfer deadline, presumably as an investment for the future.

Clubs	Signing Date	Transfer Fee	APPEARANCES				GOALS			
			Lge	FL Cup	FA Cup	Others	Lge	FL Cup	FA Cup	Others
Rotherham United	7.90	–	17+3	1	4	2	1			
Sheffield Wednesday*	3.92	£80,000								

WEBB Neil John

Born: Reading, 30 July 1963

Height: 6'1" Weight: 13.2

International Honours: E Yth, E "U21"-3, E"B", E-26

Position/Skill factor: A gifted midfielder with great vision for defence splitting passes and a talent for scoring goals, which puts many forwards to shame.

Neil Webb

Career History: Started his football career as an associated schoolboy with Reading in September 1978, following in the footsteps of his father, Doug, who had previously been a forward at Elm Park between 1956-1967. Signed as an apprentice on leaving school in June 1979, he made his FL debut at Mansfield Town on 16 February 1980 and was a regular first teamer by the time he turned professional in November 1980. Early in his career he demonstrated the knack of getting into the penalty area to score vital goals. In 1981-82 he was the "Royals'" leading scorer with 15 FL goals (including six penalties), ahead of Kerry Dixon! Transferred to Portsmouth in the summer of 1982, he played a major role in "Pompey's" Third Division Championship triumph of 1982-83 and was leading scorer with 16 FL goals in 1984-85 when they missed promotion to Division One by a whisker, on goal difference. Sadly for Portsmouth fans, they lost their brightest star for a surprisingly modest fee to Nottingham Forest in the summer of 1985. He immediately proved that he was quite at home in the First Division, scoring 14 FL goals in each of his first two seasons at the City Ground. In 1987-88 he won his first England cap, coming on for Glenn Hoddle against West Germany on 9 September 1987 and became a regular choice during 1987-88. Like most of his colleagues, however, he suffered a miserable European Championship in West Germany 1988, being substituted in the first match against the Irish Republic and taking little further part in the competition. Won his first major club honour with a League Cup winners medal in 1989, scoring one of the goals in Forest's 3-1 victory over Luton Town, but was disappointed in the FA Cup, losing in the Semi-Final to Liverpool for the second consecutive season. Followed the path of several Forest stars, by joining Manchester United in the summer of 1989, but after only four games with his new club, he suffered an achilles tendon injury in a vital World Cup qualifying game in Sweden, which not only ruled him out for most of the season, but also, many feel, prevented him reaching the heights of international stardom. He returned to action late in the season and played in the 1990 FA Cup Final where his lofted pass in the replay against Crystal Palace, set up Lee Martin for the winning goal. Played for most of the 1990-91 campaign, but weight problems had reduced his mobility and his lack of pace reduced his goal scoring capacity. A member of the League Cup Final team against Sheffield Wednesday, he was substituted as United slid to a surprise defeat. By 1991-92 his England career seemed over, but Graham Taylor, searching for some midfield guile in the enforced absence of Paul Gascoigne, recalled him to the England squad for the match against France in February. Although out of favour with his club manager, Alex Ferguson, at the the end of the season, he did enough to win selection for the England squad for the European Championship Finals in Sweden. While not making the starting line-up for the first two games, in a desperate last throw of the dice, Taylor included him in the team for the last vital match against Sweden on the ground where his England career seemed to have ended three years previously. Unfortunately, along with the rest of his colleagues, he was blown away in Sweden's second half "blitzkreig" as England went out of the competition 2-1 to the host nation.

Clubs	Signing Date	Transfer Fee	APPEARANCES				GOALS			
			Lge	FL Cup	FA Cup	Others	Lge	FL Cup	FA Cup	Others
Reading	11.80	–	65+7	2+2	2		22			
Portsmouth	7.82	£83,000	123	9	6		34	3	1	
Nottingham Forest	6.85	£250,000	146	21	13	6	47	4	2	4
Manchester United*	6.89	£1,500,000	70+4	13	9	9	8	1	1	1

WEBSTER Kenneth (Ken) Darren

Born: Hammersmith, 2 March 1973

Height: 5'9" Weight: 12.12

International Honours: E Yth

Position/Skill factor: Enthusiastic right-back, who can also play in the centre of the defence. Quick, strong and aggressive, with a very powerful right foot.

Career History: Yet to make his FL debut, he has been a professional at Arsenal for just over one year, having earlier come through the ranks as an associated schoolboy (November 1988) and as a trainee (July 1989).

Clubs	Signing Date	Transfer Fee	APPEARANCES				GOALS			
			Lge	FL Cup	FA Cup	Others	Lge	FL Cup	FA Cup	Others
Arsenal*	3.91	–								

WEGERLE Roy Connon

Born: Johannesburg, South Africa, 19 March 1964

Height: 5'8" Weight: 10.2

International Honours: USA Int

Position/Skill factor: Striker with a wonderful talent. Good controlling and passing ability, with silky skills to match. He can twist and turn defenders inside out and is capable of scoring spectacular goals. A natural athlete, he also possesses great pace.

Career History: Discovered playing in South Africa by the former Ipswich goalkeeper, Roy Bailey, he had a brief trial with Manchester United before heading for the USA and a university scholarship. After joining NASL side, Tampa Bay Rowdies, he created such a good impression that Chelsea eventually signed him during the 1986 close season, following a successful trial period. Made his FL debut as a substitute for Keith Jones in a 2-2 draw at Everton on 8 November 1986 and played seven full matches that season, scoring against Queens Park Rangers and Wimbledon. Appeared mostly on the wing for Chelsea, but never enjoyed much of a run in two seasons at Stamford Bridge, nor did an end of season loan with Swindon in 1987-88 lead to anything. Transferred to Luton Town in the summer of 1988, he established a regular place as a front runner and started to show glimpses of his true potential, particularly in the team's fine League Cup run, when he scored twice in a 3-1 victory over Manchester City in the Fourth Round and in both legs of the Semi-Final against West Ham. Sadly for Luton, the final was lost 3-1 to Nottingham Forest, despite a half-time lead. After two FL goals in 15 games in 1989-90, he was transferred to Queens Park Rangers for a truly astonishing fee of £1 million – astonishing in view of his limited experience and previous valuations. Although he looked a quality player for Rangers, six goals in 19 FL games did not seem to justify the fee. However, it made more sense in 1990-91 when he was outstanding and finished the season as leading scorer with 18 FL goals. His goals included one at Leeds when he cut in from the right touch-line, dribbled round or past six United players, before scoring with a low drive. In truth, the shot was less impressive than the run, but the goal was deservedly chosen as "Goal of the Season" by the ITV panel of experts. In 1991-92 after scoring only five goals in 23 appearances, he was sold to ambitious Blackburn Rovers. Kenny Dalglish signed him to replace the injured Mike Newell and to keep Rovers' promotion campaign on course. The gamble failed, as Rovers lost seven of the first nine games he played in and fell from the first place to outside the Play-Offs zone and after only two goals in 12 games he was dropped. Although Rovers recovered just in time to reach the Play-Offs and eventually win them, he played no further part in the proceedings and his future at Ewood Park remains in some doubt. However, having taken USA nationality, he played his first match for the USA national team at the end of the season, after waiting three years to see if he would be selected for the England team. He and team-mate, John Harkes of Sheffield Wednesday, were major factors in the USA's amazing victory in a four team tournament, including Italy, The Republic of Ireland and Portugal.

Clubs	Signing Date	Transfer Fee	APPEARANCES				GOALS			
			Lge	FL Cup	FA Cup	Others	Lge	FL Cup	FA Cup	Others
Chelsea	6.86	£100,000	15+8		1+1	2+1	3		1	
Swindon Town	3.88	Loan	7				1			
Luton Town	7.88	£75,000	39+6	10	1	2+1	10	8		
Q.P.R.	12.89	£1,000,000	71+4	5	11	1	29	1	1	
Blackburn Rovers*	3.92	£1,200,000	9+3				2			

WETHERALL David

Born: Sheffield, 14 March 1971

Height: 6'3" Weight: 12.0

International Honours: E Sch

Position/Skill factor: Strong tackling central defender who is also very good in the air.

Career History: Signed for Sheffield Wednesday as an associated schoolboy in May 1987, having represented England schools, he eventually turned professional at Hillsborough during the 1989 close season. Surprisingly sold to Leeds United two years later for a six figure fee, along with Jon Newsome, another promising "Owls'" youngster and without a first team game to his name, he made his FL debut as a substitute in a 2-2 draw against Arsenal at Elland Road on 3 September 1991, his only appearance during a season in which the club would ultimately win the League Championship. Clearly an investment for the future, he is currently studying at university.

Clubs	Signing Date	Transfer Fee	APPEARANCES				GOALS			
			Lge	FL Cup	FA Cup	Others	Lge	FL Cup	FA Cup	Others
Sheffield Wednesday	7.89	–								
Leeds United*	7.91	£125,000	0+1							

WHELAN Philip (Phil) James

Born: Stockport, 7 March 1972

Height: 6'4" Weight: 14.1

Position/Skill factor: A central defender who looks the part, he is good in the air and passes the ball with confidence.

Career History: A highly thought of youngster, he signed professional for Ipswich Town straight from school during the 1990 close season. Following an early season Zenith Cup outing in 1991-92, he made his FL debut away to Southend United on 4 April 1992, standing in for the injured Dave Linighan in central defence and remarkably, for a defender, scored a goal in a 2-1 victory. Even more remarkably, he scored again in his second game and all-in-all, showed much composure in his eight end of season games for a youngster coming into the team at a critical stage, as Town swept to the Second Division Championship and promotion to the Premier League.

Clubs	Signing Date	Transfer Fee	APPEARANCES				GOALS			
			Lge	FL Cup	FA Cup	Others	Lge	FL Cup	FA Cup	Others
Ipswich Town*	7.90	–	8			1	2			

WHELAN Ronald (Ronnie)

Born: Dublin, 25 September 1961

Height: 5'9" Weight: 10.13

International Honours: IR "U21"-1, IR-42

Position/Skill factor: The anchor man in midfield, his forté is to break up the opposition's attacks with timely interceptions and release the ball quickly to his partners with short passes. Frequently inconspicuous during matches, his value to the team is out of all proportion to the time he spends on the ball and is most noticeable when he is not playing!

Career History: Son of a former international, who never played in the Football League, he was spotted by Liverpool, playing for the League of Ireland team, Home Farm and was quickly snapped up and brought to Anfield early in 1979-80. Waited patiently for 18 months to make his FL debut, which came when he was called in to replace the injured Ray Kennedy against Stoke City on 3 April 1981 and he scored in a 3-0 win. Won a regular place in Liverpool's midfield from November 1981 at the expense of Ray Kennedy on the left side and enjoyed an outstanding first season as a regular, scoring ten FL goals and two in the 1982 League Cup Final against Tottenham. The first in the 87th minute taking the match into extra-time and his second with nine minutes remaining, clinching the "Reds'" 3-1 victory. It was the second of Liverpool's four consecutive League Cup triumphs and in the 1983 Final against Manchester United, once again, he popped up to score the winner in extra-time. In addition to his three League Cup winners medals, he has won seven League Championship medals in 1981-82, 1982-83, 1983-84, 1985-86, 1987-88 and 1989-90, two FA Cup winners medals in 1986 and 1989 and a European Cup winners medal in 1984, plus a finalists medal in 1985, despite a career riddled with injury problems which have often restricted his appearances. An infrequent scorer after his early exploits, he has occasionally been deployed as the forward run midfielder, most notably in a match against Coventry in April 1986, when he scored his only senior hat-trick in a 5-0 victory. In 1987-88, he was switched from his traditional left side duties to his present more pivotal role just in front of the back four, in place of the

injured Jan Molby and his long term knee injury incurred in a match against Everton in February 1991, coupled with the loss of his midfield partner, Steve McMahon, was a critical factor in Liverpool's late season collapse. An Irish Republic international since his debut as substitute against Czechoslovakia on 29 April 1981 – shortly after his Liverpool debut – his appearances have been limited both by injury and his club commitments. Selected for both the European Championship Finals in West Germany 1988 and World Cup Finals in Italy 1990, he will always be remembered for his bicycle-kick volley against the Soviet Union in the former competition, which was considered to be "goal of the tournament" until van Basten's effort in the Final. Sadly troubled by injury, he played little part in the Republic's remarkable progress to the World Cup Quarter-Finals in Italy. In 1991-92, he made no fewer than four unsuccessful comebacks from his knee injury. Broke down early in the season against Everton and did not reappear until the vital FA Cup Sixth Round match in March against Aston Villa, when he seemed almost back to top form. However, he was missing for the next three games, but returned in time for the first Semi-Final against Portsmouth and captured the headlines again with his tap-in equalising goal three minutes from the end of extra-time. Injured again in the replay, he returned once more for the final League game at Hillsborough, only to break down and lose his chance of a third FA Cup Final appearance. It seems doubtful that he can carry on much longer, which would be not only a personal tragedy, but also a terrible loss for his club. Although what he does for Liverpool appears simple there is no one in the current squad who can adequately replace him.

Clubs	Signing Date	Transfer Fee	APPEARANCES				GOALS			
			Lge	FL Cup	FA Cup	Others	Lge	FL Cup	FA Cup	Others
Liverpool*	10.79	–	311+11	46+4	41+1	37+2	45	14	7	6

WHITE David

Born: Manchester,
30 October 1967

Height: 6'1"

Weight: 12.9

International Honours:
E Yth, E "U21"-6, E"B"

Position/Skill factor: One of the most exciting forwards in the modern game, he loves to run with the ball at defences and scores spectacular goals from prodigious distances and acute angles.

Career History: Discovered on Manchester City's doorstep, he signed associated schoolboy forms in December 1981, before joining the club on a YTS scheme in June 1984, on leaving school. After turning professional early in 1985-86, he had to wait nearly a year to make his FL debut as a substitute at Luton Town on 27 September 1986. However, he did well enough to hold down a place on the right-wing for short spells, although the club sank into the Second Division at the end of the season. Sprang to fame in 1987-88, in a City team brimming with brilliant

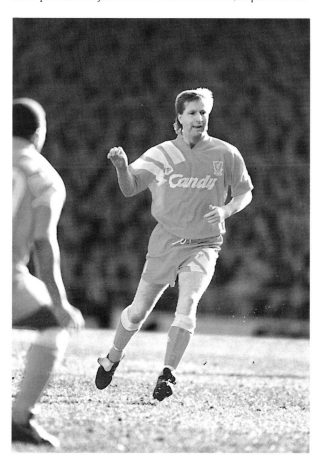

youngsters, which frequently ripped Second Division defences to shreds, most notably in a 10-1 mauling of Huddersfield in November, in which White, along with two colleagues, scored a hat-trick – possibly a unique occurrence in FL history. Sadly, the team lacked the experience to sustain a challenge, finishing eighth, but the following season promotion was achieved, with White playing in all but one game, as he did in 1989-90 when City struggled successfully to hold onto their First Division status. Always noted for his confident surging runs and powerful shooting, he was switched from the wing to central striker by manager Peter Reid in January 1990, following the signing of Mark Ward. It proved to be an inspired move as he formed a dangerous partnership with Niall Quinn which brought him 16 FL goals in 1990-91. Top scorer in 1991-92 with 19 FL goals, his haul included two against Liverpool in an early season 2-1 victory and another brace in the return match at Anfield in December – an achievement possibly without parallel in the last 30 years – and he rounded off the season with a last match hat-trick at Oldham. In any other country, a player with such confidence on the ball and such powerful shooting ability would be an automatic choice for the national team, but the nearest he came to the England side in 1991-92 was a single substitute appearance for the "B" team.

Clubs	Signing Date	Transfer Fee	APPEARANCES				GOALS			
			Lge	FL Cup	FA Cup	Others	Lge	FL Cup	FA Cup	Others
Manchester City*	10.85	–	215+12	17+2	17	9	64	9	1	2

WHITE Thomas (Tom) Hudson

Born: Auckland, New Zealand,
6 November 1974

Height: 5'9" Weight: 12.0

International Honours: NZ Yth Int

Position/Skill factor: Constructive sweeper who comes out of defence to pass the ball constructively.

Career History: Recently joined Liverpool from New Zealand junior football, he has yet to make a first team appearance.

Clubs	Signing Date	Transfer Fee	APPEARANCES				GOALS			
			Lge	FL Cup	FA Cup	Others	Lge	FL Cup	FA Cup	Others
Liverpool*	12.91	–								

WHITEHOUSE Dane Lee

Born: Sheffield,
14 October 1970

Height: 5'8"

Weight: 10.12

Position/Skill factor: Hard working left sided midfield player, who can also link up well with the attack when required.

Career History: Locally born and bred, he first joined Sheffield United as an associated schoolboy in November 1985 and continued to progress through the club as a trainee (July 1987), before turning professional during the 1989 close season. Still a trainee when he stepped out on the left-wing to make his FL debut in a 2-1 win at Blackpool on 15 October 1988, he made only limited progress, however, over the next two seasons. Was a regular member of the first team squad in 1991-92, enjoying an extended run on the left-wing and also showed he had an eye for goal scoring opportunities with seven FL goals, including two in an away win over Chelsea and three cup goals. Likely to progress in 1992-93.

Clubs	Signing Date	Transfer Fee	APPEARANCES				GOALS			
			Lge	FL Cup	FA Cup	Others	Lge	FL Cup	FA Cup	Others
Sheffield United*	7.89	–	37+18	3	6+3	3	8	1		2

WHITTON Stephen (Steve) Paul

Born: East Ham, 4 December 1960

Height: 6'0" Weight: 12.7

Position/Skill factor: Midfield, winger, or forward, he is a great striker of the ball, especially with the right foot. On the flanks, he can deceive 'keepers with outswinging crosses. Powerful in the air and an expert penalty taker.

Career History: One of many east-London youngsters discovered by Coventry City, he signed as an associated schoolboy in June 1976, before moving up as an apprentice (April 1977) and later joining the professional ranks during the 1978 close season. Just over a year later, he made his FL debut in midfield at Highfield Road against Tottenham Hotspur on 29 September 1979 and subsequently made six substitute appearances that season. He did not breakthrough until the beginning of 1981-82 when he started as a forward, before losing his place to Mark Hateley and returning to the team in March on the right-wing. The following term he was a regular choice on the wing and finished the season as the "Sky Blues'" top scorer with 12 FL goals. At the end of 1982-83 he returned to his native east-end to join the "Hammers", but in three seasons at Upton Park, was never able to establish a regular place. Returned to the midlands in the summer of 1986 to join Birmingham City, recently relegated to Division Two, after spending two months on loan to the "Blues" the previous season. At St Andrews he was converted to a central striker, top scoring with 14 FL goals in his second season. In 1988-89, the club was relegated to the Third Division, but before the axe fell, he surprisingly was back in the First Division with Sheffield Wednesday, although unable to improve the "Owls'" dismal scoring record that season. Tried out in midfield at the beginning of 1989-90, without success, he was replaced by new signing, John Sheridan. And for the remainder of his Hillsborough career, made only occasional appearances as a substitute, until rescued from obscurity by his former West Ham manager, John Lyall, who signed him for Ipswich Town.

Scored in his first two games for Town, but then lost form and his place. After several disappointing seasons, he enjoyed probably the best time of his career in 1991-92 while operating in midfield, missing only two FL games and guiding Ipswich to the Second Division Championship.

Clubs	Signing Date	Transfer Fee	APPEARANCES				GOALS			
			Lge	FL Cup	FA Cup	Others	Lge	FL Cup	FA Cup	Others
Coventry City	9.78	–	64+10	3+2	3		21		2	
West Ham United	7.83	£175,000	35+4	6	1		6	2		
Birmingham City	1.86	Loan	8				2			
Birmingham City	8.86	£60,000	94+1	7+1	5	3	28	4		1
Sheffield Wednesday	3.89	£275,000	22+10	3	0+1	0+1	4	4		
Ipswich Town*	1.91	£150,000	53	2	5	4	11		1	

WHITWORTH Neil Anthony

Born: Wigan, 12 April 1972

Height: 6'2" Weight: 12.6

International Honours: E Yth.

Position/Skill factor: Strong tackling central defender with plenty of pace, who is also very good in the air.

Career History: Signed as a trainee by Wigan Athletic in July 1988, he made his FL debut at Springfield Park against Leyton Orient on 10 February 1990 and following just one more appearance as a substitute, he was transferred to Manchester United during the 1990 close season, before he had signed a professional contract for Wigan. Made his United debut at right-back away to Southampton on 13 March 1991, but has not been required for first team duty since. To gain more experience he was loaned to both Preston North End and Barnsley during 1991-92. Very impressive in central defence at Oakwell, Barnsley manager, Mel Machin, was eager to sign him permanently.

Clubs	Signing Date	Transfer Fee	APPEARANCES				GOALS			
			Lge	FL Cup	FA Cup	Others	Lge	FL Cup	FA Cup	Others
Wigan Athletic	7.88	–	1+1							
Manchester United*	7.90	£45,000	1							
Preston North End	1.92	Loan	6							
Barnsley	2.92	Loan	11							

WHYTE Christopher (Chris) Anderson

Born: Islington, 2 September 1961

Height: 6'1" Weight: 11.10

International Honours: E "U21"-4

Position/Skill factor: Central defender who is strong in the air. Very quick, he likes to intercept balls and make good early passes to his midfield players.

Career History: After signing professional forms for Arsenal early in 1979-80, having been an associated schoolboy since May 1977, he made his FL debut two

years later at Highbury against Manchester City on 17 October 1981 and held his place throughout the rest of the season, forming a strong central defensive partnership with David O'Leary. A regular choice in 1982–83, he won selection for the England Under 21 team and appeared to have a glittering future. However, in 1983–84, he lost his place first to Colin Hill and then to Tommy Caton and his career went into a tailspin. Loaned to Crystal Palace at the beginning of 1984–85, he did well but no transfer materialised and he spent the rest of the season in the Arsenal reserves. After a handful of appearances in midfield during 1985–86, he was amazingly granted a free transfer. Even more amazingly he received no offer from an English club, or perhaps he chose to start a new career in the USA Indoor Soccer League (MISL), which is more akin to five-a-side football than the real game. Spent two years in the USA, firstly with New York Express and later with Los Angeles Lazers, before returning home. Though many have tried, very few English players have made successful comebacks to League football after playing American indoor soccer. Happily for Whyte, however, he was offered a trial by West Bromwich Albion manager, Ron Atkinson, which he successfully completed and hardly missed a game over the next two seasons. However, 1989–90 was a poor season for the "Baggies", who avoided relegation from the Second Division by a whisker. Therefore, it was something of a surprise when he was signed by newly promoted Leeds United, immediately forming a strong central defensive partnership with Chris Fairclough as an ever present in 1990–91. Absent for only one game in 1991–92, he became the proud winner of a League Championship medal – an honour he could not even have dreamed about five years earlier in the USA.

Clubs	Signing Date	Transfer Fee	APPEARANCES				GOALS			
			Lge	FL Cup	FA Cup	Others	Lge	FL Cup	FA Cup	Others
Arsenal	9.79	–	86+4	14	5	3+1	8	2		
Crystal Palace	8.84	Loan	13	4						
Los Angeles (NASL)	7.86	–								
W.B.A.	8.88	–	83+1	5	5	2	7	2		
Leeds United*	6.90	£400,000	79	12	5	5	4	1		

WHYTE David Antony

Born: Greenwich, 20 April 1971

Height: 5'9" Weight: 10.6

Position/Skill factor: Striker with pace, he uses excellent control to twist and turn defenders inside the penalty area.

Career History: Discovered by Crystal Palace playing for non-League Greenwich Borough, the same club that nurtured Ian Wright, he signed professional for the "Eagles" early in 1989. Having made his FL debut as a substitute in a 1-1 draw at Wimbledon on Boxing Day 1991, after two prior substitute appearances in the Zenith and League Cups, his first full appearance came on 1 February at home to Coventry and he scored in both of his next two games. Rested by manager Steve Coppell in March, he ended the season on loan to south London neighbours, Charlton Athletic, scoring on his debut for the Second Division club.

Clubs	Signing Date	Transfer Fee	APPEARANCES				GOALS			
			Lge	FL Cup	FA Cup	Others	Lge	FL Cup	FA Cup	Others
Crystal Palace*	2.89	–	7+4	1+2		0+1	1	1		
Charlton Athletic	3.92	Loan	7+1				2			

WIDDRINGTON Christopher (Chris)

Born: Newcastle, 1 October 1971

Height: 5'8" Weight: 11.1

Position/Skill factor: Competitive midfield player who likes to battle and looks as though he might develop into a captain. Keeping his passes simple, he doesn't give the ball away often.

Career History: Yet another north-easterner on Southampton's books, he first signed as an associated schoolboy in February 1987, before coming south as a trainee on leaving school in July 1988. Making good progress, he joined the "Saints'" professional staff during the 1990 close season, where his abilities were confined to the reserve side in 1990–91. While still awaiting a first team opportunity and in order to gain experience, he had a spell on loan at Wigan Athletic early in 1991–92, making his FL debut for the "Latics" at Springfield Park against Hull City on 14 September 1991. He proved a versatile player, operating at full-back, in central defence and in midfield, during his eight games for the Lancashire club. After returning to the Dell, he made his "Saints'" debut in late season, away to Everton on 1 April, deputising for Alan Shearer, while playing as fifth defender.

Clubs	Signing Date	Transfer Fee	APPEARANCES				GOALS			
			Lge	FL Cup	FA Cup	Others	Lge	FL Cup	FA Cup	Others
Southampton*	5.90	–	2+1							
Wigan Athletic	9.91	Loan	5+1	2						

WILCOX Jason Malcolm

Born: Farnworth, 15 March 1971

Height: 5'10"

Weight: 11.6

Position/Skill factor: A left-winger with pace and two useful feet, although favouring his left, who can go past defenders in order to produce telling crosses.

Career History: Showing great potential, he first joined Blackburn Rovers as an associated schoolboy in June 1986, before progressing through the ranks as a trainee (July 1987) and later as a professional (June 1989). Came out for his FL debut at home to Swindon Town on 16 April 1990, his only appearance in 1989–90, but played 18 times during the following season. Established a regular first team place in 1991–92, playing in 38 FL games, but was switched from the left to the right-wing from November onwards.

Clubs	Signing Date	Transfer Fee	APPEARANCES				GOALS			
			Lge	FL Cup	FA Cup	Others	Lge	FL Cup	FA Cup	Others
Blackburn Rovers*	6.89	–	49+8	2		1	4			

WILDER Christopher (Chris) John

Born: Stocksbridge, 23 September 1967

Height: 5'10"

Weight: 10.8

Position/Skill factor: Right-back who is constructive in possession, often playing short passes into his front men and getting forward to join up with the attack.

Career History: Failed to make the grade at Southampton, having been at the Dell since July 1984 as an apprentice, before turning professional and was signed on a free transfer by Sheffield United in the summer of 1986. Made his FL debut in the right-back position at Shrewsbury

Town on 24 January 1987 and played a further ten consecutive League matches before being injured. Shared the right-back slot with Andy Barnsley in 1987–88 and with Brian Smith in 1988–89, when the "Blades" were promoted back to Division Two. Out of favour in 1989–89, he was loaned out to Walsall, but returned to the team in late season and played the last three matches in central defence as United clinched promotion to Division One. After providing cover for John Pemberton in 1990–91, he played only five early season games in 1991–92, before further loan periods with Charlton Athletic and Leyton Orient.

Clubs	Signing Date	Transfer Fee	APPEARANCES				GOALS			
			Lge	FL Cup	FA Cup	Others	Lge	FL Cup	FA Cup	Others
Southampton	9.85	–								
Sheffield United*	8.86	–	89+4	8+1	7	3	1			
Walsall	11.89	Loan	4		1	2				
Charlton Athletic	10.90	Loan	1							
Charlton Athletic	11.91	Loan	2							
Leyton Orient	2.92	Loan	16			1	1			

WILKINS Raymond (Ray) Colin

Born: Hillingdon, 14 September 1956

Height: 5'8" Weight: 11.2

International Honours: E Sch, E Yth, E "U21"-1, E "U23"-2, E-84

Position/Skill factor: One of the most creative midfield players in the country, he sees passes early and invariably

picks the right option. Still capable of running a game from central midfield and can still hit great through balls.

Career History: The son of George, an inside-forward with Brentford, Nottingham Forest and Leeds United, before and after the war, he also had two brothers playing in recent times. The elder, Graham, played for Chelsea, Brentford and Southend United, while younger brother, Dean, assisted Queens Park Rangers, Leyton Orient and Brighton & Hove Albion. Eventually to become Chelsea's youngest ever captain, Ray first came to Stamford Bridge as an associated schoolboy in September 1970, before making his FL debut after signing as an apprentice in July 1972. Made his FL debut as a substitute for David Webb in a 3-0 win at home to Norwich City on 26 October 1973, six days after turning professional and had become a first team regular by the end of 1974–75, coinciding with the club being relegated to the Second Division. Became a great crowd favourite in six seasons at Stamford Bridge with his aggressive midfield play and spectacular goals and captained his team to promotion back to Division One in 1976–77. Sadly, he was unable to stop Chelsea's slide back to Division Two in 1978–79 and it was the cause of much dismay, tinged with resignation, when he moved to Manchester United in the summer of 1979. By then he was already a regular choice for England, after making his international debut against Italy on 25 May 1976 in an end of season tournament in New York, USA. Spent five good years at Old Trafford, but with only an FA Cup winners medal in 1983 to show for it, although United came close to winning the League Championship in his first season (1979–80), two points behind Champions, Liverpool and again in 1981–82 and 1983–84, as well as reaching the League Cup Final in 1983. Much less adventurous at Old Trafford than at Stamford Bridge, he scored remarkably few goals. But one in the first FA Cup Final game against Brighton & Hove Albion in 1983 will be remembered for ever – a curling 30 yard shot, which ranks as one of the greatest Cup Final goals, although it did not bring immediate victory, United winning 4-0 at the second attempt, following a 2-2 draw. Became the subject of controversy in the early 1980s, his admirers claiming that he never gave the ball away and his detractors retorting that this was because he passed the ball sideways! In 1984 he joined the exodus to Italy, although remaining an England regular and team captain, participating in two World Cup Final series in Spain 1982 and Mexico 1986. Sadly, the latter proved to be his "swansong" in an England shirt – sent off in the second disappointing game against Morocco for allegedly remonstrating with the referee (hardly credible for such a composed and disciplined player), he took no further part in the competition. He enjoyed three good years with AC Milan before losing his place and moving to French club, Paris St Germain, in the summer of 1987. However, he hardly got a game in the French team and was rescued by Graham Souness, who signed him for Glasgow Rangers in the November. Hardly missed a game in two years at Ibrox Park and won Scottish League Championship and Skol Cup winners medals in 1988–89. Returning to his native city in November 1989, joining Queens Park Rangers, he did not miss a single game in his first two seasons at Loftus Road – a tribute to his amazing stamina and durability at the age of 35. Injured in the first match of 1991-92, he returned in November with the "R's" at the foot of the First Division and guided them to mid-table respectability. Moreover, he scored a goal against Sheffield Wednesday with a remarkably controlled lob on the volley, which opposition manager, Trevor Francis, claimed could only be scored by a player of the highest class. It isn't clear how much longer Wilkins can continue playing, but his place among the "greats" of post-war English football is assured.

Clubs	Signing Date	Transfer Fee	APPEARANCES				GOALS			
			Lge	FL Cup	FA Cup	Others	Lge	FL Cup	FA Cup	Others
Chelsea	10.73	–	176+3	6+1	11+1		30	2	2	
Manchester United	8.79	£825,000	158+2	14+1	10	9	7	1	1	1
A. C. Milan (Italy)	7.84	£1,500,000								
Paris St. Germain (Fr)	7.87	–								
Glasgow Rangers	11.87	£250,000								
Q.P.R.*	11.89	–	87+1	5	10	2	4		2	1

WILKINSON Ian Matthew

Born: Warrington, 2 July 1973

Height: 5'11" Weight: 13.4

Position/Skill factor: Very agile and a good shot stopper, he is a goalkeeper who really works on his fitness in order to succeed at the highest level

Career History: A Manchester United professional acquisition during the 1991 close season, he had been with the club since August 1987 as an associated schoolboy and latterly as a trainee (June 1989). Still to make his FL debut, he was given a run out in a League Cup match at Cambridge United on 25 September 1991 that finished all square at 1-1, but was won 4-1 on aggregate by United.

Clubs	Signing Date	Transfer Fee	APPEARANCES				GOALS			
			Lge	FL Cup	FA Cup	Others	Lge	FL Cup	FA Cup	Others
Manchester United*	6.91	–		1						

WILKINSON Paul

Born: Louth,
30 October 1964

Height: 6'0"

Weight: 11.0

International Honours:
E "U21"-4

Position/Skill factor: Athletic striker who chases lost causes and is excellent in the air.

Career History: Came to Grimsby Town while still at school, signing associated schoolboy forms in February 1980, before becoming an apprentice in July 1981 and eventually graduating to the professional ranks early in 1982-83. After spending a relatively short period, acclimatising to the rigours of his new career, he made his FL debut at Blundell Park as a substitute against Charlton Athletic on 25 January 1983 and opened his account immediately, scoring in a 1-1 draw. Won a regular place in 1983–84, forming an effective partnership with Kevin Drinkell and was joint leading scorer in 1984-85 with 14

FL goals, plus four in competitions. A goal he scored at Goodison Park in November to knock Everton out of the League Cup was clearly instrumental in his move to the same club later in the season and shortly afterwards he won his first England Under 21 cap. Became an instant hero at Goodison Park, scoring the winner against arch rivals, Liverpool, in only his second full game, but hardly got a "look-in" the following season as understudy to Graham Sharp and Gary Lineker. Had the chance to establish himself in 1986-87, after Lineker's departure to Barcelona, but failed to take it and although he qualified for a League Championship medal, he had already signed for Nottingham Forest when the "Toffees" clinched the Championship. Sadly made little impact at the City Ground and after just over one year he moved on to Second Division Watford. Enjoyed three outstanding seasons at Vicarage Road, from a personal point of view, playing in all but four games in that period and top scoring in each season with 19, 15 and 18 goals, respectively. Transferred to Middlesbrough in the summer of 1991, he played a major role in the Teeside club's remarkable season, reaching the Semi-Final of the League Cup, before falling to Manchester United after extra-time and clinching promotion to the Premier League in the last match of the season. Played in every single game of "Boro's" 59 match campaign in 1991-92, without once being substituted and finished as the top scorer in all competitions, with 15 FL and nine cup goals. Appropriately, he scored the winning goal in the 77th minute of the final game away to Wolverhampton Wanderers, which clinched second place in Division Two.

Clubs	Signing Date	Transfer Fee	APPEARANCES				GOALS			
			Lge	FL Cup	FA Cup	Others	Lge	FL Cup	FA Cup	Others
Grimsby Town	10.82	–	69+2	10	4+2		27	5	1	
Everton	3.85	£250,000	19+12	3+1	3	6+2	6	7	1	1
Nottingham Forest	3.87	£200,000	32+2	3	4+1	1	5	1	2	
Watford	8.88	£300,000	133+1	4	8+1	8	52	1		3
Middlesbrough*	8.91	£550,000	46	8	4	2	15	3	4	2

WILL James Alexander

Born: Turriff, 7 October 1972

Height: 6'2" Weight: 13.13

International Honours: S Sch, S Yth,
S "U21"-3

Position/Skill factor: Goalkeeper with a powerful build, who reacts well to through balls into the penalty area and is a good shot stopper.

Career History: After gaining Scottish schoolboy international caps, he joined Arsenal as a trainee in July 1989 and on making the necessary progress, signed as a professional at Highbury early in 1990–91. Now third choice 'keeper, behind David Seaman and Allan Miller, he still awaits a first team appearance, but has already been recognised at Under 21 level by Scotland.

Clubs	Signing Date	Transfer Fee	APPEARANCES				GOALS			
			Lge	FL Cup	FA Cup	Others	Lge	FL Cup	FA Cup	Others
Arsenal*	11.90	–								

WILLIAMS Brett

Born: Dudley,
19 March 1968

Height: 5'10"

Weight: 11.11

Position/Skill factor: A left-back who favours his right foot, he has good passing ability and intercepts well.

Career History: A Nottingham Forest discovery, he first came to the City Ground as an associated schoolboy in January 1983, before leaving school and joining the club as an apprentice in July 1984. Made his FL debut on Boxing Day 1985 in a 1-0 win at Birmingham City, six days prior to turning professional and stayed in the side until replaced by Stuart Pearce towards the end of the season. Has stayed in the shadow of Pearce for all of his career to date, making only infrequent appearances each season and being forced to look for first team action on loan to other clubs. In 1991–92 he enjoyed a little bit of the Forest success story, when Stuart Pearce was injured towards the end of the season, deputising in seven FL games and also appearing in the League Cup Final against Manchester United. Sadly for him, Forest lost narrowly 1-0, thus he only received a losers medal.

Clubs	Signing Date	Transfer Fee	APPEARANCES				GOALS			
			Lge	FL Cup	FA Cup	Others	Lge	FL Cup	FA Cup	Others
Nottingham Forest	12.85	–	34	3	3					
Stockport County	3.87	Loan	2							
Northampton Town	1.88	Loan	3+1							
Hereford United	9.89	Loan	14	1	1	1				
Oxford United*	2.92	Loan	7							

WILLIAMS Lee

Born: Birmingham, 3 February 1973

Height: 5'7" Weight: 11.0

International Honours: E Yth

Position/Skill factor: Midfield player. Not very big, but he has good balance, can use both feet well and is a very useful passer of the ball.

Career History: Locally born and bred, he first came to Aston Villa as a 15-year-old associated schoolboy in November 1988. On leaving school, he signed as a trainee in July 1989 and had progressed to the club's professional ranks by early 1991. Has yet to make his first team debut.

Clubs	Signing Date	Transfer Fee	APPEARANCES				GOALS			
			Lge	FL Cup	FA Cup	Others	Lge	FL Cup	FA Cup	Others
Aston Villa*	1.91	–								

WILLIAMS Michael (Mike) Anthony

Born: Bradford, 21 November 1969

Height: 5'8" Weight: 10.6

Position/Skill factor: Hard working right-winger, or midfield player, with plenty of pace. Also has good ability on the ball.

Career History: Signed by Sheffield Wednesday from local Northern Counties (East) League club, Maltby MW, following trials with a number of clubs, he has yet to make a first team appearance for the "Owls".

Clubs	Signing Date	Transfer Fee	APPEARANCES				GOALS			
			Lge	FL Cup	FA Cup	Others	Lge	FL Cup	FA Cup	Others
Sheffield Wednesday*	2.91	–								

WILLIAMS Paul Anthony

Born: Stratford,
16 August 1965

Height: 5'7"

Weight: 10.3

International Honours:
E "U21"-4

Position/Skill factor: Striker with tremendous pace over the first ten yards, he seems to come alive in the penalty area.

Career History: Played non-League football in east London with Aveley, Clapton and Woodford Town, before signing for Charlton Athletic, following a successful trial early in 1987. Having once despaired of ever playing top class football, he made his FL debut as a substitute at Wimbledon on 1 September 1987. Loaned to Third Division Brentford shortly afterwards, he caused a stir by scoring six goals in eight games, including a hat-trick against Notts County in the Sherpa Van Trophy. Establishing himself in 1988–89, he was the "Valiants'" leading scorer with 13 FL, plus four cup goals and at the end of the season he was included in the England Under 21 squad for the annual tournament in France. He was also leading scorer in 1989–90 with ten FL goals (out of 31), as Charlton slid back to the Second Division. In the summer of 1990, he moved to Sheffield Wednesday and played in every FL game of the "Owls'" promotion campaign, scoring 15 FL goals in a strong forward partnership with David Hirst. Back in the First Division, his place came under threat from Nigel Jemson, signed from Nottingham Forest, but he saw off the challenge and ended 1991-92 as a first choice striker in a team which achieved its highest FL placing for 30 years and qualified for the UEFA Cup.

Clubs	Signing Date	Transfer Fee	APPEARANCES				GOALS			
			Lge	FL Cup	FA Cup	Others	Lge	FL Cup	FA Cup	Others
Charlton Athletic	2.87	£12,000	74+8	6	6+1		23	3	3	
Brentford	10.87	Loan	7			1	3			3
Sheffield Wednesday*	8.90	£700,000	71+15	10+3	3+2	3	24	3		

WILSON Barry

Born: Kirkcaldie, 16 February 1972

Height: 5'11" Weight: 11.7

Position: Right-winger

Career History: A recent Southampton acquisition, who was so highly thought of that in order to obtain his services, the "Saints" had to pay the Scottish junior side, Ross County, a record fee for an outgoing player. Making his reputation as a key figure in the side that won the Highland League title last season, he will look to make an early breakthrough in 1992-93.

Clubs	Signing Date	Transfer Fee	APPEARANCES				GOALS			
			Lge	FL Cup	FA Cup	Others	Lge	FL Cup	FA Cup	Others
Southampton*	6.92	£45,000								

WILSON Carl Nicholas

Born: Dublin, 18 November 1973

Height: 5'9" Weight: 10.12

Position/Skill factor: A midfielder who can play anywhere down the left hand side of the pitch. A strong tackler with a very good left foot, he also has boundless energy.

Career History: Born in the Republic of Ireland, he joined Coventry City on leaving school and played in the club's youth side, before turning professional on his 17th birthday. A useful looking prospect, he has yet to receive a first team call-up.

Clubs	Signing Date	Transfer Fee	APPEARANCES				GOALS			
			Lge	FL Cup	FA Cup	Others	Lge	FL Cup	FA Cup	Others
Coventry City*	11.90	–								

WILSON Clive

Born: Manchester, 13 November 1961

Height: 5'7"

Weight: 10.0

Position/Skill factor: Predominately a left-back, he can also play in midfield and on the left-wing. Has a cultured left foot and is a lovely passer of the ball. A good attacking player, he is very comfortable when going forward.

Career History: Christened Euclid Aklana, he was discovered by Manchester City while playing in local junior soccer and following trials at Maine Road, signed professional forms at the tail-end of 1979. Had to wait two years before making his FL debut, but when the opportunity finally came, he impressed when wearing the number three shirt at home to Wolverhampton Wanderers on 28 December 1981. No further appearances for City in 1982–83, but he gained first team experience in two loan periods with Chester City, the first for one month and the latter for three months. Had to wait until November 1983 for his next City game, but ended the season in possession of the left-back shirt. Made a breakthrough in 1984–85, playing in midfield for the first 27 games of City's promotion season, only to lose his place in February and was in-and-out of the team the following season. Not until 1986–87 did he firmly establish a first team place at left-back, playing in every FL game, only to see his team slide back to the Second Division. And with Andy Hinchcliffe waiting in the wings, City allowed him to join Chelsea at the end of the season. After playing in the first 25 games of 1987–88 on the left-wing, he lost his place and for the remainder of his stay at Stamford Bridge he could never quite nail down a permanent first team slot, although he won a Second Division Championship medal in 1988–89. Transferred to west London neighbours, Queens Park Rangers, in the summer of 1990, he started 1991-92 in a midfield role, but soon lost his place and was passed over for the remainder of the season. After three highly disappointing seasons, he was given a chance at left-back by new manager, Gerry Francis, in the third game of 1991–92 and to his credit held his place throughout.

Clubs	Signing Date	Transfer Fee	APPEARANCES				GOALS			
			Lge	FL Cup	FA Cup	Others	Lge	FL Cup	FA Cup	Others
Manchester City	12.79	–	107+2	10	2	5	9	2		
Chester City	9.82	Loan	21				2			
Chelsea	5.87	£250,000	68+13	3+3	4	10+2	5			
Q.P.R.*	7.90	£450,000	51+2	6	2	2+1	4			

WILSON Daniel (Danny) Joseph

Born: Wigan, 1 January 1960

Height: 5'6"

Weight: 11.4

International Honours: NI-25

Position/Skill factor: Good all-round midfield player with an excellent work rate. He puts opponents under pressure on one hand and on the other, is very constructive. A lovely striker of the ball, he can change the direction of play when it suits.

Career History: Came to Bury in 1977–78 from Wigan Athletic, then in the Northern Premier League, having been earlier registered with Sunderland as an associated schoolboy (April 1975). After making his FL debut as a substitute at Cambridge United on 8 November 1977, he settled in as a regular the following season, being ever present throughout the 1978–79 campaign. Following Bury's relegation to Division Four at the end of 1979–80, he was transferred to Chesterfield and formed a midfield partnership with Phil Bonnyman which almost carried the Derbyshire club to promotion in 1980–81. Considered by many to be their finest post-war player, his absence through injury for some vital end of season games probably scuppered their chances. Two seasons later, with the club struggling both on and off the field, he was virtually "given away" to Nottingham Forest. After his departure, the "Spireites" totally collapsed, winning scarcely another game all season. Nor did he fare much better. After ten games for Forest, he was dropped from the first team and never reappeared. Transferred to Brighton & Hove Albion in November 1983, following a short loan period with Scunthorpe United, he was an instant success scoring ten FL goals before the end of the season. However, in four seasons at the Goldstone Ground, he was unable to lift the "Seagulls" back to Division One, or prevent their relegation to Division Three at the end of 1986–87. It was during that season that he made his international debut for Northern Ireland against Turkey in November 1986 and he has been a regular selection ever since. Returning to the First Division in the summer of 1987, when signing for Luton Town, he won his first major honour when helping the "Hatters" to their remarkable League Cup victory over Arsenal in April 1988 and went back to Wembley the following year in the same competition, only to lose to Nottingham Forest. After three seasons at Kenilworth Road, during which he missed only six FL games, he joined the club he had helped to relegate – Sheffield Wednesday – when Luton won their last game of 1989–90, while the "Owls" lost theirs. Assisted Wednesday to promotion at the first attempt and also played in his third League Cup Final in four years, as the underdogs defeated Manchester United 1-0. Enjoyed another fine season in 1991–92, despite losing his place in mid-season. Returning in February, he was a driving force in midfield, with John Sheridan missing for much of that time, as the "Owls" stayed on well to finish in third place.

Clubs	Signing Date	Transfer Fee	APPEARANCES				GOALS			
			Lge	FL Cup	FA Cup	Others	Lge	FL Cup	FA Cup	Others
Bury	9.77	–	87+3	4	11		8		2	
Chesterfield	7.80	£100,000	100	8	9		13	1	1	
Nottingham Forest	1.83	£50,000	9+1			0+1	1			
Scunthorpe United	10.83	Loan	6				3			
Brighton & H.A.	11.83	£100,000	132+3	7	10	3	33	3	1	2
Luton Town	7.87	£150,000	110	20	8	4	24	3	2	
Sheffield Wednesday*	8.90	£200,000	70+2	14	2+1	2+1	9	1		

WILSON Gregory (Greg) James

Born: Ashton-under-Lyne, 11 November 1972

Height: 5'10" Weight: 10.12

Position/Skill factor: Very skilful midfield player with two good feet, who strikes the ball well and can really pass.

Career History: One for the future, he has been at Oldham Athletic as an associated schoolboy (November 1986), as a trainee (August 1989) and as a professional since the 1991 close season. Has yet to make a first team appearance.

Clubs	Signing Date	Transfer Fee	APPEARANCES				GOALS			
			Lge	FL Cup	FA Cup	Others	Lge	FL Cup	FA Cup	Others
Oldham Athletic*	7.91	–								

WILSON Terence Terry

Born: Broxburn,
8 February 1969

Height: 6'0"

Weight: 10.10

International Honours:
S "U21"-4

Position/Skill factor: Can play in both midfield or central defence. Always looks to pass and is at his most effective when bringing the ball out of defence.

Career History: One of the many current Nottingham Forest squad who have progressed through the club's junior ranks, he first came to the City Ground as an apprentice in August 1985. Almost 18 months after turning professional, he made his FL debut as a substitute in a 3-3 draw at home to Southampton on 2 September 1987 and following two further substitute appearances, made his full League debut at Coventry City, scoring in a 3–0 victory. He then held his place in midfield to the end of the season – a remarkable performance for a young professional in a team which not only was challenging for the League Championship, but also reached the FA Cup Semi-Final. Lost his place to Steve Hodge early in 1988–89, but returned in December as a central defender in place of injured Colin Foster. A useful squad player, he covered for both central defence and midfield slots in 1989–90 and 1990–91. Unfortunately, a second injury sustained in March 1991, virtually ruled him out of contention in 1991–92. To ease his path back to first team duty he was loaned out to struggling Newcastle United in the Second Division, but it was a futile exercise as the "Magpies" sacked Ossie Ardiles in his first week at St James' Park and new manager, Kevin Keegan, was not interested in using him. Played his first game for Forest in over a year in their last match of the season and will be hoping for better fortune in 1992–93.

Clubs	Signing Date	Transfer Fee	APPEARANCES				GOALS			
			Lge	FL Cup	FA Cup	Others	Lge	FL Cup	FA Cup	Others
Nottingham Forest*	4.86	–	89+11	11+2	10+1	6	9		2	
Newcastle United	1.92	Loan	2							

WINTERBURN Nigel

Born: Nuneaton, 11 December 1963

Height: 5'10" Weight: 10.7

International Honours: E Yth, E "U21"-1, E-1

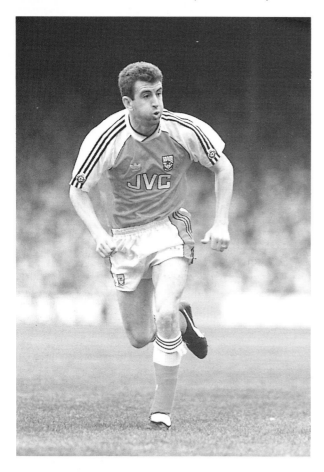

Position/Skill factor: Tough tackling left-back who likes to get forward to supply accurate crosses to the attack. Has a good left foot, can play short or long passes and is also noted for his very long throws.

Career History: Gained England Youth honours while an apprentice (May 1980) with Birmingham City, but in two years as a professional at St Andrews he failed to make the first team and was given a free transfer. Joined Wimbledon, following a unsuccessful trial at Oxford United (August 1983) and immediately made his FL debut at Bolton Wanderers on 27 August 1983, missing only three games throughout the season. In four seasons at Plough Lane he was a fixture at left-back and was absent for only seven FL games in that period, assisting the "Dons" to two promotions, to Division Two in 1983–84 and to the First Division in 1985–86, when he also won an England Under 21 cap. Transferred to Arsenal at the end of 1986–87, he had to play second fiddle to Kenny Sansom at first, but had a good run in the team in both full-back positions in the second-half of the season. Dislodged Sansom from the left-back slot at the start of 1988–89 and played in every game of the "Gunners'" remarkable last gasp League Championship triumph. Won his one and only England cap in November 1989, coming on as substitute against Italy and was ever present again in 1990–91 when winning his second League Championship medal. Although he missed only one

League match all season, neither he nor his team enjoyed the best of times in 1991–92, but the terrific end of the season flourish suggests that further honours will not be long delayed.

Clubs	Signing Date	Transfer Fee	APPEARANCES				GOALS			
			Lge	FL Cup	FA Cup	Others	Lge	FL Cup	FA Cup	Others
Birmingham City	8.81	–								
Wimbledon	8.83	–	164+1	13	12	2	8			
Arsenal*	5.87	£407,000	169+1	19	17	9	4	2		

WINTERS Jason

Born: Oakham, 15 September 1971

Height: 6'0" Weight: 11.8

International Honours: E Yth

Position/Skill factor: Brave young goalkeeper who will improve with experience. Already a good long kicker, upfield.

Career History: An England youth international, he was surprisingly released by Chelsea in September 1991, having been on the club's books as an associated schoolboy (June 1987), Trainee (August 1988) and a professional (May 1990). Started a three month trial with Ipswich Town in December 1991 and signed a contract in March 1992, after receiving coaching from former West Ham and England keeper, Phil Parkes, who is on the staff at Portman Road. Will start the 1992–93 season as understudy to Craig Forrest and will be hoping for an early first team opportunity.

Clubs	Signing Date	Transfer Fee	APPEARANCES				GOALS			
			Lge	FL Cup	FA Cup	Others	Lge	FL Cup	FA Cup	Others
Chelsea	5.90	–								
Ipswich Town*	3.92	–								

WISE Dennis Frank

Born: Kensington, 16 December 1966

Height: 5'6" Weight: 9.5

International Honours: E "U21"-1, E"B", E-5

Position/Skill factor: Winger who normally operates on the right flank and is a great crosser of the ball. Always likely to cause goalkeepers problems as he can either drive them in, or bend them away. Top class penalty taker.

Career History: Having been an associated schoolboy (January 1981) and an apprentice (July 1983) with Southampton, he was released without being offered professional terms and was snapped up by Wimbledon at the end of 1984-85. Made his FL debut in the final match of the season at Plough Lane as a substitute against Cardiff City on 11 May 1985 and played just four times during the "Dons'" successful promotion campaign in 1985–86, before securing a regular place for himself during the following term. Rose to national fame in 1987–88 during

displays for the Vauxhall Opel League side, Grays Athletic, having had previous experience with Yeading and Uxbridge, he signed for Crystal Palace in October 1990 and went straight into their reserve side. Ten months later, without ever receiving a first team opportunity, he was transferred along with Garry Thompson, to fellow Londoners, Queens Park Rangers, in the first week of the 1991–92 season. It was a strange signing, since Rangers already possessed six experienced central defenders and seemed to be overstocked in that department. Loaned out to Millwall in November 1991, he did not get a game. However, he was luckier with Plymouth Argyle. When making his FL debut for the "Pilgrims" against Leicester City on 11 January 1992, he scored in the second minute of the game, which would have been remarkable for a forward, but for a defender, it must surely be a record! Played twice more before he returned to Loftus Road.

Clubs	Signing Date	Transfer Fee	APPEARANCES				GOALS			
			Lge	FL Cup	FA Cup	Others	Lge	FL Cup	FA Cup	Others
Crystal Palace	10.90	£10,000								
Q.P.R.	8.91	£125,000								
Plymouth Argyle*	1.92	Loan	3				1			

Wimbledon's FA Cup run, scoring the winner against Luton in the Semi-Final and cleverly flighting a free-kick from which Laurie Sanchez headed the only goal to defeat Liverpool in the Cup Final. Also netted ten FL goals that season, second only to John Fashanu in the scoring lists. While most of his Cup Final colleagues then deserted Wimbledon, he remained two more years at Plough Lane, missing only four FL games during that period and demonstrating his ability to snap up vital goals. In the summer of 1990, near neighbours Chelsea made an irresistible offer and he moved to Stamford Bridge where he has enjoyed two good seasons in spite of some disciplinary problems caused by his aggressive temperament. Called up by Graham Taylor for his England debut in a vital European Championship qualifying match in Turkey on 1 May 1991, he scored the only goal to secure two priceless points. Subsequently played against the Soviet Union and gained three further caps on the summer tour of Australasia. Finished 1991–92 as Chelsea's leading scorer with 11 goals, mainly from set plays, while the club's recognised strikers, Clive Allen apart, invariably failed to take full advantage of chances going begging in the penalty area.

Clubs	Signing Date	Transfer Fee	APPEARANCES				GOALS			
			Lge	FL Cup	FA Cup	Others	Lge	FL Cup	FA Cup	Others
Wimbledon	3.85	–	127+8	14	11	5	26		3	
Chelsea*	7.90	£1,600,000	70+1	9	5	5	21	3	2	2

WITTER Anthony (Tony) Junior

Born: London, 12 August 1965

Height: 6'1" Weight: 12.7

Position/Skill factor: A central defender whose tremendous pace makes him difficult to beat on the ground, he is also good in the air.

Career History: Following some impressive early season

WOAN Ian Simon

Born: Heswall,
14 December 1967

Height: 5'10"

Weight: 11.9

Position/Skill factor: A talented left footed player, he can play in any position on the left flank. Never allowing himself to be hurried, he can both chip balls, or drive them in and has a lovely touch and a wide range of passing skills..

Career History: Starting as an associated schoolboy (October 1984) with Everton, he later went into non-League football with Heswall, Caernarfon, Newtown and Runcorn, from where Nottingham Forest signed him in March 1990. Introduced as a substitute, he made his FL debut for Forest in a 6-2 victory at Norwich City on 2 January 1991. Won a place in the Forest team on the left-wing at the end of the season and one of his three FL goals was a peach of a volley which ended Liverpool's hopes of retaining the League Championship. Nevertheless, he was a surprise selection, along with two other inexperienced youngsters (Gary Charles and Lee Glover) for the 1991 FA Cup Final against Tottenham Hotspur and although Forest took the lead, their lack of experience was painfully obvious in the second-half and extra-time as "Spurs" ground their way to a 2-1 victory. Out of favour at the start of 1991–92, he had several brief runs in the team, sharing the left-wing slot with new signing, Kingsley Black, without establishing himself as a permanent fixture.

Clubs	Signing Date	Transfer Fee	APPEARANCES				GOALS			
			Lge	FL Cup	FA Cup	Others	Lge	FL Cup	FA Cup	Others
Nottingham Forest*	3.90	£80,000	29+4	3+1	3+1	3	8			1

WOOD Stephen (Steve) Alan

Born: Bracknell, 2 February 1963

Height: 6'0" **Weight:** 11.9

Position/Skill factor: Good central defender. With two useful feet, he can pass both short and long. Never seems hurried and when he wins the ball, he invariably comes out of defence looking to make a worthwhile pass.

Career History: Came to Reading as an associated schoolboy in May 1979, before signing for the club as an apprentice, just three months later, in August 1979. Made his FL debut while still an apprentice at Southend United on 25 February 1980, deputising for the injured Steve Hetzke and was given one more outing in the side, prior to turning professional. Won a regular place in 1981–82, but was absent injured for the second half of 1982–83 when the "Royals" were relegated to Division Four. Returned in September 1983 to assist his team back to Division Three at the first attempt and was ever present for the next two seasons, winning a Third Division Championship medal in 1985–86 as Reading reached the Second Division for the first time since 1931. After one further season at Elm Park, he joined Millwall in the summer of 1987. Although injured after only seven FL games for the "Lions", he returned in February 1988 to help lift his team from fifth place to the Second Division Championship and Millwall's first ever sojourn in the top flight. A regular in the "Lions'" first season in Division One, but in-and-out the following season as they collapsed in the second half – doomed to relegation long before the end. Back in favour in 1990–91, he was injured in January and played no further part in the Second Division campaign when Millwall lost their chance of promotion in the Play-Offs. Early in 1991–92, he left the Den for the Dell and a second chance of First Division football with Southampton. However, with six central defenders already on the "Saints'" books, competition for the two (or three) first team slots was intense. After losing his place in January, he did not return until the last two games of the season.

Clubs	Signing Date	Transfer Fee	APPEARANCES				GOALS			
			Lge	FL Cup	FA Cup	Others	Lge	FL Cup	FA Cup	Others
Reading	2.81	–	216+3	10	15	4	9			
Millwall	6.87	£80,000	108+2	10	10	3+1				
Southampton*	10.91	£400,000	15		1	4			1	

WOODING Timothy (Tim) David

Born: Wellingborough, 5 July 1973

Height: 6'0" **Weight:** 12.0

Position/Skill factor: Tough tackling central defender, or

full-back, who can also pass the ball well.

Career History: Signed professional forms for Norwich City in the 1991 close season, having been with the club since becoming a trainee in September 1989. He was a regular in the reserves during 1991–92 and hopes to break into the first team next season.

Clubs	Signing Date	Transfer Fee	APPEARANCES				GOALS			
			Lge	FL Cup	FA Cup	Others	Lge	FL Cup	FA Cup	Others
Norwich City*	8.91	–								

WOODMAN Andrew (Andy) John

Born: Camberwell, 11 August 1971

Height: 6'1" **Weight:** 12.4

Position/Skill factor: Strongly built goalkeeper who comes out well for crosses and is brave to a fault. Good right footed kicker.

Career History: A Crystal Palace professional since the 1989 close season, he first came to the club as an associated schoolboy in October 1985, before signing as a trainee on leaving school in July 1987. As the third choice goalkeeper behind Nigel Martyn and Perry Suckling he has still to receive a first team opportunity after three years in the professional ranks and for first team experience he was loaned to Diadora League clubs, Carshalton Athletic and Bognor Regis Town, in 1991–92. Following the departure of Perry Suckling in the summer of 1992, he will start the new season as deputy to Nigel Martyn and will be hoping for an early break into the first team.

Clubs	Signing Date	Transfer Fee	APPEARANCES				GOALS			
			Lge	FL Cup	FA Cup	Others	Lge	FL Cup	FA Cup	Others
Crystal Palace*	6.89	–								

WOODS Christopher (Chris) Charles Eric

Born: Boston, 14 November 1959

Height: 6'2" **Weight:** 13.5

International Honours: E Yth, E "U21"-6, E-34

Position/Skill factor: Top class, experienced goalkeeper. Technically very sound, he possesses lightning reflexes, is agile, has big safe hands and judges crosses to perfection. Also marshals his defences well.

Career History: Currently England's first choice 'keeper, he started out with Nottingham Forest as an associated schoolboy in September 1975, before becoming an apprentice on leaving school in June 1976 and graduating as a professional just six months later. Sprang to fame in 1977–78 when Forest, newly promoted to Division One, ran away with the League Championship. However, he played no part in that particular triumph, but starred in the club's first ever League Cup victory. Early in the sea-

Chris Woods

son, Brian Clough had signed Peter Shilton from Stoke City and sold previous first choice John Middleton to Derby, leaving him as sole cover. However, Shilton was ineligible for the League Cup, having previously played in the competition for Stoke and he played in every match from the Third Round through to the Cup Final. One of the youngest and certainly least experienced players to appear in a Wembley Cup Final, it was a big test, particularly against the country's strongest team, Liverpool. However, after making a great save from Kenny Dalglish in the first minute, he performed impeccably and thanks to the protection of a well marshalled defence, was rarely troubled in either of the two matches, which saw Forest triumph 1–0 in a replay, after a 0–0 draw at Wembley. The following season he was selected for the England Under 21 team – the first player to be so honoured without a FL appearance to his name. Clearly too good a player to remain as understudy to the indestructible Peter Shilton, he was allowed to join Queens Park Rangers, then in Division Two, in the summer of 1979 and made his FL debut in the first game of the new season at home to Bristol Rovers on 18 August 1979, keeping a clean sheet in a 2-0 victory. An automatic first choice at Loftus Road for one and a half seasons, he inexplicably lost his place to John Burridge in December 1980 and was sold to Norwich City in the summer of 1981, after ending the season on loan at Carrow Road. Ever present in four of his five seasons with the "Canaries", he was absent for only four FL games, all in 1984–85, when winning his second League Cup winners medal after Norwich defeated Sunderland 1–0. At the end of the season, on tour with the England team, he won his first cap against the USA on 16 June 1985 and since that date was recognised as first choice deputy to Peter Shilton until the latter's retirement from international football in 1990. Although relegated in 1984–85, Norwich came back as Second Division Champions at the first attempt, but he did not stay for their next stint of First Division football, being one of the first English internationals to join the exodus to Graham Souness' re-created Glasgow Rangers' team. In five years at Ibrox Park he won four Scottish League Championship medals and four Skol League Cup medals and never lost his place except for injuries. However, in 1991, Rangers reduced their contingent of English players to avoid problems with the UEFA ruling on "foreigners" in European competition and he was sold to newly promoted Sheffield Wednesday. Curiously, his arrival was not universally welcomed by the "Owls'" supporters, some of whom were fans of the displaced Kevin Pressman and perhaps unfairly, he bore the brunt of the criticism for Wednesday's heavy defeats to Leeds (1-6) and Arsenal (1-7) and the two losses to arch-rivals, Sheffield United. Despite these disasters, Wednesday finished third and all but "stole" the League Championship "at the death". Since 1990, he has been England's undisputed first choice 'keeper and was one of the few players whose reputation remained intact, following the European Finals in Sweden during the summer.

Clubs	Signing Date	Transfer Fee	APPEARANCES				GOALS			
			Lge	FL Cup	FA Cup	Others	Lge	FL Cup	FA Cup	Others
Nottingham Forest	12.76	–		7						
Q.P.R.	7.79	£250,000	63	8	1					
Norwich City	3.81	£225,000	216	26	19	6				
Glasgow Rangers	6.86	£600,000								
Sheffield Wednesday*	8.91	£1,200,000	41	4	2	2				

WOODS Kenneth

Born: Liverpool, 15 April 1974

Height: 5'10" Weight: 12.5½

Position: Forward.

Career History: Signed professional forms for Everton during the 1992 close season, having come to Goodison as a trainee in June 1990. No first team experience.

Clubs	Signing Date	Transfer Fee	APPEARANCES				GOALS			
			Lge	FL Cup	FA Cup	Others	Lge	FL Cup	FA Cup	Others
Everton*	6.92	–								

WOODS Raymond (Ray) Guy

Born: Birkenhead, 7 June 1965

Height: 5'11"

Weight: 11.0

Position/Skill factor: Old fashioned right-winger who hugs the touchline and likes to have the ball at his feet so he can take defenders on. Has plenty of pace and can produce telling crosses.

Career History: A remarkable "rags-to-riches" story, which should serve as an inspiration to all young footballers who are thrown on the scrapheap, he joined Tranmere Rovers as an apprentice in July 1981, having been with the club on associated schoolboy forms since November 1980. Made his FL debut as a substitute at Bristol Rovers on 18 January 1983, while still an apprentice, but found it difficult to hold down a place and only appeared occasionally, before being freed and signing for Bangor City of the Northern Premier League in November 1984. He then had spells with Northwich Victoria and Runcorn both of the Alliance Premier League (Now Vauxhall Conference) and with Caernarfon Town of the NPL, before joining the all-conquering Colne Dynamoes club in 1988. Ironically, because the east Lancashire team carried a squad of no fewer than 25 full time professionals, he could not get a game with them and it was pure chance that his former manager at Tranmere Rovers, Brian Hamilton, invited him for a trial with Wigan Athletic. After eight end of season games in 1988–89, he was offered a contract, but no sooner had he started his FL comeback than it was ended again by a groin injury, which ruled him out for the whole of 1989–90. To his credit, Hamilton kept faith with him and when he shone in two FA Cup games with Coventry City in January 1991, he was immediately signed up by the "Sky Blues'" manager, Terry Butcher. In two years, including one out of action, he had graduated from Colne Dynamoes' reserve team to the First Division! He seized the opportunity gratefully and after making his Coventry debut on 2 March 1991, held his place to the end of the season. Sadly plagued by injuries in 1991–92, he made only a handful of appearances in the first-half of the season and when fit again was ignored by new City manager, Don Howe, in favour of Sean Flynn

Clubs	Signing Date	Transfer Fee	APPEARANCES				GOALS			
			Lge	FL Cup	FA Cup	Others	Lge	FL Cup	FA Cup	Others
Tranmere Rovers	6.83	–	9+5				2			
Bangor City	11.84	–								
Northwick Victoria	7.85	–								
Runcorn	.85	–								
Caernarfon Town	.86	–								
Colne Dynamoes	.88	–								
Wigan Athletic	2.89	–	25+3	2	4	2	3		1	
Coventry City*	1.91	£200,000	21	1			1			

WOODS Daragh William (Billy)

Born: Cork, 24 October 1973

Height: 5'11" Weight: 12.6

Position: Striker.

Career History: Signed professional forms for Coventry City during the 1992 close season, having come to the club as a trainee in August 1991. No first team experience.

Clubs	Signing Date	Transfer Fee	APPEARANCES				GOALS			
			Lge	FL Cup	FA Cup	Others	Lge	FL Cup	FA Cup	Others
Coventry City*	6.92	–								

WOODTHORPE Colin John

Born: Ellesmere Port, 13 January 1969

Height: 5'11"

Weight: 11.8

Position/Skill factor: Left-back who likes to get forward, he is also a good man-for-man marker, if required.

Career History: Started his football career in the lower reaches with Chester City as an associated schoolboy in September 1985 and on leaving school he signed for the club as a trainee on 23 August 1986, making his FL debut exactly a week later at Bury in a 1-1 draw. Impressed enough to be taken on as a full professional the following month, by the end of the season he was a first team regular at left-back, with 30 appearances under his belt. Remained first choice left-back at Sealand Road until the end of 1989–90, a season he was an ever present. His form warranted a higher grade of football and during the summer he was signed by Norwich City, as understudy to Mark Bowen, but did not make his FL debut for the

"Canaries" until the last match of 1990–91. After occasional first team outings in 1991–92, he forced his way into the team at the expense of Bowen in February 1992 and held his place for most of the remainder of the campaign, playing in the later rounds of the "Canaries'" FA Cup run up to the disappointing Semi-Final "knock-out" by Sunderland.

Clubs	Signing Date	Transfer Fee	APPEARANCES				GOALS			
			Lge	FL Cup	FA Cup	Others	Lge	FL Cup	FA Cup	Others
Chester City	9.86	–	154+1	10	8+1	18	6			1
Norwich City*	7.90	£175,000	13+3	0+2	4	0+1	1			

WORTHINGTON Nigel

Born: Ballymena, 4 November 1961

Height: 5'10"

Weight: 12.6

International Honours: NI Yth, NI-37

Position/Skill factor: Experienced left sided player, used mainly at left-back or in midfield. Supplies quality crosses to the front men when he gets forward and is also corner kick specialist.

Career History: Has proved to be a most consistent performer since the then Notts County manager, Jimmy Sirrel, crossed the Irish Sea to sign him from Ballymena United during the 1981 close season. After making his FL debut on 26 September 1981 at Wolverhampton Wanderers, he only played once more that season, but firmly established himself in 1982–83, missing just one match. In February 1984, his former manager at Meadow Lane, Howard Wilkinson, brought him to Hillsborough to join Sheffield Wednesday in order to assist their successful drive to promotion and First Division status for the first time since 1970. At the end of the season on 22 May 1984, he won his first cap for Northern Ireland against Wales in the penultimate match of the ill-fated Home Championship and has been a regular international selection since then, including a visit to Mexico for the World Cup Finals in 1986. Apart from a one year hiatus from September 1985 to September 1986, when eclipsed by Glynn Snodin and Chris Morris, he has been a regular first choice for the "Owls" and absent only through injury. Since the arrival of Phil King in November 1989, he has switched from left-back to left midfield, although he covers for the absence of his left flank partner and often interchanges with him, so it is difficult to say which is his true position. In 1990–91, he assisted the "Owls" to Division One, after their quite undeserved relegation the previous season and was a member of the team that carried a cup back to Hillsborough for the first time since 1935 – the League Cup after a shock 1-0 victory over favourites, Manchester United. Had a good first season back in the First Division in 1991-92, as the "Owls" finished in third place, playing 34 FL games and scoring five goals.

Clubs	Signing Date	Transfer Fee	APPEARANCES				GOALS			
			Lge	FL Cup	FA Cup	Others	Lge	FL Cup	FA Cup	Others
Notts County	7.81	£100,000	62+5	11	4		4			
Sheffield Wednesday*	2.84	£125,000	264+3	31	20	6	10			

WRIGHT Alan Geoffrey

Born: Ashton-under-Lyne, 28 September 1971

Height: 5'4"

Weight: 9.4

International Honours: E Sch, E Yth

Position/Skill factor: A left-back with the skill and pace of a winger, who uses it when getting forward to produce lovely crosses. Great in the air for his size.

Career History: A tremendous prospect who joined Blackpool as a trainee in August 1988, following excellent displays for England schoolboys, he soon graduated to professional status, winning England youth honours on the way. Prior to that, however, he became the youngest player to play for the "Seasiders" when he made his FL debut as a substitute at home to Chesterfield on 2 May 1988 at the tender age of 16 years and 217 days. He made his first team breakthrough in April 1989, on the left-wing and the following season played on both flanks as a full-back and in midfield. After the departure of Steve Morgan to Plymouth, he established a fixed position at left-back, appearing in all but the opening game of 1990–91. After 57 consecutive FL appearances for the "Seasiders", he became Kenny Dalglish's first and so far, most successful signing for Blackburn Rovers early in 1991-92. Looked totally at ease in the Second Division, missing only one game out of 34, before assisting Rovers through the Play-Offs to the Premier League.

Clubs	Signing Date	Transfer Fee	APPEARANCES				GOALS			
			Lge	FL Cup	FA Cup	Others	Lge	FL Cup	FA Cup	Others
Blackpool	4.89	–	91+7	10+2	8	11+2				
Blackburn Rovers*	10.91	£400,000	32+1		2	3	1			

WRIGHT Dale Christopher

Born: Middlesbrough, 21 December 1974

Height: 6'1" Weight: 12.2½

Position/Skill factor: Strong central defender who is a very good passer of the ball.

Career History: A Nottingham Forest professional since December 1991, he first came to the City Ground as an associated schoolboy in March 1990, before graduating as a trainee in August 1991. Has yet to receive a first team call-up.

Clubs	Signing Date	Transfer Fee	APPEARANCES				GOALS			
			Lge	FL Cup	FA Cup	Others	Lge	FL Cup	FA Cup	Others
Nottingham Forest*	12.91	–								

WRIGHT Ian Edward

Born: Woolwich, 3 November 1963

Height: 5'11" Weight: 11.11

International Honours: E"B", E-5

Position/Skill factor: Livewire striker who twists and turns well around the box and shoots early with either foot. Very quick, he loves to run at defenders.

Career History: A natural goalscorer who, after signing for Crystal Palace from Greenwich Borough during the 1985 close season, continued to score at a good rate. Was immediately introduced to first team football, making his FL debut as a substitute at Selhurst Park against Huddersfield Town on 31 August 1985 and at the end of the season, he had scored nine goals in 32 League appearances (16 as a substitute). In 1986–87 he was joint top scorer with only eight FL goals from 38 games. For ten seasons, Palace had been voted as one of the lowest scoring teams in the Football League, but with a stern defence. All that changed in 1987–88 when they were the highest scoring Second Division team with 86 goals, although the defence "leaked" 59. Was it a change of tactics, or simply the birth of the lethal Mark Bright–Ian Wright partnership? Whatever the case, he scored 20 FL goals (plus three in the cups) to Bright's 24 and the following season the totals were reversed (24 to Wright and 20 to Bright), as Palace swept to promotion through the Play-Offs. He scored the winning goal against Swindon in the Play-Off Semi-Final and two goals, including the winner three minutes from the end of extra-time, against Blackburn in the Final. Unsurprisingly, perhaps, the goals dried up in the First Division as Palace struggled to hold on to their new status, but thanks to a succession of favourable FA Cup draws against lowly opposition the side reached the Semi-Final where they amazingly defeated Liverpool 4-3 after extra-time. Having suffered a broken leg twice during the season, he played little part in the FA Cup run and was hardly match-fit for the Final against Manchester United. Nevertheless, he was selected as a substitute and after coming on in the 69th minute, he turned the match upside-down with two quite brilliant goals. Firstly, he turned the United defence inside-out to score a solo goal which took the match into extra-time and then scored with a magnificent header from a John Salako cross to put Palace 3-2 ahead. United fought back to force a replay and it was a surprise when he was left on the bench again. In a bitter, bruising and bad tempered replay, Palace showed none of the enterprise of the first match and lost 1-0, Wright's introduction coming too late to make any difference to the game. Back to full fitness in 1990–91, he played in every FL game, top scoring with 15 goals as Palace achieved their highest ever FL placing (third). He also won his first England cap against Cameroon on 6 February 1991 and played three more games that season, including the summer tour of Australasia. After scoring five goals in eight FL games at the start of 1991–92, he was transferred to Arsenal for a massive fee. Normally strikers with large transfer fees round their neck take time to settle with a new club. Wright, however, wasted no time, scoring an equaliser at Leicester in the League Cup tie in his first game, a hat-trick at Southampton in his FL debut for Arsenal and further goals in his third and fourth games. A few weeks later, he scored all four Arsenal goals in a 4-2 victory over Everton and continued to score consistently throughout the season, which he rounded off nicely with another hat-trick against Southampton's tough defence in the final match of the season. The final analysis showed that he was Arsenal's leading scorer with 24 FL goals from 30 games, plus two cup goals and that he was the First

Division's leading scorer with 29 goals. In normal circumstances he would have been an automatic selection for England. Instead he made a solitary appearance as substitute in England's warm-up programme and was passed over for inclusion in the England squad for Sweden in favour of Alan Shearer and his club colleague, Alan Smith, by then out of favour with Arsenal.

Clubs	Signing Date	Transfer Fee	APPEARANCES				GOALS			
			Lge	FL Cup	FA Cup	Others	Lge	FL Cup	FA Cup	Others
Crystal Palace	8.85	–	206+19	19	9+2	19+2	90	9	3	16
Arsenal*	9.91	£2,500,000	30	3			24	2		

WRIGHT Jeremy Howard

Born: Dewsbury, 3 October 1973

Height: 5'7" Weight: 10.8

Position: Midfield player.

Career History: Came up through the Sheffield Wednesday junior ranks to sign professional forms during the 1992 close season, having been at Hillsborough as an associated schoolboy (January 1988) and as a trainee (July 1990). No first team experience as yet.

Clubs	Signing Date	Transfer Fee	APPEARANCES				GOALS			
			Lge	FL Cup	FA Cup	Others	Lge	FL Cup	FA Cup	Others
Sheffield Wednesday*	6.92	–								

WRIGHT Mark

Born: Dorchester-on-Thames,
1 August 1963

Height: 6'3" Weight: 12.1

International Honours: E "U21"-4, E-42

Position/Skill factor: Central defender who never seems hurried and always gives himself time on the ball. Attacks the ball in the air in both penalty areas. Extremely constructive, he passes the ball accurately and carries it forward confidently.

Career History: Having signed professional for Oxford United on his 17th birthday, after playing in the youth side, he had to wait a little over a year before making his FL debut at the Manor Ground against Bristol City on 17 October, 1981, deputising for Gary Briggs. After just ten more first team games for Oxford he was used as a "makeweight" in a complicated deal which took him and Keith Cassells to Southampton in exchange for Trevor Hebberd and George Lawrence. It seemed a strange deal at the time, but "Saints'" manager, Lawrie McMenemy, clearly knew what he was doing. While Cassells never made the grade at The Dell, Wright became a fixture in central defence from the start of the 1982–83, after making his "Saints'" debut (as a forward!) in April 1982. He was selected for the England Under 21 side in 1982–83 and graduated to the national team in 1983–84, winning his first cap against Wales at Wrexham on 2 May 1984. Became an England regular the following season, but was unavailable for the 1986 World Cup Finals in Mexico due to a broken leg suffered in the FA Cup Semi-Final against Liverpool. After five good years at the Dell, apart from a well publicised "fracas" with Lawrie McMenemy, he joined Peter Shilton in moving to Derby County as part of owner Robert Maxwell's drive to establish the "Rams" as a First Division force. For a while all went well as Derby reached fifth place in 1988–89, but then Maxwell lost all interest in the club, which "withered on the vine", unable either to buy or sell players. Meanwhile, however, he was a tower of strength in central defence and continued his England career up to the European Championship Finals in West Germany 1988. Although he played well, he could not escape some of the "flak" arising from van Basten's hat-trick for the Netherlands, which knocked England out of the competition and he was not chosen at all in 1988–89. However, he picked up his England career again in 1990 and was one of the heroes of the 1990 World Cup campaign in Italy in which England started as "duffers" and returned as heroes, after reaching the Semi-Final and only losing to eventual World Champions, West Germany, on penalties, with Wright deployed as a sweeper for the first time during the campaign. Back home, the dam finally burst at Derby and the team sank without trace to the foot of the First Division, doomed to relegation long before the end of the season. Even Wright himself wilted under the pressure, most notably in a humiliat-

Mark Wright

ing 7-1 home defeat by Liverpool which, perhaps fortunately for him, new "Reds'" manager to be, Graham Souness, did not witness. During the summer of 1991 he was sold, along with team-mate Dean Saunders, to Liverpool, to enable Derby to finally pay off Maxwell and start anew. While there was no doubt about his class and ability, there was considerable doubt among "Reds'" fans of his discipline and self-control (after three sending-offs with Derby). These questions were not immediately answered as he was injured in his second game for the "Reds" and missed the first three months of the campaign. However, when he returned to the team in late November, he was magnificent, getting his head, by hook or by crook, to every high ball in the penalty area and bringing an air of authority and confidence to a defence which had been "ball watching" for at least two seasons. Under his influence, the side embarked on a run of seven victories and three draws in ten FL games, which carried them from mid-table to third place. Sadly, further injury in the second leg of the UEFA Cup Quarter-Final, not only cost Liverpool any hope of saving the tie (Genoa scoring the "killer" goal ten minutes after he departed), but also deprived the club of his services for most of the remaining matches. Fortunately he was able to return for the FA Cup Semi-Final games against Portsmouth and the Final against Sunderland. No honour was more richly deserved than when he captained the "Reds" to a 2-0 victory. Sadly, his season ended on a sour note. Having already angered Graham Taylor by joining the Liverpool victory celebrations in their home city instead of the national party for Hungary, he (or his club) failed to inform the England manager in good time of a recurrence of the leg problem aggravated in the match against Finland and did not link up with the team in Malmo.

Clubs	Signing Date	Transfer Fee	APPEARANCES				GOALS			
			Lge	FL Cup	FA Cup	Others	Lge	FL Cup	FA Cup	Others
Oxford United	8.80	–	8+2		1					
Southampton	3.82	£80,000	170	25	17	10	7	2	1	1
Derby County	8.87	£760,000	144	12	6	7	10			
Liverpool*	7.91	£2,200,000	21	1	9	4				

YALLOP Frank Walter

Born: Watford, 4 April 1964

Height: 5'11" Weight: 11.3

International Honours: E Yth, Canadian Int.

Position/Skill factor: Very experienced right-back, who drops off his opponents well and makes himself hard to beat. A good steady passer.

Career History: Spotted by Ipswich Town playing in schools football, he initially came to Portman Road as an apprentice in September 1980 and made steady progress into the club's professional ranks. Eventually, after a wait of over two years, he made his FL debut at Everton on 17 March 1984, when deputising for George Burley, but it wasn't until 1985-86 that he won a regular place in the team at full-back. Sadly for him, it coincided with the Town's relegation to Division Two. He became first choice right-back at Portman Road for the next five seasons, although occasionally filling in on the left side, or in central defence. In 1990-91, he was selected for the Canadian national team, presumably qualified by parentage. Coincidentally, the only other Canadian international in the Football League, is his teammate, Craig Forrest.

Having appeared in all but one FL match during the previous season, it was strange that he lost his place early in 1991-92. He remained a member of the first team squad until January, but subsequently played no further part in Ipswich's successful Second Division Championship campaign.

Clubs	Signing Date	Transfer Fee	APPEARANCES				GOALS			
			Lge	FL Cup	FA Cup	Others	Lge	FL Cup	FA Cup	Others
Ipswich Town*	1.82	–	238+17	18+1	12+2	19+1	4	1		

YORKE Dwight

Born: Tobago, West Indies, 3 November 1971

Height: 5'10"

Weight: 11.12

International Honours: Trinidad & Tobago Int

Position/Skill factor: Exciting forward who can play on either wing, where he can use his pace to advantage, or up front as a striker. A natural athlete with lovely balance, he has a good left foot.

Career History: Created such a good impression when playing for his country against Aston Villa on a summer tour, that Graham Taylor moved in quickly to sign him from his club, Signal Hill, in return for a substantial fee. Following a short period acclimatising at Villa Park, he made his FL debut as a substitute at Crystal Palace on 24 March 1990. Made further appearances in 1990-91 under new manager Jozef Venglos and when the latter was replaced by Ron Atkinson in the summer of 1991, he was the only Taylor signing to escape the "axe". He enjoyed an outstanding season in 1991-92, until "running out of steam" late in the season. Top scored with 11 FL goals, plus five in the cup competitions, including several headers, a flighted cross-cum-shot which floated into the net off a post and a brilliant solo goal against Southampton in late December when he dribbled 30 yards, beating two defenders to finish off with a curling low drive. He also scored a first-half hat-trick at Derby in the FA Cup Fourth Round. If he can recapture the form he showed in the middle part of last season, Villa should be a team worth watching.

Clubs	Signing Date	Transfer Fee	APPEARANCES				GOALS			
			Lge	FL Cup	FA Cup	Others	Lge	FL Cup	FA Cup	Others
Aston Villa*	11.89	£120,000	35+17	3	7	1	13		5	1

YOUDS Edward (Eddie) Paul

Born: Liverpool, 3 May 1970

Height: 6'0" Weight: 11.0

Position/Skill factor: Good looking central defender who is useful in the air and will look to come out from the back in order to pass the ball, rather than clear his lines..

Career History: Local born player, he first joined Everton as a 14-year-old associated schoolboy in April 1985. On leaving school, he went to Goodison as a trainee in June 1986 and progressed to the "Toffees'" professional ranks during the 1988 close season. Games were hard to come by and in order to gain experience he had a couple of spells out on loan, making his FL debut as a substitute in his only League appearance for Cardiff City at Bolton Wanderers on 20 January 1990. Later, the same season, he joined Wrexham on loan and played a major role in saving the Welsh club's Football League status. When he joined the "Robins" they were not only bottom of the Fourth Division, but so far behind the 23rd club as to be lost beyond recall. However, nine victories and two draws, in the space of 13 games, hauled the team to safety. Naturally, Brian Flynn, the Wrexham manager, was eager to sign him permanently, but Colin Harvey felt that he still had a future with Everton. The following term he made his Everton FL debut as substitute away to Norwich on 22 December and his full debut at right-back in the next match, finishing the season with six more games under his belt. However, failing to make any further breakthrough in 1991–92, he was transferred to Ipswich Town, debuting at right-back away to Derby County on 16 November. Tragically he broke his leg in that game and has not played since.

Clubs	Signing Date	Transfer Fee	APPEARANCES				GOALS			
			Lge	FL Cup	FA Cup	Others	Lge	FL Cup	FA Cup	Others
Everton	6.88	–	5+3	0+1		1				
Cardiff City	12.89	Loan	0+1		0+1					
Wrexham	2.90	Loan	20				2			
Ipswich Town*	11.91	£250,000	1							

YOUNG Eric

Born: Singapore, 25 March 1960

Height: 6'2"

Weight: 13.0

International Honours: W-10

Position/Skill factor: Solid tackling central defender who intercepts well and is difficult to pass, with those long legs of his, he always seems to get a foot in. Big and brave in the air, he is particularly dangerous at set pieces..

Career History: Was with Slough Town in the Isthmian League, before joining Brighton & Hove Albion in November 1982. Took a while to settle, but made his FL debut early the following season at Blackburn Rovers on 24 September 1983 and immediately became a key member of the "Seagulls'" defence, linking well with former England defender, Steve Foster. A first team regular, barring injury, for four seasons at the Goldstone Ground, he left Brighton at the end of 1986–87 when the "Seagulls"

were relegated to Division Three, joining Wimbledon, newly promoted to the First Division. He ended the 1987–88 season with an FA Cup winners medal as the "Dons" achieved a shock victory over favourites, Liverpool. In his three seasons at Plough Lane, he won a reputation as an extremely physical, combative player, frequently in trouble with referees. However, that did not prevent him being selected for Wales, an obscure criteria, making his international debut against Costa Rica on 20 May 1990 as part of the Central American team's warm up programme for the 1990 World Cup Finals in Italy. He remained a fairly regular choice over the next two years, but in the summer of 1990 he was transferred to south London neighbours, Crystal Palace, where he became an automatic fixture in the heart of the "Eagles'" defence. Made 30 FL appearances during 1991–92, again in partnership with Andy Thorn – scoring vital winning goals in a League match against Liverpool and in the Zenith Cup when Queens Park Rangers were beaten 3-2 at Loftus Road in the Third Round.

Clubs	Signing Date	Transfer Fee	APPEARANCES				GOALS			
			Lge	FL Cup	FA Cup	Others	Lge	FL Cup	FA Cup	Others
Brighton & H.A.	11.82	£10,000	126	8	11	2	10		1	
Wimbledon	7.87	£70,000	96+3	12	6+1	7	9		1	
Crystal Palace*	8.90	£850,000	64	12	4	8	4	1		1

YOUNG Michael Samuel

Born: Chester-le-Street, 15 March 1973

Height: 5'10" **Weight:** 11.0

Position/Skill factor: A naturally left footed left-winger who has both pace and stamina.

Career History: Released by Newcastle United at the end of his trainee contract, after signing in June 1989, he joined Middlesbrough in April 1991 and turned professional during the close season. Made his FL debut as a substitute at Ayresome Park against Southend United on 2 November 1991 and will be looking to make a "breakthrough" this coming season.

Clubs	Signing Date	Transfer Fee	APPEARANCES				GOALS			
			Lge	FL Cup	FA Cup	Others	Lge	FL Cup	FA Cup	Others
Middlesbrough*	7.91	–	0+1			0+1				

YOUNG Neil Anthony

Born: Harlow, 31 August 1973

Height: 5'8" **Weight:** 11.7

Position/Skill factor: Strong tackling full-back who loves getting forward to join up with play.

Career History: Signed professional forms for Tottenham Hotspur during the 1991 close season, having been on the club's books as a trainee since August 1989 and has yet to turn out for the first team.

Clubs	Signing Date	Transfer Fee	APPEARANCES				GOALS			
			Lge	FL Cup	FA Cup	Others	Lge	FL Cup	FA Cup	Others
Tottenham Hotspur*	7.91	–								